S0-BYV-819

by

Rav Shimon bar Yochai

From The Book of Avraham

with

The Sulam Commentary

by

Rav Yehuda Ashlag

The First Ever Unabridged
English Translation with Commentary

Published by

The Kabbalah Centre International Inc.
Dean Rav S. P. Berg Shlita

Edited and Compiled by
Rabbi Michael Berg

Published by
The Kabbalah Centre International Inc.

155 E. 48th St., New York, NY 10017
1062 S. Robertson Blvd., Los Angeles, CA 90035

Director Rav Berg

First Printing 2001
Revised Edition 2008

Printed in USA

ISBN: 1-57189-158-7

With much love to Bill, my past husband of many years;
May the light of the Zohar elevate your soul and bring much happiness to you—and to all who are connecting to the Zohar;

May your souls be elevated and may you have much happiness as well.

APPLYING THE POWER OF THE ZOHAR

The Zohar is a book of great mystical power and wisdom. It is Universally recognized as the definitive work on the Kabbalah – and it is also so Much more.

The Zohar is a wellspring of spiritual energy, a fountainhead of metaphysical power that not only reveals and explains, but literally brings blessing, protection, and well-being into the lives of all those who read or peruse its sacred texts. All that is required is worthy desire, the certainty of a trusting heart, and an open and receptive mind. Unlike other books, including the great spiritual texts of other traditions, The Zohar is written in a kind of code, through which metaphors, parables, and cryptic language at first conceal but ultimately reveal the forces of creation.

As electrical current is concealed in wire and cable before disclosing itself as an illuminated light bulb, the spiritual Light of the Creator is wrapped in allegory and symbolism throughout the Aramaic text of the Zohar. And while many books contain information and knowledge, the Zohar both expresses and embodies spiritual Light. The very letters on its pages have the power to bring spiritual wisdom and positive energy into every area of our lives.

As we visually scan the Aramaic texts and study the accompanying insights that appear in English, spiritual power is summoned from above – and worlds tremble as Light is sent forth in response.

It's primary purpose is not only to help us acquire wisdom, but to draw Light from the Upper Worlds and to bring sanctification into our lives. Indeed, the book itself is the most powerful of all tools for cleansing the soul and connecting to the Light of the Creator. As you open these pages, therefore, do not make understanding in the conventional sense your primary goal.

Although you may not have a knowledge of Aramaic, look first at the Aramaic text before reading the English. Do not be discouraged by difficulties with comprehension. Instead, open your heart to the spiritual transformation the Zohar is offering you.

Ultimately, the Zohar is an instrument for refining the individual soul – for removing darkness from the earth – and for bringing well being and blessing to our fellow man.

Its purpose is not only to make us intellectually wise, but to make us spiritually pure.

Glossary of Hebrew words

Torah

Also known as the Five Books of Moses, the Torah is considered to be the physical body of learning, whereas the Zohar is the internal soul. The literal stories of the Torah conceal countless hidden secrets.` The Zohar is the Light that illuminates all of the Torah's sublime mysteries.

Beresheet	Genesis
Shemot	Exodus
Vayikra	Leviticus
Bemidbar	Numbers
Devarim	Deuteronomy

Prophets

Amos	Amos
Chagai	Haggai
Chavakuk	Habakkuk
Hoshea	Hosea
Malachi	Malachi
Melachim	Kings
Michah	Micah
Nachum	Nahum
Ovadyah	Obadiah
Shmuel	Samuel
Shoftim	Judges
Tzefanyah	Zephaniah
Yechezkel	Ezekiel
Yehoshua	Joshua
Yeshayah	Isaiah
Yirmeyah	Jeremiah
Yoel	Joel
Yonah	Jonah
Zecharyah	Zechariah

Writings

Daniel	Daniel
Divrei Hayamim	Chronicles
Eicha	Lamentations
Ester	Esther
Ezra	Ezra
Nechemiah	Nehemiah
Iyov	Job
Kohelet	Ecclesiastes
Mishlei	Proverbs
Rut	Ruth
Sir Hashirim	Songs of Songs
Tehilim	Psalms

The Ten Sfirot – Emanations

To conceal the blinding *Light* of the Upper World, and thus create a tiny point into which our universe would be born, ten *curtains* were fabricated. These ten *curtains* are called Ten Sfirot. Each successive Sfirah further reduces the emanation of *Light*, gradually dimming its brilliance to a level almost devoid of *Light* – our physical world known as *Malchut*. The only remnant of Light remaining in this darkened universe is a *pilot light* which sustains our existence. This Light is the life force of a human being and the force that gives birth to stars, sustains suns and sets everything from swirling galaxies to busy ant hills in motion. Moreover, the Ten Sfirot act like a prism, refracting the Light into many *colors* giving rise to the diversity of life and matter in our world.

The Ten Sfirot are as follows:

Keter	Crown
Chochmah	Wisdom
Binah	Understanding
Da'at	Knowledge
Zeir Anpin	Small Face,
	(includes the next six Sfirot):
Chesed	Mercy (Chassadim - plural)
Gvurah	Judgment (Gvurot - Plural)
Tiferet	Splendor
Netzach	Victory (Eternity)
Hod	Glory
Yesod	Foundation
Malchut	Kingdom

The Partzufim - Spiritual forms

One complete structure of the Ten Sfirot creates a *Partzuf* or Spiritual Form. Together, these forces are the building blocks of all reality. As water and sand combine to create cement, the Ten Sfirot combine to produce a Spiritual Form *[Partzuf]*. Each of the Spiritual Forms below are therefore composed of one set of Ten Sfirot.

These Spiritual Forms are called:

Atik	Ancient
Atik Yomin	Ancient of Days
Atika Kadisha	Holy Ancient
Atik of Atikin	Anceint of Ancients
Aba	Father
Arich Anpin	Long Face
Ima	Mother
Nukva	Female
Tevunah	Intelligence
Yisrael Saba	Israel Grandfather
Zachar	Male

These names are not meant to be understood literally. Each represents a unique spiritual force and building block, producing a substructure and foundation for all the worlds make up reality.

The Five Worlds

All of the above Spiritual Forms *[Partzufim]* create one spiritual world. There are Five Worlds in total that compose all reality, therefore, five sets of the above Spiritual Forms are required.

Our physical world corresponds to the world of: Asiyah – Action

Adam Kadmon	Primordial Man
Atzilut	Emanation
Briyah	Creation
Yetzirah	Formation
Asiyah	Action

The Five Levels of the soul

Nefesh	First, Lowest level of Soul
Ruach	Second level of Soul
Neshamah	Third level of Soul
Chayah	Fourth level of Soul
Yechidah	Highest, fifth level of Soul

Names of God

As a single ray of white sunlight contains the seven colors of the spectrum, the one Light of the Creator embodies many diverse spiritual forces. These different forces are called *Names of God.* Each Name denotes a specific attribute and spiritual power. The Hebrew letters that compose these Names are the interface by which these varied Forces act upon our physical world. The most common Name of God is the Tetragrammaton (the four letters, *Yud Hei Vav Hei* יהוה.) Because of the enormous power that the Tetragrammaton transmits, we do not utter it aloud. When speaking of the Tetragrammaton, we use the term *Hashem* which means, *The Name.*

Adonai, El, Elohim, Hashem, Shadai, Eheyeh, Tzevaot, Yud Hei Vav Hei

People

Er	The son of Noach
Rabbi Elazar	The son of Rabbi Shimon bar Yochai
Rabbi Shimon bar Yochai	Author of the Zohar
Shem, Cham, Yefet	Noach's children
Shet	Seth
Ya'akov	Jacob
Yishai	Jesse (King David's father)
Yitzchak	Isaac
Yosef	Joseph
Yitro	Jethro
Yehuda	Judah

Angels

Angels are distinct energy components, part of a vast communication network running through the upper worlds. Each unique Angel is responsible for transmitting various forces of influence into our physical universe.

Adriel, Ahinael, Dumah (name of Angel in charge of the dead), Gabriel, Kadshiel, Kedumiel, Metatron, Michael, Rachmiel,

Raphael, Tahariel, Uriel

Nations

Nations actually represent the inner attributes and character traits of our individual self. The nation of Amalek refers to the doubt and uncertainty that dwells within us when we face hardship and obstacles. Moab represents the dual nature of man. Nefilim refers to the sparks of Light that we have defiled through our impure actions, and to the negative forces that lurk within the human soul as a result of our own wrongful deeds.

Amalek, Moab, Nefilim

General

Aba	Father Refers to the male principle and positive force in our universe. Correlates to the proton in an atom.
Arvit	The Evening prayer
Chayot	Animals
Chupah	Canopy (wedding ceremony)
Et	The
Avadon	Hell
Gehenom	Hell
Sheol	Hell The place a soul goes for purification upon leaving this world.
Ima	Mother The female principle and minus force in our universe. Correlates to the electron in an atom.
Kiddush	Blessing over the wine
Klipah	Shell (negativity)
Klipot	Shells (Plural)
Kriat Sh'ma	The Reading of the Sh'ma
Mashiach	Messiah
Minchah	The Afternoon prayer
Mishnah	Study
Mochin	Brain, Spiritual levels of Light
Moed	A designated time or holiday
Negev	The south of Israel
Nukva	Female
Partzuf	Face
Shacharit	The Morning prayer
Shamayim	Heavens (sky)
Shechinah	The Divine presence, The female aspect of the Creator
Tefilin	Phylacteries
The Dinur river	The river of fire
Tzadik	Righteous person
Zion	Another name for Jerusalem
Yisrael	The land of Israel The nation of Israel or an individual Israelite
Zohar	Splendor

The Hebrew vowels

Chirik אִ, Cholam אוֹ אֹ, Kamatz אָ, Patach אַ, Segol אֶ, Sh'va אְ, Shuruk אוּ אֻ, Tzere אֵ.

The Twelve Tribes

Asher, Dan, Ephraim, Gad, Issachar, Judah, Levi, Menasheh, Naphtali, Reuben, Shimon, Zebulun

Jewish Holidays

Rosh Hashanah	The Jewish New Year
Yom Kippur	Day of Atonement
Sukkot	Holiday of the Booths
Shmini Atzeret	The day of Convocation
Simchat Torah	Holiday on which we dance with the Torah
Pesach	Passover
Shavout	Holiday of the Weeks

כרך ו

פרשת וישב, מקץ, ויגש

Vol. VI

Vayeshev, Miketz, Vayigash

A Prayer from The Ari

To be recited before the study of the Zohar

Ruler of the universe, and Master of all masters, The Father of mercy and forgiveness, we thank You, our God and the God of our fathers, by bowing down and kneeling, that You brought us closer to Your Torah and Your holy work, and You enable us to take part in the secrets of Your holy Torah. How worthy are we that You grant us with such big favor, that is the reason we plead before You, that You will forgive and acquit all our sins, and that they should not bring separation between You and us.

And may it be your will before You, our God and the God of our fathers, that You will awaken and prepare our hearts to love and revere You, and may You listen to our utterances, and open our closed heart to the hidden studies of Your Torah, and may our study be pleasant before Your Place of Honor, as the aroma of sweet incense, and may You emanate to us Light from the source of our soul to all of our being. And, may the sparks of your holy servants, through which you revealed Your wisdom to the world, shine.

May their merit and the merit of their fathers, and the merit of their Torah, and holiness, support us so we shall not stumble through our study. And by their merit enlighten our eyes in our learning as it stated by King David, The Sweet Singer of Israel: “Open my eyes, so that I will see wonders from Your Torah” (Tehilim 119:18). Because from His mouth God gives wisdom and understanding.

“May the utterances of my mouth and the thoughts of my heart find favor before You, God, my Strength and my Redeemer” (Tehilim 19:15).

Vayeshev

Names of articles

1. "And Jacob dwelt"

A Synopsis

Rabbi Chiya opens a discussion about the most significant choice that each of us must make: whether to follow the Evil Inclination – a force present and persuasive from the moment of human conception – or the Good Inclination, which does not express itself until a person is thirteen years of age. A righteous individual, we learn, is one who does not put credence in the Evil Inclination, but rather, waits for the arrival of the Good.

While those who follow the Evil Inclination shall certainly suffer in the World to Come, the righteous are made to suffer trials and afflictions in this world, precisely because they do not associate with the Other Side, whose realm this is. Yet God will the deliver the righteous from all ills. As He did for Jacob, God protects the righteous from severe judgment by removing them from the world at the time of judgment, or by postponing judgment.

The Relevance of this Passage

Living in a dimension of time and space, we invariably fall under the delusion that our negative behavior bears fruit, while positive deeds go unrewarded. This illusion is fueled by our concept of time, which delays both judgement and reward. Our concepts of space and separation redirect due judgments and Light to different areas of our lives. Thus, we might behave unethically in business and reap financial reward. Judgement might then be directed towards our health, but we may fail to see a connection, believing instead that life is chaotic and random. Likewise, we might conduct our business affairs justly and honorably, yet profits fail to rise. However, we fail to notice that our children – who represent true fulfillment – have suddenly drawn closer to us. Or previous negative behavior may have destined us for chaos involving an auto accident [God Forbid], but the Light generated from a sharing action performed many years earlier averts catastrophe, without any awareness on our part of what might have been. All this is intended to allow us to exercise free will and to play an active role in our own fulfillment. This passage illuminates the forces of cause and effect, so that we may live with them in harmony. We gain time protection, time to change our ways before the severe judgments owed us are executed.

1. וַיֵּשֶׁב יַעֲקֹב בְּאֶרֶץ מְגוּרֵי אָבִיו בְּאֶרֶץ כְּנָעַן. רִבִּי חִיָּיא פָּתַח וְאָמַר, רַבּוֹת רָעוֹת צַדִּיק וּמִכֻּלָּם יַצִּילֶנּוּ יי׳. תָּא חֲזֵי, כַּמָּה מְקַטְרְגִין אִית לֵיהּ

לְבַּר נָשׁ, מִיּוֹמָא דְּקוּדְשָׁא בְּרִיךְ הוּא יְהַב בֵּיהּ נִשְׁמָתָא בְּהַאי עַלְמָא, דְּכֵיוָן דְּנָפֵיק בַּר נָשׁ לַאֲוִירָא דְּעַלְמָא, מִיָּד אִזְדַּמַּן לְאִשְׁתַּתְּפָא בַּהֲדֵיהּ יֵצֶר הָרָע, כְּמָה דְּאִתְּמָר, דִּכְתִיב לַפֶּתַח חַטָּאת רוֹבֵץ וגו'. וּכְדֵין אִשְׁתַּתַּף בַּהֲדֵיהּ יֵצֶר הָרָע.

1. "And Jacob dwelt in the land in which his father sojourned, in the land of Canaan" (Beresheet 37:1). Rabbi Chiya opened the discussion with the verse: "Many are the afflictions of the righteous, and Hashem delivers him out of them all" (Tehilim 34:20). Come and behold: how many enemies a man must face from the day that the Holy One, blessed be He, gives him a soul in this world. As soon as man comes into the world, the Evil Inclination is immediately ready to join him, as it is written: "sin crouches at the door" (Beresheet 4:7), because that is when the Evil Inclination associates with him.

2. וְתָא חֲזֵי דְּהָכֵי הוּא, דְּהָא בְּעִירֵי, מִיּוֹמָא דְּאִתְיַלִּידוּ, כֻּלְּהוּ נָטְרֵי גַּרְמַיְיהוּ, וְעָרְקִין מִן גּוֹ נוּרָא, וּמִן כָּל אַתְרִין בִּישִׁין. וּבַר נָשׁ, מִיָּד אָתֵי לַאֲרָמָא גַּרְמֵיהּ גּוֹ נוּרָא, בְּגִין דְּיֵצֶר הָרָע שָׁארֵי בְּגַוֵּיהּ, וּמִיָּד אַסְטֵי לֵיהּ לְאָרְחָא בִישָׁא.

2. Come and behold: this is true. From the day of birth, beasts protect themselves by fleeing from fire and evil places. WHEN HE IS BORN, man immediately flings himself into the fire because the Evil Inclination dwells within him and immediately prompts him to follow the path of evil.

3. וְאוֹקִימְנָא, דִּכְתִיב טוֹב יֶלֶד מִסְכֵּן וְחָכָם מִמֶּלֶךְ זָקֵן וּכְסִיל אֲשֶׁר לֹא יָדַע לְהִזָּהֵר עוֹד. טוֹב יֶלֶד: דָּא הוּא יֵצֶר טוֹב, דְּהוּא יֶלֶד, מִיּוֹמִין זְעִירִין עִמֵּיהּ דְּבַר נָשׁ, דְּהָא מִתְּלֵיסַר שְׁנִין וָאֵילָךְ, כְּמָה דְּאִתְּמָר.

3. For we have learned that it says: "Better is a poor and wise child than an old and foolish king who knows not how to take care of himself" (Kohelet 4:13). "Better is a child," because a child represents the Good Inclination; it has been with man for only a short time. Since the age of thirteen years and onward, IT IS WITH MAN, as we have already learned.

4. מִמֶּלֶךְ זָקֵן וּכְסִיל, מִמֶּלֶךְ: דָּא הוּא יֵצֶר הָרָע, דְּאִיהוּ אִקְרֵי מֶלֶךְ,

וְשַׁלִּיט בְּעָלְמָא עַל בְּנֵי נָשָׁא. זָקֵן וּכְסִיל, דְּאִיהוּ זָקֵן וַדַּאי, כְּמָה דְּאוֹקְמוּהָ, דְּכַד אִתְיְלִיד בַּר נָשׁ וְנָפִיק לַאֲוִירָא דְעָלְמָא, אִיהוּ אִזְדַּמַּן עִמֵּיהּ דְּבַר נָשׁ, וְעַ"ד אִיהוּ מֶלֶךְ זָקֵן וּכְסִיל.

4. In the verse: "...than an old and foolish king" (Kohelet 4:13), "king" refers to the Evil Inclination which is called a 'king' and 'ruler of people in the world'. It is certainly "old," and "foolish," because as soon as man is born and comes into the world, it lives with him. Hence, it is an "old and foolish king."

5. אֲשֶׁר לֹא יָדַע לְהִזָּהֵר עוֹד, לְהַזְהִיר לָא כְתִיב, אֶלָּא לְהִזָּהֵר, בְּגִין דְּאִיהוּ כְּסִיל, וַעֲלֵיהּ אֲמַר שְׁלֹמֹה ע"ה, וְהַכְּסִיל בַּחֹשֶׁךְ הוֹלֵךְ, דְּהָא מֵסּוּסִיתָא דְּחֹשֶׁךְ קָא אַתְיָא, וְלֵית לֵיהּ נְהוֹרָא לְעָלְמִין.

5. Further it reads: "…who knows not how to take care of himself." It is not written: 'to take care of others', but, "to take care of himself." Why? Because it is foolish. About it, Solomon said: "and the fool walks in darkness" (Kohelet 2:14), because it comes from the refuse of darkness and will never have light. BUT HE WHO DOES NOT KNOW HOW TO TAKE CARE OF OTHERS IS NOT YET CONSIDERED FOOLISH.

6. רִבִּי שִׁמְעוֹן אֲמַר, תָּא חֲזֵי, כְּתִיב טוֹב יֶלֶד מִסְכֵּן וְחָכָם, מַאן יֶלֶד מִסְכֵּן, הָא אוֹקְמוּהָ וְאִתְּמָר, דְּאִיהוּ יֵצֶר טוֹב, אֲבָל טוֹב יֶלֶד, הה"ד נַעַר הָיִיתִי גַּם זָקַנְתִּי, וְדָא הוּא נַעַר, דְּאִיהוּ יֶלֶד. מִסְכֵּן: דְּלֵית לֵיהּ מִגַּרְמֵיהּ כְּלוּם. וְאַמַּאי אִקְרֵי נַעַר. בְּגִין דְּאִית לֵיהּ חַדְתּוּ דְסִיהֲרָא, דְּמִתְחַדְּשָׁא תָּדִיר, וְתָדִיר אִיהוּ יֶלֶד מִסְכֵּן, כְּמָה דַּאֲמָרָן. וְחָכָם: בְּגִין דְּחָכְמָה שַׁרְיָא בֵּיהּ.

6. Rabbi Shimon said: Come and behold. It is written: "Better is a poor and wise child." AND HE ASKS: Who is a poor child? AND HE REPLIES: It has been explained, and we learned he is the Good Inclination. But "better is a child," as it is written: "I have been young, and now am old" (Tehilim 37:25). This is the lad who is a poor child and owns nothing. Why is he called a lad? Because he is constantly renewed, like the moon. He is also "a wise child," because wisdom dwells within him.

7. מִמֶּלֶךְ זָקֵן, דָּא הוּא יֵצֶר הָרַע, כְּמָה דְּאִתְּמַר, דְּהָא מִן יוֹמָא דַּהֲוָה, לָא נְפַק מִמְּסָאֲבוּתֵיהּ לְעָלְמִין, וְאִיהוּ כְּסִיל, דְּכָל אָרְחוֹי אִינוּן לְאֹרַח בִּישָׁא, וְאָזֵיל וְסָטֵי לִבְנֵי נָשָׁא, וְלָא יָדַע לְאִזְדַּהֲרָא, וְאִיהוּ אָתֵי עִם בַּר נָשׁ בְּתִסְקוּפִין, בְּגִין לְאַסְטָאָה לוֹן מֵאֹרַח טָבָא, לְאֹרַח בִּישָׁא.

7. "Than an old...king" refers to the Evil Inclination, WHICH STANDS IN CONTRAST TO METATRON AND IS CALLED A 'SCOUNDREL'. As we have learned, it never departed from its impure ways from the day it was created. It is foolish, as all its ways lead to evil. It deludes people and does not know how to take care of itself. It accuses people falsely and misleads them from the path of good to the path of wickedness.

8. תָּא חֲזֵי, עַל דָּא אַקְדִּים עִם בַּר נָשׁ בְּיוֹמָא דְּאִתְיְלִיד, בְּגִין דִּיהֵימִין לֵיהּ, דְּהָא כַּד אָתֵי יֵצֶר טוֹב, לָא יָכִיל בַּר נָשׁ לְמֶהֱימְנָא לֵיהּ, וְדָמֵי עֲלֵיהּ כְּמָטוֹלָא, כְּגַוְונָא דָּא תָּנִינָן, מַאן הוּא רָשָׁע עָרוּם, דָּא הוּא מַאן דְּאַקְדִּים לְאַטְעֲנָא מִלּוֹי לְקַמֵּי דַּיְינָא, עַד לָא יֵיתֵי חַבְרֵיהּ מָארֵי דְּדִינָא, כד"א צַדִּיק הָרִאשׁוֹן בְּרִיבוֹ וגו'.

8. Come and behold: this is why THE EVIL INCLINATION comes early TO JOIN with man, from the day he is born, so that man will believe in it. Later, when the Good Inclination arrives, man will find it difficult to believe in it, AND ITS WORDS will seem burdensome. Similarly, we have learned that he who is a subtle evilmonger hastens to plead his case in front of a judge before the arrival of his colleague, the litigant, as written: "The one who pleads first seems to be in the right" (Mishlei 18:17).

9. כְּגַוְונָא דָּא הַאי רָשָׁע עָרוּם, כד"א וְהַנָּחָשׁ הָיָה עָרוּם, וְהוּא אַקְדִּים וְשָׁרֵי עִמֵּיהּ דְּבַר נָשׁ, עַד לָא יֵיתֵי חַבְרֵיהּ לְאַשְׁרָאָה עֲלֵיהּ. וּבְגִין דְּאִיהוּ אַקְדִּים, וְהָא אַטְעִין טַעֲנָתֵיהּ עִמֵּיהּ, כַּד אָתֵי חַבְרֵיהּ דְּאִיהוּ יֵצֶר הַטּוֹב, אַבְאֵישׁ לֵיהּ לְבַר נָשׁ בַּהֲדֵיהּ, וְלָא יָכֵיל לְזַקְפָא רֵישֵׁיהּ, כְּאִילוּ אַטְעֵין עַל כִּתְפֵיהּ, כָּל מָטוֹלִין דְּעָלְמָא, בְּגִין הַהוּא רָשָׁע עָרוּם דְּאַקְדִּים

עִמֵּיהּ, וְע״ד אָמַר שְׁלֹמֹה וְחָכְמַת הַמִּסְכֵּן בְּזוּיָה, וּדְבָרָיו אֵינָם נִשְׁמָעִים, בְּגִין דְּהָא אַקְדִּים אָחֳרָא.

9. This evil monger IS THE EVIL INCLINATION. As writte, "The serpent was craftier" (Beresheet 3:2). He, too, hurries to dwell in man before his colleague, THE GOOD INCLINATION, comes to dwell in him. And because he arrived early to plead his case, when, his colleague, who is the Good Inclination, comes later, it is difficult for man to unite with it! And he cannot raise his head, as if he carried on his shoulders all the burdens of the world. All this is because the Evil One came first. Of this, Solomon said, "The Poor man's wisdom is despised and his words are not heard" (Kohelet 9:16), because the other one arrived earlier.

10. וְע״ד, כָּל דַּיָּינָא דְּקַבֵּיל מִבַּר נָשׁ מִלָּה, עַד לָא יֵיתֵי חַבְרֵיהּ, כְּאִילּוּ מְקַבֵּל עֲלֵיהּ טַעֲוָוא אָחֳרָא לִמְהֵימְנוּתָא, אֶלָּא וּבָא רֵעֵהוּ וַחֲקָרוֹ, וְדָא הוּא אֹרַח דְּבַר נָשׁ זַכָּאָה, דְּהָא בַּר נָשׁ זַכָּאָה, דָּא הוּא דְּלָא הֵימִין לְהַהוּא רָשָׁע עָרוּם דְּיֵצֶר הָרָע, עַד דְּיֵיתֵי חַבְרֵיהּ דְּאִיהוּ יֵצֶר טוֹב. וּבְגִין דָּא, בְּנֵי נָשָׁא אִינוּן כָּשְׁלִין לְעָלְמָא דְּאָתֵי.

10. Subsequently, for any judge who accepts the words of a litigant before his colleague arrives, it is as if he accepts another deity to believe in. But, "his neighbor comes forward, and sifts his case" (Mishlei 18:17), WHICH MEANS ONLY AFTER HIS COLLEAGUE COMES SHOULD HE HEAR HIS WORDS. This is the way of a righteous man because a righteous man does not believe the subtle evilmonger, who is the Evil Inclination, even if he hastens to plead his case before the arrival of his colleague, the Good Inclination. SO IT FULFILLS THE VERSE: "AND HIS NEIGHBOR COMES FORWARD, AND SIFTS HIS CASE." And with this act, people fail TO MERIT the World to Come.

11. אֲבָל הַהוּא זַכָּאָה, דְּאִיהוּ דָּחִיל לְמָארֵיהּ, כַּמָּה בִּישִׁין סָבִיל בְּהַאי עָלְמָא, בְּגִין דְּלָא יְהֵימָן, וְלָא יִשְׁתַּתַּף בְּהַהוּא יֵצֶר הָרָע, וְקוּדְשָׁא בְּרִיךְ הוּא שֵׁזֵיב לֵיהּ מִכֻּלְּהוּ, הה״ד רַבּוֹת רָעוֹת צַדִּיק וּמִכֻּלָּם יַצִּילֶנּוּ יי׳. רַבּוֹת רָעוֹת לַצַּדִּיק לָא כְּתִיב אֶלָּא צַדִּיק, בְּגִין דְּקוּדְשָׁא בְּרִיךְ הוּא

אִתְרְעֵי בֵּיהּ, וּבְגִין כָּךְ, קוּדְשָׁא בְּרִיךְ הוּא אִתְרְעֵי בְּהַהוּא בַּר נָשׁ, וְשֵׁזִיב לֵיהּ מִכֹּלָּא, בְּהַאי עַלְמָא וּבְעַלְמָא דְאָתֵי, זַכָּאָה חוּלָקֵיהּ.

11. But the righteous man who fears his Master suffers many afflictions in this world in order not to believe in and join the Evil Inclination. And the Holy One, blessed be He, saves him from them all. As it is written: "Many are the afflictions of the righteous, and Hashem delivers him out of them all" (Tehilim 34:20). Note that it is literally written: "Many afflictions to the righteous," and not 'BUT MANY ARE THE AFFLICTIONS OF the righteous.' THIS SIGNIFIES THAT WHOEVER SUFFERS MANY AFFLICTIONS IS RIGHTEOUS because the Holy One, blessed be He, cares for him– BECAUSE THE AFFLICTIONS HE SUFFERS ALIENATE HIM FROM THE EVIL INCLINATION. For this reason, the Holy One, blessed be He, cares for this man and delivers him from all in this world and the World to Come. Happy is his lot.

12. תָּא חֲזֵי, כַּמָּה בִּישִׁין עָבְרוּ עֲלֵיהּ דְּיַעֲקֹב, בְּגִין דְּלָא יִתְדַּבַּק בְּהַהוּא יֵצֶר הָרָע, וְיִתְרַחֵק מֵחוּלָקֵיהּ, וּבְגִין כָּךְ סָבִיל כַּמָּה עֳנָשִׁין, כַּמָּה בִּישִׁין, וְלָא שָׁקִיט. פָּתַח וְאָמַר, לֹא שָׁלַוְתִּי וְלֹא שָׁקַטְתִּי וְלֹא נַחְתִּי וַיָּבֹא רֹגֶז. תָּא חֲזֵי, כַּמָּה בִּישִׁין סָבְלִין צַדִּיקַיָּא בְּהַאי עַלְמָא, בִּישִׁין עַל בִּישִׁין, כְּאֵבִין עַל כְּאֵבִין, בְּגִין לְמִזְכֵּי לוֹן לְעַלְמָא דְאָתֵי.

12. Come and behold: how many afflictions befell Jacob to keep him from becoming infected by the Evil Inclination and to keep it distant from his lot. That is why he suffered punishments and afflictions, and had no quiet repose. He said: "I had no repose, nor had I rest, nor was I quiet; yet trouble came" (Iyov 3:26). Come and behold: how many afflictions do the righteous suffer in this world. Trouble after trouble, pain after pain, so that they can merit the World to Come.

13. יַעֲקֹב כַּמָּה סָבִיל, בִּישִׁין עַל בִּישִׁין תָּדִיר, כד"א לֹא שָׁלַוְתִּי: בְּבֵיתָא דְלָבָן, וְלָא יָכֵילְנָא לְאִשְׁתֵּזָבָא מִנֵּיהּ. וְלֹא שָׁקַטְתִּי: מֵעֵשָׂו, מֵהַהוּא צַעֲרָא דְּצִעֵר לִי, הַהוּא מְמַנָּא דִילֵיהּ, וּלְבָתַר דְּחִילוּ דְעֵשָׂו. וְלֹא נַחְתִּי: מִן דִּינָה, וּמִן שְׁכֶם.

13. How many afflictions did Jacob have to suffer! As it is written: "I had no repose" in Laban's house, and I could not escape from him. "Nor had I rest" because of that suffering that Esau's minister inflicted on me. And after that, there was the fear of Esau HIMSELF. "Nor was I quiet," on account of Dinah and Shchem.

14. וַיָּבֹא רֹגֶז: דָּא רוֹגְזָא וְעִרְבּוּבְיָא דְיוֹסֵף, דְּאִיהוּ קַשְׁיָא מִכֻּלְּהוּ, מִגּוֹ רְחִימוּתָא דְיַעֲקֹב לְגַבֵּי דְיוֹסֵף, דְּאִיהוּ רָזָא דִבְרִית, עָאל בְּמִצְרַיִם, בְּגִין דִּלְבָתַר כְּתִיב, וָאֶזְכֹּר אֶת בְּרִיתִי לְאִשְׁתַּכָּחָא שְׁכִינְתָּא תַּמָּן בַּהֲדֵיהּ.

14. "Yet trouble came." It was the trouble and confusion about Joseph, which was the hardest affliction of all. Why? Because Jacob loved Joseph, who is the secret of the Covenant through which JACOB entered Egypt. THAT IS WHY JACOB LOVED HIM SO MUCH, BECAUSE after this, it is written: "I remembered my covenant" (Beresheet 9:15). THE WHOLE REDEMPTION WAS FOR HIS SAKE, because the Shechinah was there with him, WITH THE COVENANT, WHO IS JOSEPH. THUS, THE CONFUSION ABOUT JOSEPH WAS HARDER ON HIM THAN ALL OTHER AFFLICTIONS THAT BEFELL HIM.

15. וַיֵּשֶׁב יַעֲקֹב בְּאֶרֶץ מְגוּרֵי אָבִיו בְּאֶרֶץ כְּנָעַן, רִבִּי יוֹסֵי פְּתַח הַצַּדִּיק אָבַד וְאֵין אִישׁ שָׂם עַל לֵב וְאַנְשֵׁי חֶסֶד נֶאֱסָפִים בְּאֵין מֵבִין כִּי מִפְּנֵי הָרָעָה נֶאֱסַף הַצַּדִּיק. הַצַּדִּיק אָבַד, בִּזְמְנָא דְקוּדְשָׁא בְּרִיךְ הוּא אַשְׁגַּח בְּעַלְמָא, וְלָא הֲוֵי עַלְמָא כִּדְקָא יָאוֹת, וְאִזְדַּמַּן דִּינָא לְשַׁרְיָא עַל עַלְמָא, כְּדֵין קוּדְשָׁא בְּרִיךְ הוּא, נָטֵיל זַכָּאָה דְּאִשְׁתַּכַּח בֵּינַיְיהוּ, בְּגִין דְּיִשְׁרֵי דִּינָא עַל כֻּלְּהוּ אָחֳרָנִין, וְלָא יִשְׁתַּכַּח מַאן דְּיָגֵין עֲלַיְיהוּ.

15. "And Jacob dwelt in the land in which his father had sojourned, in the land of Canaan." Rabbi Yosi opened the discussion with the verse: "The righteous perishes, and no man lays it to heart: and merciful men are taken away, none considering that the righteous is taken away from the evil to come" (Yeshayah 57:1). "The righteous perishes" when the Holy One, blessed be He, looks on the world and it is not as it should be, and Judgment falls on the world. Then the righteous among them is taken away so that the Judgment will fall only on the others, who will have no protection.

16. דְּהָא כָּל זִמְנָא דְּזַכָּאָה שָׁארֵי בְּעָלְמָא, דִּינָא לָא יָכִיל לְשַׁלְטָאָה עַל עָלְמָא. מְנָלָן מִמֹּשֶׁה, דִּכְתִּיב וַיֹּאמֶר לְהַשְׁמִידָם לוּלֵי מֹשֶׁה בְחִירוֹ עָמַד בַּפֶּרֶץ לְפָנָיו וגו'. וּבְגִין כָּךְ, קוּדְשָׁא בְּרִיךְ הוּא, נָטֵיל לְזַכָּאָה מִבֵּינַיְיהוּ, וְסַלֵּיק לֵיהּ מֵעָלְמָא, וּכְדֵין אִתְפְּרַע וְגָבֵי דִילֵיהּ. סוֹפֵיהּ דִּקְרָא, כִּי מִפְּנֵי הָרָעָה נֶאֱסַף הַצַּדִּיק, עַד דְּלָא יֵיתֵי רָעָה לְשַׁלְטָאָה עַל עָלְמָא, נֶאֱסַף הַצַּדִּיק. דָּבָר אַחֵר, כִּי מִפְּנֵי הָרָעָה: דָּא יֵצֶר הָרָע.

16. As long as the righteous dwells in this world, Judgment can not be handed down on it. What is the origin of this principle? Moses, as it is written: "He said that He would destroy them, had not Moses His chosen one stood before Him in the breach" (Tehilim 106:23). Thus, the Holy One, blessed be He, takes the righteous from among them and elevates them from this world. Only then does He receive His due retribution from the others – as the last part of the passage reads: "The righteous is taken away from the evil to come." THIS MEANS THAT before evil comes to rule the world, the righteous is taken away. Another explanation is that "from the evil" refers to the Evil Inclination, WHICH CORRUPTED AND MISLED THE WORLD.

17. תָּא חֲזֵי, יַעֲקֹב שְׁלִימוּ דַּאֲבָהָן הֲוָה, וְאִיהוּ קָאֵי לְקַיְּימָא בְּגָלוּתָא, אֲבָל מִגּוֹ דְּאִיהוּ צַדִּיק, אִתְעַכַּב דִּינָא, דְּלָא שָׁלְטָא בְּעָלְמָא, דְּהָא כָּל יוֹמֵי דְיַעֲקֹב, לָא שָׁרָא דִּינָא עַל עָלְמָא, וְכַפְנָא אִתְבַּטְּלַת.

17. Come and behold: Jacob was the perfection of the Fathers. He was about to be sent into exile, but he was righteous, so Judgment was withheld and did not control the world. Thus, Judgment did not befall the world through all of Jacob's days, and the famine ended.

18. וְאוּף הָכֵי בְּיוֹמוֹי דְיוֹסֵף, דְּאִיהוּ דְּיוּקְנָא דַּאֲבוֹי, לָא שְׁרָא גָלוּתָא, בְּגִין דְּאִיהוּ אָגֵין עֲלַיְיהוּ, כָּל יוֹמוֹי, כֵּיוָן דְּאִיהוּ מֵת, מִיַּד שְׁרָא עֲלַיְיהוּ גָלוּתָא, כד"א וַיָּמָת יוֹסֵף וגו', וּסְמִיךְ לֵיהּ, הָבָה נִתְחַכְּמָה לוֹ. וּכְתִיב וַיְמָרֲרוּ אֶת חַיֵּיהֶם בַּעֲבוֹדָה קָשָׁה בְּחֹמֶר וּבִלְבֵנִים וגו'.

18. Similarly, in the days of Joseph, who had his father's image, exile was avoided because he protected them throughout his life. But when he died, exile immediately befell them, as it is written: "And Joseph died..." (Shemot 1:6) which is followed by, "Come, let us deal wisely with them" (Ibid. 10), and "they made their lives bitter with hard bondage, in mortar, and in brick..." (Ibid. 14).

19. כְּגַוְונָא דָא, בְּכָל אֲתַר דְּשַׁרְיָא זַכָּאָה בְּעַלְמָא, בְּגִינֵיהּ קוּדְשָׁא בְּרִיךְ הוּא יָגֵין עַל עַלְמָא, וְכָל זִמְנָא דְּאִיהוּ קַיָּים, דִּינָא לָא שָׁרְיָא עַל עַלְמָא, וְהָא אִתְּמָר.

19. Similarly, wherever a righteous person dwells in the world, the Holy One, blessed be He, protects the world for his sake. And as long as he is alive, Judgment cannot befall the world, as we have learned.

20. תָּא חֲזֵי, וַיֵּשֶׁב יַעֲקֹב בְּאֶרֶץ מְגוּרֵי אָבִיו, מַאי מְגוּרֵי אָבִיו, כד"א מָגוֹר מִסָּבִיב, דְּכָל יוֹמוֹי הֲוָה דָחֵיל וַהֲוָה בִּדְחִילוּ. וַיֵּשֶׁב יַעֲקֹב בְּאֶרֶץ מְגוּרֵי אָבִיו. רִבִּי אֶלְעָזָר אֲמַר, דְּאִתְקַשַּׁר וִיתֵיב, בְּהַהוּא אֲתַר דְּאִתְאֲחֵיד בַּחֹשֶׁךְ. אֶרֶץ מְגוּרֵי אָבִיו דַּיְיקָא. בְּאֶרֶץ כְּנָעַן, אִתְקַשַּׁר אַתְרָא בְּאַתְרֵיהּ. מְגוּרֵי אָבִיו: דָּא דִינָא קַשְׁיָא. בְּאֶרֶץ מְגוּרֵי אָבִיו, כְּמָה דְּאִתְּמָר הַהוּא דִינָא רַפְיָא, דְּאִיהִי אֶרֶץ, דְּאִתְאַחֵיד מִן דִּינָא קַשְׁיָא, וּבֵיהּ אִתְיַשֵּׁב יַעֲקֹב, וְאִתְאַחֵיד בֵּיהּ.

20. Come and behold, it is written: "And Jacob dwelt in the land in which his father sojourned" (Beresheet 37:1). HE ASKS: What is meant by "his father sojourned (Heb. *megurei*)"? AND HE REPLIED: Terror (Heb. *magor*) from every side, because he was anxious and afraid all his days. Rabbi Elazar said: "And Jacob dwelt" in this place that was unified with darkness. "The land in which his father sojourned" means precisely THIS PANIC AND FEAR OF HIS FATHER, ISAAC, WHO IS THE LEFT COLUMN. "In the land of Canaan" alludes to a place connected to its proper location, WHICH MEANS THAT THE NUKVA IS CALLED 'LAND.' WHEN SHE IS CONNECTED TO THE LEFT COLUMN, WHO WAS THE FATHER OF JACOB, SHE IS CALLED THE 'LAND OF CANAAN'. As it was said, a place attached to its proper location, WHICH MEANS THAT THE LAND OF CANAAN IS CONNECTED TO THE LAND OF HIS FATHER'S SOJOURNING, WHICH IS THE LEFT COLUMN. "His father sojourned" is Harsh Judgment, AS IT IS THE SECRET OF THE LEFT

COLUMN OF ZEIR ANPIN. The "land in which his father sojourned" is A LAND OF Weak Judgment, as we have learned. This is land that is joined with and emerges from Harsh Judgment, WHICH IS THE LEFT COLUMN. Jacob dwelt in, and held on to, this land.

2. "These are the generations of Jacob"

A Synopsis

Here follows a discussion of the significance of Joseph as the first-named in the list of "the generations of Jacob." Also, Rabbi Aba comments on the importance of the number seventeen in relation to Jacob and Joseph.

The Relevance of this Passage

Joseph corresponds to the Sfirah of Yesod, the portal and gateway through which all the Light of the Upper Worlds flows into our world. The Patriarchs, Abraham, Isaac, and Jacob denote this supernal realm, whereas Joseph signifies the funnel through which the sacred Light emerges into physical reality. Here, we connect ourselves to this "cosmic funnel" where we receive the Divine and effulgent Light that shines in the Upper Worlds. The number seventeen is the numerical value of the Hebrew word for good [*tov*]. Thus, forces of goodness are amassed and drawn into our lives through the mystical powers attached to the number seventeen, as expounded upon in this passage.

21. אֵלֶּה תּוֹלְדוֹת יַעֲקֹב יוֹסֵף וגו׳, בָּתַר דְּאִתְיַשֵּׁב יוֹסֵף בְּיַעֲקֹב, וְאִזְדַּוַּוג שִׁמְשָׁא בְּסִיהֲרָא, כְּדֵין שָׁרָא לְמֶעְבַּד תּוֹלְדוֹת, וּמַאן אִיהוּ דַּעֲבֵיד תּוֹלְדוֹת, אַהֲדַר וַאֲמַר יוֹסֵף, דְּהָא הַהוּא נָהָר דְּנָגִיד וְנָפִיק, אִיהוּ עָבֵיד תּוֹלְדוֹת, בְּגִין דְּלָא פָּסְקִין מֵימוֹי לְעָלְמִין, וְאִיהוּ עָבֵיד תּוֹלְדוֹת בְּהַאי אֶרֶץ, וּמִנֵּיהּ נָפְקִין תּוֹלְדוֹת לְעַלְמָא.

21. "These are the generations of Jacob: Joseph..." (Beresheet 37:2). After Joseph settled in Jacob, and the sun – WHICH IS ZEIR ANPIN – mated with the moon – WHICH IS THE NUKVA – he began to produce generations. And who is he that brings forth offspring? The scripture continues saying, "Joseph." For the river that flows and comes out OF EDEN IS YESOD THAT IS DESIGNATED JOSEPH. It is he who is the progenitor of the offspring because his waters never cease to flow!

22. דְּהָא שִׁמְשָׁא, אַף עַל גָּב דְּאִתְקָרַב בְּסִיהֲרָא, לָא עָבֵיד אִיבִּין, בַּר הַהוּא דַּרְגָּא דְּאִקְרֵי צַדִּי״ק, וְיוֹסֵף אִיהוּ דַּרְגָּא דְיַעֲקֹב לְמֶעְבַּד אִיבִּין, וּלְאַפָּקָא תּוֹלָדִין לְעַלְמָא, וּבְגִין כָּךְ כְּתִיב, אֵלֶּה תּוֹלְדוֹת יַעֲקֹב יוֹסֵף.

22. The sun, WHO IS ZEIR ANPIN, unites with the moon, THE NUKVA, but can only bear fruit on the grade that is called 'Righteous', and on no other grade – NAMELY YESOD. THUS, IT IS CALLED Joseph, who is the grade of Jacob, who can bear fruit and bring forth generations to the world. Thus, it is written: "These are the generations of Jacob: Joseph..."

23. אֵלֶּה תּוֹלְדוֹת יַעֲקֹב יוֹסֵף, כָּל מַאן דַּהֲוָה מִסְתַּכֵּל בִּדְיוֹקְנָא דְּיוֹסֵף, הֲוָה אֲמַר, דְּדָא הוּא דְיוֹקְנָא דְּיַעֲקֹב. תָּא חֲזֵי, דִּבְכֻלְּהוּ בְּנֵי יַעֲקֹב, לָא כְּתִיב אֵלֶּה תּוֹלְדוֹת יַעֲקֹב רְאוּבֵן, בַּר יוֹסֵף, דִּדְיוֹקְנֵיהּ דָמֵי, לִדְיוֹקְנָא דַּאֲבוֹי.

23. "These are the generations of Jacob: Joseph..." ANOTHER INTERPRETATION IS THAT anyone who gazed at the facial image of Joseph thought it was the facial image of Jacob. Come and behold: it is not written THIS WAY when referring to any other children of Jacob. FOR EXAMPLE, IT IS NOT WRITTEN: 'These are the generations of Jacob: Reuben...' OR 'SHIMON' ETC. Only in reference to Joseph IS IT WRITTEN: "THESE ARE THE GENERATIONS OF JACOB: JOSEPH..." THE REASON IS THAT the facial image of Joseph was the same as his father's image.

24. בֶּן שְׁבַע עֶשְׂרֵה שָׁנָה. אֲמַר רִבִּי אַבָּא, רָמַז לֵיהּ קוּדְשָׁא בְּרִיךְ הוּא דְּהָא כַּד אִתְאֲבֵיד מִנֵּיהּ יוֹסֵף, בֶּן שְׁבַע עֶשְׂרֵה שְׁנִין הֲוָה, וְכָל אִינוּן יוֹמִין דְּאִשְׁתָּאֲרוּ, דְּלָא חָמָא לֵיהּ לְיוֹסֵף, הֲוָה בָּכֵי עַל אִינוּן שְׁבַע עֶשְׂרֵה שְׁנִין, וְכַמָּה דַּהֲוָה בָּכֵי עֲלֵיהּ, קוּדְשָׁא בְּרִיךְ הוּא יְהַב לֵיהּ, שְׁבַע עֶשְׂרֵה שְׁנִין אָחֳרָנִין, דְּאִתְקַיֵּים בְּאַרְעָא דְמִצְרַיִם, בְּחֵדוּ בִּיקָרָא וּבִשְׁלִימוּ דְּכֹלָּא, בְּרֵיהּ יוֹסֵף הֲוָה מַלְכָּא, וְכָל בְּנוֹי קַמֵּיהּ הֲווֹ, אִינוּן שְׁבַע עֶשְׂרֵה שְׁנִין, הֲווֹ חַיִּין לְגַבֵּיהּ, וּבְגִין כָּךְ בֶּן שְׁבַע עֶשְׂרֵה שָׁנָה הֲוָה אִיהוּ, כַּד אִתְאֲבֵיד מִנֵּיהּ.

24. "Joseph being seventeen years old" (Beresheet 37:2). Rabbi Aba said that the Holy One, blessed be He, indicated to Jacob that Joseph was seventeen years old at the time he was lost. All the days that remained AFTER HE REACHED SEVENTEEN YEARS OF AGE, during which time he did not see Joseph, Jacob was crying over him. Because he was crying during those years, the Holy One, blessed be He, gave him another seventeen years, during which he lived in the land of Egypt with happiness, honor, and fulfillment. His son, Joseph, was king and all his sons were there before him. Those seventeen years were considered as life for him. Hence, the text informs us that Joseph was seventeen years of age when he lost him.

3. "For the work of a man shall He pay back to him..."

A Synopsis

Rabbi Chiya addresses the problem of why some righteous individuals enjoy prosperity, good health, and happiness, while others endure terrible suffering. The mystery revealed to explain this emphasizes the crucial role of *mazal* (lit. 'fortune, luck'). Whether sinful or righteous, all individuals shall suffer who receive their souls from the Nukva (moon) during the period when she is defective. God compensates those righteous who suffer in this world, by ensuring their merit in the World to Come; their suffering in this world is the result of their souls' misfortune. While we may endeavor to reason why there is such disparity in the fortunes of men, Kabbalah explains that a righteous soul actually chooses the moment of birth and the physical body into which it will incarnate. The righteous will often purposely choose a life of suffering in order to help correct the sins of the generation, thus preventing great judgement and destruction. This section underscores the importance of the strength of the soul of the righteous. God's judgment rests on this strength, and not on physical or material qualities.

The Relevance of this Passage

The physical body is of the same shape and structure in all human beings. However, the internal Vessel – a man's Desire to Receive – is of different measure in each person. For example, a person endowed with a large Vessel may have the power to accumulate enormous wealth. Yet on a purely physical level, there is no distinguishing trait that hints at a wealthy man's financial capabilities and business acumen. In similar fashion, the soul of a single righteous individual may be far greater than millions of sinful people of the same generation. The suffering endured by this lone Righteous individual can therefore balance all the negativity generated by the actions of others. Through the merit Light of the righteous souls, whose Light shines so radiantly through this passage, we can help correct the effects of our own negative actions; moreover, our own Vessel is expanded, so that our efforts toward righteousness compensate for the sins of others.

25. רִבִּי חִיָּיא פְּתַח וַאֲמַר, לָכֵן אַנְשֵׁי לֵבָב שִׁמְעוּ לִי חָלִלָה לָאֵל מֵרֶשַׁע וְשַׁדַּי מֵעָוֶל. כִּי פֹּעַל אָדָם יְשַׁלֶּם לוֹ וּכְאֹרַח אִישׁ יַמְצִאֶנּוּ. תָּא חֲזֵי, כַּד בָּרָא קוּדְשָׁא בְּרִיךְ הוּא עַלְמָא, עֲבַד לֵיהּ עַל דִּינָא, וְעַל דִּינָא אִתְקַיַּים, וְכָל עוֹבָדִין דְּעַלְמָא, אִינוּן קָיְימִין בְּדִינָא, בַּר דְּקוּדְשָׁא בְּרִיךְ הוּא בְּגִין

לְקַיְּימָא עַלְמָא וְלָא יִתְאֲבִיד, פָּרִישׂ עֲלֵיהּ רַחֲמֵי, וְאִינּוּן רַחֲמֵי מְעַכְּבֵי לְדִינָא, דְּלָא יִשְׁתְּצֵי עַלְמָא, וְעַל רַחֲמֵי אִתְנַהֵיג עַלְמָא, וְאִתְקַיַּים בְּגִינֵיהּ.

25. Rabbi Chiya opened the discussion with the verse: "Therefore listen to me you men of understanding: Far be it from El to do wickedness and from Shadai to commit iniquity. For the work of a man shall He pay back to him, and according to his ways will He cause to befall every man" (Iyov 34:10). Come and behold: when the Holy One, blessed be He, created the world, He created it by Judgment, and it exists upon Judgment. All worldly affairs exist according to the principles of Judgment. Nevertheless, to support the world and prevent its destruction, the Holy One, blessed be He, spreads Mercy over it. This Mercy tempers Judgment, so that it does not put an end to the world. Thus, the world acts according to Mercy, and endures due to it.

26. וְאִי תֵּימָא דְּקוּדְשָׁא בְּרִיךְ הוּא עָבֵיד דִּינָא בְּבַר נָשׁ בְּלָא דִינָא, הָא אִתְּמָר, דְּכַד דִּינָא שַׁרְיָא עֲלֵיהּ דְּבַר נָשׁ, כַּד אִיהוּ זַכָּאָה, בְּגִין רְחִימוּתָא דְקוּדְשָׁא בְּרִיךְ הוּא בֵּיהּ אִיהִי, כְּמָה דְאִתְּמָר, דְּהָא קוּדְשָׁא בְּרִיךְ הוּא רְחֵים עֲלֵיהּ בִּרְחִימוּ, לְקָרְבָא לֵיהּ לְגַבֵּיהּ, מְתַבַּר גּוּפָא, בְּגִין לְשַׁלְטָאָה נִשְׁמָתָא, וּכְדֵין אִתְקְרֵיב בַּר נָשׁ לְגַבֵּיהּ בִּרְחִימוּ, כִּדְקָא יָאוּת. וְנִשְׁמָתָא שָׁלְטָא, וְגוּפָא אִתְחַלָּשׁ.

26. And if you say that the Holy One, blessed be He, judges man without justice, we have learned that when Judgment prevails on man and he is righteous, it is because of the love of the Holy One, blessed be He. As we have learned, when the Holy One, blessed be He, feels pity for a man, it is to bring the man closer to Him. The Holy One, blessed be He, breaks the body so as to give the soul total control. Then man can come closer to Him with love, as is fitting, and the soul controls man while his body is weakened!

27. וּבַעְיָא גּוּפָא חוּלְשָׁא, וְנַפְשָׁא תַּקִּיפָא, דְּאִתְתַּקַּף בְּתְקִיפוּ, וּכְדֵין אִיהוּ רְחִימָא דְקוּדְשָׁא בְּרִיךְ הוּא. כְּמָה דַּאֲמָרוּ חַבְרַיָּיא, יְהַב קוּדְשָׁא בְּרִיךְ הוּא לַצַּדִּיק צַעֲרָא בְּעַלְמָא דֵין, בְּגִין לְמִזְכֵּי לֵיהּ לְעַלְמָא דְאָתֵי.

3. "For the work of a man shall He pay back to him..."

27. A man needs to have a weak body and a strong soul that shall grow stronger still. Then he is beloved by the Holy One, blessed be He. According to the friends, the Holy One, blessed be He, causes sorrow to the righteous in this world so that the righteous may merit the World to Come.

28. וְכַד נִשְׁמָתָא חַלְשָׁא, וְגוּפָא תַּקִיפָא, אִיהוּ שָׂנְאֵיהּ דְּקוּדְשָׁא בְּרִיךְ הוּא, דְּלָא אִתְרְעֵי בֵּיהּ, לָא יָהֵיב לֵיהּ צַעֲרָא בְּהַאי עַלְמָא, אֶלָּא אוֹרְחוֹי מִתְתַּקְנָן, וְהוּא בִּשְׁלִימוּ יַתִּיר, בְּגִין דְּאִי עָבַד צְדָקָה, אוֹ טִיבוּ, קוּדְשָׁא בְּרִיךְ הוּא מְשַׁלֵּם לֵיהּ אַגְרֵיהּ בְּהַאי עַלְמָא, וְלָא יֶהֱוֵי לֵיהּ חוּלַק בְּהַהוּא עַלְמָא, וְדָא הוּא דְּתִרְגֵּם אוּנְקְלוּס וּמְשַׁלֵּם לְשׂוֹנְאָיו וגו', וּמְשַׁלֵּם לְשַׂנְאוֹהִי טַבְוָון דְּאִינוּן וגו', וּבְגִין כָּךְ הַהוּא זַכָּאָה דְּאִתְבַּר תָּדִיר, אִיהוּ רְחִימָא דְקוּדְשָׁא בְּרִיךְ הוּא, וְהַנֵּי מִילֵי, כַּד בָּדַק וְלָא אַשְׁכַּח חוֹבָא בִידֵיהּ, דְּאִתְעַנַּשׁ עֲלֵיהּ.

28. When the soul is weak and the body strong, man is hated by the Holy One, blessed be He, who does not care for him. Therefore, He inflicts no suffering on him in this world. His life runs smoothly and perfectly, for if this man gives alms or performs a kindness, the Holy One, blessed be He, rewards him in this world so that he will have no portion in the World to Come. This is why Onkelos translated the verse: "And He repays them that hate Him to their face" (Devarim 7:10) as 'And He repays them that Hate him in this world.' Thus, the righteous person, who always experiences pain, is beloved by the Holy One, blessed be He. This is true only if he is found to have committed no sin that merits punishment.

29. הָכָא אִית לְאִסְתַּכָּלָא בְּכַמָּה סִטְרִין, בְּכַמָּה סִטְרִין, חַד, דְּהָא חָמִינָן דִּשְׁכִינְתָּא לָא שַׁרְיָא בַּאֲתַר עֲצִיבוּ, אֶלָּא בַּאֲתַר דְּאִית בֵּיהּ חֶדְוָה, אִי חֶדְוָה לֵית בֵּיהּ, לָא שַׁרְיָא שְׁכִינְתָּא בְּהַהוּא אֲתַר, כד"א וְעַתָּה קְחוּ לִי מְנַגֵּן וְהָיָה כְּנַגֵּן הַמְנַגֵּן וַתְּהִי עָלָיו רוּחַ אֱלֹהִים, דְּהָא שְׁכִינְתָּא, וַדַּאי לָא שַׁרְיָא בַּאֲתַר עֲצִיבוּ. מְנָלָן, מִיַּעֲקֹב, דִּבְגִין דַּהֲוָה עָצִיב עֲלֵיהּ דְּיוֹסֵף, אִסְתַּלְקַת שְׁכִינְתָּא מִנֵּיהּ, כֵּיוָן דְּאָתָא לֵיהּ חֶדְוָה דִּבְשׂוֹרָה דְיוֹסֵף, מִיָּד וַתְּחִי רוּחַ יַעֲקֹב אֲבִיהֶם. הָכָא בְּהַאי זַכָּאָה דְּאִתָּבַר, כֵּיוָן דְּאִיהוּ חַלָּשָׁא. וְאִתְּבַר בְּמַכְאוֹבִין, אָן הוּא חֶדְוָה, דְּהָא

אִיהוּ בַּעֲצִיבוּ, וְלֵית עִמֵּיהּ חֶדְוָה כְּלָל.

29. There are several aspects to this matter. First, we see that the Shechinah does not dwell in a place of sorrow, but only in a place of joy. If a place has no joy, the Shechinah will not abide there. This is echoed in the verse: "But now bring me a minstrel. And it came to pass, when the minstrel played, that the hand of Hashem came upon him" (II Melachim 3:15); for assuredly the Shechinah does not dwell in a place of sadness. From where do we derive this principle? We learn this from Jacob, from whom the Shechinah departed during the time he mourned Joseph. When joy came upon him with the good news about Joseph, immediately, "the spirit of Jacob their father revived" (Beresheet 45:27). THERE IS A MYSTERY HERE, for where is joy in a Righteous man who is broken by troubles and is weak and suffering? Surely he must be saddened with no joy at all.

30. וְחַד, דְּהָא חָמִינָן, כַּמָּה רְחִימִין הֲווֹ צַדִּיקַיָּא קַמֵּי קוּדְשָׁא בְּרִיךְ הוּא, וְלָא אִתְּבְרוּ בְּמַרְעִין, וְלָא בְּמַכְאוֹבִין, וְלָא אִתְחַלַּשׁ גּוּפָא דִּלְהוֹן לְעָלְמִין, אַמַּאי לָאו אִלֵּין כְּאִלֵּין, דְּאִלֵּין אִתְּבְרוּ, וְאִלֵּין קַיְימֵי בְּגוּפַיְיהוּ, כִּדְקָא יָאוּת.

30. WE MUST LOOK into another matter, for many just men who are beloved of the Holy One, blessed be He, do not suffer bodily pain or diseases; their bodies never weaken. Why are they not as the other righteous men? WHY IS THERE A DIFFERENCE BETWEEN those who were physically broken and those who were healthy?

31. וְאִ״ת, דְּהָא אִלֵּין דְּקַיְימוּ בְּקִיּוּמָא כִּדְקָא יָאוּת, בְּגִין דְּאִינּוּן צַדִּיקֵי בְּנֵי צַדִּיקֵי אִינְהוּ, כְּמָה דְּאוֹקְמוּהָ, וְאִלֵּין אָחֳרָנִין, צַדִּיקֵי, וְלָאו בְּנֵי צַדִּיקֵי, הָא קָא חָמִינָן, צַדִּיקֵי בְּנֵי צַדִּיקֵי, דְּהָא אֲבוֹי דְּדִין זַכָּאָה בַּר זַכָּאָה, וְאִיהוּ זַכָּאָה, אַמַּאי אִתְּבַר גּוּפֵיהּ בְּמַכְאוֹבִין, וְכָל יוֹמוֹי בְּצַעֲרָא.

31. It is said that those who live well are righteous, the children of righteous men, as has already been explained, while the others, WHOSE BODIES WERE CRUSHED, are righteous, but are not children of righteous men. Yet we see Righteous men whose fathers are righteous, EVEN whose fathers were of righteous men, YET THEY STILL SUFFER MUCH PAIN. Why do they suffer bodily pain and spend their days in grief?

32. אֶלָּא הָכָא רָזָא אִיהוּ, דְּהָא כָּל עוֹבָדוֹי דְּקוּדְשָׁא בְּרִיךְ הוּא בְּקְשׁוֹט וּזְכוּ כִּי פֹעַל אָדָם יְשַׁלֶּם לוֹ וּכְאֹרַח אִישׁ יַמְצִיאֶנּוּ. אַשְׁכַּחְנָא בְּסִפְרֵי קַדְמָאֵי, רָזָא חָדָא, וּלְגַבֵּיהּ רָזָא אָחֳרָא, חַד דְּאִיהוּ תְּרֵין, דְּהָא אִית זִמְנִין, דְּסִיהֲרָא אִיהִי בִּפְגִימוּ, וְשַׁרְיָא בְּדִינָא, וְשִׁמְשָׁא לָא אִשְׁתַּכַּח גַּבָּהּ, וּבְכָל זִמְנָא וּבְכָל שַׁעְתָּא, אִית לָהּ לַאֲפָקָא נִשְׁמָתִין בִּבְנֵי נָשָׁא, כְּמָה דְּלָקְטָא בְּקַדְמֵיתָא, וַאֲפֵיקַת לוֹן הַשְׁתָּא, בְּזִמְנָא דְּאִיהִי קָיְימָא בְּדִינָא, הַאי מַאן דְּנָקִיט לָהּ בְּהַהוּא זִמְנָא, לֶיהֱוֵי תָּדִיר בִּגְרִיעוּתָא, וּמִסְכֵּנוּתָא אָזְלָא לְגַבֵּיהּ, וְאִתְּבַר תָּדִיר בְּדִינָא, כָּל יוֹמוֹי דְבַר נָשׁ, בֵּין חַיָּיבָא, בֵּין זַכָּאָה, בַּר דִּצְלוֹתָא, בָּטֵיל כָּל גִּזְרֵי דִינִין, וְיָכֵיל לְסַלְקָא בִּצְלוֹתָא.

32. There is a mystery here, for all the works of the Holy One, blessed be He, are according to Truth and Justice. "For the work of a man shall he pay back to him, and according to his ways will he cause to befall every man" (Iyov 34:11). I found in ancient books a mystery, and another mystery REVEALED within it – thus, one mystery which is two SECRETS. There are times when the moon, THE NUKVA, is defective and under Judgment, and the sun, ZEIR ANPIN, is hidden from her. She releases souls to give to men, which she first gathered FROM ZEIR ANPIN AT ANY TIME. THEREFORE, she releases THOSE SOULS, EVEN AT A DEFECTIVE TIME, when she is under Judgment. Whoever receives such a soul will always be in want and poverty, ever broken under Judgment and throughout all his life – be he just or wicked. Only prayer annuls all judgmental sentences. A MAN can avert them through prayer.

33. וְהַהוּא זִמְנָא דְּקָיְימָא הַהוּא דַּרְגָּא בִּשְׁלִימוּ, וְהַהוּא נָהָר דְּנָגֵיד וְנָפֵיק אִשְׁתַּמַּשׁ בָּהּ, כְּדֵין הַהוּא נִשְׁמָתָא, דְּנָפְקַת וְאִתְדַּבְּקַת בֵּיהּ בְּהַהוּא בַּר נָשׁ, הַהוּא בַּר נָשׁ אִשְׁתַּלֵּים בְּכֹלָּא, בְּעוֹתְרָא, בִּבְנִין, בִּשְׁלִימוּ דְגוּפָא.

33. When that grade, THE NUKVA, is complete, and the river which flows and comes out FROM EDEN, YESOD, unites with her, the soul that she releases cleaves to man. He is complete in all – in riches, children and a healthy body.

34. וְכֹלָּא בְּגִין הַהוּא מַזָּלָא, דְּנָגֵיד וְנָפֵיק, וְאִתְחַבַּר בְּהַהוּא דַּרְגָּא, לְאִשְׁתַּלְמָא בֵּיהּ, וּלְאִתְבָּרְכָא מִנֵּיהּ, וְעַל דָּא, כֹּלָּא בְּמַזָּלָא תַּלְיָא מִלְּתָא. וְעַל דָּא תָּנִינָן, בָּנֵי חַיֵּי וּמְזוֹנֵי, לָאו בִּזְכוּתָא תַּלְיָא מִלְּתָא, אֶלָּא בְּמַזָּלָא תַּלְיָא מִלְּתָא, דְּהָא בִּזְכוּתָא לָאו אִיהוּ, אֶלָּא עַד דְּאִתְמַלְיָא וְאִתְנְהֵיר מִן מַזָּלָא.

34. All this depends upon *mazal* ('constellation, luck'), YESOD, which is drawn to and attached to that grade, THE NUKVA, for Her to be perfected and blessed by it. Therefore, all depends upon Mazal. We have learned that "children, life and livelihood do not depend upon merit but upon mazal." There is no merit until THE NUKVA is filled and shines from mazal, WHICH IS YESOD.

35. וּבְגִין כָּךְ, כָּל אִינוּן דְּאִתְבָּרוּ בְּהַאי עַלְמָא, וְאִינוּן זַכָּאֵי קְשׁוֹט, כֻּלְּהוּ אִתְבָּרוּ בְּהַאי עַלְמָא, וְאִתְדָּנוּ בְּדִינָא, מ״ט, בְּגִין דְּהַהִיא נַפְשָׁא גָּרְמָא לְהוּ, וְעַל דָּא, חָיֵיס עֲלַיְיהוּ קוּדְשָׁא בְּרִיךְ הוּא לְעַלְמָא דְּאָתֵי.

35. Therefore, all those who are sentenced according to justice and crushed in this world, yet are also truly righteous, suffer by reason of the soul (Nefesh) THAT THEY RECEIVED FROM THE NUKVA WHILE SHE WAS DEFECTIVE. Therefore, the Holy One, blessed be He, has compassion for them in the World to Come.

36. רִבִּי אֶלְעָזָר אָמַר, כָּל מַה דְּעָבֵיד קוּדְשָׁא בְּרִיךְ הוּא, בְּדִינָא אִיהוּ, בְּגִין לְדַכָּאָה לְהַהִיא נַפְשָׁא, לְאַיְיתָאָה לָהּ לְעַלְמָא דְּאָתֵי, דְּכָל עוֹבָדוֹי דְּקוּדְשָׁא בְּרִיךְ הוּא, אִינוּן בְּדִינָא וּקְשׁוֹט, וּבְגִין לְאַעֲבָרָא מִנֵּיהּ הַהוּא זוּהֲמָא, דְּקַבֵּילַת בְּהַאי עַלְמָא, וְע״ד אִתָּבַר הַהוּא גּוּפָא וְאִתְדְּכִיאַת נַפְשָׁא, וּבְגִין כָּךְ, קוּדְשָׁא בְּרִיךְ הוּא עָבֵיד לְהַהוּא זַכָּאָה, דְּיִסְבּוֹל יִסּוּרִין וּמַכְאוֹבִין בְּהַאי עַלְמָא, וְיִתְנְקֵי מִכֹּלָּא וְיִזְכֶּה לְחַיֵּי עָלְמָא. וְעַל

דָּא כְּתִיב יי׳ צַדִּיק יִבְחָן וַדַּאי וְהָא אִתְּמָר.

36. Rabbi Elazar said that the Holy One, blessed be He, does everything according to Justice. IF HE BRINGS SUFFERING ON A RIGHTEOUS MAN, HE DOES SO to purify that soul (Nefesh) and bring it to the World to Come, for all the deeds of the Holy One, blessed be He, are true and just. To remove from the soul the filth it accumulated in this world, the body is crushed and the soul cleansed. Therefore the Holy One, blessed be He, brings pain to the just man, so that he will be cleansed from all sins and thereby merit life in the World to Come. As it is written: "Hashem tries the righteous" (Tehilim 11:5), as we have already learned.

4. "Only he shall not go in to the veil"

A Synopsis

Rabbi Shimon discourses on the spiritual significance of, and the benefits enjoyed by, those who receive their souls from the realm of Malchut when she is defective.

The Relevance of this Passage

The energy arising out of these verses helps reduce the pain and suffering that we endure as a result of negative deeds in present and past lives. Meditating to share this energy with others helps to reduce their pain and suffering as well. The spiritual benefits associated with the Moon's positive aspects are aroused in our life, and the negative influences arising from the Moon are averted.

37. רָבִּי שִׁמְעוֹן פְּתַח, אַךְ אֶל הַפָּרֹכֶת לֹא יָבֹא וְאֶל הַמִּזְבֵּחַ לֹא יִגָּשׁ כִּי מוּם בּוֹ וְלֹא יְחַלֵּל אֶת מִקְדָּשַׁי כִּי אֲנִי יי׳ מְקַדְּשׁוֹ. אַךְ אֶל הַפָּרֹכֶת לֹא יָבֹא. תָּא חֲזֵי, בְּהַהִיא שַׁעְתָּא דְּהַהוּא נָהָר דְּנָגֵיד וְנָפֵיק אַפֵּיק כָּל אִינוּן נִשְׁמָתִין, וְאִתְעֲבָרַת נוּקְבָא, כֻּלְּהוּ קַיְימִין לְגוֹ, בְּקוֹרְטָא דִלְגוֹ בְּסִיטוֹ קוֹרְטָא.

37. Rabbi Shimon opened the discussion with the verse: "Only he shall not go in to the veil, nor come near the to altar, because he has a blemish; that he profane not My holy places: for I, Hashem, do sanctify them" (Vayikra 21:23). "He shall not go in to the veil." Come and behold: at the time the river is flowing and comes out FROM EDEN, WHICH IS YESOD, and issues the souls TO THE NUKVA, the Nukva conceives WITH THEM. And they all abide WITHIN HER in a room within a room, where the walls are covered with wallpaper or carpets.

38. וְכַד סִיהֲרָא אִתְפְּגִים, בְּהַהוּא סִטְרָא דְּחִוְיָא בִישָׁא, כְּדֵין כָּל אִינוּן נִשְׁמָתִין דְּנָפְקִין, אַף עַל גָּב דְּכֻלְּהוּ דַּכְיָין, וְכֻלְּהוּ קַדִּישִׁין, הוֹאִיל וְנָפְלוּ בִּפְגִימוּ, בְּכָל אִינוּן אַתְרֵי דְּמָטוּ אִינוּן נִשְׁמָתִין, כֻּלְּהוּ אִתָּבְרוּ, וְאִתְפְּגִימוּ בְּכַמָּה צַעֲרִין, בְּכַמָּה כְּאֵבִין, וְאִילֵּין אִינוּן דְּאִתְרְעֵי בְּהוֹ קוּדְשָׁא בְּרִיךְ הוּא, לְבָתַר דְּאִתָּבְרוּ, וְאַף עַל גָּב דְּנִשְׁמָתִין בַּעֲצִיבוּ, וְלָא בְּחֶדְוָון.

38. When the moon is rendered defective by the same aspect of the evil serpent, all the souls that are issued AT THAT TIME, although they were all pure and sacred, since they emerged at a defective time, THE BODIES WITH WHICH the Souls came are crushed, and suffer pains and afflictions. The Holy One, blessed be He, cares for AND LOVES those who are broken, although their souls are sad instead of joyous.

39. רָזָא דְמִלָּה שַׁרְיָין כְּגַוְונָא דִלְעֵילָא, גוּפָא אִתְפְּגִים, וְנִשְׁמָתָא לְגוֹ כְּגַוְונָא דִלְעֵילָא, וְדָא כְּגַוְונָא דְּדָא, וּבְגִין כָּךְ, אִלֵּין אִינּוּן דְּבַעְיָין לְחַדְתוּתֵי בְּחַדְתוּתָא דְסִיהֲרָא, וְעַל אִלֵּין כְּתִיב וְהָיָה מִדֵּי חֹדֶשׁ בְּחָדְשׁוֹ וּמִדֵּי שַׁבָּת בְּשַׁבַּתּוֹ יָבֹא כָל בָּשָׂר לְהִשְׁתַּחֲוֹת לְפָנַי אָמַר יי׳, כָּל בָּשָׂר וַדַּאי, דְּאִלֵּין יִתְחַדְתוּן בְּכֹלָּא. וּבָעְיָין לְחַדְתוּתֵי בְּחַדְתוּתָא דְסִיהֲרָא.

39. The secret is that they remain as above IN THE NUKVA. When the body is flawed, the soul inside remains the same AS IN THE NUKVA. BECAUSE THE SOUL RESIDED WITHIN THE FLAWED NUKVA, IT RESIDES NOW WITHIN THE FLAWED BODY. The one state resembles the other. Therefore, they are renewed like the moon, as it is written: "And it shall come to pass, that every new moon, and every Shabbat, shall all flesh come to bow down to the ground before Me, says Hashem" (Yeshayah 66:23). "All flesh" assuredly, for they are in need of renewal along with the moon.

40. וְאִלֵּין אִינּוּן בְּשׁוּתָּפוּתָא חָדָא בְּסִיהֲרָא, פְּגִימִין בְּהַהוּא פְּגִימוּ דִילָהּ, וּבְגִין כָּךְ אִיהִי שַׁרְיָא בְּגַוַּויְיהוּ תָּדִיר, דְּלָא שָׁבְקָא לוֹן, כד״א וְאֶת דַּכָּא וּשְׁפַל רוּחַ, וּכְתִיב קָרוֹב יי׳ לְנִשְׁבְּרֵי לֵב, לְאִינּוּן דְּסָבְלֵי עִם סִיהֲרָא הַהוּא פְּגִימוּ, אִינּוּן קְרֵיבִין לָהּ תָּדִיר, וְעַל דָּא לְהַחֲיוֹת לֵב נִדְכָּאִים, בְּאִינּוּן חַיִּים דְּאַתְיָין לָהּ לְאִתְחַדְתָא, יְהֵא לוֹן חוּלָקְהוֹן, אִינּוּן דְּסָבְלֵי עִמָּהּ, יִתְחַדְתוּן עִמָּהּ.

40. THOSE RIGHTEOUS are the constant companions of the moon, THE NUKVA, and have the identical defects. She therefore dwells always within them and never leaves them, as it is written: "him also that is of a contrite and humble spirit" (Yeshayah 57:15) and, "Hashem is near to them who are of a broken heart" (Tehilim 34:19) – THAT IS, to those who suffered from the same defect as the moon, those who are always near her. "And He saves such as are of a contrite spirit" (Ibid.), by giving them a portion of the life flowing INTO THE NUKVA for renewal, because they who suffered with her shall also be renewed with her.

41. וְאִלֵּין אִקְרוּן יִסּוּרִין שֶׁל אַהֲבָה, שֶׁל אַהֲבָה אִינוּן, וְלָא מִנֵּיהּ דְּהַהוּא בַּר נָשׁ. שֶׁל אַהֲבָה אִינוּן, דְּאִתְפַּגֵּם נְהוֹרָא שֶׁל אַהֲבָה זוּטָא, דְּאִתְדַּחְיָיא מֵאַהֲבָה רַבָּה. בְּגִין כָּךְ אִלֵּין אִינוּן חֲבֵרִים מְשׁוּתָּפִים בַּהֲדָהּ. זַכָּאָה חוּלַקְהוֹן בְּעָלְמָא דֵּין, וּבְעָלְמָא דְאָתֵי, דְּאִינוּן זָכוּ לְהַאי, לְמֶהֱוֵי חֲבֵרִים בַּהֲדָהּ, עֲלַיְיהוּ כְּתִיב לְמַעַן אַחַי וְרֵעָי וגו'.

41. Those DEFECTS FROM WHICH THE RIGHTEOUS SUFFER are called 'sufferings of love', because they are caused by love and not by the man himself. They are of love because the light of the smaller love was impaired when rejected by the greater love. Therefore, THE RIGHTEOUS are her companions and share HER FLAW. Happy is their portion in this world and in the World to Come, for they merited to be her friends, as it is written of them: "For my brethren and companions' sakes..." (Tehilim 122:8).

5. "Behold, My servant shall prosper"

A Synopsis

In this complex and difficult section, an aspect of the relationship between Zeir Anpin [the upper world] and Malchut [our Lower World] at the time of the latter's creation is revealed, further explaining why the wicked often seem to prosper while the good suffer. The mystery of the title verse is discussed, revealing that at the end of the period of Correction, faith shall be rekindled in men, and Malchut – presented here as the moon – will once more be warmed and illuminated by the Light. There follows a detailed analysis of Torah verses. In question and answer form, the hidden meaning of the verses is revealed as a parable of the yearning for union by opposites, such as male and female. This is one of the Zohar's major themes. Through the story of Joseph and Jacob, we are shown that male and female are meant to be together as one: "For blessings abide only where male and female are united." Malchut is then described with the same attributes as the male: He is wise, for example, whereas She is wisdom; He is mighty, She is might; He is a King; She is a Kingdom. The male is then described with the same attributes as the Nukva, in a profound exposition of apparent duality that governs material creation. Finally, by suggesting a subtle link between the violation of kosher laws regarding the consumption of living flesh and the illicit yearning of one sex for the other, Rabbi Yehuda resolves a discussion about the meaning of the term "an evil report."

The Relevance of this Passage

The mystical power of these words enriches and deepens our marital relationships, while also helping the unmarried to merit the appearance of their true soulmate. It further arouses the Light of the Upper World to radiate in our physical existence. This Light also helps cleanse prior negative sexual experiences and thoughts.

42. פְּתַח וַאֲמַר, הִנֵּה יַשְׂכִּיל עַבְדִּי יָרוּם וְנִשָּׂא וְגָבַהּ מְאֹד. זַכָּאָה חוּלָקְהוֹן דְּצַדִּיקַיָּיא, דְּקוּדְשָׁא בְּרִיךְ הוּא גָּלֵי לוֹן אָרְחֵי דְאוֹרַיְיתָא, לְמֵהַךְ בְּהוֹ. תָּא חֲזֵי, הַאי קְרָא רָזָא עִלָּאָה אִיהוּ, הִנֵּה יַשְׂכִּיל עַבְדִּי וְאוֹקְמוּהָ. אֲבָל תָּא חֲזֵי, כַּד בְּרָא קוּדְשָׁא בְּרִיךְ הוּא עַלְמָא, עֲבַד לָהּ לְסִיהֲרָא, וְאַזְעֵר לָהּ נְהוֹרָהָא, דְּהָא לֵית לָהּ מִגַּרְמָהּ כְּלוּם, וּבְגִין דְּאַזְעֵירַת גַּרְמָהּ, אִתְנַהֲרָא בְּגִין שִׁמְשָׁא, וּבְתוֹקְפָא דִּנְהוֹרִין עִלָּאִין.

42. He opened the discussion with the verse: "Behold, My servant shall prosper, he shall be exalted and extolled, and be very high" (Yeshayah 52:13). Happy is the portion of the righteous, to whom the Holy One, blessed be He, revealed the ways of the Torah, so they may follow them. Come and behold: the verse, "Behold, my servant shall prosper," contains a supernal mystery, which has already been explained. Yet come and behold: when the Holy One, blessed be He, created the universe – THE SECRET OF ZEIR ANPIN AND NUKVA – He made the moon AND ENDOWED HER WITH THE SAME STATURE AS THAT OF ZEIR ANPIN. LATER, He decreased her lights in such a way that she had nothing of her own, SAVE WHAT SHE RECEIVED FROM ZEIR ANPIN. Because she made herself small, she shone from the sun, SIGNIFED BY ZEIR ANPIN, by the power of the Supernal Lights IN IT.

43. וּבִזְמְנָא דַּהֲוָה בֵּי מַקְדְּשָׁא קַיָּים, יִשְׂרָאֵל הֲווֹ מִשְׁתַּדְּלִין בְּקוּרְבָּנִין וְעִלָּוָון, וּפוּלְחָנִין דַּהֲווֹ עָבְדִין, כַּהֲנֵי וְלֵיוָאֵי וְיִשְׂרְאֵלֵי, בְּגִין לְקַשְׁרָא קִשְׁרִין וּלְאַנְהָרָא נְהוֹרִין.

43. While the Temple existed, Yisrael diligently proceeded with sacrifices, offerings and rituals performed by the priests, Levites and the children of Yisrael, creating unification and causing the lights to shine WITHIN THE NUKVA.

44. וּלְבָתַר דְּאִתְחָרַב בֵּי מַקְדְּשָׁא, אִתְחַשַּׁךְ נְהוֹרָא, וְסִיהֲרָא לָא אִתְנְהֵירַת מִן שִׁמְשָׁא, וְשִׁמְשָׁא אִסְתַּלַּק מִנָּהּ, וְלָא אִתְנְהָרָא, וְלֵית לָךְ יוֹמָא, דְּלָא שָׁלְטָא בֵּיהּ לְוָוטִין, וְצַעֲרִין וּכְאֵבִין, כְּמָה דְאִתְּמָר.

44. After the Temple was destroyed, the light darkened and the moon, THE NUKVA, no longer shone from the sun, ZEIR ANPIN. The sun withdrew from her and did not shine. Therefore, as we have learned, no day passes without curses, sorrow, and pain.

45. וּבְהַהוּא זִמְנָא, דְּמְטֵי זִמְנָא דְּסִיהֲרָא לְאִתְנַהֲרָא, מַה כְּתִיב, הִנֵּה יַשְׂכִּיל עַבְדִּי, עֲלֵיהּ דְּסִיהֲרָא אִתְּמָר, הִנֵּה יַשְׂכִּיל עַבְדִּי, דָּא הוּא רָזָא דִּמְהֵימְנוּתָא, הִנֵּה יַשְׂכִּיל: דְּאִתְּעַר אִתְעֲרוּתָא לְעֵילָא, כְּמַאן דְּאָרַח רֵיחָא, וְאָתֵי לְאִתְעָרָא וּלְאִסְתַּכָּלָא.

45. When the time comes for the moon to shine WITH HER OWN STRENGTH, AT THE END OF CORRECTION, then it is written: "Behold, My servant shall prosper," which is an allusion to the moon. "Behold, My servant shall prosper," refers to the secret of the faith, WHICH IS THE NUKVA. The words, "shall prosper," refer to the Supernal Awakening – WHICH WILL RESEMBLE a man who smells an odor and becomes alert and attentive.

46. יָרוּם: מִסִּטְרָא דִנְהוֹרָא עִלָּאָה דְּכָל נְהוֹרִין. יָרוּם: כד"א וְלָכֵן יָרוּם לְרַחֶמְכֶם. וְנִשָּׂא: מִסִּטְרָא דְאַבְרָהָם. וְגָבַהּ: מִסִּטְרָא דְיִצְחָק. מְאֹד: מִסִּטְרָא דְיַעֲקֹב. וְאַף עַל גַּב דְּאוֹקְמוּהָ, וְכֹלָּא חַד בְּרָזָא דְחָכְמְתָא.

46. "He shall be exalted," means that THE NUKVA SHALL BE FILLED from that facet of the light that is superior to all the lights, INDICATING KETER. "He shall be exalted" – as in, "and therefore will He be exalted, that He may have mercy upon you" (Yeshayah 30:18) – REFERS TO THE LIGHT OF KETER; "and extolled," on the side of Abraham, SIGNIFIES CHESED. "And be high," on the side of Isaac, MEANS GVURAH, while "very," on the side of Jacob, IS TIFERET. THIS MEANS THAT THE NUKVA WILL THUS BE FILLED BY ALL THESE GRADES. And although this has already been explained DIFFERENTLY, all is one in the secret of wisdom.

47. וּבְהַהוּא זִמְנָא, יִתְעַר קוּדְשָׁא בְּרִיךְ הוּא אִתְעֲרוּתָא עִלָּאָה, לְאַנְהָרָא לָהּ לְסִיהֲרָא כִּדְקָא יָאוּת, כד"א וְהָיָה אוֹר הַלְּבָנָה כְּאוֹר הַחַמָּה וְאוֹר הַחַמָּה יִהְיֶה שִׁבְעָתַיִם כְּאוֹר שִׁבְעַת הַיָּמִים. וּבְגִין כָּךְ יִתּוֹסַף בָּהּ רוּחַ עִלָּאָה, וּבְגִין כָּךְ יִתְעָרוּן כְּדֵין כָּל אִינוּן מֵיתַיָּא דְּאִינוּן גּוֹ עַפְרָא.

47. At that time, the Holy One, blessed be He, will intensify energy above so as to shine well upon the moon, THE NUKVA. As it is written: "Moreover the light of the moon shall be as the light of the sun, and the light of the sun shall be sevenfold, as the light of seven days" (Yeshayah 30:26). Thus will Supernal Light be added to her own. Then all the dead, BURIED in the dust, will be stirred INTO LIFE.

48. וְדָא הוּא עַבְדִּי, רָזָא דְמַפְתְּחָן דְּמָארֵיהּ בִּידֵיהּ, כד"א וַיֹּאמֶר

אַבְרָהָם אֶל עַבְדּוֹ, דָּא סִיהֲרָא כְּמָה דְאִתְּמָר, מטטרו״ן דְּאִיהוּ עָבַד שְׁלִיחָא דְּמָארֵיהּ.

48. He calls him "servant" (masculine form), THOUGH THIS ALLUDES TO THE NUKVA, for the secret path to his Master's keys is in his hand. THUS, THE PERFECTION OF THE NUKVA IS MADE KNOWN THROUGH HIM, HER MESSENGER. The same applies to the verse: "And Abraham said to the...servant," (Beresheet 24:2) who is the moon, NAMELY THE NUKVA, as we have learned. AND SHE IS REVEALED THROUGH Metatron, the servant messenger of his Master. THEREFORE THE WORD "SERVANT" WAS USED IN BOTH PLACES.

49. זְקַן בֵּיתוֹ, כד״א נַעַר הָיִיתִי גַּם זָקַנְתִּי. הַמּוֹשֵׁל בְּכָל אֲשֶׁר לוֹ, בְּגִין דְּכָל גְּוָונִין אִתְחֲזוּן בֵּיהּ, יָרוֹ״ק, וְחִוָּו״ר, וְסוּמָ״ק.

49. "The eldest of his house" (Beresheet 24:2), REFERS TO METATRON, WHO IS CALLED 'OLD', as in "I have been young, and now am old" (Tehilim 37:25). THE MINISTER OF THE WORLD 'WHO IS METATRON?' SAID THIS PHRASE. "That ruled over all that he had" (Beresheet 24:2), as all the colors: green, white, and red, are reflected in him.

50. שִׂים נָא יָדְךָ תַּחַת יְרֵכִי, דָּא הוּא צַדִּיק, רָזָא דְמִלָּה, קִיּוּמָא דְעַלְמָא, דְּהָא כְּדֵין, הַאי עֶבֶד מְמַנָּא בְּרָזָא עִלָּאָה, לַאֲחָיָיא לוֹן לְדַיְירֵי עַפְרָא, וְיִתְעֲבֵיד שְׁלִיחָא בְּרוּחָא דִלְעֵילָא, וְלַאֲתָבָא רוּחִין וְנִשְׁמָתִין לְאַתְרַיְיהוּ, לְאִינוּן גּוּפֵי דְּאִתְבָּלוּ וְאִתְרְקָבוּ תְּחוֹת עַפְרָא.

50. "Put, I pray you, your hand under my thigh" (Ibid.) refers to the Righteous, NAMELY, TO YESOD. Since he is the existence AND LIFE of the world WHEN HE HOLDS ON TO YESOD, this servant is appointed to bring life to the dwellers of the dust. And he becomes perfected through the supernal spirit to return spirits and souls to their places, in the decayed and putrefied cadavers underneath the ground.

51. וְאַשְׁבִּיעֲךָ בַּיי׳ אֱלֹהֵי הַשָּׁמַיִם. וְאַשְׁבִּיעֲךָ, מַאי וְאַשְׁבִּיעֲךָ. לְאִתְלַבְּשָׁא בְּרָזָא דִּשְׁבַע נְהוֹרִין עִלָּאִין, דְּאִינּוּן רָזָא דִשְׁלִימוּ עִלָּאָה.

אֲשֶׁר לֹא תִקַּח אִשָּׁה דָּא הוּא גוּפָא דִּתְחוֹת עַפְרָא, דְּאִית לֵיהּ קִיּוּמָא לַאֲקָמָא מֵעַפְרָא, דְּכָל אִינוּן דְּאִתְקְבָרוּ בָהּ, וְזָכוּ לְאִתְקְבָרָא בְּאַרְעָא דְיִשְׂרָאֵל, אִינוּן יִתְעָרוּן בְּקַדְמֵיתָא, כְּמָה דְאוּקִימְנָא, דִּכְתִיב יִחְיוּ מֵתֶיךָ, בְּקַדְמֵיתָא אִלֵּין מֵתִין דְּאַרְעָא דְיִשְׂרָאֵל. נְבֵלָתִי יְקוּמוּן, אִינוּן מֵתִין דִּשְׁאָר אַרְעָאן. וְעַל דָּא, לְאִינוּן גּוּפֵיהוֹן דְּיִשְׂרָאֵל דְּאִתְקְבָרוּ תַּמָּן, וְלָא לְגוּפֵי דִּשְׁאָר עַמִּין עע״ז, דְּאִסְתָּאֲבָא אַרְעָא מִינַּיְיהוּ.

51. "And I will make you swear by Hashem, the Elohim of heaven" (Beresheet 24:3). HE SAID THAT IT IS WRITTEN: "And I will make you swear." What is the meaning of, "I will make you swear"? HE ANSWERS THAT IT MEANS he will be clothed in the secret of the seven Supernal Lights – CHESED, GVURAH, TIFERET, NETZACH, HOD, YESOD AND MALCHUT – FOR they are the secret of supernal perfection. ACCORDING TO HIS EXPLANATION, "SWEAR," DERIVED FROM THE ROOT *SHIN BET AYIN,* IS DERIVED FROM 'SEVEN' (Heb. *sheva*: Shin-Bet-Ayin). "That you shall not take a wife," refers to the body underneath the ground, IN THE GRAVE, which now rises from the dust AND IS CALLED A 'WIFE'. All those who were buried and deserved to be interred in the land of Yisrael shall be the first to rise to life, as has been explained in relation to the verse: "The dead men of your people shall live" (Yeshayah 26:19), referring to the dead in the land of Yisrael. THEN, "my dead body shall arise" (Ibid.), meaning the dead outside Yisrael. For all that, only the bodies of Yisrael, buried IN THE LAND OF YISRAEL, shall rise, but not bodies from other nations, which defile the land.

52. וְעַל דָּא אֲשֶׁר לֹא תִקַּח אִשָּׁה לִבְנִי. מַאי לִבְנִי. דְּכָל נִשְׁמָתִין דְּעַלְמָא דְּנָפְקֵי מֵהַהוּא נָהָר דְּנָגֵיד וְנָפֵיק, אִינוּן בְּנִין לְקוּדְשָׁא בְּרִיךְ הוּא, וְעַל דָּא אֲשֶׁר לֹא תִקַּח אִשָּׁה: דָּא גוּפָא. לִבְנִי: דָּא נִשְׁמָתָא. מִבְּנוֹת הַכְּנַעֲנִי: אִלֵּין גּוּפִין דְּעַמִּין עע״ז, דְּזַמִּין קוּדְשָׁא בְּרִיךְ הוּא לְנַעֲרָא לוֹן מֵאַרְעָא קַדִּישָׁא, כד״א וְיִנָּעֲרוּ רְשָׁעִים מִמֶּנָּה. כְּמַאן דִּמְנַעֵר טַלִּיתָא מִזּוּהֲמָא דִילָהּ.

52. Therefore, in the verse: "That you shall not take a wife to my son," what is meant by "my son"? HE ANSWERS THAT all the souls in the world that come from the river which flows out FROM EDEN, WHICH IS YESOD, are the children of the Holy One, blessed be He. Therefore, "that you shall not take a wife," means a body; "to my son" refers to the soul; "of the daughters of the Canaan," are the bodies of the heathen nations, which the Holy One, blessed be He, will shake out of the Holy Land. As it is written: "That the wicked might be shaken out of it" (Iyov 38:13), as dirt is shaken out of a garment.

53. כִּי אֶל אַרְצִי וְאֶל מוֹלַדְתִּי תֵּלֵךְ. אַרְצִי: דָּא הִיא אַרְעָא קַדִּישָׁא, דְּאִיהוּ קַדְמָאָה לְכָל שְׁאָר אַרְעִין, כְּמָה דְּאִתְּמָר. וְע״ד כִּי אֶל אַרְצִי וְאֶל מוֹלַדְתִּי, כֵּיוָן דַּאֲמַר אֶל אַרְצִי, מַהוּ וְאֶל מוֹלַדְתִּי, אֶלָּא אֶל אַרְצִי, כְּמָה דְאִתְּמָר, וְאֶל מוֹלַדְתִּי אִלֵּין אִינּוּן יִשְׂרָאֵל.

53. "But you shall go to my country, and to my kindred" (Beresheet 24:4). In this verse, "my country" is the Holy Land, which precedes all other countries, as we have learned. Of the verse, "But you shall go to my country, and to my kindred," HE ASKS: WHY REPEAT "my kindred" after saying, "my country?" HE ANSWERS: "My country" is THE HOLY LAND, as we said and "my kindred" are Yisrael!

54. תָּא חֲזֵי, מַה כְּתִיב, וַיִּקַּח הָעֶבֶד, כְּמָה דְאִתְּמָר. עֲשָׂרָה גְּמַלִּים: אִלֵּין אִינּוּן עֲשָׂרָה דַּרְגִּין, דְּהַאי עֶבֶד שָׁלְטָא עֲלַיְיהוּ, כְּגַוְונָא דִלְעֵילָּא. מִגְּמַלֵּי אֲדֹנָיו: דְּאִינּוּן כְּהַהוּא גַּוְונָא מַמָּשׁ, כְּמָה דְאִתְּמָר, וְהַאי עֶבֶד שָׁלְטָא וְאִתְתַּקַּן בְּהוֹ.

54. It is written: "And the servant took..." (Beresheet 24:10). As we have learned, THIS IS A REFERENCE TO METATRON; "ten camels" are the ten grades, which the servant governs. They are a likeness to the above, LIKE THE GRADES OF ATZILUT. "Of the camels of his master" means they bear a likeness to his master's camels – THAT IS, THE GRADES OF THE NUKVA OF ATZILUT, HIS MASTER, as we have learned. And this servant rules over them and is established through them.

55. וְכָל טוּב אֲדֹנָיו בְּיָדוֹ: כָּל הַהוּא טִיבוּ רֵיחִין עִלָּאִין, דְּנָפְקֵי מִגּוֹ אִינּוּן נְהוֹרִין וּבוֹצִינִין עִלָּאִין. וְכָל טוּב אֲדוֹנָיו, הַהוּא שִׁמּוּשָׁא

דְּשִׁמְשָׁא, דְּאִתְמַשְׁכָא בָּהּ בְּסִיהֲרָא.

55. "For all the goods of his master were in his hand" (Beresheet 24:10), refers to the goodness and the lofty fragrance issued from the Supernal Lights and candles. ANOTHER EXPLANATION OF, "for all the goods of his master were in his hand," is that it refers to the union of the sun, ZEIR ANPIN, which is attracted to the moon, THE NUKVA. FOR THROUGH HIM OCCURS THE UNION OF MALE AND FEMALE.

56. וַיָּקָם וַיֵּלֶךְ אֶל אֲרַם נַהֲרַיִם: דָּא אֲתַר דְּאַרְעָא קַדִּישָׁא, דְּבָכַת תַּמָּן רָחֵל, כַּד חָרֵיב בֵּי מַקְדְּשָׁא. וַיַּבְרֵךְ הַגְּמַלִּים מִחוּץ לָעִיר אֶל בְּאֵר הַמָּיִם, לְאִתְתַּקְפָא חֵילָהָא בְּתוּקְפָהָא כִּדְקָא יָאוֹת, עַד לָא תֵּיעוֹל לַאֲקָמָא לוֹן לְאִינּוּן גּוּפִין.

56. "And he arose, and went to Aram-naharayim" (Beresheet 24:10), the place in the Holy Land where Rachel wept when the Temple was destroyed. "And he made his camels kneel down outside the city by a well of water" (Beresheet 24:11), for he wanted to add to her strength before raising and reviving the bodies.

57. לְעֵת עֶרֶב, מַאי לְעֵת עֶרֶב. דָּא עֶרֶב שַׁבָּת, דְּאִיהוּ זִמְנָא דְּאֶלֶף שְׁתִיתָאָה. לְעֵת עֶרֶב: כד"א, וְלַעֲבוֹדָתוֹ עֲדֵי עָרֶב. וּכְתִיב כִּי יִנָּטוּ צִלְלֵי עָרֶב.

57. In the verse: "At the time of evening" (Beresheet 24:11), WHAT TIME IS REFERRED TO? HE REPLIED: It is Shabbat eve, NAMELY YESOD, the era of the sixth millennium. FOR THE SIX DAYS OF CREATION ARE THE SECRETS OF 6,000 YEARS AND THE SIXTH DAY, SHABBAT EVE, CORRESPONDS TO THE SIXTH MILLENNIUM, ON WHICH DAY RESURRECTION WILL OCCUR. In the phrase, "At the time of evening," WHY SAY "TIME"? IT SHOULD HAVE SAID, 'AT EVENING.' HE ANSWERS: It conveys the meaning of, "And to his labor until the evening" (Tehilim. 104:23), and "For the shadows of the evening are lengthened" (Yirmeyah 6:4). THESE VERSES ARE THE SECRETS OF THE JUDGMENTS REVEALED DURING THE EVENING. "AT THE TIME OF EVENING" ALSO ALLUDES TO THE SECRET

OF YESOD, WHICH THE SERVANT HAS MENDED.

58. לְעֵת צֵאת הַשּׁוֹאֲבוֹת: דְּהַהוּא זִמְנָא, זְמִינִין לְמֵיקַם וְלַאֲחָיָיא בְּקַדְמֵיתָא, מִכָּל שְׁאָר בְּנֵי עַלְמָא, אִינּוּן דְּשָׁאֲבֵי מֵימוֹי דְאוֹרַיְיתָא, בְּגִין דְּאִתְעַסְּקוּ לְשָׁאֲבָא מִמֵּימֵי דְאוֹרַיְיתָא, וְאִתְתַּקָּפוּ בְּאִילָנָא דְחַיֵּי, וְאִינּוּן יִפְקוּן בְּקַדְמֵיתָא, דְּאִילָנָא דְחַיֵּי גָּרְמָא לוֹן דְּיְקוּמוּן בְּקַדְמֵיתָא, כְּמָא דְאִתְּמָר.

58. In the verse: "At the time that the women go out to draw water" (Beresheet 24:11), they draw the water of the Torah. At that time, they will be resurrected before any other man because, by drawing the water of the Torah, they are strengthened by the Tree of Life. Thus, they will come out first at the resurrection of the dead, as the Tree of Life causes them to be the first to rise.

59. וּבְנוֹת אַנְשֵׁי הָעִיר יוֹצְאוֹת, מַאי יוֹצְאוֹת. כד״א, וְאֶרֶץ רְפָאִים תַּפִּיל, דְּזַמִּינָא אַרְעָא לְמִפְלַט מִנָּהּ, כָּל גּוּפִין דְּאִינּוּן בְּגַוָּוהּ, וְעַל דָּא כְּתִיב יוֹצְאוֹת. לִשְׁאוֹב מַיִם: לְנַטְלָא נִשְׁמָתָא, וּלְקַבְּלָא לָהּ כִּדְקָא יָאוֹת, מְתַקְּנָא מֵאַתְרָהּ, כִּדְקָא חָזֵי.

59. "And the daughters of the men of the city come out" (Beresheet 24:13). HE ASKS: What is meant by "come out?" HE ANSWERS: It has the same meaning as: "and the earth shall cast out the shades of the dead" (Yeshayah 26:19). That is, it will cast out all the bodies that are in it. Therefore, it is written: "come out," WHICH ALLUDES TO THE BODIES THAT WILL BE CAST OUT BY THE EARTH AT THE TIME OF RESURRECTION. The words, "to draw water," MEAN to accept and properly receive a soul so that it will be perfected.

60. וְהָיָה הַנַּעֲרָה אֲשֶׁר אֹמַר אֵלֶיהָ הַטִּי נָא כַדֵּךְ וְאֶשְׁתֶּה, בְּגִין דְּהָא אִתְּמָר, דְּכָל אִינּוּן נִשְׁמָתִין דְּעַלְמָא, דְּאִתְקָיְימוּ בְּהַאי עַלְמָא, וְאִשְׁתַּדָּלוּ לְמִנְדַּע לְמָארֵיהוֹן בְּרָזָא דְחָכְמְתָא עִלָּאָה, אִיהִי סָלְקַת וְאִתְקָיְימַת בְּדַרְגָּא עִלָּאָה, עַל כָּל אִינּוּן דְּלָא אִתְדַּבְּקוּ, וְלָא יָדְעוּ,

וְאִינוּן אִתְקְיָימוּן בְּקַדְמֵיתָא. וְדָא הוּא שְׁאֵלְתָּא, דְּקָאִים הַהוּא עֶבֶד לְמִנְדַּע וּלְמִשְׁאַל, בַּמֶּה אִתְעַסְקַת הַהִיא נִשְׁמָתָא, בְּהַאי עָלְמָא.

60. "And let it come to pass that the girl to whom I shall say, 'Let down your pitcher, I pray you, that I may drink'..." (Beresheet 24:14). We have learned that every soul that strove in this world to know its Master by means of the mysteries of divine wisdom, will rise to the highest grade – a grade higher than all the souls who neither conceived nor attained knowledge. These will be the first to revive. This is the question that the servant wished to ask so that he could determine what the soul dealt with in this world, AND THUS LEARN WHETHER IT IS WORTHY OF BEING RESURRECTED FIRST. THIS IS THE MEANING OF, "LET DOWN YOUR PITCHER, I PRAY YOU, THAT I MAY DRINK."

61. וְאָמְרָה אֵלַי גַּם אַתָּה שְׁתֵה, אַנְתְּ בָּעֵי לְמִשְׁתֵּי וּלְאִתְשַׁקְיָא בְּקַדְמֵיתָא וּבַתְרָךְ וְגַם לִגְמַלֶּיךָ אַשְׁקֶה, בְּגִין דְּכָל אִינוּן שְׁאָר רְתִיכִין, אַף עַל גָּב דְּאִתְשַׁקְיָין מֵהַאי דַּרְגָּא, כֻּלְּהוּ אִתְשַׁקְיָין מִפּוּלְחָנָא דְצַדִּיקַיָּיא, דְּיָדְעֵי פּוּלְחָנָא דְמָארֵיהוֹן כִּדְקָא יָאוּת. דְּצַדִּיקַיָּיא יָדְעֵי לְסַפְּקָא לְכָל דַּרְגָּא וְדַרְגָּא כִּדְקָא יָאוּת, וְעַל דָּא וְגַם לִגְמַלֶּיךָ אַשְׁקֶה, וַדַּאי הִיא הָאִשָּׁה אֲשֶׁר הוֹכִיחַ יי׳ לְבֶן אֲדֹנִי. וַדַּאי הַהִיא אִיהוּ גוּפָא, דְּאִזְדַּמַּן לְהַהִיא נִשְׁמָתָא עִלָּאָה.

61. "And she will say to me 'You may also drink'..." (Beresheet 24:44). You need to drink and receive water yourself first. After [I have served] you: "I will also draw for your camels," because these other Chariots, although they are watered through this grade, are watered mainly from the worship of the righteous, who know well how to serve their Master. For the righteous know how to nourish each grade properly. Therefore, if she says, "I will also draw for your camels," then "she shall be the woman whom Hashem has appointed for my master's son," the body which is surely appointed to that Supernal Soul.

62. תָּא חֲזֵי, דְּהָא אִתְּמָר דְּתֵיאוּבְתָּא דִדְכוּרָא לְגַבֵּי נוּקְבָא, עָבֵיד נִשְׁמָתָא, וְתֵיאוּבְתָּא דְנוּקְבָא לְגַבֵּי דְכוּרָא, סָלְקָא וְאִתְעָרַב בַּהֲדָהּ דִּלְעֵילָּא, וְאִתְכְּלֵיל דָּא בְּדָא, וְעָבֵיד נִשְׁמָתָא, וּבְגִין כָּךְ הִיא הָאִשָּׁה,

דָּא הוּא גוּפָא וַדַּאי, דְּאִיהוּ זְמִינָא, לְהַהוּא רְעוּתָא דְנִשְׁמָתָא, דְּנָפְקָא מִן דְּכוּרָא.

62. Come and behold: we learned that the male yearns for the female, BY WHICH THE ILLUMINATION OF CHOCHMAH IS DRAWN FROM THE NUKVA, and a soul is created. The female yearns for the male, BY WHICH CHASSADIM ARE DRAWN FROM THE MALE, who rises and mingles WITH THE SOUL upward. Thus, they become included within one another, THE CHOCHMAH OF THE FEMALE WITH THE CHASSADIM OF THE MALE. This forms the soul, THAT IS, COMPLETES IT. From this procedure, THE SERVANT DIVINED THAT IF SHE SAYS 'DRINK' (WHICH ALLUDES TO DRAWING THE CHOCHMAH), "I WILL ALSO DRAW FOR YOUR CAMELS," NAMELY CONTINUING THE FLOW OF CHASSADIM – then she is indeed the woman, the body, who will execute the wishes of the soul issuing from the male, WHICH IS ZEIR ANPIN, INCLUDING BOTH CHOCHMAH AND CHASSADIM.

63. וְאִינוּן גּוּפִין זְמִינִין לְאַתְעָרָא בְּקַדְמֵיתָא כִּדְאֲמָרָן. וּלְבָתַר דְּאִלֵּין יְקוּמוּן, יְקוּמוּן כָּל אָחֳרָנִין דְּבִשְׁאָר אַרְעָאן, וְיִתְקַיְּימוּן בְּקִיּוּמָא שְׁלִים, וְיִתְחַדְּתוּן בְּחַדְתוּתָא דְּסִיהֲרָא, וְיִתְחַדֵּשׁ עַלְמָא כְּמִלְּקַדְּמִין, וּכְדֵין כְּתִיב בְּהַהוּא זִמְנָא יִשְׂמַח יי׳ בְּמַעֲשָׂיו.

63. These bodies will be raised TO LIFE earlier, as we have said. After these are revived, all other bodies outside Yisrael will be raised into perfect existence and resurrected with the renewal of the moon, FOR THE LIGHT OF THE MOON WILL THEN BE AS THE LIGHT OF THE SUN. The world will then be renewed as before. At that time, it is written: "Let Hashem rejoice in His works" (Tehilim 104:31).

64. וּבְגִין כָּךְ, הִנֵּה יַשְׂכִּיל עַבְדִּי, לְאַהֲדָרָא נִשְׁמָתִין כָּל חַד וְחַד לְאַתְרֵיהּ. יָרוּם וְנִשָּׂא וְגָבַהּ מְאֹד, מִסִּטְרָא דְּכָל אִינוּן דַּרְגִּין עִלָּאִין כִּדְקָאֲמָרָן.

64. Therefore, "Behold, My servant shall prosper," MEANS THAT THE SERVANT, METATRON, WILL KNOW how to return each soul to its own place, THAT IS, TO THE BODY WORTHY OF IT, as was said. "He shall be exalted and extolled, and be very high" (Yeshayah 52:13), on the side of all those supernal grades.

65. כַּאֲשֶׁר שָׁמְמוּ עָלֶיךָ רַבִּים כֵּן מִשְׁחַת מֵאִישׁ מַרְאֵהוּ וְתֹאֲרוֹ מִבְּנֵי אָדָם, תָּא חֲזֵי, דְּהָא אִתְּמָר, דְּכַד אִתְחָרַב בֵּי מַקְדְּשָׁא, וּשְׁכִינְתָּא אִתְגְּלֵי בְּגוֹ אַרְעָאן נוּכְרָאִין בֵּינַיְיהוּ, מַה כְּתִיב, הֵן אֶרְאֶלָּם צָעֲקוּ חוּצָה מַלְאֲכֵי שָׁלוֹם מַר יִבְכָּיוּן, כֻּלְּהוּ בְּכוֹ עַל דָּא, וּקְשִׁירוּ בְּכִיָּה וְאֶבְלָא, וְכָל דָּא עֲלָה דִּשְׁכִינְתָּא דְּאִתְגַּלְיָיא מֵאַתְרָהּ, וְכַמָּה דְּאִיהִי מִשְׁתַּנִּית מִכְּמָה דַּהֲוַת, אוּף הָכֵי בַּעֲלָהּ, לָא נָהֵיר נְהוֹרֵיהּ, וְאִשְׁתַּנֵּי מִכְּמָה דַּהֲוָה, דִּכְתִּיב חָשַׁךְ הַשֶּׁמֶשׁ בְּצֵאתוֹ, וְעַל דָּא כְּתִיב כֵּן מִשְׁחַת מֵאִישׁ מַרְאֵהוּ.

65. "Just as many were astonished at you, saying, 'Surely his visage is too marred to be that of a man, and his form to be that of the sons of man'" (Yeshayah 52:14). Come and behold: we have learned that when the Temple was destroyed and the Shechinah exiled to foreign countries, it is written: "Behold, the mighty ones shall cry outside; ambassadors of peace shall weep bitterly" (Yeshayah 33:7). They all wept for her, they mourned and grieved for the Shechinah who went from her place into exile. EXILE changes Her and Her husband, ZEIR ANPIN, WHO withholds his light, FOR THERE IS NO ONE TO SHINE UPON, as it is written: "The sun shall be darkened in his going forth" (Yeshayah 13:10). Therefore, "his visage is too marred to be that of a man." Another explanation of the verse, "Surely his visage is too marred to be that of a man," is that it refers to the servant METATRON, WHO AT THE TIME OF EXILE WAS changed in form and colors, WHICH WERE GREEN, WHITE, RED.

66. דָּבָר אַחֵר כֵּן מִשְׁחַת מֵאִישׁ מַרְאֵהוּ, מֵהַאי עֶבֶד, דְּאִשְׁתַּנֵּי דְיוֹקְנֵיהּ וּגְוָונֵיהּ מִכְּמָה דַּהֲוָה. דָּבָר אַחֵר כֵּן מִשְׁחַת מֵאִישׁ מַרְאֵהוּ, כד"א אַלְבִּישׁ שָׁמַיִם קַדְרוּת וְשַׂק אָשִׂים כְּסוּתָם. דְּהָא מִיּוֹמָא דְּאִתְחָרַב בֵּי מַקְדְּשָׁא, לָא קָיְימוּ שָׁמַיִם בִּנְהוֹרָא דִּלְהוֹן, וְרָזָא דְּמִלָּה, בִּרְכָאן לָא שָׁרְיָין, אֶלָּא בַּאֲתַר דְּאִשְׁתַּכָּחוּ דְּכַר וְנוּקְבָא, וְאוּקְמוּהָ כד"א זָכָר וּנְקֵבָה בְּרָאָם וַיְבָרֶךְ אֹתָם. וּבְגִין כָּךְ מִשְׁחַת מֵאִישׁ מַרְאֵהוּ.

66. Yet another explanation of, "Surely his visage is too marred to be that of a man," is that it has the same meaning as the verse: "I clothe the heavens with blackness, and I make sackcloth their covering" (Yeshayah 50:3). From the day the Temple was destroyed, the heavens, MEANING ZEIR ANPIN, did not hold their light. The secret is that blessings dwell only where there are Male and Female, as has been explained in relation to the verse: "Male and Female He created them. And Elohim blessed them" (Beresheet 1:27-28). But in exile, where male and female are not united, it is written: "His visage is too marred to be that of a man."

67. וְדָא הוּא כְּמָה דִכְתִיב, הַצַּדִּיק אָבַד, אָבוּד אוֹ נֶאֱבַד, לֹא נֶאֱמַר, אֶלָּא אָבַד, דְּלָא שַׁרְיָין בִּרְכָאן, אֶלָּא בַּאֲתַר דְּאִשְׁתַּכָּחוּ דְּכַר וְנוּקְבָה כַּחֲדָא, כְּמָה דְּאִתְּמָר.

67. It is similar to the meaning of: "The righteous perished" (Yeshayah 57:1), which does not read 'perishes' or 'will perish', but rather "perished" ('is lost'), WHICH MEANS THAT THE RIGHTEOUS LOST HIS BLESSINGS. For blessings abide only where male and female are united.

68. בְּגִין דָּא, בְּהַהוּא זִמְנָא, דְּלָא אִשְׁתַּכַּח דְּכוּרָא בַּהֲדָהּ, וּכְדֵין כָּל אִינוּן נִשְׁמָתִין דְּנָפְקֵי, כֻּלְּהוּ הֲוֵי לְהוֹ שְׁנוּיָא, מִכְּמָה דַּהֲווֹ בְּזִמְנָא דְּשִׁמְשָׁא אִתְחַבַּר בְּסִיהֲרָא, כְּמָה דְּאִתְּמָר. וְעַל דָּא אֵלֶּה תּוֹלְדוֹת יַעֲקֹב יוֹסֵף וגו' וְאִתְּמָר.

68. Therefore, when the male is not with the female, the souls released FROM HER are different than those issued when the sun, ZEIR ANPIN, was united with the moon, THE NUKVA, as we learned. FOR AS ZEIR ANPIN AND NUKVA WERE CHANGED DURING THE EXILE, SO THE SOULS OF THEIR OFFSPRING WERE DIFFERENT FROM THE PREVIOUS ONES. Of this, it is written: "These are the generations of Jacob: Joseph..." (Beresheet 37:2). AFTER JOSEPH BECAME LIKE JACOB AND THE SUN UNITED WITH THE MOON, THE VIRTUE OF THE SOULS IS ELEVATED. BUT THEY CHANGE DURING EXILE.

69. וְהוּא נַעַר, בְּגִין דְּלָא מִתְפָּרְשִׁין לְעָלְמִין, צַדִּי"ק וְצֶדֶ"ק כַּחֲדָא

אִינוּן, כְּמָה דְּאִיהִי אִתְקְרִיאַת בִּשְׁמָא דִּדְכוּרָא, הָכֵי נָמֵי אִתְקְרֵי אִיהוּ, בִּשְׁמָא דִּילָהּ, דִּכְתִּיב וְהוּא נַעַר.

69. "...and the lad..." (Beresheet 37:2) means that because their union is never broken, the Righteous, WHICH IS YESOD, and Righteousness, WHICH IS THE NUKVA, are constantly together. The Nukva is described with the same attributes as the male, WITH THE ADDITION OF THE FEMALE SUFFIX. FOR EXAMPLE: HE IS WISE, SHE IS WISDOM; HE IS MIGHTY, SHE IS MIGHT; HE IS A KING; SHE IS A KINGDOM. And the male is described with the same attributes as the Nukva. As it is written: "And the lad (Heb. *na'ar*)..."; AS THE NUKVA IS CALLED 'GIRL' (HEB. *NA'ARAH*), SO IS Yesod CALLED 'LAD'.

70. אֶת בְּנֵי בִלְהָה וְאֶת בְּנֵי זִלְפָּה, בְּכֻלְּהוּ קַיְימָא לְחַדְתָּא לוֹן כִּדְקָא יָאוֹת, וּלְאִשְׁתַּעְשְׁעָא לוֹן בְּחֶדְוָה דִּילֵיהּ. דְּכֻלְּהוּ עַנְפִּין, וְכֻלְּהוּ עָלִין, כֻּלְּהוּ אִתְבָּרְכִין בְּחֶדְוָה דִּילֵיהּ.

70. "...with the sons of Bilhah, and the sons of Zilpah" (Beresheet 37:2). JOSEPH is found within them, all TWELVE TRIBES, EVEN IN THE SONS OF THE HANDMAIDS, THE HIND PARTS OF THE SHECHINAH. He renews them appropriately and delights them with his mirth, for all branches and leaves OF THE SHECHINAH are blessed by his joy; THAT IS, EVEN THE HIND PARTS OF THE SHECHINAH, WHICH ARE CALLED 'LEAVES' – IN ACCORDANCE WITH THE VERSE: "WHOSE LEAF SHALL NOT WITHER" (YECHEZKEL 47:12) – ARE PERFECTED THROUGH HIM.

71. אֵלֶּה תּוֹלְדוֹת יַעֲקֹב יוֹסֵף, כְּמָה דְּאִתְּמָר, דְּכָל דְּיוֹקְנָא דְּיַעֲקֹב, הֲוָה בֵּיהּ בְּיוֹסֵף, וְכָל מַה דְּאֵירַע לְהַאי, אֵירַע לְהַאי, וְתַרְוַויְיהוּ כַּחֲדָא אָזְלֵי, וְדָא הוּא רָזָא דְּאָת ו"ו, דְּאָזְלֵי תַּרְוַויְיהוּ כַּחֲדָא, בְּגִין דְּאִינוּן רָזָא חֲדָא, וּדְיוֹקְנָא חֲדָא.

71. "And these are the generations of Jacob: Joseph..." (Beresheet 37:2). We have learned that Jacob's image was reproduced in Joseph. Thus, everything that happened to Jacob also happened to Joseph. They shared the same path, according to the secret of the letter *Vav* – THE FIRST *VAV* BEING

THE SECRET OF JACOB, TIFERET AND THE SECOND, THE FULLY SPELLED *VAV*, BEING THE SECRET OF JOSEPH, YESOD. And they walk together – AS THEY SOUND LIKE ONE WHEN THE *VAV* IS PRONOUNCED – because they share one meaning and image.

72. וַיָּבֵא יוֹסֵף אֶת דִּבָּתָם רָעָה, הָא אוֹקְמוּהָ, דַּהֲוָה אֲמַר לַאֲבוּי עֲלַיְיהוּ, דַּהֲווֹ אָכְלֵי שַׁיְיפָא מִבַּעֲלֵי חַיִּין, כַּד אִינוּן חַיִּין. וַיָּבֵא יוֹסֵף אֶת דִּבָּתָם רָעָה, וְכִי הָא בְּמִנְיינָא הֲווֹ, אִינוּן בְּנֵי שְׁפָחוֹת, הֵיךְ הֲווֹ מְזַלְזְלִין בְּהוֹן בְּנֵי לֵאָה וְהֵיךְ הֲווֹ אָכְלִין אֵבָר מִן הַחַי, וַהֲווֹ עָבְרִין עַל פִּקּוּדָא דְמָארֵיהוֹן, דְּהָא פַּקִּיד עַל בְּנֵי נֹחַ פִּקּוּדָא דָא, כד״א אַךְ בָּשָׂר בְּנַפְשׁוֹ דָמוֹ לֹא תֹאכֵלוּ, וְאִינוּן הֲווֹ אָכְלֵי לֵיהּ, וְעָבְרִין עַל פִּקּוּדָא דְמָארֵיהוֹן. אֶלָּא, יוֹסֵף הֲוָה קָאֲמַר, וְעַל דָּא אִתְעַנַּשׁ.

72. "…and Joseph brought to his father their evil report" (Beresheet 37:2). As has been explained, he told his father that they ate raw meat cut from a living animal. HE INSISTED THAT the sons of the handmaids were part of the twelve tribes. Thus, how could the sons of Leah treat them with contempt and also eat flesh from a living animal, thereby transgressing the commandment of their Master to the sons of Noah? As it is written: "But flesh with its life, which is its blood, you shall not eat" (Beresheet 9:4). Could they have eaten and thus transgressed their Master's commandment? HE ANSWERS: Joseph told this BY HIS OWN INVENTION, and was therefore punished for it.

73. רִבִּי יְהוּדָה אֲמַר, אֶת דִּבָּתָם רָעָה, כְּמָה דְאוֹקְמוּהָ, דְּיַהֲבֵי עֵינַיְיהוּ בִּבְנוֹת אַרְעָא, וְדָא הוּא דִּבָּתָם רָעָה לֵינְקָא לְכָל אִינוּן דַּרְגִּין דְּלָא קַדִּישִׁין, דְּאַתְיָין מִסִּטְרָא מְסָאֲבָא.

73. According to one explanation, Rabbi Yehuda said: Joseph's "evil report" is that they cast their eyes upon the daughters of the land, which is CONSIDERED TO BE evil because IT ALLOWED the unholy grades of the Side of Defilement to nourish.

6. "Now Israel loved Joseph"

A Synopsis

Using the story of Joseph and his many-colored coat as an analogy, Rabbi Elazar discusses the spiritually privileged position of the children of Israel and the enmity this inspires in idolatrous nations. We learn that Jacob's love for Joseph over his brothers, and the coat that he gave Joseph, was the immediate cause of the Exile itself, which is, in turn, shown to be a parable of human history.

The Relevance of this Passage

The children of Israel are designated as the Chosen People in response to the measure of their internal Vessel – the Desire to Receive – which is more intense than that of other nations. For this reason, they are the channel through which the Light of The Creator emerges into our world. When the Desire to Receive is directed towards the self alone, there is a lack of Light in our world, and this instigates negative repercussions from other nations. These other nations sense the lack of Light, which creates enmity between them and the children of Israel, and is ultimately the cause for the continuing Exile. Thus, Exile is both a personal and an historical occurrence. When the hardships of life reach their extreme, this is a spiritual connection to the Exile of the children of Israel, which exists to this very day. The Exile is also an effect of our failure to direct our desires towards positive and sharing causes. The spiritual forces of liberation present in this passage can hasten both our personal redemption and also the Final Redemption of the entire world.

74. וְיִשְׂרָאֵל אָהַב אֶת יוֹסֵף מִכָּל בָּנָיו כִּי בֶן זְקֻנִים הוּא לוֹ וְעָשָׂה לוֹ כְּתֹנֶת פַּסִּים. רִבִּי אֶלְעָזָר פָּתַח וַאֲמַר, לֵךְ עַמִּי בֹּא בַחֲדָרֶיךָ וּסְגֹר דְּלָתְךָ בַּעֲדֶךָ חֲבִי כִמְעַט רֶגַע עַד יַעֲבָר זָעַם. לֵךְ עַמִּי בֹּא בַחֲדָרֶיךָ. תָּא חֲזֵי, כַּמָּה קוּדְשָׁא בְּרִיךְ הוּא רָחִים לוֹ לְיִשְׂרָאֵל, וּבְגִין רְחִימוּתָא דִלְהוֹן, דִּרְחֵים לוֹן עַל כָּל עַמִּין עעכו"ם, אַזְהַר לוֹן, וּבָעֵי לְנַטְרָא לוֹן, בְּכָל מַה דְּאִינוּן עָבְדִין.

74. "Now Israel loved Joseph more than all his children, because he was the son of his old age; and he made him a striped coat" (Beresheet 37:3). Rabbi Elazar began the discussion with the verse: "Come, My people, enter you into your chambers, and shut your doors about you: hide yourself for a little moment, until the indignation be overpast" (Yeshayah 26:20). Come and behold: how much did the Holy One, blessed be He, love Yisrael? He had more love for them than for all the other heathen nations. Thus, He warned them and guarded them in their actions.

75. תָּא חֲזֵי, תְּלַת זִמְנִין אִית בְּיוֹמָא, דְּדִינָא שַׁרְיָא בְּעַלְמָא, וְכַד אָתֵי הַהוּא זִמְנָא, מִבָּעֵי לֵיהּ לְבַר נָשׁ, לְאִזְדַּהֲרָא, וּלְאִסְתַּמְרָא, דְּלָא יִפְגַּע בֵּיהּ הַהוּא דִּינָא, וְאִינּוּן זִמְנִין יְדִיעָן, וְהָא אוֹקְמוּהָ.

75. Come and behold: Judgment hovers about the world three times a day. During these times, it behooves a man to take heed and be watchful lest Judgment shall fall on him. This is so at specific times, as has already been explained.

76. בְּגִין דְּהָא כַּד סָלֵיק צַפְרָא, אַבְרָהָם אִתְּעַר בְּעַלְמָא, וְאָחִיד לֵיהּ לְדִינָא לְקַשְׁרָא לֵיהּ בַּהֲדֵיהּ, וּבְשֵׁירוּתָא דִּתְלַת שָׁעֵי קַמַּיְיתָא, נָטֵיל דִּינָא מֵאַתְרֵיהּ, לְאִתְעָרָא בֵּיהּ בְּיַעֲקֹב, עַד דְּאִתְעַר צְלוֹתָא דְמִנְחָה, דְּאַהֲדַר דִּינָא לְאַתְרֵיהּ, וְאִתְעַר דִּינָא דִּלְתַתָּא, לְאִתְקַשְּׁרָא בְּדִינָא דִּלְעֵילָא, דְּהָא כְּדֵין אִתְקַשַּׁר דִּינָא בְּדִינָא, וּבָעֵי לְאִזְדַּהֲרָא.

76. The three times are when morning comes and Abraham is awakened into the world, where he holds on to Judgment, so that he is attached to it. Within the first three hours, Judgment is driven from its place to be awakened within Jacob, until the time is come for Minchah. Then, the lower Judgment is stirred to be attached to the upper Judgment. Then one Judgment joins another, and it behooves us to be on our guard.

77. תוּ, כַּד דִּינָא אִתְּעַר בְּעַלְמָא, וּמוֹתָא אִשְׁתַּכַּח בְּמָתָא, לָא לִיבָּעֵי לֵיהּ לְבַר נָשׁ לְמֵיהַךְ יְחִידָאי בְּשׁוּקָא, וְהָא אוֹקִימְנָא מִלֵּי, אֶלָּא בָּעֵי לְאַסְגָּרָא גַּרְמֵיהּ, דְּלָא יִפּוֹק לְבַר, כְּמָה דְּאוֹקְמוּהָ בְּנֹחַ, דְּאַסְגַּר גַּרְמֵיהּ בְּתֵיבוּתָא, דְּלָא יִשְׁתַּכַּח קַמֵּי מְחַבְּלָא.

77. Moreover, when Judgment is upon the world and death is in the marketplace, no man should walk alone in a public place, as has been explained elsewhere. Man should shut himself in and never venture out, as

Noah did when he shut himself in the ark to avoid being found in the presence of the Angel of Destruction.

78. וְעַל דָּא, לֵךְ עַמִּי בֹּא בַחֲדָרֶיךָ, אַסְגַּר גַּרְמָךְ. וּסְגֹר דְּלָתְךָ בַּעֲדֶךָ, דְּלָא יִתְחֲזֵי קַמֵּיהּ דִּמְחַבְּלָא. חֲבִי כִּמְעַט רֶגַע עַד יַעֲבָר זַעַם, דְּבָתַר דְּאַעֲבַר דִּינָא לֵית לֵיהּ רְשׁוּ לִמְחַבְּלָא לְחַבָּלָא.

78. Therefore: "Come, My people, enter you into your chambers…" (Yeshayah 26:20) MEANS shut yourself inside YOUR HOUSE, "and shut your doors about you," so as not to be seen by the Destroying Angel. "Hide yourself for a little moment, until the anger be overpast," because after the Judgment has past, the Angel of Destruction has no permission to harm you.

79. תָּא חֲזֵי, דְּקוּדְשָׁא בְּרִיךְ הוּא בְּגִין רְחִימוּתָא דְּאִיהוּ רָחֵים לוֹן לְיִשְׂרָאֵל, וְקָרֵיב לוֹן לְגַבֵּיהּ, כָּל שְׁאָר עַמִּין עכו"ם שָׂנְאִין לוֹן לְיִשְׂרָאֵל, בְּגִין דְּאִינוּן מִתְרַחֲקִין, וְיִשְׂרָאֵל קְרֵיבִין.

79. Come and behold: it is the affection that the Holy One, blessed be He, harbors for Yisrael and His drawing them near Him THAT CAUSES the other heathen nations to hate Yisrael. For they are kept away from the Holy One, blessed be He, while Yisrael are near.

80. וְתָא חֲזֵי, בְּגִין רְחִימוּתָא דִּרְחֵים יַעֲקֹב לְיוֹסֵף יַתִּיר מֵאֲחוֹי, אַף עַל גָּב דְּכֻלְּהוּ הֲווֹ לֵיהּ אַחִין, מַה כְּתִיב וַיִּתְנַכְּלוּ אֹתוֹ לַהֲמִיתוֹ, כָּל שֶׁכֵּן עַמִּין עוֹבְדֵי עֲבוֹדַת כּוֹכָבִים וּמַזָּלוֹת לְיִשְׂרָאֵל.

80. Come and behold: as a result of the exceptional love Jacob had for Joseph, his brothers "conspired against him to slay him" (Beresheet 37:18). How much more do the idolatrous nations HATE Yisrael BECAUSE OF THE LOVE THAT THE HOLY ONE, BLESSED BE HE, HAS FOR YISRAEL ABOVE THEM!

81. תָּא חֲזֵי כַּמָּה גָּרֵים לֵיהּ הַהוּא רְחִימוּתָא דִּרְחֵים לֵיהּ יַתִּיר, דְּגָרַם לֵיהּ דְּאִתְגְּלֵי מֵאֲבוֹי, וְאִתְגְּלֵי אֲבוֹי בַּהֲדֵיהּ, וְגָרַם לְהוֹ גָלוּתָא,

וְלִשְׁכִינְתָּא דְאִתְגַּלְיָא בֵּינַיְיהוּ, וְאַף עַל גָּב דְאִתְגְּזֵירַת גְּזֵרָה, וְאוֹקְמוּהָ דִבְגִין כְּתֹנֶת פַּסִּים דַּעֲבַד לֵיהּ יַתִּיר, מַה כְּתִיב וַיִּרְאוּ אֶחָיו.

81. Come and behold what this love, which Jacob had for Joseph OVER HIS BROTHERS, caused. JOSEPH was exiled from his father, who then joined him. By this action, he brought exile upon the tribes and the Shechinah. Although it was decreed IN THE COVENANT BETWEEN THE PIECES, THE REASON, NEVERTHELESS, WAS THAT HE LOVED HIM BETTER THAN HIS BROTHERS. It has been explained that all this happened because of the many-colored coat he made him, as it is written: "And when his brethren saw...THEY HATED HIM, AND COULD NOT SPEAK PEACEABLY TO HIM" (Beresheet 37:4).

7. “And Joseph dreamed a dream”

A Synopsis

Rabbi Chiya discusses dreams as a form of divine revelation. Situated beneath Prophecy and Vision in the hierarchy of revelatory experiences, dreams comprise a mixture of truth and falsehood, and serve as an admonition to the dreamer. Once given, the interpretation of a dream can influence both its meaning and its fulfillment. According to Rabbi Shimon, the dreamer's awareness and interpretation is not necessary for fulfillment. The interpretation of Joseph's dream by his brothers, whereby they sealed their fate, warns us not to dismiss our dreams too quickly or to share them with those who are not friends.

The Relevance of this Passage

Reading this section raises awareness of the vital information dreams often provide to help in our spiritual development. We learn to protect ourselves against negative dream interpretations and their manifestation.

82. וַיַּחֲלֹם יוֹסֵף חֲלוֹם וגו׳, רִבִּי חִיָּיא פְּתַח וַאֲמַר, וַיֹּאמֶר שִׁמְעוּ נָא דְבָרָי אִם יִהְיֶה נְבִיאֲכֶם יי׳ בַּמַּרְאָה אֵלָיו אֶתְוַדָּע בַּחֲלוֹם אֲדַבֶּר בּוֹ. תָּא חֲזֵי, כַּמָּה דַרְגִּין לְדַרְגִּין עֲבַד קוּדְשָׁא בְּרִיךְ הוּא, וְכֻלְּהוּ קָיְימֵי דָא עַל דָא, דַּרְגָּא עַל דַּרְגָּא, דָּא לְעֵיל מִן דָּא, וְכֻלְּהוּ יָנְקִין אִלֵּין מִן אִלֵּין, כִּדְקָא חָזֵי לוֹן, אִלֵּין מִימִינָא וְאִלֵּין מִשְּׂמָאלָא, וְכֻלְּהוּ אִתְמַנָּן אִלֵּין עַל אִלֵּין, כֹּלָּא כִּדְקָא יָאוּת.

82. “And Joseph dreamed a dream” (Beresheet 37:5). Rabbi Chiya opened the discussion with the verse: “And he said, ‘Hear now My words: If there be a prophet among you, I, Hashem, make Myself known to him in a vision, and speak to him in a dream’” (Bemidbar 12:6). Come and behold: how many grades of prophecy the Holy One, blessed be He, formed. They stand upon each other, one grade superior to another, higher than the other. They all nourish each other according to their ability, some from the right and some from the left, as is proper.

83. תָּא חֲזֵי, כָּל נְבִיאֵי דְעַלְמָא כֻּלְּהוּ יָנְקֵי מִסִּטְרָא חָדָא, מִגּוֹ תְּרֵין דַּרְגִּין יְדִיעָן, וְאִינוּן דַּרְגִּין הֲווֹ אִתְחַזְיָין בְּגוֹ אַסְפַּקְלַרְיָא דְּלָא נָהֲרָא, דִּכְתִיב בַּמַּרְאָה אֵלָיו אֶתְוַדָּע, מַאי הוּא מַרְאָה, כְּמָה דְאִתְּמָר חֵיזוּ דְּכָל

גְּוָונִן אִתְחַזְיָין בְּגַוָּוהּ, וְדָא הִיא אַסְפַּקְלַרְיָא דְּלָא נָהֲרָא. בַּחֲלוֹם אֲדַבֶּר בּוֹ, דָּא הוּא חַד מִשִּׁתִּין בִּנְבוּאָה, כְּמָה דְּאוֹקְמוּהָ, וְאִיהוּ דַּרְגָּא שְׁתִיתָאָה מֵהַהוּא דַּרְגָּא דִּנְבוּאָה, וְאִיהוּ דַּרְגָּא דְּגַבְרִיאֵל, דִּמְמַנָּא עַל חֶלְמָא, וְהָא אִתְּמָר.

83. Come and behold: the prophets in the world are all nourished from one aspect, from two known grades, NETZACH AND HOD, which are seen within the mirror (Heb. *mar'ah*) that has no reflection, WHICH IS THE NUKVA. As it is written: "I, Hashem make Myself known to him in a vision (Heb. *mar'eh*)" (Bemidbar 12:6). This is the mirror that reflects all the colors, NAMELY WHITE, RED, AND GREEN, WHICH REPRESENT THE THREE COLUMNS OF ZEIR ANPIN; it is known as the 'dull mirror'. The phrase: "And speak to him in a dream" (Ibid.), refers to the sixtieth part of prophecy. As has been explained, it is Gabriel's grade, the sixth grade BENEATH the grade of prophecy, who supervises dreams.

84. תָּא חֲזֵי, כָּל חֶלְמָא דְּאִיהוּ כִּדְקָא יָאוֹת, מֵהַאי דַּרְגָּא קָא אַתְיָא, וְעַל דָּא, לֵית לָךְ חֶלְמָא, דְּלָא יִתְעָרְבוּן עִמֵּיהּ מִלִּין כְּדִיבִין, כְּמָה דְּאוֹקִימְנָא, וּבְגִין כָּךְ, מִנַּיְיהוּ קְשׁוֹט, וּמִנַּיְיהוּ כְּדִיבָן, וְלֵית לָךְ חֶלְמָא, דְּלָא אִית בֵּיהּ מֵהַאי גִּיסָא וּמֵהַאי גִּיסָא.

84. Come and behold: every well-formed dream proceeds from that grade OF THE ANGEL GABRIEL. BECAUSE IT IS FROM AN ANGEL, every dream includes some lies. Therefore, parts of dreams are true and parts are false; no dream is without both.

85. וּבְגִין דְּאִית בֵּיהּ בְּחֶלְמָא כֹּלָּא כִּדְאֲמָרָן, כָּל חֶלְמִין דְּעָלְמָא, אָזְלִין בָּתַר פִּשְׁרָא דְּפוּמָא, וְאוֹקְמוּהָ דִּכְתִיב, וַיְהִי כַּאֲשֶׁר פָּתַר לָנוּ כֵּן הָיָה, מ"ט, בְּגִין דְּאִית בֵּיהּ בְּחֶלְמָא כְּדִיבוּ וּקְשׁוֹט, וּמִלָּה שָׁלְטָא עַל כֹּלָּא, וּבְגִין כָּךְ, בָּעֵי חֶלְמָא פִּשְׁרָא טָבָא. רִבִּי יְהוּדָה אָמַר, בְּגִין דְּכָל חֶלְמָא, מִדַּרְגָּא דִּלְתַתָּא אִיהוּ, וְדִבּוּר שָׁלְטָא עֲלֵיהּ, וּבְגִין כָּךְ כָּל חֶלְמָא אָזְלָא בָּתַר פִּשְׁרָא.

85. Because a dream has both TRUE AND FALSE ELEMENTS, all the dreams in the world follow verbal interpretations, as was explained in relation to the verse: "And it came to pass, as he interpreted to us, so it was" (Beresheet 41:13); FOR IT COMES TO PASS ACCORDING TO ITS OWN INTERPRETATION. What is the reason? A dream contains truth and lies; hence, the words of interpretation prevail over everything, IN THAT THEY DETERMINE WHETHER THE TRUE OR THE FALSE PART SHALL PREVAIL. A dream therefore needs a favorable interpretation. Rabbi Yehuda said that because a dream is of a lower grade, THAT OF THE ANGEL GABRIEL, and speech, THE SECRET OF THE NUKVA, has power OVER THE ANGEL, dreams follow their own interpretations – WHICH COME FROM THE ASPECT OF SPEECH AND PROCEED FROM THE NUKVA, CALLED 'SPEECH', RULING OVER THE ANGEL GABRIEL'.

86. פְּתַח וַאֲמַר, בַּחֲלוֹם חֶזְיוֹן לַיְלָה בִּנְפֹל תַּרְדֵּמָה עַל אֲנָשִׁים בִּתְנוּמוֹת עֲלֵי מִשְׁכָּב אָז יִגְלֶה אֹזֶן אֲנָשִׁים וּבְמֹסָרָם יַחְתֹּם. תָּא חֲזֵי, כַּד סָלֵיק בַּר נָשׁ לְעַרְסֵיהּ, מִבָּעֵי לֵיהּ, לְאַמְלָכָא עֲלֵיהּ מַלְכוּתָא דִשְׁמַיָּא בְּקַדְמֵיתָא, וּלְבָתַר יֵימָא חַד פְּסוּקָא דְרַחֲמֵי, וְאוֹקְמוּהָ חַבְרַיָּיא, בְּגִין דְּהָא כַּד בַּר נָשׁ נָאִים עַל עַרְסֵיהּ, הָא נִשְׁמָתֵיהּ נַפְקָא מִנֵּיהּ, וְאָזְלָא וְשָׁטְיָא לְעֵילָא, כָּל חַד וְחַד כְּפוּם אָרְחֵיהּ וְהָכֵי סְלֵיקַת, כְּמָה דְאִתְּמָר.

86. He opened with the verse: "In a dream, in a vision of the night, when deep sleep falls upon men, in slumbering upon the bed, then He opens the ears of men, and with discipline seals their instruction" (Iyov 33:15-16). Come and behold: when man lies in his bed, he should first acknowledge the Kingdom of Heaven over him, then utter a verse of mercy. The friends explained that when a man sleeps in his bed, his soul leaves him to soar above, each soul according to its own way.

87. מַה כְּתִיב בַּחֲלוֹן חֶזְיוֹן לַיְלָה, כַּד בְּנֵי נָשָׁא שָׁכְבֵי בְּעַרְסַיְיהוּ נָיְימִין, וְנִשְׁמָתָא נָפְקַת מִנַּיְיהוּ, הה"ד בִּתְנוּמוֹת עֲלֵי מִשְׁכָּב, אָז יִגְלֶה אֹזֶן אֲנָשִׁים, וּכְדֵין קוּדְשָׁא בְּרִיךְ הוּא אוֹדַע לָהּ לְנִשְׁמָתָא, בְּהַהוּא דַרְגָּא דְקַיְימָא עַל חֶלְמָא, אִינּוּן מִלִּין דִּזְמִינִין לְמֵיתֵי עַל עַלְמָא, אוֹ אִינּוּן מִלִּין, כְּפוּם אִינּוּן הִרְהוּרִין דְּלִבֵּיהּ, בְּגִין דְּבַר נָשׁ נָטֵיל אָרְחָא דְתוֹכָחֵי דְעָלְמָא.

87. When people fall asleep in their beds, the soul departs. "In slumbering upon the bed, then He opens the ears of men." Thus, the Holy One, blessed be He, reveals to the soul through the grade in charge of dreams, NAMELY GABRIEL, what will happen in the world in the future, or that which corresponds to his innermost thoughts, THAT IS, TRUTH, LIES, OR BOTH. Thus, through admonition, a man receives knowledge of things to come. FOR THIS REASON, HE IS TOLD OF FUTURE EVENTS.

88. בְּגִין דְּהָא לָא מוֹדָעִין לֵיהּ לְבַר נָשׁ, בְּעוֹד דְּאִיהוּ קָאִים בְּתוֹקְפָּא דְגוּפָא, כִּדְקָאֲמָרָן, אֶלָּא מַלְאָכָא אוֹדַע לְנִשְׁמָתָא, וְנִשְׁמָתָא לְבַר נָשׁ, וְהַהוּא חֶלְמָא אִיהוּ מִלְּעֵילָּא, כַּד נִשְׁמָתִין נָפְקִין מִגּוּפֵי, וְסָלְקִין כָּל חַד וְחַד כְּפוּם אָרְחֵיהּ.

88. A man is not given this knowledge while the body is strong. The angel informs the soul, and the soul informs the man. The dream comes TO THE SOULS from above, when the souls depart from the body and ascend, each according to its merit.

89. וְכַמָּה דַּרְגִּין עַל דַּרְגִּין, בְּרָזָא דְחֶלְמָא, כֻּלְּהוּ בְּרָזָא דְחָכְמְתָא. וְתָא חֲזֵי, חֲלוֹם דַּרְגָּא חָדָא, מַרְאָה דַּרְגָּא חָדָא, נְבוּאָה דַּרְגָּא חָדָא, וְכֻלְּהוּ דַּרְגִּין לְדַרְגִּין אִלֵּין עַל אִלֵּין.

89. How many grades are in the secret of the dream, in the secret of wisdom? Come and behold: a dream is one grade, a vision is another, and a prophecy a third. All these grades are in ascending order; THE DREAM IS BENEATH VISION, AND VISION IS BENEATH PROPHECY.

90. וַיַּחֲלֹם יוֹסֵף חֲלוֹם וַיַּגֵּד לְאֶחָיו וַיּוֹסִפוּ עוֹד שְׂנֹא אֹתוֹ, עַל חֲלוֹמוֹתָיו. מֵהָכָא, דְּלָא מִבָּעֵי לֵיהּ לְבַר נָשׁ לְמֵימַר חֶלְמֵיהּ, בַּר לְהַהוּא בַּר נָשׁ דְּרָחֵים לֵיהּ, וְאִי לָאו, אִיהוּ גָּרֵים לֵיהּ, דְּאִי הַהוּא חֶלְמָא מִתְהַפֵּךְ לְגַוְונָא אָחֳרָא, אִיהוּ גָּרֵים לְסַלָּקָא.

90. "And Joseph dreamed a dream, and told it to his brethren: and they hated him yet the more" (Beresheet 37:5). From this, we learn that a man should tell his dream only to someone who loves him. If the listener does not LOVE HIM, he shall bring evil upon him; for if the dream changes, he is the reason that THE TRUE MEANING OF THE DREAM is not fulfilled, BECAUSE OF HIS INCORRECT INTERPRETATION.

91. תָּא חֲזֵי, דְּיוֹסֵף אִיהוּ אֲמַר חֶלְמָא לַאֲחוּהִי, וְעַל דָּא גָּרְמוּ לֵיהּ לְסַלָּקָא חֶלְמֵיהּ, תְּרֵין וְעֶשְׂרִין שְׁנִין דְּאִתְעַכַּב, רִבִּי יוֹסֵי אֲמַר, מְנָלָן, דִּכְתִיב וַיּוֹסִיפוּ עוֹד שְׂנֹא אוֹתוֹ, מַאי שְׂנֹא אוֹתוֹ, דְּגָרְמוּ לֵיהּ קִטְרוּגִין בְּדָא.

91. Come and behold: Joseph told his dream to his brothers WHO DID NOT LOVE HIM, and so fulfillment of the dream was delayed 22 years. Rabbi Yosi asks: How do we know THAT HATRED PREVENTED THE DREAM FROM BEING CARRIED OUT? From the words: "and they hated him yet the more" (Beresheet 37:8). This hatred caused accusations to be brought against him, AND THE DREAM WAS DELAYED FOR 22 YEARS.

92. מַה כְּתִיב וַיֹּאמֶר אֲלֵיהֶם שִׁמְעוּ נָא הַחֲלוֹם הַזֶּה אֲשֶׁר חָלָמְתִּי, דְּבָעָא מִנַּיְיהוּ דְּיִשְׁמְעוּן לֵיהּ. וְאִיהוּ אוֹדַע לְהוֹ הַהוּא חֶלְמָא, דְּאִלְמָלֵא אִינוּן דְּאַהֲפָכוּ לֵיהּ לְגַוְונָא אָחֳרָא, הָכֵי אִתְקַיַּים, וְאִינוּן אֲתִיבוּ וַאֲמָרוּ הֲמָלֹךְ תִּמְלֹךְ עָלֵינוּ אִם מָשׁוֹל תִּמְשֹׁל בָּנוּ, מִיָּד אֲמָרוּ לֵיהּ פִּשְׁרָא דְחֶלְמָא, וְגָזְרוּ גְּזֵרָה, וּבְגִין כָּךְ וַיּוֹסִיפוּ עוֹד שְׂנֹא אוֹתוֹ.

92. It is written: "And he said to them, 'Hear, I pray you, this dream which I have dreamed'" (Beresheet 37:6). He begged them to listen to him and recounted the dream, yet were it not for them, who gave the dream a different meaning, it would have come true. But they answered: "'Shall you indeed reign over us? Or shall you indeed have dominion over us?'" (Beresheet 37:8). In their answer, they gave its interpretation, AND TURNED ITS MEANING OF REIGN AND DOMINION INTO SOMETHING ELSE. They decreed THAT HE SHOULD NOT REIGN OVER THEM, and it is therefore written: "And they hated him yet the more," MEANING THEY CAUSED ACCUSATIONS TO BE BROUGHT AGAINST HIM.

93. ר׳ חִיָּיא וְרִבִּי יוֹסֵי, הֲווּ שְׁכִיחֵי קַמֵּיהּ דְּר׳ שִׁמְעוֹן, אֲמַר רִבִּי חִיָּיא,

הָא תָּנִינָן חֶלְמָא דְּלָא אִתְפַּשַּׁר, כְּאִגַּרְתָּא דְּלָא מִתְקַרְיָא, אִי בְּגִין דְּאִתְקַיַּים וְאִיהוּ לָא יָדַע, אוֹ דְּלָא אִתְקַיַּים כְּלָל. אֲמַר לֵיהּ אִתְקַיַּים וְלָא אִתְיְידַע, דְּהָא הַהוּא חֶלְמָא, חֵילָא תַּלְיָא עֲלֵיהּ, וְאִיהוּ לָא אִתְיְדַע, וְלָא יְדִיעַ אִי אִתְקַיַּים, אִי לָא אִתְקַיַּים.

93. Rabbi Chiya and Rabbi Yosi were with Rabbi Shimon. Rabbi Chiya said: We have learned an uninterpreted dream resembles an unopened letter. HE ASKS: Does this mean that the dream comes true without the dreamer being conscious of it, or that it does not come true at all? He answers: IT MEANS THAT the dream comes true, but the dreamer does not know it. For there is a power dwelling upon the dream WHICH FORCES IT TO COME TRUE. Only the dreamer is not aware whether the dream comes true or not, JUST AS ONE DOES NOT KNOW THE CONTENTS OF AN UNOPENED LETTER.

94. וְלֵית לָךְ מִלָּה בְּעַלְמָא, דְּעַד לָא יֵיתֵי לְעַלְמָא, דְּלָאו אִיהוּ תַּלְיָיא בְּחֶלְמָא, אוֹ עַל יְדָא דִּכְרוֹזָא, דְּהָא אִתְּמַר, דְּכָל מִלָּה וּמִלָּה עַד לָא יֵיתֵי לְעַלְמָא, מַכְרְזֵי עֲלֵיהּ בִּרְקִיעַ, וּמִתַּמָּן אִתְפַּשַּׁט בְּעַלְמָא, וְאִתְיְהֵיב עַל יְדָא דִּכְרוֹזָא, וְכֹלָּא בְּגִין דִּכְתִּיב כִּי לֹא יַעֲשֶׂה יי׳ אֱלֹהִים דָּבָר כִּי אִם גָּלָה סוֹדוֹ אֶל עֲבָדָיו הַנְּבִיאִים, בִּזְמְנָא דִּנְבִיאִים אִשְׁתַּכָּחוּ בְּעַלְמָא, וְאִי לָאו, אַף עַל גַּב דִּנְבוּאָה לָא שַׁרְיָא, חַכִּימֵי עֲדִיפֵי מִנְּבִיאִים, וְאִי לָא, אִתְיְהֵיב בְּחֶלְמָא, וְאִי לָאו, בְּצִפְּרֵי שְׁמַיָּא מִשְׁתַּכְּחֵי מִלָּה, וְהָא אוֹקְמוּהָ.

94. Everything that happens in the world depends on a dream or a proclamation before it becomes reality. We have learned that before any matter enters the world, a proclamation resounds in heaven, from where it is spread throughout the world. It is done by a crier, as it is written: "Surely Hashem Elohim will do nothing without revealing His secret to His servants the prophets" (Amos 3:7). This was when there were prophets in the world. When the prophets were gone, sages took their places who rank higher. And when THE SAGES were gone, the future was announced by a dream – and if not BY A DREAM, through birds in the sky, as has been already explained.

8. "And his brothers went to feed"

A Synopsis

This section touches upon the role of providence in the story of Joseph and especially of his sale into slavery–since, when Joseph's brothers sold him, they were in collaboration with the Shechinah.

The Relevance of this Passage

The longest and strongest master-slave relationship is that between man and his ego. All of us are in bondage to our reactive whims and egocentric desires. We are also prisoners of other people's perceptions of us. Our ego is our taskmaster – and the ego is so good at its job, most of us don't even realize we are in bondage. Therefore, the Light of The Creator will send us challenging opportunities to provoke our ego and highlight our self-centeredness. The Light of this passage opens our eyes and shows us the way to freedom by allowing us to recognize life's hardships for what they really–opportunities to rise above the power of impulse and effect inner transformation.

95. וַיֵּלְכוּ אֶחָיו לִרְעוֹת אֶת צֹאן אֲבִיהֶם בִּשְׁכֶם. רִבִּי שִׁמְעוֹן אֲמַר, לִרְעוֹת צֹאן אֲבִיהֶם מִבָּעֵי לֵיהּ, מַאי אֶ"ת. נָקוּד מִלְּעֵילָּא, לְאַסְגָּאָה עִמְהוֹן שְׁכִינְתָּא, דְּאִיהִי עִמְּהוֹן שַׁרְיָא, בְּגִין דְּאִינוּן הֲווֹ עֲשָׂרָה, דְּהָא יוֹסֵף לָא הֲוָה עִמְּהוֹן, וּבִנְיָמִין אִיהוּ זְעִיר בְּבֵיתָא, וּבְגִין כָּךְ אִינוּן הֲווֹ עֲשָׂרָה, וְכַד אָזְלוּ, הֲוַת שְׁכִינְתָּא בֵּינַיְיהוּ, וְעַל דָּא נָקוּד מִלְּעֵילָּא.

95. "And his brothers went to feed their father's flock in Shchem" (Beresheet 37:12). Rabbi Shimon asks: Why is the particle *Et* ('the') added? HE ANSWERS: THE PREPOSITION *Et* has dots over it, which represent the Shechinah, FOR THE SHECHINAH, NAMED *'ET'*, dwelt with them as they were a group of ten. WHEREVER THERE ARE TEN MEN, THE SHECHINAH HOVERS ABOVE THEM. They were ten because Joseph was not with them and little Binyamin was at home. When they went, the Shechinah was among them, for which reason there are dots ABOVE THE PARTICLE *ET*.

96. וּבְגִין כָּךְ בִּזְמְנָא דְּזַבִּינוּ לֵיהּ לְיוֹסֵף, אִשְׁתַּתָּפוּ כֻּלְּהוּ בַּהֲדֵי שְׁכִינְתָּא, וְאַשְׁתִּיפוּ לָהּ בַּהֲדַיְיהוּ, כַּד עֲבִידוּ אוֹמָאָה, וְעַד דְּאִתְגַּלְיָיא מִלָּה דְּיוֹסֵף, לָא שַׁרְיָא שְׁכִינְתָּא עֲלֵיהּ דְּיַעֲקֹב.

96. For that reason, they were in collaboration with the Shechinah when they sold Joseph; they made Her a partner to their oath and made Her vow NOT TO REVEAL THE SALE OF JOSEPH. Thus, until THE SALE OF Joseph was made known, the Shechinah did not rest upon Jacob.

97. וְאִי תֵּימָא דִּשְׁכִינְתָּא לָא אִשְׁתַּכְּחַת עִמְּהוֹן, תָּא חֲזֵי, דִּכְתִּיב שֶׁשָּׁם עָלוּ שְׁבָטִים שִׁבְטֵי יָהּ עֵדוּת לְיִשְׂרָאֵל לְהוֹדוֹת לְשֵׁם יי׳, כֻּלְּהוּ צַדִּיקֵי וַחֲסִידֵי, קִיּוּמָא דְּכָל עַלְמָא, קִיּוּמָא אִינּוּן לְעֵילָּא וְתַתָּא.

97. If you say that the Shechinah was not with THE TRIBES, come and behold the verse: "There the tribes used to go up, the tribes of Yah, an appointed practice for Yisrael to give thanks to the name of Hashem" (Tehilim 122:4). They were all just and pious, the sustenance of the inhabitants of the world, FOR THE WHOLE WORLD ENDURED THANKS TO THEM both above and below, IN THE UPPER AND LOWER WORLDS.

9. “O Jerusalem, built”

A Synopsis

This section begins with a brief discussion of the preordained roles of David and Solomon in the construction of the temple, and then proceeds to address the relationship between the terrestrial Jerusalem and the heavenly Jerusalem. It is, we see, mirrored by the relationship of the children of Israel to the Upper and Lower Worlds.

The Relevance of this Passage

Our planet contains many spiritual energy centers that serve as portals through which the supernal Light of the Upper World flows into our dimension. Israel is the energy center of the entire planet. The city of Jerusalem is the energy source of Israel. The Temple is the primal source of energy for Jerusalem, and the Holy of Holies is the Fountainhead of spiritual energy for the Temple. Reading this passage connects us to Jerusalem, the Temple and ultimately, to the Holy of Holies. It ensures that all our prayers, deeds, and meditations draw their Light from this wellspring of spiritual energy.

98. פְּתַח וַאֲמַר שָׂמַחְתִּי בְּאוֹמְרִים לִי בֵּית יי׳ נֵלֵךְ. הַאי קְרָא אוֹקְמוּהָ, דְּדָוִד הֲוָה עִם לִבֵּיהּ לְמִבְנֵי בֵּיתָא, כד״א וַיְהִי עִם לְבַב דָּוִד אָבִי לִבְנוֹת בַּיִת לְשֵׁם יי׳ וגו׳. וּלְבָתַר מַה כְּתִיב, רַק אַתָּה לֹא תִבְנֶה הַבַּיִת כִּי אִם בִּנְךָ הַיּוֹצֵא מֵחֲלָצֶיךָ הוּא יִבְנֶה הַבַּיִת לִשְׁמִי, וְכָל יִשְׂרָאֵל הֲווֹ יָדְעֵי דָא, וַהֲווֹ אָמְרוּ, אֵימָתַי יָמוּת דָּוִד, וְיָקוּם שְׁלֹמֹה בְּרֵיהּ וְיִבְנֶה בֵּיתָא, וּכְדֵין עוֹמְדוֹת הָיוּ רַגְלֵינוּ בִּשְׁעָרַיִךְ יְרוּשָׁלִַם, כְּדֵין נֵיסַק וְנַקְרִיב תַּמָּן קָרְבָּנִין.

98. He then quoted the verse: “I was glad when they said to me, ‘Let us go into the house of Hashem’” (Tehilim 122:4). It has been explained that David said this when he set his heart on building the Temple, as it is written: “And it was in the heart of David, my father, to build a house for the name of Hashem, the Elohim of Yisrael” (I Melachim 8:17). But then it is written: “Yet you shall not build the house; but your son that shall come forth out of your loins, he shall build the house to My Name” (Ibid. 19). All Yisrael knew that and asks: When will David die so that his son Solomon can rise and build the Temple, as “our feet are standing within your gates, O Jerusalem” (Tehilim 122:2), and we will go up to offer sacrifices?

99. וְעִם כָּל דָּא, אַף עַל גָּב דַּהֲווֹ אָמְרוּ אֵימָתַי יָמוּת סָבָא דָא, כְּדֵין

שְׂמַחְתִּי וְחֶדְוָה הֲוָה לִי, בְּגִין בְּרִי, דַּהֲווֹ אָמְרֵי דִבְרִי יָקוּם תְּחוֹתִי, לְמִגְמַר פִּקּוּדָא לְמִבְנֵי בֵּיתָא, כְּדֵין שָׁרֵי וְשַׁבַּח לָהּ, וַאֲמַר יְרוּשָׁלַיִם הַבְּנוּיָה כְּעִיר שֶׁחֻבְּרָה לָּהּ יַחְדָּו.

99. For all that they used to ask, ‘When will this old man die?’ David was nevertheless “glad,” and rejoiced on account of his son, who, it was said, would reign in his stead and carry out the building the Temple. Then he began to praise THE SHECHINAH, saying: “O Jerusalem, built as a city that is joined together” (Tehilim 122:3).

100. תְּנַן, עָבַד קוּדְשָׁא בְּרִיךְ הוּא יְרוּשָׁלַיִם לְתַתָּא, כְּגַוְונָא דִלְעֵילָּא, וְדָא מִתְתַּקְנָא, לָקֳבֵל דָּא, דִּכְתִיב מָכוֹן לְשִׁבְתְּךָ פָּעַלְתָּ יי'. הַבְּנוּיָה: דְּזַמִּין קוּדְשָׁא בְּרִיךְ הוּא לְנַחֲתָא לָהּ יְרוּשָׁלַיִם דִּלְעֵילָּא כִּדְקָא יָאוֹת, וּבְגִין כָּךְ הַבְּנוּיָה. שֶׁחֻבְּרָה לָּהּ יַחְדָּו, וְהָא אוֹקְמוּהָ, שֶׁחֻבְּרָה שֶׁחִבְּרוּ מִבָּעֵי לֵיהּ. אֶלָּא דְּאִתְחַבְּרַת אִמָּא בִּבְרַתָּא, וַהֲווֹ כַּחֲדָא, וְאוֹקְמוּהָ.

100. We learned that the Holy One, blessed be He, formed the terrestrial Jerusalem, THE NUKVA, in the image of the heavenly Jerusalem, BINAH, with each facing the other, FOR THE NUKVA IS ESTABLISHED WITH ALL THE IMPLEMENTS OF BINAH. As it is written: “In the place, Hashem, which You have made for you to dwell in” (Shemot 15:17). “Built” means that the Holy One, blessed be He, will cause Jerusalem to descend from above, completely BUILT. Therefore, HE SAYS “built.” “That is joined together,” as has already been explained. HE SAID: It should have been ‘are joined’, IN THE PLURAL. HE ANSWERS: The mother, BINAH, joined her daughter, THE NUKVA, and they became as one. HENCE IT IS WRITTEN IN THE SINGULAR, as has been explained.

101. וְאִתְּמָר. שֶׁשָּׁם עָלוּ שְׁבָטִים, אִלֵּין אִינּוּן קִיּוּמָא דְעַלְמָא, וְתִקּוּנָא דְעַלְמָא תַּתָּאָה, וְלָא תֵימָא דְעַלְמָא תַּתָּאָה בִּלְחוֹדוֹי, אֶלָּא אֲפִילּוּ דְעַלְמָא עִלָּאָה, דִּכְתִיב שִׁבְטֵי יָהּ עֵדוּת לְיִשְׂרָאֵל, לְיִשְׂרָאֵל דַּיְיקָא, בְּגִין דְּאִינּוּן קִיּוּמָא לְתַתָּא, סַהֲדוּתָא אִינּוּן לְעֵילָּא, וְכֹלָּא לְהוֹדוֹת לְשֵׁם יי', לְאוֹדָאָה שְׁמֵיהּ דְּקוּדְשָׁא בְּרִיךְ הוּא, לְכָל סִטְרִין, דִּכְתִיב לְהוֹדוֹת לְשֵׁם יי'.

9. "O Jerusalem, built"

101. "There the tribes used to go up..." (Tehilim 122:4). They sustain the world and support the lower world. And not just the lower world, but also the upper world, as it is written: "The tribes of Yah, an appointed practice (also: 'testimony') for Yisrael" – precisely, "for Yisrael." Because the children of Yisrael support the lower world, they bear testimony above IN THE UPPER WORLD. All this is to thank the Holy One, blessed be He, on all sides, as it is written: "To give thanks to the name of Hashem" (Ibid.).

10. "And a certain man found him"

A Synopsis

This section addresses the role of providence in the sale of Joseph to the Egyptians and illustrates our inability to interpret events and their causal relationships as positive or negative, since we are ignorant of their role in God's preordained design.

The Relevance of this Passage

The selling of Joseph into slavery, and his subsequent rise from the status of prisoner to the second in command of Egypt, alludes to our ability to take control over the physical reality and triumph over our most base desires, thereby freeing our souls. The strength to accomplish this is aroused within us by the liberating Light set aflame by these Kabbalistic verses. In addition, we become more cognizant of our limited perspectives on life, particularly when hardships strike. Just as Joseph's imprisonment was a dire and tragic predicament that was eventually turned into triumph, our afflictions can be transformed into conquests given the right state of enlightened consciousness. That is, the foresight and wisdom to see beyond the immediate circumstances. Enlightenment is thus awakened in us by the lessons and Light emitted through the luminous letters of the Hebrew language appearing in this passage.

102. וַיִּמְצָאֵהוּ אִישׁ וְהִנֵּה תֹעֶה בַּשָּׂדֶה וַיִּשְׁאָלֵהוּ הָאִישׁ לֵאמֹר מַה תְּבַקֵּשׁ. מַה כְּתִיב לְעֵילָּא, וַיֹּאמֶר יִשְׂרָאֵל אֶל יוֹסֵף הֲלוֹא אַחֶיךָ רֹעִים בִּשְׁכֶם לְכָה וְאֶשְׁלָחֲךָ אֲלֵיהֶם. וְכִי יַעֲקֹב שְׁלֵימָא, דַּהֲוָה רָחֵים לֵיהּ לְיוֹסֵף מִכָּל בְּנוֹי, וְהוּא יָדַע דְּכָל אֲחוֹי הֲווֹ סָנְאִין לֵיהּ, אַמַּאי שַׁדַּר לֵיהּ לְגַבַּיְיהוּ, אֶלָּא אִיהוּ לָא חָשִׁיד עֲלַיְיהוּ, דַּהֲוָה יָדַע דְּכֻלְּהוּ הֲווֹ זַכָּאִין, וְלָא חָשִׁיד לוֹן, אֶלָּא גָּרֵים קוּדְשָׁא בְּרִיךְ הוּא כָּל דָּא, בְּגִין לְקַיְּימָא גְּזֵרָה דִּגְזַר בֵּין הַבְּתָרִים.

102. "And a certain man found him, and behold, he was wandering in the field; and the man asked him, saying, 'What are you seeking?'" (Beresheet 37:15). It is written earlier: "And Yisrael said to Joseph, 'Do not your brothers feed the flock in Shchem? Come, and I will send you to them'" (Ibid. 13). Why did the perfected Jacob, who loved Joseph better than his other sons and knew that his brothers hated him, send Joseph to them? HE ANSWERS: Because he knew they were righteous, he did not distrust them.

The Holy One, blessed be He, caused all this to carry out the decree He made TO ABRAHAM in the Covenant, between the pieces.

103. אַשְׁכַּחְנָא בְּסִפְרֵי קַדְמָאֵי, דְּבָעְיָין אִלֵּין בְּנֵי יַעֲקֹב, לְשַׁלְטָאָה עֲלוֹי, עַד לָא יֵחוֹת לְמִצְרַיִם, דְּאִילּוּ הוּא יֵחוֹת לְמִצְרַיִם וְאִינוּן לָא שָׁלְטוּ בֵּיהּ בְּקַדְמֵיתָא, יָכְלֵי מִצְרָאֵי לְשַׁלְטָאָה לְעָלְמִין עֲלַיְיהוּ דְּיִשְׂרָאֵל, וְאִתְקַיְימָא בֵּיהּ בְּיוֹסֵף, דְּאִזְדַּבַּן לְעַבְדָּא, וְאִינוּן שָׁלְטוּ עֲלוֹי, וְאַף עַל גַּב דְּיוֹסֵף הֲוָה מַלְכָּא לְבָתַר, וּמִצְרָאֵי הֲווֹ עַבְדִין לֵיהּ, אִשְׁתַּכָּחוּ יִשְׂרָאֵל דְּשָׁלְטוּ עַל כֻּלְּהוּ.

103. We have found it stated in ancient books that it was imperative that the sons of Jacob have mastery over Joseph before he descended to Egypt. For if he had gone there before they dominated him, the Egyptians would have ruled over Yisrael in perpetuity, AND YISRAEL WOULD NOT HAVE BEEN ABLE TO LEAVE. THEREFORE, it came to pass that HIS BROTHERS were Joseph's masters and sold him as a slave. THUS, when Joseph was later crowned king of Egypt, Yisrael ruled over them all. FOR THEY OBTAINED MASTERY OVER JOSEPH, THEIR KING, BY SELLING HIM TO BE A SLAVE. IT WAS AS IF THEY RULED OVER THE EGYPTIANS THEMSELVES. THIS WEAKENED EGYPTIAN POWER AND ENABLED YISRAEL TO BE FREED FROM IT.

104. תָּא חֲזֵי, דְּיוֹסֵף דְּאִיהוּ בְּרִית עִלָּאָה, כָּל זִמְנָא דְּאִתְקַיַּים בְּרִית, שְׁכִינְתָּא אִתְקַיַּים בַּהֲדַיְיהוּ דְּיִשְׂרָאֵל בִּשְׁלָם, כִּדְקָא יָאוֹת, כֵּיוָן דְּאִסְתַּלַּק יוֹסֵף בְּרִית עִלָּאָה מֵעָלְמָא, כְּדֵין בְּרִית, שְׁכִינְתָּא, וְיִשְׂרָאֵל כֻּלְּהוּ בְּגָלוּתָא נָפְקוּ, וְהָא אוֹקִימְנָא דִּכְתִּיב, וַיָּקָם מֶלֶךְ חָדָשׁ עַל מִצְרַיִם אֲשֶׁר לֹא יָדַע אֶת יוֹסֵף, וְכֹלָּא הֲוָה מֵעִם קוּדְשָׁא בְּרִיךְ הוּא, כִּדְקָא יָאוֹת.

104. Come and behold: Joseph was the Supernal Covenant, YESOD OF ZEIR ANPIN, and as long as the Covenant, JOSEPH, endured, the Shechinah lived within Yisrael in peace. Once Joseph, the Supernal Covenant, was gone from the world AND SOLD AS A SLAVE, the Covenant, the Shechinah, and Yisrael all went into exile. This has been explained in connection with the verse: "Now there arose a new king over Egypt, who knew not Joseph"

(Shemot 1:8). THIS INDICATES THAT HIS RANK HAD BEEN REVOKED AND HE WENT INTO EXILE. The Holy One, blessed be He, caused all this, and it happened as it had to.

105. תָּא חֲזֵי, וַיִּמְצָאֵהוּ אִישׁ, דָּא גַּבְרִיאֵל, וְאוֹקְמוּהָ כְּתִיב הָכָא וַיִּמְצָאֵהוּ אִישׁ, וּכְתִיב הָתָם וְהָאִישׁ גַּבְרִיאֵל אֲשֶׁר רָאִיתִי בֶחָזוֹן בַּתְּחִלָּה. וְהִנֵּה תוֹעֶה, בְּכֹלָּא תּוֹעֶה, דְּאַבְטַח עַל אֲחוֹי, דַּהֲוָה מִתְבַּע אַחְוָה דִלְהוֹן, וְלָא אַשְׁכַּח, וְתָבַע לְהוֹ, וְלָא אַשְׁכַּח. וְעַל דָּא תוֹעֶה בְּכֹלָּא, וְעַל דָּא וַיִּשְׁאָלֵהוּ הָאִישׁ לֵאמֹר מַה תְּבַקֵּשׁ.

105. "And a certain man found him" refers to Gabriel. It has been explained here that it is written: "And a certain man found him," and elsewhere it is written: "The man Gabriel, whom I had seen in the vision at the beginning" (Daniel 9:21). BY ANALOGY, WE LEARN THAT THE MAN IN THE FIRST SENTENCE IS ALSO GABRIEL, and "he was wandering" (Beresheet 37:15) in every way, for trusting his brothers, for seeking fraternity but not obtaining it, and for looking for them without finding them. Therefore, "the man asked him, saying, 'What are you seeking?'"

11. “I seek my brothers...”

A Synopsis

Rabbi Yehuda interprets the title quotation to indicate Joseph’s intimate association with righteousness and the Shechinah. We are also shown how Joseph’s enduring love and loyalty toward his brothers provide a human demonstration of God’s compassionate love for the children of Israel.

The Relevance of this Passage

The drama of human existence is more than a one-act play. It’s a production that encompasses many lifetimes, where credits and debits accrue according to our actions. Therefore, forgiving those who have inflicted harm upon us really has nothing to do with the other person. Kabbalistically, the people who hurt us in life are messengers. Everything that befalls us is a result of our prior deeds. The consequences of our actions eventually return through the agency of others, in order to help us achieve spiritual growth and correction. The strength to display compassion and forgiveness, even when we feel it is not deserved, is stimulated by the words of this passage.

106. וַיֹּאמֶר אֶת אַחַי אָנֹכִי מְבַקֵּשׁ וגו׳. וַיֹּאמֶר הָאִישׁ נָסְעוּ מִזֶּה וגו׳ ר׳ יְהוּדָה פָּתַח, מִי יִתֶּנְךָ כְּאָח לִי יוֹנֵק שְׁדֵי אִמִּי אֶמְצָאֲךָ בַחוּץ אֶשָּׁקְךָ גַּם לֹא יָבוּזוּ לִי. הַאי קְרָא אוֹקְמוּהָ חַבְרַיָּא, אֲבָל הַאי קְרָא, כְּנֶסֶת יִשְׂרָאֵל אֲמָרוֹ לְמַלְכָּא דִשְׁלָמָא דִילֵיהּ, מִי יִתֶּנְךָ כְּאָח לִי, כְּיוֹסֵף עַל אֲחוֹי, דַּאֲמַר וְעַתָּה אַל תִּירָאוּ אָנֹכִי אֲכַלְכֵּל אֶתְכֶם וְאֶת טַפְּכֶם, יְהַב לוֹן מְזוֹנָא, וְזָן לְהוֹ בְּכַפְנָא. בְּגִין כָּךְ מִי יִתֶּנְךָ כְּאָח לִי.

106. “And he said, ‘I seek my brothers’...And the man said, ‘They are departed from here.’” Rabbi Yehuda quoted the verse: “O that you were as my brother, that sucked the breasts of my mother! when I should find you outside, I would kiss you; and none would scorn me” (Shir Hashirim 8:1). This verse has already been explained by the friends. The Congregation of Yisrael, THE NUKVA, said to the King to whom peace belongs, TO ZEIR ANPIN: “O that you were as my brother,” as Joseph was to his brothers. Joseph said to them, “’Now therefore fear not: I will nourish you, and your little ones’” (Beresheet 50:21) and he provided for them in time of famine. Therefore, THE CONGREGATION OF YISRAEL SAID TO ZEIR ANPIN, “O that you were as my brother,” AS JOSEPH WAS TO HIS BROTHERS.

107. דָּבָר אֲחֵר מִי יִתֶּנְךָ כְּאָח לִי, דָּא יוֹסֵף לְגַבָּהּ דִּשְׁכִינְתָּא, דְּאִתְאַחַד עִמָּהּ וְאִתְדַּבַּק בַּהֲדָהּ. יוֹנֵק שְׁדֵי אִמִּי, דְּהָא כְּדֵין אַחְוָה וּשְׁלִימוּ בַּהֲדַיְיהוּ. אֶמְצָאֲךָ בַחוּץ, גּוֹ גָּלוּתָא, דְּאִיהוּ בְּאַרְעָא אָחֳרָא. אֶשָּׁקְךָ, בְּגִין לְאִתְדַּבְּקָא רוּחָא בְּרוּחָא. גַּם לֹא יָבוּזוּ לִי, אַף עַל גַּב דַּאֲנָא בְּאַרְעָא אָחֳרָא.

107. According to another explanation of "O that you were as my brother...," Joseph, YESOD, said this to the Shechinah, whom he joined and to whom he cleaved. "...that sucked the breasts of my mother..." means that WHEN SHE RECEIVES MOCHIN FROM IMA, there is friendship and unity between them. "I should find you outside," in exile in a strange land; "I would kiss you," to merge her spirit with his; "...and none would scorn me" –'although I am in a foreign land'.

108. תָּא חֲזֵי, דְּיוֹסֵף אַף עַל גָּב דַּאֲחוֹי לָא הֲווֹ לֵיהּ כְּאַחִין, כַּד נְפַל בִּידַיְיהוּ, אִיהוּ הֲוָה לוֹן כְּאַחָא, כַּד נְפָלוּ בִּידֵיהּ, וְהָא אוֹקְמוּהָ דִּכְתִיב וַיְנַחֵם אוֹתָם וַיְדַבֵּר עַל לִבָּם, בְּכֹלָּא דִּבֵּר עַל לִבַּיְיהוּ.

108. Come and behold: although Joseph's brothers did not act as his brothers when he fell into their hands, he was a brother to them when they fell into his hands. This is understood from the verse: "And he comforted them and spoke kindly to them" (Beresheet 50:21); he spoke kindly in every WAY UNTIL THEY BELIEVED HIM.

12. There is anger, and there is anger

A Synopsis

This section provides a discussion on the two species of anger, one blessed and the other cursed. Rabbi Shimon then explains the ritual of cleansing the hands each morning, and why this sanctification is necessary.

The Relevance of this Passage

At times we must exert judgement or anger that is rooted in love and sharing. Positive anger is a form of love, as when a parent disciplines a child out concern for the child's safety. Ego-based anger, however, creates negative energy. If a parent punishes a child as an expression of inner frustration, this anger is cursed. One version of anger generates love; the other creates darkness. The words that reveal these truths help us attain the wisdom to mete out anger rooted in love, which is, therefore, blessed with the Light of The Creator.

109. וְתָא חֲזֵי מַה כְּתִיב, וַיֹּאמְרוּ אִישׁ אֶל אָחִיו, דָּא שִׁמְעוֹן וְלֵוִי, דְּאִינּוּן הֲווֹ אַחִין וַדַּאי בְּכֹלָּא, בְּגִין דְּקָא אָתוֹ מִסִּטְרָא דְּדִינָא קַשְׁיָא, וּבְגִין כָּךְ, רוּגְזָא דִּלְהוֹן, אִיהוּ רוּגְזָא דִּקְטָלָא בְּעַלְמָא, כד"א אָרוּר אַפָּם כִּי עָז וְעֶבְרָתָם כִּי קָשָׁתָה.

109. Come and behold: "And they said one to another (lit. 'a man to his brother')" (Beresheet 37:19). These are Shimon and Levi, who were brothers in every respect, because they both came from the side of Harsh Judgment, and their anger was therefore murderous anger, as it is written: "Cursed be their anger, for it was fierce; and their wrath, for it was cruel" (Beresheet 49:7).

110. תָּא חֲזֵי רָזָא דְּמִלָּה, אִית רוּגְזָא וְאִית רוּגְזָא. אִית רוּגְזָא דְּאִיהוּ מְבָרְכָא מֵעֵילָּא וּמִתַּתָּא, וְאִקְרֵי בָּרוּךְ, כְּמָה דְּאִתְּמָר דִּכְתִּיב בָּרוּךְ אַבְרָם לְאֵל עֶלְיוֹן קוֹנֵה שָׁמַיִם וָאָרֶץ, וְהָא אוֹקְמוּהָ. וְאִית רוּגְזָא, דְּאִיהִי אִתְלַטְיָא לְעֵילָּא וְתַתָּא, כְּמָה דְּאִתְּמָר דְּאִקְרֵי אָרוּר, דִּכְתִּיב אָרוּר אַתָּה מִכָּל הַבְּהֵמָה וּמִכָּל חַיַּת הַשָּׂדֶה. אָרוּר אַפָּם כִּי עָז.

110. Come and behold the secret of this matter. There are two kinds of anger. One kind of anger is blessed above and below, and is called 'blessed', as we learned from the verse: "Blessed be Abram of the most high El, possessor of heaven and earth" (Beresheet 14:19). It has already been explained THAT ALTHOUGH ABRAHAM WAS ENGAGED IN WAR AND KILLED PEOPLE, IT WAS STILL SAID OF HIM, 'BLESSED BE ABRAM,' BECAUSE HE SANCTIFIED THE NAME OF HEAVEN IN DOING IT. Another kind of anger is cursed above and below, and we have learned that it is called 'cursed', as it is written: "You are cursed above all cattle" (Beresheet 3:14), and "Cursed be their anger."

111. וְעַל רָזָא דָא, אִית תְּרֵין טוּרִין, דִּכְתִיב וְנָתַתָּ אֶת הַבְּרָכָה עַל הַר גְּרִיזִים וְאֶת הַקְּלָלָה עַל הַר עֵיבָל, לָקֳבֵיל אִלֵּין תְּרֵין דַּרְגִּין, וְעַל דָּא, דָּא אִקְרֵי אָרוּר וְדָא אִקְרֵי בָּרוּךְ, וְשִׁמְעוֹן וְלֵוִי אִינוּן מִסִּטְרָא דְדִינָא קַשְׁיָא, וּמִן סִטְרָא דְדִינָא קַשְׁיָא תַּקִּיפָא, נָפְקַת רוּגְזָא דְאִתְלַטְיָא.

111. Two mountains rely on this mystery, as it is written: "That you shall put the blessing upon mount Gerizim, and the curse upon mount Eval" (Devarim 11:29). They correspond to the two grades, THE ONE CALLED 'BLESSED' AND THE OTHER 'CURSED'. OF THESE MOUNTAINS AS WELL, one is called 'cursed' and the other 'blessed'. Shimon and Levi are from the side of Harsh Judgment, and from this harsh and rigorous Judgment, the accursed anger, WHICH IS CALLED 'CURSED', is issued.

112. וְתָא חֲזֵי, מִסִּטְרָא דְדִינָא קַשְׁיָא, נָפְקֵי רוּגְזָא לִתְרֵי סִטְרִין, חַד דְּאִתְבָּרַךְ, וְחַד דְּאִתְלַטְיָא. חַד בָּרוּךְ, וְחַד אָרוּר. כְּגַוְונָא דָא, מִסִּטְרָא דְיִצְחָק, נָפְקוּ תְּרֵין בְּנִין, חַד מְבוֹרָךְ וְחַד דְּאִתְלַטְיָא לְעֵילָּא וְתַתָּא, דָּא אִתְפָּרַשׁ לְסִטְרֵיהּ, וְדָא אִתְפָּרַשׁ לְסִטְרֵיהּ, דָּא דִּיּוּרֵיהּ בְּאַרְעָא קַדִּישָׁא, וְדָא דִּיּוּרֵיהּ בְּטוּרָא דְשֵׂעִיר, דִּכְתִיב אִישׁ יוֹדֵעַ צַיִד אִישׁ שָׂדֶה. דָּא אַתְרֵיהּ בַּאֲתַר דְּמִדְבְּרָא וְחָרְבָא וּשְׁמָמָה, וְדָא יוֹשֵׁב אֹהָלִים. וְכֹלָּא כְּגַוְונָא דְאִיצְטְרִיךְ.

112. Come and behold: from the side of Harsh Judgment, anger travels in two directions, one blessed and the other accursed. Similarly, two sons issued from Isaac, the one blessed and the other accursed, above and below. Each went to his own side. One dwelled in the Holy Land, while the other was in the mount of Seir, as "a cunning hunter, a man of the field"

(Beresheet 25:27). One dwelled in a place of desolation and ruin, while the other was "dwelling in tents," as it should be.

113. וּבְגִין כָּךְ, תְּרֵין דַּרְגִּין אִינּוּן: בָּרוּךְ וְאָרוּר, דָּא לְסִטְרֵיהּ, וְדָא לְסִטְרֵיהּ, מֵהַאי נָפְקִין כָּל בִּרְכָאן דְעָלְמִין לְעֵילָּא וְתַתָּא, וְכָל טִיבוּ, וְכָל נְהִירוּ, וְכָל פּוּרְקָן, וְכָל שֵׁזָבוּתָא. וּמֵהַאי נָפְקִין, כָּל לְוָוטִין, וְכָל חַרְבָא, וְכָל דָּמָא, וְכָל שְׁמָמָא, וְכָל בִּישִׁין, וְכָל מְסָאֲבוּ דְעָלְמָא.

113. Therefore, each of the two grades, blessed and cursed, goes to its own side. From the former come all the blessings in the world from above and below – all goodness, illumination, redemption, and salvation. From the latter comes all the curse, ruin, blood, waste, evil, and all that is defiled in the world.

114. רַבִּי שִׁמְעוֹן פָּתַח וַאֲמַר, אֶרְחַץ בְּנִקָּיוֹן כַּפָּי וַאֲסוֹבְבָה אֶת מִזְבַּחֲךָ ה', הַאי קְרָא אוּקְמוּהָ. אֲבָל תָּא חֲזֵי רָזָא דְמִלָּה הָכָא, דְּהָא לֵית לָךְ בַּר נָשׁ בְּעָלְמָא, דְּלָא טָעֵים טַעְמָא דְמוֹתָא בְּלֵילְיָא, וְרוּחַ מְסָאֲבָא שַׁרְיָא עַל הַהוּא גוּפָא, מַאי טַעְמָא, בְּגִין דְּנִשְׁמְתָא קַדִּישָׁא, אִסְתַּלְּקַת מִנֵּיהּ דְּבַר נָשׁ, וְנָפְקַת מִנֵּיהּ. וְעַל דְּנִשְׁמְתָא קַדִּישָׁא נָפְקַת וְאִסְתַּלְּקַת מִנֵּיהּ, שַׁרְיָא רוּחָא מְסָאֲבָא עַל הַהוּא גוּפָא, וְאִסְתָּאַב.

114. Rabbi Shimon quoted the verse: "I wash my hands in innocence: so I compass Your altar, Hashem" (Tehilim 26:6). This has already been explained, yet come and behold: the mystery is that no man in the world avoids tasting death at night. As a result, the Spirit of Defilement hovers above his body. The reason is that the Holy Soul leaves him at that time and, once it leaves, the Spirit of Defilement hovers above his body, and he is defiled.

115. וְכַד נִשְׁמְתָא אִתְהַדְּרַת לְגוּפָא, אִתְעֲבַר הַהוּא זוּהֲמָא, וְהָא אִתְּמָר דִּידוֹי דְּבַר נָשׁ, זוּהֲמָא דִמְסָאֲבוּ אִשְׁתָּאַר בְּהוּ, וְעַל דָּא לָא יַעֲבַר יְדוֹי עַל עֵינוֹי, בְּגִין דְּהַהוּא רוּחַ מְסָאֲבָא שַׁרְיָא עֲלוֹי, עַד דְּנָטֵיל לוֹן, וְכַד נָטֵיל יְדוֹי כִּדְקָא חֲזֵי, כְּדֵין אִתְקַדַּשׁ, וְאִקְרֵי קָדוֹשׁ.

115. When the soul returns to the body, the filth passes away; yet it remains on the hands. Thus, a man should not pass his hands across his eyes since the Spirit of Defilement rests on them until they are washed. When a man properly washes them, he is then sanctified and called 'holy'.

116. וְהֵיךְ בָּעֵי לְאִתְקַדְּשָׁא. בָּעֵי חַד כְּלִי לְתַתָּא, וְחַד כְּלִי מִלְּעֵילָּא, בְּגִין דְּיִתְקַדַּשׁ מֵהַהוּא דִּלְעֵילָּא, וְהַהוּא דִּלְתַתָּא דְּיָתֵיב בְּזוּהֲמָא דִּמְסָאֲבוּ בֵּיהּ, וְדָא כְּלִי לְקַבְּלָא מְסָאֲבוּ, וְדָא לְאִתְקַדְּשָׁא מִנֵּיהּ, דָּא בָּרוּךְ, וְדָא אָרוּר, וְלָא בָּעְיָין אִינוּן מַיִין דְּזוּהֲמָא, לְאוֹשְׁדָא לוֹן בְּבֵיתָא, דְּלָא יִקְרַב בְּהוֹ בַּר נָשׁ, דְּהָא בְּהוֹ מִתְכַּנְּשֵׁי סִטְרָא דִּלְהוֹן, וְיָכֵיל לְקַבְּלָא נִזְקָא מֵאִינוּן מַיִין מְסָאֲבִין.

116. HE ASKS: How should we sanctify ourselves WITH HAND WASHING? HE RESPONDED THAT we need a vessel beneath and a vessel above. To be sanctified from the vessel above, the vessel below must receive the filth of impurity and hold the contaminated WATER, while the vessel ABOVE is used for sanctification, AS ITS WATER IS POURED ON THE HANDS. The one ABOVE is blessed, and the one BENEATH is cursed. We must not empty the impure water within the house so that no one will come near it, for HARMFUL SPIRITS gather to it and a man might be harmed by the unclean water.

117. וְעַד דְּיִתְעֲבַר זוּהֲמָא מִן יְדוֹי, לָא יְבָרֵךְ, וְאוֹקִימְנָא. וּבְגִין כָּךְ, בַּר נָשׁ עַד לָא יְקַדֵּשׁ יְדוֹי בְּצַפְרָא, אִקְרֵי טָמֵא, כֵּיוָן דְּאִתְקַדַּשׁ אִקְרֵי טָהוֹר, וּבְגִין כָּךְ, לָא יִטּוֹל, אֶלָּא מִן יְדָא דְּאִדְכֵּי בְּקַדְמֵיתָא, דִּכְתִיב וְהִזָּה הַטָּהוֹר עַל הַטָּמֵא דָּא אִקְרֵי טָהוֹר, וְדָא אִקְרֵי טָמֵא.

117. A man should not say a blessing before he removes the filth from his hands. It has been explained that a man is called 'unclean' before he washes his hands in the morning. Once he washes his hands, he is called 'pure'. Therefore, a man's hands should be washed only by the hands of a man who was cleansed before, as it is written: "And the clean person shall sprinkle upon the unclean" (Bemidbar 19:19). He WHO ALREADY WASHED HIS HANDS is called 'pure', while he WHO HAS NOT is called 'impure'.

118. בְּגִין כָּךְ, חַד כְּלִי לְעֵילָא, וְחַד כְּלִי לְתַתָּא, דָּא קַדִּישָׁא, וְדָא מְסָאֲבָא. וּמֵאִינוּן מַיִין אָסִיר לְמֶעְבַּד בְּהוֹ מִידֵי, אֶלָּא בָּעֵי לְאוֹשְׁדָא לוֹן, בַּאֲתַר דִּבְנֵי נָשָׁא לָא עָבְרִין עֲלַיְיהוּ, וְלָא יָבִית לוֹן בְּבֵיתָא, דְּהָא כֵּיוָן דְּאִתּוֹשְׁדָן בְּאַרְעָא, רוּחָא מְסָאֲבָא אִשְׁתַּכַּח תַּמָּן, וְיָכֵיל לְנַזְקָא, וְאִי חָפַר לוֹן מִדְרוֹן תְּחוֹת אַרְעָא דְּלָא יִתְחֲזוּן, שַׁפִּיר.

118. Therefore, the vessel above is pure, and the vessel below is impure. It is forbidden to put the impure water to any use; it needs be emptied where no one shall use it or pass over it. It must not be kept in the house at night, for once it is spilt on the ground, the Spirit of Defilement abides there and might cause harm. It is considered wise to dig a hole for it under the ground, where it can flow unseen.

119. וְלָא יָהֵיב לוֹן לִנְשֵׁי חֲרָשַׁיָּא, דְּיֵכְלוּן לְאַבְאָשָׁא בְּהוֹ לִבְנֵי נָשָׁא, בְּגִין דְּאִינוּן מַיִין דְּאִתְלַטְיָין, וְקוּדְשָׁא בְּרִיךְ הוּא בָּעֵי לְדַכָּאָה לוֹן לְיִשְׂרָאֵל, וּלְמֶהֱוֵי קַדִּישִׁין, דִּכְתִיב וְזָרַקְתִּי עֲלֵיכֶם מַיִם טְהוֹרִים וּטְהַרְתֶּם מִכֹּל טֻמְאוֹתֵיכֶם וּמִכָּל גִּלּוּלֵיכֶם אֲטַהֵר אֶתְכֶם.

119. It must not be given to witches who may use it to harm people, because it is water that causes the curse. The Holy One, blessed be He, wishes to purify Yisrael and make the people holy, as it is written: "Then will I sprinkle clean water upon you, and you shall be clean" (Yechezkel 36:25).

13. "And that pit was empty; there was no water in it"

A Synopsis

This section opens with a description of the rich rewards of studying Torah, both in this world and the World to Come. Those who neglect study, we are told, receive punishment. As Rabbi Yehuda points out, the children of Israel were exiled from the Holy Land because they abandoned the Torah. The discussion moves from various interpretations of the "empty pit" to the actions of Joseph's brothers–including Reuben's repentance and redemption, the punishment of Jacob, and the removal of Judah as king of the tribe.

The Relevance of this Passage

Kabbalistic concepts of retribution are not based on a Creator who metes out penalties and rewards. The Light of The Creator is a Divine Force whose only attributes are sharing and goodness. This can be compared to an electrical current – which can bring light to a city, or can be destructive if we carelessly poke a finger into a wall socket. Our own free will determines whether we short-circuit [receive punishment] or turn on the "light switch" [gain reward]. The Torah is a blueprint to show us how the universe is "wired," so that we harness spiritual forces in a positive and productive way. This wisdom and enlightenment comes to us through the intricate "wiring" of the words that compose these passages, and the spiritual Light they emit.

120. וַיִּקָּחֻהוּ וַיַּשְׁלִכוּ אֹתוֹ הַבֹּרָה וְהַבּוֹר רֵק אֵין בּוֹ מָיִם. רִבִּי יְהוּדָה פָּתַח וַאֲמַר, תּוֹרַת ה׳ תְּמִימָה מְשִׁיבַת נָפֶשׁ. כַּמָּה אִית לוֹן לִבְנֵי נָשָׁא לְאִשְׁתַּדְלָא בְּאוֹרַיְיתָא, דְּכָל מַאן דְּאִשְׁתַּדַּל בְּאוֹרַיְיתָא, לֶהֱוֵי לֵיהּ חַיִּים בְּעַלְמָא דֵין, וּבְעַלְמָא דְאָתֵי, וְזָכֵי בִּתְרֵין עָלְמִין, וַאֲפִילוּ מַאן דְּאִשְׁתַּדַּל בְּאוֹרַיְיתָא, וְלָא יִשְׁתַּדַּל בָּהּ לִשְׁמָהּ, כִּדְקָא יָאוּת, זָכֵי לַאֲגַר טַב בְּעַלְמָא דֵין, וְלָא דָיְינִין לֵיהּ בְּהַהוּא עַלְמָא.

120. "And they took him, and cast him into a pit: and that pit was empty; there was no water in it" (Beresheet 37:24). Rabbi Yehuda opened the discussion with the verse: "The Torah of Hashem is perfect, restoring the soul" (Tehilim 19:8). Men should endeavor to study the Torah as much as possible, for whoever does so gains life in this world and in the World to Come, and he merits both worlds. Even he who strives to study the Torah, but does it for worldly reasons, merits reward in this world and escapes Judgment in the next.

121. וְתָא חֲזֵי, כְּתִיב אֹרֶךְ יָמִים בִּימִינָהּ בִּשְׂמֹאלָהּ עֹשֶׁר וְכָבוֹד. אֹרֶךְ יָמִים, בְּהַהוּא דְּאִשְׁתַּדַּל בְּאוֹרַיְיתָא לִשְׁמָהּ, דְּאִית לֵיהּ אֹרֶךְ יָמִים בְּהַהוּא עַלְמָא, דְּבֵיהּ אוֹרְכָא דְיוֹמִין, וְאִינוּן יוֹמִין, אִינוּן יוֹמִין וַדַּאי, תַּמָּן אִיהוּ רָחֲצָנוּ דִקְדוּשָּׁא דִלְעֵילָּא, דְּאִתְרְחֵיץ בַּר נָשׁ בְּהַאי עַלְמָא לְאִשְׁתַּדְּלָא בְּאוֹרַיְיתָא, לְאִתְתַּקְּפָא בְּהַהוּא עַלְמָא, בִּשְׂמֹאלָהּ עוֹשֶׁר וְכָבוֹד, אֲגַר טַב וְשַׁלְוָה אִית לֵיהּ בְּהַאי עַלְמָא.

121. Come and behold, it is written: "Length of days is in her right hand; and in her left hand are riches and honor" (Mishlei 3:16). "Length of days," refers to that person who endeavors to study the Torah for its own sake, for he has length of days in a world of long days, SIGNIFYING THE EVERLASTING WORLD. These days, which are found in the everlasting world, are certainly days. THIS MEANS THAT THEY ARE SURELY GOOD AND WORTHY DAYS. In addition, there is the certainty of sacredness above, NAMELY THE HOPED FOR REWARD. A man who trusts in this world should study the Torah diligently to be happy in the EVERLASTING world. "And in her left hand are riches and honor," for he receives good reward and peace in this world.

122. וְכָל מַאן דְּיִשְׁתַּדַּל בְּאוֹרַיְיתָא לִשְׁמָהּ, כַּד נָפֵיק מֵהַאי עַלְמָא, אוֹרַיְיתָא אָזְלָא קַמֵּיהּ, וְאַכְרְזַת קַמֵּיהּ, וַאֲגִינַת עֲלֵיהּ, דְּלָא יִקְרְבוּן בַּהֲדֵיהּ מָארֵיהוֹן דְּדִינָא. כַּד שָׁכֵיב גּוּפָא בְּקִבְרָא, הִיא נָטְרַת לֵיהּ. כַּד נִשְׁמָתָא אָזְלָא לְאִסְתַּלְּקָא לְמֵיתַב לְאַתְרָהּ, אִיהִי אָזְלָא קַמָּהּ דְּהַהִיא נִשְׁמָתָא, וְכַמָּה תַּרְעִין אִתְּבְרוּ מִקַּמָּהּ דְּאוֹרַיְיתָא, עַד דְּעָאלַת לְדוּכְתָּהּ, וְקַיְּימָא עֲלֵיהּ דְּבַר נָשׁ, עַד דְּיִתְּעַר, בִּזְמְנָא דִּיקוּמוּן מֵתַיָּיא דְעַלְמָא, וְאִיהִי מַלְּפָא סַנֵּיגוֹרָא עֲלֵיהּ.

122. Whoever studies the Torah for its own sake will find that when he passes from the world, the Torah goes before him with proclamations and protects him from approaching accusers. When the body lies in the grave, it guards him and when the soul departs to ascend to its place, it precedes the soul. Many CLOSED gates are thrown open before the Torah until it brings THE SOUL to its place. THE TORAH stands by that man when the dead are resurrected, and speaks in his favor.

123. הה"ד בְּהִתְהַלֶּכְךָ תַּנְחֶה אֹתָךְ בְּשָׁכְבְּךָ תִּשְׁמֹר עָלֶיךָ וַהֲקִיצוֹתָ הִיא תְשִׂיחֶךָ. בְּהִתְהַלֶּכְךָ תַּנְחֶה אֹתָךְ, כְּמָה דְּאִתְּמָר. בְּשָׁכְבְּךָ תִּשְׁמֹר עָלֶיךָ, בְּשַׁעְתָּא דְּשָׁכֵיב גּוּפָא בְּקִבְרָא, דְּהָא כְּדֵין בְּהַהוּא זִמְנָא, אִתְדָּן גּוּפָא בְּקִבְרָא, וּכְדֵין אוֹרַיְיתָא אֲגִינַת עֲלֵיהּ. וַהֲקִיצוֹתָ הִיא תְשִׂיחֶךָ, כְּמָא דְּאִתְּמָר, בִּזְמְנָא דְּיִתְעָרוּן מֵתֵי עַלְמָא מִן עַפְרָא. הִיא תְשִׂיחֶךָ, לְמֶהֱוֵי סַנֵּיגוֹרְיָא עֲלָךְ.

123. "When you walk, it shall lead you; when you lie down, it shall keep you and when you awake, it shall talk with you" (Mishlei 6:22). "When you walk, it shall lead you," refers to THE TORAH THAT GOES BEFORE HIM WHEN HE DIES as we explained. "When you lie down, it shall keep you," refers to the interval when the body lies in the grave, for at that time the body is judged and sentenced and the Torah acts in its defense. "And when you awake, it shall talk with you," refers to the time at which the dead rise TO LIFE from the dust. "It shall talk with you," means it will speak in your defense.

124. רִבִּי אֶלְעָזָר אֲמַר, הִיא תְשִׂיחֶךָ. מַאי הִיא תְשִׂיחֶךָ. בְּגִין, דְּאַף עַל גָּב דְּהַשְׁתָּא יְקוּמוּן מֵעַפְרָא, אוֹרַיְיתָא לָא יִתְנְשֵׁי מִנְּהוֹן, דְּהָא כְּדֵין יִנְדְּעוּן כָּל הַהִיא אוֹרַיְיתָא דִּשְׁבָקוּ, כַּד אִסְתַּלְקוּ מֵהַאי עַלְמָא, הַהִיא אוֹרַיְיתָא נְטִירָא מֵהַהוּא זִמְנָא, וְתֵיעוֹל בְּמֵעַיְיהוּ כְּמִלְּקַדְּמִין, וְאִיהִי תְּמַלֵּל בְּמֵעַיְיהוּ

124. Rabbi Elazar quoted the verse: "It shall talk with you." What does this mean? HE ANSWERS: It means that although they have just risen from the dust, they will remember the Torah THEY STUDIED BEFORE THEIR DEATH. They will know all they studied before departing from the world. It penetrates inside them and speak in their innermost parts. THIS MEANS THAT IT DOES NOT COME BACK SLOWLY, AS IS THE NATURE OF THOUGHT, BUT AT ONCE, AS IN DRESSING, AS IS THE NATURE OF THE VISCERA.

125. וְכָל מִלִּין מִתְתַּקְּנָן יַתִּיר מִכְּמָה דַּהֲווֹ בְּקַדְמֵיתָא, דְּהָא כָּל אִינּוּן מִלִּין, דְּאִיהוּ לָא יָכֵיל לְאַדְבָּקָא לוֹ כִּדְקָא יָאוֹת, וְאִיהוּ אִשְׁתַּדַּל בְּהוֹ,

וְלָא אִתְדַּבַּק בְּהוֹ, כֻּלְּהוּ עָאלִין בְּמֵעוֹי מִתְתַּקְּנָן, וְאוֹרַיְיתָא תְּמַלֵּל בֵּיהּ, הה"ד וַהֲקִיצוֹתָ הִיא תְשִׂיחֶךָ. רִבִּי יְהוּדָה אָמַר, כְּגַוְונָא דָא, כָּל מַאן דְּאִשְׁתַּדַּל בְּאוֹרַיְיתָא בְּהַאי עַלְמָא, זָכֵי לְאִשְׁתַּדְּלָא בָּהּ לְעַלְמָא דְאָתֵי, וְהָא אִתְּמָר.

125. And everything shall be clearer than it was before HE DIED, for whatever he did not grasp well THEN, whatever he strove to understand yet did not successfully grasp, is now clear in his innermost parts. And the Torah speaks within him. This is the meaning of the verse: "And when you awake, it shall talk with you." Rabbi Yehuda said that whoever studied the Torah diligently in this world deserves to be occupied with it in the World to Come.

126. תָּא חֲזֵי, הַהוּא בַּר נָשׁ דְּלָא זָכֵי לְאִשְׁתַּדְּלָא בְּהַאי עַלְמָא בְּאוֹרַיְיתָא, וְאִיהוּ אָזֵיל בַּחֲשׁוֹכָא, כַּד נָפֵיק מֵהַאי עַלְמָא, נָטְלִין לֵיהּ, וְעָאלִין לֵיהּ לַגֵּיהִנֹּם, אֲתַר תַּתָּאָה, דְּלָא יְהֵא מְרַחֵם עֲלֵיהּ, דְּאִקְרֵי בּוֹר שָׁאוֹן, טִיט הַיָּוֵן, כד"א, וַיַּעֲלֵנִי מִבּוֹר שָׁאוֹן מִטִּיט הַיָּוֵן וַיָּקֶם עַל סֶלַע רַגְלַי כּוֹנֵן אֲשׁוּרָי.

126. Come and behold: a man who did not have the merit to be occupied with the Torah in this world walks in darkness. When he passes from the world, he is put in the lowest place in Gehenom, where no one pities him, a place described as a "gruesome pit", a "miry clay," as it is written: "He brought me up also out of the gruesome pit, out of the miry clay, and set my feet upon a rock, and established my footsteps" (Tehilim 40:3).

127. וּבְגִין כָּךְ, הַהוּא דְּלָא אִשְׁתַּדַּל בְּאוֹרַיְיתָא בְּהַאי עַלְמָא, וְאִתְטַנַּף בְּטִנּוּפֵי עַלְמָא, מַה כְּתִיב, וַיִּקָּחֻהוּ וַיַּשְׁלִיכוּ אֹתוֹ הַבֹּרָה, דָּא הוּא גֵּיהִנֹּם, אֲתַר דְּדַיְינִין לְהוֹ, לְאִינּוּן דְּלָא אִשְׁתַּדְּלוּ בְּאוֹרַיְיתָא, וְהַבּוֹר רֵק, כְּמָה דְאִיהוּ הֲוָה רֵק, מַאי טַעְמָא, בְּגִין דְּלָא הֲוָה בֵּיהּ מַיִם.

127. It is therefore written of he who does not study the Torah in this world, but besmirches himself with the filth of this world: "And they took him, and cast him into a pit" (Beresheet 37:24), into Gehenom, where those who do not study the Torah are sentenced. "And the pit was empty" (Ibid.); it is empty, because there was no water in it – THAT IS, TORAH, CALLED 'WATER'.

128. וְתָא חֲזֵי כַּמָּה הוּא עוֹנְשָׁא דְּאוֹרַיְיתָא, דְּהָא לָא אִתְגָּלוּ יִשְׂרָאֵל מֵאַרְעָא קַדִּישָׁא, אֶלָּא בְּגִין דְּאִסְתַּלָּקוּ מֵאוֹרַיְיתָא, וְאִשְׁתְּבָקוּ מִינָהּ, הה"ד, מִי הָאִישׁ הֶחָכָם וְיָבֵן אֶת זֹאת וגו', עַל מָה אָבְדָה הָאָרֶץ וגו'. וַיֹּאמֶר ה' עַל עָזְבָם אֶת תּוֹרָתִי וגו'. רִבִּי יוֹסֵי אָמַר מֵהָכָא, לָכֵן גָּלָה עַמִּי מִבְּלִי דָעַת.

128. Come and behold the punishment for neglecting the study of the Torah. Yisrael were exiled from the Holy Land, only for being removed from and leaving the Torah. This is explained by the verse, "Who is the wise man, that may understand this? Why does the land perish…? Because they have forsaken My Torah which I set before them" (Yirmeyah 9:11-12). Rabbi Yosi said: "Therefore My people are gone into captivity, because they have no knowledge" (Yeshayah 5:13), NAMELY, OF THE TORAH.

129. בְּגִין כָּךְ, כֹּלָּא קַיְימָא עַל קִיּוּמָא דְּאוֹרַיְיתָא, וְעַלְמָא לָא אִתְקַיַּים בְּקִיּוּמֵיהּ, אֶלָּא בְּאוֹרַיְיתָא, דְּאִיהוּ קִיּוּמָא דְּעָלְמִין, עֵילָּא וְתַתָּא, דִּכְתִּיב, אִם לֹא בְרִיתִי יוֹמָם וָלַיְלָה חֻקּוֹת שָׁמַיִם וָאָרֶץ לֹא שָׂמְתִּי.

129. Hence, everything is based on the existence of the Torah, and the world only endures by means of the Torah, which sustains the worlds above and below. As it is written: "If my Covenant be not day and night, it were as if I had not appointed the ordinances of heaven and earth…" (Yirmeyah 33:25).

130. וַיִּקָּחֻהוּ וַיַּשְׁלִיכוּ אוֹתוֹ הַבּוֹרָה, רָמַז, עַל דְּאַרְמִיאוּ לֵיהּ לְגוֹ מִצְרָאֵי, אֲתַר דְּלָא אִשְׁתַּכַּח רָזָא דִּמְהֵימְנוּתָא כְּלָל. רִבִּי יִצְחָק אָמַר, אִי נְחָשִׁין וְעַקְרַבִּין הֲווֹ בֵּיהּ, אַמַּאי כְּתִיב בִּרְאוּבֵן, לְמַעַן הַצִּיל אוֹתוֹ מִיָּדָם לַהֲשִׁיבוֹ אֶל אָבִיו, וְכִי לָא חַיֵּישׁ רְאוּבֵן לְהַאי, דְּהָא אִינּוּן נְחָשִׁין וְעַקְרַבִּין יִנַּזְקוּן לֵיהּ, וְאֵיךְ אָמַר לַהֲשִׁיבוֹ אֶל אָבִיו, וּכְתִיב לְמַעַן הַצִּיל אוֹתוֹ.

13. "And that pit was empty; there was no water in it"

130. "And they took him, and cast him into a pit" (Beresheet 37:24). This alludes to the fact that LATER they cast him into Egypt, where the secret of the faith does not abide. WATER IS THE SECRET OF THE FAITH, AND WHEN IT IS WRITTEN: "AND THE PIT WAS EMPTY," IT REFERS TO A LACK OF THE SECRET OF THE FAITH. Rabbi Yitzchak said: If there were snakes and scorpions in the pit – ACCORDING TO THE SAGES, IT DID NOT CONTAIN WATER, BUT IT DID CONTAIN SNAKES AND SCORPIONS – why is it written of Reuben, "He might save him out of their hands" (Ibid. 22)? Did not Reuben fear that the snakes and scorpions would harm Joseph? If so, how did he plan "to deliver him back to his father…that he might save him"?

131. אֶלָּא, חָמָא רְאוּבֵן, דִּנְזָקָא אִשְׁתַּכַּח בִּידַיְיהוּ דַּאֲחוֹי, בְּגִין דְּיָדַע כַּמָּה שָׂנְאִין לֵיהּ, וּרְעוּתָא דִלְהוֹן לְקַטְלָא לֵיהּ, אֲמַר רְאוּבֵן, טַב לְמִנְפַּל לֵיהּ לְגוֹ גּוּבָא דִּנְחָשִׁין וְעַקְרַבִּין, וְלָא יִתְמְסַר בִּידָא דְּשַׂנְאוֹי, דְּלָא מְרַחֲמֵי עֲלֵיהּ. מִכָּאן אָמְרוּ, יַפִּיל בַּר נָשׁ גַּרְמֵיהּ לְאֶשָּׁא, אוֹ לְגוּבָא דִּנְחָשִׁין וְעַקְרַבִּין, וְלָא יִתְמַסַּר בִּידָא דְּשַׂנְאוֹי.

131. HE REPLIED THAT Reuben saw that Joseph would surely come to harm in their hands, for he knew how much they hated him and wished to kill him. Reuben thought it was better to cast him into the pit of snakes and scorpions than to deliver him to his enemies, who have no compassion for him. Thus, the saying: "Rather should a man throw himself into a fire or a pit full of serpents and scorpions, than be delivered into the hands of his enemies."

132. בְּגִין, דְּהָכָא אֲתַר דִּנְחָשִׁים וְעַקְרַבִּים, אִי אִיהוּ צַדִּיקָא, קוּדְשָׁא בְּרִיךְ הוּא יַרְחִישׁ לֵיהּ נִיסָּא, וּלְזִמְנִין דִּזְכוּ דַּאֲבָהָן מְסַיְּיעִין לֵיהּ לְבַר נָשׁ, וְיִשְׁתְּזֵיב מִנַּיְיהוּ, אֲבָל כֵּיוָן דְּיִתְמַסַּר בִּידָא דְּשַׂנְאוֹי, זְעִירִין אִינּוּן דְּיָכְלִין לְאִשְׁתֵּזָבָא.

132. For if a man is righteous here in a place of snakes and scorpions, the Holy One, blessed be He, performs miracles for him, or sometimes he is saved by the merit of his fathers. But once delivered into the hands of enemies, few escape.

133. וּבְגִין כָּךְ אֲמַר לְמַעַן הַצִּיל אוֹתוֹ מִיָּדָם. מִיָּדָם דַּיְיקָא, וְלָא כְתִיב

לְמַעַן הַצִּיל אוֹתוֹ וְתוּ לָא, אֶלָּא אֲמַר רְאוּבֵן, יִשְׁתְּזֵיב מִן יְדַיְיהוּ, וְאִי יְמוּת בְּגוּבָא יְמוּת, וּבְגִין כָּךְ כְּתִיב וַיִּשְׁמַע רְאוּבֵן וַיַּצִּילֵהוּ מִיָּדָם.

133. Therefore, he said: "That he might save him out of their hands," (Beresheet 37:22) not simply 'that he might save him', but rather, "out of their hands." Reuben said to himself, 'may he be saved from them, and if he dies, it is BETTER FOR HIM to die in the pit.' It is therefore written: "And Reuben heard it, and he delivered him out of their hands." HE SAVED HIM ONLY FROM DYING BY THEIR HANDS, EVEN THOUGH HE MIGHT HAVE DIED IN THE PIT.

134. תָּא חֲזֵי, כַּמָּה חֲסִידוּתֵיהּ דִּרְאוּבֵן, דִּבְגִין דְּיָדַע, דְּשִׁמְעוֹן וְלֵוִי, שׁוּתְּפוּתָא וַחֲכִימוּתָא וְחַבְרוּתָא דִּלְהוֹן קַשְׁיָא אִינוּן, דְּכַד אִתְחַבָּרוּ בִּשְׁכֶם, קָטְלוּ כָּל דְּכוּרָא, לָא דַּי לוֹן, אֶלָּא דְּנָטְלִין נָשִׁין וָטַף, וְכַסְפָּא וְדַהֲבָא, וְכָל בְּעִירֵי, וְכָל מָאנֵי דִּיקָר, וְכָל מַאן דְּאִשְׁתַּכַּח בְּקַרְתָּא, וְלָא דַּי כָּל דָּא, אֶלָּא דַּאֲפִילוּ כָּל מַה דִּבְחַקְלָא נָטְלוּ, דִּכְתִיב וְאֵת אֲשֶׁר בָּעִיר וְאֵת אֲשֶׁר בַּשָּׂדֶה לָקָחוּ.

134. Come and behold the piety of Reuben. He knew that Shimon and Levi were ruthless when they joined forces and cunning. When they joined against Shchem, they killed all the males. They were not satisfied, so they took the women and the little ones, gold and silver, and all beasts and precious vessels – in short, everything that was to be found in the city. Yet even this was not enough, so they took what was in the field, as it is written: "And that which was in the city, and that which was in the field they took" (Beresheet 34:28).

135. אֲמַר, וּמַה קַרְתָּא רַבָּתָא כִּי הַאי, לָא אִשְׁתְּזֵיב מִנְּהוֹן, אִלְמָלֵא רַבְיָא דָא יִפּוֹל בִּידַיְיהוּ, לָא יַשְׁאֲרוּן מִנֵּיהּ אוּמְצָא בְּעָלְמָא, וְעַל דָּא אֲמַר, טַב לְאִשְׁתְּזָבָא מִנַּיְיהוּ, דְּלָא יַשְׁאֲרוּן מִנֵּיהּ אִשְׁתָּאֲרוּתָא בְּעָלְמָא, וְלָא יֶחֱמֵי אַבָּא מִנֵּיהּ כְּלוּם לְעָלְמִין.

135. Reuben said, 'If such a great city did not escape them, then if this boy falls in their hands, not a shred of flesh will remain. Therefore, it is better to save him from them, for they will leave no sign of him for my father to see.'

136. וְהָכָא, אִי יְמוּת, לָא יָכְלִין לֵיהּ, וְיִשְׁתָּאַר כָּל גּוּפֵיהּ שְׁלִים, וַאֲתֵיב לֵיהּ לְאַבָּא שְׁלִים, וְעַל דָּא לְמַעַן הַצִּיל אוֹתוֹ מִיָּדָם לַהֲשִׁיבוֹ אֶל אָבִיו, אַף עַל גָּב דִּימוּת הָתָם. וּבְגִין כָּךְ אֲמַר הַיֶּלֶד אֵינֶנּוּ, וְלָא אֲמַר אֵינֶנּוּ חַי, אֶלָּא אֲמַר אֵינֶנּוּ אֲפִילוּ מֵת.

136. ‘Even if he dies IN THE PIT, his brothers will not prevail against him. His body will remain intact and I will return him whole to my father.’ Therefore, it is written: “that he might save him out of their hands, to deliver him back to his father.” ‘I WILL BE ABLE TO RETURN HIM TO MY FATHER even though he will die there.’ He therefore said, “The child is not” (Beresheet 37:30), instead of ‘not alive’, because he was not even dead.

137. תָּא חֲזֵי, מַאי דַּעֲבַד, דְּאִיהוּ בְּחָכְמְתָא הֲוָה, שַׁתֵּיף גַּרְמֵיהּ בַּהֲדַיְיהוּ, דִּכְתִיב לֹא נַכֶּנּוּ נָפֶשׁ, וְלָא כְתִיב לָא תַכּוּהוּ, וְאִיהוּ לָא הֲוָה תַּמָּן, כַּד אִזְדַּבַּן יוֹסֵף, דְּהָא כֻּלְּהוּ מְשַׁמְּשֵׁי לַאֲבוּהוֹן, כָּל חַד וְחַד יוֹמָא חַד, וְהַהוּא יוֹמָא דִּרְאוּבֵן הֲוָה, וְע״ד בָּעָא, דִּבְהַהוּא יוֹמָא דַּהֲוָה שִׁמּוּשָׁא דִּילֵיהּ, לָא יִתְאֲבֵיד יוֹסֵף, וּבְגִין כָּךְ כְּתִיב, וַיָּשָׁב רְאוּבֵן אֶל הַבּוֹר וְהִנֵּה אֵין יוֹסֵף בַּבּוֹר וַיִּקְרַע אֶת בְּגָדָיו. וְהִנֵּה אֵין יוֹסֵף דַּיְיקָא, אֲפִילוּ מִית, מִיַּד וַיָּשָׁב אֶל אֶחָיו וַיֹּאמֶר הַיֶּלֶד אֵינֶנּוּ.

137. Come and behold what Reuben did. He wisely joined them and said, “Let us not kill him” (Beresheet 37:21), instead of ‘Do not you take his life’, for he was not there when Joseph was sold. They each then attended their father for one day. When it was Reuben’s day, he did not want Joseph to perish. It is therefore written: “And Reuben returned to the pit and, behold, Joseph was not in the pit” – NOT EVEN DEAD – “and he rent his clothes.” Immediately, “he returned to his brothers, and said, ‘The child is not’.”

138. וַאֲפִילוּ רְאוּבֵן, לָא יָדַע מֵהַהוּא זְבִינָא דְּיוֹסֵף, וְהָא אוֹקְמוּהָ דְּאִשְׁתַּתֵּיף בְּהוֹ שְׁכִינְתָּא, וְע״ד, לָא יָדַע רְאוּבֵן, מֵהַהוּא זְבִינָא דְּיוֹסֵף, וְלָא אִתְגַּלְיָיא לֵיהּ, עַד הַהוּא זִמְנָא, דְּאִתְגְּלֵי יוֹסֵף לַאֲחוֹהִי.

138. Even Reuben was not informed of the sale of Joseph. It has already been explained that the Shechinah was a partner IN THE VOW NOT TO REVEAL THE SALE OF JOSEPH. Therefore Reuben did not know of it, and it was not revealed to him until Joseph made himself known to his brothers!

139. תָּא חֲזֵי, כַּמָּה גָּרֵים לֵיהּ לִרְאוּבֵן, בְּגִין דְּאִיהוּ אִשְׁתַּדַּל לַאֲחָיָיא לֵיהּ לְיוֹסֵף, מַה כְּתִיב, יְחִי רְאוּבֵן וְאַל יָמוֹת וגו׳. דְּהָא בְּגִין דָּא אַף עַל גָּב דְּיָדַע דְּאִשְׁתְּקִיל בְּכֵירוּתֵיהּ מִנֵּיהּ, וְאִתְיְהֵיב לְיוֹסֵף, אִשְׁתַּדַּל לַאֲחַיָּיא לֵיהּ, וְצַלֵּי מֹשֶׁה וַאֲמַר, יְחִי רְאוּבֵן וְאַל יָמוֹת, וְאִתְקַיֵּים בְּעַלְמָא דֵין, וְאִתְקַיֵּים בְּעַלְמָא דְאָתֵי. מַאי טַעְמָא, בְּגִין דָּא, וּבְגִין דַּעֲבַד תְּשׁוּבָה מֵהַהוּא עוֹבָדָא. דְּכָל מַאן דְּעָבֵיד תְּשׁוּבָה, קוּדְשָׁא בְּרִיךְ הוּא קַיֵּים לֵיהּ, בְּעַלְמָא דֵין, וּבְעַלְמָא דְאָתֵי.

139. Come and behold what Reuben attained in trying to save Joseph's life. It is written: "Let Reuben live, and not die" (Devarim 33:6). For although he knew that the birthright was taken from him and given to Joseph, nevertheless he tried to save his life. Therefore Moses prayed for him, saying, "Let Reuben live, and not die," and be supported in this world and in the World to Come. What is the reason - it is this SAVING JOSEPH'S LIFE and repenting for DEFILING HIS FATHER'S BED! If a man repents his sins, the Holy One, blessed be He, will revive him in this world and in the World to Come.

140. תָּא חֲזֵי, מַה כְּתִיב וַיִּקְחוּ אֶת כְּתֹנֶת יוֹסֵף וגו׳, הָא אוּקְמוּהָ, דִּבְגִין דִּדְמָא דְשָׂעִיר, דַּמְיָא לִדְמָא דְבַר נָשׁ. אֲבָל תָּא חֲזֵי, אַף עַל גָּב דְּמִלָּה אַתְיָא כִּדְקָא חָזֵי, קוּדְשָׁא בְּרִיךְ הוּא מְדַקְדֵּק בְּצַדִּיקַיָּיא, אֲפִילּוּ כְּחוּט הַשַּׂעֲרָה.

140. Come and behold: "And they took Joseph's coat..." (Beresheet 37:31). It has been explained that this is because a goat's blood resembles human blood. Yet come and behold: even when an act is well executed – WITHOUT COMMITTING ANY SIN – the Holy One, blessed be He, is strict with the righteous, even to a hair's breadth.

141. יַעֲקֹב עָבַד עוֹבָדָא כִּדְקָא יָאוֹת, בְּמַאי בְּגִין דְּאַקְרֵיב לְגַבֵּי אֲבוֹי

שָׂעִיר, דְּאִיהוּ סִטְרָא דְּדִינָא קַשְׁיָא, וְעִם כָּל דָּא, בְּגִין דְּאִיהוּ אַקְרֵיב שָׂעִיר, וְאַכְחֵישׁ לֵיהּ לַאֲבוֹי, דְּאִיהוּ סִטְרָא דִּילֵיהּ, אִתְעֲנַשׁ בְּהַאי שָׂעִיר אָחֳרָא, דְּאַקְרִיבוּ לֵיהּ בְּנוֹי דְּמָא דִּילֵיהּ.

141. Jacob did well to kill a goat for his father. Yet by offering a goat, which comes from the side of Harsh Judgment, he weakened THE ASPECT OF THE STRICT JUDGMENT OF his father since he is of its aspect, AS ISAAC TOO PERTAINS TO SEVERE JUDGMENT. AND ALTHOUGH THE JUDGMENT TOOK HOLD OF THE GOAT, Jacob was punished in that his sons brought its blood before him.

142. בְּאִיהוּ כְּתִיב, וְאֵת עוֹרוֹת גְּדָיֵי הָעִזִּים הִלְבִּישָׁה עַל יָדָיו וְעַל חֶלְקַת צַוָּארָיו, בְּגִין כָּךְ וַיִּטְבְּלוּ אֶת הַכֻּתֹּנֶת בַּדָּם, אַקְרִיבוּ לֵיהּ כְּתוֹנְתָּא, לְאַכְחָשָׁא לֵיהּ, וְכֹלָּא דָּא לָקֳבֵל דָּא, אִיהוּ גָּרִים דִּכְתִיב וַיֶּחֱרַד יִצְחָק חֲרָדָה גְּדוֹלָה עַד מְאֹד, בְּגִין כָּךְ גָּרְמוּ לֵיהּ, דְּחָרַד חֲרָדָה, בְּהַהוּא זִמְנָא, דִּכְתִיב הַכֶּר נָא הַכְּתֹנֶת בִּנְךָ הִיא אִם לֹא.

142. It is written OF JACOB: "And she put the skins of the kids of the goats upon his hands, and upon the smooth of his neck" (Beresheet 27:16). Therefore it is said OF HIS SONS: "And they dipped the coat in the blood" (Beresheet 37:31). This was measure for measure. Since he caused that "Isaac trembled very much" (Ibid. 33), HIS SONS made him tremble when they said, "'Know now whether it be your son's coat or not'" (Ibid. 32).

143. רִבִּי חִיָּיא אֲמַר, בֵּיהּ כְּתִיב, הַאַתָּה זֶה בְּנִי עֵשָׂו אִם לֹא. לֵיהּ כְּתִיב, הַכְּתֹנֶת בִּנְךָ הִיא אִם לֹא. וּבְגִין כָּךְ, קוּדְשָׁא בְּרִיךְ הוּא מְדַקְדֵּק בְּהוּ בְּצַדִּיקַיָּא, בְּכָל מַה דְּאִינוּן עָבְדִין.

143. Rabbi Chiya said, it is written concerning him (Jacob): "Are you my son Esau or not" (Beresheet 27:21), and addressing him (they said), "is it your son's coat or not" (Beresheet 37:32). This is because the Holy One, blessed be He, is strict with the righteous to a hair's breadth in everything they do.

144. רִבִּי אַבָּא אֲמַר, כֵּיוָן דְּחָמוּ כֻּלְּהוּ שִׁבְטִין, הַהוּא צַעֲרָא דַּאֲבוּהוֹן,

אִתְנֶחָמוּ וַוַדַּאי, וִיהִיבוּ גַּרְמַיְיהוּ עֲלֵיהּ דְּיוֹסֵף, דְּיִפְדּוּן לֵיהּ, אִלְמָלֵא יִשְׁכְּחוּן לֵיהּ, כֵּיוָן דְּחָמוּ דְּלָא יָכִילוּ, אַהֲדָרוּ לְגַבֵּיהּ דִּיהוּדָה, וְאַעֲבָרוּ לֵיהּ מֵעֲלַיְיהוּ, בְּגִין דְּאִיהוּ הֲוָה מַלְכָּא עֲלַיְיהוּ, אַעֲבָרוּהוּ מֵעֲלַיְיהוּ, מַה כְּתִיב וַיְהִי בָּעֵת הַהִיא וַיֵּרֶד יְהוּדָה וגו׳.

144. Rabbi Aba said that when the tribes saw their father's grief, they surely regreted SELLING JOSEPH and determined to rescue him if they could find him. When they saw they could not RESCUE HIM, they turned to Judah, WHO ADVISED THEM TO SELL HIM and rejected him from among them. For he now was their king, and when they deposed him, it is written: "And it came to pass at that time, that Judah went down from his brothers" (Beresheet 38:1).

14. Zion and Jerusalem

A Synopsis

Here, Rabbi Yehuda discusses the creation of the universal structure that issued from Zion, the central point of faith and perfection. While Zion and Jerusalem are one, they represent the two grades of judgment and mercy. Through Binah, which correlates to understanding, the attributes of mercy and judgment are commingled and reconciled in the world.

The Relevance of this Passage

Throughout life, our actions disrupt and misalign the supernal forces that embody the attributes of judgement and mercy. This occurs on both a personal and universal level, in line with individual and collective actions of humanity. Consequently, judgement may occur in place of mercy; the world may seem especially hard and judgmental toward us. In response, we may find ourselves overreacting to situations where we'd normally respond with restraint and patience. Balancing these two attributes in our behavior is vital.

An example of judgement and mercy is illustrated by the following parent-child situation. A child terribly misbehaves. The parent becomes extremely upset and immediately spanks the youngster. The parent reacted to the situation, and the act of judgement was rooted in selfish frustration. The child might attempt to change his behavior, but he does so only out of fear. Kabbalistically, the parent needs to balance judgement with mercy. That is, sharing and care for the child must be the intent behind any disciplinary action. The parent might still gently spank the child, but out of love and concern, rather than anger and frustration. The child's motivation for change will now be rooted in love and respect, not fear.

If a soul descends into a human being from the lineage of Abraham [Right Column], it is said that the person's nature will be shaped and influenced by the quality of mercy. If a soul descends from the lineage of Isaac [Left Column], the individual is imbued with a greater proportion of judgement in his nature, and behavior is influenced in that direction.

Reading this section helps balance the forces of judgement and mercy in our interactions with the world. Moreover, these verses open us to the Light so that we ourselves can be worthy of mercy, rather than judgement, when the time comes for them to appear in our lives.

145. רִבִּי יְהוּדָה פָּתַח וַאֲמַר, וַיַּרְעֵם בַּשָּׁמַיִם יי׳ וְעֶלְיוֹן יִתֵּן קוֹלוֹ בָּרָד

וְגַחֲלֵי אֵשׁ. תָּא חֲזֵי, כַּד בָּרָא קוּדְשָׁא בְּרִיךְ הוּא עַלְמָא, אַתְקִין לֵיהּ שִׁבְעָה סְמָכִין, עַל מַה דְּקַיְימָא, וְכֻלְּהוּ סְמָכִין, קַיְימֵי בְּחַד סָמְכָא יְחִידָאי, וְהָא אוֹקְמוּהָ דִּכְתִיב חָכְמוֹת בָּנְתָה בֵיתָהּ חָצְבָה עַמּוּדֶיהָ שִׁבְעָה, וְאִלֵּין כֻּלְּהוּ, אִינּוּן קַיְימֵי בְּחַד דַּרְגָּא מִנַּיְיהוּ, דְּאִקְרֵי צַדִּיק יְסוֹד עוֹלָם.

145. Rabbi Yehuda quoted the verse: "Hashem also thundered in the heavens, and the highest gave His voice; hail and coals of fire" (Tehilim 18:14). Come and behold: when the Holy One, blessed be He, created the universe, THAT IS, WHEN THE HOLY ONE, BLESSED BE HE, EMANATED THE NUKVA, CALLED 'WORLD', He made seven pillars for it BY ILLUMINATING ON HER WITH THE SEVEN SFIROT: CHESED, GVURAH, TIFERET, NETZACH, HOD, YESOD AND MALCHUT OF ZEIR ANPIN. All of them are supported by one single pillar, NAMELY YESOD OF ZEIR ANPIN'. In the verse: "Wisdom has built her house, she has hewn out her seven pillars" (Mishlei 9:1), it was explained that they all stand on one grade called 'YESOD OF ZEIR ANPIN'; "the righteous is an everlasting foundation" (Mishlei 10:25).

146. וְעַלְמָא כַּד אִתְבְּרֵי, מֵהַהוּא אֲתַר אִתְבְּרֵי, דְּאִיהוּ שִׁכְלוּלָא דְּעַלְמָא וְתִקּוּנוֹי, דְּאִיהוּ חַד נְקוּדָה דְּעַלְמָא, וְאֶמְצָעִיתָא דְּכֹלָּא, וּמַאן אִיהוּ, צִיּוֹן, דִּכְתִיב מִזְמוֹר לְאָסָף אֵל אֱלֹהִים יי׳ דִּבֶּר וַיִּקְרָא אֶרֶץ מִמִּזְרַח שֶׁמֶשׁ עַד מְבוֹאוֹ. וּמֵאָן אֲתַר, מִצִּיּוֹן, דִּכְתִיב מִצִּיּוֹן מִכְלַל יוֹפִי אֱלֹהִים הוֹפִיעַ, מֵהַהוּא אֲתַר, דְּאִיהוּ סִטְרָא דְּשִׁכְלוּלָא דִּמְהֵימְנוּתָא שְׁלֵימָתָא כִּדְקָא יָאוֹת, וְצִיּוֹן תַּקִּיפוּ וּנְקוּדָה דְּכָל עַלְמָא, וּמֵהַהוּא אֲתַר אִשְׁתַּכְלַל כָּל עַלְמָא וְאִתְעֲבֵיד, וּמִגַּוֵּיהּ כָּל עַלְמָא אִתְּזָן.

146. When the universe was created, it issued from the spot that included the world with its improvements, which the point in the middle of the world, which is Zion, THE INNER YESOD OF THE NUKVA. As it is written: "A psalm of Asaf. The mighty one, El, Elohim Hashem, has spoken and called the earth from the rising of the sun to the going down thereof" (Tehilim 50:1). Where did He speak from? From Zion, as it is written: "Out of Zion, the perfection of beauty, Elohim has shone forth" (Tehilim 50:2), the place that constructs faith to perfection. Zion is the strength, THE SECRET OF THE ILLUMINATION OF CHOCHMAH, and the point of the whole world – THAT IS THE SECRET OF THE LIGHT OF CHASSADIM – on which the world has been constructed BY THE CHOCHMAH IN IT, and wherein it is nourished, BY THE LIGHT OF CHASSADIM IN IT.

147. וְתָּא חֲזֵי, וַיַּרְעֵם בַּשָּׁמַיִם ה׳ וְעֶלְיוֹן יִתֵּן קוֹלוֹ וגו׳, כֵּיוָן דַּאֲמַר וַיַּרְעֵם בַּשָּׁמַיִם ה׳ אַמַּאי כְּתִיב וְעֶלְיוֹן יִתֵּן קוֹלוֹ, הָא הָכָא רָזָא דִּמְהֵימְנוּתָא דַּאֲמִינָא דְּצִיּוֹן אִיהוּ שִׁכְלוּלָא וְשַׁפִּירוּ דְּעַלְמָא, וְעַלְמָא מִנֵּיהּ אִתְּזָן, בְּגִין דִּתְרֵין דַּרְגִּין אִינוּן, וְאִינוּן חַד, אִינוּן: צִיּוֹן וִירוּשָׁלַם, דָּא דִּינָא, וְדָא רַחֲמֵי, וְתַרְוַויְיהוּ חַד, מֵהָכָא דִּינָא וּמֵהָכָא רַחֲמֵי.

147. Come and behold: after stating, "Hashem also thundered in the heavens" (Tehilim 18:14), why add, "and the Highest gave His voice," WHICH IS REDUNDANT? RABBI YEHUDA ANSWERS: Here is the secret of the faith I mentioned. For Zion constructs and beautifies the world, and the world is nourished by Zion FROM ITS TWO ASPECTS, NAMELY CHOCHMAH AND CHASSADIM. This is similar to the two grades that are one, namely Zion and Jerusalem; the former of Judgment and the latter of Mercy, and both are one. Judgment is issued from one, and Mercy is issued from the other.

148. מֵעֵילָּא לְעֵילָּא נָפְקָא קוֹל דְּאִשְׁתְּמַע, לְבָתַר דְּהַהוּא קוֹל נָפְקָא וְאִשְׁתְּמַע, נָפְקֵי דִּינִין, וְאָרְחֵי דְּדִינָא וְרַחֲמֵי נָפְקִין וּמִתְפָּרְשָׁן מִתַּמָּן, וַיַּרְעֵם בַּשָּׁמַיִם ה׳, דָּא בֵּי דִּינָא בְּרַחֲמֵי. וְעֶלְיוֹן: אַף עַל גָּב דְּלָא אִשְׁתְּכַּח וְלָא אִתְיְידַע, כֵּיוָן דְּהַהוּא קוֹל נָפֵיק, כְּדֵין אִשְׁתַּכַּח כֹּלָּא, דִּינָא וְרַחֲמֵי, הה״ד וְעֶלְיוֹן יִתֵּן קוֹלוֹ, כֵּיוָן דְּיִתֵּן קוֹלוֹ, כְּדֵין בָּרָד וְגַחֲלֵי אֵשׁ, מַיָא וְאֶשָּׁא.

148. From high up, REFERRING TO BINAH, a voice resounds. THIS IS THE CENTRAL RECONCILING COLUMN OF BINAH. When it is heard, WHEN IT RECONCILES THE NUKVA, AND THE LIGHTS OF RIGHT AND LEFT ARE HEARD THAT IS, ILLUMINATE, Judgments issue forth FROM THE NUKVA and the paths of Judgment and Mercy may be seen diverging. "Hashem also thundered in the heavens," refers to the Merciful Court. And although the highest, BINAH, may be neither found nor known, because the same voice comes out AND RECONCILES RIGHT AND LEFT, all is then under Judgment and Mercy. THAT IS, IT SUSTAINS THE ILLUMINATION OF THE RIGHT AND LEFT COLUMNS. So it is written: "And the Highest gave His voice" (Tehilim 18:14). ONCE IT GAVE HIS VOICE, AS THE HIGHEST, BINAH, GIVES ITS VOICE TO THE NUKVA AND RECONCILES HER TWO COLUMNS. Then came "hail and coals of fire" – water and fire.

149. תָּא חֲזֵי, בְּשַׁעְתָּא דְּאִתְיְלֵיד יְהוּדָה, מַה כְּתִיב, וַתַּעֲמֹד מִלֶּדֶת, בְּגִין דְּדָא הוּא יְסוֹדָא רְבִיעָאָה מֵאִינוּן אַרְבַּע, דְּאִינוּן רְתִיכָא עִלָּאָה, סַמְכָא חַד, מֵאִינוּן אַרְבַּע סַמְכִין, מַה כְּתִיב בֵּיהּ, וַיְהִי בָּעֵת הַהִיא וַיֵּרֶד יְהוּדָה מֵאֵת אֶחָיו דַּהֲוָה מַלְכָּא עֲלַיְיהוּ, מַאי טַעְמָא, בְּגִין דְּיוֹסֵף נָחֲתוּ לֵיהּ לְמִצְרַיִם כִּדְקָאֲמָרָן.

149. Come and behold: when Judah was born, it was written: "And she left off bearing" (Beresheet 29:35). This refers to the fourth of the four foundations, CALLED CHESED, GVURAH, TIFERET AND MALCHUT', because they are the Supernal Chariot OF BINAH, and this is one of the four legs OF THE THRONE, CALLED MALCHUT. THEREFORE, IT WAS WRITTEN WITH REGARD TO HIM, "AND SHE LEFT OFF BEARING," FOR HE IS THE LAST SFIRAH, MALCHUT. It is written of him: "And it came to pass at that time, that Judah went down from his brothers" (Beresheet 38:1). He was their king, BEING MALCHUT, BUT AFTER SELLING JOSEPH, HE WAS DEPOSED. Why? Because Joseph was brought down to Egypt.

15. "And he called his name Er"

A Synopsis

The interconnection of the upper and lower worlds is exemplified in this section concerning the fate of Judah's firstborn son, Er. Judah's fall and descent, we're told, signify the descent and obscuring of the moon and the supernal Light; consequently, his son was born of the Side of Defilement, and was therefore later slain by the Lord.

The Relevance of this Passage

In order to grow spiritually and bring greater fulfillment to our lives, we must abolish all the character traits within us that emerge from the side of Defilement and Darkness. The end of darkness occurs the instant the 'Light' is turned on – which, in turn, occurs at the moment we peruse these profound words of wisdom.

150. וַיַּרְא שָׁם יְהוּדָה בַּת אִישׁ כְּנַעֲנִי. וְכִי כְּנַעֲנִי הֲוָה, אֶלָּא הָא אוּקְמוּהָ חַבְרַיָּיא. וַתַּהַר וַתֵּלֶד בֵּן וַיִּקְרָא אֶת שְׁמוֹ עֵר, תְּלַת בְּנִין הֲווֹ לֵיהּ לִיהוּדָה, וְלָא אִשְׁתָּאֲרוּ מִנַּיְיהוּ בַּר חַד, וְדָא הוּא שֵׁלָה.

150. "And Judah saw there a daughter of a certain Canaanite" (Beresheet 38:2). HE ASKS: Was he Canaanite? DID NOT THE FATHERS AVOID MARRYING AMONG THE CANAANITES? HE REPLIES: It has been explained by the friends THAT THE WORD CANAANITE MEANS 'MERCHANT'. "And she conceived, and bore a son, and he called his name Er" (Ibid. 3). Judah had three sons, but only one, Shelah, remained. THE MEANING OF "JUDAH WENT DOWN," IS THAT HE BEGOT SONS AND BURIED THEN, WHICH IS A DESCENT AND PUNISHMENT.

151. רִבִּי אֶלְעָזָר, וְרִבִּי יוֹסֵי, וְרִבִּי חִיָּיא, הֲווֹ אָזְלֵי בְּאָרְחָא. אֲמַר רִבִּי יוֹסֵי לְרִבִּי אֶלְעָזָר, אַמַּאי כְּתִיב בִּבְנוֹי דִּיהוּדָה בְּקַדְמָאָה, וַיִּקְרָא אֶת שְׁמוֹ עֵר, וּבִתְרֵין אָחֳרָנִין כְּתִיב, וַתִּקְרָא אֶת שְׁמוֹ אוֹנָן, וַתִּקְרָא אֶת שְׁמוֹ שֵׁלָה.

151. Rabbi Elazar, Rabbi Yosi, and Rabbi Chiya were walking along the road. Rabbi Yosi asks Rabbi Elazar: Why is it written in relation to Judah's firstborn: "And he called his name Er," USING THE MALE PRONOUN, and of the other two sons, "she called his name Onan," and "she called his name

Shelah," USING THE FEMALE PRONOUN?

152. אָמַר לוֹ תָּא חֲזֵי, הַאי פָּרְשָׁתָא רָזָא עִלָּאָה אִיהוּ, וְכֹלָּא אִיהוּ כִּדְקָא חָזֵי. וַיֵּרֶד יְהוּדָה מֵאֵת אֶחָיו, דְּהָא אִתְכַּסְיָא סִיהֲרָא, וְנָחֲתַת מִדַּרְגָּא דִּתְקִנָּא, לְגוֹ דַּרְגָּא אוֹחֲרָא דְּאִתְחַבַּר בֵּיהּ חִוְיָא, כד"א וַיֵּט עַד אִישׁ עֲדֻלָּמִי וּשְׁמוֹ חִירָה.

152. He said to him: Come and behold. This portion contains a profound secret, and all is proper. "Judah went down from his brothers" because the moon, THE NUKVA, became obscure and descended from the upright grade to another grade to which the serpent is attached. It is written: "And turned into a certain Adullamite, whose name was Chirah."

153. וַתַּהַר וַתֵּלֶד בֵּן וַיִּקְרָא אֶת שְׁמוֹ עֵר, וְאִיהוּ רַע, וְכֹלָּא חַד, דְּאַתְיָא מִסִּטְרָא דְיֵצֶר הָרָע. וּבְגִין כָּךְ כְּתִיב, וַיִּקְרָא אֶת שְׁמוֹ, וְלָא כְתִיב וַיִּקְרָא שְׁמוֹ בְּיַעֲקֹב כְּתִיב, וַיִּקְרָא שְׁמוֹ, דְּקוּדְשָׁא בְּרִיךְ הוּא קָרָא לֵיהּ יַעֲקֹב, וְהָכָא אֶ"ת, לְאַסְגָּאָה דַּרְגָּא אָחֳרָא דְּזוּהֲמָא דִּמְסָאֲבָא אִתְיְלֵיד, וְדָא הוּא עֵר רַע, וְכֹלָּא חַד.

153. "And she conceived, and bore a son; and he called his name Er (*Ayin Resh*)" (Beresheet 38:3). He was evil (Heb. *Resh Ayin*) – which amounts to the same thing, FOR 'EVIL' AND *ER* ARE SPELLED WITH THE SAME HEBREW LETTERS. Because he came from the side of the Evil Inclination, it is written: "And he called (Heb. *et)* his name Er." The particle *Et* adds yet another grade of filth of defilement, from which he was born. This is why Er and *Ra* ('evil') are identical, NAMELY, SPELLED WITH THE SAME HEBREW LETTERS!

154. לְבָתַר לָא אִתְבַּסַּם אַתְרָא, עַד דַּאֲתָא שֵׁלָה, דַּהֲוָה עִקָּרָא דְּכֻלְּהוּ. מַה כְּתִיב וַיְהִי עֵר בְּכֹר יְהוּדָה רַע בְּעֵינֵי ה', כְּתִיב הָכָא רַע, וּכְתִיב הָתָם, כִּי יֵצֶר לֵב הָאָדָם רַע מִנְּעוּרָיו, רַע: דְּאוֹשִׁיד דָּמִין, אוֹשִׁיד זַרְעָא עַל אַרְעָא, וּבְגִין כָּךְ וַיְמִיתֵהוּ ה', מַה כְּתִיב בַּתְרֵיהּ, וַיֹּאמֶר יְהוּדָה לְאוֹנָן בֹּא אֶל אֵשֶׁת אָחִיךָ וגו'.

15. "And he called his name Er"

154. With the second son, the place was not yet mitigated AND RETURNED TO HOLINESS. That happened only when Shelah, who was the most important of them all, came. It is written: "And Er, Judah's firstborn, was wicked in the sight of Hashem" (Beresheet 38:7), and "for the inclination of man's heart is evil from his youth" (Beresheet 8:21). THERE IT MEANS 'SPILLING SEMEN IN VAIN'; THUS, HERE IT MEANS HE WAS SPILLING blood, for he spilt semen on the ground. That is why "Hashem slew him" (Ibid.). Then, "Judah said to Onan, 'Go in to your brother's wife...'"

16. "Go in to your brother's wife, and perform the duty of a brother in law"

A Synopsis

Rabbi Shimon begins by discussing the responsibility of the righteous man to beget children in order to ensure a place for his soul in the World to Come. By perpetuating the image of the Holy King through offspring, the righteous man may prevent the reincarnation of his soul. Thus, the section addresses the necessity of marriage and of levirate marriage. We are also reminded of the futility and vanity of the individual who endeavors to provide only for himself, without creating a family.

The Relevance of this Passage

A dark room becomes progressively brighter with each lighting of a new candle. Every soul that comes into this world is likened to a candle. Though true reality, which is our ultimate destination, offers immortality and endless fulfillment, during the course of human spiritual evolution, the Light is temporarily dimmed. Immortality is relegated to the act of procreation and childbearing, which ensures the ongoing entrance of new souls into this world for the purpose of bringing about the final correction of humanity. In other words, the chain of humanity is immortal, while the individual body remains perishable and finite. All men live for the existence of the chain until such time as humanity completes its spiritual correction and transformation. At that juncture, the force of immortality will expand and bring endless life. This transformation, the final redemption, is hastened by bringing new souls into this world, whose Light, through the path of Torah, helps diminish darkness and death and accelerate the process of correction. This Light is also generated through the spiritual influences that radiate from these ancient Hebrew verses.

155. וַיֹּאמֶר יְהוּדָה לְאוֹנָן בֹּא אֶל אֵשֶׁת אָחִיךָ וגו׳. רִבִּי שִׁמְעוֹן פְּתַח וַאֲמַר הַעִירוֹתִי מִצָּפוֹן וַיַּאת מִמִּזְרַח שֶׁמֶשׁ יִקְרָא בִשְׁמִי וְיָבֹא סְגָנִים כְּמוֹ חֹמֶר וּכְמוֹ יוֹצֵר יִרְמָס טִיט. תָּא חֲזֵי, כַּמָּה אִינוּן בְּנֵי נָשָׁא טִפְּשִׁין, דְּלָא יָדְעִין וְלָא מִסְתַּכְּלִין לְמִנְדַּע אָרְחוֹי דְקוּדְשָׁא בְּרִיךְ הוּא, דְּהָא כֻּלְּהוּ נַיְימִין, דְּלָא מִתְעָרֵי, שֵׁינְתָא בְּחוֹרֵיהוֹן.

155. "And Judah said to Onan, 'Go in to your brother's wife'..." (Beresheet 38:21). Rabbi Shimon then quoted: "'I have raised up one from the north, and he is come from the rising of the sun, and he shall call upon my name; and he shall come upon princes as upon mortar, and as the potter treads clay" (Yeshayah 41:25). Come and behold: how foolish are men who neither know nor care for the ways of the Holy One, blessed be He. They are all asleep, and sleep never leaves their eye sockets.

156. תָּא חֲזֵי, קוּדְשָׁא בְּרִיךְ הוּא עֲבַד לֵיהּ לְבַר נָשׁ, כְּגַוְונָא דִלְעֵילָּא, כֹּלָּא אִיהוּ בְּחָכְמְתָא, דְּלֵית לָךְ שַׁיְיפָא וְשַׁיְיפָא בְּבַר נָשׁ, דְּלָא קָיְימָא בְּחָכְמְתָא עִלָּאָה, דְּהָא כֵּיוָן דְּאִתְתַּקַּן כָּל גּוּפָא, בְּשַׁיְיפוֹי כִּדְקָא יָאוֹת, קוּדְשָׁא בְּרִיךְ הוּא אִשְׁתַּתַּף בַּהֲדֵיהּ, וְאָעֵיל בֵּיהּ נִשְׁמָתָא קַדִּישָׁא, בְּגִין לְאוֹלָפָא לֵיהּ לְבַר נָשׁ, לְמֵהַךְ בְּאָרְחוֹי דְּאוֹרַיְיתָא, וּלְמִיטַר פִּקּוּדוֹי, בְּגִין דְּיִתְתַּקַּן בַּר נָשׁ כִּדְקָא יָאוֹת.

156. Come and behold: the Holy One, blessed be He, wisely created man in the image of above. There is neither a member nor an organ within man that was not created by Divine Wisdom, AS EACH ORGAN ALLUDES TO A SPECIFIC GRADE. After the body is complete with all its members, the Holy One, blessed be He, joins them and inserts a sacred soul to teach the man to tread the paths of the Torah and keep its commandments, so that the man will be properly perfected IN ACCORDANCE WITH THE APHORISM: 'A MAN'S SOUL SHALL TEACH HIM.'

157. וּבְגִין דְּאִית בֵּיהּ נִשְׁמָתָא קַדִּישָׁא, מִבָּעֵי לֵיהּ לְבַר נָשׁ, לְאַסְגָּאָה דְּיוֹקְנָא דְמַלְכָּא עִלָּאָה בְּעַלְמָא. וְרָזָא דָא, דְּהָא הַהוּא נָהָר דְּנָגֵיד וְנָפֵיק, לָא פָּסְקָן מֵימוֹי לְעָלְמִין, וְעַל דָּא מִבָּעֵי לֵיהּ לְבַר נָשׁ, דְּלָא יַפְסִיק נַהֲרָא וּמְקוֹרָא דִּילֵיהּ בְּהַאי עָלְמָא. וְכָל זִמְנָא דְּבַר נָשׁ לָא יַצְלַח בְּהַאי עַלְמָא קוּדְשָׁא בְּרִיךְ הוּא עָקַר לֵיהּ, וְנָטַע לֵיהּ בְּכַמָּה זִמְנִין כְּמִלְּקַדְּמִין.

157. Now that the sacred soul is within him, HE IS WORTHY OF BEGETTING CHILDREN IN THE IMAGE AND LIKENESS OF THE BLESSED ONE. Therefore, a man should multiply to perpetuate the image of the highest King in the universe. The secret of this is the river which issues forth,

SUPERNAL YESOD, whose water never stops. Similarly, a man should never stop the flowing of his river and the source in this world, BUT SHOULD BEGET CHILDREN. When a man is unsuccessful IN BEGETTING CHILDREN in this world, the Holy One, blessed be He, uproots him FROM THIS WORLD and replants him again and again. THAT IS, HE DIES AND IS BORN AGAIN INTO THE WORLD UNTIL HE SUCCEEDS IN BEGETTING CHILDREN.

158. תָּא חֲזֵי מַה כְּתִיב, הַעִירוֹתִי מִצָּפוֹן וַיַּאת, הַעִירוֹתִי: דָּא אִתְעֲרוּתָא, דְּזִוּוּגָא דְּבַר נָשׁ בְּהַאי עַלְמָא, דְּאִיהוּ אִתְעֲרוּתָא מִסִּטְרָא דְּצָפוֹן. וַיַּאת: דָּא הִיא נִשְׁמָתָא קַדִּישָׁא, דְּאַתְיָא מִלְּעֵילָּא, וְקוּדְשָׁא בְּרִיךְ הוּא מְשַׁדַּר לָהּ מִלְּעֵילָּא, אַתְיָא בְּהַאי עַלְמָא, וְעָאלַת בְּגוֹ בְּנֵי נָשָׁא, כִּדְקָאֲמָרָן.

158. Come and behold, it is written: "I have raised up one from the North, and he is come" (Yeshayah 41:25). "I have raised up," refers to a man's desire to mate in this world, which is raised by the north side FROM THE LEFT, FOR THE DESIRE TO MATE COMES FROM THE LEFT. "And he is come," refers to the sacred soul, which comes from above, sent by the Holy One, blessed be He, into this world, where it enters people.

159. מִמִּזְרַח שֶׁמֶשׁ: דָּא אֲתַר דְּהַהוּא נָהָר דְּנָגֵיד וְנָפֵיק, דְּמִתַּמָּן נָפְקַת נִשְׁמָתָא, וְאִתְנְהֵירַת. וְיָבֹא סְגָנִים. אִלֵּין אִינּוּן חֵילִין דְּעָלְמָא, דְּאַתְיָין בְּגִין הַהוּא אִתְעֲרוּתָא דְּנִשְׁמָתִין. כְּמוֹ חוֹמֶר כְּגַוְונָא דְּאִתְעַר בַּר נָשׁ, בְּגוּפָא.

159. "...from the rising of the sun..." (Ibid.) The place from which the river issues forth is TIFERET, THE ABODE OF YESOD, from which the soul comes and is born then and shines, AS ALL SOULS COME FROM THE UNION OF TIFERET AND MALCHUT. "And he shall come upon princes" (Ibid.), means that the armies of the world – THE NUKVA CALLED 'WORLD', WHOSE ARMIES ARE ANGELS – come with the stirring of the souls, NAMELY, ARE BORN WITH THEM. AND, "as upon mortar" (Ibid.), means as a man awakening into his body, WHICH IS CALLED 'MORTAR'.

160. דְּהָא בְּגִין דָּא, קוּדְשָׁא בְּרִיךְ הוּא עָבֵיד זִוּוּגִין, וְאַטֵּיל נִשְׁמָתִין

בְּעַלְמָא, וְחַבְרוּתָא אִשְׁתַּכַּח לְעֵילָּא וְתַתָּא, וּמְקוֹרָא דְּכֹלָּא הוּא בָּרוּךְ. וּבְגִין כָּךְ, קוּדְשָׁא בְּרִיךְ הוּא עֲבַד לֵיהּ לְבַר נָשׁ, בְּגִין לְאִשְׁתַּדְּלָא בְּאָרְחוֹי, וְלָא יַפְסִיק מְקוֹרֵיהּ וּמַבּוּעָא דִילֵיהּ לְעָלְמִין.

160. Therefore, the Holy One, blessed be He, couples souls and sends them into this world, causing union between above and below, and thus the source of all is blessed. Therefore, the Holy One, blessed be He, created man so that he will strive to walk in His ways and never stop his river, RATHER HE WILL BEGET CHILDREN.

161. וְכָל מַאן דְּפָסֵיק מְקוֹרֵיהּ, כַּד נָפֵיק מֵהַאי עַלְמָא, הַהוּא בַּר נָשׁ לָא עָאל בְּפַרְגּוֹדָא, וְלָא נָטֵיל חוּלַק בְּהַהוּא עַלְמָא. תָּא חֲזֵי, כְּתִיב לֹא תֹהוּ בְרָאָהּ לָשֶׁבֶת יְצָרָהּ, דְּקוּדְשָׁא בְּרִיךְ הוּא בְּגִין דָּא עֲבַד לֵיהּ לְבַר נָשׁ כִּדְקָא יָאוֹת, כִּדְאֲמָרָן, וְקוּדְשָׁא בְּרִיךְ הוּא, עֲבַד טִיבוּ עִם עַלְמָא. תָּא חֲזֵי, מַה כְּתִיב, וַיּוֹסֶף אַבְרָהָם וַיִּקַּח אִשָּׁה וּשְׁמָהּ קְטוּרָה, רָזָא, דְּנִשְׁמָתָא אָתַת לְאִתְתַּקָּנָא, כְּמִלְקַדְּמִין.

161. He whose source is dried up AND DOES NOT BEGET CHILDREN cannot enter the presence of the Holy One, blessed be He, when he passes from the world, and he does not participate in that world. Come and behold, it is written: "He did not create it a waste land; He formed it to be inhabited" (Yeshayah 45:18). Therefore, He created man IN THE LIKENESS OF ABOVE, for the Holy One, blessed be He, is kind to the world. Come and behold, it is written: "Then again Abraham took a wife, and her name was Kturah" (Beresheet 25:1). This is the secret of the soul returning INTO A BODY to be perfected.

162. תָּא חֲזֵי, הַהוּא גוּפָא, מַה כְּתִיב, וַה' חָפֵץ דַּכְּאוֹ הֶחֱלִי אִם תָּשִׂים אָשָׁם נַפְשׁוֹ יִרְאֶה זֶרַע יַאֲרִיךְ יָמִים וְחֵפֶץ ה' בְּיָדוֹ יִצְלָח. וַה' חָפַץ דַּכְּאוֹ, הַאי קְרָא אִית לְאִסְתַּכָּלָה בֵּיהּ, אַמַּאי חָפֵץ, בְּגִין דְּיִתְדַּכֵּי. אִם תָּשִׂים אָשָׁם, אִם יָשִׂים אָשָׁם מִבָּעֵי לֵיהּ, מַאי אִם תָּשִׂים. אֶלָּא לְנִשְׁמָתָא אַהֲדַר מִלָּה, אִי הַהִיא נִשְׁמָתָא בַּעְיָא לְאִתְתַּקָּנָא כִּדְקָא יָאוֹת, יִרְאֶה זֶרַע, בְּגִין דְּהַהִיא נִשְׁמָתָא אָזְלַת וְשָׁאטַת, וְאִיהִי זְמִינָא

לְאָעֲלָא בְּהַהוּא זֶרַע, דְּאִתְעַסַּק בָּהּ בַּר נָשׁ בִּפְרִיָּה וּרְבִיָּה, וּכְדֵין יַאֲרִיךְ יָמִים, וְחֵפֶץ ה׳ דָּא אוֹרַיְיתָא, בִּידֵיהּ אַצְלַח.

162. Come and behold: it is written of the body, "But it pleased Hashem to crush man by disease: if his soul shall consider it a recompense for guilt, he shall see his seed, he shall prolong his days, and the purpose of Hashem shall prosper in his hand" (Yeshayah 53:10). We have to study this verse further. Why does it so please HIM? HE ANSWERS: Because it purifies him! HE ASKS: Why the feminine gender INSTEAD OF THE MASCULINE in the verse, "If his soul shall consider (feminine) it a recompense for guilt"? HE ANSWERS: Because the phrase, "shall consider," alludes to the soul. THUS, if the soul wishes to perfect herself properly, then "he shall see his seed," because the soul roams around without rest and is destined to enter the seed of a man who observed THE COMMANDMENT OF being fruitful and multiplying. He shall then "prolong his days...and the purpose of Hashem," referring to the study of the Torah, "shall prosper in his hand." BUT IF HE DID NOT HAVE CHILDREN, THE TORAH DOES NOT HELP HIM.

163. תָּא חֲזֵי, אַף עַל גָּב דְּבַר נָשׁ אִשְׁתַּדַּל בְּאוֹרַיְיתָא יְמָמָא וְלֵילְיָא, וּמְקוֹרֵיהּ וּמַבּוּעֵיהּ קָיְימָא בֵּיהּ לְמַגָּנָא, לֵית לֵיהּ אֲתַר לַאֲעָלָא לְפַרְגּוֹדָא, וְהָא אִתְּמָר, דְּבֵירָא דְמַיָּא, אִי הַהוּא מְקוֹרָא וּמַבּוּעָא לָא עָאל בֵּיהּ, לָאו אִיהוּ בְּאֵר, דְּבֵירָא וּמְקוֹרָא כַּחֲדָא אִינוּן, וְרָזָא חָדָא אִיהוּ וְאוֹקִימְנָא.

163. Come and behold: if a man studies the Torah day and night, but does not use his source and fountain TO BEGET CHILDREN, he is not permitted in the presence of the Holy One, blessed be He. We have learned that a well of water is no well unless the source feeds it, for the well and the source are of one secret. And we have explained THAT WHOEVER HAS NO CHILDREN IS JUDGED AS IF THE SOURCE DID NOT FLOW INTO HIM, NAMELY DID NO WORK WITHIN HIM.

164. כְּתִיב, שָׁוְא לָכֶם מַשְׁכִּימֵי קוּם מְאַחֲרֵי שֶׁבֶת אוֹכְלֵי לֶחֶם הָעֲצָבִים כֵּן יִתֵּן לִידִידוֹ שֵׁנָה. תָּא חֲזֵי, כַּמָּה חֲבִיבִין אִינוּן מִלֵּי דְאוֹרַיְיתָא, דְּכָל מִלָּה וּמִלָּה דְאוֹרַיְיתָא, אִית בֵּיהּ רָזִין עִלָּאִין קַדִּישִׁין, וְהָא אִתְּמָר, דְּכַד

16. "Go in to your brother's wife, and perform the duty of a brother in law"

יָהַב קוּדְשָׁא בְּרִיךְ הוּא אוֹרַיְיתָא לְיִשְׂרָאֵל, כָּל גְּנִיזִין עִלָּאִין קַדִּישִׁין, כֻּלְּהוּ יְהַב לְהוֹ בְּאוֹרַיְיתָא, וְכֻלְּהוּ אִתְיְיהִיבוּ לְהוֹ לְיִשְׂרָאֵל, בְּשַׁעְתָּא דְּקַבִּילוּ אוֹרַיְיתָא בְּסִינַי.

164. It is written: "It is vain for you to rise up early, to sit up late, to eat the bread of sadness; for truly to His beloved He gives tranquillity" (Tehilim 127:2). Come and behold: how precious are the words of the Torah, for each contains high and holy mysteries. We have learned that when the Holy One, blessed be He, gave Yisrael the Torah, He included within it all the holy and supernal mysteries that were given to Yisrael when they received the Torah on Mount Sinai.

166. תָּא חֲזֵי, שָׁוְא לָכֶם מַשְׁכִּימֵי קוּם, אִלֵּין אִינּוּן יְחִידִים דְּאִשְׁתַּכָּחוּ דְּלָאו אִינּוּן דְּכַר וְנוּקְבָא כִּדְקָא יָאוֹת, וְאַקְדְּמָן בְּצַפְרָא לַעֲבִידְתַּיְיהוּ, כְּמָה דְאַתְּ אָמֵר, יֵשׁ אֶחָד וְאֵין שֵׁנִי וגו', וְאֵין קֵץ לְכָל עֲמָלוֹ. מְאַחֲרֵי שֶׁבֶת: מְאַחֲרִין נַיְיחָא, כְּמָה דְאַתְּ אָמֵר, כִּי בוֹ שָׁבַת, בְּגִין דְּאִתְּתָא לְגַבֵּי בַּר נָשׁ, אִיהִי נַיְיחָא לְגַבֵּיהּ וַדַּאי.

165. Come and behold: "It is vain for you to rise early," refers to single men WITHOUT WIVES who are not as they should be, without union with a woman. They rise up early to do their work, as is manifest in the verse: "There is one alone, without a companion…yet there is no end of all his labor" (Kohelet 4:8). "…to sit up late…" refers to those who retire late, WHO ARE LATE TO MARRY, FOR IT MEANS 'REST', as in "because in it He rested" (Beresheet 2:3); for a woman is considered a repose for man.

166. אוֹכְלֵי לֶחֶם הָעֲצָבִים, מַאי לֶחֶם הָעֲצָבִים, דְּכַד בַּר נָשׁ אִית לֵיהּ בְּנִין, הַהוּא נַהֲמָא דְּאָכֵיל, אָכֵיל לֵיהּ בְּחֶדְוָה, וּבִרְעוּתָא דְלִבָּא, וְהַהוּא דְּלֵית לֵיהּ בְּנִין, הַהוּא נַהֲמָא דְּאָכֵיל, אִיהוּ נַהֲמָא דַּעֲצִיבוּ. וְאִלֵּין אִינּוּן אוֹכְלֵי לֶחֶם הָעֲצָבִים וַדַּאי.

166. Of the verse, "To eat the bread of sadness" (Tehilim 127:2), HE ASKS: What is the bread of sadness? HE ANSWERS THAT when a man has children, he eats his bread joyously, with a glad heart. If he does not have children, he eats the bread of sadness. These are assuredly those who "eat the bread of sadness."

167. כֵּן יִתֵּן לִידִידוֹ שֵׁנָה, מַאי יִתֵּן לִידִידוֹ, דָּא הוּא דִּמְקוֹרֵיהּ מְבָרַךְ, דְּקוּדְשָׁא בְּרִיךְ הוּא יְהַב לֵיהּ שֵׁינָה בְּהַהוּא עַלְמָא, כד"א וְשָׁכַבְתָּ וְעָרְבָה שְׁנָתֶךָ. בְּגִין דְּאִית לֵיהּ חוּלָקָא בְּעַלְמָא דְאָתֵי, בְּגִין דְּהַהוּא בַּר נָשׁ שָׁכֵיב, וְיִתְהַנֵּי בְּהַהוּא עַלְמָא דְאָתֵי כִּדְקָא יָאוּת.

167. HE ASKS: What is meant by the verse, "For truly to His beloved He gives tranquillity" (Tehilim 127:2)? HE ANSWERS: To whom whose source is blessed WITH CHILDREN, the Holy One, blessed be He, gives sleep in this world, in accordance with the verse, "You shall lie down, and your sleep shall be sweet" (Mishlei 3:24). This is because he has a part in the World to Come, and he therefore lies IN THE GRAVE and enjoys the World to Come.

168. יֵשׁ אֶחָד וְאֵין שֵׁנִי וגו'. יֵשׁ אֶחָד: דָּא הוּא בַּר נָשׁ דְּאִיהוּ יְחִידָאי בְּעַלְמָא, לָא יְחִידָאי כִּדְקָא יָאוּת, אֶלָּא דְּאִיהוּ בְּלָא זִוּוּגָא. וְאֵין שֵׁנִי: דְּלֵית עִמֵּיהּ סֶמֶךְ. גַּם בֵּן דְּיוֹקִים שְׁמֵיהּ בְּיִשְׂרָאֵל לָא שָׁבַק. וְאָח לְאַיְיתָאָה לֵיהּ לְתִקּוּנָא.

168. "There is one alone without a companion" (Kohelet 4:8), refers to the man who is alone in the world, but not appropriately; HE IS without a wife. He is "without a companion," having no wife to help him. "…he has neither son…" to preserve his name in Yisrael after him, "nor brother" to amend for him BY LEVIRATE MARRIAGE.

169. וְאֵין קֵץ לְכָל עֲמָלוֹ, דְּאִיהוּ עָמֵל תָּדִיר, דְּאַקְדֵּים יְמָמָא וְלֵילְיָא. גַּם עֵינוֹ לֹא תִשְׂבַּע עֹשֶׁר, וְלֵית לֵיהּ לִבָּא לְאַשְׁגָּחָא, וּלְמֵימַר לְמִי אֲנִי עָמֵל, וּמְחַסֵּר אֶת נַפְשִׁי מִטּוֹבָה. וְאִי תֵּימָא דִּבְגִין דְּיֵיכוֹל וְיִשְׁתֵּי יַתִּיר, וְיַעֲבֵד מִשְׁתַּיָא בְּכָל יוֹמָא תָּדִיר, לָאו הָכֵי, דְּהָא נַפְשָׁא לָא אִתְהַנֵּי מִנֵּיהּ, אֶלָּא וַדַּאי אִיהוּ מְחַסֵּר לְנַפְשֵׁיהּ, מִטִּיבוּ דִּנְהוֹרָא דְעַלְמָא דְאָתֵי, בְּגִין דְּדָא הִיא נַפְשָׁא חַסְרָא, דְּלָא אִשְׁתַּלֵּימַת כִּדְקָא יָאוּת. תָּא חֲזֵי,

כַּמָּה חָס קוּדְשָׁא בְּרִיךְ הוּא עַל עוֹבָדוֹי, בְּגִין דְּקָא בָּעֵי דְּיִתְתַּקַּן, וְלָא יִתְאֲבֵיד מֵהַהוּא עַלְמָא דְּאָתֵי, כִּדְקָאֲמָרָן.

169. "…yet there is no end of all his labor…" (Ibid.) means that he labors constantly, from early day to night. "Neither is his eye satisfied with riches" (Ibid.), and he has not the sense to ask, "For whom then do I labor, and bereave my soul of good?" It may be said that if he toils to have more food and drink to feast every day, this is not so, because the soul does not derive any enjoyment from it. Assuredly, he denies his soul good, of the light of the World to Come, because the soul is defective; that is, it is not properly perfected. Come and behold: how compassionate is the Holy One, blessed be He, toward His creatures, IN BRINGING HIM BACK IN ANOTHER INCARNATION SO HE CAN PERFECT HIMSELF. For He wishes him to be perfected and not to be cut off from the World to Come.

170. רִבִּי חִיָּיא בָּעָא, הַאי דְּאִיהוּ זַכָּאָה שְׁלֵימָא, וְאִשְׁתַּדַּל בְּאוֹרַיְיתָא יוֹמֵי וְלֵילֵי, וְכָל עוֹבָדוֹי לִשְׁמָא דְּקוּדְשָׁא בְּרִיךְ הוּא, וְלָא זָכָה לִבְנִין בְּהַאי עַלְמָא, כְּגוֹן דְּאִשְׁתַּדַּל בְּהוֹ וְלָא זָכָה, אוֹ דַּהֲווֹ לֵיהּ וּמִיתוּ, מַה אִינוּן לְעַלְמָא דְּאָתֵי. אָמַר לוֹ רִבִּי יוֹסֵי, עוֹבָדוֹי, וְהַהִיא אוֹרַיְיתָא, קָא מָגִינָן עֲלֵיהּ, לְהַהוּא עַלְמָא.

170. Rabbi Chiya asks: What is the position in the World to Come of a thoroughly righteous man who engages in the study of the Torah day and night and devotes all his deeds to the Name of the Holy One, blessed be He, yet does not have children in this world? Or a man who tries but can not have children, or has children who die? Rabbi Yosi replied: His deeds and the Torah protect him, so he is worthy of the World to Come.

171. אֲמַר רִבִּי יִצְחָק, עֲלַיְיהוּ, וְעַל אִינוּן זַכָּאֵי קְשׁוֹט, עֲלַיְיהוּ כְּתִיב, כֹּה אָמַר ה׳ לַסָּרִיסִים אֲשֶׁר יִשְׁמְרוּ אֶת שַׁבְּתוֹתַי וּבָחֲרוּ בַּאֲשֶׁר חָפָצְתִּי וּמַחֲזִיקִים בִּבְרִיתִי, מַה כְּתִיב בַּתְרֵיהּ וְנָתַתִּי לָהֶם בְּבֵיתִי וּבְחוֹמוֹתַי יָד וָשֵׁם טוֹב מִבָּנִים וּמִבָּנוֹת שֵׁם עוֹלָם אֶתֵּן לוֹ אֲשֶׁר לֹא יִכָּרֵת, בְּגִין דְּאִלֵּין אִית לוֹן חוּלָקָא לְעַלְמָא דְּאָתֵי. אֲמַר לֵיהּ רִבִּי יוֹסֵי, יָאוּת הוּא וְשַׁפִּיר.

171. Rabbi Yitzchak said: It is written of them and of the truly just: "For thus says Hashem to the eunuchs that keep My Shabbatot, and choose the things that please Me, and take hold of My Covenant. And to them will I give in My house and within My walls a memorial better than sons and daughters: I will give them an everlasting name, that shall not be cut off" (Yeshayah 56:4-5), for they have a portion in the World to Come. Rabbi Yosi said to him: This is good and well; THAT IS, HE AGREED WITH HIM.

172. תָּא חֲזֵי, זַכָּאָה שְׁלִים דַּהֲווֹ כָּל אִלֵּין בֵּיהּ, וְאִשְׁתְּלֵים כִּדְקָא יָאוֹת, וּמִית בְּלָא בְּנִין, וְהָא קָא יָרִית דוּכְתֵּיהּ בְּהַהוּא עַלְמָא, אִתְּתֵיהּ בָּעְיָא לִיבוּמֵי, אוֹ לָא. אִי תֵּימָא דִּלְבָּעֵי לִיבוּמֵי, הָא בְּרֵיקַנְיָא אִיהוּ, דְּהָא אַתְרֵיהּ קָא יָרִית בְּהַהוּא עַלְמָא.

172. Come and behold: a thoroughly righteous man who attained all THE AFOREMENTIONED VIRTUES and reached perfection, but died without children, inherits his place in the World to Come. HE ASKS: Does his wife have to marry his brother or not? If she does, it is in vain, FOR HE DOES NOT NEED HIS BROTHER TO PERFECT HIM, having already attained his place in the World to Come!

173. אֶלָּא, וַדַּאי בָּעְיָא לִיבוּמֵי, בְּגִין דְּלָא יַדְעִינָן אִי הֲוָה שְׁלִים בְּעוֹבָדוֹי אִי לָאו. וְהִיא אִי אִתְיַיבְּמַת, לָא הֲוָה בְּרֵיקַנְיָא, בְּגִין דַּאֲתַר אִית לֵיהּ לְקוּדְשָׁא בְּרִיךְ הוּא, דְּהָא בַּר נָשׁ הֲוָה בְּעַלְמָא, וּמִית בְּלָא בְּנִין, וּפוּרְקָא לָא הֲוֵי לֵיהּ בְּעַלְמָא, כֵּיוָן דְּמִית הַאי זַכָּאָה שְׁלִים, וְאִתְּתֵיה אִתְיַיבְּמַת, וְאִיהוּ אַתְרֵיהּ יָרֵית, אֲתָא הַהוּא בַּר נָשׁ וְאִשְׁתַּלֵּים הָכָא, וּבֵין כָּךְ וּבֵין כָּךְ, קוּדְשָׁא בְּרִיךְ הוּא אֲתַר זַמִּין לֵיהּ לְעַלְמָא, עַד דְּיֵימוּת הַאי זַכָּאָה שְׁלִים, וְיִשְׁתְּלֵים אִיהוּ בְּעַלְמָא, הה"ד כִּי בְעִיר מִקְלָטוֹ יֵשֵׁב עַד מוֹת הַכֹּהֵן הַגָּדוֹל וגו'.

173. HE ANSWERS: Assuredly his wife should marry his brother, for we can not tell whether he was whole in his deeds or not. If his wife marries his brother, it is not in vain, EVEN IF HE ATTAINED PERFECTION. For the Holy One, blessed be He, keeps a place FOR THOSE WHO DIE WITHOUT CHILDREN OR A BROTHER TO MARRY THEIR WIFE. When a thoroughly righteous man dies and his wife marries his brother, he has already inherited his place AND DOES NOT NEED THE CORRECTION OF THE LEVIRATE MARRIAGE. Then comes a man WHO DIED CHILDLESS, WITHOUT A REDEEMER IN THE WORLD, and is perfected by the marriage OF THE RIGHTEOUS MAN'S WIFE. In the meanwhile, the Holy One, blessed be He, prepares a place FOR THE MAN WITHOUT THE REDEEMER until the righteous man dies. Then, he may be perfected in the world THROUGH A LEVIRATE MARRIAGE. This is the meaning of the verse: "Because he should have remained in the city of his refuge until the death of the high priest" (Bemidbar 35:28).

174. וְדָא הוּא דְּתָנִינָן, בְּנִין זְמִינִין אִינוּן לְצַדִּיקַיָּא בְּמִיתַתְהוֹן, בְּחַיֵּיהוֹן לָא זָכוּ, וּבְמִיתַתְהוֹן זָכוּ, וּבְגִין כָּךְ כָּל עוֹבָדוֹי דְּקוּדְשָׁא בְּרִיךְ הוּא כֻּלְּהוּ קְשׁוֹט וּזְכוּ, וְחָיֵיס עַל כֹּלָּא.

174. In relation to this, we have learned that the righteous are destined to have children through their death; THAT IS, THE CHILDREN OF THE LEVIRATE MARRIAGE WHO PERFECT THOSE WHO HAVE DIED CHILDLESS AND WITHOUT A BROTHER. They attain in their deaths what they did not attain during their lives. Hence, all the works of the Holy One, blessed be He, are true, just, and compassionate toward all, EVEN THOSE WHO HAVE NO BROTHER.

175. פָּתַח וַאֲמַר טוֹבִים הַשְּׁנַיִם מִן הָאֶחָד אֲשֶׁר יֵשׁ לָהֶם שָׂכָר טוֹב בַּעֲמָלָם, אִלֵּין אִינוּן דְּמִתְעַסְּקִין בְּהַאי עַלְמָא, לְאוֹלָדָא בְּנִין, דְּאִינוּן בְּנִין דִּשְׁבָקוּ, בְּגִינֵיהוֹן אִית לוֹן אֲגַר טַב בְּהַאי עַלְמָא, וּבְגִינֵיהוֹן יַרְתִּין אֲבָהָן דִּלְהוֹן, חוּלָקָא בְּהַהוּא עַלְמָא, וְאוֹקְמוּהָ.

175. He began by quoting the verse: "Two are better than one because they have a good reward for their labor" (Kohelet 4:9). This refers to those who strive to beget children in this world. For the sake of the children they leave after them, they receive a good reward in this world. For their sake, their fathers inherit a portion of the World to Come.

176. תָּא חֲזֵי, קוּדְשָׁא בְּרִיךְ הוּא נָטַע אִילָנִין בְּהַאי עַלְמָא, אִי אַצְלָחוּ

יָאוֹת, לָא אַצְלָחוּ, אַעֲקַר לוֹן, וְשָׁתַל לוֹן, אֲפִילּוּ כַּמָּה זִמְנִין, וּבְגִין כָּךְ, כָּל אָרְחוֹי דְּקוּדְשָׁא בְּרִיךְ הוּא, כֻּלְּהוּ לְטַב וּלְאַתְקָנָא עָלְמָא.

176. Come and behold: the Holy One, blessed be He, plants trees in the world. If they grow well, it is good; if they do not, He uproots them and replants them SOMEWHERE ELSE as many times as required. Such are the ways of the Holy One, blessed be He, in tending to the good and to the correction of the world.

177. בֹּא אֶל אֵשֶׁת אָחִיךָ וְיַבֵּם אוֹתָהּ, דְּהָא יְהוּדָה וְכֻלְּהוּ שִׁבְטִין, הֲווֹ יָדְעֵי דָּא, וְעִקָּרָא דְמִלְּתָא, וְהָקֵם זֶרַע, בְּגִין דְּהַהוּא זֶרַע, אִצְטְרִיךְ לְאִתְתַּקָּנָא מִלָּה, וּלְמִגְלַם גּוֹלָמָא, לְתִקּוּנָא, דְּלָא יִתְפְּרַשׁ גִּזְעָא מִשָּׁרְשֵׁיהּ כִּדְקָא יָאוֹת, הֲדָא הוּא דִכְתִיב וְאָדָם עַל עָפָר יָשׁוּב.

177. "Go in to your brother's wife, and perform the duty of a brother-in-law" (Beresheet 38:8) IS REDUNDANT, for Judah and the other tribes knew this. The ONLY important thing he told him was, "and raise up seed", for seed was needed for purification and for preparing an embryo to receive the remedy, so that the stock would not be severed from the root. This is the meaning of: "and man shall return to dust" (Iyov 34:15).

178. וְכַד מִתְתַּקַּן לְבָתַר כִּדְקָא יָאוֹת, אִלֵּין מִשְׁתַּבְּחִין בְּהַהוּא עַלְמָא, בְּגִין דְּקוּדְשָׁא בְּרִיךְ הוּא אִתְרְעֵי בְּהוֹ, וּבְגִין כָּךְ כְּתִיב, וְשַׁבֵּחַ אֲנִי אֶת הַמֵּתִים שֶׁכְּבָר מֵתוּ דַּיְיקָא, מִן הַחַיִּים אֲשֶׁר הֵמָּה חַיִּים עֲדֶנָה. מַאי עֲדֶנָה, כד"א אַחֲרֵי בְּלוֹתִי הָיְתָה לִי עֶדְנָה. וּכְתִיב יָשׁוּב לִימֵי עֲלוּמָיו.

178. Having been bettered properly AFTER THE SAID INCARNATION, they are well valued in the World to Come, for they please the Holy One, blessed be He. It is therefore written: "So I praised the dead that are already dead more than the living that are yet (Heb. *adenah*) alive" (Kohelet 4:2). FOR THEY COME BACK TO LIFE AND RETURN TO A TENDER AGE. The word "*adenah*" as in, "After I am grown old shall I have pleasure (Heb. *ednah*)" (Beresheet 18:12), and "he shall return to the days of his youth" (Iyov 33:24), MEANS THE DAYS OF YOUTH AND PLEASURE TO WHICH HE RETURNED IN INCARNATION.

16. "Go in to your brother's wife, and perform the duty of a brother in law"

179. וְטוֹב מִשְּׁנֵיהֶם אֵת אֲשֶׁר עֲדֶן לֹא הָיָה אֲשֶׁר לֹא רָאָה אֶת הַמַּעֲשֶׂה הָרַע אֲשֶׁר נַעֲשָׂה תַּחַת הַשָּׁמֶשׁ. וְטוֹב מִשְּׁנֵיהֶם אֶת אֲשֶׁר עֲדֶן לֹא הָיָה, דְּלָא שָׁב לִימֵי עֲלוּמָיו, וְלָא אִצְטְרִיךְ לְאִתְתַּקָּנָא, וְלָא סָבִיל חוֹבִין קַדְמָאֵי, בְּגִין דְּקוּדְשָׁא בְּרִיךְ הוּא יְהַב לֵיהּ אֲתַר מְתַקְּנָא בְּהַהוּא עַלְמָא, כִּדְקָא יָאוֹת.

179. "…but better than both of them is he who has not yet been, who has not seen the evil work that is done under the sun" (Kohelet 4:3), refers to he who has not returned to his youth AND BEEN REINCARNATED. HE IS A THOROUGHLY RIGHTEOUS PERSON, who does not need a new incarnation to achieve perfection and is not burdened by former sins, like one incarnated who suffers for sins he committed in former life. The Holy One, blessed be He, prepared for him a fitting place in the World to Come.

180. תָּא חֲזֵי, מַה כְּתִיב, וּבְכֵן רָאִיתִי רְשָׁעִים קְבוּרִים וגו', כְּמָה דְּאִתְּמָר, בְּגִין דְּקוּדְשָׁא בְּרִיךְ הוּא עָבִיד טִיבוּ, וְלָא בָּעָא לְשֵׁיצָאָה עַלְמָא, אֶלָּא כְּמָה דְּאִתְּמָר, וְכָל אָרְחוֹי כֻּלְּהוּ קְשׁוֹט וּזְכוּ, לְאוֹטָבָא לְהוֹ בְּהַאי עַלְמָא, וּבְעַלְמָא דְּאָתֵי. זַכָּאָה חוּלַקְהוֹן דְּצַדִּיקַיָּיא, דְּאִינוּן אָזְלֵי בְּאֹרַח קְשׁוֹט, עֲלַיְיהוּ כְתִיב, צַדִּיקִים יִרְשׁוּ אָרֶץ.

180. Come and behold, it is written: "And so I saw the wicked buried, and come to their rest" (Kohelet 8:10), as we said THAT THEY WERE BORN AGAIN TO MEND THEIR DEEDS. For the Holy One, blessed be He, is kind and does not want the world to perish, BUT PREFERS TO REFORM THE WICKED THROUGH REINCARNATION. All His ways are true and gracious and benefit them in this world and in the World to Come. Happy is the portion of the righteous who walk the true path, of whom it is written: "The righteous shall inherit the land" (Tehilim 37:29).

17. “And the thing which he did displeased Hashem...”

A Synopsis

This section addresses the sin which, we’re told, defiles man most in this world and in the World to Come: masturbation. This judgment is not based upon moral or ethical principles, but rather upon the metaphysical structure of the Upper Worlds. The dark forces that challenge us throughout our spiritual development derive their strength and sustenance from the Light they steal from us. Thus, when we react or behave with intolerance towards others, the Light we lose strengthens the Evil Inclination. Masturbation is condemned for the simple reason that a man’s seed is the substance that is closest in form to the Light of The Creator. It is raw, naked energy, and therefore requires concealment when it is revealed in our physical world. This concealment takes place when a man’s seed is used for the direct purpose of creating life. Moreover, sexual relations between a man and wife express the ultimate in sharing, with both parties imparting pleasure to one another. In this loving and protected environment, the Light and power of a man’s sperm cannot be appropriated or defiled by the Evil Inclination. The spilling of a man’s seed is an act that is done for immediate self-gratification. Consequently, negative forces immediately appropriate this Light and our lives grow a little bit darker. Hardships and misfortunes in life – whether emotional, financial, marital, or otherwise – result from a lack of spiritual Light. We also learn of the great rewards in the World to Come for a man who has trained his children to draw close to God and live by the spiritual wisdom of Torah.

The Relevance of this Passage

When a man refrains from pleasuring himself through the wanton spilling of his seed, his spiritual life force grows increasingly stronger. This manifests in many ways, including more intense sexual desire for his mate, and greater emotional stability and inner peace. The Light of this passage helps to cleanse and eradicate the dark forces that attach to us as a result of our sexually self-gratifying actions. This Light helps us to recognize the spiritual benefits associated with directing our carnal desires towards sharing pleasure with our mate, and drawing the Light of The Creator into this darkened world.

181. וַיֵּרַע בְּעֵינֵי ה׳ אֲשֶׁר עָשָׂה וַיָּמֶת גַּם אֹתוֹ. רִבִּי חִיָּיא פְּתַח בַּבֹּקֶר זְרַע אֶת זַרְעֶךָ וְלָעֶרֶב אַל תַּנַּח יָדְךָ וגו׳. תָּא חֲזֵי, כַּמָּה אִתְחֲזֵי לֵיהּ לְבַר נָשׁ, לְאִזְדַּהֲרָא מֵחוֹבוֹי וּלְאִזְדַּהֲרָא בְּעוֹבָדוֹי קַמֵּי קוּדְשָׁא בְּרִיךְ הוּא,

בְּגִין דְּכַמָּה שְׁלִיחָן וְכַמָּה מְמַנָּן אִינוּן בְּעַלְמָא, דְּאִינוּן אָזְלִין וְשָׁיְיטָן, וְחָמָאן עוֹבָדֵיהוֹן דִּבְנֵי נָשָׁא, וְסָהֲדִין עֲלוֹי, וְכֹלָּא בְּסִפְרָא כְּתִיבִין.

181. "And the thing which he did displeased Hashem: So He slew him also" (Beresheet 38:10). Rabbi Chiya opened the discussion with the verse: "In the morning sow your seed, and in the evening do not withhold your hand" (Kohelet 11:6). Come and behold: it behooves man much to be careful lest he sin and to be heedful in his actions before the Holy One, blessed be He. For there are numerous messengers and chieftains in the world who roam about observing the deeds of man and bearing testimony of him, recording everything in a book.

182. וְתָא חֲזֵי, בְּכָל אִינוּן חוֹבִין דְּאִסְתָּאַב בְּהוֹ בַּר נָשׁ בְּהַאי עַלְמָא, דָּא אִיהוּ חוֹבָא דְּאִסְתָּאַב בֵּיהּ בַּר נָשׁ יַתִּיר בְּהַאי עַלְמָא, וּבְעַלְמָא דְּאָתֵי, מַאן דְּאוֹשִׁיד זַרְעֵיהּ בְּרֵיקַנְיָא, וְאַפֵּיק זַרְעָא לְמַגָּנָא, בִּידָא אוֹ בְּרַגְלָא וְאִסְתָּאַב בֵּיהּ, כְּמָה דְּאַתְּ אָמֵר כִּי לֹא אֵל חָפֵץ רֶשַׁע אָתָּה לֹא יְגוּרְךָ רָע.

182. Come and behold: of all the sins that defile a man in this world, that which defiles him the most in this world and in the World to Come is spilling his semen in vain. Letting it out in vain by the hand or leg brings impurity on man, as it is written: "For you are not an El that has pleasure in wickedness: nor shall evil dwell with You" (Tehilim 5:5).

183. בְּג"ד, לָא עָאל לְפַרְגּוֹדָא, וְלָא חָמֵי סֵבֶר אַפֵּי עַתִּיק יוֹמִין, כְּמָה דְּתָנִינָן, כְּתִיב הָכָא לֹא יְגוּרְךָ רָע, וּכְתִיב וַיְהִי עֵר בְּכוֹר יְהוּדָה רַע בְּעֵינֵי ה', וּבְגִין כָּךְ כְּתִיב, יְדֵיכֶם דָּמִים מָלֵאוּ. זַכָּאָה חוּלָקֵיהּ דְּבַר נָשׁ דְּדָחִיל לְמָארֵיהּ, וִיהֵא נְטִיר מֵאוֹרַח בִּישָׁא, וְיַדְכֵּי גַּרְמֵיהּ, לְאִשְׁתַּדָּלָא בִּדְחִילוּ דְּמָארֵיהּ.

183. He therefore does not come inside the curtain OF THE HOLY ONE, BLESSED BE HE, or behold the presence of Atik Yomin, as is learned from the verses: "Nor shall evil dwell with You," and "And Er, Judah's firstborn, was wicked in the sight of Hashem" (Beresheet 38:7). BOTH VERSES

INDICATE THAT HE DOES NOT BEHOLD THE FACE OF HASHEM. Hence, it is written: "Your hands are full of blood" (Yeshayah 1:15), WHICH REFERS TO LETTING SEMEN BY THE HAND, WHICH IS LIKENED TO SHEDDING BLOOD. Happy is the portion of the man who fears Hashem and is guarded from the evil path, and purifies himself to be occupied in the fear of his Master.

184. תָּא חֲזֵי, בַּבֹּקֶר זְרַע אֶת זַרְעֶךָ, הַאי קְרָא אוֹקְמוּהָ, בַּבֹּקֶר: דָּא הוּא, בְּזִמְנָא דְּבַר נָשׁ אִתְקַיַּים בְּחֵילֵיהּ, וִיהֵא בְּעוּלֵימוֹ, כְּדֵין אִשְׁתַּדַּל לְאוֹלָדָא בְּנִין, בְּאִיתְּתָא דְּחַזְיָא לֵיהּ, דִּכְתִּיב בַּבֹּקֶר זְרַע אֶת זַרְעֶךָ.

184. The verse, "In the morning sow your seed" (Kohelet 11:6), has already been explained. The morning is the time of man's strength and youth. He should then strive to beget children with the wife appropriate for him, according to the verse: "In the morning sow your seed."

185. דְּהָא כְּדֵין זִמְנָא אִיהוּ, כד"א, כְּחִצִּים בְּיַד גִּבּוֹר כֵּן בְּנֵי הַנְּעוּרִים, בְּגִין דְּיָכִיל לְמֵילַף לְהוֹ אָרְחוֹי דְקוּדְשָׁא בְּרִיךְ הוּא, וִיהֵא לֵיהּ אַגְרָא טָבָא לְעַלְמָא דְאָתֵי, דִּכְתִּיב אַשְׁרֵי הַגֶּבֶר אֲשֶׁר מִלֵּא אֶת אַשְׁפָּתוֹ מֵהֶם לֹא יֵבֹשׁוּ כִּי יְדַבְּרוּ אֶת אוֹיְבִים בַּשָּׁעַר. לֹא יֵבוֹשׁוּ בְּהַהוּא עַלְמָא, בְּזִמְנָא דְמָארֵיהוֹן דְּדִינָא יֵיתוּן לְקַטְרְגָא עֲלוֹי, דְּלֵית לָךְ אַגְרָא טָבָא בְּהַהוּא עַלְמָא, כְּהַהוּא דְאוֹלִיף לֵיהּ לִבְרֵיהּ דְּחִילוּ דְמָרֵיהּ, בְּאָרְחוֹי דְאוֹרַיְיתָא.

185. Then it is his time TO BEGET CHILDREN, as it is written: "As arrows in the hand of a mighty man, so are the children of one's youth" (Tehilim 127:4). Then he is able to teach them the ways of the Holy One, blessed be He, and to receive good reward for the World to Come, as it is written: "Happy is the man that has his quiver full of them, they shall not be put to shame, but they shall speak with their enemies in the gate" (Ibid. 5). "They shall not be put to shame" in the World of Truth when the Accusers bring accusations on them, for there is no better reward in that world then THE REWARD of he who teaches his child the fear of Hashem in the ways of the Torah.

186. תָּא חֲזֵי, מַה אָמַר בְּאַבְרָהָם דִּכְתִיב כִּי יְדַעְתִּיו לְמַעַן אֲשֶׁר יְצַוֶּה אֶת בָּנָיו וְאֶת בֵּיתוֹ אַחֲרָיו וְשָׁמְרוּ דֶּרֶךְ ה׳ לַעֲשׂוֹת צְדָקָה וּמִשְׁפָּט, וְעַל דָּא הַהוּא זְכוּ קָיְימָא לֵיהּ בְּהַהוּא עַלְמָא, לְגַבֵּי כָּל מָארֵיהוֹן דְּדִינָא.

186. Come and behold: it is written about Abraham, "For I know him, that he will command his children and his household after him, and they shall keep the way of Hashem, to do justice and judgment" (Beresheet 18:19). This merit stood him well in the World to Come against all Accusers.

187. וּבְגִין כָּךְ בַּבֹּקֶר זְרַע אֶת זַרְעֶךָ וְלָעֶרֶב אַל תַּנַּח יָדֶךָ אֲפִילּוּ בְּיוֹמֵי דְזִקְנָה, דְּאִיהוּ זִמְנָא דְסִיב בַּר נָשׁ, מַה כְּתִיב אַל תַּנַּח יָדֶךָ, לָא יִשְׁבּוֹק מִלְּאוֹלָדָא בְּהַאי עַלְמָא, מַאי טַעְמָא, בְּגִין דְּלָא תֵדַע אֵיזֶה יִכְשַׁר הֲזֶה אוֹ זֶה לִפְנֵי הָאֱלֹהִים, בְּגִין דִּיקוּמוּן בְּגִינֵיהּ בְּהַהוּא עַלְמָא.

187. It is therefore written: "In the morning sow your seed, and in the evening do not withhold your hand" (Kohelet 11:6). Even in old age, CALLED 'EVENING', it is written: "Do not withhold your hand" from begetting children. Why? "For you know not which shall prosper, whether this of that," before Elohim, and which will defend them in the World of Truth.

188. וְעַל דָּא כְתִיב, הִנֵּה נַחֲלַת ה׳ בָּנִים, דָּא צְרוֹרָא דְנִשְׁמָתָא, סִטְרָא דְעַלְמָא דְאָתֵי, וּלְהַאי נַחֲלָה. מַאן זָכֵי לֵיהּ לְבַר נָשׁ לְאַעָלָא בְּהַהוּא נַחֲלַת ה׳, בָּנִים, אִינּוּן בְּנִין, זָכָאן לֵיהּ לְנַחֲלַת ה׳, וְעַל דָּא זַכָּאָה הַהוּא בַּר נָשׁ, דְּזָכֵי לוֹן דְּיוֹלִיף לוֹן אָרְחוֹי דְאוֹרַיְיתָא, כְּמָה דְּאִתְּמָר.

188. Hence it is written: "Lo, children are the heritage of Hashem" (Tehilim 127:3). This is the 'bundle of LIFE' OF the soul, THE SECRET OF THE VERSE, "YET THE SOUL OF MY LORD SHALL BE BOUND IN THE BOND OF LIFE" (I SHMUEL 25:29), CONSIDERED AS the World to Come and called 'heritage' BY THE SCRIPTURE. Who causes man to merit the heritage of Hashem? Children do. The children cause man to merit the heritage of Hashem! Therefore, happy is the man who has children to whom he may teach the ways of the Torah.

18. "And she put off her widow's garments..."

A Synopsis

This section explains the actions of Ruth and Tamar, two women who lost their first husbands and later conceived through levirate marriage. We learn that both acted piously and with the help of God, because the fruitful seed of Judah was established through them.

The Relevance of this Passage

This story concerns the eventual birth of King David and the Messiah. What's most relevant to the reader is the Messianic Light concealed inside the passage. A simple reading of the text sets the Light aglow, helping to hasten the emergence of the Messiah within us, and in turn, the arrival of the global Messiah and Final Redemption.

189. וַתָּסַר בִּגְדֵי אַלְמְנוּתָהּ מֵעָלֶיהָ וגו׳, תָּא חֲזֵי, תָּמָר בַּת כֹּהֵן הֲוַת, וְכִי ס״ד דְּאִיהִי אָזְלָא בְּגִין לְאַזְנָאָה עִם חָמוּהָ, דְּהָא אִיהִי צְנִיעוּתָא אִשְׁתַּכְּחַת בָּהּ תָּדִיר. אֶלָּא אִיהִי צַדֶּקֶת הֲוַת, וּבְחָכְמָה עָבְדַת הַאי, דְּהָא אִיהִי לָא אַפְקָרַת גַּרְמָהּ לְגַבֵּיהּ, אֶלָּא בְּגִין דִּידִיעָה יָדְעַת, וְחָכְמְתָא אִסְתַּכָּלַת, וְע״ד אִיהִי אָתַת לְגַבֵּיהּ, לְמֶעְבַּד טִיבוּ וּקְשׁוֹט, וְעַל דָּא אָתַת וְאִשְׁתַּדְּלַת בְּעִסְקָא דָּא.

189. "And she put off her widow's garments..." (Beresheet 38:14). Come and behold: could it be that Tamar, a priest's daughter, who was always modest, would commit incest with her father-in-law? HE ANSWERS: She was a righteous woman and did this with wisdom. She was not lewd, but wise, AND KNEW WHAT WOULD BECOME OF IT. SHE approached him to do kindness and truth by him.

190. תָּא חֲזֵי, בְּגִין דְּאִיהִי יָדְעַת יְדִיעָה, וְאִשְׁתַּדְּלַת בְּעִסְקָא דָּא, קוּדְשָׁא בְּרִיךְ הוּא עֲבַד סִיּוּעָא תַּמָּן בְּהַהוּא עוֹבָדָא, וְאִתְעֲבָרַת מִיָּד, וְכֹלָּא הֲוָה מִנֵּיהּ. וְאִי תֵּימָא, אַמַּאי לָא אַיְיתֵי קוּדְשָׁא בְּרִיךְ הוּא אִינוּן בְּנִין מֵאִתְּתָא אוּחֲרָא, אַמַּאי מִן דָּא. אֶלָּא, וַדַּאי אִיהִי אִצְטְרִיכָא לְעוֹבָדָא דָּא, וְלָא אִתְּתָא אָחֳרָא.

190. Come and behold: because she knew what would become of her efforts, the Holy One, blessed be He, aided her in the act, and she conceived immediately. All this was from THE HOLY ONE, BLESSED BE HE. It may be wondered why the Holy One, blessed be He, did not use another woman to bear these sons, but this one, TAMAR. HE ANSWERS: Assuredly, she was needed for this and no other woman would do.

191. תְּרֵין נָשִׁין הֲווֹ, דְּמִנַּיְיהוּ אִתְבְּנֵי זַרְעָא דִיהוּדָה, וַאֲתוֹ מִנַּיְיהוּ דָּוִד מַלְכָּא, וּשְׁלֹמֹה מַלְכָּא, וּמַלְכָּא מְשִׁיחָא. וְאִלֵּין תְּרֵין נָשִׁין, דָּא כְּגַוְונָא דְּדָא, תָּמָר וְרוּת, דְּמִיתוּ בַּעֲלַיְיהוּ בְּקַדְמֵיתָא, וְאִינוּן אִשְׁתַּדְּלוּ לְעוֹבָדָא דָא.

191. The seed of Judah was established with two women, who bore King David, King Solomon, and Messiah. The two women, Tamar and Rut, resembled each other. Both Tamar and Rut lost their first husbands and replaced them through similar efforts.

192. תָּמָר אִשְׁתַּדְּלַת לְגַבֵּי חָמוּהָ, דְּאִיהוּ קָרִיב יַתִּיר לִבְנוֹי דְּמִיתוּ, מַאי טַעְמָא אִיהִי אִשְׁתַּדְּלַת לְגַבֵּיהּ, דִּכְתִיב כִּי רָאֲתָה כִּי גָדַל שֵׁלָה וְהִיא לֹא נִתְּנָה לוֹ לְאִשָּׁה. וּבְגִין דָּא, אִשְׁתַּדְּלַת בְּעוֹבָדָא דָא, לְגַבֵּי חָמוּהָ.

192. Tamar approached her father-in-law, who was next of kin to his dead sons AND THUS WORTHY OF TAKING HER IN LEVIRATE MARRIAGE. The reason for her act is stated in the verse: "For she saw that Shelah was grown, and she was not given to him to wife" (Beresheet 38:14). She therefore did this by her father-in-law.

193. רוּת מִית בַּעֲלָהּ, וּלְבָתַר אִשְׁתַּדְּלַת בְּעוֹבָדָא דָא, לְגַבֵּיהּ דְּבֹעַז, דִּכְתִיב, וַתְּגַל מַרְגְּלוֹתָיו וַתִּשְׁכָּב, וְאִשְׁתַּדְּלַת בַּהֲדֵיהּ, וּלְבָתַר אוֹלֵידַת לֵיהּ לְעוֹבֵד. וְאִי תֵּימָא אַמַּאי לָא נָפִיק עוֹבֵד מֵאִתְּתָא אָחֳרָא, אֶלָּא וַדַּאי הִיא אִצְטְרִיכַת וְלָא אִתְּתָא אָחֳרָא. וּמִתְּרֵין אִלֵּין אִתְבְּנֵי וְאִשְׁתַּכְלַל זַרְעָא דִיהוּדָה, וְתַרְוַויְיהוּ בְּכַשְׁרוּת עָבְדוּ, לְמֶעְבַּד טִיבוּ עִם אִינוּן מֵיתַיָּיא, לְאִתְתַּקְּנָא עַלְמָא לְבָתַר.

193. Rut's first husband died AS DID THAT OF TAMAR, and then she did the deed by Boaz, as it is written: "And uncovered his feet, and laid herself down" (Rut 3:7). She then gave birth to Oved. You might ask why Oved was not born to another woman, INSTEAD OF IN THIS MANNER. HE ANSWERS: Assuredly, it was necessary that she, and not any other woman, bore him. From these two, the seed of Judah was built and established. Both did well and brought kindness upon the dead, so they would later be perfected in the world.

194. וְדָא הוּא כְּמָה דְּאִתְּמָר, וְשַׁבֵּחַ אֲנִי אֶת הַמֵּתִים שֶׁכְּבָר מֵתוּ, דְּהָא כַּד הֲווֹ חַיִּין בְּקַדְמֵיתָא לָא הֲוָה בְהוֹ שִׁבְחָא, וְתַרְוַויְיהוּ אִשְׁתַּדְּלוּ לְמֶעְבַּד טִיבוּ וּקְשׁוֹט עִם אִנּוּן מֵיתַיָּיא, וְקוּדְשָׁא בְּרִיךְ הוּא סַיֵּיעַ בְּהַהוּא עוֹבָדָא, וְכֹלָּא הֲוָה כִּדְקָא יָאוֹת, זַכָּאָה אִיהוּ מַאן דְּאִשְׁתַּדַּל בְּאוֹרַיְיתָא יְמָמָא וְלֵילְיָא, כד"א, וְהָגִיתָ בּוֹ יוֹמָם וָלַיְלָה לְמַעַן תִּשְׁמֹר לַעֲשׂוֹת כְּכָל הַכָּתוּב בּוֹ כִּי אָז תַּצְלִיחַ אֶת דְּרָכֶיךָ וגו'.

194. This is the explanation of the verse: "So I praised the dead that are already dead" (Kohelet 4:2). As long as THE HUSBANDS OF TAMAR AND RUT were alive, there was no praise to their name. After they died, THEIR WIVES WERE TAKEN IN LEVIRATE MARRIAGE AND THE KINGDOM OF DAVID, SOLOMON, AND MESSIAH DESCENDED FROM THEM. Both TAMAR AND RUT did kindness and truth by the dead, and the Holy One, blessed be He, helped them in the very act. Thus, all is fitting as it should be. Happy is he who studies the Torah day and night, as it is written: "But you shall meditate therein day and night, that you may observe to do according to all that is written in it: for then you shall make your way prosperous, and then you shall have good success" (Yehoshua 1:8).

19. "And Joseph was brought down to Egypt..."

A Synopsis

This section begins by interpreting the phrasing of the title quotation as indicating God's approval of this act; it was necessary in order to fulfill His announcement to Abraham.
A discussion follows concerning the legions of angels who sing praises to the glory of God throughout the night. It is the role of the children of Israel to offer praises to God through litanies three times daily. In this way, God is glorified both day and night, from above and below. Rabbi Shimon next offers two explanations of the phrase, "who commands the sun," in the context of Jacob and Joseph. One explanation interprets this as an allusion to Joseph, when he was sold. The other understands it to be concerned with Jacob, when his sons showed him evidence of Joseph's death.

The Relevance of this Passage

In the course of spiritual development, we sometimes have to fail in order to build a greater vessel that can hold all the Light that awaits us as we ascend to the next level. This is what happened to Joseph when he was "brought down to Egypt." Egypt is a code word for darkness and disconnection from the Light of The Creator. Reading these passages helps attune us to the angelic hierarchies and the spiritual energy forces they transmit. These forces give us power to rise when we fall, strength to stand after we stumble – and this serves to increase the size of our vessel, so that we can receive even greater Light in our lives. These verses also help us expand our vessel so that it is not necessary for us to fall quite so far down or to stumble quite so often.

195. וְיוֹסֵף הוּרַד מִצְרַיְמָה וַיִּקְנֵהוּ פּוֹטִיפַר וגו'. מַאי הוּרַד. דְּאִסְתַּכַּם קוּדְשָׁא בְּרִיךְ הוּא בְּהַהוּא עוֹבָדָא, לְקַיְּימָא גְּזֵרָה דִילֵיהּ דִּגְזַר בֵּין הַבְּתָרִים, דִּכְתִיב יָדוֹעַ תֵּדַע כִּי גֵר יִהְיֶה זַרְעֲךָ וגו'. וַיִּקְנֵהוּ פּוֹטִיפַר לְסִטַר חֲטָאָה קָנָה לֵיהּ.

195. In the verse, "And Joseph was brought down to Egypt; and Potifar bought him" (Beresheet 39:1), why is it written: "brought down" RATHER THAN 'WENT DOWN TO EGYPT'? HE ANSWERS: The Holy One, blessed be He, consented to the act OF SELLING JOSEPH TO EGYPT, so that the decree He made between the pieces would be fulfilled, as it is written: "Know surely that your seed shall be a stranger" (Beresheet 15:13). "And Potifar bought him," to commit sin with him, NAMELY SODOMY.

196. פְּתַח וְאָמַר, הָאוֹמֵר לַחֶרֶס וְלֹא יִזְרָח וּבְעַד כֹּכָבִים יַחְתֹּם. תָּא חֲזֵי שִׁבְעָה כֹּכְבַיָּא עֲבַד קוּדְשָׁא בְּרִיךְ הוּא בִּרְקִיעָא, וְכָל רְקִיעָא וּרְקִיעָא, אִית בֵּיהּ כַּמָּה שַׁמָּשִׁין מְמַנִּין, לְשַׁמָּשָׁא לֵיהּ לְקוּדְשָׁא בְּרִיךְ הוּא.

196. He quoted the verse: "Who commands the sun, and it rises not; and seals up the stars" (Iyov 9:7). Come and behold: the Holy One, blessed be He, made seven stars in the firmament THAT CORRESPOND TO THE SEVEN SFIROT: CHESED, GVURAH, TIFERET, NETZACH, HOD, YESOD AND MALCHUT. Each firmament contains numerous attendants who wait upon the Holy One, blessed be He.

197. בְּגִין דְּלֵית לָךְ שַׁמָּשָׁא, אוֹ מְמַנָּא, דְּלֵית לֵיהּ פּוּלְחָנָא וְשִׁמּוּשָׁא לְמָארֵיהּ, וְקַיְימֵי כָּל חַד וְחַד, עַל הַהוּא שִׁמּוּשָׁא דְּאִתְפַּקְּדָא בֵּיהּ, וְכָל חַד יָדַע עֲבִידְתֵּיהּ לְשַׁמָּשָׁא.

197. There is no attendant or appointee who does not have a specific task and service to perform for the Holy One, blessed be He, and each knows his own task.

198. מִנְּהוֹן מְשַׁמְּשֵׁי בִּשְׁלִיחוּתָא דְּמָרֵיהוֹן, וְאִתְפַּקְּדָן בְּעַלְמָא עַל כָּל עוֹבָדֵיהוֹן דִּבְנֵי נָשָׁא, וּמִנְּהוֹן דְּקָא מְשַׁבְּחִין לֵיהּ, וְאִינוּן אִתְפַּקְּדָן עַל שִׁירָתָא, וְאַף עַל גָּב דְּאִינוּן אִתְפַּקְּדָן בְּהַאי, לֵית לָךְ כָּל חֵילָא בִּשְׁמַיָּא, וְכֹכָבִין וּמַזָּלֵי, דְּכֻלְּהוּ לָא מְשַׁבְּחָן לֵיהּ לְקוּדְשָׁא בְּרִיךְ הוּא.

198. Some act as their Master's messengers, appointed in this world to oversee men's deeds. There are those who sing CHANTS AND HYMNS before Him, and those in charge of poetry. And even they are in charge of poetry, there is no host, no star or constellation that does not praise the Holy One, blessed be He.

199. דְּהָא בְּשַׁעְתָּא דְּעָאל לֵילְיָא, כְּדֵין אִתְפַּרְשָׁן תְּלַת סִטְרִין מַשִּׁרְיָין, לִתְלַת סִטְרֵי עַלְמָא, וּבְכָל סִטְרָא וְסִטְרָא, אֶלֶף אַלְפִין, וְרִבּוֹא, וְכֻלְּהוּ מְמַנָּן עַל שִׁירָתָא.

199. For when night falls, three legions are divided into the three directions of the world, each containing thousands and tens of thousands OF ANGELS, whose task it is to sing.

200. תְּלַת מַשִׁרְיָין אִינוּן, וְחַד חֵיוָתָא קַדִּישָׁא מְמַנָּא עֲלַיְיהוּ, וְקַיְימָא עֲלַיְיהוּ, וְכֻלְּהוּ קָא מְשַׁבְּחָן לֵיהּ לְקוּדְשָׁא בְּרִיךְ הוּא, עַד דְּאָתֵי צַפְרָא, כַּד אָתֵי צַפְרָא, כָּל אִינוּן דְּבִסְטַר דָּרוֹם, וְכָל כֹּכְבַיָּא דְּנָהֲרֵי, כֻּלְּהוּ מְשַׁבְּחָן, וְאָמְרֵי שִׁירָתָא לְקוּדְשָׁא בְּרִיךְ הוּא, כד"א, בְּרָן יַחַד כֹּכְבֵי בֹקֶר וַיָּרִיעוּ כָּל בְּנֵי אֱלֹהִים. בְּרָן יַחַד כֹּכְבֵי בֹקֶר, אִלֵּין כֹּכְבַיָּא דְּבִסְטַר דָּרוֹם, כד"א וַיַּשְׁכֵּם אַבְרָהָם בַּבֹּקֶר. וַיָּרִיעוּ כָּל בְּנֵי אֱלֹהִים, אִלֵּין אִינוּן, דְּבִסְטַר שְׂמָאלָא, דְּאִתְכְּלִילוּ בִּימִינָא.

200. There are three hosts OF ANGELS and one living creature, THE NUKVA, that stands in charge of them. They all praise the Holy One, blessed be He, until morning comes, when those of the south side and the luminous stars, THE ANGELS, praise and recite poetry before the Holy One, blessed be He. It is written: "When the morning stars sang together, and all the sons of Elohim shouted for joy" (Iyov 38:7). "The morning stars" are the stars on the south side, NAMELY CHESED, as it is written: "And Abraham went early in the morning" (Beresheet 19:27). "All the sons of Elohim shouted for joy," refers to the stars on the left side, which are included within the right.

201. וּכְדֵין צַפְרָא נָהִיר, וְיִשְׂרָאֵל נָטְלֵי שִׁירָתָא, וּמְשַׁבְּחָן לֵיהּ לְקוּדְשָׁא בְּרִיךְ הוּא, בִּימָמָא, תְּלַת זִמְנִין בִּימָמָא, לָקֳבֵל תְּלַת זִמְנִין דְּלֵילְיָא, וְקַיְימִין אִלֵּין לָקֳבֵיל אִלֵּין, עַד דְּיִסְתַּלַּק יְקָרָא דְּקוּדְשָׁא בְּרִיךְ הוּא, בִּימָמָא וּבְלֵילְיָא כִּדְקָא יָאוֹת, וְקוּדְשָׁא בְּרִיךְ הוּא אִסְתַּלַּק בְּהוֹ בְּשִׁית אִלֵּין.

201. When daylight breaks, Yisrael sing the praises of the Holy One, blessed be He, three times a day, corresponding to the three night WATCHES. They stand before each other until the glory of the Holy One, blessed be He, is duly risen day and night. The Holy One, blessed be He, ascends by means of the six LITANIES, THREE IN THE DAY AND THREE AT NIGHT.

202. הַהוּא חֵיוָתָא קַדִּישָׁא, דְּקַיְימָא עֲלַיְיהוּ לְעֵילָּא, קַיְימָא עַל יִשְׂרָאֵל לְתַתָּא, בְּגִין לְאַתְקָנָא כֹּלָּא כִּדְקָא יָאוֹת, מַה כְּתִיב בָּהּ, וַתָּקָם בְּעוֹד לַיְלָה וַתִּתֵּן טֶרֶף לְבֵיתָהּ וְחֹק לְנַעֲרוֹתֶיהָ. וַתִּתֵּן טֶרֶף לְבֵיתָהּ אִלֵּין אִינּוּן מַשִּׁירְיָין דִּלְעֵילָּא, וְחֹק לְנַעֲרוֹתֶיהָ, אִלֵּין מַשִּׁרְיָין דְּיִשְׂרָאֵל לְתַתָּא, וּבְגִין כָּךְ יְקָרָא דְקוּדְשָׁא בְּרִיךְ הוּא אִסְתַּלַּק מִכָּל סִטְרִין, מֵעֵילָּא וּמִתַּתָּא. וְעַל דָּא כֹּלָּא הוּא בִּרְשׁוּתֵיהּ קַיְימָא, וְכֹלָּא אִיהוּ בִּרְעוּתֵיהּ.

202. The living creature that stands above them, THE NUKVA, also stands on Yisrael below to properly fix everything, as it is written: "She rises also while it is yet night, and gives food to her household, and a portion to her maidens" (Mishlei 31:15). "And gives food to her household," refers to the upper THREE hosts and, "a portion to her maidens," alludes to the camp of Yisrael below. Thus the glory of the Holy One, blessed be He, is extolled on every side, above and below; everything exists by His permission and according to His wish.

203. הָאוֹמֵר לַחֶרֶס וְלֹא יִזְרָח. רִבִּי שִׁמְעוֹן אֲמַר, דָּא יוֹסֵף. וּבְעַד כּוֹכָבִים יַחְתּוֹם, אִלֵּין אִינּוּן אֲחוֹי, דִּכְתִיב בְּהוֹ, וַאֲחַד עָשָׂר כּוֹכָבִים מִשְׁתַּחֲוִים לִי. דָּבָר אַחֵר הָאוֹמֵר לַחֶרֶס, דָּא יַעֲקֹב, בְּשַׁעְתָּא דַּאֲמָרוּ לוֹ הַכֶּר נָא. וְלֹא יִזְרָח, בְּשַׁעְתָּא דְּאִסְתַּלְּקַת שְׁכִינְתָּא מִנֵּיהּ. וּבְעַד כֹּכָבִים יַחְתּוֹם, בְּגִין בְּנוֹי, אִתְחַתַּם וְאִסְתֵּים נְהוֹרָא דִּילֵיהּ, שִׁמְשָׁא אִתְחַשַּׁךְ, וְכֹכְבַיָּא לָא נְהִירוּ, בְּגִין דְּיוֹסֵף אִתְפָּרַשׁ מֵאֲבוֹי. וְתָא חֲזֵי מֵהַהוּא יוֹמָא דְּהַהוּא עוֹבָדָא דְיוֹסֵף, אִתְפְּרַשׁ יַעֲקֹב מִשִּׁמּוּשָׁא דְּעַרְסָא, וְאִשְׁתָּאַר אֲבֵלָא, עַד הַהוּא יוֹמָא דְּאִתְבַּשַּׂר בְּשׂוֹרָה דְיוֹסֵף.

203. "...who commands the sun, and it rises not..." (Iyov 9:7). Rabbi Shimon says this refers to Joseph WHEN HE WAS SOLD INTO EGYPT. "And seals up the stars" are his brothers, about whom it is written: "And the eleven stars bowed down to me" (Beresheet 37:9). In another explanation, "Who commands the sun," refers to Jacob at the time he was told: "know now WHETHER IT BE YOUR SON'S COAT OR NOT" (Beresheet 37:32). "...and it rises not..." means when the Shechinah was gone from him; "and seals up the stars," means his sons, as his light was sealed and closed upon him because of them. The sun darkened and the stars did not shine because Joseph was separated from his father. Come and behold: since Joseph was sold, Jacob abstained from marital intercourse and remained in mourning until he heard the good tidings of Joseph.

20. "And Hashem was with Joseph"

A Synopsis

Rabbi Yosi quotes the verse, "For The Creator loves justice," in order to lead a discussion on the protection that God offers the righteous. Through the examples of David and Joseph, both of whom walked "through the valley of the shadow of death," we are shown that God never abandons the righteous. In His mercy, He even guards the wicked, who, we learn, receive blessings and are sustained by the spiritual elevation of the righteous. Ultimately, though, we see that fortunate, indeed, are the righteous in this world and in the World to Come.

The Relevance of this Passage

Kabbalistically, mercy represents the concept of time. Time is defined as the distance between cause and effect; the separation between action and reaction; the space between deed and dividend; the span between a person's behavior and the inevitable repercussion; the divide between crime and consequence. Within this gap, it is hoped that a person becomes enlightened to the senselessness of negative ways, and recognizes the rewards of spiritual growth and positive, unselfish behavior. Time, however, can cause us to mistakenly believe that goodness goes unrewarded, while the wicked go unpunished. Yet time merely creates a delay – a window of opportunity in which our free will can earn us fulfillment, transformation, and recognition of the cause-and-effect principle that is at work in our world. Without time, a person would be instantly punished the moment he sinned. The wicked would be obliterated the moment they transgressed. They would lose the opportunity to change their ways and partake of the endless fulfillment in the World to Come. Mercy [time] is awarded to the wicked on the merit of the righteous who love humanity unconditionally. Awareness and a deeper understanding of mercy and the cause-and-effect principle are aroused within us through the merit of the righteous, whose spiritual power surges through this passage.

204. וַיְהִי ה׳ אֶת יוֹסֵף וַיְהִי אִישׁ מַצְלִיחַ וַיְהִי בְּבֵית אֲדוֹנָיו וגו׳. רִבִּי יוֹסֵי פָּתַח, כִּי ה׳ אֹהֵב מִשְׁפָּט וְלֹא יַעֲזֹב אֶת חֲסִידָיו לְעוֹלָם נִשְׁמָרוּ. הַאי קְרָא אוֹקְמוּהָ בְּאַבְרָהָם, אֶת חֲסִידָיו, חֲסִידוֹ כְּתִיב, וְהָא אִתְּמָר.

204. "And Hashem was with Joseph, and he was a successful man; and he was in the house of his master the Egyptian" (Beresheet 39:2). Rabbi Yosi opened the discussion with the verse: "For Hashem loves justice, and forsakes not His pious ones; they are preserved forever" (Tehilim 37:28). It has been explained that this refers to Abraham, because "His pious ones" is spelled 'pious one' IN THE SINGULAR, as has already been explained.

205. תָּא חֲזֵי, בְּכָל אֲתַר דְּצַדִּיקַיָּא אָזְלֵי, קוּדְשָׁא בְּרִיךְ הוּא נָטִיר לוֹן, וְלָא שָׁבֵיק לוֹן. דָּוִד אֲמַר, גַּם כִּי אֵלֵךְ בְּגֵיא צַלְמָוֶת לֹא אִירָא רָע כִּי אַתָּה עִמָּדִי שִׁבְטְךָ וּמִשְׁעַנְתֶּךָ וגו', בְּכָל אֲתַר דְּצַדִּיקַיָּא אָזְלֵי, שְׁכִינְתָּא אָזְלָא עִמְּהוֹן, וְלָא שָׁבֵיק לוֹן.

205. Come and behold: wherever the Righteous go, the Holy One, blessed be He, protects them and never abandons them. As David said, "Even though I walk through the valley of the shadow of death, I will fear no evil: for You are with me; Your rod and Your staff" (Tehilim 23:4). For wherever the Righteous go, the Shechinah never leaves them.

206. יוֹסֵף אָזַל בְּגֵיא צַלְמָוֶת, וְנָחֲתוּ לֵיהּ לְמִצְרַיִם, שְׁכִינְתָּא הֲוַת עִמֵּיהּ, הה"ד, וַיְהִי ה' אֶת יוֹסֵף, וּבְגִין דַּהֲוַת עִמֵּיהּ שְׁכִינְתָּא, בְּכָל מַה דַּהֲוָה עָבִיד, הֲוָה מַצְלַח בִּידֵיהּ. דַּאֲפִילוּ מַאי דַּהֲוָה בִּידֵיהּ, וַהֲוָה תָּבַע לֵיהּ מָארֵיהּ בְּגַוְונָא אָחֳרָא, הֲוָה מִתְהַפֵּךְ בִּידֵיהּ, לְהַהוּא גַּוְונָא דִּרְעוּתָא דְּמָארֵיהּ הֲוָה רָעֵי בֵּיהּ, כד"א וַיַּרְא אֲדוֹנָיו כִּי ה' אִתּוֹ וְכָל אֲשֶׁר הוּא עוֹשֶׂה ה' מַצְלִיחַ בְּיָדוֹ, מַצְלִיחַ בְּיָדוֹ וַדַּאי, כִּי ה' אִתּוֹ.

206. When Joseph walked the valley of the shadow of death and was brought down to Egypt, the Shechinah was with him, as it is written: "And Hashem was with Joseph" (Beresheet 39:2). Because the Shechinah was with him, whatever he did in his hand prospered. If he had something in his hand, but his master asked for something else, what was in his hand would turn into that which his master wanted, as it is written: "And his master saw that Hashem was with him, and that Hashem made all that he did prosper in his hand" (Ibid. 3). Assuredly, it "did prosper in his hand," for Hashem was with him.

207. תָּא חֲזֵי, וַיֵּדַע אֲדֹנָיו כִּי ה' אִתּוֹ לָא כְּתִיב, אֶלָּא וַיַּרְא אֲדֹנָיו, דְּהָא בְּעֵינוֹי הֲוָה חָמֵי, עוֹבָדָא דְּנִסִּין בְּכָל יוֹמָא, דְּקוּדְשָׁא בְּרִיךְ הוּא

עָבֵיד בִּידֵיהּ, וְעַל דָּא וַיְבָרֶךְ ה׳ אֶת בֵּית הַמִּצְרִי בִּגְלַל יוֹסֵף. קוּדְשָׁא בְּרִיךְ הוּא נָטֵיר לוֹן לְצַדִּיקַיָּא, וּבְגִינֵהוֹן נָטַר לוֹן לְרַשִׁיעַיָּא, דְּהָא רַשִׁיעַיָּא מִתְבָּרְכִין בְּגִינֵהוֹן דְּצַדִּיקַיָּא. כְּגַוְונָא דָא, כְּתִיב וַיְבָרֶךְ ה׳ אֶת בֵּית עוֹבֵד אֱדוֹם הַגִּתִּי בַּעֲבוּר אֲרוֹן הָאֱלֹקִים.

207. Come and behold, it is not written: 'And his master knew that Hashem was with him,' but rather "And his master saw." THIS TEACHES US THAT he saw with his own eyes the miracles that the Holy One, blessed be He, performed by His hand. Therefore, "Hashem blessed the Egyptian house for Joseph's sake" (Beresheet 39:5). The Holy One, blessed be He, preserves the righteous. For their sakes, He also protects the wicked as they are blessed for the sake of the righteous. This is said in the verse: "Hashem has blessed the house of Oved Edom...because of the ark of Elohim" (II Shmuel 6:12).

208. צַדִּיקַיָּא, אָחֳרָנִין מִתְבָּרְכִין בְּגִינַייהוּ, וְאִינוּן לָא יָכְלוּ לְאִשְׁתֵּזָבָא בִּזְכוּתַייהוּ, וְהָא אוֹקְמוּהָ. יוֹסֵף אִתְבָּרֵךְ מָארֵיהּ בְּגִינֵיהּ, וְאִיהוּ לָא יָכֵיל לְאִשְׁתֵּזָבָא בִּזְכוּתֵיהּ מִנֵּיהּ, וּלְנָפְקָא לְחֵירוּ.

208. Other people are blessed for the sake of the righteous, but they themselves can not be saved by their own merits. This has been explained: Joseph's master has been blessed for his sake, yet Joseph could not be saved by his merits and gain his freedom.

209. וּלְבָתַר אָעֵיל לֵיהּ בְּבֵית הַסֹּהַר, כד״א עִנּוּ בַכֶּבֶל רַגְלוֹ בַּרְזֶל בָּאָה נַפְשׁוֹ, עַד דִּלְבָתַר קוּדְשָׁא בְּרִיךְ הוּא אַפֵּיק לֵיהּ לְחֵירוּ, וְשַׁלְטֵיהּ עַל כָּל אַרְעָא דְמִצְרָיִם. וּבְגִין כָּךְ כְּתִיב, וְלֹא יַעֲזֹב אֶת חֲסִידָיו לְעוֹלָם נִשְׁמָרוּ, חֲסִידוֹ כְּתִיב וְאִתְּמַר, וְקוּדְשָׁא בְּרִיךְ הוּא אָגֵין עֲלַייהוּ דְּצַדִּיקַיָּא, בְּעַלְמָא דֵין וּבְעַלְמָא דְאָתֵי, דִּכְתִיב וְיִשְׂמְחוּ כָל חוֹסֵי בָךְ לְעוֹלָם יְרַנֵּנוּ וְתָסֵךְ עָלֵימוֹ וְיַעְלְצוּ בְךָ אוֹהֲבֵי שְׁמֶךָ.

209. He was later put in prison, as it is written: "Whose foot they hurt with fetters; he was laid in iron" (Tehilim 105:18). Subsequently, the Holy One, blessed be He, set him free and made him ruler over Egypt. Thus, it is written: “For Hashem loves justice and forsakes not His pious ones; they are preserved forever” (Tehilim 37:28). ‘Pious’ is spelled to read ‘pious one’ has already been explained, and the Holy One, blessed be He, protects the righteous in this world and in the World to Come, as it is written: “But let all those that put their trust in You rejoice: let them ever shout for joy, because You do defend them; and let those who love Your name be joyful in You” (Tehilim 5:12).

21. "His master's wife cast her eyes"

A Synopsis

This section pointedly reminds us that we must constantly be on guard to avoid being led astray by the Evil Inclination. As the Accusers assail man daily, he must cleave to the dimension and Sfirah known as Gvurah to become mightier than the Evil Inclination. As the rabbis point out, Joseph exemplifies this endeavor. He exposed himself to unfounded accusations because of the enormous care he took over his personal appearance. The rabbis next address the importance of guarding and preserving the Holy Covenant. The Covenant, we're told, upholds heaven and Earth. When it is properly guarded, God showers the world with blessings, but if God's judgment finds the world full of wicked people, heaven and earth will dry up and their natural, life-sustaining functions will cease.

The Relevance of this Passage

A reading of this section strengthens our resistance to evil and vain impulses, and steels our resolve to pursue positive change, for the sake of our soul and for all humankind. The collective intolerant, self-centered actions of man can become so great that they create a mass of negativity that literally blocks the Light from flowing into our world. Our connection to this passage helps dissolve this blockage, to allow the penetration of the Light.

210. וַיְהִי אַחַר הַדְּבָרִים הָאֵלֶּה וַתִּשָּׂא אֵשֶׁת אֲדֹנָיו אֶת עֵינֶיהָ אֶל יוֹסֵף. רִבִּי חִיָּיא פָּתַח וַאֲמַר, בָּרְכוּ ה׳ מַלְאָכָיו גִּבּוֹרֵי כֹחַ עוֹשֵׂי דְבָרוֹ לִשְׁמוֹעַ בְּקוֹל דְּבָרוֹ. תָּא חֲזֵי, כַּמָּה אִצְטְרִיךְ לֵיהּ לְבַר נָשׁ לְאִסְתַּמְרָא מֵחוֹבוֹי, וּלְמֵיהַךְ בְּאֹרַח מִתְתַּקְנָא, בְּגִין דְּלָא יִסְטֵי לֵיהּ הַהוּא יֵצֶר הָרָע, דְּאִיהוּ מְקַטְרְגָא לֵיהּ כָּל יוֹמָא וְיוֹמָא, כְּמָה דְאִתְּמָר.

210. "And it came to pass after these things that his master's wife cast her eyes upon Joseph" (Beresheet 39:7). Rabbi Chiya began the discussion with the verse: "Bless Hashem, you angels of His, you mighty in strength who perform His bidding, hearkening to the voice of His word" (Tehilim 103:20). Come and behold: a man should be very careful to avoid sinning and should walk the path of righteousness so as not to be led astray by the Evil Inclination, who daily brings accusations against him.

211. וּבְגִין דְּאִיהוּ מְקַטְרְגָא לֵיהּ תָּדִיר, בָּעֵי בַּר נָשׁ לְאִתְתַּקְפָא עֲלֵיהּ,

וּלְאִסְתַּלְּקָא עֲלֵיהּ, בַּאֲתַר תַּקִּיפוּ, דְּבָעֵי לְמֶהֱוֵי גָּבַר עֲלֵיהּ, וּלְאִשְׁתַּתְּפָא בַּאֲתַר דִּגְבוּרָה, בְּגִין דְּכַד בַּר נָשׁ אַתְקֵף עֲלֵיהּ, כְּדֵין אִיהוּ בִּסְטַר גְּבוּרָה, וְאִתְדַּבַּק בֵּיהּ לְאִתְתַּקְּפָא, וּבְגִין דְּהַהוּא יֵצֶר הָרָע תַּקִּיף, בָּעֵי בַּר נָשׁ דִּיהֵא תַּקִּיף מִינֵיהּ.

211. Because the Evil Inclination constantly accuses him, it behooves a man to overcome it and stand firmly, SO THAT THE EVIL INCLINATION CANNOT MOVE HIM. Man must be mightier than it and be attached to the place of Gvurah ('might'), for when man overpowers it, he cleaves to the side of Gvurah and is strengthened. Because the Evil Inclination is mighty, it behooves a man to be mightier.

212. וְאִלֵּין בְּנֵי נָשָׁא דְּאִתְתַּקְּפוּ עֲלֵיהּ, אִקְרוּן גִּבּוֹרֵי כֹּחַ, לְאִשְׁתַּכְּחָא זִינָא עִם זִינֵיהּ, וְאִלֵּין אִינוּן מַלְאָכָיו דְּקוּדְשָׁא בְּרִיךְ הוּא, דְּאַתְיָין מִסִּטְרָא דִגְבוּרָה קַשְׁיָא, לְאִתְתַּקְּפָא עֲלֵיהּ, גִּבּוֹרֵי כֹּחַ עוֹשֵׂי דְבָרוֹ. בָּרְכוּ ה׳ מַלְאָכָיו, כְּיוֹסֵף, דְּאִקְרֵי צַדִּיק וְגִבּוֹר וּנְטַר בְּרִית קַדִּישָׁא דְּאִתְרְשִׁים בְּגַוֵּיהּ.

212. Those who overcome it are described as "mighty in strength," as they are with their own kind FOR BY OVERCOMING THE MIGHTY ONE, THEY BECOME AS MIGHTY AS IT. These are the angels of the Holy One, blessed be He, NAMELY THE RIGHTEOUS, who come from the side of Harsh Gvurah to overcome THE EVIL INCLINATION. THEY ARE CALLED the "mighty in strength who perform His bidding" (Tehilim 103:20). "Bless Hashem, you angels of His," such as Joseph, who was called 'righteous' and 'mighty' and preserved the Holy Covenant, which was imprinted upon him.

213. רִבִּי אֶלְעָזָר אָמַר, וַיְהִי אַחַר הַדְּבָרִים הָאֵלֶּה, מַאי הִיא, הָא אוֹקְמוּהָ, אֲתַר דָּא דְּיִצָּה״ר מְקַטְרֵג, דְּאִיהוּ דַּרְגָּא אַחַר הַדְּבָרִים. בְּגִין דְּיוֹסֵף יְהַב לֵיהּ דּוּכְתָּא לְקַטְרָגָא, דַּהֲוָה יוֹסֵף מְסַלְסֵל בְּשַׂעֲרֵיהּ, וְאַתְקֵין גַּרְמֵיהּ, וְקַשֵּׁיט לֵיהּ, כְּדֵין אִתְיְהֵיב דּוּכְתָּא לַיִצָּה״ר לְקַטְרְגָא, דַּאֲמַר וּמַה אֲבוֹי דְּאִיהוּ מִתְאַבֵּל עֲלֵיהּ, וְיוֹסֵף מְקַשֵּׁיט גַּרְמֵיהּ, וּמְסַלְסֵל בְּשַׂעֲרֵיהּ, כְּדֵין אִתְגָּרֵי בֵּיהּ דּוּבָּא וְקַטְרֵיג לֵיהּ.

213. Rabbi Elazar asks: What is THE MEANING OF THE VERSE, "And it came to pass after these things" (Beresheet 39:7)? HE SAYS: It has been explained that the place from which the Evil Inclination brings forth accusations is the grade CALLED "after these things." Joseph gave it an opening for accusations, so THE EVIL INCLINATION said that Joseph's father was mourning over him and that he, Joseph, adorned himself and curled his hair. Thus, it aroused against him the bear, NAMELY POTIFAR'S WIFE, and it assailed him.

214. וַיְהִי אַחַר הַדְּבָרִים הָאֵלֶּה. תָּא חֲזֵי, בִּזְמְנָא דְקוּדְשָׁא בְּרִיךְ הוּא אַשְׁגַּח בֵּיהּ בְּעַלְמָא, לְמֵידַן יָתֵיהּ, וְאַשְׁכַּח חַיָּיבִין בְּעַלְמָא, מַה כְּתִיב, וְעָצַר אֶת הַשָּׁמַיִם וְלֹא יִהְיֶה מָטָר וְהָאֲדָמָה לֹא תִתֵּן אֶת יְבוּלָהּ, וּכְדֵין וַאֲבַדְתֶּם מְהֵרָה, דְּהָא בְּגִין חוֹבִין דִּבְנֵי נָשָׁא, שְׁמַיָּא וְאַרְעָא אִתְעֲצָרוּ, וְלָא נָהֲגֵי נִמּוּסֵיהוֹן כִּדְקָא יָאוּת.

214. "And it came to pass after these things." Come and behold: when the Holy One, blessed be He, inspects the world to judge it and finds wicked people therein, then "He shut up the heavens, that there be no rain, and that the land yield not its fruit" and then "you perish quickly" (Devarim 11:17). Because of the sins of men, the heavens and earth stop performing their natural functions.

215. וְתָא חֲזֵי, אִינוּן דְּלָא נָטְרוּ לְהַאי קְיָימָא דְקוּדְשָׁא, גָּרְמֵי פְּרִישׁוּ בֵּין יִשְׂרָאֵל לַאֲבוּהוֹן דְּבִשְׁמַיָּא, בְּגִין דִּכְתִיב וְסַרְתֶּם וַעֲבַדְתֶּם אֱלֹהִים אֲחֵרִים וְהִשְׁתַּחֲוִיתֶם לָהֶם, וּכְתִיב וְעָצַר אֶת הַשָּׁמַיִם וְלֹא יִהְיֶה מָטָר. דְּהַאי אִיהוּ כְּמַאן דְּסָגִיד לֵאלָהָא אָחֳרָא, דִּמְשַׁקֵּר בְּהַאי אָת קְיָימָא קַדִּישָׁא.

215. Come and behold: those who do not keep the Holy Covenant cause separation between the children of Yisrael and their Father in heaven. For it is written: "And you turn aside, and serve other Elohim, and worship them; and then Hashem's anger be inflamed against you and He shut up the heavens, that there be no rain" (Devarim 11:16-17). He WHO GUARDS NOT THE COVENANT is equal to a person who serves other Elohim, for he is false to the Holy Covenant.

216. וְכַד קְיָימָא קַדִּישָׁא אִתְנְטִיר בְּעָלְמָא כִּדְקָא יָאוּת, כְּדֵין קוּדְשָׁא בְּרִיךְ הוּא יָהֵיב בִּרְכָאן לְעֵילָּא, לְאִתְרְקָא בְּעָלְמָא, כד"א, גֶּשֶׁם נְדָבוֹת תָּנִיף אֱלֹהִים נַחֲלָתְךָ וְנִלְאָה אַתָּה כוֹנַנְתָּהּ. גֶּשֶׁם נְדָבוֹת, דָּא גֶּשֶׁם דִּרְעוּתָא, כַּד אִתְרְעֵי קוּדְשָׁא בְּרִיךְ הוּא בִּכְנֶסֶת יִשְׂרָאֵל, וּבָעֵי לַאֲרָקָא לָהּ בִּרְכָאן, כְּדֵין נַחֲלָתְךָ וְנִלְאָה אַתָּה כוֹנַנְתָּהּ.

216. When the holy Covenant is well kept in the world, the Holy One, blessed be He, pours blessings from above, which are showered over the world, as it is written: "You Elohim, did send a plentiful rain, whereby You did strengthen Your inheritance when it languished" (Tehilim 68:10). The "plentiful rain" is a rain of favor that pours when the Holy One, blessed be He, is favorable toward the Congregation of Yisrael and desires to pour blessings upon it. Then, "You did strengthen Your inheritance when it languished."

217. נַחֲלָתְךָ: אִינּוּן יִשְׂרָאֵל, דְּאִינּוּן אַחְסַנְתֵּיהּ דְּקוּדְשָׁא בְּרִיךְ הוּא, כד"א, יַעֲקֹב חֶבֶל נַחֲלָתוֹ. וְנִלְאָה: דָּא כְּנֶסֶת יִשְׂרָאֵל, דְּאִיהִי נִלְאָה בְּאַרְעָא אָחֳרָא, דְּאִיהִי צַחְיָא לְמִשְׁתֵּי, וּכְדֵין אִיהִי נִלְאָה. וְכַד הַהוּא גֶּשֶׁם דִּרְעוּתָא אִתְיְהֵיב, כְּדֵין אַתָּה כּוֹנַנְתָּהּ.

217. Your inheritance is Yisrael, the inheritance of the Holy One, blessed be He, as it is written: "Jacob is the lot of His inheritance" (Devarim 32:9). The 'languishing' is the Congregation of Yisrael which languishes in a strange land. It is thirsty for water BUT CANNOT SLAKE ITS THIRST and is thus weary. With favorable rain then, "You did strengthen."

218. וְעַל דָּא, שְׁמַיָּא וְאַרְעָא, וְכָל חֵילֵיהוֹן, כֻּלְּהוּ קַיְימָא עַל קִיּוּמָא דָּא, דִּכְתִּיב אִם לֹא בְרִיתִי יוֹמָם וָלַיְלָה חֻקּוֹת שָׁמַיִם וָאָרֶץ לֹא שָׂמְתִּי. וּבְגִין כָּךְ, בָּעֵי לְאִזְדַּהֲרָא בְּדָא, וְהָא אוֹקְמוּהָ. וּבְגִין כָּךְ כְּתִיב, וַיְהִי יוֹסֵף יְפֵה תֹאַר וִיפֵה מַרְאֶה, וּבַתְרֵיהּ כְּתִיב וַתִּשָּׂא אֵשֶׁת אֲדֹנָיו אֶת עֵינֶיהָ אֶל יוֹסֵף.

218. Thus, the heavens, the earth, and all their armies are all established on the principles of the Covenant, as it is written: "If my covenant be not day and night, it were as if I had not appointed the ordinances of heaven and earth" (Yirmeyah 33:25). We should guard it, as has already been explained. It is therefore first written: "And Joseph was of beautiful form and fair to look upon," and then, "his master's wife cast her eyes upon Joseph," WHICH MEANS THAT BECAUSE HE WAS NOT ON HIS GUARD, BUT ADORNED HIMSELF BY CURLING HIS HAIR, AND WAS GOOD LOOKING AND WELL FAVORED, HIS MASTER'S WIFE CAST HER EYES UPON HIM.

22. "...she spoke to Joseph day by day"

A Synopsis

This section discusses the struggle of the individual to resist the seduction of the Evil Inclination. God has provided certain devices that preserve us from accusations of the Evil Side. The most important of these is, of course, the Torah. Those who study the Torah for its own sake, we are told, shall inherit both the upper and lower worlds, and will rejoice when God finally banishes the Evil Inclination from this world. Those who succumb to the Defiled Side, however, shall be punished in Gehenom, or Hell. There they shall weep with anguish that they did not overcome the Evil Inclination.

The Relevance of this Passage

Physical creation came about when the collective souls of man rejected the endless Light of Fulfillment that was originally bestowed upon them by The Creator. We did this in order to gain the opportunity to earn and create this fulfillment through our own effort. Moreover, just as an athlete requires competition to give meaning to the concept of victory, the Evil Inclination was created to challenge us during this process. The Torah represents the path to victory over our Evil Inclination, not from a strictly religious standpoint, but from a spiritual perspective. The Torah, through the lens of Kabbalah, is a tool that imbues us with strength and courage to conquer our negative impulses – even those that may have been barely noticeable. A reading of these passages provides us with spiritual strength to reject the temptation of the ego-based desires that are our true adversaries in life.

219. וַיְהִי כְּדַבְּרָהּ אֵלָיו יוֹם יוֹם. רִבִּי אֶלְעָזָר פָּתַח וַאֲמַר, לִשְׁמָרְךָ מֵאֵשֶׁת רָע וגו', זַכָּאִין אִינוּן צַדִּיקַיָּא, דְּיָדְעֵי אָרְחוֹי דְּקוּדְשָׁא בְּרִיךְ הוּא, לְמֵיזַל בְּהוֹ, בְּגִין דְּאִינוּן מִשְׁתַּדְּלֵי בְּאוֹרַיְיתָא יְמָמָא וְלֵילְיָא, דְּכָל מַאן דְּאִשְׁתַּדַּל בְּאוֹרַיְיתָא יוֹמֵי וְלֵילֵי, אַחְסֵין תְּרֵין עָלְמִין: עַלְמָא עִלָּאָה, וְעַלְמָא תַּתָּאָה. אַחְסֵין הַאי עַלְמָא, אַף עַל גַּב דְּלָא אִתְעַסַּק בָּהּ בַּר נָשׁ לִשְׁמָהּ, וְאַחְסֵין הַהוּא עַלְמָא עִלָּאָה, כַּד אִתְעַסַּק בָּהּ בַּר נָשׁ לִשְׁמָהּ.

219. "And it came to pass, as she spoke to Joseph day by day" (Beresheet 39:10). Rabbi Elazar began the discussion with the verse: "To keep you from the evil woman" (Mishlei 6:24). Happy are the righteous who know the paths of the Holy One, blessed be He, and tread them, for they are occupied in the study of the Torah day and night. And whoever is occupied with the Torah day and night inherits two worlds, the upper and the lower. He inherits this world even though he does not study the Torah for its own sake, and inherits the upper world if he does study it for its own sake.

220. תָּא חֲזֵי, מַה כְּתִיב אֹרֶךְ יָמִים בִּימִינָהּ בִּשְׂמֹאלָהּ עֹשֶׁר וְכָבוֹד, אֹרֶךְ יָמִים בִּימִינָהּ, מַאן דְּאָזֵיל לִימִינָא דְאוֹרַיְיתָא, אַרְכָא דְחַיִּין אִיהוּ לְעַלְמָא דְאָתֵי, דְּזָכֵי תַּמָּן לִיקָרָא דְאוֹרַיְיתָא, דְּאִיהוּ יְקָרָא וְכִתְרָא, לְאִתְעַטְּרָא עַל כֹּלָּא, דְּכִתְרָא דְאוֹרַיְיתָא בְּהַהוּא עַלְמָא אִיהוּ. בִּשְׂמֹאלָהּ עֹשֶׁר וְכָבוֹד, בְּהַאי עַלְמָא, דְּאַף עַל גַּב דְּלָא אִתְעַסַּק בָּהּ לִשְׁמָהּ, זָכֵי בְּהַאי עַלְמָא בְּעוּתְרָא וִיקָרָא.

220. Come and behold, it is written: "Length of days is in her right hand; and in her left hand are riches and honor" (Mishlei 3:16). "Length of days is in her right hand," means that whoever walks to the right of the Torah, THAT IS STUDIES THE TORAH FOR ITS OWN SAKE has length of days in the World to Come, where he attains the glory of the Torah. This is the Glory and Crown which adorn everything, for the crown of the Torah abides only in the World to Come. "And in her left hand are riches and honor," in this world, as even he who does not study the Torah for its own sake merits riches and honor in this world.

221. דְּהָא רִבִּי חִיָּיא, כַּד אָתָא מֵהָתָם, לְאַרְעָא דְיִשְׂרָאֵל קָרָא בְּאוֹרַיְיתָא, עַד דַּהֲווֹ אַנְפּוֹי נְהִירִין כְּשִׁמְשָׁא, וְכַד הֲווֹ קַיְימִין קַמֵּיהּ כָּל אִינוּן דְּלָעָאן בְּאוֹרַיְיתָא, הֲוָה אֲמַר, דָּא אִשְׁתַּדַּל בְּאוֹרַיְיתָא לִשְׁמָהּ, וְדָא לָא אִשְׁתַּדַּל לִשְׁמָהּ, וַהֲוָה צַלֵּי עַל הַהוּא דְּאִתְעַסַּק לִשְׁמָהּ, דְּלֶיהֱוֵי הָכֵי תָּדִיר, וְיִזְכֵּי לְעַלְמָא דְאָתֵי, וְצַלֵּי עַל הַהוּא דְּלָא אִתְעַסַּק בָּהּ לִשְׁמָהּ, דְּיֵיתֵי לְאִתְעַסְּקָא בָּהּ לִשְׁמָהּ, וְיִזְכֵּי לְחַיֵּי עָלְמָא.

221. When Rabbi Chiya came FROM BABYLON to the land of Yisrael, he read the Torah until his face shone like the sun. Those who studied the Torah stood before him, and he would say this one studied it for its own sake and this one did not. He would pray for the one who studied it for its own sake, prayed that he would do so always and merit the World to Come. And he prayed for he who did not study it for its own sake, that he would come to do so and thereby merit everlasting life.

222. יוֹמָא חַד, חָמָא חַד תַּלְמִיד, דַּהֲוָה לָעֵי בְּאוֹרַיְיתָא, וְאַנְפּוֹי מוֹרִיקָן, אֲמַר וַדַּאי מְהַרְהֵר בְּחֶטְאָה אִיהוּ דְּנָא, אָחֵיד לֵיהּ לְקַמֵּיהּ, וְאַמְשֵׁיךְ עֲלֵיהּ בְּמִלִּין דְּאוֹרַיְיתָא, עַד דְּאִתְיַישַּׁב רוּחֵיהּ בְּגַוֵּיהּ, מִן הַהוּא יוֹמָא וּלְהָלְאָה, שַׁוֵּי עַל רוּחֵיהּ, דְּלָא יִרְדּוֹף בָּתַר אִינוּן הִרְהוּרִין בִּישִׁין, וְיִשְׁתַּדַּל בְּאוֹרַיְיתָא לִשְׁמָהּ.

222. One day, he saw a student who studied the Torah. The student's face was pale. He said to himself that he assuredly contemplates sin. He made him come before him and spoke to him the words of the Torah until he composed himself. From that day on, the student resolved not to seek evil thoughts, but to study the Torah for its own sake

223. אֲמַר רִבִּי יוֹסֵי, כַּד חָמֵי בַּר נָשׁ דְּהִרְהוּרִין בִּישִׁין אַתְיָין לְגַבֵּיהּ, יִתְעַסַּק בְּאוֹרַיְיתָא, וּכְדֵין יִתְעַבְרוּן מִנֵּיהּ. אֲמַר רִבִּי אֶלְעָזָר, כַּד הַהוּא סִטְרָא בִּישָׁא אָתֵי לְמִפְתֵּי לֵיהּ לְבַר נָשׁ, יְהֵא מָשֵׁיךְ לֵיהּ לְגַבֵּי אוֹרַיְיתָא, וְיִתְפְּרַשׁ מִנֵּיהּ.

223. Rabbi Yosi said that when a man notices that he is assailed by evil thoughts, he should study the Torah and they will pass. Rabbi Elazar said that when the Evil Side comes to crush man, he should draw it toward the Torah and it will part from him.

224. תָּא חֲזֵי, דְּהָא תָּנִינָן, דְּכַד הַאי סִטְרָא בִּישָׁא. קָיְימָא קַמֵּיהּ דְּקוּדְשָׁא בְּרִיךְ הוּא, לְאַסְטָאָה עַל עַלְמָא, בְּגִין עוֹבָדִין בִּישִׁין. קוּדְשָׁא בְּרִיךְ הוּא חָס עַל עַלְמָא, וְיָהֵיב עֵיטָא לִבְנֵי נָשָׁא, לְאִשְׁתֵּזָבָא מִנֵּיהּ, וְלָא יָכֵיל לְשַׁלְטָאָה עֲלֵיהוֹן, וְלָא עַל עוֹבָדֵיהוֹן, וּמַאי אִיהוּ עֵיטָא, לְאִשְׁתַּדְּלָא בְּאוֹרַיְיתָא, וְאִשְׁתֵּזָבוּ מִנֵּיהּ, מְנָלָן, דִּכְתִּיב כִּי נֵר מִצְוָה וְתוֹרָה אוֹר וְדֶרֶךְ חַיִּים תּוֹכְחוֹת מוּסָר, מַה כְּתִיב בַּתְרֵיהּ לִשְׁמָרְךָ

מֵאֵשֶׁת רָע מֵחֶלְקַת לָשׁוֹן נָכְרִיָּה.

224. Come and behold: we have learned that when the Evil Side stands before the Holy One, blessed be He, and indicts the world for its evil sins, the Holy One, blessed be He, pities the world and advises men on how to be saved from it, so it will not control them or their deeds. The advice is to escape the Evil Side by studying the Torah diligently. HE ASKS: How do we know this? HE ANSWERS: From the verse, "For Your commandment is a lamp; and Torah is light; and reproofs of instruction are the way of life," which is followed by the verse: "To keep you from the evil woman, from the smoothness of the tongue of an alien" (Mishlei 6:23-24). THE TORAH THEN PRESERVES ONE FROM THE EVIL INCLINATION.

225. וְדָא הוּא סִטְרָא מְסָאֲבָא, סִטְרָא אָחֳרָא, דְּאִיהִי קַיְימָא תָּדִיר קַמֵּיהּ קוּדְשָׁא בְּרִיךְ הוּא, לְאַסְטָאָה עַל חוֹבֵיהוֹן דִּבְנֵי נָשָׁא, וְקַיְימָא תָּדִיר לְאַסְטָאָה לְתַתָּא לִבְנֵי נָשָׁא. קַיְימָא תָּדִיר לְעֵילָּא, בְּגִין לְאַדְכָּרָא חוֹבֵיהוֹן דִּבְנֵי נָשָׁא, וּלְאַסְטָאָה לוֹן עַל עוֹבָדֵיהוֹן, וּבְגִין דְּאִתְיְהִיבוּ בִּרְשׁוּתֵיהּ, כְּמָה דַּעֲבַד לֵיהּ לְאִיּוֹב.

225. The Side of Defilement, the Other Side, is always before the Holy One, blessed be He, blaming men for their transgressions. It also stands below to accuse men for their sins. HE EXPLAINED THAT it stands above to remind men of their sins and to accuse them for their deeds, because they were given over to its power, as was Job WHEN THE HOLY ONE, BLESSED BE HE, SAID TO THE SATAN: "HE IS IN YOUR HAND" (IYOV 2:6).

226. וְכֵן קַיְימָא עֲלַיְיהוּ לְאַסְטָאָה, וּלְאַדְכָּרָא חוֹבֵיהוֹן, בְּכָל מַה דַּעֲבָדוּ, בְּאִינוּן זִמְנִין דְּקוּדְשָׁא בְּרִיךְ הוּא קַיְימָא עֲלַיְיהוּ בְּדִינָא, כְּדֵין קָאֵים לְאַסְטָאָה לוֹן, וּלְאַדְכָּרָא חוֹבֵיהוֹן, וְקוּדְשָׁא בְּרִיךְ הוּא חָס עֲלַיְיהוּ דְּיִשְׂרָאֵל, וִיהַב לוֹן עֵיטָא לְאִשְׁתֵּזָבָא מִנֵּיהּ, וּבַמֶּה, בַּשּׁוֹפָר בְּיוֹמָא דְּרֹאשׁ הַשָּׁנָה, וּבְיוֹמָא דְּכִפּוּרֵי בְּשָׂעִיר הַמִּשְׁתַּלֵּחַ, דְּיָהֲבִין לֵיהּ, בְּגִין לְאִתְפָּרְשָׁא מִנַּיְיהוּ, וּלְאִשְׁתַּדְּלָא בְּהַהוּא חוּלָקֵיהּ, וְהָא אוֹקְמוּהָ.

226. It also accuses them and when the Holy One, blessed be He, judges them ON ROSH HASHANAH (THE JEWISH NEW YEAR) AND YOM KIPPUR

(DAY OF ATONEMENT), it remembers every sin and deed. It stands over them and brings accusations, but the Holy One, blessed be He, pities Yisrael and advises them on how to escape the Evil Side. How? By blowing the *Shofar* on Rosh Hashanah day and giving of the scapegoat on Yom Kippur, so the Evil One will leave them and busy himself with the portion GIVEN HIM.

227. תָּא חֲזֵי, מַה כְּתִיב, רַגְלֶיהָ יוֹרְדוֹת מָוֶת שְׁאוֹל צְעָדֶיהָ יִתְמוֹכוּ. וּבְרָזָא דִּמְהֵימְנוּתָא מַה כְּתִיב דְּרָכֶיהָ דַרְכֵי נוֹעַם וְכָל נְתִיבוֹתֶיהָ שָׁלוֹם. וְאִלֵּין אִינוּן אָרְחִין וּשְׁבִילִין דְּאוֹרַיְיתָא, וְכֹלָּא חַד, הַאי שָׁלוֹם, וְהַאי מָוֶת, וְכֹלָּא הִפּוּכָן דָּא מִן דָּא.

227. Come and behold, it is written: "Her feet go down to death; her steps take hold of Sheol" (Mishlei 5:5). Of the secret of the faith it is said, "Her ways are ways of pleasantness, and all her paths are peace" (Mishlei 3:17). These are the ways and paths of the Torah, and all are one; THAT IS, THE ROADS – THOSE OF DEFILEMENT AND THOSE OF HOLINESS – ARE ALL ONE. The one is of Peace, and the other is of Death. And they are complete opposites to each other, FOR EACH AND EVERY PATH LEADING TO DEFILEMENT HAS AN OPPOSING PATH LEADING TO HOLINESS.

228. זַכָּאָה חוּלַקְהוֹן דְּיִשְׂרָאֵל, דְּאִינוּן מִתְדַּבְּקִין בֵּיהּ בְּקוּדְשָׁא בְּרִיךְ הוּא כִּדְקָא חָזֵי, וְיָהֵיב לוֹן עֵיטָא לְאִשְׁתֵּזָבָא מִכָּל סִטְרִין אָחֳרָנִין דְּעַלְמָא, בְּגִין דְּאִינוּן עַמָּא קַדִּישָׁא לְאַחְסַנְתֵּיהּ וְחוּלָקֵיהּ, וְעַל דָּא יָהֵיב לוֹן עֵיטָא בְּכֹלָּא. זַכָּאִין אִינוּן בְּעַלְמָא דֵין, וּבְעַלְמָא דְאָתֵי.

228. Happy is the portion of Yisrael who cleave faithfully to the Holy One, blessed be He, for He advises them on how to be saved from all the other sides in the world. Because they are a Holy Nation – His lot and portion– He helps them in every THING. Happy are they in this world and in the World to Come.

229. תָּא חֲזֵי, כַּד הַאי סִטְרָא בִּישָׁא, נָחַת וְשָׁאַט בְּעַלְמָא, וְחָמֵי עוֹבָדִין דִּבְנֵי נָשָׁא, דְּאִינוּן כֻּלְּהוּ סָטְאִין אָרְחַיְיהוּ בְּעַלְמָא, סָלֵיק לְעֵילָא, וְאַסְטֵין לוֹן, וְאִלְמָלֵא דְקוּדְשָׁא בְּרִיךְ הוּא חָיֵיס עַל עוֹבָדֵי יְדוֹי, לָא

יִשְׁתָּאֲרוּן בְּעַלְמָא.

229. Come and behold: the Evil Side comes down to hover about the world, and when it sees the deeds of men who deviated from their ways in the world, it goes up to accuse them. And were it not for the Holy One, blessed be He, who feels pity for His creatures, they would not remain in the world.

230. מַה כְּתִיב וַיְהִי כְּדַבְּרָהּ אֶל יוֹסֵף יוֹם יוֹם. כְּדַבְּרָהּ: דְסָלְקָא וְסָאטֵי בְּכָל יוֹמָא וְיוֹמָא, וַאֲמַר קַמֵּי קוּדְשָׁא בְּרִיךְ הוּא, כַּמָּה בִּישִׁין, כַּמָּה דִּלְטוּרִין, בְּגִין לְשֵׁיצָאָה בְּנֵי עַלְמָא.

230. It is written: "And it came to pass, as she spoke to Joseph day by day" (Beresheet 39:10). "As she spoke," REFERS TO THE EVIL SIDE, who daily ascends to bring accusations before the Holy One, blessed be He, SINCE JOSEPH ALLUDES TO THE HOLY ONE, BLESSED BE HE, as well as evil reports and slander, in order to destroy men.

231. מַה כְּתִיב, וְלֹא שָׁמַע אֵלֶיהָ לִשְׁכַּב אֶצְלָהּ לִהְיוֹת עִמָּהּ. וְלֹא שָׁמַע אֵלֶיהָ, בְּגִין דְּאִיהוּ חָיֵיס עַל עַלְמָא. לִשְׁכַּב אֶצְלָהּ, מַהוּ לִשְׁכַּב אֶצְלָהּ. בְּגִין לְנָסְבָא שָׁלְטָנוּ, לְשַׁלְטָאָה עַל עַלְמָא, וְשָׁלְטָנוּ לָא שָׁלְטָא, עַד דְּאִתְיְהֵיב לֵיהּ רְשׁוּ.

231. It is written: "that he hearkened not to her, to lie by her, or to be with her" (Beresheet 39:10). "He hearkened not to her," because THE HOLY ONE, BLESSED BE HE, is compassionate towards the world; "to lie by her" means to allow it to rule over the world, for it cannot govern without permission.

232. דָּבָר אַחֵר לִשְׁכַּב אֶצְלָהּ: כד"א וּלְאִישׁ אֲשֶׁר יִשְׁכַּב עִם טְמֵאָה. לִהְיוֹת עִמָּהּ: לְמֵיהַב לָהּ רִבוּ, וּבִרְכָאן, וְסַיַּיעְתָּא, דְּאִלְמָלֵא סִיּוּעָא הֲוָה לָהּ מִלְעֵילָא, לָא אִשְׁתָּאַר בְּעַלְמָא אֲפִילּוּ חַד, אֲבָל בְּגִין דְּקוּדְשָׁא בְּרִיךְ הוּא חָיֵיס עַל עַלְמָא, אִשְׁתָּאַר עַלְמָא בְּקִיּוּמֵיהּ.

232. Another explanation of the phrase, "to lie by her," has the same meaning as: "and of him that lies with her that is unclean" (Vayikra 15:33). "...to be with her..." means to give it power, blessings, and help. Were it not for the help it obtained from above, not one man would remain in the world. But the Holy One, blessed be He, pities the world AND HELPS IT WHEN THE OTHER SIDE RULES THE WORLD, so the world continues to exist.

233. ר׳ אַבָּא אֲמַר, כֹּלָּא אִיהוּ אָרְחָא חָדָא, אֲבָל יצה״ר, הוּא דְקָא אָזֵיל וּמְפַתֵּי לוֹן לִבְנֵי נָשָׁא, בְּגִין לְאַסְטָאָה אָרְחַיְיהוּ, וּלְאִתְדַּבְּקָא בְּהוֹ, בְּכָל יוֹמָא וְיוֹמָא, וּבְכָל עִידָן וְעִידָן, סָטֵי לֵיהּ לְבַר נָשׁ, מֵאָרְחָא דִקְשׁוֹט, בְּגִין לְדַחְיָיא לֵיהּ, מֵאָרְחָא דְחַיֵּי, לְאַמְשָׁכָא לֵיהּ לַגֵּיהִנֹּם.

233. Rabbi Aba said: THE TWO EXPLANATIONS are really the same, but the Evil Inclination roams about seducing men, diverting their paths and cleaving to them. Each day, it seduces men from the Path of Truth and pushes them from the Path of Life to Gehenom.

234. זַכָּאָה אִיהוּ, מַאן דְעָבֵיד וְנָטֵיר אָרְחוֹי וּשְׁבִילוֹי, בְּגִין דְּלָא יִתְדַּבַּק בֵּיהּ, הַיְינוּ דִכְתִיב וַיְהִי כְּדַבְּרָהּ אֶל יוֹסֵף יוֹם יוֹם וְלֹא שָׁמַע אֵלֶיהָ, כַּמָּה דְאִיהִי אֲמָרַת לֵיהּ בְּכָל יוֹמָא, דְּהָא רוּחַ מְסָאֲבָא, יֵצֶר הָרָע, אִיהוּ מְפַתֵּי לֵיהּ לְבַר נָשׁ, בְּכָל יוֹמָא, לִשְׁכַּב אֶצְלָהּ, גּוֹ גֵּיהִנֹּם, וּלְאִתְדָּנָא תַּמָּן, לִהְיוֹת עִמָּהּ.

234. Happy is he whose deeds ARE GOOD, who keeps his ways so that THE EVIL INCLINATION shall not be attached to him, as it is written: "And it came to pass, as she spoke to Joseph day by day that he hearkened not to her" (Beresheet 39:10). HE DID NOT HEARKEN to what she said to him daily, as the Spirit of Defilement, which is the Evil Inclination, seduces man every day "to lie by her" in Gehenom, and thus be sentenced there "to be with her."

235. תָּא חֲזֵי, כַּד בַּר נָשׁ אִתְדַּבַּק בְּהַהוּא סִטְרָא, אִתְמְשַׁךְ אֲבַתְרָהּ, וְאִסְתָּאַב עִמָּהּ בְּהַאי עַלְמָא, וְאִסְתָּאַב עִמָּהּ בְּעַלְמָא אָחֳרָא. תָּא חֲזֵי, הַאי סִטְרָא מְסָאֲבָא, מְנוּוְלָא אִיהוּ, לִכְלוּכָא אִיהוּ, כְּדִכְתִיב, צֵא

תֹּאמַר לוֹ, צוֹאָה מַמָּשׁ, וּבֵיהּ אִתְדָּן מַאן דְּאַסְטֵי אָרְחוֹי מִן אוֹרַיְיתָא, וּבֵיהּ אִתְדָּנוּ אִינּוּן חַיָּבִין דְּעַלְמָא, דְּלֵית לוֹן מְהֵימְנוּתָא בְּקוּדְשָׁא בְּרִיךְ הוּא.

235. Come and behold: when a man cleaves to that side, he is drawn after it. He defiles himself with it in this world and in the next. Come and behold: the Side of Impurity is dirty and filthy, as it is written: "You shall say to it, 'Get you hence (Heb. *tze*)'" (Yeshayah 30:22). Actual excrement is implied (Heb. *tzoah*), and with 'EXCREMENT', we proclaim that whoever turns from the ways of the Torah is condemned to excrement, to which were sentenced all the wicked people in the world who had no faith in the Holy One, blessed be He.

236. מַה כְּתִיב וַיְהִי כְּהַיּוֹם הַזֶּה וַיָּבֹא הַבַּיְתָה לַעֲשׂוֹת מְלַאכְתּוֹ וְאֵין אִישׁ מֵאַנְשֵׁי הַבַּיִת שָׁם בַּבָּיִת. וַיְהִי כְּהַיּוֹם הַזֶּה: יוֹמָא דְיִצה"ר שָׁלְטָא בְּעַלְמָא, וְנָחֲתָא לְאַסְטָאָה לִבְנֵי נָשָׁא. אֵימָתַי, יוֹמָא דְּאָתֵי בַּר נָשׁ לַאֲתָבָא בִּתְיוּבְתָּא עַל חוֹבוֹי, אוֹ לְאִשְׁתַּדְּלָא בְּאוֹרַיְיתָא, וּלְמֶעְבַּד פִּקּוּדֵי דְאוֹרַיְיתָא, וּכְדֵין בְּהַהוּא זִמְנָא נָחֲתָא, בְּגִין לְאַסְטָאָה לִבְנֵי עָלְמָא.

236. It is written: "And it came to pass about this day, that he went into the house to do his work; and there was none of the men of the house there within" (Beresheet 39:11). "This day" is when the Evil Inclination rules over the world and goes down to lead men astray. HE ASKS: When will that be? HE ANSWERS: When men repent their sins or study the Torah and observe its precepts, THE EVIL INCLINATION comes down to lead them astray AND THUS PREVENT THEIR REPENTANCE AND OCCUPATION WITH THE TORAH AND ITS PRECEPTS.

237. וַיָּבֹא הַבַּיְתָה לַעֲשׂוֹת מְלַאכְתּוֹ, בְּגִין לְאִשְׁתַּדְּלָא בְּאוֹרַיְיתָא, וּלְמֶעְבַּד פִּקּוּדֵי דְאוֹרַיְיתָא, דְּאִיהוּ מְלַאכְתּוֹ דְּבַר נָשׁ בְּהַאי עַלְמָא, וְכֵיוָן דַּעֲבִידְתָּא דְּבַר נָשׁ בְּהַאי עַלְמָא, הוּא עֲבִידְתָּא דְקוּדְשָׁא בְּרִיךְ הוּא, בָּעֵי לֵיהּ לְבַר נָשׁ, לְמֶהֱוֵי תַּקִּיפָא כְּאַרְיָא בְּכָל סִטְרוֹי, בְּגִין דְּלָא

יִשְׁלוֹט עֲלוֹי סִטְרָא אָחֳרָא, וְלָא יָכֵיל לְמִפְתֵּי לֵיהּ, מַה כְּתִיב וְאֵין אִישׁ, לֵית גְּבַר דִּיקוּם לְקִבְלֵיהּ דְּיֵצֶר הָרָע, וְיִגַּח בֵּיהּ קְרָבָא כִּדְקָא יָאוֹת.

237. "He went into the house to do his work," to study the Torah and observe its precepts, which are man's work in this world. Because a man's work in this world is the service of the Holy One, blessed be He, NAMELY THE STUDY OF THE TORAH AND ITS PRECEPTS, a man should be as strong as a lion on all sides, so that the Other Side will not have power over him and seduce him. It is written: "And there was none of the men," namely nobody to rise before the Evil Inclination and wage war against it.

238. מַאי אוֹרְחֵיהּ דְּיֵצֶר הָרָע, כֵּיוָן דְּחָמֵי דְּלֵית בַּר נָשׁ קָאֵים לְקִבְלֵיהּ, וּלְאַגָּחָא בֵּיהּ קְרָבָא, מִיָּד, וַתִּתְפְּשֵׂהוּ בְּבִגְדוֹ לֵאמֹר שִׁכְבָה עִמִּי. וַתִּתְפְּשֵׂהוּ בְּבִגְדוֹ, בְּגִין דְּכַד שַׁלִּיט יצה"ר עֲלֵיהּ דְּבַר נָשׁ, אַתְקֵין לֵיהּ, וְקַשֵּׁיט לֵיהּ לְבוּשׁוֹי, מְסַלְסֵל בְּשַׂעֲרֵיהּ, הה"ד וַתִּתְפְּשֵׂהוּ בְּבִגְדוֹ לֵאמֹר שִׁכְבָה עִמִּי: אִתְדַּבַּק עִמִּי.

238. When it sees no one standing against it, it is the way of the Evil Inclination to wage war with it immediately: "She caught him by his garment, saying, 'Lie with she'". "She caught him by his garment," because when the Evil Inclination obtains mastery over man, HE FIRST adorns and mends his clothes and curls his hair, as it is written: "She caught him by his garment, saying, 'Lie with me'" and cleave to me.

239. מַאן דְּאִיהוּ זַכָּאָה, אִתְתַּקַּף לְקִבְלֵיהּ, וְאַגַּח בֵּיהּ קְרָבָא, מַה כְּתִיב, וַיַּעֲזֹב בִּגְדוֹ בְּיָדָהּ וַיָּנָס וַיֵּצֵא הַחוּצָה, יִשְׁבּוֹק לֵיהּ, וְיִתְתַּקַּף לְקִבְלֵיהּ. וְיֵעֲרוֹק מִנֵּיהּ, בְּגִין לְאִשְׁתֵּזָבָא מִנֵּיהּ, וְלָא יִשְׁלוֹט עֲלוֹי.

239. The Righteous stands against it and engages in war against him (Beresheet 39:12). It is written: "And he left his garment in her hand, and fled, and went outside." He should leave it, be strong against it, flee from it, and escape it so that it will have no power over him.

240. אֲמַר רִבִּי יִצְחָק, זְמִינִין אִינוּן צַדִּיקַיָּא, לְמֶחֱמֵי לְיֵצֶר הָרָע, כְּחַד

טוּרָא רַבְרְבָא, וְיִתְמְהוּן, וְיֵימְרוּן אֵיךְ יָכֵילְנָא לְאִכַּפְיָא, לֵיהּ לְטוּרָא רַבְרְבָא הָדֵין עִלָּאָה. וּזְמִינִין רַשִׁיעַיָּא, לְמֶחֱמֵי לֵיהּ לְיֵצֶר הָרָע, דַּקִּיק כְּחוּטָא דְּשַׂעֲרָא, וְיִתְמְהוּן וְיֵימְרוּן, הֵיךְ לָא יָכֵילְנָא לְאִכַּפְיָא לְחוּטָא דְשַׂעֲרָא כְּדָא דַּקִּיק, אִלֵּין יִבְכּוּן, וְאִלֵּין יִבְכּוּן, וְקוּדְשָׁא בְּרִיךְ הוּא יְבַעֵר לֵיהּ מֵעַלְמָא, וְיִכּוֹס לֵיהּ לְעֵינַיְיהוּ, וְלָא יִשְׁלוֹט עוֹד בְּעַלְמָא, וְיֶחֱמוּן צַדִּיקַיָּא וְיֶחֱדוּן, כד״א, אַךְ צַדִּיקִים יוֹדוּ לִשְׁמֶךָ יֵשְׁבוּ יְשָׁרִים אֶת פָּנֶיךָ.

240. Rabbi Yitzchak said that IN THE FUTURE, the righteous will see the Evil Inclination as a high mountain and wonder how we could have conquered such a high and huge mountain. The wicked will see the Evil Inclination as a thread that is as thin as a hair. They will marvel and ask: How could we not have overcome such a tiny thread of hair? These weep, and the others weep. The Holy One, blessed be He, will sweep the wicked from the world and slay it before their eyes, so it will not have dominion over the world anymore. The Righteous will see it and rejoice, as it is written: "Surely the righteous shall give thanks to Your name: the upright shall dwell in Your presence" (Tehilim 140:14).

23. “The butler of the king of Egypt and his baker...”

A Synopsis

In this section we learn that God regulates the order of nature so He may execute His divine purpose, which is to bestow infinite pleasure to His Creation upon humanity’s completion of spiritual transformation. Rabbi Yehuda opens a discussion on the superior position of man in the hierarchy of the animal kingdom. Man, we’re told, retains dominion over all species as long as his divine image is not tainted by sin. This point is exemplified by the story of Daniel in the lions’ den. We should, therefore, guard against sin and examine our actions every day so that we may repent for any sins we have committed. The text then turns to an examination of God’s role in enabling Joseph to achieve greatness because he was righteous. We learn that Joseph was able to provide interpretations of dreams only because he entrusted the task of interpreting them to God.

The Relevance of this Passage

We have the divine capacity to consider others before ourselves, and even to sacrifice our own lives for the good of others. This is a uniquely human trait and a mark of humanity’s spiritual superiority throughout Creation. However, if we are intolerant and insensitive to one another, we utterly lose our spiritual value. This passage removes intolerance and judgement of others. It awakens compassion, respect, and sensitivity toward our fellow human beings, especially during moments of hostility and conflict. This passage further assists us in more clearly identifying and more sincerely trusting the many hidden roles played by The Creator in our lives. The purpose of these many roles is to bring Light into the world through human actions and interactions.

241. וַיְהִי אַחַר הַדְּבָרִים הָאֵלֶּה חָטְאוּ מַשְׁקֵה מֶלֶךְ מִצְרַיִם וגו׳. ר׳ יְהוּדָה פְּתַח הֲיִשְׁאַג אַרְיֵה בַּיַּעַר וְטֶרֶף אֵין לוֹ הֲיִתֵּן כְּפִיר קוֹלוֹ מִמְּעוֹנָתוֹ בִּלְתִּי אִם לָכָד. הֲיִשְׁאַג אַרְיֵה בַּיַּעַר, תָּא חֲזֵי כַּמָּה אִית לוֹן לִבְנֵי נָשָׁא, לְאַשְׁגָּחָא בְּפוּלְחָנָא דְקוּדְשָׁא בְּרִיךְ הוּא, דְּכָל מַאן דְּאִשְׁתַּדַּל בְּאוֹרַיְיתָא, וּבְפוּלְחָנָא דְקוּדְשָׁא בְּרִיךְ הוּא, דַּחֲלְתֵּיהּ וְאֵימָתֵיהּ הוּא עַל כֹּלָּא.

241. “And it came to pass after these things, that the butler of the king of Egypt...” (Beresheet 40:1). Rabbi Yehuda opened with the verse: “Will a lion roar in the forest, when he has no prey? Will a young lion cry out of his den, if he has taken nothing?" (Amos 3:4) Come and behold: how careful should a man be in worshipping the Holy One, blessed be He, for whoever is assiduous in studying the Torah and serving the Holy One, blessed be He, is feared by all.

242. דְּהָא כַּד בְּרָא קוּדְשָׁא בְּרִיךְ הוּא עַלְמָא, עֲבַד כָּל בִּרְיָין דְּעַלְמָא, כָּל חַד וְחַד בִּדְיוֹקְנֵיהּ כִּדְקָא חָזֵי לֵיהּ, וּלְבָתַר בְּרָא לֵיהּ לְבַר נָשׁ, בִּדְיוֹקְנָא עִלָּאָה, וְשַׁלְטֵיהּ עַל כֻּלְּהוּ, בִּדְיוֹקְנָא דָא, דְּכָל זִמְנָא דְּבַר נָשׁ קָאֵי בְּעַלְמָא, כָּל אִינוּן בִּרְיָין דְּעַלְמָא זָקְפִין רֵישָׁא, וּמִסְתַּכְּלָן בִּדְיוֹקְנָא עִלָּאָה דְּבַר נָשׁ, כְּדֵין כֻּלְּהוּ דַּחֲלִין וְזָעִין מִקַּמֵּיהּ, כד"א וּמוֹרַאֲכֶם וְחִתְּכֶם יִהְיֶה עַל כָּל חַיַּת הָאָרֶץ וְעַל כָּל עוֹף הַשָּׁמַיִם וגו', וְהַנֵּי מִילֵּי, כַּד מִסְתַּכְּלָן וְחָמָאן בֵּיהּ, הַאי דְּיוֹקְנָא, וְנִשְׁמְתָא בֵּיהּ.

242. For when the Holy One, blessed be He, created the universe, He made all the creatures in the world in their appropriate shape. He then created man in the supernal image and made him ruler, by power of this image, over all creatures. As long as man continues in the world, all creatures look up to him, and when they see the Supernal Image of man, they feel dread and tremble before him, as it is written: "And the fear of you and the dread of you shall be upon every beast of the earth, and upon every bird" (Beresheet 9:2). This is true only when they look and see in him the Supernal Image and the soul IS in him.

243. אֲמַר ר' אֶלְעָזָר, אַף עַל גָּב דְּנִשְׁמְתָא לָאו בֵּיהּ, צַדִּיקַיָּא לָא מִשְׁתַּנְיָין, מִכְּמָה דַּהֲוָה דְּיוֹקְנְהוֹן בְּקַדְמֵיתָא, וְכַד בַּר נָשׁ לָא אָזֵיל בְּאָרְחוֹי דְּאוֹרַיְיתָא, הַאי דְּיוֹקְנָא קַדִּישָׁא אִתְחַלַּף לֵיהּ, וּכְדֵין חֵיוַת בְּרָא, וְעוֹפָא דִּשְׁמַיָּא, יָכְלִין לְשַׁלְטָאָה עֲלֵיהּ, בְּגִין דְּאִתְחַלַּף לֵיהּ הַאי דְּיוֹקְנָא קַדִּישָׁא, אִתְחַלַּף לֵיהּ הַאי דְּיוֹקְנָא דְּבַר נָשׁ.

243. Rabbi Elazar said that the image of the Righteous does not change, even when the soul is not in them. When a man does not walk in the ways of the Torah, his sacred image is altered, and the beasts of the field and the birds in the sky then prevail against him. When the sacred image was changed, so was the image of man, WHO THEN RECEIVED THE IMAGE OF THE OTHER ANIMALS, SO THAT CREATURES ARE NO LONGER FEARFUL OF HIM AND CAN HAVE POWER OVER HIM.

244. וְתָא חֲזֵי, קוּדְשָׁא בְּרִיךְ הוּא אַחְלַף עוֹבָדִין דִּלְעֵילָא וְתַתָּא, בְּגִין לְאַהֲדְרָא מִלִּין לְאַתְרַיְיהוּ, וּלְאִשְׁתַּכְּחָא רְעוּתֵיהּ בְּכָל עוֹבָדֵי דְעַלְמָא. דָנִיֵּאל לָא אִשְׁתַּנֵּי דְיוֹקְנֵיהּ, כַּד אַפִּילוּ לֵיהּ בְּגוֹבָא דְאַרְיְוָתָא, וּבְגִין כָּךְ אִשְׁתֵּזִיב. אָמַר רַבִּי חִזְקִיָּה, אִי הָכֵי, הָא כְּתִיב אֱלָהִי שְׁלַח מַלְאֲכֵיהּ וּסֲגַר פּוּם אַרְיָוָתָא וְלָא חַבְּלוּנִי, מַשְׁמַע דִּבְגִין מַלְאָכָא דְּאַסְגַּר לְפוּמַיְיהוּ, לָא אִתְחַבַּל.

244. Come and behold: the Holy One, blessed be He, alters the deeds above and below. THAT IS, HE SWITCHES THE SACRED IMAGE ABOVE AND THE IMAGE OF MAN BELOW to bring matters back to their roots, AS THEY WERE BEFORE THE SIN OF THE TREE OF KNOWLEDGE, so that His wish shall abide in all the world's deeds. BY RETRIBUTION, ALL THE DEEDS IN THE WORLD IMPROVE. Daniel's image was not changed when he was cast into the lions' den and, because of that, he was saved. Rabbi Chizkiya asks: If this is true, why is it written: "My Elohim has sent his angel, and he has shut the lions' mouths, that they have no hurt me" (Daniel 6:23). It sounds as if he was not hurt because of the angels who shut the lions' mouths, AND NOT BECAUSE OF HIS SACRED IMAGE.

245. אָמַר לוֹ, בְּגִין דָא, לָא אִתְחַבַּל, דְּהָא הַהוּא דְיוֹקְנֵיהּ דְּבַר נָשׁ זַכָּאָה, אִיהוּ מַלְאָכָא מַמָּשׁ, דִּסְגִיר פּוּמָא, וְקָשִׁיר לוֹן, לְנַטְרָא לֵיהּ, דְּלָא יְחַבְּלוּן לֵיהּ, וּבְגִין כָּךְ, אֱלָהִי שְׁלַח מַלְאֲכֵיהּ, הַהוּא דְּכָל דְּיוֹקְנִין דְּעָלְמָא מִתְחַקְּקָן בֵּיהּ, וְאִיהוּ אַתְקֵיף דְיוֹקְנִי בִּי, וְלָא יָכִילוּ לְשַׁלְטָאָה בִּי, וּסֲגַר פּוּמַיְיהוּ, וְע״ד שְׁלַח מַלְאֲכֵיהּ וַדַּאי.

245. He said to him: Daniel was not hurt because the sacred image of a Righteous man is the very angel who shut the LIONS' mouths and shackled them to keep Daniel safe. Therefore, DANIEL SAID: "My Elohim has sent an angel" (Daniel 6:23). This refers to that angel upon whom all the images of the world are engraved. He strengthened the image in me, so that the lions could not overpower me, and he shut their mouths. Assuredly, He sent His angel.

246. וְהַאי מַלְאֲכָא, הַהוּא דְּכָל דְּיוֹקְנִין מִתְחַקְּקָן בֵּיהּ. דִּכְתִיב יָדִין בַּגּוֹיִם מָלֵא גְוִיּוֹת, אִיהוּ דְּלָא אִשְׁתַּנֵּי קַמֵּיהּ כָּל דְּיוֹקְנִין דְּעַלְמָא, וְעַל דָּא מִבָּעֵי לֵיהּ לְבַר נָשׁ, לְאִסְתַּמְּרָא אָרְחוֹי וּשְׁבִילוֹי, בְּגִין דְּלָא יֶחֱטָא קַמֵּיהּ דְּמָארֵיהּ, וְיִתְקַיֵּים בִּדְיוֹקְנָא דְאָדָם.

246. This is the one angel upon whom all the images are engraved. HE IS THE SECRET OF THE NUKVA, CALLED 'ANGEL', FROM WHOM ALL THE SHAPES IN THE WORLD ARE ISSUED. It is written: "He judges among the nations: their land is full of dead bodies" (Tehilim 110:6), FOR ALL THE SHAPES OF THE BODIES ARE BEFORE HIM BECAUSE no shape can change itself before him. Thus, it behooves a man to guard his ways and paths so as not to sin before his Master, and thereby retain the image of Adam.

247. תָּא חֲזֵי, יְחֶזְקֵאל נָטַר פּוּמֵיהּ מִמַּאֲכָלֵי דְאִיסּוּרֵי, דִּכְתִיב וְלָא בָּא בְּפִי בְּשַׂר פִּגּוּל, זָכָה וְאִקְרֵי בֶּן אָדָם. דָּנִיֵּאל מַה כְּתִיב בֵּיהּ, וַיָּשֶׂם דָּנִיֵּאל עַל לִבּוֹ אֲשֶׁר לֹא יִתְגָּאַל בְּפַת בַּג הַמֶּלֶךְ וּבְיֵין מִשְׁתָּיו, זָכָה הוּא, וְאִתְקַיֵּים בִּדְיוֹקְנֵיהּ דְּאָדָם, בְּגִין דְּכָל מִלִּין דְּעַלְמָא, כֻּלְּהוּ דַּחֲלִין מִקַּמֵּי דְּיוֹקְנָא דְאָדָם, דְּאִיהוּ שַׁלִּיטָא עַל כֻּלְּהוּ, וְאִיהוּ מַלְכָּא עַל כֹּלָּא.

247. Come and behold: Ezekiel guarded his mouth against forbidden food, as it is written: "Nor did loathsome meat ever come into my mouth" (Yechezkel 4:14). He therefore merited being named the son of Adam. It is written of Daniel: "But Daniel purposed in his heart that he would not defile himself with the portion of the king's food, nor with the wine which he drank" (Daniel 1:8). He then merited preserving the image of Adam. For all the beings in the world were fearful of the image of Adam, who ruled over them all and was king over all.

248. אָמַר רַבִּי יוֹסֵי, בְּגִין דָּא, אִצְטְרִיךְ לֵיהּ לְבַר נָשׁ, לְאִסְתַּמְּרָא מֵחוֹבוֹי, וְלָא יִסְטֵי לִימִינָא וְלִשְׂמָאלָא. וְעִם כָּל דָּא, בָּעֵי לֵיהּ לְבַר נָשׁ, לְמִבְדַּק בְּחוֹבוֹי, בְּכָל יוֹמָא וְיוֹמָא, דְּהָא כַּד בַּר נָשׁ קָאֵים מֵעַרְסֵיהּ,

תְּרֵין סַהֲדִין קָיְימִין קַמֵּיהּ, וְאָזְלֵי בַּהֲדֵיהּ, כָּל יוֹמָא.

248. Rabbi Yosi said that a man should beware of sinning and not deviate right or left. ALTHOUGH HE GUARDS HIMSELF, he should search himself daily for sins. For when a man rises from his bed, two witnesses stand before him and accompany him the whole day.

249. בָּעֵי בַּר נָשׁ לְמֵיקַם, אִינּוּן סַהֲדֵי אָמְרִין לֵיהּ, בְּשַׁעְתָּא דְּאַפְתַּח עֵינוֹי, עֵינֶיךָ לְנֹכַח יַבִּיטוּ וְעַפְעַפֶּיךָ יַיְשִׁירוּ נֶגְדֶּךָ. קָם וְאַתְקִין רַגְלוֹי לְמֵהַךְ, אִינּוּן סַהֲדִין אָמְרִין לֵיהּ, פַּלֵּס מַעְגַּל רַגְלֶךָ וגו'. וְעַל דָּא כַּד אָזֵיל בַּר נָשׁ, בְּכָל יוֹמָא, בָּעֵי לֵיהּ לְאִסְתַּמְּרָא מֵחוֹבוֹי.

249. When a man wishes to rise, he opens his eyes and the witnesses say to him, "Let your eyes look right on, and let your eyelids look straight before you" (Mishlei 4:25). When he prepares himself to go, they say to him, "Make even the path of your foot" (Ibid. 26). Thus, when a man walks, he should guard against his sins the whole day.

250. בְּכָל יוֹמָא וְיוֹמָא, כַּד אָתֵי לֵילְיָא, בָּעֵי לְאִסְתַּכְּלָא, וּלְמִבְדַּק, בְּכָל מַה דַּעֲבַד כָּל הַהוּא יוֹמָא, בְּגִין דְּיֵיתוּב מִנַּיְיהוּ, וְיִסְתַּכֵּל בְּהוֹ תָּדִיר, בְּגִין דְּיֵיתוּב קַמֵּי מָארֵיהּ, כְּמָה דְּאַתְּ אָמֵר וְחַטָּאתִי נֶגְדִּי תָמִיד, בְּגִין דְּיֵיתוּב מִנַּיְיהוּ.

250. When night falls, he should examine and search his actions for that day to repent for his deeds. He should always search them so he can repent before his Master, as it is written: "And my sin is ever before me" (Tehilim 51:5).

251. וְתָא חֲזֵי, בִּזְמְנָא דַּהֲווֹ יִשְׂרָאֵל בְּאַרְעָא קַדִּישָׁא, לָא אִשְׁתַּכַּח בִּידַיְיהוּ חוֹבָא, כְּמָה דְּאוֹקְמוּהָ, בְּגִין דְּאִינּוּן קָרְבָּנִין, דַּהֲווֹ מְקָרְבִין בְּכָל יוֹמָא, הֲווֹ מְכַפְּרֵי עֲלַיְיהוּ. הַשְׁתָּא דְּאִתְגָּלוּן יִשְׂרָאֵל מֵאַרְעָא, וְלֵית מַאן דִּמְכַפֵּר עֲלַיְיהוּ, אוֹרַיְיתָא הִיא מְכַפְּרָא עֲלַיְיהוּ, וְעוֹבָדִין דְּכַשְׁרָן, בְּגִין דִּשְׁכִינְתָּא עִמְּהוֹן בְּגָלוּתָא, וּמַאן דְּאִיהוּ לָא מִסְתַּכַּל בְּאָרְחוֹי דְּקוּדְשָׁא

בְּרִיךְ הוּא, גָּרֵים לִשְׁכִינְתָּא לְאִתְכַּפְיָא בְּגוֹ עַפְרָא, כד״א יַשְׁפִּילֶנָּה יַשְׁפִּילָהּ עַד אֶרֶץ וגו׳.

251. Come and behold: as long as Yisrael were in the Holy Land, they had no sin on their hands, because – as has been explained – of the sacrifices they offered daily that atoned for their sins. Once Yisrael is exiled from the Holy Land, and there was nothing to atone for them, the Torah and their good deeds atoned for them. Because the Shechinah is with them in exile, whoever does not care for the ways of the Holy One, blessed be He, causes the Shechinah to bend to the dust, as it is written: "He lays it low, even to the ground" (Yeshayah 26:5).

252. אָמַר רַבִּי יִצְחָק, וְכֵן מַאן דְּאִשְׁתַּדַּל בְּאוֹרַיְיתָא, וּבְעוֹבָדִין דְּכַשְׁרָן, גָּרֵים לָהּ לכנ״י, לַאֲרָמָא רֵישָׁא בְּגוֹ גָּלוּתָא. זַכָּאָה חוּלָקֵיהוֹן, דְּאִינוּן דְּמִשְׁתַּדְּלֵי בְּאוֹרַיְיתָא יְמָמָא וְלֵילֵי.

252. Rabbi Yitzchak said that he who devotes himself to the Torah and to good deeds causes the Congregation of Yisrael, THE SHECHINAH, to lift up its head in exile. Happy is the portion of those who devote themselves to the Torah day and night.

253. תָּא חֲזֵי, גִּלְגֵּל קוּדְשָׁא בְּרִיךְ הוּא גִּלְגּוּלִין בְּעַלְמָא, בְּגִין לַאֲרָמָא רֵישָׁא דְצַדִּיקַיָּיא, דְּהָא בְּגִין דְּיָרֵים יוֹסֵף רֵישֵׁיהּ בְּעַלְמָא, עַל דְּאִשְׁתַּכַּח זַכָּאָה קַמֵּיהּ, אַרְגֵּיז רִבּוֹנָא עַל עַבְדוֹי, כד״א חָטְאוּ מַשְׁקֵה מֶלֶךְ מִצְרַיִם וְהָאוֹפֶה לַאֲדוֹנֵיהֶם לְמֶלֶךְ מִצְרַיִם, וְכֹלָּא בְּגִין לַאֲרָמָא רֵישָׁא דְיוֹסֵף זַכָּאָה. וְתָא חֲזֵי, עַל יְדָא דְחֶלְמָא, אִתְכַּפְיָיא מֵעִם אֲחוֹי, וְעַל יְדָא דְחֶלְמָא אִתְרַבֵּי עַל אֲחוֹי, וְאִתְרַבֵּי עַל כָּל עַלְמָא.

253. Come and behold: the Holy One, blessed be He, transforms matters in the world so as to lift the heads of the righteous. To enable Joseph to raise his head for being righteous before Him, He caused the master to be angry with his servants, as it is written: "The butler of the king of Egypt, and his baker, offended their lord the king of Egypt" (Beresheet 40: 1). All this happened to lift the head of Joseph the righteous. Come and behold: he was humiliated by his brothers through a dream. He obtained greatness over his brothers and was raised above the whole world through a dream, NAMELY BY THE DREAM OF PHARAOH.

254. **וַיַּחַלְמוּ חֲלוֹם שְׁנֵיהֶם אִישׁ חֲלוֹמוֹ בְּלַיְלָה אֶחָד אִישׁ כְּפִתְרוֹן וגו', תָּא חֲזֵי, דְּהָא אִתְּמָר דְּכָל חֶלְמִין אָזְלִין בָּתַר פּוּמָא, יוֹסֵף כַּד פָּשַׁר לְהוֹ חֶלְמָא, אַמַּאי פָּשַׁר לְהַאי פִּשְׁרָא טָבָא, וּלְהַאי פִּשְׁרָא בִּישָׁא. אֶלָּא, אִינוּן חֶלְמִין עֲלֵיהּ דְּיוֹסֵף הֲוָה, וּבְגִין דְּיָדַע מִלָּה עַל עִקָּרָא וְשָׁרְשָׁא דִילָהּ, בְּגִין כָּךְ פָּשַׁר חֶלְמָא לְהוֹ כְּמָה דְאִצְטְרִיךְ. לְכָל חַד וְחַד פָּשַׁר לְהוֹן פִּשְׁרָא, לְאַהֲדָרָא מִלָּה עַל אַתְרֵיהּ.**

254. “And they dreamed a dream, both of them, each man on the same night, each man according to the interpretation of his dream” (Beresheet 40:5). Come and behold: we have learned that all dreams follow their interpretation. IN THIS RESPECT, HE ASKS: When Joseph interpreted their dreams, why did he give one a good interpretation and another a bad one? WHY DID NOT HE GIVE THEM BOTH A GOOD INTERPRETATION? HE ANSWERS: The two dreams concerned Joseph, and because he knew the root of every matter, he interpreted their dreams accordingly, and gave them meaning, so as to return each matter to its own place AND ROOT.

255. **מַה כְּתִיב וַיֹּאמֶר אֲלֵיהֶם יוֹסֵף הֲלֹא לֵאלֹהִים פִּתְרוֹנִים סַפְּרוּ נָא לִי, מַאי טַעְמָא, בְּגִין דְּהָכֵי מִבָּעֵי לֵיהּ לְמִפְשַׁר חֶלְמָא, לְפָקְדָא פִּשְׁרָא לְקוּדְשָׁא בְּרִיךְ הוּא, בְּגִין דְּתַמָּן אִיהוּ קִיּוּמָא דְּכֹלָּא, וּבֵיהּ קָיְימָא פִּשְׁרָא.**

255. It is written: “And Joseph said to them, ‘Do not interpretations belong to Elohim? tell me them, I pray you’” (Ibid. 8). HE ASKS: Why DID HE SPEAK THUS? HE ANSWERS: This is the way a dream should be interpreted, by entrusting the interpretation to the Holy One, blessed be He. For the existence of everything is there, and therein lies the interpretation.

256. **תָּא חֲזֵי, הָא אִתְּמָר, דְּדַרְגָּא דְחֶלְמָא לְתַתָּא אִיהוּ, וְאִיהוּ דַרְגָּא שְׁתִיתָאָה, בְּגִין דְּהָא מֵאֲתַר דִּנְבוּאָה שַׁרְיָא, עַד הַאי דַּרְגָּא דְחֶלְמָא,**

שִׁיתָּא דַרְגִּין אִינּוּן, וְסָלְקָא פִּישְׁרָא מִדַּרְגָּא דְחֶלְמָא, לְדַרְגָּא אָחֳרָא. חֶלְמָא אִיהוּ דַרְגָּא דִלְתַתָּא, וּפִשְׁרָא קַיְימָא עֲלַיְיהוּ, וּפִישְׁרָא קַיְימָא בְּדִבּוּר, וְעַל דָּא בְּדִבּוּר קַיְימָא מִלָּה, דִּכְתִיב הֲלֹא לֵאלֹהִים פִּתְרוֹנִים, הֲלֹא לֵאלֹהִים וַדַּאי.

256. Come and behold: we have learned that the dream's grade is the sixth below prophecy. For between the grade of prophecy and the grade of dreams lie six grades, and interpretation ascends from the dream's grade into another one. HE EXPLAINS THAT the dream is a low grade OF GABRIEL, and interpretation is established by it, for it depends upon speech –THE NUKVA – as it is written: "Do not interpretations belong to Elohim"; assuredly, "to Elohim," WHICH IS THE NUKVA CALLED 'ELOHIM'.

24. “Let a double portion of your spirit be upon me”

A Synopsis

We learn that whoever contemplates the image of his master in the spirit of wisdom shall gain an additional measure of spirit. Thus Elisha, Elijah’s heir by right, was granted the power to perform a double achievement with the same spirit, if he could penetrate to the deepest core of the spirit that Elijah had bequeathed at the moment Elijah was taken from him. Joseph also received illumination in this way. This allowed him to interpret the symbolism of the dreams of the chief wine steward and the chief baker, and to grasp the significance these dreams held for the children of Israel. The chief wine steward’s dream, it is explained, belonged to “the grade of the moon in lightness” and was thus under the rule of Zeir Anpin; while the chief baker’s dream belonged to “the grade of the moon in darkness” and thus came under the rule of the Evil One.

The Relevance of this Passage

Here we receive a powerful connection to the souls of the righteous, which gives us the ability to ascend to spiritual heights unattainable by ordinary men. Moreover, we begin to recognize our spirit’s ceaseless yearning for re-union with The Creator, coupled with the wisdom to find our way back to Him

257. תָּא חֲזֵי מַה כְּתִיב וַיְסַפֵּר שַׂר הַמַּשְׁקִים אֶת חֲלוֹמוֹ לְיוֹסֵף וגו׳. רִבִּי אֶלְעָזָר פָּתַח וַאֲמַר, וַיְהִי בְּעָבְרָם וְאֵלִיָּהוּ אָמַר אֶל אֱלִישָׁע שְׁאַל מָה אֶעֱשֶׂה לָּךְ בְּטֶרֶם אֶלָּקַח מֵעִמָּךְ וַיֹּאמֶר אֱלִישָׁע וִיהִי נָא פִּי שְׁנַיִם בְּרוּחֲךָ אֵלָי. הָכָא אִית לְאִסְתַּכְּלָא, וְהַאי קְרָא תְּוָוהָא אִיהוּ, וְאֵלִיָּהוּ אָמַר אֶל אֱלִישָׁע שְׁאַל מָה אֶעֱשֶׂה לָּךְ, וְכִי בִּרְשׁוּתֵיהּ קַיְימָא, וְהָא בִּרְשׁוּתֵיהּ דְּקוּדְשָׁא בְּרִיךְ הוּא אִיהוּ. וְתוּ, דֶּאֱלִישָׁע הָכֵי נָמֵי אִיהוּ הֲוָה יָדַע, מַאי טַעְמָא אָמַר, וִיהִי נָא פִּי שְׁנַיִם בְּרוּחֲךָ אֵלָי.

257. Come and behold the verse: “And the chief butler told his dream to Joseph” (Beresheet 40:9). Rabbi Elazar opened with the verse: “And it came to pass, when they had gone over, that Elijah said to Elisha, ‘Ask what I shall do for you, before I am taken away from you.’ And Elisha said, ‘I pray you, let a double portion of your spirit be upon me’” (II Melachim 2:9). We must study this verse, for the words are surprising. “Elijah said to Elisha, ‘Ask what I shall do for you.’” It was not for him, but for the Holy One, blessed be He, to grant wishes. Moreover, Elisha also knew HE COULD NOT GRANT HIS REQUEST, ONLY THE HOLY ONE, BLESSED BE HE, COULD. Why did he ask, "I pray you, let a double portion of your spirit be upon me?"

258. אֶלָּא וַדַּאי, מַאן דְּאָחִיד בִּשְׁמַיָּא וְאַרְעָא, וְכָל עָלְמִין, הֵיךְ לָא יְהֵא בִּרְשׁוּתֵיהּ דָּא, וַדַּאי אֵלִיָּהוּ, וּשְׁאָר צַדִּיקִים, קוּדְשָׁא בְּרִיךְ הוּא עָבִיד רְעוּתְהוֹן דְּצַדִּיקַיָּיא תָּדִיר, דִּכְתִיב, רְצוֹן יְרֵאָיו יַעֲשֶׂה, וְכָל שֶׁכֵּן דְּהַהוּא רוּחָא קַדִּישָׁא, דִּדְרֵי עֲלֵיהּ, יָרֵית לֵיהּ לְצַדִּיקָא דֶּאֱלִישָׁע, דַּהֲוָה שַׁמָּשָׁא דִילֵיהּ, וְהָא קוּדְשָׁא בְּרִיךְ הוּא אָמַר לוֹ וְאֶת אֱלִישָׁע בֶּן שָׁפָט מֵאָבֵל מְחוֹלָה תִּמְשַׁח לְנָבִיא תַּחְתֶּיךָ, וְעַל דָּא הֲוָה לֵיהּ לֶאֱלִישָׁע לְיָרְתָא לֵיהּ.

258. HE ANSWERS THAT He who held heaven and earth and the whole world in His grip could perform this wish. It is a certainty that the Holy One, blessed be He, always fulfills the wishes of Elijah and the other righteous, as it is written: "He will fulfill the desire of those who fear him" (Tehilim 145:19). This is all the more true of he, upon whom the Holy Spirit dwells, who bequeaths it to Elisha the righteous. For Elisha was his servant AND WAS WORTHY OF BEING HIS HEIR, as was expressly said by the Holy One, blessed be He: "And Elisha the son of Shafat of Avel-mecholah shall you anoint to be prophet in your place" (I Melachim 19:16). Elisha was then his heir apparent.

259. פִּי שְׁנַיִם בְּרוּחֲךָ, מַאי פִּי שְׁנַיִם בְּרוּחֲךָ אֵלַי, וְכִי סַלְקָא דַעְתָּךְ, דְּעַל חַד תְּרֵין שָׁאֵיל, וּמַה דְּלָא הֲוָה בִּרְשׁוּתֵיהּ, הֵיךְ שָׁאַל מִינֵּיהּ. אֶלָּא, אִיהוּ לָא שָׁאֵיל רוּחַ עַל חַד תְּרֵין, אֶלָּא הָכֵי שָׁאַל מִינֵּיהּ, בְּהַהוּא רוּחָא דַּהֲוָה לֵיהּ, דְּיַעֲבִיד תְּרֵין נִמּוּסִין בְּעָלְמָא, בְּהַהוּא רוּחָא.

259. "...double portion of your spirit be upon me" (II Melachim 2:9). HE ASKS: What does this mean? Could it possibly mean that he asks two for one, THAT IS, THAT HIS SPIRIT WILL BE DOUBLE ELIJAH'S SPIRIT? How could he have asked of him for something that he did not possess, AS NO ONE CAN GIVE WHAT HE DOES NOT HAVE? HE REPLIES THAT he did not ask for two spirits for the one he had, but that the same spirit he had perform twice as many miracles AS ELIJAH PERFORMED.

260. מַה כְּתִיב וַיֹּאמֶר הִקְשִׁיתָ לִשְׁאוֹל אִם תִּרְאֶה אוֹתִי לֻקָּח מֵאִתָּךְ יְהִי לְךָ כֵן וְאִם אַיִן לֹא יִהְיֶה. מַאי טַעְמָא אִם תִּרְאֶה אוֹתִי. אֶלָּא, אֲמַר לֵיהּ, אִם תֵּיכוּל לְמֵיקַם עַל עִקָּרָא דְרוּחָא דִּשְׁבַקְנָא לָךְ, בְּשַׁעְתָּא דְּאִתְנְסֵיבְנָא מִינָךְ, יְהֵא לָךְ כְּדֵין, דְּהָא כָּל הַהוּא עִקָּרָא דְרוּחָא בְּשַׁעְתָּא דְיִסְתַּכֵּל בֵּיהּ, כַּד חָמֵי לֵיהּ לְאֵלִיָּהוּ, יֶהֱוֵי דְבֵיקוּתָא בֵּיהּ, כִּדְקָא יָאוּת.

260. It is written: "And he said, 'You have asked a hard thing: nevertheless, if you see me when I am taken from you, it shall be so for you; but if not, it shall not be so'" (II Melachim 2:10). WHY DID HE MAKE HIS REQUEST CONDITIONAL? HE ANSWERS THAT he said to him: 'If you could understand the essence of the spirit that I leave you when I am taken from you, it shall be yours.' For the essence of the spirit that he discerns while looking at Elijah is something he should well cleave to.

261. תָּא חֲזֵי, הַאי מַאן דְּאִסְתַּכַּל בְּמָה דְאוֹלִיף מֵרַבֵּיהּ, וְחָמֵי לֵיהּ בְּהַהוּא חָכְמְתָא, יָכִיל לְאִתּוֹסְפָא בְּהַהוּא רוּחָא יַתִּיר. תָּא חֲזֵי, דְּהָא יוֹסֵף בְּכָל מַה דְּאִיהוּ עָבֵיד, הֲוֵי חָמֵי בְּרוּחָא דְחָכְמְתָא, לְהַהוּא דְיוֹקְנָא דַּאֲבוֹי, הֲוָה מִסְתַּכֵּל. וּבְגִין כָּךְ הֲוָה מִסְתַּיְּיעָא לֵיהּ מִלְּתָא, וְאִתּוֹסְפָא לֵיהּ רוּחָא אָחֳרָא, בִּנְהִירוּ עִלָּאָה יַתִּיר.

261. Come and behold: he who looks into what he learned from his Rabbi and sees in him the wisdom HE LEARNED FROM HIM could receive an additional portion of spirit. Come and behold: in whatever he did, Joseph would see the spirit of wisdom in his father's image. He therefore succeeded in what he did, and another spirit of a superior illumination was added to him.

262. בְּשַׁעְתָּא דַּאֲמַר לֵיהּ הַהוּא רָשָׁע, וְהִנֵּה גֶּפֶן לְפָנַי, אִזְדַּעְזַע יוֹסֵף, דְּלָא הֲוָה יָדַע עַל מַה תֵּיתֵי מִלָּה, כֵּיוָן דַּאֲמַר וּבַגֶּפֶן שְׁלֹשָׁה שָׂרִיגִים, מִיָּד אִתְּעַר רוּחֵיהּ, וְאִתּוֹסַף בִּנְהִירוּ, וְאִסְתַּכַּל בִּדְיוֹקְנָא דַּאֲבוֹי, כְּדֵין אִתְנְהִיר רוּחֵיהּ, וְיָדַע מִלָּה.

262. When that wicked man said to him, "Behold, a vine was before me" (Beresheet 40:9), Joseph trembled because he did not know what it meant. But when he added, "And on the vine were three tendrils" (Ibid. 10), his spirit rose and received additional illumination. He looked at his father's image and his spirit shone because he understood its meaning.

263. מַה כְּתִיב, וּבַגֶּפֶן שְׁלֹשָׁה שָׂרִיגִם. אֲמַר יוֹסֵף, הָא וַדַּאי בְּשׂוֹרָה דְחֶדְוָה בִּשְׁלִימוּ אִיהוּ, מַאי טַעְמָא, בְּגִין דְּהַאי גֶּפֶן עַל כְּנֶסֶת יִשְׂרָאֵל אִתְחֲזֵי לֵיהּ, וְאִתְבַּשַּׂר יוֹסֵף בְּהַאי. וּבַגֶּפֶן שְׁלֹשָׁה שָׂרִיגִם: אִלֵּין אִינּוּן תְּלָתָא דַרְגִּין עִלָּאִין, דְּנָפְקֵי מֵהַאי גֶּפֶן, כַּהֲנֵי לֵיוָאֵי וְיִשְׂרְאֵלֵי.

263. It is written: "And on the vine were three tendrils." Joseph said: 'This is assuredly an altogether good tiding', for the vine indicated the Congregation of Yisrael, THE NUKVA. Joseph was informed THAT HER TIME CAME TO RULE, "and on the vine were three tendrils" that allude to the three supernal grades that came out of the vine: the priests, Levites, and Yisrael – CHESED, GVURAH, AND TIFERET OF ZEIR ANPIN, WHICH SHINE WITHIN THE NUKVA WHEN SHE IS WHOLE.

264. וְהִיא כְפוֹרַחַת עָלְתָה נִצָּהּ, דְּהָא בְּגִינֵיהוֹן, סָלְקָא כְּנֶסֶת יִשְׂרָאֵל, וְאִתְבָּרְכַת מֵעִם מַלְכָּא עִלָּאָה. הִבְשִׁילוּ אַשְׁכְּלוֹתֶיהָ עֲנָבִים, אִלֵּין אִינּוּן צַדִּיקַיָּא דְעַלְמָא, דְּאִינּוּן כַּעֲנָבִים מְבוּשָּׁלִים כִּדְקָא חָזֵי. דָּבָר אֲחֵר הִבְשִׁילוּ אַשְׁכְּלוֹתֶיהָ עֲנָבִים, דָּא הוּא יַיִן דְּאִתְנְטִיר בְּעִנְבַיְיהוּ, מִשֵּׁשֶׁת יְמֵי בְרֵאשִׁית.

264. "...and it was as though it budded, and its blossoms shot forth" (Beresheet 40:10). For their sake, the Congregation of Yisrael mounts TO ZEIR ANPIN and is blessed by the Supernal King, ZEIR ANPIN; "and its clusters brought forth ripe grapes," refers to the righteous men in the world, who are likened to ripened grapes. Another explanation of the verse, "and its clusters brought forth ripe grapes," is that it refers to the wine preserved in its grapes since the six days of Creation.

265. עַד הָכָא אִתְבַּשַּׂר יוֹסֵף בְּחֶלְמֵיהּ, מִכָּאן וּלְהָלְאָה חֶלְמָא אִיהוּ דִילֵיהּ, בְּגִין דְּאִית חֶלְמִין לֵיהּ, וּלְאַחֲרָנִין. וָאֶקַּח אֶת הָעֲנָבִים, דְּאִיהוּ

לֵיהּ לְגַרְמֵיהּ.

265. Thus far was Joseph informed by this dream OF THE CHIEF BUTLER. The rest of the dream OF THE CHIEF BUTLER is his. Some dreams are for the dreamer as well as for others; THAT IS, PART OF THEM REVEALS FUTURE EVENTS FOR THE DREAMER, AND ANOTHER PART FUTURE EVENTS FOR OTHERS. "...and I took the grapes..." refers to himself – NOT TO JOSEPH.

266. תָּנִינָן, הַאי מַאן דְּחָמֵי עִנְבִין חִוָּורִין בְּחֶלְמָא, סִימָן יָפֶה לוֹ, אוּכְמֵי לָא, מַאי טַעְמָא, בְּגִין דְּאִיהוּ רָזָא דִתְרֵין דַּרְגִּין יְדִיעָן, אִינוּן אוּכְמֵי וְחִוָּורֵי, הַאי אִיהוּ טַב, וְהַאי אִיהוּ דְּלָא טַב, וְכֻלְּהוּ עִנְבִין בְּרָזָא דִמְהֵימְנוּתָא תַּלְיָין, וְע״ד מִתְפַּרְשָׁן בְּחָכְמְתָא, הֵן לְטַב, הֵן לְבִישׁ, אִלֵּין צְרִיכִין רַחֲמֵי, וְאִלֵּין אַשְׁגָּחוּתָא דְרַחֲמֵי.

266. We have learned that whoever sees white grapes in his dream sees a good sign for himself. Black grapes are not A GOOD SIGN. What is the reason for this? There are two grades, black and white. One is good and the other is not, FOR WHITE INDICATES MERCY AND BLACK INDICATES JUDGMENT. All grapes, BOTH WHITE AND BLACK, depend on the secret of the faith, THE NUKVA. According to wisdom, their meanings are explained as either good or evil. The BLACK ONES indicate the need for Mercy, and THE WHITE indicates the providential care of Mercy.

267. תָּא חֲזֵי, אָדָם הָרִאשׁוֹן, אִנְתְּתֵיהּ סָחֲטָא לֵיהּ עִנְבִין, וּגְרֵימַת לֵיהּ מוֹתָא, וּלְכָל יִשְׂרָאֵל, וּלְכָל עַלְמָא. נֹחַ אֲתָא לְהַנֵּי עִנְבִין, וְלָא אִתְנְטַר כִּדְקָא יָאוּת, מַה כְּתִיב, וַיֵּשְׁתְּ מִן הַיַּיִן וַיִּשְׁכָּר וַיִּתְגַּל בְּתוֹךְ אָהֳלֹה, בְּהֵ״א. בְּנֵי אַהֲרֹן, שָׁתוֹ חַמְרָא מִנַּיְיהוּ, וְקָרִיבוּ קָרְבָּנָא בְּהַהוּא חַמְרָא, וּמִיתוּ, וְהָא אִתְּמָר. וּבְגִין כָּךְ כְּתִיב, עֲנָבֵימוֹ עִנְּבֵי רֹאשׁ אַשְׁכְּלוֹת מְרוֹרוֹת לָמוֹ, בְּגִין דְּאִינוּן עִנְבִין גָּרְמֵי הַאי.

267. Come and behold: Adam's wife pressed him grapes and brought death upon him, Yisrael, and the whole world. When Noah came upon these grapes, he was not well guarded, as it is written: "He drank of the wine, and was drunk; and he was uncovered within his tent" (Beresheet 9:21). The sons of Aaron drank wine PRESSED FROM THESE GRAPES and offered a sacrifice while still under its influence. Consequently they died, as has been already explained. It is therefore written: "Their grapes are grapes of gall, their clusters are bitter" (Devarim 32:32). It is written thus because of what the grapes caused.

268. חָמָא עִנְבִין, דְּאִינּוּן טָבִין, בְּהַהוּא כֶּרֶם, דְּקָא סָלְקִין נַיְיחָא וְרֵיחָא בְּדַרְגִּין שְׁלֵימִין, כִּדְקָא יָאוֹת. וְע״ד יוֹסֵף יָדַע מִלָּה, וְאִסְתַּכַּל בְּעִקָּרָא, וּפְשַׁר חֶלְמָא עַל בּוּרְיֵיהּ. בְּגִין דְּאִתְבַּשַּׂר בְּהַהוּא חֶלְמָא, כִּדְקָא יָאוֹת. וּבְגִין כָּךְ פָּשַׁר פִּשְׁרָא לְטַב, וְאִתְקַיַּים הָכֵי.

268. THE CHIEF BUTLER saw IN HIS DREAM good grapes, NAMELY WHITE GRAPES, in the vineyard, where they sent forth pleasantness and fragrance in perfectly whole grades. Joseph therefore knew it, looked into the root OF THE MATTER, and solved it thoroughly. Because he received good tidings by that dream, he interpreted it favorably, and so it came to pass.

269. מַה כְּתִיב. וַיַּרְא שַׂר הָאוֹפִים כִּי טוֹב פָּתָר וַיֹּאמֶר אֶל יוֹסֵף אַף אֲנִי בַּחֲלוֹמִי וְהִנֵּה שְׁלֹשָׁה סַלֵּי חֹרִי עַל רֹאשִׁי. תָּא חֲזֵי, אֲרוּרִין אִינּוּן רַשִׁיעַיָּא, דְּכָל עוֹבָדֵיהוֹן כֻּלְּהוֹן לְבִישׁ, וְכָל אִינּוּן מִלִּין דְּאִינּוּן אָמְרִין, כֻּלְּהוּ לְבִישׁ, וּלְאַבְאָשָׁא.

269. Come and behold, it is written: "When the chief baker saw that the interpretation was good, he said to Joseph, 'I also (Heb. *af*) in my dream, behold: I had three baskets of white bread on my head'" (Beresheet 40:16). Damned are the wicked, whose every deed is for evil, whose every speech is uttered for evil and to cause evil.

270. כֵּיוָן דִּפְתַח פּוּמֵיהּ בְּאַף, מִיָּד דָּחֵיל יוֹסֵף, וְיָדַע דְּכָל מִלּוֹי אִינּוּן לְאַבְאָשָׁא, וּבְשׂוֹרָה דְּבִישׁ בְּפוּמֵיהּ. וְהִנֵּה שְׁלֹשָׁה סַלֵּי חֹרִי עַל רֹאשִׁי, כְּדֵין יָדַע יוֹסֵף, דְּאִתְבַּשַּׂר עַל חֲרִיבוּ דְּבֵי מַקְדְּשָׁא, וְיִשְׂרָאֵל בְּגָלוּתָא, דְּיִתְגָּלוּן מֵאַרְעָא קַדִּישָׁא.

270. He opened his speech with the word "*af* (also: 'anger')" IN THE SENTENCE, "I ALSO IN MY DREAM..." Immediately, Joseph was seized with fright, for he knew that all his words were of evil intent and that he bore evil tidings. By the verse: "Behold, I had three baskets of white bread on my head," Joseph knew that he was informed of the destruction of the Temple and the exile of Yisrael from the Holy Land.

271. חָמֵי מַה כְּתִיב, וּבַסַּל הָעֶלְיוֹן מִכָּל מַאֲכַל פַּרְעֹה מַעֲשֵׂה אוֹפֶה וְהָעוֹף אוֹכֵל אוֹתָם מִן הַסַּל מֵעַל רֹאשִׁי אִלֵּין אִינּוּן שְׁאָר עַמִּין, דְּמִתְכַּנְשֵׁי עֲלַיְיהוּ דְּיִשְׂרָאֵל, וְקָטְלֵי לוֹן, וְחָרְבֵי בֵּיתַיְיהוּ, וּמְפַזְּרֵי לוֹן לְאַרְבַּע סִטְרֵי דְּעַלְמָא, וְכֹלָּא אִסְתַּכַּל יוֹסֵף, וְיָדַע דְּהַהוּא חֶלְמָא עַל יִשְׂרָאֵל, כַּד יְהוֹן בְּחִיּוּבָא קַמֵּי מַלְכָּא, מִיָּד פָּשַׁר לֵיהּ פִּשְׁרָא לְבִישׁ, וְאִתְקַיַּים בֵּיהּ.

271. Come and behold: "And in the uppermost basket there was all manner of Pharaoh's baked food; and the birds did eat them out of the basket upon my head" (Beresheet 40:17). This refers to the other nations, who will gather upon Yisrael to kill them, destroy their homes, and scatter them to the four winds of the world. Joseph saw all this and knew that this dream alluded to Yisrael, who would be guilty before the King. He then interpreted his dream in an evil sense, which was fulfilled.

272. וְתָּא חֲזֵי, תְּרֵין דַּרְגִּין אִלֵּין, דְּקָא חָמָא הַאי, וְחָמָא הַאי, דָּא חָמָא כַּד סָלֵיק, וְקָא שַׁלִּיט דַּרְגָּא עִלָּאָה, וְאִתְנְהֵיר סִהֲרָא. וְדָא חָמָא, דְּאִתְחַשַּׁךְ וְשַׁלִּיט עֲלָהּ חִיְוְיָא בִישָׁא, וּבְגִין כָּךְ אִסְתַּכַּל יוֹסֵף בְּהַהוּא חֶלְמָא, וּפָשַׁר לֵיהּ פִּשְׁרָא לְבִישׁ. וְע"ד, כֹּלָּא בְּפִישְׁרָא קָיְימָא, וְדָא וְדָא חָמוּ, בְּאִלֵּין תְּרֵין דַּרְגִּין, דְּשַׁלִּיט דָּא, וְשַׁלִּיט דָּא.

272. Come and behold: there were two grades that they had seen. THE CHIEF BUTLER saw the supernal grade, ZEIR ANPIN, ascending to rule, and the moon, THE NUKVA, shining. THE CHIEF BAKER saw darkness and the evil serpent ruling over THE NUKVA. Joseph therefore looked into the dream and gave it an evil interpretation. Thus, all depends on interpretation. The two of them saw the two grades RULING OVER THE NUKVA, ZEIR ANPIN,

OR THE EVIL SERPENT. Either the one rules, ZEIR ANPIN, or that EVIL One, THE SERPENT, does.

25. "Create in me a clean heart, Elohim..."

A Synopsis

Rabbi Yehuda begins a discussion of the steadfast spirit of Messiah, which King David invoked to preserve himself from the spirit of confusion, whose task is leading people astray. Rabbi Yosi and Rabbi Elazar then discuss in some detail Ahab's crime against Navot, along with the verse, "the lying spirit in the mouth of the prophets." This spirit was not that of Navot, as has been presumed, but rather, the lying spirit which continually ascends and descends to distract people from life's true goal. King David, because he knew full well the rewards of the righteous, often made supplication in order that he might be guarded from defilement by powerful Accusers of this world.

The Relevance of this Passage

Far worse than lying to others is the act of lying to ourselves. It is in our nature to believe our own false tales and then attempt to promote these distortions in the world. Self-deception is the greatest of all deceptions, because our intentions might very well be good. When sunlight shines through the window pain, the dust floating in the air is suddenly revealed. Spiritual Light has the same effect on our negative qualities, which so often remain hidden. Purposefully perusing these passages removes prevarication, so that the true purpose of our existence – identifying and eliminating negative aspects of our character – shines brightly in our lives. It is of equivalent effect to David's supplications, summoning the Light to guard us from the ever-present dangers of self-deception, and allowing us to grow in righteousness and wisdom.

273. רִבִּי יְהוּדָה פָּתַח, לֵב טָהוֹר בְּרָא לִי אֱלֹקִים וְרוּחַ נָכוֹן חַדֵּשׁ בְּקִרְבִּי, הַאי קְרָא אוֹקְמוּהָ, אֲבָל לֵב טָהוֹר, כד״א, וְנָתַתָּ לְעַבְדְּךָ לֵב שׁוֹמֵעַ וגו׳, וּכְתִיב וְטוֹב לֵב מִשְׁתֶּה תָּמִיד, וּבְגִין כָּךְ לֵב טָהוֹר וַדַּאי.

273. Rabbi Yehuda opened the discussion with the verse: "Create in me a clean heart, Elohim, and renew a steadfast spirit within me" (Tehilim 51:12). This verse has already been expounded upon, yet the "clean heart" has the same meaning as in the verses: "Give therefore Your servant an understanding heart" (I Melachim 3:9), and "but he that is of a merry heart has a continual feast" (Mishlei 15:15). For that reason, his heart is assuredly clean.

274. וְרוּחַ נָכוֹן חַדֵּשׁ בְּקִרְבִּי, דָּא הוּא רוּחַ נָכוֹן וַדַּאי כד״א, וְרוּחַ אֱלֹקִים מְרַחֶפֶת עַל פְּנֵי הַמָּיִם, וְאִתְּעָרוּ, זֶה רוּחוֹ שֶׁל מָשִׁיחַ, וְאִתְּעָרוּ, וְרוּחַ חֲדָשָׁה אֶתֵּן בְּקִרְבְּכֶם, וְצַלֵּי דָּוִד, הַהוּא רוּחַ נָכוֹן, חַדֵּשׁ בְּקִרְבִּי.

274. "…and renew a steadfast spirit within me." This is surely the steadfast spirit mentioned in the verse: "And a spirit from Elohim moved over the surface of the waters" (Beresheet 1:2). It has been said that this is the spirit of Messiah, ABOUT WHICH IT IS WRITTEN: "A new spirit will I put within you" (Yechezkel 36:26). David therefore asked, "and renew a steadfast spirit" – THE SPIRIT OF MESSIAH – "within me."

275. בְּגִין דְּאִית מִסִּטְרָא אָחֳרָא, לֵב טָמֵא, וְרוּחַ עִוְעִים, דְּאַסְטֵי לִבְנֵי עַלְמָא, וְדָא הוּא רוּחַ טֻמְאָה, דְּאִקְרֵי רוּחַ עִוְעִים, כד״א, ה׳ מָסַךְ בְּקִרְבָּהּ רוּחַ עִוְעִים, וְעַל דָּא וְרוּחַ נָכוֹן חַדֵּשׁ בְּקִרְבִּי. מַאי חָדָשׁ. דָּא חִדּוּשָׁא דְּסִיהֲרָא, בְּשַׁעְתָּא דְּאִתְחַדַּשׁ סִיהֲרָא, דָּוִד מֶלֶךְ יִשְׂרָאֵל חַי וְקַיָּם וּבְגִין כָּךְ חָדָשׁ.

275. For on the Other Side, there is a defiled heart and a spirit of confusion that provokes humans to transgress. This is the Defiled Spirit, called "the spirit of confusion," as it is written: "Hashem has mingled a spirit of confusion in the midst of her" (Yeshayah 19:14). Therefore David requested, "renew a steadfast spirit within me." HE ASKS: What does "renew" imply? HE ANSWERS: It refers to the renewal of the moon – THAT IS, THE RENEWAL OF THE UNION BETWEEN THE NUKVA AND ZEIR ANPIN. Because at the time that the moon is renewed, it is proven that David, King of Yisrael – SYMBOLIC OF THE NUKVA – is considered alive and well, HAVING ATTAINED MOCHIN OF THE LIGHT OF CHAYAH. Therefore, he asked to be renewed, IMPLYING THE RENEWAL OF THE UNION WITH ZEIR ANPIN.

276. רִבִּי אֶלְעָזָר, וְרִבִּי יוֹסֵי הֲווֹ אָזְלֵי בְּאָרְחָא, אֲמַר רִבִּי יוֹסֵי לְר׳ אֶלְעָזָר, הַאי דִּכְתִיב, וַיֵּצֵא הָרוּחַ וַיַּעֲמֹד לִפְנֵי ה׳ וַיֹּאמֶר אֲנִי אֲפַתֶּנּוּ וַיֹּאמֶר ה׳ אֵלָיו בַּמָּה וַיֹּאמֶר אֵצֵא וְהָיִיתִי רוּחַ שֶׁקֶר בְּפִי כָּל נְבִיאָיו וַיֹּאמֶר תְּפַתֶּה וְגַם תּוּכָל צֵא וַעֲשֵׂה כֵן. וְתָנִינָן, דַּהֲוָה רוּחַ נָבוֹת

הַיִּזְרְעֵאלִי, וְכִי נִשְׁמָתִין, כֵּיוָן דְּסָלְקִין וְקַיְימִין לְעֵילָּא, אִינוּן יָכְלִין לַאֲתָבָא בְּהַאי עַלְמָא, וּמִלָּה תְּמִיהָה, דַּאֲמַר אֵצֵא וְהָיִיתִי רוּחַ שֶׁקֶר בְּפִי וגו'.

276. As they were walking together, Rabbi Yosi asks Rabbi Elazar about the verse: "And there came forth a spirit, and stood before Hashem, and said, 'I will persuade him.' And Hashem said to him, 'With what?' And he said, 'I will go out, and I will be a lying spirit in the mouth of all his prophets.' And He said, 'You shall persuade him, and prevail also: go out, and do so'" (I Melachim 22:21-22). We have learned that this was the spirit of Navot the Yizraeli. HE ASKS: Could it be that the souls, after ascending and staying above, return to this world? It is astonishing that he said, "I will go out and I will be a lying spirit..."

277. וְתוּ מַ"ט אִתְעֲנַשׁ עֲלֵיהּ אַחְאָב, דְּהָא דִינָא דְאוֹרַיְיתָא, דְּשַׁוֵּי שְׁמוּאֵל, קַמַּיְיהוּ דְיִשְׂרָאֵל, הָכֵי הוּא. דִּכְתִיב, אֶת שְׂדוֹתֵיכֶם וְכַרְמֵיכֶם וְזֵיתֵיכֶם הַטּוֹבִים יִקָּח, וְאִי אַחְאָב נָטַל הַהוּא כֶּרֶם בְּנָבוֹת, דִּינָא הֲוָה. וְתוּ דַּהֲוָה יָהֵיב לֵיהּ כַּרְמָא אָחֳרָא, אוֹ דַּהֲבָא, וְלָא בָעָא.

277. Also, why was Ahab punished for what he did? It was a law decreed by Samuel to Yisrael, as it is written: "And he will take your fields, and your vineyards, and your best oliveyards" (I Shmuel 8:14). If Ahab took the vineyard from Navot, he was within his rights. Moreover, Ahab offered him a vineyard or gold in exchange, but he refused. WHY, THEREFORE, WAS HE PUNISHED?

278. אָמַר לוֹ יָאוּת שְׁאַלְתְּ, תָּא חֲזֵי, הַאי רוּחַ דְּקָאֲמָרוּ דְּאִיהוּ רוּחַ דְּנָבוֹת, הָכָא אִית לְאִסְתַּכָּלָא, וְכִי רוּחָא דְנָבוֹת, יָכֵיל לְסַלְּקָא וּלְקַיְּימָא קַמֵּיהּ דְּקוּדְשָׁא בְּרִיךְ הוּא, לְמִתְבַּע שִׁקְרָא, דִּכְתִיב וַיֵּצֵא הָרוּחַ. וְאִי צַדִּיקָא הוּא, אֵיךְ יִבָּעֵי שִׁקְרָא בְּהַהוּא עַלְמָא, דְּאִיהוּ עַלְמָא דִקְשׁוֹט, וּמַה בְּהַאי עַלְמָא, לָא בָעֵי זַכָּאָה שִׁקְרָא, בְּהַהוּא עַלְמָא לָא כ"ש. וְאִי לָאו זַכָּאָה אִיהוּ, הֵיךְ יָכֵיל לְקַיְּימָא קַמֵּי קוּדְשָׁא בְּרִיךְ הוּא.

278. Rabbi Elazar replied: This is well asked. Come and behold: we have to look at the assumption that this was Navot's spirit. Could his spirit have risen and stood in the presence of the Holy One, blessed be He, and asked to lie, as it is written: "And there came a spirit…'I WILL GO OUT, AND I WILL BE A LYING SPIRIT'" (I Melachim 22:22). If he were righteous, how could he have asked to lie in that world, which is the World of Truth? A righteous man will not ask to lie in this world, let alone in that world. And if he were not righteous, how could he have stood in the presence of the Holy One, blessed be He?

279. אֶלָּא וַדַּאי נָבוֹת לָאו זַכָּאָה הֲוָה כ"כ, לְקַיְימָא קַמֵּי קוּדְשָׁא בְּרִיךְ הוּא, אֶלָּא רוּחָא אָחֳרָא הֲוָה, דְּשָׁלְטָא בְּעַלְמָא, דְּדָא הוּא רוּחָא דְּקָיְימָא תָּדִיר, וְסָלְקָא קַמֵּי קוּדְשָׁא בְּרִיךְ הוּא, וְדָא הוּא דְּאַסְטֵי לִבְנֵי עַלְמָא בְּשִׁקְרָא, וּמַאן דְּאִיהוּ רָגִיל בְּשִׁקְרָא, אִשְׁתַּדַּל תָּדִיר בְּשִׁקְרָא, וְעַל דָּא אֲמַר אֵצֵא וְהָיִיתִי רוּחַ שֶׁקֶר וגו', וְע"ד קוּדְשָׁא בְּרִיךְ הוּא אָמַר לוֹ צֵא, וַעֲשֵׂה כֵן, פּוּק מֵהָכָא, כְּמָה דְּאוֹקְמוּהָ דִּכְתִיב, דּוֹבֵר שְׁקָרִים לֹא יִכּוֹן לְנֶגֶד עֵינָי. וּבְגִין דָּא אִיהוּ רוּחַ שֶׁקֶר וַדַּאי.

279. But surely Navot was not righteous enough to stand before the Holy One, blessed be He. It is another spirit that rules over the world, the spirit that always ascends to stand before the Holy One, blessed be He – NAMELY, THE SATAN. He is the one who leads men astray by lying, FOR HE LIES BY THE HOLY NAME. He is wont to lie and constantly resorts to lies. Therefore he said, "I will go out, and I will be a lying spirit." The Holy One, blessed be He, replied, "Go out, and do so." Get you hence, for it has been explained that "He that tells lies shall not remain in my sight" (Tehilim 101:7). He is therefore assuredly a Lying Spirit.

280. וְתוּ. עַל מַה דְּקָטַל לֵיהּ לְנָבוֹת, וְנָטַל כַּרְמָא דִילֵיהּ, קָטוֹלָא אַמַּאי קָטֵיל לֵיהּ. אֶלָּא עַל דְּקָטֵיל לֵיהּ בְּלָא דִינָא אִתְעֲנַשׁ. קָטַל לֵיהּ בְּלָא דִינָא, וּנְסֵיב כַּרְמָא דִילֵיהּ. וּבְגִין כָּךְ כְּתִיב, הֲרָצַחְתָּ וְגַם יָרָשְׁתָּ, וְע"ד אִתְעֲנַשׁ. וְתָא חֲזֵי, כַּמָּה אִינוּן בְּנֵי נָשָׁא בְּעַלְמָא, דְּאַסְטֵי לוֹן הַאי רוּחַ שִׁקְרָא בְּשִׁקְרָא, וְשַׁלִּיט אִיהוּ בְּעַלְמָא, בְּכַמָּה סִטְרִין, וּבְכַמָּה עוֹבָדִין וְהָא אוֹקִימְנָא מִלֵּי.

280. Further, WE HAVE TO EXPLAIN WHY HE WAS PUNISHED. IT WAS BECAUSE he killed Navot. If he already took his vineyard, why kill him? It was because he killed him without cause that he was punished. He first killed unjustly and then took his vineyard. Thus, it is written: "Have you killed, and also taken possession?" (I Melachim 21:19). Therefore he was punished. Come and behold: there are innumerable people in the world, whom the Lying Spirit has led astray. He has dominion over the world, using several devices and actions, as we have already explained.

281. וְע״ד, דָּוִד מַלְכָּא בָּעָא לְאִסְתַּמְרָא מִנֵּיהּ, וּבָעָא לַאֲפָקָא מִגּוֹ מְסָאֲבוּ, דִּכְתִּיב לֵב טָהוֹר בְּרָא לִי אֱלֹקִים וְרוּחַ נָכוֹן חַדֵּשׁ בְּקִרְבִּי, דָּא הוּא רוּחַ נָכוֹן, וְאָחֳרָא אִיהוּ רוּחַ שֶׁקֶר, וְע״ד תְּרֵין דַּרְגִּין אִינוּן, חַד קַדִּישָׁא, וְחַד מְסָאֲבָא.

281. King David therefore wished to be guarded from THE LYING SPIRIT and to be removed from impurity, as it is written: "Create in me a clean heart, Elohim, and renew a steadfast spirit within me." This is the steadfast spirit; the other is the Lying Spirit. Thus there are two grades, the one holy, THE STEADFAST SPIRIT, and the other impure, THE LYING SPIRIT.

282. פָּתַח וַאֲמַר, וַה׳ נָתַן קוֹלוֹ לִפְנֵי חֵילוֹ כִּי רַב מְאֹד מַחֲנֵהוּ וְכִי עָצוּם עוֹשֵׂה דְבָרוֹ וגו׳, הַאי קְרָא אוּקְמוּהָ. אֲבָל וַה׳, בְּכָל אֲתַר הוּא וּבֵי דִינֵיהּ. נָתַן קוֹלוֹ דָּא הוּא קָלָא, דִּכְתִּיב, קוֹל דְּבָרִים, וּכְתִיב הָתָם, לֹא אִישׁ דְּבָרִים, מַאן אִישׁ דְּבָרִים. כד״א אִישׁ הָאֱלֹקִים. לִפְנֵי חֵילוֹ. אִלֵּין אִינוּן יִשְׂרָאֵל.

282. He opened with the verse: "And Hashem utters His voice before His army: for His camp is very great: for he is mighty who executes His word" (Yoel 2:11). This verse has already been explained, yet wherever "and Hashem (*Vav*-Yud Hei Vav Hei)" is mentioned, IT ALLUDES TO ZEIR ANPIN and His court of Justice, THE NUKVA – HE "utters His voice." This is the voice referred to in the verses: "The voice of words" (Devarim 4:12), and "I am not a man of words" (Shemot 4:10), because the man of words is, "the man of Elohim" (Devarim 33:1); " before His army," refers to Yisrael.

283. כִּי רַב מַחֲנֵהוּ: כד"א הֲיֵשׁ מִסְפָּר לִגְדוּדָיו, דְּכַמָּה מְמַנָּן וּשְׁלִיחָן אִית לֵיהּ לְקוּדְשָׁא בְּרִיךְ הוּא, וְכֻלְּהוּ קַיְימֵי לְאַסְטָאָה עֲלַיְיהוּ דְּיִשְׂרָאֵל. וְעַל דָּא קוּדְשָׁא בְּרִיךְ הוּא אִזְדַּמַּן קַמַּיְיהוּ דְּיִשְׂרָאֵל, בְּגִין לְנַטְרָא לְהוֹ, וְלָא יָכִילוּ לְקַטְרְגָא לְהוֹ.

283. "...for His camp is very great..." is similar to the verse: "Is there any number to His armies?" (Iyov 25: 3). For there are countless chieftains and messengers to the Holy One, blessed be He, all ready to bring accusations against Yisrael. The Holy One, blessed be He, therefore came before Yisrael, AS WAS STATED ABOVE "AND HASHEM UTTERS HIS VOICE BEFORE HIS ARMY," to guard them against the accusations.

284. כִּי עָצוּם עוֹשֵׂה דְּבָרוֹ, מַאן עָצוּם, דָּא הוּא זַכָּאָה, הַהוּא דְּאִשְׁתַּדַּל בְּאוֹרַיְיתָא קַדִּישָׁא, יְמָמָא וְלֵילֵי. דָּבָר אַחֵר, כִּי עָצוּם, דָּא הוּא מְקַטְרְגָא, דְּאִשְׁתַּכַּח קַמֵּי קוּדְשָׁא בְּרִיךְ הוּא, וְאִיהוּ תַּקִּיפָא כְּפַרְזְלָא. תַּקִּיפָא כְּטִינָרָא. עוֹשֵׂה דְּבָרוֹ: דְּנָטִיל רְשׁוּת מִלְּעֵילָּא וְנָטֵיל נִשְׁמָתָא מִתַּתָּא.

284. "...for he is mighty who executes His word." HE ASKS: Who is mighty? HE REPLIES: It is the righteous who is occupied with the Torah day and night. Another explanation is that "mighty" refers to the Accuser who is always before the Holy One, blessed be He, strong as iron, strong as a stone. He "executes His word." After receiving permission above FROM THE HOLY ONE, BLESSED BE HE, he takes away the soul below.

285. כִּי גָדוֹל יוֹם ה' וְנוֹרָא מְאֹד וּמִי יְכִילֶנּוּ, דְּאִיהוּ שַׁלִּיט עַל כֹּלָּא, וְעִלָּאָה וְתַקִּיפָא עַל כֻּלְּהוּ, וְכֻלְּהוּ תְּחוֹת שָׁלְטָנֵיהּ. זַכָּאִין אִינוּן צַדִּיקַיָּיא דְּקוּדְשָׁא בְּרִיךְ הוּא אִתְרְעֵי בְּהוֹ תָּדִיר, לְזַכָּאָה לוֹן לְעָלְמָא דְּאָתֵי, וּלְמֶחֱדֵי לְהוֹ בְּחֵידוּ דְּצַדִּיקַיָּיא, דִּזְמִינִין לְמֶחֱדֵי בֵּיהּ בְּקוּדְשָׁא בְּרִיךְ הוּא, דִּכְתִיב, וְיִשְׂמְחוּ כָל חוֹסֵי בָךְ לְעוֹלָם יְרַנֵּנוּ וְתָסֵךְ עָלֵימוֹ וְיַעְלְצוּ בְךָ אוֹהֲבֵי שְׁמֶךָ.

285. “For the day of Hashem is great and very terrible; and who can abide it” (Yoel 2:11). He is ruler over all, high and mighty, and everything is subject to His dominion. Happy are the righteous, to whom the Holy One, blessed be He, desires always to give merit in the World to Come and to enable them to participate in the joy in the Holy One, blessed be He, of the righteous in the future to come. It is written: “But let all those that put their trust in You rejoice: Let them ever shout for joy, because You do defend them: and let those who love Your Name be joyful in You” (Tehilim 5:12).

בָּרוּךְ ה׳ לְעוֹלָם אָמֵן וְאָמֵן.

Blessed be Hashem for ever, Amen and Aamen.

Miketz

Names of the articals

1. "He puts an end to darkness"

A Synopsis

Rabbi Chiya introduces a discussion on the secret nature of good and evil. Rabbi Shimon then defines evil as "the end of the left"; that is, the lack of "remembrance" or connection between the Left and Right Columns. The friends relate this phenomenon to the dreams of Joseph and the Pharaoh. Joseph's dream of a river signifies the end of darkness and evil, and the beginning of peace and plenty.

The Relevance of this Passage

The energy arising from the mystical shapes of the Hebrew letters enlightens us to the severity of our negative actions and their consequences. Negative behavior rooted in the Left Column refers to selfish indulgence without regard or concern for others. Awareness and careful management of both Columns – of receiving and of sharing – bring lasting Light to our lives. Inattention to either Column creates imbalance. Sharing without receiving [Right Column without Left Column], for example, quickly depletes our resources. If we share water from a glass without replenishment, the glass will soon be empty. Receiving without sharing is like casting a dehydrated man into the middle of a raging sea. Though he is in desperate need of water, overabundance eventually drowns him. Reading this section has a stabilizing effect on our spirituality and on the decisions we make. Intuitively, we begin making that strike a delicate balance between knowing when to share and when to receive.

1. וַיְהִי מִקֵּץ, רִבִּי חִיָּיא פְּתַח וַאֲמַר, קֵץ שָׂם לַחֹשֶׁךְ וּלְכָל תַּכְלִית הוּא חוֹקֵר אֶבֶן אֹפֶל וְצַלְמָוֶת, הַאי קְרָא אִתְּמָר, קֵץ שָׂם לַחֹשֶׁךְ, דָּא אִיהוּ קֵץ דִּשְׂמָאלָא, דְּאִיהוּ שָׁאט בְּעַלְמָא, וְשָׁאט לְעֵילָא, וְקָיְימָא קַמֵּי קוּדְשָׁא בְּרִיךְ הוּא, וְאַסְטֵי, וְקַטְרֵיג עַל עַלְמָא, וְהָא אִתְּמָר. וּלְכָל תַּכְלִית הוּא חוֹקֵר, דְּהָא כָּל עוֹבָדוֹי לָאו אִינוּן לְטַב, אֶלָּא לְשֵׁיצָאָה תָּדִיר, וּלְמֶעְבַּד כְּלָיָה בְּעָלְמָא.

1. "And it came to pass at the end of two years" (Beresheet 41:1). Rabbi Chiya opened the discussion with the verse, "He puts an end to darkness, and searches out all perfection: the stone of darkness and the shadow of death" (Iyov 28:3). "He puts an end to darkness" is the end of the left, WHICH IS NOT INCLUDED WITHIN THE RIGHT; IT IS THE SATAN, THE ANGEL OF DEATH. He hovers about the world AND INCITES PEOPLE TO

SIN; he hovers above and stands before the Holy One, blessed be He, and blames and accuses the world. As it is written, he "searches out all perfection (Heb. *tachlit*)," for his deeds are not intended to achieve good, but rather to exterminate (Heb. *lechalot*) and bring extinction to the world, AS HE TAKES THE SOULS OF MEN AND KILLS THEM.

2. אֶבֶן אֹפֶל וְצַלְמָוֶת, דָּא אֶבֶן נֶגֶף, דְּבָהּ כָּשְׁלִין חַיָּיבִין, וְקַיְּימָא בְּהַאי דְּאִקְרֵי, אֶרֶץ עֵפָתָה כְּמוֹ אֹפֶל. תָּא חֲזֵי אִית אֶרֶץ חַיִּים לְעֵילָּא, וְהַאי אִיהוּ אֶרֶץ יִשְׂרָאֵל. וְאִית אֶרֶץ לְתַתָּא וְנִקְרָא אֹפֶל וְצַלְמָוֶת, אֹפֶל דְּנַפְקָא מֵאֶרֶץ עֵפָתָה. מַאי אֶבֶן אֹפֶל וְצַלְמָוֶת, דָּא הוּא קֵץ, דְּאִיהוּ מִסִּטְרָא דְחֹשֶׁךְ, זוּהֲמָא דְּדַהֲבָא, וְהָא אִתְּמָר.

2. "... the stone of darkness and the shadow of death" refers to a stumbling stone, NAMELY THE SATAN, WHO IS CALLED A STUMBLING STONE BECAUSE the wicked stumble and sin on it. It abides in that which is called "a land of gloom, as darkness itself" (Iyov 10:22). Come and behold: There is the land of the living above, which is the land of Yisrael, NAMELY, THE NUKVA OF ZEIR ANPIN. And there is a land below called "darkness and the shadow of death," namely the darkness that is issued from the land of gloom, WHICH IS THE NUKVA OF THE KLIPAH. What are "the stone of darkness and the shadow of death?" They are the end, on the side of darkness. They are THE SATAN, the dross of gold, as we have already learned.

3. תָּא חֲזֵי, כַּמָּה אִית לוֹן לִבְנֵי נָשָׁא, לְאִסְתַּכָּלָא בְּפוּלְחָנָא דְקוּדְשָׁא בְּרִיךְ הוּא, וּלְאִשְׁתַּדְּלָא בְּאוֹרַיְיתָא, יְמָמָא וְלֵילֵי, בְּגִין דְּיִנְדְּעוּן וְיִסְתַּכְּלוּן בְּפוּלְחָנֵיהּ, דְּהָא אוֹרַיְיתָא אִיהִי מַכְרְזָא בְּכָל יוֹמָא קַמֵּיהּ דְּבַר נָשׁ וְאָמְרָה, מִי פֶּתִי יָסוּר הֵנָּה חֲסַר לֵב וְאָמְרָה לוֹ, וְהָא אוֹקִימְנָא מִלֵּי.

3. Come and behold how much it behooves men to look into the worship of the Holy One, blessed be He, and strive to study the Torah day and night, so they will know and behold His worship. For the Torah proclaims every day before men, saying, "Whoever is simple, let him turn in here: as for him that lacks understanding, she says to him" (Mishlei 9:4). We have already explained this matter.

4. וְכַד בַּר נָשׁ אִשְׁתַּדַּל בְּאוֹרַיְיתָא, וְאִתְדַּבַּק בָּהּ, זָכֵי לְאִתְתַּקְפָא בְּאִילָנָא דְחַיֵּי, דִּכְתִיב עֵץ חַיִּים וגו'. וְתָא חֲזֵי, כַּד בַּר נָשׁ אִתְתַּקַּף בְּאִילָנָא דְחַיֵּי בְּהַאי עָלְמָא, אִתְתַּקַּף בֵּיהּ לְעָלְמָא דְאָתֵי, דְּהָא כַּד נִשְׁמָתִין נָפְקִין מֵהַאי עָלְמָא, הָכֵי אִתְתַּקְּנָן לְהוֹ דַּרְגִּין לְעָלְמָא דְאָתֵי.

4. When a man studies the Torah and cleaves to it, he is strengthened in the Tree of Life, WHICH IS ZEIR ANPIN, as it is written: "a Tree of Life..." (Mishlei 3:18). Come and behold: When a man is strengthened in the Tree of Life in this world, he is strengthened in it for the World to Come. And when the souls leave this world, grades are prepared for them in the World to Come.

5. תָּא חֲזֵי, אִילָנָא דְחַיֵּי, אִיהוּ בְּכַמָּה דַרְגִּין מִתְפָּרְשָׁן דָּא מִן דָּא, וְכֻלְּהוּ חַד. דְּהָא בְּאִילָנָא דְחַיֵּי, אִית דַּרְגִּין אִלֵּין עַל אִלֵּין, עַנְפִּין, וְעָלִין, קְלִיפִין, גּוּפָא דְאִילָנָא, שָׁרְשִׁין. וְכֹלָּא הוּא אִילָנָא. כְּגַוְונָא דָא, כָּל מַאן דְּאִשְׁתַּדַּל בְּאוֹרַיְיתָא, אִיהוּ אִתְתַּקַּן וְאִתְתַּקַּף בְּאִילָנָא דְחַיֵּי.

5. Come and behold: The Tree of Life is divided into several grades, but they are all unified into one. For in the Tree of Life there are grades upon grades – branches, leaves, husks, the trunk, and the roots. All of them are the tree. In the same manner, whoever strives to study the Torah is strengthened and improved by the Tree of Life, NAMELY, IN THE TRUNK OF THE TREE.

6. וְכָל בְּנֵי דִמְהֵימְנוּתָא יִשְׂרָאֵל, כֻּלְּהוֹן מִתְתַּקְּפִין בְּאִילָנָא דְחַיֵּי, כֻּלְּהוּ אֲחִידִין בְּאִילָנָא מַמָּשׁ, מִנְּהוֹן בְּהַהוּא גּוּפָא דְבֵיהּ, מִנְּהוֹן אֲחִידָן בְּעַנְפִּין, מִנְּהוֹן בְּעָלִין, מִנְּהוֹן בְּשָׁרְשִׁין, אִשְׁתַּכָּחוּ דְּכֻלְּהוּ אֲחִידָן בְּאִילָנָא דְחַיֵּי. וְאִינוּן דְּמִשְׁתַּדְּלִין בְּאוֹרַיְיתָא כֻּלְּהוּ אֲחִידָן בְּגוּפָא דְאִילָנָא. וּבְגִין כָּךְ, מַאן דְּאִשְׁתַּדַּל בְּאוֹרַיְיתָא, אִיהוּ אָחִיד בְּכֹלָּא, וְהָא אוֹקְמוּהָ וְאִתְּמָר.

6. All those of the faith, Yisrael, are strengthened by the Tree of Life. They all hold onto the tree, but some of them hold on to the trunk, some to the branches, some to the leaves, and some to the roots. It seems, therefore, that they hold onto the Tree of Life. All of those who are occupied in the study of the Torah hold to the trunk of the tree, and for that reason, he who studies the Torah holds onto the whole tree, BECAUSE THE TREE TRUNK INCLUDES ALL OF IT. This has already been explained.

7. וַיְהִי מִקֵּץ, מַאי מִקֵּץ. רִבִּי שִׁמְעוֹן אָמַר, אֲתַר דְּלֵית בָּהּ זְכִירָה. וְדָא הוּא קֵץ דִּשְׂמָאלָא, מַאי טַעְמָא, בְּגִין דִּכְתִיב כִּי אִם זְכַרְתַּנִי אִתְּךָ כַּאֲשֶׁר יִיטַב לָךְ. וְכִי הָכֵי אִתְחֲזֵי לֵיהּ לְיוֹסֵף צַדִּיקָא, דְּאִיהוּ אֲמַר כִּי אִם זְכַרְתַּנִי אִתְּךָ, אֶלָּא כֵּיוָן דְּאִסְתַּכַּל יוֹסֵף בְּחֶלְמֵיהּ, אֲמַר וַדַּאי חֶלְמָא דִּזְכִירָה אִיהוּ, וְאִיהוּ טָעָה בְּהַאי, דְּהָא בֵּיהּ בְּקוּדְשָׁא בְּרִיךְ הֲוֵי כֹּלָּא.

7. "And it came to pass at the end." HE ASKS: What is the meaning of "the end?" Rabbi Shimon replied that this is a place in which there is no remembrance – the end of the left. What does this mean? For it is written, "But think of me (lit. 'remember') when it shall be well with you" (Beresheet 40:14). HE ASKS: Is it proper for Joseph the righteous to say, "But remember me." AND HE ANSWERS, When Joseph looked at the dream, he said, 'This is assuredly a dream of remembrance' – but he was wrong, because it all came from the Holy One, blessed be He.

8. וְע"ד אֲתַר דַּהֲוָה בֵּיהּ נַשְׁיוּ קָם קַמֵּיהּ, מַה כְּתִיב וְלֹא זָכַר שַׂר הַמַּשְׁקִים אֶת יוֹסֵף וַיִּשְׁכָּחֵהוּ. כֵּיוָן דַּאֲמַר וְלֹא זָכַר שַׂר הַמַּשְׁקִים, מַהוּ וַיִּשְׁכָּחֵהוּ. אֶלָּא וַיִּשְׁכָּחֵהוּ אֲתַר דְּאִית בֵּיהּ שִׁכְחָה, וְדָא הוּא קֵץ דְּסִטְרָא דְּחֹשֶׁךְ. שְׁנָתַיִם יָמִים, מַאי שְׁנָתַיִם. דְּתָב דַּרְגָּא, לְדַרְגָּא דְּאִית בֵּיהּ זְכִירָה.

8. Therefore, the place of forgetfulness rose against him. It is written: "Nevertheless the chief butler did not remember Joseph, but forgot him". HE ASKS: If it is said "the chief butler did not remember," why then add "but forgot him"? HE ANSWERS, "but forgot him" indicates the place in which there is forgetfulness, which is CALLED the end on the side of darkness. HE ASKS: What are the two years? AND HE ANSWERS: The grade of forgetfulness returned after that time to the grade in which there is remembrance.

9. וּפַרְעֹה חוֹלֵם וְהִנֵּה עוֹמֵד עַל הַיְאֹר, דָּא חֶלְמָא דְיוֹסֵף הֲוָה, בְּגִין דְּכָל נָהָר דְּיוֹסֵף הַצַּדִּיק אִיהוּ, וְרָזָא דָּא הֲוֵי, הַאי מַאן דְּחָמֵי נָהָר בְּחֲלוֹם, חָמֵי שָׁלוֹם, דִּכְתִיב הִנְנִי נוֹטֶה אֵלֶיהָ כְּנָהָר שָׁלוֹם.

9. "...that Pharaoh dreamed: and behold, he stood by the river" concerns the dream of Joseph, NAMELY A DREAM OF REMEMBRANCE THAT REFERS TO JOSEPH, because every river is part of Joseph the Righteous. This is the hidden meaning of the thought that whoever sees a river in his dream sees peace, WHICH IS THE GRADE OF YESOD, THAT IS, JOSEPH, as it is written, "I will extend peace to her like a river" (Yeshayah 66:12), SO "RIVER" ALLUDES TO JOSEPH.

2. "And it came to pass at the end of two years"

A Synopsis

Here the rabbis discuss Joseph's sojourn in Egypt. Joseph is compared to King David, who at a later time occupied a similar position in relation to the world above and the world below. "The king by justice establishes the land but he who exacts gifts overthrows it." The king is the Pharaoh of Mosess' time. His lack of faith and his inability to interpret the true meaning of his dream bring destruction to his realm.

The Relevance of this Passage

Joseph's sojourn in Egypt is a metaphor for the soul's human incarnation in the material world. Joseph represents the soul, and Egypt, the negativity of the body. King David also represents the realm of Malchut, our lower dimension. Man's spiritual work is to rise above the temptations of material existence by removing the blinders that prevent us from recognizing the Divinity in the world, the foolishness of our negative behavior, and the consequences of our negative deeds. This elevated consciousness is stimulated by reading this section.

10. וַיְהִי מִקֵּץ שְׁנָתַיִם. רִבִּי חִיָּיא פָּתַח וַאֲמַר, מֶלֶךְ בְּמִשְׁפָּט יַעֲמִיד אֶרֶץ וְאִישׁ תְּרוּמוֹת יֶהֶרְסֶנָּה, תָּא חֲזֵי, כַּד בָּרָא קוּדְשָׁא בְּרִיךְ הוּא עַלְמָא עִלָּאָה, אַתְקִין כֹּלָּא כִּדְקָא יָאוּת, וְאַפֵּיק נְהוֹרִין עִלָּאִין מְנַהֲרִין לְכָל סִטְרִין, וְכֹלָּא אִיהוּ חַד, וּבָרָא שָׁמַיִם דִּלְעֵילָּא, וְאֶרֶץ דִּלְעֵילָּא, לְאִתְתַּקְנָא כֻּלְּהוּ כַּחֲדָא, לְתוֹעַלְתָּא דְתַתָּאֵי.

10. "And it came to pass at the end of two years." Rabbi Chiya opened the discussion with the verse: "The king by justice establishes the land: but he who exacts gifts overthrows it" (Mishlei 29:4). Come and behold: When the Holy One, blessed be He, created the upper world, BINAH, He made everything properly and created bright lights that shone in all directions. THESE REPRESENT THE THREE COLUMNS, and all is united into one. He created heaven above, WHICH IS ZEIR ANPIN, and the earth below, WHICH IS THE NUKVA, to combine as one – BINAH, ZEIR ANPIN, AND NUKVA – to benefit the lower beings.

11. תָּא חֲזֵי, מֶלֶךְ בְּמִשְׁפָּט יַעֲמִיד אֶרֶץ, מַאן מֶלֶךְ. דָּא קוּדְשָׁא בְּרִיךְ הוּא. בְּמִשְׁפָּט: דָּא יַעֲקֹב, דְּאִיהוּ קִיּוּמָא דְאַרְעָא, וְעַל דָּא ו׳ אִתְּזָן מִן

ה' עִלָּאָה, ה' תַּתָּאָה אִתְּזָנַת מִן ו', דְּקִיּוּמָא דְּאַרְעָא אִיהוּ בְּמִשְׁפָּט, דְּהָא מִשְׁפָּט יַעֲמִיד אֶרֶץ בְּכָל תִּקּוּנוֹי, וְזָן לָהּ.

11. Come and behold: In the verse, "The king by justice establishes the land", who is the king? He is the Holy One, blessed be He – BINAH. The words "by justice" refer to Jacob, THAT IS, ZEIR ANPIN, who forms the foundation of the land. Therefore the letter *Vav* IN THE NAME YUD HEI VAV HEI, WHICH IS ZEIR ANPIN, is sustained by the upper *Hei* IN THE NAME YUD HEI VAV HEI, WHICH IS BINAH. The lower *Hei* IN THE NAME YUD HEI VAV HEI, WHICH IS THE NUKVA, is sustained by the *Vav*, WHICH IS ZEIR ANPIN, because "justice establishes the land" with all its needs and nourishes it.

12. דָּבָר אֲחֵר, מֶלֶךְ: דָּא קוּדְשָׁא בְּרִיךְ הוּא. בְּמִשְׁפָּט: דָּא יוֹסֵף, יַעֲמִיד אֶרֶץ: דִּכְתִיב וְכָל הָאָרֶץ בָּאוּ מִצְרַיְמָה לִשְׁבּוֹר אֶל יוֹסֵף, וּבְגִין דְּקוּדְשָׁא בְּרִיךְ הוּא אִתְרְעֵי בֵּיהּ בְּיַעֲקֹב, עֲבַד לֵיהּ לְיוֹסֵף שַׁלִּיטָא עַל אַרְעָא.

12. Another explanation of "the king" is that it refers to the Holy One, blessed be He, while justice refers to Joseph, "who established the land" as it is written: "And all countries (lit. 'and all the land') came to Egypt to Joseph to buy provisions" (Beresheet 41:57). Because the Holy One, blessed be He, favored Jacob, He made him governor of all the land.

13. רַבִּי יוֹסֵי אָמַר, מֶלֶךְ: דָּא יוֹסֵף. בְּמִשְׁפָּט יַעֲמִיד אֶרֶץ: דָּא יַעֲקֹב, דְּהָא עַד לָא אָתָא יַעֲקֹב לְמִצְרַיִם, לָא הֲוָה קִיּוּמָא בְּאַרְעָא, מִגּוֹ כַּפְנָא. כֵּיוָן דְּאָתָא יַעֲקֹב לְמִצְרַיִם, בִּזְכוּתֵיהּ אִסְתַּלַּק כַּפְנָא, וְאִתְקַיַּים אַרְעָא.

13. Rabbi Yosi said: "The king" is Joseph and "by justice" is Jacob, because as long as Jacob did not come to Egypt, the land was beset by famine. After Jacob came to Egypt by his merit, the famine was gone and the land was established.

14. דָּבָר אֲחֵר מֶלֶךְ בְּמִשְׁפָּט יַעֲמִיד אֶרֶץ: דָּא דָּוִד מַלְכָּא, דִּכְתִיב וַיְהִי

דָּוִד עוֹשֶׂה מִשְׁפָּט וּצְדָקָה לְכָל עַמּוֹ, וְאִיהוּ קַיֵּים אַרְעָא, וּבִזְכוּתֵיהּ קָיְימָא לְבָתַר דְּנָא. וְאִישׁ תְּרוּמוֹת יֶהֶרְסֶנָּה: דָּא רְחַבְעָם.

14. Another explanation is that "The king by justice establishes the land" refers to King David, as it is written: "And David reigned over all Yisrael; and David executed judgment and righteousness to all his people" (II Shmuel 8:15). He established the land DURING HIS LIFETIME, and by his merit, it stood AFTER HIS DEMISE. THE PHRASE, "but he who exacts gifts overthrows it" refers to Rechav'am.

15. תָּא חֲזֵי, קוּדְשָׁא בְּרִיךְ הוּא בְּגִינֵיהוֹן דְּצַדִּיקַיָּא, אַף עַל גַּב דְּפוּרְעֲנוּתָא אִתְגְּזַר עַל עָלְמָא, מִתְעַכְּבָא בְּגִינֵיהוֹן, וְלָא שָׁלְטָא עַל עָלְמָא. כָּל יוֹמוֹי דְּדָוִד מַלְכָּא, אִתְקָיְימָא אַרְעָא בְּגִינֵיהּ, לְבָתַר דְּמִית אִתְקָיְימָא בִּזְכוּתֵיהּ, דִּכְתִיב וְגַנּוֹתִי עַל הָעִיר הַזֹּאת לְהוֹשִׁיעָהּ לְמַעֲנִי וּלְמַעַן דָּוִד עַבְדִּי. כְּגַוְונָא דָּא, כָּל יוֹמוֹי דְּיַעֲקֹב, וְכָל יוֹמוֹי דְּיוֹסֵף, לָא שָׁלְטָא פּוּרְעֲנוּתָא בְּעַלְמָא.

15. Come and behold: For the sake of the righteous, the Holy One, blessed be He, did not impose punishment that had been decreed on the world, so it will not have sway over the world. All the days of King David, the land was established for his sake. After he died, it continued because of his merit, as it is written: "and I will defend this city for my own sake, and for my servant David's sake" (II Melachim 20:6). Similarly, no punishment was inflicted on the world during all the days of Jacob and all the days of Joseph, AS THE FAMINE CEASED FOR THEIR SAKES AND THE ENSLAVING BY EGYPT WAS DELAYED.

16. תָּא חֲזֵי מֶלֶךְ בְּמִשְׁפָּט יַעֲמִיד אֶרֶץ: דָּא יוֹסֵף. וְאִישׁ תְּרוּמוֹת יֶהֶרְסֶנָּה: דָּא פַּרְעֹה, דְּהָא בְּגִין דְּאַקְשֵׁי לִבֵּיהּ לְגַבֵּי דְּקוּדְשָׁא בְּרִיךְ הוּא, חָרֵיב אַרְעָא דְּמִצְרַיִם, וּבְקַדְמֵיתָא עַל יְדָא דְּיוֹסֵף אִתְקַיַּים אַרְעָא, בְּהַהוּא חֶלְמָא דְּחָלַם, דִּכְתִיב וַיְהִי מִקֵּץ שְׁנָתַיִם יָמִים וגו'.

16. Come and behold: The verse, "The king by justice establishes the land" refers to Joseph, "but he who exacts gifts overthrows it" refers to Pharaoh.

Because Pharaoh hardened his heart against the Holy One, blessed be He, the land of Egypt was destroyed. Before that, the land was thriving through Joseph, in accordance with Pharaoh's dream, as it is written, "And it came to pass at the end of two years..."

17. וַיְהִי מִקֵּץ וגו'. ר' אֶלְעָזָר פָּתַח וַאֲמַר, חַי ה' וּבָרוּךְ צוּרִי וְיָרוּם אֱלֹהֵי יִשְׁעִי. אֱלוֹהֵי כְּתִיב, בְּוי"ו. הַאי קְרָא אִית לְאִסְתַּכָּלָא בֵּיהּ, חַי ה': דָּא חַי צַדִּיקָא יְסוֹדָא דְעַלְמָא, דְּאִקְרֵי חַי דְעָלְמִין. וּבָרוּךְ צוּרִי: דָּא הוּא דִכְתִיב בָּרוּךְ ה' צוּרִי, וְדָא עַלְמָא דְאִתְקַיַּים עֲלֵיהּ צַדִּיקָא דָא. וְיָרוּם אֱלֹהֵי יִשְׁעִי. וְיָרוּם: דָּא עַלְמָא עִלָּאָה. אֱלוֹהֵי בְּוא"ו: דָּא שָׁמַיִם, כד"א הַשָּׁמַיִם שָׁמַיִם לַה'.

17. Rabbi Elazar opened the discussion with the verse, "Hashem lives; and blessed is my Rock; and let the Elohim (Heb. *Elohai*) of my salvation be exalted" (Tehilim 18:47). "Elohai" is spelled with a *Vav*. This verse requires careful study. The phrase, "Hashem lives" refers to the Righteous, the foundation of the world, NAMELY, YESOD OF ZEIR ANPIN, who is referred to as the life of the worlds. The phrase "and blessed is my Rock" is the meaning of "Blessed be Hashem my Rock" (Tehilim 144:1). The world, THAT IS, THE NUKVA, is sustained by the generosity of the Righteous, WHICH IS YESOD OF ZEIR ANPIN. IN THE VERSE, "Let the Elohim of my salvation be exalted": "exalted" refers to the upper world, NAMELY BINAH, and "Elohai" with a *Vav* is heaven, NAMELY ZEIR ANPIN, as it is written: "The heavens are the heavens of Hashem" (Tehilim 115:16).

18. תָּא חֲזֵי בָּרוּךְ אֲדֹנָ"י יוֹם יוֹם יַעֲמָס לָנוּ, בָּרוּךְ אֲדֹנָ"י, בְּאָלֶ"ף דָּלֶ"ת נוּ"ן יוּ"ד, וְהַאי קְרָא רָזָא דְחָכְמְתָא אִיהוּ. יוֹם יוֹם: אֵלּוּ שְׁנָתַיִם יָמִים, כד"א וַיְהִי מִקֵּץ שְׁנָתַיִם יָמִים. וּפַרְעֹה חוֹלֵם וְהִנֵּה עוֹמֵד עַל הַיְאוֹר, רָזָא אִיהוּ, כְּמָה דְאִתְּמָר דָּא יוֹסֵף, דְּנָהָר דָּא, יוֹסֵף הַצַּדִּיק הוּא.

18. Come and behold: "Blessed be Adonai who day by day bears our burden" (Tehilim 68:20). The name Adonai is spelled *Aleph-Dalet-Nun-Yud*, WHICH ALLUDES TO THE NUKVA. This verse contains the mystery of wisdom. "Day by day" is the secret of "two years (lit. 'two years' days')", WHICH ARE THE TWO GRADES BINAH AND ZEIR ANPIN, FOR THE NUKVA

IS BLESSED ONLY BY THEM. This is as it is written: "And it came to pass at the end of two years that Pharaoh dreamed: and behold, he stood by the river." We have already learned this secret; it means Joseph, because the words, "a river" refer to Joseph the Righteous.

19. וְהִנֵּה מִן הַיְאוֹר עוֹלוֹת שֶׁבַע פָּרוֹת יְפוֹת מַרְאֶה וּבְרִיאוֹת בָּשָׂר וַתִּרְעֶינָה בָּאָחוּ. וְהִנֵּה מִן הַיְאוֹר, דְּהָא מִנָּהָר דָּא אִתְבָּרְכָאן כָּל אִינוּן דַּרְגִּין דִּלְתַתָּא, בְּגִין דְּהַהוּא נָהָר דְּנָגֵיד וְנָפֵיק, אִיהוּ אַשְׁקֵי וְזָן לְכֹלָּא, וְיוֹסֵף אִיהוּ נָהָר, לְאִתְבָּרְכָא כָּל אַרְעָא דְמִצְרַיִם בְּגִינֵיהּ.

19. The verse, "And, behold, there came up out of the river seven cows, well favored, and fat of flesh, and they fed in the reed grass" reads "out of the river" because from this river, WHICH IS YESOD, all the grades below are blessed, because the river that flows from Eden, WHICH IS BINAH, waters and sustains everything. And Joseph, WHO IS YESOD, is a river, and the whole land of Egypt is blessed for his sake.

20. וְתָא חֲזֵי, הַהוּא נָהָר שֶׁבַע דַּרְגִּין אִתְשַׁקְיָין וְאִתְבָּרְכָן מִנֵּיהּ, וְאִלֵּין אִינוּן יְפוֹת מַרְאֶה וּבְרִיאוֹת בָּשָׂר. וַתִּרְעֶינָה בָּאָחוּ: בְּחִבּוּרָא בְּאַחֲוָותָא דְּלָא אִשְׁתַּכַּח בְּהוֹ פֵּרוּדָא, וְכֻלְּהוּ לְשַׁבְחָא קָיְימִין, דְּהָא כָּל הַנֵּי דַּרְגִּין שֶׁבַע דְּקָאֲמָרָן, רָזָא אִיהוּ, כד"א וְאֵת שֶׁבַע הַנְּעָרוֹת הָרְאוּיוֹת לָתֵת לָהּ מִבֵּית הַמֶּלֶךְ וגו'. וְע"ד שֶׁבַע פָּרוֹת יְפוֹת מַרְאֶה, וְלָקֳבֵל דָּא כְּתִיב, שִׁבְעַת הַסָּרִיסִים הַמְשָׁרְתִים אֶת פְּנֵי הַמֶּלֶךְ וגו'.

20. Come and behold: From that river, NAMELY YESOD, the seven grades OF THE NUKVA, CHESED, GVURAH, TIFERET, NETZACH, HOD, YESOD AND MALCHUT IN HER, THAT WERE EXTENDING FROM HER, AND WERE SITUATED IN THE WORLD OF BRIYAH are watered and blessed by it. These are THE SEVEN "well favored, and fat of flesh" COWS, who "fed in the reed grass." THAT IS, they fed together in friendship, and there was no separation among them. All of them stand to be praised, FOR THERE IS NO NOURISHMENT FOR THE OTHER SIDE, for these seven grades are the mystery of the verse: "and the seven maids chosen to be given her, out of the king's house" (Ester 2:9), WHICH REFERS TO THE SEVEN TEMPLES OF BRIYAH, ALL OF WHICH ARE PRAISEWORTHY. And so are the "seven cows well favored," ALL TO BE PRAISED. In contrast, "the seven chamberlains who served in the presence of the king" (Tehilim 1:10) ARE NOT TO BE WHOLLY PRAISED, FOR THEY INCLUDE A PORTION OF THE POWERS OF DEFILEMENT, WHICH IS THE SECRET OF THE SEVEN LEAN COWS.

21. רִבִּי יִצְחָק אֲמַר, שֶׁבַע פָּרוֹת הַטּוֹבוֹת, דַּרְגִּין אִינוּן עִלָּאִין עַל אָחֳרָנִין. וְשֶׁבַע הַפָּרוֹת הָרָעוֹת, דַּרְגִּין אָחֳרָנִין דִּלְתַתָּא. אִלֵּין מִסִּטְרָא דִקְדוּשָּׁה, וְאִלֵּין מִסִּטְרָא דִּמְסָאֲבָא.

21. Rabbi Yitzchak said: The seven good cows are grades, superior to other grades, whereas the seven ill-favored cows are the grades below. THE UPPER ONES are on the side of holiness, and THE LOWER BEINGS on the side of defilement.

22. שֶׁבַע הַשִּׁבֳּלִים, רִבִּי יְהוּדָה אֲמַר, אִלֵּי קַדְמָאֵי, אִינוּן טָבִין, בְּגִין דְּאִינוּן מִסִּטְרָא דִימִינָא, דִּכְתִיב בֵּיהּ כִּי טוֹב, וְאִלֵּין בִּישִׁין אִינוּן לְתַתָּא מִנַּיְיהוּ. שֶׁבַע הַשִּׁבֳּלִים אִינוּן מִסִּטְרָא דְּדַכְיוּ, וְאִלֵּין מִסִּטְרָא דִּמְסָאֲבוּ, וְכֻלְּהוּ דַּרְגִּין קָיְימִין אִלֵּין עַל אִלֵּין, וְאִלֵּין לָקֳבֵל אִלֵּין, וְכֻלְּהוּ קָא חָמָא פַּרְעֹה בְּחֶלְמֵיהּ.

22. "...the seven ears of grains:" Rabbi Yehuda said that the first SEVEN EARS are good, because they are of the right side, about which it is written, "it was good." The ill and thin SEVEN EARS are beneath them. The seven GOOD ears are on the side of purity, and the ILL ones are on the side of impurity. These grades all stand on top of each other – against each other. Pharaoh saw all of them in his dream.

23. אָמַר רָבִּי יֵיסָא, וְכִי לְהַהוּא חַיָּיבָא דְּפַרְעֹה אַחְזְיָין לֵיהּ כָּל הַנֵּי. אָמַר לוֹ ר' יְהוּדָה, כְּגַוְונָא דִּלְהוֹן חָמָא, דְּכַמָּה דַּרְגִּין עַל דַּרְגִּין, אִלֵּין לָקֳבֵל אִלֵּין, וְאִלֵּין עַל אִלֵּין, וְאִיהוּ חָמָא בְּאִינוּן דַּרְגִּין דִּלְתַתָּא.

23. Rabbi Yesa asks: How could they have shown the evil Pharaoh all these grades? Rabbi Yehuda answers, He only saw their likeness, NOT THE GRADES THEMSELVES. For there are grades upon grades, all stand on top of each other, of which Pharaoh saw only their images.

24. וְהָא תָּנִינָן, דְּהָא כְּמָה דְּאִיהוּ בַּר נָשׁ, הָכֵי אַחְזְיוּ לֵיהּ בְּחֶלְמֵיהּ, וְהָכֵי חָמֵי, וְנִשְׁמָתָא הָכֵי סָלְקַת לְאִשְׁתְּמוֹדְעָא, כָּל חַד וְחַד כְּפוּם דַּרְגֵּיהּ כִּדְקָא חָזֵי לֵיהּ, וּבְגִין כָּךְ פַּרְעֹה חָמָא כִּדְקָא חָזֵי לֵיהּ, וְלָא יַתִּיר.

24. We have already learned that a man is shown things in his dreams according to his character. As his soul ascends, he will perceive that which he deserves according to his grade. Pharaoh, therefore, saw what he was worthy of seeing and no more.

25. וַיְהִי מִקֵּץ וגו׳, רִבִּי חִזְקִיָּה פְּתַח וַאֲמַר לַכֹּל זְמַן וְעֵת לְכָל חֵפֶץ תַּחַת הַשָּׁמָיִם. תָּא חֲזֵי, כָּל מַה דַּעֲבַד קוּדְשָׁא בְּרִיךְ הוּא לְתַתָּא, לְכֹלָּא שַׁוֵּי זִמְנָא וּזְמַן קָצוּב, זְמַן שַׁוֵּי לִנְהוֹרָא וְלַחֲשׁוֹכָא, זִמְנָא שַׁוֵּי לִנְהוֹרָא דִּשְׁאָר עַמִּין, דְּאִינוּן שָׁלְטִין הַשְׁתָּא עַל עַלְמָא. וְזִמְנָא שַׁוֵּי לַחֲשׁוֹכָא, דְּאִיהוּ גָּלוּתָא דְּיִשְׂרָאֵל, תְּחוֹת שָׁלְטָנוּתָא דִּלְהוֹן, זִמְנָא שַׁוֵּי קוּדְשָׁא בְּרִיךְ הוּא לְכֹלָּא, בְּגִין כָּךְ לַכֹּל זְמַן וְעֵת לְכָל חֵפֶץ. מַאי וְעֵת לְכָל חֵפֶץ. זִמְנָא וְעִדָּן הוּא לְכֹלָּא, לְכָל הַהוּא רְעוּתָא דְּאִשְׁתַּכַּח לְתַתָּא.

25. "And it came to pass in the end." Rabbi Chizkiah began with the verse: "To everything there is a season, and a time to every purpose under the heaven" (Kohelet 3:1). Come and behold what the Holy One, blessed be He, did below: He set a time for everything, and fixed a term for it. He fixed a term for light and darkness. He set a time for light for all nations EXCEPT YISRAEL, which now have mastery over the world, and He set time for darkness, when Yisrael are in exile and under the dominion of other nations. The Holy One, blessed be He, appointed a season for all and, therefore: "To everything there is a season, and a time to every purpose." HE ASKS: What is the meaning of, "and a time to every purpose?" HE REPLIES: It means a time and season for everything that is below, that is, all the goodness found below has a set time and season.

26. דָּבָר אַחֵר וְעֵת לְכָל חֵפֶץ, מַאי עֵת. כְּדִכְתִיב עֵת לַעֲשׂוֹת לַיְיָ׳ הֵפֵרוּ תּוֹרָתֶךָ. וּכְתִיב וְאַל יָבֹא בְכָל עֵת אֶל הַקֹּדֶשׁ. וְאִיהוּ דַּרְגָּא מְמַנָּא, וְהָא אוֹקְמוּהָ. וּבְגִין כָּךְ עֵת אִיהוּ מְמַנָּא, לְכָל חֵפֶץ תַּחַת הַשָּׁמָיִם. וַיְהִי מִקֵּץ

שְׁנָתַיִם יָמִים, מִסִּטְרָא דְהַהוּא קֵץ דְּחֹשֶׁךְ, חָמָא פַּרְעֹה בְּחֶלְמֵיהּ, וּמִתַּמָּן יָדַע וְאִתְגְּלֵי לֵיהּ הַהוּא חֶלְמָא.

26. Another explanation for "...and a time to every purpose." HE ASKS: What is "time?" HE ANSWERS, It is the same as mentioned in the verses: "It is time to act for Hashem: they have made void Your Torah" (Tehilim 119:126) and "that he come not at all times into the holy place" (Vayikra 16:2). This is the grade appointed TO LEAD THE WORLD, NAMELY, THE NUKVA, and has already been explained. Therefore, the scriptures explain that "time", THE NUKVA, is appointed over "every purpose under the heaven." "And it came to pass at the end of two years" refers to the side of the end of darkness, FOR HE SET AN APPOINTED TIME FOR LIGHT AND DARKNESS, that Pharaoh had seen in his dream. This is where he derived his knowledge from, and the dream was revealed to him.

3. "His spirit was troubled"

A Synopsis

This passage deals with Pharaoh's troubled spirit, caused by his inability to interpret his dream. The rabbis compare Pharaoh's state of mind to that of Nevuchnetzar during the Babylonian captivity. Rabbi Yitzchak maintains that kings and other heads of state are occasionally granted glimpses of the hidden world usually only provided to the prophets of Israel.

The Relevance of this Passage

Each night our soul ascends to higher realms, where it receives dream messages that can influence us in our spiritual endeavors. Depending on our actions and interactions during the previous day, these messages can advance or hinder our efforts. Positive actions arouse prophetic messages of truth, while negative behavior invokes deceitful messages and disingenuous dreams. Here we receive assistance in making positive use of our sleep, so that our dreams can provide reliable glimpses of the future.

27. וַיְהִי בַבֹּקֶר וַתִּפָּעֶם רוּחוֹ וַיִּשְׁלַח וַיִּקְרָא אֶת כָּל חַרְטֻמֵּי מִצְרַיִם וְאֶת כָּל חֲכָמֶיהָ וגו׳. וַתִּפָּעֶם רוּחוֹ. מַאי וַתִּפָּעֶם. רִבִּי יוֹסֵי אֲמַר, הָא אוֹקְמוּהָ בְּפַרְעֹה כְּתִיב וַתִּפָּעֶם, וּבִנְבוּכַדְנֶצַּר כְּתִיב וַתִּתְפָּעֶם, וְאוֹקְמוּהָ דְּהָא בְּפַרְעֹה כְּתִיב וַתִּפָּעֶם, בְּגִין דַּהֲוָה יָדַע חֶלְמָא, וּפִשְׁרָא לָא הֲוָה יָדַע, אֲבָל נְבוּכַדְנֶצַּר, חָמָא חֶלְמָא, וְחָמָא פִּשְׁרָא, וְאִתְנְשֵׁי כֹּלָּא מִנֵּיהּ.

27. "And it came to pass in the morning that his spirit was troubled (Heb. *vatipaem*)." HE ASKS: What does *vatipaem* mean? Rabbi Yosi said: It has already been explained. Of Pharaoh, it is written, *vatipaem*, and of Nebuchadnezzar, it is written, "his spirit was troubled (Heb. *vatitpaem*)" (Daniel 2:1). Pharaoh is described as *vatipaem* because he comprehended the dream but not its interpretation. Nebuchadnezzar, on the other hand, saw the dream and its interpretation, but forgot everything. IT IS THEREFORE WRITTEN *VATITPAEM* (WITH AN EXTRA *TET*).

28. אֲבָל תָּא חֲזֵי, וַתִּפָּעֶם רוּחוֹ, כד״א לְפַעֲמוֹ, דַּהֲוָה אָתֵי רוּחָא וְאָזֵיל, וְאָתֵי וְאָזֵיל וְלָא הֲוָה מִתְיַישְׁבָא עִמֵּיהּ עֲדַיִין כִּדְקָא יָאוֹת, וְעַל דָּא כְּתִיב וַתָּחֶל רוּחַ יי׳ לְפַעֲמוֹ, דִּכְדֵין הֲוָה שֵׁירוּתָא, אוּף הָכָא רוּחֵיהּ

אִתְעַר בֵּיהּ, וְאָזֵיל וְאִתְעַר, וְלָא הֲוָה מִתְיַשְּׁבָא עִמֵּיהּ לְמִנְדַּע. נְבוּכַדְנֶצַּר וַתִּתְפָּעֶם רוּחוֹ, בְּאִתְעֲרוּתָא הֲוָה אִתְעַר עַל חַד תְּרֵין, וְאָזְלִין, וְתָיְיבִין, וְדָא הוּא כד"א כְּפַעַם בְּפַעַם, פַּעַם בְּהַאי, וּפַעַם בְּהַאי, וְלָא מִתְיַשְּׁבָא דַּעְתֵּיהּ וְרוּחֵיהּ.

28. But come and behold: "and his spirit was troubled (Heb. *vatipaem*)" corresponds to "And the spirit of Hashem began to move him (Heb. *lefa'ahmo*)" (Shoftim 13:25), for the spirit would appear and disappear, come and go, yet not settle upon him properly. It is therefore written, "And the spirit of Hashem began to move him," when THE SPIRIT just began TO INSPIRE HIM. Here also the spirit would appear and leave, then appear AGAIN, but would not settle upon him, so that he could understand. Of Nebuchadnezzar it is written, "and his spirit was troubled (Heb. *vatitpaem*)," for the inspiration, THE SPIRIT, was twice as strong, BECAUSE HE UNDERSTOOD NEITHER THE DREAM NOR ITS INTERPRETATION. THE SPIRITS would come and go, as it is written, "as on previous occasions (Heb. *kefa'am befa'am,* lit. 'as time to time')" (I Shmuel 3:10), now upon this and now upon that, but his mind was not settled.

29. וַיִּשְׁלַח וַיִּקְרָא אֶת כָּל חַרְטוּמֵי מִצְרַיִם, אִלֵּין חָרָשִׁין. וְאֶת כָּל חֲכָמֶיהָ, אִלֵּין חַכִּימִין בְּטַיְירָא, וְכֻלְּהוּ הֲווֹ מִסְתַּכְּלָן לְמִנְדַּע וְלָא יָכִילוּ לְאַדְבְּקָא.

29. The verse: "and he sent and called for all the magicians of Egypt," refers to the sorcerers; "and all her wise men" refers to the astrologers. They all tried to understand, but could not.

30. אָמַר רִבִּי יִצְחָק, אַף עַל גָּב דְּאִתְּמָר דְּלָא אַחְזְיָין לֵיהּ לְבַר נָשׁ אֶלָּא בְּהַהוּא דַּרְגָּא דִילֵיהּ, שָׁאנֵי לְמַלְכִים, דְּאַחְזְיָין לוֹן מִלִּין עִלָּאִין, וּמְשַׁנְיָין מִבְּנֵי נָשָׁא אָחֳרָנִין, כְּמָה דְמַלְכָּא דַּרְגֵּיהּ עִלָּאָה עַל כָּל שְׁאָר אָחֳרָנִין, הָכֵי נָמֵי אַחֲזִיאוּ לֵיהּ בְּדַרְגָּא עִלָּאָה עַל כָּל שְׁאָר אָחֳרָנִין, כד"א אֵת אֲשֶׁר הָאֱלֹהִים עוֹשֶׂה הֶרְאָה אֶת פַּרְעֹה. אֲבָל לִשְׁאָר בְּנֵי נָשָׁא לָא גָּלֵי לוֹן קוּדְשָׁא בְּרִיךְ הוּא, מַה דְּאִיהוּ עָבֵד, בַּר לִנְבִיאֵי, אוֹ לַחֲסִידֵי, אוֹ לְחַכִּימֵי דָּרָא, וְהָא אוּקְמוּהָ.

3. "His spirit was troubled"

30. Rabbi Yitzchak said: Although we have learned that a man is shown only what is appropriate to his grade, this is not true for kings. They are shown supernal things that are different from those that other people ARE SHOWN. Because a king is of a superior grade than other men, that which he is shown is of a higher grade than the rest, as it is written, "what the Elohim are about to do He has declared to Pharaoh" (Beresheet 41:25). But to other men, the Holy One, blessed be He, does not reveal His works. He reveals them only to the prophets, the pious, and the wise men of the ages, as has already been explained.

31. תָּא חֲזֵי, כְּתִיב אוֹתִי הֵשִׁיב עַל כַּנִּי וְאוֹתוֹ תָּלָה, מִכָּאן דְּחֶלְמָא אָזֵיל בָּתַר פִּישְׁרָא, הֵשִׁיב עַל כַּנִּי מַאן, אֶלָּא דָּא יוֹסֵף. וְאוֹתוֹ תָּלָה, בְּהַהוּא פִּישְׁרָא דְּקָא פָּשַׁר לֵיהּ, וּכְתִיב וַיְהִי כַּאֲשֶׁר פָּתַר לָנוּ כֵּן הָיָה.

31. Come and behold: It is written, "me he restored to my office, and him he hanged" (Beresheet 41:13). From this, we understand that a dream follows its interpretation. Who is referred to in the phrase, "me he restored to my office?" It is Joseph. Also JOSEPH hanged him because of his interpretation of the dream, and so it is written: "And it came to pass, as he interpreted to us, so it was" (Ibid.).

4. "And they brought him hastily out of the dungeon"

A Synopsis

This passage discourses on the allegorical meaning of Pharaoh's elevation of Joseph. Rabbi Aba maintains that the verse reveals the benefits of standing in awe of God and of studying Torah at night. The text then moves to a discussion of Ecclesiastes (Kohelet). It points out that while we cannot control what comes into our eyes and ears, we can control what comes out of our mouths. Therefore, speak not evil. A discussion follows on the nature of time, the timing of good deeds, the valuable lessons to be learned from our mistakes, and the dilemma of those caught in an evil time.

The Relevance of this Passage

Words are vessels that draw particular blends of energy into our lives. Human speech possesses power that can directly influence the world around us. Hence, we should take great care in choosing what we say. Although we are initially given an unlimited amount of time to live in this world and accomplish our spiritual purpose, every negative word decreases the length of our stay. Positive words do not add time to our lives, but they also do not detract from it. This passage helps us use our speech for spiritual purposes, so that our words inspire Light in others instead of adding darkness to the world.

32. וַיִּשְׁלַח פַּרְעֹה וַיִּקְרָא אֶת יוֹסֵף וַיְרִיצֻהוּ מִן הַבּוֹר וגו'. רִבִּי אַבָּא פְּתַח וַאֲמַר רוֹצֶה יי' אֶת יְרֵאָיו אֶת הַמְיַחֲלִים לְחַסְדּוֹ. כַּמָּה קוּדְשָׁא בְּרִיךְ הוּא, אִתְרְעֵי בְּהוֹ בְּצַדִּיקַיָּא, בְּגִין דְּצַדִּיקַיָּא אִינוּן עַבְדִּין שְׁלָמָא לְעֵילָּא, וְעַבְדֵי שְׁלָמָה לְתַתָּא, וְאָעֲלִין כַּלָּה בְּבַעֲלָהּ, וּבְגִין כָּךְ קוּדְשָׁא בְּרִיךְ הוּא אִתְרְעֵי בְּהוֹ, בְּאִנּוּן דְּדַחֲלִין לֵיהּ וְעָבְדִין רְעוּתֵיהּ.

32. "Then Pharaoh sent and called Joseph, and they brought him hastily out of the dungeon." Rabbi Aba opened the discussion with the verse, "Hashem takes pleasure in those who fear Him, in those who hope for His mercy" (Tehilim 147:11). How much the Holy One, blessed be He, delights in the righteous, for they make peace above IN ABA AND IMA, they make peace below IN ZEIR ANPIN AND NUKVA, and they bring the bride to her husband. The Holy One, blessed be He, is therefore pleased with those who fear Him and abide by His wish.

33. לַמְיַחֲלִים לְחַסְדּוֹ, מַאן אִינוּן מְיַחֲלִים לְחַסְדּוֹ, הֱוֵי אֵימָא אִינוּן

דְּמִשְׁתַּדְּלֵי בְּאוֹרַיְיתָא בְּלֵילְיָא, וְאִשְׁתַּתְּפוּ בַּהֲדֵי שְׁכִינְתָּא, וְכַד אָתֵי צַפְרָא, אִינוּן מְחַכָּאן לְחַסְדּוֹ, וְהָא אוֹקְמוּהָ, בְּזִמְנָא דְּבַר נָשׁ אִשְׁתַּדַּל בְּאוֹרַיְיתָא בְּלֵילְיָא, חוּטָא דְּחֶסֶד אִתְמְשִׁיךְ עֲלֵיהּ בִּימָמָא, כְּדִכְתִיב יוֹמָם יְצַוֶּה יי׳ חַסְדּוֹ וּבַלַּיְלָה שִׁירֹה עִמִּי. מַאי טַעְמָא יוֹמָם יְצַוֶּה יי׳ חַסְדּוֹ, מִשּׁוּם דְּבַלַּיְלָה שִׁירֹה עִמִּי. וּבְגִין כָּךְ, רוֹצֶה יי׳ אֶת יְרֵאָיו כְּתִיב, וְלֹא בִּירֵאָיו, כְּמַאן דְּרָעֵי בִּרְעוּתֵיהּ לְאַחֲרָא, וְאִתְרְעֵי לֵיהּ לְאִתְפַּיְּיסָא בַּהֲדֵיהּ, וּבְגִין כָּךְ רוֹצֶה יי׳ אֶת יְרֵאָיו, וְלֹא בִּירֵאָיו.

33. “Those who hope for His mercy.” HE ASKS: Who are “those who hope for His mercy?” HE ANSWERS, They are the ones who study the Torah at night and join the Shechinah. When morning comes, they hope for His mercy. It has already been explained that when a man studies the Torah at night, a thread of grace is drawn upon him during the day, as it is written: “Yet Hashem will command His grace in the daytime, and in the night His song shall be with me” (Tehilim 42:9). Why is it said that “Hashem will command His grace in the daytime?” Because “in the night His song shall be with me.” Hence the verse, “Hashem takes pleasure (in) those who fear Him,” uses the particle *Et* instead of “in,” BECAUSE HE IS NOT ONLY PLEASED WITH THEM, BUT ACT as one who pleases another and wishes to be at peace with him. It is therefore written: “Hashem takes pleasure (in) those who fear him” – WHICH MEANS THAT HE PLEASES AND APPEASES THEM, rather than “Hashem takes pleasure in those who fear Him,” WHICH WOULD ONLY MEAN HE IS PLEASED WITH THEM THEMSELVES.

34. כְּגַוְונָא דָא, יוֹסֵף הֲוָה עָצִיב בַּעֲצִיבוּ דְּרוּחָא, בַּעֲצִיבוּ דְּלִבָּא, דַּהֲוָה אָסִיר תַּמָּן, כֵּיוָן דְּשַׁדַּר פַּרְעֹה בְּגִינֵיהּ מַה כְּתִיב, וַיְרִיצוּהוּ אִתְפַּיְּיסוּ לֵיהּ, וְאַהֲדָרוּ לֵיהּ מִלִּין דְּחֶדְוָה, מִלִּין לְמֶחֱדֵי לִבָּא, בְּגִין דַּהֲוָה עָצִיב מִן בֵּירָא. תָּא חֲזֵי, בְּקַדְמֵיתָא נָפַל בְּבֵירָא, בְּבֵירָא אִסְתַּלַּק לְבָתַר.

34. Similarly, Joseph was sad in mind and spirit, BECAUSE he was imprisoned. Once Pharaoh had sent for him, it is written: “and they brought him hastily,” which means that he appeased him and addressed him with joyful words that gladden the heart. Why? Because he was dejected FROM SITTING in the dungeon (lit. ‘pit’). Come and behold: First he fell into a pit, and from the pit he later rose to greatness.

35. רִבִּי שִׁמְעוֹן אֲמַר, עַד לָא אֵירַע לְיוֹסֵף הַהוּא עוֹבָדָא, לָא אִקְרֵי צַדִּיק, כֵּיוָן דְּנָטַר הַהוּא בְּרִית קַיָּימָא, אִקְרֵי צַדִּיק, וְהַהוּא דַּרְגָּא דִּבְרִית קַדִּישָׁא אִתְעַטַּר בַּהֲדֵיהּ, וּמַאי דַּהֲוָה בַּבּוֹר בְּקַדְמֵיתָא, אִסְתַּלַּק בַּהֲדֵיהּ, וּכְתִיב וַיְרִיצֻהוּ מִן הַבּוֹר, אִסְתַּלַּק מִן דָּא, וְאִתְעַטַּר בִּבְאֵר מַיִם חַיִּים.

35. Rabbi Shimon said: Before the incident happened, Joseph was not called righteous. After he guarded the Holy Covenant BY NOT SINNING WITH POTIFAR'S WIFE, he was called Righteous and the grade of the Holy Covenant, YESOD, decorated him. He who was first in the dungeon, THE KLIPAH, rose from it. It is written: "and they brought him hastily out of the dungeon," for he had ascended from THE KLIPAH and was adorned with a well of living water, THE SHECHINAH.

36. וַיִּשְׁלַח פַּרְעֹה וַיִּקְרָא אֶת יוֹסֵף, לִקְרֹא לְיוֹסֵף מִבָּעֵי לֵיהּ. אֶלָּא וַיִּקְרָא אֶת יוֹסֵף: דָּא קוּדְשָׁא בְּרִיךְ הוּא, דִּכְתִיב עַד עֵת בֹּא דְבָרוֹ אִמְרַת יי׳ צְרָפָתְהוּ. עַד עֵת בֹּא דְבָרוֹ, הה״ד וַיִּקְרָא אֶת יוֹסֵף, כְּתִיב הָכָא וַיִּקְרָא אֶת יוֹסֵף, וּכְתִיב הָתָם וַיִּקְרָא אֶל מֹשֶׁה. וַיְגַלַּח וַיְחַלֵּף שִׂמְלוֹתָיו, בְּגִין יְקָרָא דְמַלְכָּא, וְהָא אוּקְמוּהָ.

36. "Then Pharaoh sent and called Joseph." HE SAID: It should have been written "to call Joseph" INSTEAD OF "AND CALLED," WHICH INTERRUPTS THE PHRASE. HE ANSWERS, It was the Holy One, blessed be He, WHO CALLED TO BRING HIM FROM THE PIT, as it is written, "until the time that His word came to pass: the word of Hashem had tested him" (Tehilim 105:19). The verse: "until the time that His word came to pass" is similar to the phrase, "and called Joseph," FOR IT WAS THE HOLY ONE, BLESSED BE HE, WHO CALLED HIM. It is written here "and called Joseph" and elsewhere "And He called to Moses" (Vayikra 1:1). IN BOTH PASSAGES, IT WAS THE HOLY ONE, BLESSED BE HE, WHO CALLED HIM. "And he shaved himself, and changed his garments" out of respect for the king, AS HE HAD TO STAND BEFORE PHARAOH.

37. ר׳ אֶלְעָזָר פָּתַח, וַיָּבֹא יִשְׂרָאֵל מִצְרַיִם וְיַעֲקֹב גָּר בְּאֶרֶץ חָם. תָּא חֲזֵי, דְּקוּדְשָׁא בְּרִיךְ הוּא מְגַלְגֵּל גִּלְגּוּלִין בְּעָלְמָא, וּמְקַיֵּים אֱסָרִין וְקִיּוּמִין, בְּגִין לְקַיְּימָא קִיּוּמָא וּגְזֵרָה דְּאִיהוּ גָּזַר.

37. Rabbi Elazar opened the discussion with the verse: "So Yisrael came into Egypt; and Jacob sojourned in the land of Ham" (Vayikra 1:23). Come and behold: The Holy One, blessed be He, directs events and fulfills vows and oaths in order to fulfill the vow and edict He decreed.

38. דְּהָא תְּנַן, אִלְמָלֵא חֲבִיבוּ וּרְחִימוּ דְּרָחֵים קוּדְשָׁא בְּרִיךְ הוּא לַאֲבָהָן, הֲוָה אִתְחֲזֵי לְנָחֲתָא יַעֲקֹב לְמִצְרַיִם בְּשַׁלְשְׁלֵי דְּפַרְזְלָא, וּבִרְחִימוּ דִּלְהוֹן, שַׁלְטֵיהּ לְיוֹסֵף בְּרֵיהּ, וַעֲבַד לֵיהּ מַלְכָּא דְּשַׁלִּיטָא עַל כָּל אַרְעָא, וְנָחֲתוּ כֻּלְּהוּ שִׁבְטִין בִּיקָרָא, וְיַעֲקֹב כְּמַלְכָּא.

38. We have learned that were it not for the fondness and affection the Holy One, blessed be He, bore for the Patriarchs, Jacob would have had to go down to Egypt in iron chains. In His love for them, He made Joseph, His son, ruler and governor over the whole land. The tribes then went to Egypt honored, and Jacob was as a king.

39. תָּא חֲזֵי, מַה כְּתִיב וַיָּבֹא יִשְׂרָאֵל מִצְרַיִם וְיַעֲקֹב גָּר בְּאֶרֶץ חָם, כֵּיוָן דִּכְתִיב וַיָּבֹא יִשְׂרָאֵל מִצְרַיִם, לָא יְדַעְנָא דְּיַעֲקֹב גָּר בְּאֶרֶץ חָם, אַמַּאי אִצְטְרִיךְ הָא. אֶלָּא וַיָּבֹא יִשְׂרָאֵל מִצְרַיִם: דָּא קוּדְשָׁא בְּרִיךְ הוּא. וְיַעֲקֹב גָּר בְּאֶרֶץ חָם: דָּא יַעֲקֹב, דְּהָא בְּגִינֵיהּ דְּיַעֲקֹב וּבְנוֹי, אֲתָא שְׁכִינְתָּא לְמִצְרַיִם, וְקוּדְשָׁא בְּרִיךְ הוּא גִּלְגֵּל גִּלְגּוּלִין, וְאָחֵית לֵיהּ לְיוֹסֵף בְּקַדְמֵיתָא, דְּבִזְכוּתֵיהּ אִתְקַיַּים בְּרִית בַּהֲדֵיהּ, וְשַׁלְטֵיהּ עַל כָּל אַרְעָא.

39. Come and behold: It is written, "So Yisrael came into Egypt; and Jacob sojourned in the land of Ham." HE ASKS: Because it is written, "So Yisrael came into Egypt," it is understood that Jacob sojourned in the land of Ham. Why should he have added it? HE REPLIES: "so Yisrael came into Egypt" refers to the Holy One, blessed be He, NAMELY, ZEIR ANPIN CALLED YISRAEL, AND "and Jacob sojourned in the land of Ham" refers to Jacob, because it was for the sake of Jacob, and his sons that the Shechinah came down to Egypt. The Holy One, blessed be He, planned events so that Joseph was brought down first; for as a result of his merit, the covenant dwelt with him and made him ruler over the whole land.

40. מַה כְּתִיב, שָׁלַח מֶלֶךְ וַיַּתִּירֵהוּ מוֹשֵׁל עַמִּים וַיְפַתְּחֵהוּ. ר' שִׁמְעוֹן

אֲמַר, כְּתִיב יי׳ מַתִּיר אֲסוּרִים וגו׳, וְהָכָא כְּתִיב, שָׁלַח מֶלֶךְ וַיַּתִּירֵהוּ, אַמַּאי מוֹשֵׁל עַמִּים וַיְפַתְּחֵהוּ. אֶלָּא שָׁלַח מֶלֶךְ: דָּא קוּדְשָׁא בְּרִיךְ הוּא. מוֹשֵׁל עַמִּים: דָּא קוּדְשָׁא בְּרִיךְ הוּא. שָׁלַח מֶלֶךְ, מֶלֶךְ עִלָּאָה שָׁלַח וַיַּתִּירֵהוּ, וּמַאן אִיהוּ דְּשָׁלַח, דָּא מַלְאָךְ הַגּוֹאֵל, דְּאִיהוּ מוֹשֵׁל עַמִּים, דְּאִיהוּ מוֹשֵׁל עַל תַּתָּאֵי. וְכֹלָּא מֵעִם קוּדְשָׁא בְּרִיךְ הוּא אִיהוּ.

40. It is written: "The king sent and loosed him: and the ruler of the people let him go free" (Tehilim 105:20). Rabbi Shimon said: It is written, "Hashem looses the prisoners" (Tehilim 146:7), and "The king sent and loosed him." Why DID HE REPEAT THE THOUGHT BY SAYING, "and the ruler of the people let him go free?" HE ANSWERS, "The king" is the Holy One, blessed be He, and the "ruler of the people" is the Holy One, blessed be He. THE MEANING OF THE VERSE IS: "The king" refers to the supernal king, ZEIR ANPIN, who "sent and loosed him." Whom did he send? The redeeming angel, THE NUKVA, who is "ruler of the people" and rules below IN THE LOWER WORLD. All comes from the Holy One, blessed be He.

41. וַיְרִיצֻהוּ חָסֵר וא״ו, וּמַאן אִיהוּ, דָּא קוּדְשָׁא בְּרִיךְ הוּא. בְּגִין דְּהָא לֵית מַאן דְּאָסִיר וּפָתַח, בַּר קוּדְשָׁא בְּרִיךְ הוּא, דִּכְתִיב יִסְגֹּר עַל אִישׁ וְלֹא יִפָּתֵחַ. וּכְתִיב וְהוּא יַשְׁקִיט וּמִי יַרְשִׁיעַ וְיַסְתֵּר פָּנִים וּמִי יְשׁוּרֶנּוּ וְעַל גּוֹי וְעַל אָדָם יָחַד, דְּהָא כֹּלָּא בֵּיהּ, וּכְתִיב וּכְמִצְבְּיֵהּ עָבֵד בְּחֵיל שְׁמַיָּא. וְדָאֲרֵי אַרְעָא וְלָא אִיתַי דִּי יְמַחֵי בִידֵיהּ וְיֵאמַר לֵיהּ מָה עֲבַדְתְּ, וּבְגִין כָּךְ כְּתִיב וַיְרִיצֻהוּ מִן הַבּוֹר וגו׳.

41. The word, *vayritzuhu* ("and they brought him hastily") is spelled without the letter *Vav* TO INDICATE THAT IT IS SINGULAR INSTEAD OF PLURAL. Who BROUGHT HIM HASTILY FROM THE DUNGEON? The Holy One, blessed be He, for there is no one else who imprisons and frees people from prison, as it is written: "He shuts up a man, and there can be no opening" (Iyov 12:14) and "When He gives quietness, who then can condemn? and when He hides His face, who then can behold Him? Whether against a nation, or against a man alike" (Iyov 34:29). For everything depends upon Him, as it is written, "and He does according to His will in the host of heaven, and among the inhabitants of the earth: and none can stay His hand, or say to Him, What do you?" (Daniel 4:32). Hence it is written: "and they (he) brought him hastily out of the dungeon," THAT IS, THE HOLY ONE, BLESSED BE HE, BROUGHT HIM HASTILY OUT OF THE DUNGEON.

42. מַאי וַיְרִיצֻהוּ. כד"א יֶעְתַּר אֶל אֱלוֹהַ וַיִּרְצֵהוּ, כְּגַוְונָא דָא וַיְרִיצֻהוּ מִן הַבּוֹר, וּלְבָתַר וַיָּבֹא אֶל פַּרְעֹה. דָּבָר אֲחֵר וַיְרִיצֻהוּ, דְּאַמְשִׁיךְ עֲלֵיהּ חוּטָא דְחֶסֶד, לְמֵיהַב לֵיהּ חִנָּא קַמֵּיהּ דְּפַרְעֹה, אֱלֹהִים יַעֲנֶה אֶת שְׁלוֹם פַּרְעֹה, בְּגִין לְאַקְדָּמָא לֵיהּ שָׁלוֹם, וּלְמִפְתַּח בְּשָׁלוֹם.

42. HE ASKS: What is the meaning of "and he brought him hastily (Heb. *vayritzuhu*)?" HE REPLIES: As "he shall pray to Eloha, and He will be favorable to him (Heb. *vayretzehu*)" (Iyov 33:26) MEANS THE HOLY ONE, BLESSED BE HE, WAS FAVORABLE TO HIM, so the verse "and he brought him hastily out of the dungeon" MEANS THAT THE HOLY ONE, BLESSED BE HE, WAS FAVORABLE TO HIM. Then he was brought before Pharaoh. Another explanation is that *vayritzuhu* IS DERIVED FROM WILL (HEB. *RATZON*) AND GRACE, for He drew upon him a thread of grace so he will find grace before Pharaoh. HE ADDRESSED HIM WITH, "Elohim shall give Pharaoh an answer of peace" to hasten to greet him and open HIS SPEECH with THE WORD "peace."

43. רִבִּי אַבָּא אָמַר, תָּא חֲזֵי, בְּהַהוּא רָשָׁע דְּפַרְעֹה, דְּאִיהוּ אָמַר, לֹא יָדַעְתִּי אֶת ה', וּפַרְעֹה חַכִּים הֲוָה מִכָּל חָרָשׁוֹי, אֶלָּא וַדַּאי שְׁמָא דֵּאלֹהִים הֲוָה יָדַע, דְּהָא כְּתִיב הֲנִמְצָא כָזֶה אִישׁ אֲשֶׁר רוּחַ אֱלֹקִים בּוֹ. וּבְגִין דְּמֹשֶׁה לָא אֲתָא לְגַבֵּיהּ אֶלָּא בִּשְׁמָא דַּה', וְלֹא בִּשְׁמָא דֵּאלֹהִים, וְדָא הֲוָה קַשְׁיָא קַמֵּיהּ מִכֹּלָּא, דְּאִיהוּ הֲוָה יָדַע דְּהָא שְׁמָא דָא אִיהוּ שַׁלִּיט בְּאַרְעָא, וּבִשְׁמָא דַּה' לָא הֲוָה יָדַע, וְעַל דָּא קַשְׁיָא קַמֵּיהּ שְׁמָא דָא.

43. Rabbi Aba said: Come and behold the wicked Pharaoh, who said: "I know not Hashem (Yud Hei Vav Hei)" (Shemot 5:2). As he was wiser than all his magicians, HOW COULD HE HAVE NOT KNOWN YUD HEI VAV HEI? HE ANSWERS, Assuredly he knew the name of Elohim, as it is written, "Can we find such a one as this is, a man in whom is the spirit of Elohim" (Beresheet 41:38). However, because Moses came before him with the name of Hashem only, it was hard for him to understand anything more, for he knew that ELOHIM was ruler over the land, but he did not know the name Hashem. Therefore he found this name difficult to grasp.

44. וְדָא הוּא דִכְתִיב וַיְחַזֵּק ה׳ אֶת לֵב פַּרְעֹה, דְּמִלָּה דָא הֲוָה אַתְקִיף לִבֵּיהּ, וְאַקְשֵׁי לֵיהּ, וְעַל דָּא מֹשֶׁה לֹא אוֹדַע לֵיהּ מִלָּה דִּשְׁמָא אָחֳרָא, אֶלָּא שְׁמָא דַּה׳ בִּלְחוֹדוֹי, וְאוֹקְמוּהָ.

44. This is why it is written, "And Hashem hardened the heart of Pharaoh." It was the word YUD HEI VAV HEI that hardened his heart and made him headstrong. Moses, therefore, spoke to him only by the name Yud Hei Vav Hei, as has already been explained.

45. פָּתַח וַאֲמַר מִי כַּה׳ אֱלֹקֵינוּ הַמַּגְבִּיהִי לָשָׁבֶת וגו׳ מִי כַּה׳ אֱלֹקֵינוּ הַמַּגְבִּיהִי לָשָׁבֶת, דְּאִסְתַּלַּק מֵעַל כָּרְסֵי יְקָרֵיהּ, וְלָא אִתְגְּלֵי לְתַתָּא, בְּשַׁעְתָּא דְּלָא אִשְׁתַּכָּחוּ זַכָּאִין בְּעָלְמָא, הָא אִיהוּ אִסְתַּלַּק מִנַּיְיהוּ, וְלָא אִתְגְּלֵי לְהוֹ. הַמַּשְׁפִּילִי לִרְאוֹת, בְּשַׁעְתָּא דְּזַכָּאִין אִינוּן דְּאִשְׁתַּכָּחוּ בְּעָלְמָא. קוּדְשָׁא בְּרִיךְ הוּא נָחִית בְּדַרְגּוֹי לְקַבְּלֵהוֹן דְּתַתָּאֵי, לְאַשְׁגָּחָא עַל עַלְמָא, לְאוֹטָבָא לְהוֹ.

45. He opened the discussion with the verse: "Who is like Hashem our Elohim, who is enthroned on high, who looks far down to behold" (Tehilim 113:5-6): "Who is like Hashem our Elohim, who is enthroned on high" MEANS THAT He rises above His Throne of Glory not to be revealed below. For when there are no righteous to be found in the world, He is gone from them and does not reveal Himself to them. The phrase: "who looks far down to behold" REFERS TO the time when the righteous are found in the world, and the Holy One, blessed be He, descends to the lower beings to take care of the world and do good by them.

46. דְּהָא כַּד זַכָּאִין לָא אִשְׁתַּכָּחוּ בְּעָלְמָא, אִיהוּ אִסְתַּלַּק, וְאַסְתִּיר אַנְפִּין מִנַּיְיהוּ, וְלָא אַשְׁגַּח עֲלַיְיהוּ, בְּגִין דְּצַדִּיקַיָּיא אִינוּן יְסוֹדָא וְקִיּוּמָא דְעָלְמָא, דִּכְתִיב וְצַדִּיק יְסוֹד עוֹלָם.

46. For when there are no righteous men in the world, He is gone, hides His face from them, and does not pay attention to them. This is because the righteous are the foundation and existence of the world, as it is written, “and the righteous is an everlasting foundation (or: the foundation of the world)” (Mishlei 10:25).

47. וְעַל דָּא קוּדְשָׁא בְּרִיךְ הוּא לָא גַּלֵּי שְׁמֵיהּ קַדִּישָׁא, בַּר לְיִשְׂרָאֵל בִּלְחוֹדוֹי, דְּאִינּוּן חוּלַק עַדְבֵיהּ וְאַחְסַנְתֵּיהּ, וְעַלְמָא פָּלֵיג לֵיהּ קוּדְשָׁא בְּרִיךְ הוּא, לִמְמַנָּן תְּרֵיסִין, וְהָא אִתְּמָר דִּכְתִיב בְּהַנְחֵל עֶלְיוֹן גּוֹיִם וגו׳. וּכְתִיב כִּי חֵלֶק ה׳ עַמּוֹ יַעֲקֹב חֶבֶל נַחֲלָתוֹ.

47. The Holy One, blessed be He, therefore revealed His Holy Name to Yisrael alone, who are His portion, lot and inheritance. The Holy One, blessed be He, divided the world among the mighty chieftains, THE SEVENTY MINISTERS. This we have learned from the verse: “He set the borders of the people... For Hashem’s portion is His people; Jacob is the lot of His inheritance” (Devarim 32: 8-9).

48. רִבִּי חִיָּיא וְרִבִּי יוֹסֵי הֲווֹ אָזְלֵי בְּאָרְחָא, אָמַר רָבִּי יוֹסֵי לְרִבִּי חִיָּיא תְּוַוהְנָא עַל הַאי דְּקָאֲמַר שְׁלֹמֹה, כָּל מִלּוֹי סְתִימִין וְלָא אִתְיָידְעוּן, דְּהָא קֹהֶלֶת סְתִים סְתִימִין.

48. Rabbi Chiya and Rabbi Yosi were walking together. Rabbi Yosi said: I wonder about the words of King Solomon, for all his speeches are obscure, and the words of Kohelet are vague.

49. פְּתַח וַאֲמַר כָּל הַדְּבָרִים יְגֵעִים לֹא יוּכַל אִישׁ לְדַבֵּר לֹא תִשְׂבַּע עַיִן לִרְאוֹת וְלֹא תִמָּלֵא אֹזֶן מִשְּׁמוֹעַ, כָּל הַדְּבָרִים יְגֵעִים. וְכִי כָּל הַדְּבָרִים יְגֵעִים אִינּוּן לְמַלָּלָא, דְּקָאֲמַר לֹא יוּכַל אִישׁ לְדַבֵּר. וְלֹא תִשְׂבַּע עַיִן לִרְאוֹת. וְלֹא תִמָּלֵא אֹזֶן מִשְּׁמוֹעַ, מ״ט אִלֵּין. אֶלָּא בְּגִין דִּתְרֵין מִנְּהוֹן, וְאִינּוּן עַיְינִין וְאוּדְנִין, לָא קַיָּימִין בִּרְשׁוּתֵיהּ דְּבַר נָשׁ, וּפוּמָא אִיהוּ בִּרְשׁוּתֵיהּ, וְכָל אִלֵּין תְּלַת לָא יָכְלִין לְאַשְׁלָמָא כֹּלָּא, וּלְאַדְבָּקָא כֹּלָּא.

49. He began with the verse, “All things are full of weariness; man cannot utter it: the eye is not satisfied with seeing, nor the ear filled with hearing”

(Kohelet 1:8): HE ASKS: If "all things are full of weariness," are they all too weary to speak? SOME THINGS CLEARLY ARE NOT. He also quoted the verse: "man cannot utter it: the eye is not satisfied with seeing, nor the ear filled with hearing." Why did precisely these occur to him? HE ANSWERS, Two of them – eyes and ears – are not under a man's control; the mouth, however, is under his control. THUS, HE TEACHES US THAT ALTHOUGH THESE ORGANS COMPRISE ALL THE FACULTIES OF MAN, the tree AND SIMILAR ONES cannot comprehend and conceive everything. THE QUESTION IS THEREFORE SETTLED, FOR "ALL THINGS ARE FULL OF WEARINESS" MEANS THAT THE EYES, EARS, AND MOUTH CANNOT COMPREHEND EVERYTHING.

50. **אֲמַר ר׳ חִיָּיא, הָכֵי הוּא, דְּדִבּוּרָא דְּבַר נָשׁ לָא יָכֵיל לְמַלָּלָא, וְעַיְינִין לְמֶחֱמֵי, וְאוּדְנִין לְמִשְׁמַע, וְאֵין כָּל חָדָשׁ תַּחַת הַשֶּׁמֶשׁ. וְתָא חֲזֵי אפי׳ בִּרְיָין וְקַסְטוֹרִין, דַּעֲבַד קוּדְשָׁא בְּרִיךְ הוּא תַּחַת הַשֶּׁמֶשׁ, לָא יָכְלִין לְמַלָּלָא כָּל מִלִּין דְּעַלְמָא, וְעֵינָא לָא יָכֵיל. לְמִשְׁלַט וּלְמֶחֱמֵי, וְאוּדְנָא לְמִשְׁמָע. וּבְגִין כָּךְ שְׁלֹמֹה דַּהֲוָה יָדַע כָּל מִלָּה, הֲוָה אֲמַר דָּא.**

50. Rabbi Chiya said: It is so. A man's speech cannot utter, nor the eyes see and the ears hear "and there is nothing new under the sun" (Kohelet 1:9). Come and behold: Even the ghosts and spirits that the Holy One, blessed be He, formed under the sun cannot say all that there is in the world, nor can the eye see or the ear hear. Solomon, who knew everything, therefore said this.

51. **וְתָא חֲזֵי, כָּל עוֹבָדִין דְּעַלְמָא, בְּכַמָּה קַסְטְרִין תַּלְיָין, וְכָל בְּנֵי עַלְמָא לָא יָדְעִין, וְלָא מַשְׁגִּיחִין עַל מַה קָּיְימֵי בְּעַלְמָא, וַאֲפִילּוּ שְׁלֹמֹה מַלְכָּא, דַּהֲוָה חֲכָמִים מִכָּל בְּנֵי עַלְמָא, לָא יָכֵיל לְקָיְימָא בְּהוּ.**

51. Come and behold: All actions in the world depend on many chieftains, FOR THERE IS NOT ONE HERB BELOW THAT HAS NOT A CHIEF OVER IT, WHO STRIKES IT AND COMMANDS, "GROW." Yet all the people in the world do not know or care about THEIR ROOTS OR why they are in the world. For even King Solomon, who was wiser than any other man, could not grasp them.

52. **פְּתַח וַאֲמַר, אֶת הַכֹּל עָשָׂה יָפֶה בְעִתּוֹ גַּם אֶת הָעוֹלָם, נָתַן בְּלִבָּם**

מִבְּלִי אֲשֶׁר לֹא יִמְצָא הָאָדָם אֶת הַמַּעֲשֶׂה אֲשֶׁר עָשָׂה הָאֱלֹקִים וגו'. תָּא חֲזֵי, זַכָּאִין אִינוּן דְּמִשְׁתַּדְּלֵי בְּאוֹרַיְיתָא וְיָדְעֵי לְאִסְתַּכְּלָא בְּרוּחָא דְחָכְמְתָא. אֶת הַכֹּל עָשָׂה יָפֶה בְעִתּוֹ, כָּל עוֹבָדִין דַּעֲבַד קוּדְשָׁא בְּרִיךְ הוּא בְּעַלְמָא, בְּכָל עוֹבָדָא וְעוֹבָדָא, אִית דַּרְגָּא מְמַנָּא עַל הַהוּא עוֹבָדָא בְּעַלְמָא, הֵן לְטַב הֵן לְבִישׁ. מִנְּהוֹן דַּרְגִּין לִימִינָא, וּמִנְהוֹן דַּרְגִּין לִשְׂמָאלָא, אָזֵיל בַּר נָשׁ לִימִינָא, הַהוּא עוֹבָדָא דְּעָבֵיד, הַהוּא דַרְגָּא מְמַנָּא לְהַהוּא סִטְרָא, וְעָבֵיד לֵיהּ סִיּוּעָא, וְכַמָּה אִינוּן דִּמְסַיְּיעֵי לֵיהּ. אָזַל בַּר נָשׁ לִשְׂמָאלָא, וְעָבֵיד עוֹבָדוֹי, הַהוּא עוֹבָדָא דְּעָבֵיד, מְמַנָּא אִיהוּ לְהַהוּא סִטְרָא, וְקָא מְקַטְרֵג לֵיהּ, וְאוֹבִיל לֵיהּ לְהַהוּא סִטְרָא, וְאַסְטֵי לֵיהּ. וּבְגִין כָּךְ, הַהוּא עוֹבָדָא דְּעָבֵיד בַּר נָשׁ כִּדְקָא חָזֵי, הַהוּא מְמַנָּא דִסְטַר יְמִינָא, קָא מְסַיֵּיעַ לֵיהּ, וְדָא הוּא בְּעִתּוֹ, יָפֶה בְּעִתּוֹ, דְּהַהוּא עוֹבָדָא מִתְקַשְּׁרָא בְּעִתּוֹ, כִּדְקָא חָזֵי לֵיהּ.

52. He opened the discussion by quoting: "He has made every thing beautiful in its time: also He has set the world in their heart, so that no man can find out the work which the Elohim has made" (Kohelet 3:11): Come and behold: Happy are those who study the Torah and know how to observe with the spirit of wisdom. "He has made every thing beautiful in its time" REFERS TO all the works that the Holy One, blessed be He, performed in the world. Over every action in the world there is a grade in charge, either for good or for evil. THESE ARE THE 28 TIMES MENTIONED BY KOHELET, FOURTEEN FOR GOOD ON THE RIGHT IN THE SECRET OF THE SHECHINAH, AND FOURTEEN FOR EVIL ON THE LEFT, IN THE SECRET OF THE OTHER SIDE THAT PUNISHES MEN. From them, some grades go to the right and some to the left. When a man goes to the right, the deed he performs, the grade appointed over that RIGHT side, gives him help and he has many helpers. If a man goes to the left and performs a certain deed, the chief of the LEFT side denounces him for that deed, conducts him to that side and leads him astray. Therefore when a man acts worthily, the chief of the right side helps him. The "in its time" referred to in the phrase, "beautiful in its time" tells us that the deed was properly connected to "its time," TO THE NUKVA CALLED TIME. THE SECRET OF THE FOURTEEN TIMES FOR GOOD IS THEIR BEING ON THE RIGHT. THROUGH THE PUNISHMENTS OF THE FOURTEEN TIMES FOR EVIL, A MAN CHOOSES THE FOURTEEN TIMES ON THE RIGHT AND CLEAVES TO THE SHECHINAH. IT

IS FOUND THEN, THAT HE HAS MADE EVERY THING BEAUTIFUL IN ITS TIME."

53. גַּם אֶת הָעוֹלָם נָתַן בְּלִבָּם. כָּל עַלְמָא, וְכָל עוֹבָדוֹי דְעַלְמָא, לָאו אִינּוּן אֶלָּא בִּרְעוּתָא דְלִבָּא, כַּד סָלֵיק בִּרְעוּתָא דְבַר נָשׁ. זַכָּאִין אִנּוּן צַדִּיקַיָּא דְּאַמְשִׁיכוּ עוֹבָדִין טָבִין, לְאוֹטָבָא לוֹן, וּלְכָל עַלְמָא, וְאִינּוּן יָדְעִין לְאִתְדַּבְקָא בְּעֵת שָׁלוֹם, וּבְחֵילָא דִצְדָקָה דְּעָבְדִין לְתַתָּא, אִינּוּן מָשְׁכִין לְהַהוּא דַרְגָּא דְּאִקְרֵי כָּל, לְאַנְהָרָא בְּעִתּוֹ.

53. "...also He has set the world in their heart." This means that the world and all its actions are not bound to holiness except through the heart's desire when desire rises in man, WHICH IS THE SECRET OF THE VERSE, "KNOW THEREFORE THIS DAY, AND CONSIDER IT IN YOUR HEART" (DEVARIM 4:39). Happy are the righteous who draw BY THEIR HEART'S DESIRE good deeds that benefit them and the whole world, and who know how to be attached to the "time of peace" (Kohelet 3:8), THAT IS, TO THE TIME OF HIGH UNION CALLED PEACE. By the strength of charity that they give below, they cause the grade called all (lit. 'everything'), YESOD, to illuminate "in its time," THE NUKVA.

54. וַוי לוֹן לְחַיָּיבַיָּא, דְּלָא יָדְעִין עֵת דְּהַהוּא עוֹבָדָא, וְלָא מַשְׁגִּיחִין לְמֶעְבַּד עוֹבָדֵיהוֹן בְּעַלְמָא עַל תִּקּוּנָא דְאִצְטְרִיךְ לֵיהּ לְעַלְמָא, וּלְאַתְקָנָא עוֹבָדָא בְּהַהוּא דַרְגָּא דְּאִתְחֲזֵי לֵיהּ, מַאי טַעְמָא, בְּגִין דְּלָא יָדְעִין.

54. Woe to the wicked who do not know the time, NAMELY THE TIME OF PEACE, for the action and do not pay attention, so that they perform their actions for the sake of needed improvement in the world and correct the deed in its appropriate grade. THIS MEANS THAT THEY DO NOT ELEVATE MAYIN NUKVIN (FEMALE WATERS) BY THEIR WORKS TO SUPERNAL UNION, WHICH IS THE SECRET OF "TIME OF PEACE." They do not do so, because they do not know this.

55. וְעַל דָּא אִתְיְיהֵב כֹּלָּא בִּרְעוּתְהוֹן דִּבְנֵי נָשָׁא, דִּכְתִיב מִבְּלִי אֲשֶׁר לֹא יִמְצָא הָאָדָם אֶת הַמַּעֲשֶׂה אֲשֶׁר עָשָׂה הָאֱלֹקִים מֵרֹאשׁ וְעַד סוֹף,

וּבְגִין כָּךְ דְּאִינוּן עוֹבָדִין לָא אִתְעֲבִידוּ לְאַתְקָנָא בְּדַרְגַּיְיהוּ כִּדְקָחָזֵי, דְּיִתְכְּלֵיל עוֹבָדָא דָא בְּדַרְגָּא דָא, כֹּלָּא כְּתִקּוּנָא אֶלָּא כְּפוּם רְעוּתָא דְּבַר נָשׁ, מַה כְּתִיב בַּתְרֵיהּ יָדַעְתִּי כִּי אֵין טוֹב בָּם כִּי אִם לִשְׂמוֹחַ וְלַעֲשׂוֹת טוֹב בְּחַיָּיו. יָדַעְתִּי כִּי אֵין טוֹב בָּם, בְּאִינוּן עוֹבָדִין, דְּלָא אִתְעֲבִידוּ כִּדְקָא יָאוֹת, כִּי אִם לִשְׂמוֹחַ, בְּכָל מַה דְּיֵיתֵי עֲלוֹי, וּלְמֵיהַב הוֹדָאָה לְקוּדְשָׁא בְּרִיךְ הוּא, וְלַעֲשׂוֹת טוֹב בְּחַיָּיו, דְּהָא אִי הַהוּא עוֹבָדָא גָּרֵים לֵיהּ בִּישָׁא, בְּגִין הַהוּא דַּרְגָּא דְּקָא מְמַנָּא עֲלוֹי, אִית לֵיהּ לְמֶחֱדֵי בֵּיהּ, וּלְאוֹדָאָה עֲלֵיהּ, דְּאִיהוּ גָּרֵים לֵיהּ לְנַפְשֵׁיהּ, וְאִיהוּ אָזֵיל בְּלָא יְדִיעָא, כְּצִיפֳּרָא דָא בְּגוֹ קוּסְטִירָא.

55. Therefore everything is given to man's desire, as it is written: "so that no man can find out the work which the Elohim has made from the beginning to the end" (Kohelet 3:11). Because these deeds were not performed with the intention of correcting them according to their appropriate grades, that is, to include the deeds in their CORRESPONDING grade, they are accomplished according to man's desire, IN STUBBORNNESS. Of this, it is written: "I know that there is nothing good in them, but to rejoice, and to do good in his life" (Ibid. 12). "I know there is nothing good in them" – in the deeds that are not properly performed WITH THE PURPOSE OF CORRECTING – "but to rejoice" at whatever comes upon him, EITHER GOOD OR BAD, to thank the Holy One, blessed be He, "and to do good in his life." HE ASKS: WHY SHOULD HE REJOICE AT EVIL? HE ANSWERS, If the deed brought evil consequences because of the grade appointed over it ON THE LEFT SIDE, he should rejoice and be thankful FOR THE EVIL HE DESERVED, for he himself caused all this by going without knowledge as a bird falling into a snare. NOW THAT HE OBTAINED KNOWLEDGE BECAUSE OF THE PUNISHMENT, HE WOULD KNOW "TO DO GOOD IN HIS LIFE." ONE SHOULD, THEREFORE, REJOICE AND BE THANKFUL FOR PUNISHMENT.

56. וְכָל דָּא מְנָלָן, דִּכְתִיב כִּי גַּם לֹא יֵדַע הָאָדָם אֶת עִתּוֹ, כַּדָּגִים הַנֶּאֱחָזִים בִּמְצוֹדָה רָעָה וְכַצִּפֳּרִים הָאֲחוּזוֹת בַּפָּח כָּהֵם יוּקָשִׁים בְּנֵי הָאָדָם לְעֵת רָעָה כְּשֶׁתִּפּוֹל עֲלֵיהֶם פִּתְאוֹם. כִּי גַּם לֹא יָדַע הָאָדָם אֶת עִתּוֹ. מַאי עִתּוֹ, עִתּוֹ דְּהַהוּא עוֹבָדָא דְּקָא עָבֵיד, כְּמָה דְּאַתְּ אָמֵר, אֶת

הַכֹּל עָשָׂה יָפֶה בְּעִתּוֹ, וּבְגִין כָּךְ אִינוּן כַּצִּפֳּרִים הָאֲחוּזוֹת בַּפָּח. וּבְגִין כָּךְ זַכָּאִין אִינוּן דְּמִשְׁתַּדְּלֵי בְּאוֹרַיְיתָא, וְיָדְעֵי אוֹרְחוֹי וּשְׁבִילוֹי דְּאוֹרַיְיתָא דְּמַלְכָּא עִלָּאָה, לְמֵיהַךְ בָּהּ בְּאֹרַח קְשׁוֹט.

56. HE ASKS: how do we know THAT A MAN IS WITHOUT KNOWLEDGE? HE ANSWERS, From the verse, "For man also knows not his time: like the fishes that are taken in an evil net, and like the birds that are caught in the snare; so are the sons of men snared in an evil time, when it falls suddenly upon them" (Kohelet 9:12). HE ASKS: What is the time in "For man also knows not his time?" HE REPLIES: "his time" of the deed he has done, as it is written: "He has made every thing beautiful in its time." He is therefore "like the birds that are caught in the snare." Happy then are those who are occupied in the study of the Torah, who know the ways and roads of the Torah of the most High King, because they can walk in it on the path of truth.

57. וְתָא חֲזֵי, לְעוֹלָם אַל יִפְתַּח בַּר נַשׁ פּוּמֵיהּ לְבִישׁ, דְּאִיהוּ לָא יָדַע מַאן נָטֵיל הַהִיא מִלָּה, וְכַד לָא יָדַע בַּר נָשׁ אִתְכְּשַׁל בָּהּ, וְצַדִּיקַיָּא כַּד פָּתְחֵי פּוּמַיְיהוּ כֻּלְּהוּ שְׁלָם. תָּא חֲזֵי, יוֹסֵף כַּד שָׁרָא לְמַלָּלָא לְפַרְעֹה, מַה כְּתִיב, אֱלֹהִים יַעֲנֶה אֶת שְׁלוֹם פַּרְעֹה. אֲמַר רִבִּי יְהוּדָה, הָא אִתְּמָר, דְּקוּדְשָׁא בְּרִיךְ הוּא חָס עַל שְׁלָמָא דְמַלְכוּתָא, כד"א וַיְצַוֵּם אֶל בְּנֵי יִשְׂרָאֵל וְאֶל פַּרְעֹה מֶלֶךְ מִצְרַיִם וְאוֹקְמוּהָ.

57. Come and behold: A man should never open his mouth to speak evil, for he knows not who receives his word, and when a man does not know, he may stumble. When the righteous open their mouths, they do so peacefully. When Joseph addressed Pharaoh, he first said, "Elohim shall give Pharaoh an answer of peace." Rabbi Yehuda said: We have learned that the Holy One, blessed be He, cares for the peace of the kingdom, as it is written: "and He gave them a charge to the children of Yisrael, and to Pharaoh the king of Egypt" (Shemot 6:13). And they explained it, MEANING TO GIVE HONOR TO PHARAOH.

5. "Since Elohim has shown you all this"

A Synopsis

Here the Zohar speculates on the hidden meaning of Joseph's successful interpretation of Pharaoh's dream, and the resulting prosperity for both himself and the people of Israel. The rabbis compare Joseph's experience to that of Daniel in Babylon. They proceed to describe Joseph's work as Pharaoh's Minister of Agriculture and Minister of Finance, and praise his wisdom and discretion in both posts. An interesting passage concerns God's ability to create demand in order to benefit those who are able to supply.

The Relevance of this Passage

A reading of this section helps us to recognize the links between causes and effects, and to govern our actions accordingly. In this way, when life makes demands on us, we can know they are only for our benefit.

58. רִבִּי חִיָּיא אֲמַר, פַּרְעֹה בָּעָא לְנַסָּאָה לֵיהּ לְיוֹסֵף, וְאַחְלַף לֵיהּ חֶלְמָא, וְיוֹסֵף בְּגִין דַּהֲוָה יָדַע דַּרְגִּין, אִסְתַּכַּל בְּכָל מִלָּה וּמִלָּה, וַאֲמַר כָּךְ חֲמֵיתָא, כָּל מִלָּה וּמִלָּה כִּדְקָא חָזֵי.

58. Rabbi Chiya said: Pharaoh wished to test Joseph and therefore mixed THE EVENTS OF his dream, but Joseph, who recognized the grades ALLUDED TO IN THE DREAM, looked into each matter and said: You have seen it this way and ARRANGED everything in a proper manner.

59. הה"ד, וַיֹּאמֶר פַּרְעֹה אֶל יוֹסֵף אַחֲרֵי הוֹדִיעַ אֱלֹהִים אוֹתְךָ אֶת כָּל זֹאת אֵין נָבוֹן וְחָכָם כָּמוֹךָ. אַחֲרֵי הוֹדִיעַ אֱלֹהִים, אַחֲרַי הֲוֵית בְּהַהִיא שַׁעְתָּא דַּחֲלָמִית חֶלְמָא, תַּמָּן הֲוֵית שְׁכִיחַ. וּבְגִין כָּךְ אֲמַר אֶת כָּל זֹאת יָדַעְתְּ חֶלְמָא הֵיךְ הֲוָה וְיָדַעְתְּ פִּשְׁרֵיהּ.

59. It is written: "And Pharaoh said to Joseph, 'Since Elohim has shown you all this, there is none so discreet and wise as you are.'" The phrase, "since Elohim has shown you" MEANS because you were there when I had this dream. Therefore, he said "all this," because you knew the dream and its interpretation.

60. אָמַר רָבִּי יִצְחָק, אִי הָכֵי יוֹסֵף אֲמַר כֹּלָּא, חֶלְמָא וּפִשְׁרָא, כְּדָנִיֵּאל

דַּאֲמַר חֶלְמָא וּפִשְׁרֵיהּ. אָמַר לוֹ לָאו הַאי כְּהַאי, יוֹסֵף אִסְתַּכַּל מִגּוֹ מִלּוּלָא דְפַרְעֹה, דַּהֲוָה אֲמַר בְּדַרְגִּין יְדִיעָן, וְחָמָא לֵיהּ דְּקָא טָעָה, וְאָמַר לוֹ לָאו הָכֵי, אֶלָּא הָכֵי הוּא, בְּגִין דְּדַרְגִּין כְּסִדְרָן אַתְיָין. אֲבָל דָּנִיֵּאל, לָא אִסְתַּכַּל מִגּוֹ מִלּוּלָא דִּנְבוּכַדְנֶצַּר כְּלוּם. וְכֹלָּא קָאֲמַר לֵיהּ חֶלְמָא וּפִשְׁרֵיהּ.

60. Rabbi Yitzchak said: If this be so, then Joseph told everything – the dream and its interpretation – just like Daniel, who told the dream and its interpretation. He said to him, There is no resemblance between the cases. Joseph looked into the words of Pharaoh, who told THE CONTENT OF HIS DREAM through certain grades, and saw he was mistaken BECAUSE HE TOLD IT NOT ACCORDING TO THE ORDER THAT PREVAILS IN THE GRADES OF THAT DREAM. He said to Pharaoh, You have not seen it this way but rather that way, for the grades have a particular order. Daniel, on the other hand, did not derive anything from Nebuchadnezzar, but rather told him everything, the dream and its interpretation.

61. מַה כְּתִיב בְּדָנִיֵּאל, אֱדַיִן לְדָנִיֵּאל בְּחֶזְוָא דִי לֵילְיָא רָזָא גְּלִי. בְּחֶזְוָא דִי לֵילְיָא, מַאן חֶזְוָא דִי לֵילְיָא, דָּא גַּבְרִיאֵל, דְּאִיהוּ חֶזְוָא חֵיזוּ מִן חֵיזוּ.

61. In relation to Daniel, the verse says: “Then was the secret revealed to Daniel in a night vision” (Daniel 2:19). HE ASKS: What is the “night vision?” HE REPLIES: It is Gabriel, who is a vision, a vision from a vision.

62. תָּא חֲזֵי, מַה כְּתִיב וְהִנֵּה כְּבוֹד אֱלֹקֵי יִשְׂרָאֵל בָּא מִדֶּרֶךְ הַקָּדִים וְקוֹלוֹ כְּקוֹל מַיִם רַבִּים. וְהָאָרֶץ הֵאִירָה מִכְּבוֹדוֹ, מַה כְּתִיב בַּתְרֵיהּ, וּכְמַרְאֵה הַמַּרְאֶה אֲשֶׁר רָאִיתִי בְּבֹאִי לְשַׁחֵת אֶת הָעִיר וּמַרְאוֹת כַּמַּרְאֶה אֲשֶׁר רָאִיתִי עַל נְהַר כְּבָר וָאֶפֹּל עַל פָּנָי. כָּל אִלֵּין מַרְאוֹת, אִינוּן שִׁית, דְּאִינוּן מַרְאוֹת, וְחֵיזוּ דְּחֶזְוָא, חֵיזוּ אִית לֵיהּ, לְאִתְחֲזָאָה בֵּיהּ גְּוָונִין דִּלְעֵילָא, וְאִתְחֲזוּן בְּהַהוּא חֵיזוּ, וְאִית חֵיזוּ לְחֵיזוּ, וְחֵיזוּ לְחֵיזוּ, דָּא עַל דָּא, וְכֻלְּהוּ קַיְימִין בְּדַרְגִּין יְדִיעָן וְשָׁלְטֵי, וְאִקְרוּן חֵיזוּ דְּלֵילְיָא, וּבְהוֹ מִתְפָּרְשִׁין כָּל חֶלְמִין דְּעָלְמָא, וְאִלֵּין אִינוּן כְּגַוְונָא דִּלְעֵילָא, עֲלַיְיהוּ.

62. Come and behold: It is written, "and behold the glory of the Elohim of Yisrael came from the way of the east: and His voice was like the sound of many waters: and the earth shone with His glory" (Yechezkel 43:2). This is followed by: "And the appearance of the earth shone with His glory. And the appearance of the vision which I saw was like the vision that I saw when I came to destroy the city: and the visions were like the vision that I saw by the river K'var, and I fell upon my face" (Yechezkel 43:3). All the visions MENTIONED IN THE VERSE correspond to six grades, which are visions. The vision of a vision, GABRIEL, has a mirror that reflects the upper hues. Thus, THE SIX MIRRORS OF THE NUKVA reflected in this mirror, GABRIEL. There are visions upon visions; every vision is on top of another and all within certain grades – CHESED, GVURAH, TIFERET, NETZACH, HOD AND YESOD – where they have dominion by the name of "night vision." All the dreams in the world are interpreted through them. They resemble those above them, THE SIX VISIONS OF THE NUKVA.

63. וּבְגִין כָּךְ, דָּנִיֵּאל בְּחֶזְוָא דְלֵילְיָא רָזָא גֲלִי. אִתְגְּלֵי לָא כְתִיב, אֶלָּא רָזָא גֲלִי, חַד מֵאִלֵּין דַּרְגִּין, גַּלֵּי לֵיהּ הַהוּא חֶלְמָא וּפִשְׁרֵיהּ. אֲבָל יוֹסֵף, מִגּוֹ מִלּוֹי דְפַרְעֹה, אִסְתַּכַּל בְּדַרְגִּין עִלָּאִין וְקָאֲמַר.

63. To Daniel, though "the secret revealed...in a night vision," he did not find it himself. Once the secret had been revealed, one of the grades of the "night vision" told him of the dream and its interpretation. But Joseph, from the words of Pharaoh, beheld the high grades TO WHICH THE DREAM ALLUDED, and revealed ITS INTERPRETATION TO PHARAOH.

64. וּבְגִין כָּךְ פַּקְדֵיהּ עַל כָּל אַרְעָא דְמִצְרַיִם, בְּגִין דְּקוּדְשָׁא בְּרִיךְ הוּא, מִדִּילֵיהּ דְּיוֹסֵף קָא יָהֵיב לֵיהּ, פּוּמָא דְלָא נָשַׁק לַעֲבֵירָה, כְּתִיב וְעַל פִּיךָ יִשַּׁק כָּל עַמִּי. יְדָא דְלָא קָרֵיב לַעֲבֵירָה, כְּתִיב וַיִּתֵּן אוֹתָהּ עַל יַד יוֹסֵף. צַוָּאר דְּלָא קָרֵיב לַעֲבֵירָה, כְּתִיב וַיָּשֶׂם רְבִיד הַזָּהָב עַל צַוָּארוֹ. גּוּפָא דְלָא קָרֵיב לַעֲבֵירָה, וַיַּלְבֵּשׁ אֹתוֹ בִּגְדֵי שֵׁשׁ. רֶגֶל דְּלָא רָכֵיב לַעֲבֵירָה, כְּתִיב וַיַּרְכֵּב אֹתוֹ בְּמִרְכֶּבֶת הַמִּשְׁנֶה אֲשֶׁר לוֹ. הַמַּחֲשָׁבָה דְּלָא חָשַׁב, נִקְרָא נָבוֹן וְחָכָם. לֵב שֶׁלֹּא הִרְהֵר, וַיִּקְרְאוּ לְפָנָיו אַבְרֵךְ. וְכֹלָּא מִדִּילֵיהּ נָטַל.

64. PHARAOH, therefore, gave him command over the whole land of Egypt, because the Holy One, blessed be He, gave Joseph from his own. Because his mouth did not kiss transgression, it is said: "according to your mouth shall my people be ruled" (Beresheet 41:40). Because his hand did not come near sinning, it is written: "and put it on Joseph's hand." Because the neck did not approach sin, it is written: "and put a gold chain about his neck." Because the body did not get nigh sin, it is written: "arrayed him in garments of fine linen." Because the foot did not ride to transgression, it is written: "he made him to ride in the second chariot which he had." Because his mind did not harbor SINFUL thought, he was called "discreet and wise" and because his heart did not reflect UPON SIN, "they cried before him *Avrech* (lit. 'bow the knee')." He received what was properly his.

65. מַה כְּתִיב, וַיֵּצֵא יוֹסֵף מִלִּפְנֵי פַרְעֹה וַיַּעֲבֹר בְּכָל אֶרֶץ מִצְרָיִם. אָמַר רִבִּי חִזְקִיָּה, מַאי טַעְמָא וַיַּעֲבוֹר בְּכָל אֶרֶץ מִצְרַיִם. בְּגִין לְשַׁלְטָאָה, דְּמַכְרְזֵי קַמֵּי הָכֵי, וּבְגִין לְמִכְנַשׁ עִבּוּרָא, בְּכָל אֲתַר וַאֲתַר. רִבִּי אֶלְעָזָר אֲמַר, כְּנַשׁ יוֹסֵף עִיבּוּר, בְּכָל אֲתַר, בְּגִין דְּלָא יִתְרַקַּב.

65. It is written, "And Joseph went out from the presence of Pharaoh and went through all the land of Egypt." Rabbi Chizkiah asks: Why did he go through all the land of Egypt? HE ANSWERS, He did so to establish his rule OVER THEM, by their crying before him *AVRECH*. Another reason was to gather grain from every district. Rabbi Elazar said: Joseph gathered the grain of every district, "THE FOOD OF THE FIELD, WHICH WAS ROUND ABOUT EVERY CITY, LAID HE UP WITHIN IT," AND NOT IN ANOTHER PLACE so it would not rot, FOR IT IS THE NATURE OF A PLACE TO PRESERVE ITS FRUIT.

66. אֲמַר רִבִּי שִׁמְעוֹן, כָּל מַה דַּעֲבַד קוּדְשָׁא בְּרִיךְ הוּא, כֹּלָּא אִיהוּ לְגַלְגְּלָא גִּלְגּוּלִין, בְּגִין דְּבָעֵי לְקָיְימָא קִיּוּמָא. תָּא חֲזֵי, כַּד בָּרָא קוּדְשָׁא בְּרִיךְ הוּא עָלְמָא, אַיְיתֵי כָּל מַה דְּאִצְטְרִיךְ עַלְמָא בְּקַדְמֵיתָא, וּלְבָתַר אַיְיתֵי לֵיהּ לְבַר נָשׁ לְעַלְמָא, וְאַשְׁכַּח מְזוֹנָא.

66. Rabbi Shimon said: The Holy One, blessed be He, created everything in such a manner AS TO BENEFIT YISRAEL. This He did because He wanted to fulfill His promise. Come and behold: When the Holy One, blessed be He, created the world, first He supplied it with its needs, and then He put man in it and gave him sustenance.

67. כְּגַוְונָא דָא, קוּדְשָׁא בְּרִיךְ הוּא אֲמַר לְאַבְרָהָם, יָדוֹעַ תֵּדַע כִּי גֵּר יִהְיֶה זַרְעֲךָ בְּאֶרֶץ לֹא לָהֶם וגו׳, וְאַחֲרֵי כֵן יֵצְאוּ בִּרְכוּשׁ גָּדוֹל, כַּד אָתָא יוֹסֵף לְאַרְעָא דְמִצְרַיִם, לָא אִשְׁתְּכַח בָּהּ רְכוּשׁ גָּדוֹל, גִּלְגֵּל גִּלְגּוּלִין, וְאַיְיתֵי כַּפְנָא עַל עַלְמָא, וְכָל עַלְמָא הֲווֹ מַיְיתִין כַּסְפָּא וְדַהֲבָא לְמִצְרַיִם, וְאִתְמְלֵי כָּל אַרְעָא דְמִצְרַיִם כַּסְפָּא וְדַהֲבָא. לְבָתַר דְּאִתְתַּקַּן כֹּלָּא רְכוּשׁ גָּדוֹל, אַיְיתֵי יַעֲקֹב לְמִצְרַיִם.

67. Similarly, the Holy One, blessed be He, said to Abraham, "Know surely that your seed shall be a stranger in a land that is not theirs...and afterwards shall they come out with great substance" (Beresheet 15:13-14). When Joseph arrived in Egypt, there was no great substance in it. TO CORRECT THIS, THE HOLY ONE, BLESSED BE HE, brought famine upon the world. People then brought silver and gold to Egypt until the land of Egypt was filled with silver and gold. After great substance was acquired, He brought Jacob to Egypt.

68. דְּהָכֵי אָרְחֵי דְקוּדְשָׁא בְּרִיךְ הוּא, בְּקַדְמֵיתָא בָּארֵי אַסְוָותָא, וּלְבָתַר מָחֵי, כָּךְ בְּקַדְמֵיתָא אַתְקִין רְכוּשׁ גָּדוֹל, וּלְבָתַר אַיְיתֵי לוֹן לְגָלוּתָא, וְע״ד גִּלְגֵּל גִּלְגּוּלִין, וְאַיְיתֵי כַּפְנָא עַל כָּל עַלְמָא, בְּגִין דְּלֵיהֱוֵי מַיְיתִין כַּסְפָּא וְדַהֲבָא כָּל עַלְמָא לְמִצְרַיִם.

68. These are the ways of the Holy One, blessed be he: He first creates the medicine and then inflicts the wound. First He brought great substance TO EGYPT, and then He brought them into exile. He arranged matters and brought famine upon the whole world so that people would bring silver and gold from all over the world into Egypt.

69. תָּא חֲזֵי, בְּגִין יוֹסֵף דְּאִיהוּ צַדִּיק, אִיהִי גָּרֵים עוֹתְרָא כַּסְפָּא וְדַהֲבָא, לְנַטְלָא יִשְׂרָאֵל, כְּדִכְתִיב וַיּוֹצִיאֵם בְּכֶסֶף וְזָהָב וְאֵין בִּשְׁבָטָיו כּוֹשֵׁל. וּמִן יְדָא דְצַדִּיק אָתָא דָא לְיִשְׂרָאֵל, וְכֹלָּא לְמִזְכֵּי לוֹן לְעַלְמָא דְאָתֵי.

69. Come and behold: For the sake of the righteous Joseph, He caused Yisrael to obtain riches – silver and gold – as it is written, "He brought them forth also with silver and gold: and there was not one who stumbled among their tribes" (Tehilim 105:37). This came upon Yisrael by the hand of a righteous man, all in order to make them merit the World to Come.

70. פָּתַח וַאֲמַר רְאֵה חַיִּים עִם אִשָּׁה אֲשֶׁר אָהַבְתָּ וגו׳. תָּא חֲזֵי, הַאי קְרָא בְּרָזָא עִלָּאָה אִיהוּ, וְאוּקְמוּהָ. רְאֵה חַיִּים: אִלֵּין חַיִּין דְעַלְמָא דְאָתֵי, דְזַכָּאָה הוּא בַּר נָשׁ דְזָכֵי בֵיהּ כִּדְקָא יָאוּת.

70. He opened the discussion with the verse: "Live joyfully with the wife whom you love" (Kohelet. 9:9). Come and behold: This verse is explained according to a supernal secret; thus, "live joyfully (lit. 'see a life')" alludes to life in the World to Come, for happy is he who merits it as he should.

71. עִם אִשָּׁה אֲשֶׁר אָהַבְתָּ: דָא כְּנֶסֶת יִשְׂרָאֵל, בְּגִין דְבָהּ כְּתִיב אַהֲבָה, דִכְתִיב וְאַהֲבַת עוֹלָם אֲהַבְתִּיךְ, אֵימָתַי. בְּשַׁעְתָּא דְסִטְרָא דִימִינָא אָחֵיד בָהּ, דִכְתִיב עַל כֵּן מְשַׁכְתִּיךְ חָסֶד.

71. The phrase, "with the wife whom you love," refers to the Congregation of Yisrael, which is referred to with love in, "I have loved you with an everlasting love" (Yirmeyah 31:3). When is that? At the time the right side takes hold of it, as it is written: "Therefore with Chesed have I drawn you" (Ibid.), CHESED BEING THE RIGHT SIDE.

72. כָּל יְמֵי חַיֵּי הֶבְלֶךָ, בְּגִין דְאִיהִי אִתְקַשְּׁרַת בַּחַיִּים, וְאִיהִי עוֹלָם דְחַיִּין שָׁרְיָין בֵּיהּ. דְהָא עַלְמָא דָא, לָא שַׁרְיָין בֵּיהּ חַיִּים, בְּגִין דְאִינוּן תַּחַת הַשֶּׁמֶשׁ, וְלָא מָטְאוּ הָכָא אִינוּן נְהוֹרִין דְהַהוּא שִׁמְשָׁא, וְאִסְתַּלָּקוּ מֵעַלְמָא, מִיּוֹמָא דְאִתְחָרֵיב בֵּי מַקְדְשָׁא, דִכְתִיב חָשַׁךְ הַשֶּׁמֶשׁ בְּצֵאתוֹ וגו׳. מַאי חָשַׁךְ הַשֶּׁמֶשׁ, דְסָלֵיק נְהוֹרֵיהּ, וְלָא נָהֵיר, כד״א הַצַּדִיק אָבַד וגו׳.

72. The verse continues with "all the days of the life of your vanity." This is because she, THE NUKVA, CALLED THE CONGREGATION OF YISRAEL

WHEN IN GREATNESS, is attached to life, NAMELY TO BINAH CALLED LIFE, which is a world full of life. For this world, THE NUKVA, is without life OF ITS OWN, being beneath the sun, ZEIR ANPIN. THUS, IT IS CALLED "LIFE OF VANITY." But the rays of the sun do not reach this world; they have been gone from this world since the day the Temple was destroyed, as it is written, "the sun shall be darkened in his going forth" (Yeshayah 13:10). Its light has gone UP and does not shine BELOW, as it is written: "The righteous perishes..." (Yeshayah 57:1). THIS REFERS TO YESOD OF ZEIR ANPIN, WHICH POURS PLENTY DOWN INTO THIS WORLD, THE NUKVA. THERE IS NEED, THEREFORE, TO DRAW LIFE TO HER FROM BINAH.

73. כִּי הוּא חֶלְקְךָ בַּחַיִּים, דָּא הוּא שִׁמְשָׁא בְּסִיהֲרָא, וּבְעִינָן לְמֵיעַל סִיהֲרָא בְּשִׁמְשָׁא וְשִׁמְשָׁא בְּסִיהֲרָא, דְּלָא לְאַפְרְשָׁא לוֹן, וְדָא הוּא חוּלָקָא דְּבַר נָשׁ, לְמֵיעַל בְּהוֹ לְעַלְמָא דְּאָתֵי.

73. The verse concludes with: "for that is your portion in life" (Kohelet 9:9), MEANING THE UNION BETWEEN the sun, ZEIR ANPIN, and the moon, THE NUKVA. THE NUKVA IS CALLED PORTION AND THE LIGHT OF THE SUN, LIFE. The sun should come into the moon and the moon into the sun, and they must not be separated. It is a man's responsibility TO EFFECT BY HIS ACTIONS THE SUPERNAL UNION, to come to them in the World to Come.

74. מַה כְּתִיב בַּתְרֵיהּ, כֹּל אֲשֶׁר תִּמְצָא יָדְךָ לַעֲשׂוֹת בְּכֹחֲךָ עֲשֵׂה כִּי אֵין מַעֲשֶׂה וְחֶשְׁבּוֹן וְדַעַת וְחָכְמָה בִּשְׁאוֹל אֲשֶׁר אַתָּה הוֹלֵךְ שָׁמָּה, הַאי קְרָא אִית לְאִסְתַּכְּלָא בֵּיהּ, כֹּל אֲשֶׁר תִּמְצָא יָדְךָ לַעֲשׂוֹת, וְכִי הוּתְּרָה רְצוּעָה, לְמֶעְבַּד בַּר נָשׁ כָּל מַה דְּיָכִיל. אֶלָּא, לַעֲשׂוֹת בְּכֹחֲךָ כְּתִיב, מַאי בְּכֹחֲךָ. דָּא נִשְׁמָתֵיהּ דְּבַר נָשׁ, דְּאִיהִי חֵילָא דְּבַר נָשׁ, לְמִזְכֵּי בָהּ לְעַלְמָא דֵין, וּלְעַלְמָא דְּאָתֵי.

74. The verse is followed by the words, "Whatever your hand finds to do, do it with your strength, for there is no work, nor device, nor knowledge, nor wisdom, in Sheol, where you go" (Kohelet 9:10). We have to study the verse, which reads: "Whatever your hand finds to do." Is there no longer any fear of punishment? Can a man do whatever he wishes and is able to do? HE ANSWERED, It is written: "Do it with your strength." Your strength is man's soul, which gives him strength to merit this world and the World to Come.

75. דָּבָר אֲחֵר בְּכֹחֲךָ: דָּא הִיא אִשָּׁה דְקָאֲמָרָן, דְּאִיהִי חֵילָא לְאִתְתַּקְּפָא בָּהּ, בְּעַלְמָא דֵין, וּבְעַלְמָא דְאָתֵי, וּבָעֵי בַּר נָשׁ לְמִזְכֵּי בָהּ בְּהַאי עַלְמָא, בְּהַאי חֵילָא, בְּגִין דְּיִתְתַּקַּף בָּהּ בְּהַהוּא עַלְמָא.

75. Another explanation is that "your strength" is the wife we mentioned, THE CONGREGATION OF YISRAEL, who is a source of strength in this world and the World to Come. A man should merit this world by means of that strength, so he will be able to draw strength from it in the World to Come.

76. מַאי טַעְמָא. בְּגִין דִּלְבָתַר דְּיִפּוֹק בַּר נָשׁ מֵהַאי עַלְמָא, לֵית בֵּיהּ חֵילָא לְמֶעְבַּד מִדֵּי, וְלוֹמַר הַשְׁתָּא מִכָּאן וּלְהָלְאָה אַעֲבֵיד עוֹבָדִין טָבִין, דְּוַדַּאי אֵין מַעֲשֶׂה וְחֶשְׁבּוֹן וְדַעַת וְחָכְמָה בִּשְׁאוֹל אֲשֶׁר וגו׳. אִי לָא זָכֵי בַּר נָשׁ בְּהַאי עַלְמָא, לָא יִזְכֵּי בֵיהּ לְבָתַר בְּהַהוּא עַלְמָא, וְאוּקְמוּהָ מַאן דְּלָא אַתְקִין זְוָודִין לְמֵיהַךְ מֵהַאי עַלְמָא, לָא יֵיכוּל בְּהַהוּא עַלְמָא, וְאִית עוֹבָדִין טָבִין דְּעָבֵיד בַּר נָשׁ בְּהַאי עַלְמָא, דְּיֵיכוּל מִנַּיְיהוּ הָכָא, וְכֹלָּא אִשְׁתָּאַר לְעַלְמָא דְאָתֵי, וּלְאִתְזְנָא מִנַּיְיהוּ.

76. Why DO WE HAVE TO STRENGTHEN OURSELVES WITH GOOD DEEDS IN THIS WORLD? Because after a man leaves this world, he has no more power to do anything. He cannot say, from now on I will perform good deeds. Assuredly, this is true "for there is no work, nor device, nor knowledge, nor wisdom, in Sheol" and if a man does not acquire merit in this world he will not do so in the World to Come. It has been explained that "he who has not laid up provisions for the journey from this world will have nothing to eat in the other world." There are some good deeds a man does in this world, whose fruit he may enjoy here in this world, but the main reward is sustenance in the World to Come.

77. תָּא חֲזֵי, יוֹסֵף זָכָה בְּהַאי עַלְמָא, וְזָכָה בְּעַלְמָא דְאָתֵי, בְּגִין דְּבָעָא לְאִתְאַחֲדָא בְּאִשָּׁה יִרְאַת יי׳, כד״א וְחָטָאתִי לֵאלֹהִים, וּבְגִין כָּךְ זָכָה

לְמִשְׁלַט בְּהַאי עָלְמָא, וְזָכָה לוֹן לְיִשְׂרָאֵל.

77. Come and behold: Joseph merited this world and merited the World to Come, because he wished to be united with a wife who feared Hashem, THE NUKVA, THE SECRET OF THIS WORLD, as it is written, "and sin against Elohim" (Beresheet 39:9), THE NUKVA CALLED ELOHIM. He, therefore, deserved to be ruler over this world and to cause Yisrael to acquire merit.

78. מַה כְּתִיב וַיְלַקֵּט יוֹסֵף אֶת כָּל הַכֶּסֶף, וְהָכֵי אִתְחֲזֵי, דְּהָא הַהוּא נָהָר דְנָגֵיד וְנָפֵיק, אִיהוּ לָקֵיט כֹּלָּא, וְכָל עוֹתְרָא בֵּיהּ קָיְימָא. וְדָא הִיא רָזָא דִכְתִיב, וַיִּתֵּן אוֹתָם אֱלֹהִים בִּרְקִיעַ הַשָּׁמַיִם, וְכֹלָּא אִיהוּ כִּדְקָא יָאוֹת, וַדַּאי יוֹסֵף בָּעֵי לְמִשְׁלַט עַל מַלְכוּתָא.

78. It is written: "And Joseph gathered all the money" (Beresheet 47:14). So it should be, for the river which flows FROM EDEN, YESOD CALLED JOSEPH, gathers everything, BY COMPRISING AND RECEIVING FROM ALL THE SFIROT, and comprises all kinds of riches. This is the secret of the verse: "And Elohim set them in the firmament of heaven" (Beresheet 1:17), FOR YESOD, CALLED FIRMAMENT, SHINES ON THE EARTH, THE SECRET OF THE NUKVA. All is as it should be, for surely Joseph, THE SECRET OF YESOD, should rule over the kingdom (Malchut,) THE NUKVA, AND SHOWER ABUNDANCE UPON HER.

79. וְתָא חֲזֵי, כְּתִיב וַיַּרְכֵּב אוֹתוֹ בְּמִרְכֶּבֶת הַמִּשְׁנֶה, מַאן מִרְכֶּבֶת הַמִּשְׁנֶה. קוּדְשָׁא בְּרִיךְ הוּא עָבֵיד לֵיהּ לַצַּדִּיק שַׁלִּיטָא, בְּגִין דְּהָא מִנֵּיהּ אִתְּזַן עָלְמָא, וְאִצְטְרִיךְ לְאִתְזָנָא, וְקוּדְשָׁא בְּרִיךְ הוּא אִית לֵיהּ רְתִיכָא עִלָּאָה, וְאִית לֵיהּ רְתִיכָא תַּתָּאָה, רְתִיכָא תַּתָּאָה אִיהִי מִרְכֶּבֶת הַמִּשְׁנֶה, וְיוֹסֵף צַדִּיק אִקְרֵי וְלֵיהּ אִתְחֲזֵי לְמֶהֱוֵי רָכֵיב עַל מִרְכֶּבֶת הַמִּשְׁנֶה אֲשֶׁר לוֹ לְקוּדְשָׁא בְּרִיךְ הוּא, וְכֹלָּא אִיהוּ בְּרָזָא עִלָּאָה, לְמֶהֱוֵי כְּגַוְונָא דִלְעֵילָא.

79. Come and behold the verse: "And he made him to ride in the second chariot which he had." HE ASKS: What is the second chariot? HE REPLIED: The Holy One, blessed be He, made the righteous governor because the world, THE NUKVA, is and should be sustained by him. The Holy One, blessed be He, has an upper Chariot – CHESED, GVURAH, TIFERET AND MALCHUT ABOVE THE CHEST OF ZEIR ANPIN – and a lower chariot – THE SECRET OF THE NUKVA. The lower Chariot is called the second chariot, and Joseph who is called righteous, NAMELY YESOD, is worthy of riding the second chariot of the Holy One, blessed be He, as everything is in the likeness of the world above.

80. תָּא חֲזֵי, וַיִּקְרְאוּ לְפָנָיו אַבְרֵךְ, מַאי אַבְרֵךְ. קְשִׁירוּ דְּאִתְקַשַּׁר שִׁמְשָׁא בְּסִיהֲרָא, וְכֹלָּא כָּרְעִין לְקָבֵל אֲתַר דָּא. וְנָתוֹן אוֹתוֹ עַל כָּל עַלְמָא, וְכֻלְּהוּ אוֹדָן לְגַבֵּיהּ, וּבְגִין דָּא כֹּלָּא בְּרָזָא עִלָּאָה אִיהוּ.

80. Come and behold: "And they cried before him Avrech." HE ASKS: What is an Avrech? HE ANSWERS, He is the connection between the sun and the moon, THE SECRET OF YESOD, WHICH JOINS ZEIR ANPIN AND THE NUKVA. Everybody kneels to that place, FOR BOWING DURING PRAYER ALLUDES TO YESOD, WHO IS CALLED BLESSED (HEB. *BARUCH*) AND IS CALLED AVRECH AFTER THE KNEELING, WHICH IS DERIVED FROM THE VERSE, "AND HE MADE HIS CAMELS KNEEL (HEB. *VAYAVRECH*)" (BERESHEET 24:11), and he rules over the whole world, THE NUKVA, and all the inhabitants of the world are thankful FOR THE PLENTY IT POURS ON THEM. All then proceeds according to the supreme mystery.

81. תָּא חֲזֵי, קוּדְשָׁא בְּרִיךְ הוּא עָבַד מַלְכוּתָא דְּאַרְעָא, כְּעֵין מַלְכוּתָא דִּרְקִיעָא, וְכֹלָּא דָּא כְּגַוְונָא דָּא. וְכָל מַה דְּאִתְעֲבֵיד בְּאַרְעָא קָיְימָא קַמֵּי קוּדְשָׁא בְּרִיךְ הוּא בְּקַדְמֵיתָא. תָּא חֲזֵי, מַלְכוּתָא קַדִּישָׁא, לָא קַבֵּיל מַלְכוּתָא שְׁלֵימָתָא, עַד דְּאִתְחַבַּר בַּאֲבָהָן, בְּגִין דְּקוּדְשָׁא בְּרִיךְ הוּא עָבַד לָהּ לְמַלְכוּ עִלָּאָה, לְאִתְנַהֲרָא מֵרָזָא דַּאֲבָהָן.

81. Come and behold: The Holy One, blessed be He, created the kingdom of the earth in the likeness of the kingdom of heaven. Thus, the one resembles the other, FOR WHATEVER IS ON EARTH HAS A COUNTERPART ROOT IN HEAVEN. Whatever is manifest on earth appeared first before the Holy One, blessed be He, IN HEAVEN. Come and behold: The holy Malchut did not reach completion until it was united with the Patriarchs, for the Holy One, blessed be He, made the upper Malchut so it would shine from the secret of the fathers.

82. וְכַד יוֹסֵף הַצַּדִּיק נָחַת לְמִצְרַיִם בְּקַדְמֵיתָא, אִיהוּ מָשִׁיךְ לָהּ לִשְׁכִינְתָּא לְבָתַר עִמֵּיהּ, דְּהָא שְׁכִינְתָּא לָא אָזְלָא אֶלָּא בַּתְרָא דְצַדִּיק, וּבְגִין כָּךְ אִתְמְשַׁךְ יוֹסֵף לְמִצְרַיִם בְּקַדְמֵיתָא, וְנָטֵיל כָּל עוּתְרָא דְעַלְמָא כִּדְקָא יָאוּת, וּלְבָתַר נָחֲתַת שְׁכִינְתָּא לְמִצְרַיִם, וְכֻלְּהוּ שִׁבְטִין בַּהֲדָהּ.

82. After Joseph the Righteous, went down to Egypt, he drew the Shechinah to him, for the Shechinah follows only the righteous. Hence, Joseph first went down to Egypt and received all the wealth of the world as he deserved. Then the Shechinah went down to Egypt with all the tribes.

83. וּבְגִינֵי כָּךְ, יוֹסֵף דְּנָטַר לֵיהּ לַבְּרִית, זָכָה לְאִתְעַטְּרָא בְּאַתְרֵיהּ, וְזָכָה לְמַלְכוּתָא דִלְעֵילָא, וּלְמַלְכוּתָא דִלְתַתָּא, וְעַל דָּא כָּל מַאן דְּנָטַר בְּרִית קַדִּישָׁא, כְּאִילוּ קַיֵּים אוֹרַיְיתָא קַדִּישָׁא כּוּלָהּ, דְּהָא בְּרִית שָׁקֵיל כְּכָל אוֹרַיְתָא.

83. By keeping the HOLY Covenant, Joseph merited to be adorned in his place, THAT IS, TO BECOME A CHARIOT TO YESOD OF ZEIR ANPIN, and attained the upper kingdom and the lower kingdom. Whoever guards the Holy Covenant, is considered to be observing the holy Torah in its entirety, for the Covenant corresponds to the whole Torah.

6. "Now Jacob saw that there were provisions in Egypt"

A Synopsis

Rabbi Chiya offers a discourse on the subject of judgment, specifically the manner through which judgment is executed in this physical world. We learn that when a man transgresses, supernal justice – the laws of cause and effect – decrees that an immediate punishment should take place. However, The Creator, ever merciful, carries our burdens for us, and thus, He inserts time into the process, delaying the consequences of our crimes. This temporary postponement gives man the opportunity to repent and atone for his iniquities. Rabbi Shimon then explicates upon the power of sadness, how it banishes the Light of The Creator from our being. It therefore behooves a man to always maintain a positive outlook and pleased perspective, especially during trying times. As the Rabbi Yesa and Rabbi Chizkiah embark on their travels, Rabbi Yesa reveals that every man has a definite and clear-cut spiritual path laid out for him. The Other Side, however, constantly diverts man from his true path so that he ends up traveling treacherous mountains, as opposed to a lush green, sun-soaked valley.

The Relevance of this Passage

When life appears to be calm and waters still, we must realize that The Creator is carrying all of our judgments for us. We should use these moments to repent and proactively uproot our negative traits. We should intensify and/or renew our commitments to the spiritual path before the weight of judgments becomes to great to bear and they come crashing down upon us without warning.

84. וַיַּרְא יַעֲקֹב כִּי יֶשׁ שֶׁבֶר בְּמִצְרַיִם וַיֹּאמֶר יַעֲקֹב לְבָנָיו וגו'. ר' חִיָּיא פָּתַח וַאֲמַר, מַשָּׂא דְבַר יי' עַל יִשְׂרָאֵל נְאֻם יי' נוֹטֶה שָׁמַיִם וְיוֹסֵד אָרֶץ וְיוֹצֵר רוּחַ אָדָם בְּקִרְבּוֹ, הַאי קְרָא אִית לְאִסְתַּכְּלָא בֵּיהּ, מַשָּׂא דְּבַר יי', בְּכָל הַנֵּי אֲתַר דְּקָאֲמַר מַשָּׂא, מַשָּׂא אַמַּאי. אֶלָּא, בְּכָל אֲתַר דְּאִיהוּ עַל דִּינָא דִּשְׁאָר עַמִּין וַאֲמַר מַשָּׂא, לְטַב. בְּכָל אֲתַר דְּאִיהוּ עַל יִשְׂרָאֵל וְאָמַר מַשָּׂא, לְבִישׁ.

84. "Now Jacob saw that there were provisions in Egypt" (Beresheet 42:1). THIS VERSE IS DIFFICULT TO UNDERSTAND, BECAUSE THE SHECHINAH LEFT HIM WHEN JOSEPH WAS SOLD. THEREFORE, HOW COULD HE HAVE SEEN THAT THERE WERE PROVISIONS IN EGYPT? Rabbi Chiya opened the discussion with the verse: "The burden of the word of Hashem concerning Yisrael. The saying of Hashem, who stretches out the heavens and lays the foundation of the earth and forms the spirit of man within him" (Zecharyah 12:1). We have to study this verse carefully. HE ASKS: What is the meaning of burden in the various passages? HE ANSWERS: Whenever the word burden is used in reference to judging other nations, the word has a good meaning; whenever it is used in a reference to Yisrael, it has an evil meaning.

85. בְּכָל אֲתַר דְּאִיהוּ עַל דִּינָא דִשְׁאָר עַמִּין, לְטַב, בְּגִין דְּמַשָּׂא מָטוּלָא אִיהוּ, כִּבְיָכוֹל מָטוּלָא אִיהוּ עֲלֵיהּ דְּקוּדְשָׁא בְּרִיךְ הוּא, שָׁלוֹם דְּעַמִּין עכו"ם, וְכַד אִתְגְּזַר דִּינָא עֲלַיְיהוּ מַעֲבַר מִנֵּיהּ הַהוּא מָטוּלָא דְּאִיהוּ סָבִיל עֲלַיְיהוּ. בְּכָל אֲתַר דְּדִינָא אִתְגְּזַר עֲלַיְיהוּ דְּיִשְׂרָאֵל, וַאֲמַר מַשָּׂא, כִּבְיָכוֹל מָטוּלָא אִיהוּ עֲלֵיהּ דְּקוּדְשָׁא בְּרִיךְ הוּא, וּבְגִין כָּךְ, מַשָּׂא מֵהַאי גִּיסָא, וּמֵהַאי גִּיסָא, מָטוּלָא אִיהוּ.

85. HE EXPLAINED, Wherever it speaks of judging the other nations, the word burden has a good meaning, because it is used literally, for the welfare of the idolatrous nations is a burden to the Holy One, blessed be He. But when judgment is upon them, He removes the burden He assumed for their sake. HENCE, WHEN BURDEN IS MENTIONED IN RELATION TO THEM, IT IS FOR GOOD. Wherever judgment has been pronounced upon Yisrael and the word "burden" is used, it is a burden on the Holy One, blessed be He, TO PUNISH YISRAEL. It is a double burden, BECAUSE IT IS A BURDEN FOR HIM WHEN HE DOES PUNISH THEM AND WHEN HE DOES NOT, IT IS A BURDEN FOR HIM. IF HE DOES NOT PUNISH THEM, THEY WILL REMAIN DEFILED BY SIN; IF HE DOES PUNISH THEM HE IS SORRY FOR THEIR TROUBLES. THEREFORE WHEN "BURDEN" IS MENTION IN REGARD TO THEM, IT IS FOR EVIL.

86. כֵּיוָן דַּאֲמַר נוֹטֶה שָׁמַיִם וְיוֹסֵד אָרֶץ, אַמַּאי אִצְטְרִיךְ וְיוֹצֵר רוּחַ אָדָם בְּקִרְבּוֹ, וְכִי לָא הֲוֵינָא יָדְעֵי, דְּאִיהוּ יוֹצֵר רוּחַ אָדָם, אֶלָּא לְאַחֲזָאָה דַּרְגָּא יְדִיעָא, דְּכָל רוּחִין וְנִשְׁמָתִין דְּעַלְמָא, בְּהַהוּא דַּרְגָּא קַיְימִין.

86. HE ASKS: After the words: "who stretches out the heavens, and lays the foundation of the earth," why is it added, "and forms the spirit of man within him?" Would not we know He "forms the spirit of man within him" IF IT WERE NOT WRITTEN? HE REPLIES: These words point at a certain grade, where all the spirits and souls of the world are found, NAMELY THE NUKVA, WHERE THE SPIRITS AND SOULS ARE, AND FROM WHOM THE LOWER BEINGS RECEIVE.

87. רַבִּי שִׁמְעוֹן אֲמַר, הַאי קְרָא קַשְׁיָא, אִי אֲמַר וְיוֹצֵר רוּחַ אָדָם וְלָא יַתִּיר יָאוֹת, אֲבָל בְּקִרְבּוֹ מַהוּ. אֶלָּא רָזָא אִיהוּ בִּתְרֵין סִטְרִין, דְּהָא מֵהַהוּא נָהָר דְּנָגִיד וְנָפֵיק, מִתַּמָּן נָפְקֵי וּפָרְחֵי נִשְׁמָתִין כֻּלְּהוּ, וְאִתְכְּנִישׁוּ בַּאֲתַר חָד, וְהַהוּא דַּרְגָּא אִיהוּ יוֹצֵר רוּחַ אָדָם בְּקִרְבּוֹ, וְהַאי כְּאִתְּתָא דְאִתְעַבְּרָא מִן דְּכוּרָא, וְהַהוּא וְלָדָא, צָרַת לָהּ בִּמְעָהָא. עַד דְּאִצְטַיֵּיר כֹּלָּא בְּצִיּוּרָא שְׁלִימוּ בִּמְעָהָא, כָּךְ וְיוֹצֵר רוּחַ אָדָם בְּקִרְבּוֹ, בְּקִרְבּוֹ קָיְימָא, עַד דְּאִתְבְּרֵי בַּר נָשׁ בְּעַלְמָא וְיָהֵיב לֵיהּ.

87. Rabbi Shimon said: This verse is difficult. If it said: "forms the spirit of man", it would suffice, but what is the meaning of "within him?" HE ANSWERS, The secret of this verse is on the two sides, YESOD AND THE NUKVA. For from the river, which flows and comes out FROM EDEN, YESOD, all the souls come out and soar into one place, THE NUKVA. That grade, YESOD, "forms the spirit of man within him," WITHIN THE NUKVA, which resembles a woman, who conceives from a man, whose fetus presses her bowels until it is fully formed in her belly. Thus, He "forms the spirit of man within him," WITHIN THE NUKVA, and THE SPIRIT stands there TO BE FORMED until man enters the world, and She gives him THE SPIRIT.

88. דָּבָר אֲחֵר, וְיוֹצֵר רוּחַ אָדָם בְּקִרְבּוֹ, בְּקִרְבּוֹ דְּאָדָם מַמָּשׁ. בְּגִין דְּכַד אִתְבְּרֵי בַּר נָשׁ, וְקוּדְשָׁא בְּרִיךְ הוּא יְהַב לֵיהּ נִשְׁמָתֵיהּ, וְנָפֵיק לַאֲוִירָא דְעַלְמָא, הַהוּא רוּחָא דִּבְגַוֵּיהּ, לָא אַשְׁכַּח גּוּפָא לְאִתְפַּשְּׁטָא בְּגַוֵּיהּ, וְקָיְימָא בְּסִטְרָא חַד בְּגַוֵּיהּ.

88. Another explanation for "forms the spirit of man within him" IS THAT IT MEANS within man himself, NOT IN THE SUPERNAL NUKVA; for when a man is created, the Holy One, blessed be He, provides him with His soul. Only then is he born into the world. The spirit finds that it does not have enough room to expand within the body, so it stands on one side, NAMELY THE RIGHT, INSTEAD OF EXPANDING RIGHT AND LEFT.

89. וְכַד בַּר נָשׁ אִתְפַּשַּׁט גּוּפֵיהּ, הַהוּא רוּחָא אִתְפַּשַּׁט, וְיָהֵיב בֵּיהּ חֵילָא, וְכֵן כְּגַוְונָא דְגוּפָא אִתְרַבֵּי, הָכֵי רוּחָא יָהֵיב חֵילָא בֵּיהּ, לְאִתְתַּקְפָא בַּר נַשׁ בַּהֲדֵיהּ, וּבְגִין כָּךְ יוֹצֵר רוּחַ אָדָם בְּקִרְבּוֹ מַמָּשׁ.

89. When a man's body grows, the spirit also grows and gives it strength. When the body grows, the spirit allots man power with which to strengthen himself. Thus, He indeed "forms the spirit of man within him."

90. וְאִי תֵּימָא יוֹצֵר רוּחַ אָדָם מַהוּ, בְּגִין דְּהַהוּא רוּחָא, אִצְטְרִיךְ חֵילָא דִלְעֵילָא יַתִּיר לְאִסְתַּיְיעָא בַּהֲדֵיהּ, וְעַל דָּא קוּדְשָׁא בְּרִיךְ הוּא אִיהוּ יוֹצֵר רוּחַ אָדָם בְּקִרְבּוֹ, וְיָהֵיב לֵיהּ סִיּוּעָא בְּבַר נָשׁ.

90. You may ask about THE MEANING OF the phrase: "forms the spirit of man within him." HE EXPLAINS, Because the spirit needs additional strength as support from above, the Holy One, blessed be He, "forms the spirit of man within him" and thus enables it TO EXPAND within man.

91. תָּא חֲזֵי, כַּד הַהוּא רוּחָא אִצְטְרִיךְ סִיּוּעָא, כְּגַוְונָא דְּאִיהוּ הַהוּא בַּר נָשׁ, וּכְגַוְונָא דְּהַהוּא גּוּפָא אִתְתַּקַּן, הָכֵי נָמֵי הַהוּא רוּחָא מְתַקְּנִין לֵיהּ, וְאוֹסְפִין לֵיהּ רוּחָא לְאִתְתַּקְּנָא, וְדָא הוּא יוֹצֵר רוּחַ אָדָם בְּקִרְבּוֹ.

91. Come and behold: When that spirit needs help, it is perfected from above in accordance with man's worth and the condition of his body. It is also given an additional spirit, FOR WHOEVER WISHES TO BE PURIFIED IS HELPED. This is the meaning of "forms the spirit of man within him." MAN IS GIVEN AN ADDITIONAL PORTION OF SPIRIT THAT IS ABLE TO EXPAND WITHIN HIS BODY.

92. וְתָא חֲזֵי כֵּיוָן דְּאִתְאֲבֵיד יוֹסֵף מֵאֲבוֹי, יַעֲקֹב אָבֵיד הַהוּא תּוֹסֶפֶת רוּחָא דַּהֲוָה לֵיהּ, וְאִסְתַּלְּקַת מִנֵּיהּ שְׁכִינְתָּא, לְבָתַר מַה כְּתִיב וַתְּחִי רוּחַ יַעֲקֹב אֲבִיהֶם, וְכִי עַד הַשְׁתָּא מִית הֲוָה. אֶלָּא הַהוּא תּוֹסֶפֶת רוּחָא

אִסְתַּלַּק מִנֵּיהּ שְׁכִינְתָּא, וְלָא הֲוָה בְּגַוֵּיהּ, בְּגִין דְּעִצְבוֹנָא דַּהֲוָה בֵּיהּ גָּרְמָא לֵיהּ, לָא הֲוָה רוּחֵיהּ בְּקִיּוּמֵיהּ, וּבְגִין כָּךְ וַתְּחִי רוּחַ יַעֲקֹב אֲבִיהֶם.

92. Come and behold: When Jacob lost Joseph, he lost the additional portion of the spirit that was in him, and the Shechinah departed from him. It is written later: "The spirit of Jacob their father revived" (Beresheet 45:27). HE ASKS: Was he dead until then? HE ANSWERS, Only the additional spirit was gone from him. His sadness caused his spirit to withdraw. The scripture, therefore, reads: "The spirit of Jacob their father revived."

93. וְהָכָא כְּתִיב וַיַּרְא יַעֲקֹב, דְּעַד כְּעָן לָא אִתְבַּשַּׂר, מְנָא הֲוָה יָדַע, אֶלָּא וַיַּרְא יַעֲקֹב, דְּחָמָא לְכָל דָּיְירֵי אַרְעָא דְּאָזְלֵי לְמִצְרַיִם, וּמַיְיתָן עִבּוּרָא.

93. It is written: "Now Jacob saw THAT THERE WERE PROVISIONS IN EGYPT," WHICH MEANS THAT HE SAW IT THROUGH THE HOLY SPIRIT. HE ASKS: But he was not yet informed THAT JOSEPH WAS ALIVE AND THE SHECHINAH WAS STILL GONE FROM HIM. How did he learn THAT THERE WERE PROVISIONS IN EGYPT? HE ANSWERS, "Jacob saw" MEANS THAT he saw the inhabitants of the country go to Egypt and bring provisions; HE DID NOT SEE THROUGH THE MEDIUM OF THE HOLY SPIRIT.

94. ר' יִצְחָק אָמַר, תָּא חֲזֵי, דָּוִד מַלְכָּא, זָכָה לְאִתְחַבְּרָא בַּאֲבָהָן, וְיָרִית דּוּכְתֵּיהּ בְּגַוַּויְיהוּ. הה"ד, אֶבֶן מָאֲסוּ הַבּוֹנִים הָיְתָה לְרֹאשׁ פִּנָּה.

94. Rabbi Yitzchak said: Come and behold: King David deserved to be united with the Patriarchs and inherited a place among them, as it is written, "The stone which the builders rejected has become the head stone of the corner" (Tehilim 118:22). (THE END IS MISSING).

95. ר' יֵיסָא וְר' חִזְקִיָּה הֲווֹ אָזְלֵי מִקַּפּוֹטְקִיָּא לְלוֹד, וַהֲוָה עִמְּהוֹן חַד יוּדָאִי, בְּמָטוֹל דְּקַפְטִירָא דְּחַמְרָא, עַד דַּהֲווֹ אָזְלֵי אֲמַר ר' יֵיסָא לְר' חִזְקִיָּה, אַפְתַּח פּוּמָךְ, וְאֵימָא חַד מִלָּה, מֵאִינּוּן מִילֵּי מַעַלְיָיתָא דְּאוֹרַיְיתָא, דְּאַתְּ אֲמַר בְּכָל יוֹמָא קַמֵּי בּוּצִינָא קַדִּישָׁא.

6. "Now Jacob saw that there were provisions in Egypt"

95. Rabbi Yesa and Rabbi Chizkiah were walking from Cappadocia to Lod with a Jew, who was carrying a skin-bottle of wine. As they were walking, Rabbi Yesa said to Rabbi Chizkiah, Open your mouth and give one of those beautiful expositions on the Torah that you deliver daily before the holy luminary.

96. פְּתַח וַאֲמַר, דְּרָכֶיהָ דַרְכֵי נוֹעַם וְכָל נְתִיבוֹתֶיהָ שָׁלוֹם. דְּרָכֶיהָ דַרְכֵי נֹעַם, אִלֵּין אָרְחִין דְּאוֹרַיְיתָא, דְּמַאן דְּאָזֵיל בְּאָרְחֵי דְאוֹרַיְיתָא, קוּדְשָׁא בְּרִיךְ הוּא אַשְׁרֵי עֲלֵיהּ נְעִימוּתָא דִשְׁכִינְתָּא, דִּי לָא תַעֲדֵי מִנֵּיהּ לְעָלְמִין. וְכָל נְתִיבוֹתֶיהָ שָׁלוֹם, דְּכֻלְּהוּ נְתִיבִין דְּאוֹרַיְיתָא כֻּלְּהוּ שְׁלָם, שְׁלַם לֵיהּ לְעֵילָּא, שְׁלָם לֵיהּ לְתַתָּא, שְׁלָם לֵיהּ בְּעַלְמָא דֵין, שְׁלָם לֵיהּ בְּעַלְמָא דְאָתֵי.

96. He opened the discussion with the verse: "Her ways are ways of pleasantness, and all her paths are peace" (Mishlei 3:17). "Her ways are ways of pleasantness" refers to the ways of the Torah; for whoever walks in them, the Holy One, blessed be He, causes the pleasantness of the Shechinah to rest upon him and never to pass away. "Her paths are peace," for all the paths of the Torah are peaceful. Thus, he enjoys peace above and below – peace in this world and in the World to Come.

97. אֲמַר הַהוּא יוּדָאי, אִיסִּירָא בְּקִיסְטְרָא בְּהַאי קְרָא אִשְׁתַּכַּח, אֲמָרוּ לֵיהּ מְנַיִן לָךְ, אֲמַר לוֹן מֵאַבָּא שְׁמַעְנָא, וְאוֹלִיפְנָא הָכָא בְּהַאי קְרָא מִלָּה. פְּתַח וַאֲמַר, הַאי קְרָא בִּתְרֵין גְּוָונִין אִיהוּ, וּבִתְרֵין סִטְרִין, קָרֵי בֵּיהּ דְּרָכִים, וְקָרֵי בֵּיהּ נְתִיבוֹת, קָרֵי בֵּיהּ נֹעַם, וְקָרֵי בֵּיהּ שָׁלוֹם. מַאן דְּרָכִים, וּמַאן נְתִיבוֹת. מַאן נֹעַם, וּמַאן שָׁלוֹם.

97. The Jew said: This verse is like a coin in the pocket BECAUSE THE HIDDEN MEANING OF THE VERSE CONTAINS A PRECIOUS SECRET. They asked him, How do you know this? He answered, I learned it from my father. He began his exposition. This verse concerns two matters, NAMELY WAYS AND PATHS, and two aspects, NAMELY PLEASANTNESS AND PEACE. HE ASKS: What are ways and what are paths? What is pleasantness and what is peace?

98. אֶלָּא דְּרָכֶיהָ דַרְכֵי נֹעַם. הַיְינוּ דִּכְתִּיב הַנּוֹתֵן בַּיָּם דָּרֶךְ, דְּהָא בְּכָל אֲתַר דְּאִקְרֵי בְּאוֹרַיְיתָא דֶּרֶךְ, הוּא אוֹרַח פְּתִיחָא לְכֹלָּא, כְּהַאי אָרְחָא, דְּאִיהוּ פְּתִיחַ לְכָל בַּר נָשׁ, כָּךְ דְּרָכֶיהָ דַרְכֵי נֹעַם, אִילֵין דְּרָכִים דְּאִינוּן פְּתִיחָן מֵאֲבָהָן, דְּכָרְאן בְּיַמָּא רַבָּא, וְעָאלִין בְּגַוֵּיהּ, וּמֵאִינוּן אוֹרְחִין מִתְפַּתְּחִין לְכָל עֵיבַר וּלְכָל סִטְרֵי עַלְמָא.

98. HE ANSWERS, "Her ways are ways of pleasantness" is referred to in the verse: "who makes a way in the sea" (Yeshayah 43:16), for wherever a way is mentioned in the Torah, it is a way open for all, a MATERIAL way accessible to everybody. Thus, "Her ways are ways of pleasantness" are the ways opened by the fathers, NAMELY, CHESED, GVURAH AND TIFERET CALLED ABRAHAM, ISAAC AND JACOB, who opened them up in the great sea and traversed it. LIGHTS SHINE from them and illuminate every corner across the whole length and breadth of the world.

99. וְהַאי נֹעַם: הוּא נְעִימוּ דְּנָפַק מֵעַלְמָא דְּאָתֵי, וּמֵעַלְמָא דְּאָתֵי נָהֲרִין כָּל בּוּצִינִין, וּמִתְפַּרְשָׁן לְכָל עֵיבַר, וְהַהוּא טִיבוּ וְהַהוּא נְהוֹרָא דְּעַלְמָא דְּאָתֵי, דְּיָנְקִין אֲבָהָן, אִקְרֵי נֹעַם. דָּבָר אֲחֵר, עַלְמָא דְּאָתֵי אִקְרֵי נֹעַם, וְכַד אִתְעַר עַלְמָא דְּאָתֵי, כָּל חֵדוּ, וְכָל טִיבוּ, וְכָל נְהוֹרִין, וְכָל חֵירוּ דְּעַלְמָא אִתְעַר, וּבְגִינֵי כָּךְ אִקְרֵי נֹעַם.

99. The pleasantness is issued from the World to Come, where all the lights shine and diverge in every direction, THAT IS, DIVERGE TO THE THREE COLUMNS – RIGHT, LEFT AND CENTRAL. The goodness and light of the World to Come, which the Patriarchs inherit, are called pleasantness. Another explanation is that the World to Come itself is called pleasantness. When it is aroused TO ILLUMINATE, every joy, goodness, light, and freedom are aroused. Thus, it is called pleasantness.

100. וְעַל דָּא תָּנִינָן, חַיָּיבִין דְּגֵיהִנֹּם, בְּשַׁעְתָּא דְּעָאל שַׁבַּתָּא, נָיְיחִין כֻּלְּהוּ, וְאִית לְהוֹ חֵירוּת וְנַיְיחָא. בְּשַׁעְתָּא דְּנָפֵיק שַׁבַּתָּא, אִית לָן לְאִתְעָרָא חֵידוּ עִלָּאָה עֲלָנָא, דְּנִשְׁתֵּזִיב מֵהַהוּא עוֹנָשָׁא דְחַיָּיבַיָּא דְּאִתְדָּנוּ מֵהַהִיא שַׁעְתָּא וּלְהָלְאָה. וְאִית לָן לְאִתְעָרָא וְלֵימָא, וִיהִי נֹעַם

יי׳ אֱלֹקֵינוּ עָלֵינוּ, דָּא הוּא נֹעַם עִלָּאָה, חֵידוּ דְּכֹלָּא, וְעַל דָּא דְּרָכֶיהָ דַּרְכֵי נֹעַם.

100. We have learned that when Shabbat comes, the wicked in Gehenom take a rest and obtain freedom and respite. At the end of Shabbat, it behooves us to arouse the supernal joy to save us from the punishment of the wicked, who are condemned from that moment onward. We should arise and say, “And let the pleasantness of Hashem our Elohim be upon us” (Tehilim 90:17), which alludes to the supernal pleasantness that cheers everything.

101. וְכָל נְתִיבוֹתֶיהָ שָׁלוֹם, מַאן נְתִיבוֹתֶיהָ. אִלֵּין אִינּוּן שְׁבִילִין דְּנָפְקִין מִלְעֵילָּא, וְכֻלְּהוּ נָקִיט לוֹן בְּרִית יְחִידָאי, דְּאִיהוּ אִקְרֵי שָׁלוֹם, שְׁלָמָא דְּבֵיתָא, וְאָעֵיל לוֹן לְיַמָּא רַבָּא, כַּד אִיהוּ בְּתוֹקְפֵיהּ, וּכְדֵין יָהֵיב לֵיהּ שְׁלָמָא, הה״ד וְכָל נְתִיבוֹתֶיהָ שָׁלוֹם. תָּא חֲזֵי, יוֹסֵף בְּרִית שָׁלוֹם הֲוָה, וַהֲוָה בְּמִצְרַיִם מַלְכָּא, וְשַׁלִּיט עַל אַרְעָא, וְיַעֲקֹב בְּגִין דְּאִסְתַּלַּק מִנֵּיהּ שְׁכִינְתָּא, לָא הֲוָה יָדַע.

101. “And all her paths are peace.” HE ASKS: What are her paths? HE REPLIES: They are the paths that descend from above, gathered by the Covenant, YESOD, which is called peace – household peace. It carries the paths into the great sea when it is agitated, and brings it peace. This is the meaning of the verse: “And all her paths are peace.” Come and behold: Joseph was the Covenant of Peace, THAT IS, HE RECEIVED THESE PATHS and became ruler over the land, but Jacob, from whom the Shechinah departed, did not know it.

102. וְעִם כָּל דָּא, יַעֲקֹב הֲוָה לֵיהּ תַּבְרָא, בְּגִין לְמִזְבַּן עִבּוּרָא בְּמִצְרַיִם, וְחָמָא דְּאִיהוּ תְּבִירָא עַל תְּבִירָא, דְּיֵיחֲתוּן בְּנוֹי לְמִצְרַיִם, וַיֹּאמֶר יַעֲקֹב לְבָנָיו לָמָּה תִּתְרָאוּ, בְּגִין דְּלָא תֶּחֱמוּן גּוּפַיְיכוּ, אֶלָּא כִּרְעֵבִין, כְּגוּבְרִין דְּלֵית לוֹן שַׂבְעָא.

102. Nevertheless, Jacob had misfortune (Heb. *shever*) so he had to buy provisions (Heb. *shever*) in Egypt, and saw misfortune (Heb. *shever*) after misfortune in his sons going down to Egypt. Hence, “Jacob said to his sons,

'Why do you look at one another?'" (Beresheet 42:1); you should show yourselves as hungry people, who have not enough to eat.

103. אָמַר ר' חִזְקִיָּה, וַדַּאי רָזָא הָכָא, דְּהָא בְּכָל זִמְנָא דְּצַעֲרָא אִיהוּ בְּעַלְמָא, לָא בָּעֵי בַּר נָשׁ, לְאַחֲזָאָה גַּרְמֵיהּ בְּשׁוּקָא, בְּגִין דְּלָא יִתְפַּס בְּחוֹבוֹי, וְעַל דָּא אֲמַר לָמָּה תִּתְרָאוּ, וְהָא אִתְּמָר.

103. Rabbi Chizkiah said: Assuredly a mystery lies here, for whenever there is sorrow in the world, a man should refrain from being seen in the marketplace, so as not to be caught for his sins. THIS IS BECAUSE HIS ACCUSERS MIGHT SEE HIM IN A PUBLIC PLACE, ACCUSE HIM, AND REVEAL HIS MISDEEDS IN ORDER TO PUNISH HIM. JACOB therefore asked them, "Why do you look at one another (also: 'why are you afraid')"; IT BEHOOVES YOU TO BE AWARE OF THE ACCUSERS. This has already been explained.

104. דָּבָר אַחֵר וַיַּרְא יַעֲקֹב כִּי יֶשׁ שֶׁבֶר בְּמִצְרַיִם, עִבּוּר מַמָּשׁ, דְּהָא קוּדְשָׁא בְּרִיךְ הוּא ע"ד שַׁדַּר כַּפְנָא בְּעַלְמָא, בְּגִין לְנַחֲתָא לְיַעֲקֹב וּבְנוֹי לְתַמָּן, וְעַל דָּא חָמָא בְּנֵי אַרְעָא, דַּהֲווֹ מַיְיתִין מִתַּמָּן עִבּוּר.

104. Another explanation of the verse: "Now Jacob saw that there were provisions in Egypt" IS THAT THE WORD *SHEVER* MEANS real provisions AND IS NOT AN ALLUSION TO A CALAMITY, AS WAS SAID EARLIER. The Holy One, blessed be He, sent famine into the world to bring Jacob and his sons there. Jacob, therefore, saw the people of the country bringing provitions from there.

105. וַיַּרְא יַעֲקֹב כִּי יֶשׁ שֶׁבֶר בְּמִצְרַיִם, בְּשַׁעְתָּא דְּמִית יִצְחָק, אָתוּ יַעֲקֹב וְעֵשָׂו לְמִפְלַג, וְעֵשָׂו נָפַק מֵחוּלָקֵיהּ דְּאַרְעָא וּמִכֹּלָּא, וְיַעֲקֹב דְּיִסְבּוֹל גָּלוּתָא יִטּוֹל כֹּלָּא, וְעַל דָּא חָמָא, הַהוּא תְּבִירָא דַּהֲוָה לֵיהּ בְּמִצְרַיִם, הוּא וּבְנוֹי, לְמִסְבַּל גָּלוּתָא, וְעַל דָּא וַיֹּאמֶר יַעֲקֹב לְבָנָיו לָמָּה תִּתְרָאוּ. מִקַּמֵּי דִּינָא דִּלְעֵילָּא, דְּלָא יִשְׁתַּכַּח עֲלַיְיכוּ מְקַטְרְגָא. וַיֹּאמֶר הִנֵּה שָׁמַעְתִּי כִּי יֶשׁ שֶׁבֶר בְּמִצְרַיִם רְדוּ שָׁמָּה, הָא אוּקְמוּהָ רד"ו, חוּשְׁבַּן דָּא הֲווֹ יִשְׂרָאֵל בְּמִצְרַיִם.

6. "Now Jacob saw that there were provisions in Egypt"

105. "Now Jacob saw that there were provitions in Egypt." When Isaac died, Jacob and Esau came to divide his inheritance. Esau renounced his share of the land and everything else BY LEAVING AND AVOIDING THE EXILE; Jacob received it all by suffering the exile; THAT IS, THIS WAS THEIR COMPROMISE. Jacob thus saw the calamity awaiting him and his sons in Egypt – the endurance of the exile. This is why Jacob asked his sons, "Why are you afraid" of the supernal justice? ARE YOU NOT AFRAID lest the accuser will find you? "I have heard that there are provitions in Egypt, go down there (Heb. *redu*)." It has already been explain that the numerical value of *redu* is 210, the number of years Yisrael stayed in Egypt.

7. "And Joseph was the governor of the land"

A Synopsis

This passage speculates on the secret meanings of Joseph's triumph in Egypt. It tells us that his victory was also one against the hidden powers of evil on the Left – that is, "the Evil Inclination."

The Relevance of this Passage

Egypt is a metaphor for the human ego, our Evil Inclination, which is rooted in the Left Column. Strength and discipline to triumph over egocentric desires and evil tendencies are summoned forth in our souls as we scan the Hebrew Letters of this passage.

106. וְיוֹסֵף הוּא הַשַּׁלִּיט עַל הָאָרֶץ וגו', ר' יֵיסָא פְּתַח וַאֲמַר, וְעַתָּה יָרוּם רֹאשִׁי עַל אוֹיְבַי סְבִיבוֹתַי וְאֶזְבְּחָה בְאָהֳלוֹ זִבְחֵי תְרוּעָה אָשִׁירָה וַאֲזַמְּרָה לַיי'. תָּא חֲזֵי, כַּד קוּדְשָׁא בְּרִיךְ הוּא אִתְרְעֵי בֵּיהּ בְּבַר נָשׁ, זָקֵיף לֵיהּ עַל כָּל בְּנֵי עַלְמָא, וְעָבֵיד לֵיהּ רֵישָׁא דְכֹלָּא, וְכֻלְּהוּ שָׂנְאוֹי אִתְכַּפְיָין תְּחוֹתוֹי.

106. "And Joseph was the governor of the land." Rabbi Yesa opened the discussion with the verse: "And now shall my head be lifted up above my enemies round about me: therefore I will offer in His tabernacle sacrifices with trumpet sound; I will sing, and I will make melody to Hashem" (Tehilim 27:6). Come and behold: When the Holy One, blessed be He, takes pleasure in a man, He raises him above all the inhabitants of the world and makes him ruler over them. All his enemies are subdued under him.

107. דָּוִד מַלְכָּא, שָׂנְאוּ לֵיהּ אֲחוֹי, דָּחוֹ לֵיהּ מִנַּיְיהוּ, קוּדְשָׁא בְּרִיךְ הוּא אָרֵים לֵיהּ, עַל כָּל בְּנֵי עַלְמָא, אָתָא חֲמוֹי עָרַק מִקַּמֵּיהּ, קוּדְשָׁא בְּרִיךְ הוּא אָרֵים לֵיהּ, עַל כָּל מַלְכוּתֵיהּ, וְכֻלְּהוּ הֲווֹ כָּרְעִין וְסָגְדִין קַמֵּיהּ. וְיוֹסֵף דָּחוּ לֵיהּ אֲחוֹי, לְבָתַר כֻּלְּהוּ כָּרְעוּ וּסְגִידוּ קַמֵּיהּ, הה"ד וַיָּבֹאוּ אֲחֵי יוֹסֵף וַיִּשְׁתַּחֲווּ לוֹ אַפַּיִם אָרְצָה.

107. King David was hated and rejected by his brothers, and the Holy One, blessed be He, raised him above all the inhabitants of the world. He fled from SAUL, his father-in-law, and the Holy One, blessed be He, raised him above all kingdoms, and everyone bowed and knelt before him. Joseph was rejected by his brothers, and afterward they all knelt and prostrated themselves before him, as it is written: "And Joseph's brothers came, and bowed themselves down before him with their faces to the earth" (Beresheet 42:6).

108. דָּבָר אֲחֵר, וְעַתָּה יָרוּם רֹאשִׁי, מַאי וְעַתָּה, כְּמוֹ וְאַתָּה. ר׳ יְהוּדָה אֲמַר, הָא אִתְּמָר, עֵת דְּאִיהוּ דַּרְגָּא עִלָּאָה, וּמַאן אִיהוּ הַהוּא עֵת. דָּא ה״א, וְאִקְרֵי עַתָּה, וְעַתָּה: דָּא אִיהוּ וּבֵי דִינֵיהּ.

108. Another explanations for "And now (Heb. *ve'ata*) shall my head be lifted up." HE ASKS: What is the meaning of *ve'ata*? HE SAYS: That of "as you (Heb. *ve'ata*)." Rabbi Yehuda said: We have learned that *et* (time) is a supernal grade; that time is the *Hei* IN THE NAME YUD HEI VAV HEI, NAMELY THE SHECHINAH called *ata* (now). *Ve'ata* WITH THE LETTER *VAV* refers to ZEIR ANPIN and His court of justice, THE NUKVA, JUST AS THE *VAV* OF *VE'ATA* ALLUDES TO ZEIR ANPIN.

109. יָרוּם רֹאשִׁי, לַאֲרָמָא לָהּ, בִּיקָרָא וּמַלְכוּתָא. עַל אוֹיְבַי סְבִיבוֹתַי, אִלֵּין שְׁאָר מַלְכֵי אַרְעָא. וְאֶזְבְּחָה בְּאָהֳלוֹ, דָּא יְרוּשָׁלַם, בְּאָהֳלוֹ דָּא אֹהֶל מוֹעֵד. זִבְחֵי תְרוּעָה, לְמִשְׁמַע כָּל עַלְמָא. אָשִׁירָה וַאֲזַמְּרָה, מֵהַהוּא סִטְרָא דִתְרוּעָה הִיא, דְּהָא מִתַּמָּן, מֵהַהוּא סִטְרָא דִתְרוּעָה, הִיא אַתְיָא שִׁירָה וְתוּשְׁבַּחְתָּא.

109. "And now shall my head be lifted up." I will lift up my head through dignity and dominion "above my enemies round about me" the other kings of the land. "Therefore I will offer in His tabernacle" refers to Jerusalem; "His tabernacle" SPELLED WITH Vav ALLUDES TO the Tent of Meeting "sacrifices with trumpet sound" that will sound throughout the world; "I will sing, and I will make melody" from the side of the trumpet sound, for from there, song and melody arise.

110. דָּבָר אֲחֵר, וְעַתָּה יָרוּם רֹאשִׁי, דָּא כְּנֶסֶת יִשְׂרָאֵל. עַל אוֹיְבַי סְבִיבוֹתַי, דָּא עֵשָׂו וְכָל אֲפַרְכִין דִּילֵיהּ. וְאֶזְבְּחָה בְּאָהֳלוֹ, אִלֵּין יִשְׂרָאֵל. זִבְחֵי תְרוּעָה, דִּכְתִיב זִבְחֵי אֱלֹקִים רוּחַ נִשְׁבָּרָה, בְּגִין לְאַעֲבָרָא דִינָא

מֵעַלְמָא. אָשִׁירָה וַאֲזַמְּרָה, לְאוֹדָאָה וּלְשַׁבְּחָא לְקוּדְשָׁא בְּרִיךְ הוּא, בְּלָא פְּסִיקוּ לְעוֹלָם.

110. According to another explanation, "And now shall my head be lifted up" refers to the Congregation of Yisrael, NAMELY THE NUKVA CALLED NOW, and the phrase: "Above my enemies round about me" refers to Esau and his ministers. "I will offer in His tabernacle" in THE MIDST OF Yisrael "sacrifices with trumpet sound (also: 'of breaking')," as it is written: "The sacrifices of Elohim are a broken spirit" (Tehilim 51:19), in order to remove Judgment from the world. "I will sing, to make melody" and I will thank the Holy One, blessed be He, continuously, forever.

111. דָּבָר אֲחֵר, וְעַתָּה יָרוּם רֹאשִׁי, בְּכֹלָּא, יֵצֶר טוֹב עַל יֵצֶר רָע, דִּכְתִּיב עַל אוֹיְבַי סְבִיבוֹתַי, דָּא יֵצֶר הָרָע, דְּאִיהוּ סַחֲרָנֵיהּ דְּבַר נָשׁ, וְאִיהוּ שָׂנְאֵיהּ בְּכֹלָּא. וְאֶזְבְּחָה בְאָהֳלוֹ זִבְחֵי תְרוּעָה, דָּא אוֹרַיְיתָא, דְּאִתְיְהִיבַת מִסִּטְרָא דְאֶשָּׁא, כְּדִכְתִּיב מִימִינוֹ אֵשׁ דָּת לָמוֹ, דְּהָא בְּגִין אוֹרַיְיתָא, יָרוּם רֵישֵׁיהּ, וְאִתְּבְרוּ כָּל שָׂנְאוֹי קָדָמוֹי, כְּדִכְתִּיב תַּכְרִיעַ קָמַי תַּחְתָּי.

111. Another explanation of "And now shall my head be lifted up" IS THAT MY HEAD IS AN ALLUSION TO THE GOOD INCLINATION. HE PRAYED that in every respect the Good Inclination SHALL BE LIFTED above the Evil Inclination, as it is written: "Above my enemies round about me", which is an allusion to the Evil Inclination that surrounds and hates man. "I will offer in His tabernacle sacrifices with trumpet sound" refers to THE STUDY OF the Torah, which was given from the side of fire, as it is written: "From His right hand went a fiery law for them" (Devarim 33:2). Through the Torah shall his head be lifted up and his enemies subjugated before him, as it is written: "You have subdued under me those who rose up against me" (Tehilim 18:40).

112. דָּבָר אֲחֵר וְעַתָּה יָרוּם רֹאשִׁי, לְאִתְכְּלָלָא בַּאֲבָהָן, דְּהָא דָּוִד מַלְכָּא, אִית לֵיהּ לְאִתְדַּבָּקָא בַּאֲבָהָן, וּכְדֵין יִתְרוֹמֵם וְסָלֵיק לְעֵילָּא, וְאִיהוּ בְּחַד קְשׁוּרָא בְּהוֹ. עַל אוֹיְבַי סְבִיבוֹתַי, אִלֵּין אִינּוּן דְּבִסְטַר שְׂמָאלָא, כֻּלְּהוּ מָארֵי דִינִין, דְּמִתְכַּוְּנִין לְחַבָּלָא, וּכְדֵין שִׁמְשָׁא אִתְחַבַּר

בְּסִיהֲרָא, וַהֲוֵי כֹּלָּא חָד.

112. Another explanation of the verse: "And now shall my head be lifted up" is that it means, that I shall be included with the fathers, for King David had cleaved to the Patriarchs in order to be united with them IN THE SECRET OF THE FOURTH LEG and to be lifted above and bound to them. "Above my enemies round about me" refers to those of the left side, all of them accusers intent upon destruction. WHEN HE IS LIFTED ABOVE THEM, the sun, ZEIR ANPIN, is united with the moon, THE NUKVA, and all becomes one.

113. תָּא חֲזֵי, כְּתִיב וְיוֹסֵף הוּא הַשַּׁלִּיט עַל הָאָרֶץ, דָּא שִׁמְשָׁא דְּשַׁלִּיט בְּסִיהֲרָא, וְנָהִיר לָהּ, וְזָן לָהּ. הוּא הַמַּשְׁבִּיר לְכָל עַם הָאָרֶץ, דְּהָא הַהוּא נָהָר דְּנָגִיד וְנָפִיק, מִנֵּיהּ אִתְזָנוּ כֻּלְּהוּ, וּמִתַּמָּן פָּרְחִין נִשְׁמָתִין לְכֹלָּא, וּבְגִין דָּא כֻּלְּהוּ סָגְדִין לְגַבֵּיהּ דְּהַהוּא אֲתַר, דְּהָא לֵית לָךְ מִלָּה בְּעָלְמָא, דְּלָא תָּלֵי בְּמַזָּלָא וְאוּקְמוּהָ.

113. Come and behold: It is written, "And Joseph was the governor of the land." JOSEPH is the sun, ZEIR ANPIN, FOR JOSEPH IS YESOD OF ZEIR ANPIN, which rules over the moon, THE NUKVA, shining upon and sustaining her. "...and he it was that sold to all the people of the land," as the river that flows and comes out FROM EDEN, YESOD CALLED JOSEPH, supplies everybody with nourishment. From there the souls OF EVERY MEN emerge. Hence, everyone bows before that place, for there is nothing in the world that does not depend upon Mazal, YESOD, as has already been explained.

8. "And Joseph recognized his brothers"

A Synopsis

The Zohar examines the nature of fear and sin, and tells us that negative sexual activity and masturbation lead to negativity and ruin. Fear and sin, it claims, allows our enemies to behave like Joseph's brothers and gives them an opportunity to punish us without mercy.

The Relevance of this Passage

A man's seminal fluids are the closest reflection of The Creator's essence in the physical world. For this reason, a man's seed brings forth life and generates profound pleasure, both of which are attributes of the Divine. However, negative forces, here to test and challenge us, need their own sustenance of Light, which they retrieve when a man wantonly spills his seed. Keeping our sexual relations within the spiritual boundaries of marriage – for the purpose of sharing with our spouse and for bringing new life into the world – protects the Light from the onslaughts of the Other Side. The result is greater fulfillment and pleasure in every area of life.

114. וַיַּכֵּר יוֹסֵף אֶת אֶחָיו וְהֵם לֹא הִכִּירוּהוּ. רִבִּי אֶלְעָזָר פָּתַח וַאֲמַר, לָמָּה אִירָא בִּימֵי רָע עֲוֹן עֲקֵבַי יְסֻבֵּנִי. תָּא חֲזֵי, תְּלַת אִינּוּן דְּדָחֲלִין וְלָא יָדְעִין מִמַּה דָּחֲלִין, וְאוּקְמוּהָ, אֲבָל אִית מַאן דְּדָחֵיל, וְלָא יָדַע מִמַּה אִיהוּ דָּחֵיל, בְּגִין אִינּוּן חֶטְאֵי, דְּלָא יָדַע דְּאִינּוּן חֲטָאִין, וְלָא אַשְׁגַּח בְּהוֹ, וְאִיהוּ דָּחֵיל מִימֵי רָע.

114. "And Joseph recognized his brethren, but they recognized him not." Rabbi Elazar quoted the verse: "Why should I fear in the days of evil, when the iniquity of my persecutors (lit. 'my heels') compasses me about" (Tehilim 49:6). Come and behold: AS WAS SAID BY THE SAGES, there are three classes of those who fear, yet do not know what they fear. But in addition to these three, there is he who fears, yet does not know what he fears, because he commits sins unknowingly. He therefore fears the days of evil.

115. מַאן אִינּוּן יְמֵי רָע, אִלֵּין אִינּוּן יוֹמִין דְּאִינּוּן אִזְדַּמְּנָן בְּהַהוּא רָע, וּמַאן אִינּוּן, דָּא יֵצֶר הָרָע, דְּאִיהוּ אִקְרֵי רָע, וְאִית לֵיהּ יוֹמִין יְדִיעָן, דְּאִתְיְהִיב לֵיהּ רְשׁוּ בְּעַלְמָא, לְאַסְטָאָה לְכָל אִינּוּן דְּמְסָאֲבֵי אָרְחַיְיהוּ,

דְּמַאן דְּאָתֵי לְאִסְתְּאֲבָא מְסָאֲבֵי לֵיהּ. וְאִלֵּין אִינּוּן אִקְרוּן יְמֵי רָע, וְאִלֵּין מְמַנָּן עַל אִינּוּן חוֹבִין דְּדָשִׁין בְּהוֹ בְּנֵי נָשָׁא בַּעֲקֵבַיְיהוּ.

115. HE ASKS: What are the days of evil? HE SAID: These are days meant for evil. It is the Evil Inclination called evil, which on certain days is given permission in the world to lead astray those who defile their ways BY SPILLING SEMEN IN VAIN. Whoever wishes to be polluted is defiled. They are called days of evil, reserved for PUNISHMENT FOR transgressions that a man treads under his heels.

116. תָּא חֲזֵי, כָּל אִינּוּן דִּמְסָאֲבֵי אָרְחַיְיהוּ, כַּמָּה חֲבִילֵי טְהִירִין, אִזְדַּמְּנָן לְגַבַּיְיהוּ, וּמְסָאֲבֵי לְהוֹ. בְּאָרְחָא דְּבָעֵי בַּר נָשׁ לְמֵיהַךְ, בְּהַהוּא אָרְחָא מְדַבְּרִין לֵיהּ מַמָּשׁ, אָתֵי בַּר נָשׁ לְאִתְדַּכָּאָה, כַּמָּה אִינּוּן דִּמְסַיְיעִין לֵיהּ.

116. Come and behold: Packs of fiends await to defile those who defile their ways. A man is led in the very way he chooses to walk. A man who wishes to be purified has many helpers.

117. הָא תָּנִינָן, דְּכַד בַּר נָשׁ קָם בְּצַפְרָא, בָּעֵי לְאַסְחָאָה יְדוֹי, מִגּוֹ נַטְלָא דְּמַיָא, דְּאִיהוּ מָאנָא לִיטּוֹל מִנֵּיהּ מַיָא, מִגּוֹ מַאן דְּאַסְחֵי יְדוֹי בְּקַדְמֵיתָא, כְּמָה דְּאוֹקְמוּהָ. וְתָא חֲזֵי, בְּגִין נַטְלָא דָא, אוֹקִימְנָא מִלָּה.

117. We have learned that when a man wakes up in the morning, he should wash his hands with a laver, AND HE SHOULD BE WASHED by someone who has already washed, as has been explained. Come and behold: We have learned all this for the sake of the laver. THIS EXPOSITION WAS MEANT TO TEACH US THAT WE NEED A LAVER TO WASH OUR HANDS IN THE MORNING.

118. וְתוּ, דְּבָעְיָא לֵיהּ לְבַר נָשׁ, לְנַטְלָא יְדָא יְמִינָא בִּשְׂמָאלָא, בְּגִין לְשַׁלְטָאָה יְמִינָא עַל שְׂמָאלָא, וְיִסְתְּחֵי יְמִינָא מִן שְׂמָאלָא, וּבְגִין כָּךְ אִיהוּ נְטִילָא, וְעַל דָּא, מַאן דְּנָטֵיל יְדוֹי, יִטּוֹל יְמִינָא בִּשְׂמָאלָא,

לְאַשְׁלָטָא יְמִינָא עַל שְׂמָאלָא, בְּגִין דְּלָא יְהֵיב דּוּכְתָּא לְיֵצֶר הָרָע לְשַׁלְטָאָה כְּלַל, וְהָא אוֹקִימְנָא.

118. We also learned that a man should wash his right hand with his left hand, SO THAT THE LEFT WILL SERVE THE RIGHT and the right will thus be stronger than the left. The right should be laved by the left. The washing is expressly intended to ensure that THE RIGHT WILL RULE OVER THE LEFT. Therefore, when washing hands, it behooves one to wash the right with the left, thus causing the right to rule over the left, so as not to give the Evil Inclination an opening to rule at all.

119. תָּא חֲזֵי, בְּשַׁעְתָּא דְדִינָא בִּישָׁא שָׁלְטָא, לָא אָתֵיב יְדֵיהּ מִלְאַבְאָשָׁא, וּבְשַׁעְתָּא דִימִינָא שָׁלְטָא עַל עַמִּין עעכו״ם, לְתַבְרָא לוֹן, חָיֵיס קוּדְשָׁא בְּרִיךְ הוּא עֲלַיְיהוּ, וְלָא שֵׁצֵי לוֹן.

119. Come and behold: When evil Judgment reigns, it does not refrain from harming EVEN THE RIGHTEOUS, FOR WHEN THE DESTROYER IS GIVEN SWAY, HE DOES NOT DISCRIMINATE BETWEEN GOOD AND EVIL. When the right rules over the idolatrous nations to break them, the Holy One, blessed be He, feels pity for them and does not destroy them. YOU MAY SEE HERE THE GREAT DIFFERENCE BETWEEN THE COMPASSION OF THE RIGHT AND THE JUDGMENT OF THE LEFT.

120. וּבְגִין כָּךְ, כָּל מַאן דְּאִיהוּ חָטֵי, בְּאִינוּן חֶטְאִין דְּדָשׁ בְּהוֹ בְּרַגְלוֹי, לָא יָדַע בְּהוֹ, וְדָחֵיל תְּדִירָא. דָּוִד מַלְכָּא הֲוָה אִסְתַּמַר תָּדִיר, מֵחוֹבִין אִלֵּין, וְכַד הֲוָה נָפֵיק לִקְרָבָא, הֲוָה מְפַשְׁפֵּשׁ לוֹן, וְעַל דָּא לָא דָחֵיל לַאֲגָחָא עִמְּהוֹן קְרָבָא.

120. Therefore, when one unknowingly commits sins that he treads under his heels, he is always afraid. King David was always guarded from such sins and, when he went to battle, he searched for them IN ORDER TO REPENT. He therefore was not afraid to wage war.

121. וְתָּא חֲזֵי, אַרְבַּע מַלְכִין הֲווֹ, מַאן דְּשָׁאֵיל דָּא, לָא שָׁאֵיל דָּא. דָּוִד אֲמַר, אֶרְדּוֹף אוֹיְבַי וְאַשִּׂיגֵם וְלֹא אָשׁוּב עַד כַּלּוֹתָם, מַאי טַעְמָא בְּגִין

דַּהֲוָה אִסְתַּמַּר מֵאִלֵּין חוֹבִין, וְלָא יָהֵיב דוּכְתָּא לְשַׂנְאוֹי לְשַׁלְטָאָה, וְעַל דָּא בָּעֵי לְמִרְדַּף אֲבַתְרַיְיהוּ תָּדִיר. וְלָא יִרְדְּפוּן אִינוּן אֲבַתְרֵיהּ, לְמִתְבַּע חוֹבוֹי, וְיִפּוֹל בִּידַיְיהוּ.

121. Come and behold: There were four kings, each of whom asked for a different thing. David said: “Let me pursue my enemies, and overtake them: neither let me turn back till they are consumed” (Tehilim 18:38). Why did he say that? Because he was guarded from sins THAT ARE TRODDEN UNDER THE HEELS and gave no opening to his enemies to rule. He therefore pursued them continuously, rather than having them chase him, catch him, and indict him for his sins.

122. אָסָא הֲוָה דָּחִיל יַתִּיר, אַף עַל גַּב דַּהֲוָה מְפַשְׁפֵּשׁ בְּחֶטְאוֹי, וְלָא כְּדָוִד מַלְכָּא, אִיהוּ בָּעֵי לְמִרְדַּף אֲבַתְרַיְיהוּ, וְלָא יַגִּיחַ לוֹן, וְיִקְטוֹל לוֹן קוּדְשָׁא בְּרִיךְ הוּא, וְכָךְ הֲוָה, דִּכְתִּיב וַיִּרְדְּפֵם אָסָא וְהָעָם אֲשֶׁר עִמּוֹ וגו׳, וּכְתִיב וַיִּגּוֹף ה׳ אֶת הַכּוּשִׁים לִפְנֵי אָסָא וְלִפְנֵי יְהוּדָה וַיָּנוּסוּ הַכּוּשִׁים. דָּוִד מַה כְּתִיב בֵּיהּ וַיַּכֵּם דָּוִד מֵהַנֶּשֶׁף וְעַד הָעֶרֶב לְמָחֳרָתָם, אֲבָל אָסָא אִיהוּ רָדִיף וְקוּדְשָׁא בְּרִיךְ הוּא מָחֵי.

122. Asa was more fearful. Although he searched for his sins, he was not AS THOROUGH as King David. He merely wished to pursue his enemies, but not to fight them, and hoped that the Holy One, blessed be He, would slay them. And so it came to pass, as it is written: “And Asa and the people who were with him pursued them. So Hashem smote the Kushim before Asa, and before Judah, and the Kushim fled” (II Divrei Hayamim 14:11-12). Of David, the scripture reads, “And David smote them from the twilight to the evening of the next day” (I Shmuel 30:17). But Asa merely pursued them, and the Holy One, blessed be He, slew them.

123. יְהוֹשָׁפָט מֶלֶךְ יְהוּדָה, אוּף הָכֵי נָמֵי הֲוָה שָׁאִיל, וַאֲמַר, לָא יָכֵילְנָא לְמִרְדַּף, וְלָא לְקַטְלָא, אֶלָּא אֲנָא אֲזַמֵּר, וְאַתְּ קְטִיל לוֹן, בְּגִין דְּלָא הֲוָה מְפַשְׁפֵּשׁ כָּל כָּךְ כְּאָסָא, וְקוּדְשָׁא בְּרִיךְ הוּא עֲבַד לֵיהּ הָכֵי, דִּכְתִּיב וּבְעֵת הֵחֵלּוּ בְרִנָּה וּתְהִלָּה נָתַן ה׳ מְאָרְבִים עַל בְּנֵי עַמּוֹן מוֹאָב וְהַר שֵׂעִיר הַבָּאִים לִיהוּדָה וַיִּנָּגֵפוּ.

123. Yehoshafat, the King of Judah, also said: I can neither pursue nor kill them, but I shall sing hymns and You shall kill them. This was because he did not examine himself as Asa did. Yet the Holy One, blessed be He, did as He was requested, as it is written: "And when they began to sing and to praise, Hashem set an ambush against the children of Amon, Moab and mount Seir who were come against Judah; and they were routed" (II Divrei Hayamim 20:22).

124. חִזְקִיָּה מֶלֶךְ יְהוּדָה, אוּף הָכֵי נָמֵי אֲמַר, אֲנָא לָא יָכֵילְנָא, לָא לְזַמָּרָא, וְלָא לְמִרְדַּף, וְלָא לַאֲגָחָא קְרָבָא, בְּגִין דְּדָחֵיל מֵאִלֵּין חוֹבִין דְּקָאֲמָרָן, מַה כְּתִיב, וַיְהִי בַּלַּיְלָה הַהוּא וַיֵּצֵא מַלְאַךְ ה׳ וַיַּךְ בְּמַחֲנֵה אַשּׁוּר מֵאָה וּשְׁמוֹנִים וַחֲמִשָּׁה אֶלֶף וַיַּשְׁכִּימוּ בַבֹּקֶר וְהִנֵּה כֻלָּם פְּגָרִים מֵתִים, וְחִזְקִיָּה הֲוָה יָתֵיב בְּבֵיתֵיהּ, וְשָׁכֵיב בְּעַרְסֵיהּ, וְקוּדְשָׁא בְּרִיךְ הוּא קָטֵיל לוֹן.

124. Hezekiah, the King of Judah, said: I can neither chant, pursue nor wage war. For he was afraid of the sins we mentioned THAT ARE TRODDEN UNDER THE HEELS. It is written: "And it came to pass that night, that the angel of Hashem went out and smote in the camp of Ashur 185,000: and when they arose early in the morning, behold, they were all dead corpses" (II Melachim 19:35). Hezekiah was then at home lying in bed, and the Holy One, blessed be He, killed them.

125. וּמַה צַדִּיקִים אִלֵּין, הֲווֹ דָּחֲלִין מֵאִלֵּין חוֹבִין, שְׁאָר בְּנֵי עַלְמָא עַל אַחַת כַּמָּה וְכַמָּה. בְּגִין כָּךְ, אִית לֵיהּ לְבַר נָשׁ לְאִסְתַּמְּרָא מֵאִלֵּין חוֹבִין, וּלְפַשְׁפְּשָׁא בְּהוֹן כִּדְקָאֲמָרָן, בְּגִין דְּלָא יִשְׁלְטוּן עֲלוֹי אִינּוּן יְמֵי רָע, דְּלָא מְרַחֲמֵי עֲלֵיהּ.

125. How fearful were these righteous men on account of their sins? How much more fearful should the inhabitants of the world be? A man should therefore always be on his guard against these sins and search for them, so that the days of evil, which have no mercy on him, will not have control over him.

126. תָּא חֲזֵי, וַיַּכֵּר יוֹסֵף אֶת אֶחָיו, בְּשַׁעְתָּא דְּנָפְלוּ בִּידֵיהּ, אִיהוּ רְחֵים

עֲלַיְיהוּ, בְּגִין דְּאִיהוּ שְׁלִים, וְהֵם לֹא הִכִּירוּהוּ, דְּאִינוּן שִׁמְעוֹן וְלֵוִי, אָתוֹ מִסִּטְרָא דְּדִינָא קַשְׁיָא, וְעַל דָּא לָא רְחִימוּ עֲלֵיהּ, דְּהָא כָּל אִינוּן מָארֵיהוֹן דְּדִינָא קַשְׁיָא, לָא מְרַחֲמֵי עֲלַיְיהוּ דִבְנֵי נָשָׁא, בְּשַׁעְתָּא דְּנָפְלֵי בִּידַיְיהוּ.

126. Come and behold: "And Joseph knew his brethren" means that when they fell into his hands, he felt pity for them, because he was whole. "...but they knew him not" REFERS TO Simeon and Levi, who came from the side of harsh Judgment and therefore did not have pity on him. For all those from the side of harsh Judgment have no pity on the people who fall into their hands. THEY ARE OF THE ASPECT OF THE DAYS OF EVIL, WHICH DO NOT PITY MEN, AS HAS ALREADY BEEN SAID.

127. וּבְגִין כָּךְ אֲמַר דָּוִד, לָמָּה אִירָא. יָרֵאתִי לָא כְתִיב, אֶלָּא אִירָא, דְּאִית לִי לְמִדְחַל מֵאִינוּן יְמֵי רָע, כִּדְקָאֲמָרָן. עֲוֹן עֲקֵבַי יְסֻבֵּנִי, מַאן עֲקֵבַי, אִלֵּין אִינוּן בְּרָזָא דִּמְהֵימְנוּתָא, דִּכְתִיב, וְיָדוֹ אוֹחֶזֶת בַּעֲקֵב עֵשָׂו, דָּא הוּא עֲקִיבָא, וְאִינוּן עֲקִיבִין דְּמִסְתַּכְּלִין בְּהוֹ תָּדִיר, בְּהַהוּא חוֹבָא דְּדָשׁ בֵּיהּ בַּר נָשׁ תָּדִיר בַּעֲקֵבוֹי.

127. David therefore said: "Why should I fear THE DAYS OF EVIL?" He did not say, "I feared" IN THE PAST TENSE, but rather "should fear" IN THE PRESENT TENSE, WHICH MEANS THAT HE IS STILL FEARFUL. THUS HE SAID: I should always fear the days of evil, as we have said: "...the iniquity of my persecutors (lit. 'my heels') compasses me about." HE ASKS: What are "my heels?" HE ANSWERS, They are in the secret of the faith, NAMELY, IN HOLINESS, as it is written: "And his hand took hold on Esau's heel" (Beresheet 25:26). ESAU'S HEEL WAS IN THE SECRET OF THE FAITH, IN HOLINESS, BECAUSE JACOB'S HAND TOOK HOLD OF IT. This heel (Heb. *akev*), OF WHICH IT IS WRITTEN: "THE INIQUITY OF MY HEELS COMPASSES ME ABOUT," represents the footprints (Heb. *akevot*) that follow the same transgression that a man constantly treads under his heels.

128. תָּא חֲזֵי, מַה כְּתִיב הוֹי מוֹשְׁכֵי הֶעָוֹן בְּחַבְלֵי הַשָּׁוְא וְכַעֲבוֹת הָעֲגָלָה חַטָּאָה. בְּחַבְלֵי הַשָּׁוְא: דְּדָשׁ בֵּיהּ בַּעֲקֵבָא, וְלָא חַיֵּישׁ עֲלֵיהּ, וּלְבָתַר אִתְתַּקַּף וְאִתְעֲבֵיד כַּעֲבוֹת הָעֲגָלָה, וְאִתְתַּקַּף הַהוּא חֶטְאָה,

וְאַסְטֵי לֵיהּ בְּהַאי עַלְמָא, וּבְעַלְמָא דְאָתֵי.

128. Come and behold the verse: "Woe to them that draw iniquity with cords of vanity, and sin as it were with a cart rope" (Yeshayah 5:18). The "cords of vanity" are the sins that he treads under his heels without thinking of it. They are then strengthened into "a cart rope." The sins become stronger and lead him astray in this world and the World to Come.

129. זַכָּאִין אִינוּן צַדִּיקַיָּיא, דְּיָדְעִין לְאִסְתַּמְּרָא מֵחוֹבֵיהוֹן, וְאִינוּן מְפַשְׁפְּשִׁין תָּדִיר בְּעוֹבָדַיְיהוּ, בְּגִין דְּלָא יִשְׁתַּכַּח עֲלַיְיהוּ מְקַטְרְגָא בְּהַאי עַלְמָא, וְלָא יִסְטוּן עֲלַיְיהוּ לְעַלְמָא דְאָתֵי, דְּהָא אוֹרַיְיתָא מְתַקְנָא לְהוֹ אָרְחִין וּשְׁבִילִין לְמֵיהַךְ בְּהוֹ, דִּכְתִיב דְּרָכֶיהָ דַרְכֵי נֹעַם וְכָל נְתִיבוֹתֶיהָ שָׁלוֹם.

129. Happy are the righteous, who know how to be guarded against their sins and always examine their deeds, so that no accuser will be found against them in this world nor turn them from their way in the World to Come. The Torah prepares for them ways and paths on which to walk, as it is written: "Her ways are ways of pleasantness, and all her paths are peace."

9. "And Joseph remembered the dreams"

A Synopsis

The commentators stress the importance of remembering one's dreams and presenting them to a sympathetic audience of friends in order to obtain a favorable interpretation. The necessity of obeying every last precept of the Torah is also discussed. The rabbis use the example of King Solomon, who ruined his posterity by disobeying the injunction against polygamy. Rabbi Yosi comments on the verse "Treasures of wickedness profit nothing." That is to say, wealth gained in an impure manner will soon disappear, but the righteous life of Torah study endures.

The Relevance of this Passage

Dreams can assist us in our spiritual development. However, our dreams should only be interpreted by someone who loves us, since the interpretation itself influences its physical manifestation. The Light of this passage helps bring loving people into our lives when the need for dream interpretation arises. In addition, the passage allows our dreams to be derived from the highest realms of the spiritual atmosphere, ensuring positive and truthful messages. Pertaining to the verse "Treasures of wickedness profit nothing," the Zohar teaches us that a narcissistic, self-serving pursuit for wealth, power, and position will ultimately lead to ruin in some area of life. The influences emanating from the Hebrew verses imbue us with wisdom and strength to resist trading away life's true fulfillment – marriage, children, friendship, and spiritual fulfillment – for the fleeting pleasure of ego gratification.

130. וַיִּזְכּוֹר יוֹסֵף אֶת הַחֲלוֹמוֹת אֲשֶׁר חָלַם לָהֶם וגו'. רִבִּי חִיָּיא פְּתַח וַאֲמַר, בִּנְפוֹל אוֹיִבְךָ אַל תִּשְׂמַח וּבִכָּשְׁלוֹ אַל יָגֵל לִבֶּךָ. תָּא חֲזֵי, קוּדְשָׁא בְּרִיךְ הוּא עֲבַד לֵיהּ לְבַר נָשׁ, דְּיִזְכֵּי לִיקָרָא דִילֵיהּ, וּלְשַׁמָּשָׁא קַמֵּיהּ תְּדִירָא, וּלְאִשְׁתַּדְּלָא בְּאוֹרַיְיתָא יְמָמָא וְלֵילֵי, בְּגִין דְּקוּדְשָׁא בְּרִיךְ הוּא אִתְרְעֵי בָּהּ בְּאוֹרַיְיתָא תָּדִיר.

130. "And Joseph remembered the dreams which he had dreamed" (Beresheet 42:9). Rabbi Chiya opened the discussion with the verse: "Do not rejoice when your enemy falls, and do not let your heart be glad when he stumbles" (Mishlei 24:17). Come and behold: The Holy One, blessed be He, created man, so that he would be worthy of His glory, serve Him always, and be occupied with the Torah day and night, because the Holy One, blessed be He, ever takes delight in the Torah.

131. וְכֵיוָן דִּבְרָא קוּדְשָׁא בְּרִיךְ הוּא לְאָדָם, יְהַב קַמֵּיהּ אוֹרַיְיתָא, וְאוֹלֵיף לֵיהּ בָּהּ לְמִנְדַּע אָרְחָהָא. מְנָלָן, דִּכְתִּיב אָז רָאָהּ וַיְסַפְּרָהּ הֱכִינָהּ וְגַם חֲקָרָהּ. וּלְבָתַר, וַיֹּאמֶר לָאָדָם הֵן יִרְאַת ה׳ הִיא חָכְמָה וְסוּר מֵרָע בִּינָה. כֵּיוָן דְּאִסְתַּכַּל בָּהּ, וְלָא נָטֵיר לָהּ, עֲבַר עַל פִּקּוּדָא דְמָארֵיהּ, וְאִתְפַּס בְּחוֹבֵיהּ.

131. When the Holy One, blessed be He, created Adam, He put the Torah before him and taught him how to know its ways. How do we know this? From the words: "Then He saw it, and declared it; He established it, yea, and searched it out," which is followed by: "And to man He said: Behold, the fear of Hashem, that is wisdom; and to depart from evil is understanding" (Iyov 28:27-28). Because he inquired into her, but did not keep her, he transgressed the command of his Master and was caught for his sin.

132. וְכָל אִינוּן דְּעָבְרוּ עַל מִלָּה חָדָא דְאוֹרַיְיתָא, אִתְפָּסוּ בָהּ. שְׁלֹמֹה מַלְכָּא, דְּאִתְחַכַּם עַל כָּל בְּנֵי עַלְמָא, עֲבַר עַל מִלָּה חָדָא דְאוֹרַיְיתָא, וְגָרֵים לֵיהּ לְאִתְעֲבָרָא מַלְכוּתֵיהּ מִנֵּיה, וּלְאִתְפַּלְגָא מַלְכוּתָא מִן בְּנוֹי, מַאן דְּאַעֲבַר עַל אוֹרַיְיתָא עַל אַחַת כַּמָּה וְכַמָּה.

132. All those who transgress one precept of the Torah are caught for it. King Solomon, who was wisest among all the people in the world, transgressed only one precept of the Torah BY HAVING MANY WIVES and caused his kingdom to pass on from him BECAUSE, AS THE SAGES SAID, ASMODEUS MADE AN IGNORANT MAN OF HIM and caused his kingdom to be divided from the time of his sons. This is even truer for those who transgress MANY PRECEPTS OF the Torah.

133. וְיוֹסֵף דַּהֲוָה יָדַע אוֹרַיְיתָא, וַאֲחוֹי נָפְלוּ בִּידֵיהּ, אַמַּאי גִּלְגֵּל עֲלַיְיהוּ כָּל גִּלְגּוּלָא דָא, וְהָא אִיהוּ יָדַע אוֹרַיְיתָא דְּאוֹלִיף לֵיהּ אֲבוֹי. אֶלָּא, ח"ו דְּיוֹסֵף גִּלְגֵּל עֲלַיְיהוּ גִּלְגּוּלִין לְנַקְמָא מִנַּיְיהוּ, אֶלָּא כָּל דָּא לָא עֲבַד, אֶלָּא לְאַיְיתָאָה לַאֲחוּהָ בִּנְיָמִן לְגַבֵּיהּ, דְּתֵיאוּבְתֵּיהּ הֲוָה לְגַבֵּיה, וְאִיהוּ לָא שָׁבַק לַאֲחוֹי לְמִנְפַּל, דְּהָא כְתִיב וַיְצַו יוֹסֵף וַיְמַלְאוּ אֶת כְּלֵיהֶם בָּר וגו׳, וְכָל דָּא בְּגִין דְּלָא יִנְפְּלוּן.

133. He asks: Joseph knew the Torah, and her words "You shall not avenge, nor bear any grudge" (Vayikra 19:18). Why then, when his brothers fell into his hands, did he bring upon them all these things, when he knew the Torah his father had taught him? He replied: Heaven forbid to think that Joseph did all this to take revenge upon them. He did it only to bring his brother Benjamin to him, for he longed for him. He did not leave his brothers wanting, as it is written: "Then Joseph gave orders to fill their sacks with grain" (Beresheet 42:25), so they would not come to grief.

134. ר׳ יְהוּדָה אֲמַר, כַּד בְּרָא קוּדְשָׁא בְּרִיךְ הוּא לְסִיהֲרָא, הֲוָה אִסְתַּכַּל בָּהּ תָּדִיר, כְּדִכְתִיב, תָּמִיד עֵינֵי ה׳ אֱלֹהֶיךָ בָּהּ, אַשְׁגָּחוּתָא דִילֵיהּ בָּהּ תָּדִיר, וּכְתִיב אָז רָאָהּ: דְּהָא שִׁמְשָׁא בְּאַשְׁגָּחוּתָא דִילֵיהּ בָּהּ, אִתְנְהִיר. וַיְסַפְּרָהּ, מַאי וַיְסַפְּרָהּ, כְּמָא דְאַתְּ אָמֵר מְקוֹם סַפִּיר אֲבָנֶיהָ.

134. Rabbi Yehuda continued with the verse: "Then He saw it..." (Iyov 28:27). When the Holy One, blessed be He, created the moon, the Nukva, He beheld her constantly, as it is written: "The eyes of Hashem your Elohim are always upon it" (Devarim 11:12), for she was constantly under His care. It is written: "Then He saw"; He saw that the sun, Zeir Anpin, by looking at the Nukva became illumined, for it receives sight, the secret of Chochmah, only when He is united with the Nukva. He asks: In the phrase: "And declared it (Heb. *vaysapera*) (Ibid.)," what does "*vaysapera*" mean? He answers, The same as in the verse: "The stones of it are the place of sapphires" (Heb. *sapir*) (Ibid. 6); it is derived from the Sfirot and illumination.

135. הֱכִינָהּ: דְּאִיהִי יָתְבָא בְּתִקּוּנָא, בִּתְרֵיסַר תְּחוּמִין, מִתְפַּלְּגָא בְּשִׁבְעִין קְסִירִין, אַתְקִין לָהּ בְּשִׁבְעָה סַמְכִין עִלָּאִין, לְאִתְנַהֲרָא וּלְיַתְבָא עַל שְׁלִימוּ. וְגַם חֲקָרָהּ: לְאַשְׁגָּחָא עֲלָהּ תָּדִיר, זִמְנָא בָּתַר זִמְנָא, דְּלָא פָּסֵיק לְעָלְמִין.

135. "He established it" together with her mendings so she would be divided into twelve groups and be given to seventy angels. He fixed for her seven supernal pillars through which she would receive lights and exist in wholeness. The phrase: "And searched it out" means He searched her out and attended to her always so that the Other Side will not

NOURISH ITSELF FROM HER.

136. וּלְבָתַר אַזְהַר לֵיהּ לְבַר נָשׁ, וַאֲמַר, וַיֹּאמֶר לָאָדָם הֵן יִרְאַת ה׳ הִיא חָכְמָה וְסוּר מֵרָע בִּינָה, דְּהַאי מִתְעַטְּרָא עַל תַּתָּאֵי, לְדַחֲלָא, וּלְמִנְדַע לֵיהּ לְקוּדְשָׁא בְּרִיךְ הוּא בְּגִינָהּ. וְסוּר מֵרָע בִּינָה, בְּרִירוּ מִפְּסָלוּתָא, דְּלָא לְמִקְרַב בַּהֲדֵיהּ, וּכְדֵין אַשְׁגָּחוּתָא דְּבִינָה, לְמִנְדַע וּלְאִסְתַּכְּלָא בִּיקָרָא דְּמַלְכָּא עִלָּאָה.

136. He then warned man thus: “And to man He said, ‘Behold, the fear of Hashem, that is wisdom; and to depart from evil is understanding’” (Iyov 28:28). Because “THE FEAR OF HASHEM,” THE NUKVA, is adorned with all the lower beings so they will learn to fear and know Hashem through her strength. SHE IS THEREFORE CHOCHMAH. And “to depart from evil is understanding (Heb. *binah*).” The separation of pollution so it will not approach HOLINESS with her, WHICH IS “DEPART FROM EVIL,” is the purpose of the existence of Binah, THAT IS, the knowledge and beholding of the glory of the highest King.

137. רִבִּי יוֹסֵי קָם בְּלֵילְיָא חַד, לְאִשְׁתַּדְּלָא בְּאוֹרַיְיתָא, וַהֲוָה תַּמָּן עִמֵּיהּ חַד יוּדָאי, דְּאָעֲרַע בֵּיהּ בְּהַהוּא בֵּיתָא. פָּתַח ר׳ יוֹסֵי וַאֲמַר, לֹא יוֹעִילוּ אוֹצְרוֹת רֶשַׁע וּצְדָקָה תַּצִּיל מִמָּוֶת. לֹא יוֹעִילוּ אוֹצְרוֹת רֶשַׁע, אִלֵּין אִינּוּן דְּלָא מִשְׁתַּדְּלֵי בְּאוֹרַיְיתָא, וְאָזְלֵי בָּתַר מִלֵּי דְּעָלְמָא, וּלְמִכְנַשׁ אוֹצְרִין דְּחִיּוּבָא, מַה כְּתִיב וְאָבַד הָעֹשֶׁר הַהוּא בְּעִנְיַן רָע, בְּגִין דְּאִינּוּן אוֹצְרוֹת רֶשַׁע.

137. Rabbi Yosi rose one night to study the Torah. There happened to be a Jew there, whom he met in that house. Rabbi Yosi opened the discussion with the verse: “Treasures of wickedness profit nothing: but righteousness (also: ‘charity’) delivers from death” (Mishlei 10:2). “Treasures of wickedness profit nothing” are those who are not occupied with the study of the Torah, but follow worldly matters and gather wicked treasures. Of them it is written, “But those riches perish by evil adventure” (Kohelet 5:13), because they are wicked treasures.

138. וּצְדָקָה תַּצִּיל מִמָּוֶת, אִלֵּין דְּמִשְׁתַּדְּלֵי בְּאוֹרַיְיתָא, וְיָדְעִין אוֹרְחָהָא

לְאִשְׁתַּדְּלָא בָּהּ, דְּהָא אוֹרַיְיתָא עֵץ חַיִּים אִקְרֵי, וְאִתְקְרִיאַת צְדָקָה, דִּכְתִיב וּצְדָקָה תִּהְיֶה לָנוּ. דָּבָר אַחֵר, וּצְדָקָה תַּצִּיל מִמָּוֶת, דָּא צְדָקָה מַמָּשׁ, וּבִתְרֵין גַּוְונִין אִיהוּ, וּבִתְרֵין סִטְרִין, קָרֵי בֵּיהּ אוֹרַיְיתָא, וְקָרֵי בֵּיהּ צְדָקָה, וְכֹלָּא חַד.

138. "But righteousness delivers from death" refers to those who are occupied with the study of the Torah and know how to study her ways, for the Torah is called the Tree of Life and Righteousness, as it is written: "And it shall be accounted righteousness in us" (Devarim 6:25). Another explanation of "but righteousness delivers from death" is that it refers to charity given to the poor. There are two ways to read and understand it: THE WORD RIGHTEOUSNESS may be understood as the Torah, or it may simply mean charity, yet all is one.

139. אֲמַר הַהוּא יוּדָאי, וְקָרֵי בֵּיהּ שָׁלוֹם, אֲמַר רִבִּי יוֹסֵי, הָכֵי הוּא וַדַּאי דְּאִקְרֵי שָׁלוֹם. קָם הַהוּא יוּדָאי, וְאִשְׁתַּתַּף בַּהֲדֵיהּ, פְּתַח הַהוּא יוּדָאי וַאֲמַר, עוֹבֵד אַדְמָתוֹ יִשְׂבַּע לָחֶם וּמְרַדֵּף רֵקִים יִשְׂבַּע רֵישׁ. הַאי קְרָא קַשְׁיָא, וְכִי שְׁלֹמֹה מַלְכָּא דְּאִיהוּ חַכִּים מִכָּל בְּנֵי עַלְמָא, הֵיךְ אֲמַר דְּיִשְׁתַּדֵּל בַּר נָשׁ לְמִפְלַח אַרְעָא, וּלְאִשְׁתַּדְּלָא אֲבַתְרֵיהּ, וְיִשְׁבּוֹק חַיֵּי עָלְמָא.

139. That Jew said: you may read IN THE WORD RIGHTEOUSNESS the meaning of peace. Rabbi Yosi said to him, Assuredly, she is called peace. The Jew rose to study THE TORAH with him. The Jew quoted the verse: "He who tills his land shall have plenty of bread: but he who follows after vain persons shall have poverty enough" (Mishlei 28:19). This verse is difficult to understand. How could King Solomon, who was the wisest of all men, say that a man should strive to cultivate the earth, till it, and neglect everlasting life?

140. אֶלָּא רָזָא אִיהוּ. פְּתַח וַאֲמַר, וַיִּקַּח ה' אֱלֹקִים אֶת הָאָדָם וַיַּנִּיחֵהוּ בְגַן עֵדֶן לְעָבְדָהּ וּלְשָׁמְרָהּ, וְאוֹקְמוּהָ בְּרָזָא דְקָרְבָּנִין אִיהוּ. תָּא חֲזֵי, לְעָבְדָהּ: דָּא מַלְכָּא עִלָּאָה. וּלְשָׁמְרָהּ: דָּא מַלְכָּא תַּתָּאָה. עַלְמָא עִלָּאָה, וְעַלְמָא תַּתָּאָה. לְעָבְדָהּ בְּרָזָא דְזָכוֹר, וּלְשָׁמְרָהּ בְּרָזָא דְשָׁמוֹר.

140. HE REPLIED: There is a mystery here. He then quoted the verse: "And Hashem Elohim took the man, and put him into the Garden of Eden to till (also: 'to worship') it and to keep" (Beresheet 2:15). It has already been explained that it refers to worship by sacrificing. Come and behold: "to till it" is the Upper King, THAT IS, IT REFERS TO THE DRAWING OF PLENTY OF BLESSINGS FROM THE UPPER KING, ZEIR ANPIN; and "to keep" is the lower king, THAT IS, IT REFERS TO THE KEEPING OF PLENTY RECEIVED BY THE LOWER KING, THE NUKVA. THE VERSE REFERS TO the upper world, ZEIR ANPIN, and the lower world, THE NUKVA. HE FURTHER EXPLAINS THAT "to till it" is in the secret of Remember, ZEIR ANPIN, and keep is in the secret of Keep, THE NUKVA. THEREFORE IN THE FIRST TABLES OF THE TESTIMONY IT IS WRITTEN: "REMEMBER THE SHABBAT DAY" (SHEMOT 20, 8), AND IN THE SECOND TABLES OF THE TESTIMONY IT IS WRITTEN, "KEEP THE SHABBAT DAY" (DEVARIM 5:12).

141. וּבְגִין כָּךְ, עוֹבֵד אַדְמָתוֹ דָּא גַּן עֵדֶן, דְּאִצְטְרִיךְ לְמֶעְבַּד וּלְמִפְלַח, וּלְאַמְשָׁכָא לָהּ בִּרְכָאן מִלְּעֵילָּא, וְכַד אִתְבָּרְכָא וְאִתְמַשְׁכָא לָהּ בִּרְכָאן מִלְּעֵילָּא, אִיהוּ נָמֵי אִתְבָּרֵךְ בַּהֲדָהּ. תָּא חֲזֵי, דְּכַהֲנָא דִּמְבָרֵךְ, מִתְבָּרֵךְ. כד"א וַאֲנִי אֲבָרְכֵם. וּבְגִין כָּךְ, עוֹבֵד אַדְמָתוֹ יִשְׂבַּע לָחֶם, דָּא הוּא מְזוֹנָא דִּלְעֵילָּא. וּמְרַדֵּף רֵקִים: מַאן דְּיִתְדַּבַּק בְּסִטְרָא אָחֳרָא, דְּאִיהוּ מְרַדֵּף רֵקִים. יִשְׂבַּע רֵישׁ וַדַּאי. אֲמַר רִבִּי יוֹסֵי, זַכָּאָה אַנְתְּ, דְּזָכִית לְהַאי מִלָּה.

141. Therefore, "He that tills his land" (Mishlei 12:11) refers to the Garden of Eden, THE NUKVA, FOR MAN should work and draw blessings on it from ZEIR ANPIN above. When it is blessed and blessings pour on it from above, MAN is blest with it. Come and behold: When the priest blesses, he is also blessed, as it is written: "and I will bless them" (Bemidbar 5:27). Hence, "He that tills his land" TO DRAW PLENTY ON THE NUKVA, "shall have plenty of bread," nourishment from above, WHICH HE EARNS BY HIS WORK, FOR HE WHO BLESSES IS BLESSED. "...but he that follows vain persons," he who cleaves to the Other Side, which follows vain persons, surely "shall have poverty enough." Rabbi Yosi said to him, Happy are you to have merited this.

142. תּוּ פָּתַח וַאֲמַר קְרָא אֲבַתְרֵיהּ, אִישׁ אֱמוּנוֹת רַב בְּרָכוֹת, דָּא הוּא

בַּר נָשׁ, דִּמְהֵימְנוּתָא דְּקוּדְשָׁא בְּרִיךְ הוּא בֵּיהּ, כְּגוֹן רִבִּי יֵיסָא סָבָא, דְּאַף עַל גָּב דַּהֲוָה לֵיהּ מֵיכְלָא דְּהַהוּא יוֹמָא לְמֵיכַל, לָא הֲוָה מַתְקִין לֵיהּ, עַד דְּשָׁאֵיל מְזוֹנֵיהּ קַמֵּי מַלְכָּא קַדִּישָׁא, לְבָתַר דְּצַלֵּי צְלוֹתֵיהּ, וְשָׁאֵיל מְזוֹנֵיהּ קַמֵּי מַלְכָּא, כְּדֵין הֲוָה מְתַקֵּין, וַהֲוָה אֲמַר תָּדִיר, לָא נְתַקֵּין, עַד דְּיִנָּתְנוּן מִבֵּי מַלְכָּא.

142. He then cited the verse that comes after THE VERSE, "HE THAT TILLS HIS LAND." IT IS, "A faithful man shall abound with blessings" (Mishlei 28:20), which alludes to a man who has faith in the Holy One, blessed be He, such as Rabbi Yesa Saba (the elder), who, though he had food for that day, did not set the table before praying for food before the Holy King. After praying and asking for nourishment from the King, he would set the table. He always said: Let us not set the table until NOURISHMENT is given from the King's house.

143. וְאָץ לְהַעֲשִׁיר לֹא יִנָּקֶה, בְּגִין דְּלָא בָּעָא לְאִשְׁתַּדְּלָא בְּאוֹרַיְיתָא, דְּאִיהִי חַיִּין דְּעָלְמָא דֵּין, וְחַיִּין דְּעַלְמָא דְּאָתֵי, הַשְׁתָּא דְּאִיהִי שַׁעְתָּא לְאִשְׁתַּדְּלָא בְּאוֹרַיְיתָא, נִשְׁתַּדֵּל.

143. "But he who makes haste to be rich shall not go unpunished" (Mishlei 28:20), because he did not want to study the Torah, which is life in this world and life in the World to Come. Now is the time to be occupied with the Torah. Let us do so.

144. פְּתַח הַהוּא גַּבְרָא בְּרָזָא דְּחֶלְמָא וַאֲמַר, וַיִּזְכּוֹר יוֹסֵף אֶת הַחֲלוֹמוֹת אֲשֶׁר חָלַם לָהֶם וגו'. וַיִּזְכּוֹר יוֹסֵף אֶת הַחֲלוֹמוֹת, וְכִי יוֹסֵף אַמַּאי אַדְכַּר לוֹן אִינוּן חֲלוֹמוֹת דְּחָלַם לְהוֹ. וּמַה סַגְיָא לֵיהּ אִלּוּ לָא אַדְכַּר לְהוֹ, דְּהָא יוֹסֵף חַכִּים הֲוָה, וּכְתִיב כָּל עָרוּם יַעֲשֶׂה בְדָעַת וּכְסִיל יִפְרֹשׂ אִוֶּלֶת.

144. The man opened with the mystery of the dream. He said: "And Joseph remembered the dreams which he had dreamed about them." HE ASKS ABOUT THE WORDS: "And Joseph remembered the dreams." Why did Joseph remember the dreams he had about them? What would have happened if he forgot them, as Joseph was wise and studied the verse, "a prudent man acts with knowledge: but a fool lays bare his folly" (Mishlei 13:16)?

145. אֲבָל, כֵּיוָן דְּחָמָא דְאִינוּן אִתּוֹ, וְסָגְדֵי לֵיהּ אַפִּין עַל אַרְעָא, כְּדֵין אִדְכַּר מִמַּה דְּחָלַם לְהוֹ, כַּד הֲוָה עִמְּהוֹן, דִּכְתִיב וְהִנֵּה קָמָה אֲלֻמָּתִי וְגַם נִצָּבָה וְהִנֵּה תְסֻבֶּינָה אֲלֻמּוֹתֵיכֶם וַתִּשְׁתַּחֲוֶינָה לַאֲלֻמָּתִי, בְּשַׁעְתָּא דְחָמָא דְּכָרְעִין אֲחוֹי קַמֵּיהּ, דִּכְתִיב וַיָּבֹאוּ אֲחֵי יוֹסֵף וַיִּשְׁתַּחֲווּ לוֹ אַפַּיִם אַרְצָה, כְּדֵין וַיִּזְכּוֹר יוֹסֵף אֶת הַחֲלוֹמוֹת אֲשֶׁר חָלַם, דְּהָא חָמָא דַּהֲווֹ קָיְימֵי.

145. HE REPLIES: When Joseph saw them bowing before him with their faces to the earth, he remembered the dream he dreamed about them, as it is written, "and, lo, my sheaf arose, and also stood upright; and, behold, your sheaves stood round about, and bowed down to my sheaf" (Beresheet 37:7). For when he saw his brothers prostrating themselves before him, as it is written, "and Joseph's brothers came, and bowed themselves down before him with their faces to the earth", then, "Joseph remembered of the dreams which he had dreamed," that is, he saw them coming true. THUS, "AND JOSEPH REMEMBERED THE DREAMS" MEANS THAT HE SAW THAT THEY CAME TRUE.

146. תּוּ, וַיִּזְכּוֹר יוֹסֵף אֶת הַחֲלוֹמוֹת אֲשֶׁר חָלַם, אַדְכַּר לוֹן, בְּגִין דְּלֵית נַשְׁיוּ קַמֵּי קוּדְשָׁא בְּרִיךְ הוּא, דְּהָא חֶלְמָא דְּאִיהוּ טָבָא, בָּעֵיבַּר נָשׁ לְאַדְכָּרָא לֵיהּ, דְּלָא יִתְנְשֵׁי, וּכְדֵין אִתְקַיַּים, דְּהָא כְּמָה דְאִתְנְשֵׁי קַמֵּיהּ דְּבַר נָשׁ, הָכֵי אִתְנְשֵׁי עֲלֵיהּ.

146. "And Joseph remembered the dreams which he had dreamed" can also mean that he was reminded of them because there is no forgetfulness before the Holy One, blessed be He. A man should remember a good dream, so it is not forgotten, for then it is realized. But if it is forgotten by him, it is forgotten ABOVE AND DOES NOT COME TRUE.

147. תָּא חֲזֵי, חֶלְמָא דְּלָא אִתְפַּשַּׁר, כְּאִגַּרְתָּא דְּלָא מִתְקַרְיָא, וְתָא חֲזֵי, בְּגִין דְּלָא אִדְכַּר, כְּמַאן דְּלָא יָדַע לֵיהּ, וְעַל דָּא, מַאן דְּאִתְנְשֵׁי מִנֵּיהּ

חֶלְמָא, וְלָא יָדַע לֵיהּ, לָא קָיְימָא עֲלֵיהּ לְאִתְקָיְימָא, וּבְגִין דָּא, יוֹסֵף הֲוָה דָּכִיר חֶלְמֵיהּ, בְּגִין לְאִתְקַיְּימָא, בְּגִין דְּלָא יִתְנְשֵׁי חֶלְמָא מִנֵּיהּ לְעָלַם, וַהֲוָה מְחַכֶּה לֵיהּ תָּדִיר. וַיֹּאמֶר אֲלֵיהֶם מְרַגְּלִים אַתֶּם, אִיהוּ דָּכִיר חֶלְמָא, אֲבָל מִלָּה לָא אֲמַר לוֹן, אֶלָּא מְרַגְּלִים אַתֶּם.

147. Come and behold: A dream that was not interpreted resembles an unopened letter, FOR THE DREAMER DOES NOT DERIVE ANY BENEFIT FROM IT. Come and behold: He who does not remember THE DREAM acts as if he did not know HOW TO INTERPRET IT. Therefore, whoever forgets his dream and cannot recall it, will find his dream unfulfilled. Joseph therefore remembered his dream and never forgot it, so it would come true. He waited for it all the time. He said to them, "You are spies" (Beresheet 42:9). Although he remembered the dream, he said nothing except, "You are spies."

148. פְּתַח ר' יוֹסֵי וַאֲמַר, כִּי בָא הַחֲלוֹם בְּרוֹב עִנְיָן וְקוֹל כְּסִיל בְּרוֹב דְּבָרִים. כִּי בָא הַחֲלוֹם בְּרוֹב עִנְיָן, הָא אוֹקְמוּהָ דְּכַמָּה אִינוּן סְמִיכִין בְּחֶלְמָא, וּמְמַנָּן דַּרְגִּין עַל דַּרְגִּין, עַד דְּחָלְמִין מִנְּהוֹן קְשׁוֹט כֻּלְּהוּ, וּמִנְּהוֹן דְּאִית בְּהוֹן קְשׁוֹט וּכְדִיבוּ. אֲבָל לְאִינוּן זַכָּאֵי קְשׁוֹט, לָא אִתְגְּלֵי לוֹן מִלִּין כְּדִיבָן כְּלוּם אֶלָּא כֻּלְּהוּ קְשׁוֹט.

148. Rabbi Yosi continued with the verse, "For a dream comes through a multitude of business; and a fool's voice is known by a multitude of words" (Kohelet 5:2). HE EXPLAINED THAT "a dream comes through a multitude of business" means there are many who help the dream endure, including chiefs and grades upon grades, for some dreams are all truth and some contain both truth and lies, THAT IS, ONE PART WILL COME TRUE AND ANOTHER WILL NOT. But the truly righteous are shown no lies in their dreams; they are shown only truth.

149. תָּא חֲזֵי, דָּנִיֵּאל מַה כְּתִיב בֵּיהּ, אֱדַיִן לְדָנִיֵּאל בְּחֶזְוָא דִי לֵילְיָא רָזָא גַּלִּי, וּכְתִיב דָּנִיֵּאל חֵלֶם חֲזָה וְחֶזְוֵי רֵאשֵׁהּ עַל מִשְׁכְּבֵיהּ בֵּאדַיִן חֶלְמָא כְתַב. וְאִי אִית בֵּיהּ מִלִּין כְּדִיבָן, אַמַּאי אִיכְתִּיב בֵּין כְּתוּבִים. אֶלָּא אִינוּן זַכָּאֵי קְשׁוֹט, בְּשַׁעְתָּא דְּנִשְׁמַתְהוֹן סָלְקִין, לָא מִתְחַבְּרָן בְּהוּ,

אֶלָּא מִלִּין קַדִּישִׁין, דְּאוֹדְעִין לֵיהּ מִלֵּי דִקְשׁוֹט, מִלִּין קַיְימָן, דְּלָא מְשַׁקְּרָן לְעָלְמִין.

149. Come and behold: It is written of Daniel, "Then to Daniel, in a vision of the night," NAMELY, IN A DREAM, "the secret was revealed" (Daniel 2:19) and "Daniel had a dream and visions of his head as he lay upon his bed: then he wrote his dream" (Daniel 7:1). Had the dream contained lies, the book of Daniel would not be among the scriptures. But when the souls of the truly righteous ascend during sleep, only holy beings join them. These holy beings tell them true words, enduring words, that never lie.

150. וְאִי תֵּימָא, הָא תְּנַן, דְּדָוִד מַלְכָּא, לָא חָמָא חֶלְמָא טָבָא, הָא אִשְׁתְּמַע דַּהֲוָה חָמֵי דָּוִד מִלִּין דְּלָא קְשׁוֹט. אֶלָּא וַדַּאי, כָּל יוֹמוֹי הֲוָה מִשְׁתַּדֵּל לְאוֹשְׁדָא דָמִין, וְאַגַּח קְרָבִין, וְכָל חֶלְמוֹי לָא הֲווֹ, אֶלָּא חֶלְמִין בִּישִׁין, חוּרְבָּא וְשׁוֹמְמוּתָא וְדָמָא וְאוֹשִׁידוּ דְּדָמִין, וְלָא חֶלְמָא דִשְׁלָם.

150. You may say that King David never had a good dream. It may be concluded that he saw untrue things. YET IN FACT HE WAS FULL OF KINDNESS AND THE GRACE OF HASHEM. HE ANSWERS, Surely it was because he spent his days shedding blood and engaging in war. Thus all his dreams were bad dreams about destruction, waste, blood, and bloodshed, and not peaceful dreams.

151. וְאִי תֵּימָא, לְבַר נָשׁ טַב אַחֲזִיאוּ לֵיהּ חֶלְמָא בִּישָׁא, הָכֵי הוּא וַדַּאי, כָּל אִינוּן בִּישִׁין דְּזַמִּינִין לְאִתְדַּבְּקָא, עַל אִינוּן דְּעָבְרֵי עַל פִּתְגָּמֵי דְאוֹרַיְיתָא, וְאִינוּן עוֹנָשִׁין דְּזַמִּינִין לְאִתְעֲנָשָׁא בְּהַהוּא עַלְמָא, כֻּלְּהוּ חָמֵי, בְּגִין דְּכָל שַׁעְתָּא יְהֵא דְחִילוּ דְמָרֵיהּ עֲלֵיהּ, וְהָא אִתְּעָרוּ, דִּכְתִּיב וְהָאֱלֹקִים עָשָׂה שֶׁיִּרְאוּ מִלְּפָנָיו, זֶה חֲלוֹם רָע. וְעַל דָּא, לְהַהוּא זַכָּאָה, אַחֲזִיוּ לֵיהּ חֶלְמָא בִּישָׁא, כְּמָה דְאִתְּמָר.

151. It may be asked how a good man could POSSIBLY be shown a bad dream. HE REPLIES: Surely all the evil is destined to cleave to those who transgress the words of the Torah, and the punishment destined for them in the world of truth was seen BY KING DAVID, so that the fear of his Master will be upon him at all times. THIS SETTLES THE QUESTION, HOW HE

COULD HAVE SEEN UNTRUE THINGS? HE SAW THEM IN RELATION TO SINNERS, FOR WHOM THEY WERE REAL. HE WAS SHOWN THIS TO AROUSE THE FEAR OF HEAVEN IN HIM. It has been said with regard to the verse, "and Elohim does it, so that men should fear before Him" (Kohelet 3:14) that it is a bad dream WHICH CAUSES A MAN TO BE FEARFUL. A righteous man is therefore shown a bad dream, as we have already said.

152. תָּא חֲזֵי, דְּהָא תָּנִינָן, דְּהַהוּא בַּר נָשׁ, דְּחָמֵי חֶלְמָא, בָּעֵי לֵיהּ לְמִפְתַּח פּוּמֵיהּ בֵּיהּ, קָמֵי בְּנֵי נָשָׁא דְּרַחֲמֵי לֵיהּ, בְּגִין דְּיִסְתַּלַּק רְעוּתָא דִּלְהוֹן לְגַבֵּיהּ לְטַב, וְיִפְתְּחוּן פּוּמַיְיהוּ לְטַב, וְיִשְׁתַּכַּח רְעוּתָא וּמִלָּה כֹּלָּא לְטַב. רְעוּתָא דְּאִיהִי מַחֲשָׁבָה, שֵׁרוּתָא דְּכֹלָּא, וּמִלָּה דְּאִיהִי סִיּוּמָא דְּכֹלָּא. וְעַל דָּא אִשְׁתַּכַּח דְּהָא שְׁלִימוּ אִיהוּ בְּרָזָא עִלָּאָה, וּבְגִין כָּךְ אִתְקַיַּים כֹּלָּא, וּבְעִינָן רְחִימִין דְּבַר נָשׁ לְאִתְקַיְּימָא בְּהַהוּא פִּשְׁרָא טָבָא, וְכֹלָּא אִיהוּ כִּדְקָא יָאוּת.

152. Come and behold; We have learned that when a man has a dream, he should speak about it. He SHOULD SEEK AN INTERPRETATION before his friends, whose wishes will be favorable toward him and whose words will be expressed for his good. Thus THEIR wishes and words will be for the good. Their wishes, which is thought, NAMELY CHOCHMAH, is the beginning of everything, OF THE SFIROT, and the word, NAMELY, MALCHUT, is the completion of everything, OF THE SFIROT. Thus it is made whole by the supernal mystery, BECAUSE OF THE PRESENCE OF THE BEGINNING AND THE END OF THE SFIROT, and all of it comes true. MOREOVER, they ask for compassion for that man and ask that the good interpretation THEY GAVE will endure. Thus all is as it should be.

153. וּבְגִין כָּךְ, קוּדְשָׁא בְּרִיךְ הוּא אוֹדַע לֵיהּ לְבַר נָשׁ, כָּל חַד וְחַד, בְּהַהוּא דַּרְגָּא דִילֵיהּ, כְּמָה דְּאִיהוּ, וּבְהַהוּא גַּוְונָא דְּכָל חַד וְחַד אֲמַר דִּיהֵא חֶלְמָא. אֲמַר הַהוּא יוּדָאי, וַדַּאי דְּחֶלְמָא לָאו אִיהוּ אֶלָּא לְבַר נָשׁ זַכָּאָה, דְּאִיהוּ חָמָא חֶלְמָא כִּדְקָא חָזֵי.

153. The Holy One, blessed be He, then informs each man IN HIS DREAM according to his worth and grade and in the same way each man interprets the dream. The Jew said: Assuredly, the dream is but for the righteous man, who sees dreams properly.

154. וְתָא חֲזֵי, דְּכַד בַּר נָשׁ נָאֵים עַל עַרְסֵיהּ, נִשְׁמָתֵיהּ נָפְקָא וְשַׁטְיָא בְּעַלְמָא לְעֵילָא, וְעָאלַת בְּאַתְרָא דְּעָאלַת, וְכַמָּה חֲבִילֵי טְהִירִין, קָיְימִין וְאָזְלִין בְּעַלְמָא, וּפָגְעִין בָּהּ בְּהַהִיא נִשְׁמָתָא, אִי זַכָּאָה הִיא, סַלְקָא לְעֵילָא וְחָמַאת מַה דְּחָמַאת, וְאִי לָאו, אִתְאַחֲדַת בְּהַהוּא סִטְרָא, וּמוֹדִיעִין לָהּ מִלִּין כְּדִיבָן, אוֹ מִלִּין דְּזַמִּינִין לְמֵיתֵי לִזְמַן קָרִיב, וְכַד אִתְעַר הַהִיא נִשְׁמָתָא דְּבֵיהּ, אִיהִי מוֹדְעָא לֵיהּ מַה דְּחָמַאת.

154. Come and behold: When a man sleeps in his bed, his soul departs and roams in the world above. It enters wherever it can, and camps of spirits that hover in the world meet the soul. If THAT MAN is righteous, THE SOUL ascends and sees whatever it sees. If he is not righteous, THE SOUL holds to the other side and is told lies or things that will happen in the near future.

155. וְעַל דָּא, לְבַר נָשׁ דְּלָאו אִיהוּ זַכָּאָה, מוֹדִיעִין לֵיהּ חֶלְמָא טָבָא, דְּלָאו אִיהוּ קְשׁוֹט, כֹּלָּא בְּגִין לְאַסְטָאָה לֵיהּ, מֵהַהוּא אֹרַח קְשׁוֹט, כֵּיוָן דְּאִיהוּ אַסְטֵי אוֹרְחֵיהּ מֵאֹרַח קְשׁוֹט, מְסָאֲבִין לֵיהּ. דְּכָל מַאן דְּאָתֵי לְאִתְדַּכָּאָה, מְדַכְּאִין לֵיהּ, וּמַאן דְּאָתֵי לְאִסְתַּאֲבָא, מְסָאֲבִין לֵיהּ, הָא וַדַּאי אִתְּמָר הָכֵי.

155. Therefore, a man who is not righteous is shown a good but untruthful dream, so that he will turn from the way of truth. Once he turns, he is defiled, for whoever comes to be purified is purified, and whoever comes to be defiled is defiled. Assuredly this is so, as we have already learned.

156. יָתְבוּ עַד דְּסָלֵיק צַפְרָא, אֲמַר רִבִּי יוֹסֵי, וַדַּאי לָא זָכַר שְׁמֵיהּ דְּיוֹסֵף, בְּאִינוּן דְּגָלִים, דִּכְתִּיב דֶּגֶל מַחֲנֵה אֶפְרַיִם, וְלָא כְּתִיב דֶּגֶל מַחֲנֵה יוֹסֵף, בְּגִין דְּאִתְגָּאֵי עַל אֲחוֹי, וְהָא אִתְּמָר.

156. They sat till dawn. Rabbi Yosi said: Surely the name of Joseph was not mentioned among the standards, as it is written, "the standard of the camp of Ephraim" (Bemidbar 2:18), rather than, "the standard of the camp of

Joseph." The reason for this is that he exalted himself above his brothers, as we have already learned.

157. אֲמַר הַהוּא יוּדָאי, וַדַּאי שְׁמַעְנָא, דְּיוֹסֵף אִיהוּ בְּעַלְמָא דִּדְכוּרָא, וְכֻלְּהוּ שִׁבְטִין בְּעַלְמָא דְנוּקְבָא אִינוּן, וְעַל דָּא לָא אִתְכְּלֵיל יוֹסֵף עִמְּהוֹן, בְּגִין דְּאִיהוּ בְּעַלְמָא דִּדְכוּרָא עִמְּהוֹן.

157. The Jew said: Surely I have heard that Joseph is of the world of the male, BEING OF YESOD OF ZEIR ANPIN, and all the tribes were of the world of the female, NAMELY THE SHECHINAH. Joseph therefore had no part in the standards, being of the world of the male.

158. מַה כְּתִיב, כֻּלָּנוּ בְּנֵי אִישׁ אֶחָד נָחְנוּ, נָחְנוּ, אֲנַחְנוּ מִבָּעֵי לֵיהּ. אַמַּאי חָסֵר א'. אֶלָּא, בְּגִין דְּרָזָא דִבְרִית לָא אִשְׁתַּכַּח עִמְּהוֹן, אִסְתַּלַּק מִתַּמָּן א', דְּהָא א' דְּכוּרָא אִיהוּ, וְעַל דָּא ב' אִיהִי נוּקְבָא, א' דְּכוּרָא. וּבְגִין דָּא, אִסְתַּלַּק א' מִתַּמָּן, וְאִשְׁתָּאֲרוּ אִינוּן נוּקְבֵי, לְגַבֵּי שְׁכִינְתָּא.

158. It is written, "We (Heb. *nachnu*) are all one man's sons" (Beresheet 42:11). HE ASKS: Why is it written *nachnu* instead of the standard form *anachnu*? Why is the *Aleph* missing? HE ANSWERS, Because the secret of the Covenant, WHICH IS JOSEPH, was not among them, the *Aleph* was gone AND IT WAS WRITTEN *NACHNU*. Thus, because the *Aleph* is male and *Bet* is female, the *Aleph*, JOSEPH, was gone and only the female LETTERS OF *NACHNU* remained with the Shechinah, WHICH CONTAINS THE SECRET OF THE TRIBES.

159. וּלְבָתַר אֲמָרוּ, כֵּנִים אֲנַחְנוּ, אִתּוֹסַף א', אֲמָרוּ וְלָא יָדְעֵי מַה קָאֲמָרוּ, בְּגִין דְּיוֹסֵף אִשְׁתַּכַּח תַּמָּן, וְאַשְׁלִימוּ מִלָּה, וַאֲמָרוּ אֲנַחְנוּ, מְנָלָן, דִּכְתִיב וַיֹּאמְרוּ שְׁנֵים עָשָׂר עֲבָדֶיךָ אַחִים אֲנַחְנוּ, וְיוֹסֵף אִיהוּ בְּחוּשְׁבָּנָא, כַּד עָאל בְּחוּשְׁבָּנָא, אֲמָרוּ אֲנַחְנוּ, וְכַד לָא עָאל בְּחוּשְׁבָּנָא, אֲמָרוּ נָחְנוּ.

159. They later said: "We (Heb. *anachnu*) are true men" (Ibid.) with the letter *Aleph* added. They said it, yet knew not what they said, for it was because of Joseph that they uttered the complete word *anachnu*. How do we know this? From the verse, "And they said, 'Your servants are twelve, we are (Heb. *anachnu*) brothers'" (Ibid. 13), including Joseph. Thus, when JOSEPH was included, they said *anachnu*, and when he was not, they said *nachnu*.

160. אֲמַר רִבִּי יוֹסֵי, כָּל הַנֵּי מִלִּין דְּקָאֲמָרָן הָכָא, קוּדְשָׁא בְּרִיךְ הוּא אִתְרְעֵי בְּהוֹ, דְּהָא שְׁכִינְתָּא לָא אַעֲדֵי מֵהָכָא, כְּדִכְתִיב אָז נִדְבְּרוּ יִרְאֵי יי׳ אִישׁ אֶל רֵעֵהוּ וַיַּקְשֵׁב יי׳ וַיִּשְׁמָע וַיִּכָּתֵב סֵפֶר זִכָּרוֹן לְפָנָיו לְיִרְאֵי יי׳ וּלְחוֹשְׁבֵי שְׁמוֹ.

160. Rabbi Yosi said: All the things we have said delighted the Holy One, blessed be He, because the Shechinah did not depart from here. This is in accordance with the verse, "Then, they who feared Hashem spoke to one another: and Hashem hearkened, and heard it, and a book of remembrance was written before Him for those who feared Hashem and took heed of His name" (Malachi 3:16).

10. "And he put them all together into custody"

A Synopsis

The verses relate the twelve signs of the zodiac to the twelve sons of Jacob and the twelve tribes of Israel. Joseph, who shows mercy to his treacherous brother, becomes a Patriarch. Rabbi Elazar speculates on the hidden meaning of this occurrence.

The Relevance of this Passage

Celestial influences arising from the twelve Signs impel, but they do not compel.

We have the power to rise above their influence. We transcend the signs and their corresponding negative influences as we visually connect with these ancient mystical texts.

161. וַיֶּאֱסֹף אוֹתָם אֶל מִשְׁמָר שְׁלֹשֶׁת יָמִים. אֲמַר רִבִּי אֶלְעָזָר, הַנֵּי תְּלַת יוֹמִין אַמַּאי. אֶלָּא הַנֵּי תְּלַת יוֹמִין, לָקֳבֵיל תְּלַת יוֹמִין דִּשְׁכֶם, דִּכְתִּיב וַיְהִי בַיּוֹם הַשְּׁלִישִׁי בִּהְיוֹתָם כּוֹאֲבִים.

161. "And he put them all together into custody for three days" (Beresheet 42:17). Rabbi Elazar asked: Why for three days? HE ANSWERS, These three days correspond to the days of Shchem, of which it is written, "And it came to pass on the third day, when they were in pain" (Beresheet 34: 25).

162. תָּא חֲזֵי מַה כְּתִיב בֵּיהּ, וַיֹּאמֶר אֲלֵיהֶם יוֹסֵף בַּיּוֹם הַשְּׁלִישִׁי זֹאת עֲשׂוּ וִחְיוּ. לְאַחֲזָאָה, דָּא עָבַד אִיהוּ, כְּמָה דְּאִינוּן עָבְדוּ בִּשְׁכֶם, דְּגָרְמוּ לְאַנְשֵׁי שְׁכֶם לְקַבְּלָא עֲלַיְיהוּ הַאי זֹאת, רָזָא דִבְרִית, וּלְבָתַר דַּעֲבָדוּ קִיּוּמָא דָא, קְטִילוּ לוֹן, וְלָא אִשְׁתָּאַר מִנְּהוֹן חַד, וְאִיהוּ מַה כְּתִיב, זֹאת עֲשׂוּ וִחְיוּ, מ"ט בְּגִין דְּאֶת הָאֱלֹקִים אֲנִי יָרֵא, נָטִיר קְיָימָא, וְכָל גִּלְגּוּלָא דָא לָא הֲוָה, אֶלָּא בְּגִינֵיהּ דְּבִנְיָמִין.

162. Come and behold: It is written with regard to this, "And Joseph said to them on the third day, 'this do, and live'". This teaches us that he did not act toward them as they did toward Shchem. They made the people of Shchem accept upon them this (Heb. *zot*) – THE NUKVA CALLED 'THIS', and the secret of the covenant, BECAUSE THE COVENANT, WHICH IS THE SECRET OF YESOD, IS ATTACHED TO HER. And when they were circumcised, they were killed and not even one witness left. But he said: It is written, "This do, and live," THAT IS, HE WILL LET THEM LIVE. The reason is that "I fear the Elohim" who keeps the Covenant. And everything he did was only for the sake of Benjamin, THAT IS, TO MAKE THEM BRING BENJAMIN.

163. וַיֹּאמְרוּ אִישׁ אֶל אָחִיו אֲבָל אֲשֵׁמִים אֲנַחְנוּ עַל אָחִינוּ וגו'. וַיֹּאמְרוּ אִישׁ אֶל אָחִיו: דָּא שִׁמְעוֹן וְלֵוִי, כְּמָה דַּהֲוָה בְּקַדְמֵיתָא, דִּכְתִיב וַיֹּאמְרוּ אִישׁ אֶל אָחִיו הִנֵּה בַּעַל הַחֲלוֹמוֹת הַלָּזֶה בָּא, מַה לְהַלָּן שִׁמְעוֹן וְלֵוִי, אוּף הָכָא שִׁמְעוֹן וְלֵוִי.

163. "And they said one to the other, truly we are guilty concerning our brother" (Beresheet 42:21). The phrase, "one to another (lit. 'man to his brother')" refers to Simeon and Levi, just as in an earlier passage, "And they said one to another, behold, this dreamer comes" (Beresheet 37:19). Both verses refer to Simeon and Levi.

164. תָּא חֲזֵי, מַאן אִישׁ. וּמַאן אָחִיו. אֶלָּא אִישׁ: דָּא שִׁמְעוֹן, כְּתִיב הָכָא אִישׁ, וּכְתִיב הָתָם וְהִנֵּה אִישׁ מִבְּנֵי יִשְׂרָאֵל בָּא, מַה לְהַלָּן מִשִּׁמְעוֹן, אוּף הָכָא נָמֵי שִׁמְעוֹן. וּבְגִין דְּאַהֲדַר בִּתְשׁוּבָה, בָּכָה וְאִתְנֶחָם עַל דָּא, וַאֲמַר לְלֵוִי, אֲבָל אֲשֵׁמִים אֲנַחְנוּ, עַל דָּא אִתְבְּנֵי מַזָּלֵיהּ שׁוֹר, כְּגַוְונָא דְּמַזְּלֵיהּ דְּיוֹסֵף שׁוֹר, דִּכְתִיב בְּכוֹר שׁוֹרוֹ הָדָר לוֹ, וּמַזָּלֵיהּ דְּשִׁמְעוֹן שׁוֹר אִיהוּ.

164. Come and behold: Who is the "man" and who is "his brother?" HE ANSWERS, The man is Simeon, who is here mentioned as man, as he is elsewhere, IN THE VERSE, "And behold, a man of the children of Yisrael came" (Bemidbar 25:6). In both verses, the man is Simeon. And since he repented, he cried and felt remorse for what he did and said to Levi, "truly we are guilty." Therefore WHEN HE REPENTED, Simeon's sign became Taurus. THERE ARE TWELVE SIGNS THAT CORRESPOND TO THE TWELVE TRIBES, ARIES TO REUBEN, TAURUS TO SIMEON, AND SO ON. Simeon's sign is Taurus, just as Joseph's sign is, as it is written, "His firstling bullock, majesty is his" (Devarim 33:17).

11. "And took from them Simeon"

A Synopsis

This passage comments on the mercy Joseph shows his brothers. The commentators assert that even idolaters are not punished if they live in peace. The secret meaning of circumcision and its relation to the Covenant are also discussed. Whoever is charitable in this world is free of harsh judgment in the next. Thus, like Joseph, we are encouraged to turn the other cheek and leave vengeance to the Lord.

The Relevance of this Passage

Judgments decreed against us are measured and meted out in accordance to the degree and severity of the judgments we pass on our friends and foes. Trust in The Creator encompasses certainty in the laws of cause and effect, which dictate that all our enemies will be correctly judged without our having to participate in the correction process. A person who has attained spiritual enlightenment accepts any wrongs committed against him as payment for negative actions he may have committed in the past. This wise perspective is stimulated by the Divine Light of this Hebrew script.

165. וְעַל דָּא וַיִּקַּח מֵאִתָּם אֶת שִׁמְעוֹן, בְּגִין דְּלָא יְקַטְרֵג בַּהֲדֵיהּ דְּלֵוִי, בְּגִין דְּשִׁמְעוֹן וְלֵוִי, כַּד מִתְחַבְּרָן תַּרְוַויְיהוּ, יָכְלֵי לְקַטְרְגָא. וַיֶּאֱסוֹר אוֹתוֹ לְעֵינֵיהֶם, הָא אוֹקְמוּהָ, לְעֵינֵיהֶם אֲסָרוֹ, וּלְבָתַר דְּנָפְקוּ הֲוָה מַאֲכִיל לֵיהּ, וּמַשְׁקֵי לֵיהּ.

165. He therefore "took from them Simeon" (Beresheet 42:24) so that he would not indict him together with Levi. For when they came together, Simeon and Levi might bring accusations. The phrase, "and bound him before their eyes" means that he arrested him only in front of their eyes. When they left, he gave him food and drink.

166. וְאִי תֵּימָא דִּרְעוּתָא דְּיוֹסֵף אִיהוּ, בְּגִין דִּכְתִיב אִם רָעֵב שׂוֹנַאֲךָ הַאֲכִילֵהוּ לֶחֶם וְאִם צָמֵא הַשְׁקֵהוּ מַיִם, אִי הָכֵי יוֹסֵף דְּאִיהוּ זַכָּאָה, הֵיכִי עָבֵיד הָכֵי, דְּהָא כְתִיב כִּי גֶחָלִים אַתָּה חוֹתֶה עַל רֹאשׁוֹ וַיְיָ׳ יְשַׁלֶּם לָךְ.

166. It may be said that Joseph acted according to the verse, "If your enemy is hungry, give him bread to eat; and if he is thirsty, give him water to drink" (Mishlei 25:21). FOR THIS REASON HE FED SIMEON, WHO WAS HIS ENEMY. How could the righteous Joseph have behaved in such a manner? As the verse ends with the words, "for you shall heap coals of fire on his head, and Hashem shall reward you." IT IS NOT SEEMLY FOR A RIGHTEOUS MAN TO TAKE REVENGE UPON HIS BROTHER.

167. אֶלָּא, ח"ו דְּיוֹסֵף לְהָכֵי הוּא דְּחָיֵישׁ, אֶלָּא כְּבַר נָשׁ לַאֲחוּי, הָכֵי נָמֵי הֲוָה עָבֵיד, אִתְנְהִיג עִמֵּיהּ בְּאַחְוָה, וְלָא בְּגַוְונָא אָחֳרָא, וְלָא עִמֵּיהּ בִּלְחוֹדוֹי, אֶלָּא עִם כָּל אֲחוֹי, כְּמָה דִכְתִיב וַיְצַו יוֹסֵף וַיְמַלְאוּ אֶת כְּלֵיהֶם בָּר וּלְהָשִׁיב כַּסְפֵּיהֶם אִישׁ אֶל שַׂקּוֹ וְלָתֵת לָהֶם צֵדָה לַדֶּרֶךְ וַיַּעַשׂ לָהֶם כֵּן, בְּגִין לְאַנְהָגָא עִמְּהוֹן בְּאַחְוָה.

167. HE ANSWERS, Heaven forbid that Joseph had such intentions. His conduct toward him was only that of a man toward his brother, and in no other way. And not to him alone, but to all his brothers he behaved so, as it is written, "Then Joseph gave orders to fill their sacks with grain, and to restore every man's money into his sack, and to give them provision for the way: and thus it was performed" (Beresheet 42:25), all to be brotherly toward them.

168. רִבִּי יוֹסֵי פָּתַח וַאֲמַר, אִם שְׁלֵמִים וְכֵן רַבִּים וְכֵן נָגֹזּוּ וְעָבָר וְעִנִּיתִיךְ לֹא אֲעַנֵּךְ עוֹד, הַאי קְרָא אוֹקְמוּהָ, דְּכַד עַמָּא כֻּלְּהוּ אִית בְּהוֹ שְׁלָם, וְלָא אִית בְּהוֹ מָארֵי דְּבָבוּ, קוּדְשָׁא בְּרִיךְ הוּא חָיֵיס עֲלַיְיהוּ, וְדִינָא לָא שָׁלְטָא בְּהוֹ, וְאַף עַל גַּב דְּכֻלְּהוּ פָּלְחֵי לְכו"ם, וְאִינוּן בִּשְׁלָם, דִּינָא לָא שַׁלִּיט עֲלַיְיהוּ, וְאוֹקְמוּהָ דִּכְתִיב חֲבוּר עֲצַבִּים אֶפְרָיִם הַנַּח לוֹ.

168. Rabbi Yosi continued with the verse, "Though they are at peace, and likewise many, even so they shall be cut down, and it shall pass away. Though I have afflicted you, I will afflict you no more" (Nachum 1:12). This verse has been explained as follows: When the people are peaceful, with no dissension in their midst, the Holy One, blessed be He, has pity on them, and Judgment has no sway. Even if they worship idols, if they are at peace, no judgment has power over them. It can also be explained in relation to the verse, "Ephraim is joined to idols: let him alone" (Hoshea 4:17). IT MEANS THAT EVEN THOUGH THEY SERVE IDOLS, IF THEY ARE JOINED, "LET HIM ALONE."

169. וְכֵן נָגֹזוּ וְעָבָר, מַאי וְכֵן נָגֹזוּ, וְנָגֹזוּ מִבָּעֵי לֵיהּ. אֶלָּא, דָּא הוּא רֵישָׁא דִקְרָא דְּאִיהוּ שְׁלֵמִים, אוּף הָכָא שְׁלָם, וּמַאי אִיהוּ, דָּא צְדָקָה, בְּגִין דִּצְדָקָה דָּא הוּא שָׁלוֹם, וּמַאן דְּאַסְגֵּי בִּצְדָקָה, אַסְגֵּי שְׁלָם לְעֵילָּא, וְאַסְגֵּי שְׁלָם לְתַתָּא, וּבְגִין כָּךְ נָגֹזוּ וְעָבָר, דְּגָזְזֵי מָמוֹנְהוֹן בִּצְדָקָה. וְעָבָר, וְעָבְרוּ מִבָּעֵי לֵיהּ, מַאי וְעָבָר. אֶלָּא דָּא הוּא דִּינָא דְרוּגְזָא, כד"א עַד יַעֲבֹר זַעַם, עָבַר דִּינָא מֵעֲלַיְיהוּ.

169. HE ASKS: What then is the meaning of the phrase, "even so they shall be cut down (also: 'shorn')?" HE ANSWERS, As it talks of peace in the beginning, here IT likewise TALKS of peace, which means charity. For charity is peace, and whoever promotes charity, promotes peace above and below. Hence the scripture reads, "even so they shall be shorn, and it shall pass away." The word "shorn" REFERS TO those who shear their money for charity. "EVEN SO" INDICATES THAT AS THE BEGINNING TALKS OF PEACE, HERE ALSO IT TALKS OF PEACE, NAMELY, CHARITY, AS HAS BEEN EXPLAINED. Of the phrase, "It shall pass away," HE ASKS: Should it have been written: "they shall pass away" IN THE PLURAL, JUST AS IT IS WRITTEN, "THEY WILL...BE CUT DOWN." Why is it written, "it shall pass away?" HE REPLIES: The subject is wrathful judgment, just as in the verse, "until the indignation be overpast" (Yeshayah 26:20); IT MEANS until judgment passes away from them.

170. דָּבָר אֲחֵר, כֹּה אָמַר יי' אִם שְׁלֵמִים, אִלֵּין יִשְׂרָאֵל, דְּקוּדְשָׁא בְּרִיךְ הוּא יְהַב לוֹן בְּרִית קַיָּימָא לְנַטְרָא לֵיהּ תָּדִיר, וּלְמֶהֱוֵי בֵּיהּ בַּר נָשׁ שְׁלִים בְּכָל סִטְרִין לְעֵילָּא וְתַתָּא. וְאִי לָא נָטֵיר לֵיהּ בַּר נָשׁ תָּדִיר, הָא אִיהוּ פָּגִים, פָּגוּם בְּכֹלָּא, מְנָלָן, דִּכְתִיב הִתְהַלֵּךְ לְפָנַי וֶהְיֵה תָמִים, מַאי תָמִים. שְׁלִים. דְּעַד לָא אִתְקַיַּים בֵּיהּ בְּרִית, אִיהוּ פָּגִים.

170. Another explanation is that the verse: "Thus says Hashem, though (if) they are a peace (also: 'whole')," refers to Yisrael, to whom the Holy One, blessed be He, gave an everlasting covenant, NAMELY, CIRCUMCISION, to keep always, so as to be whole on all sides – CHESED, GVURAH, TIFERET AND MALCUT above and below, THAT ARE NETZACH AND HOD. If man does not guard the covenant at all times, he is defective in every respect. How do we know this? From the verse, "Walk before Me, and be perfect"

(Beresheet 17:1). Perfect means whole, and we derive from this that before the covenant was established in him, BEFORE HE WAS CIRCUMCISED, he was defective.

171. וּבְגִין כָּךְ אִם שְׁלֵמִים וְכֵן רַבִּים, אִם שְׁלֵמִים דְּנָטְרֵי פִּקּוּדָא דָא, לְמֶהֱוֵי שְׁלֵימִין, דְּלָא יְהוֹן פְּגִימִין, וְכֵן רַבִּים: יִפְשׁוּן וְיִסְגּוּן בֵּיהּ, בְּגִין דְּנִשְׁמָתִין לָא נָפְקֵי לְעַלְמָא, אֶלָּא בְּהַאי בְּרִית. וְכֵן נָגֹזּוּ, הַאי אִם שְׁלֵמִים דְּנָטְרֵי לֵיהּ תָּדִיר, נָגֹזּוּ מַאן דְּאִתְגְּזַר וְקִבֵּל עֲלֵיהּ קְיָימָא דָא. וְעָבָר, מַאי וְעָבָר. הַהוּא זוּהֲמָא דְעָרְלָה, דַּהֲוָה בֵּיהּ בְּקַדְמֵיתָא.

171. Therefore, "if they be whole" MEANS if they observe the precept OF CIRCUMCISION, and are therefore whole instead of defective; "and likewise many," NAMELY they will increase and multiply, for souls come into the world only through the covenant. "And they shall be cut down" REFERS TO THE FIRST PHRASE: "If they be whole" and constantly guard THE COVENANT, namely, "they shall be cut down" those who are circumcised, and accept upon hem the covenant. "CUT DOWN" IS DERIVED FROM SHEARING AND CUTTING. Then "it shall pass away", the filth of the foreskin that was upon them.

172. דָּבָר אֲחֵר כֹּה אָמַר יי׳ אִם שְׁלֵמִים וְכֵן רַבִּים, אִלֵּין בְּנֵי יַעֲקֹב, דְּהָא כָּל זִמְנָא דַּהֲווֹ לְגַבֵּיהּ דְּיוֹסֵף, אִינוּן שְׁלֵמִים, דְּקָיְימֵי בַּהֲדֵיהּ דִּבְרִית. וְכֵן נָגֹזּוּ, דְּאָזְלוּ וְשָׁבְקוּ לֵיהּ לְיוֹסֵף וּלְשִׁמְעוֹן. וְעָבָר, כְּדֵין דִּינָא שַׁרְיָא בְּגִינַיְיהוּ, כד״א וְעָבַר יי׳ לִנְגּוֹף אֶת מִצְרַיִם.

172. Another interpretation of "Thus says Hashem, 'If they be whole and likewise many'" is that these are the children of Jacob, who, as long as they were with Joseph, were whole, because they were joined with the covenant, WHICH IS JOSEPH. "Even so they shall be cut down (Heb. *nagozu*)" MEANS when they went away and left Joseph and Simeon. *NAGOZU* IS DERIVED FROM PASSING AWAY, AS IN "IT IS SOON PAST (HEB. *GAZ*), AND WE FLY AWAY" (TEHILIM 90:10). Then "it shall pass away" means that then Judgment is passed upon them, as it is written, "and Hashem will pass through to smite Egypt" (Shemot 12:23). IN BOTH VERSES, PASS ALLUDES TO JUDGMENT.

173. תָּא חֲזֵי, אִית דִּינָא קַשְׁיָא, וְאִית דִּינָא רַפְיָא. דִּינָא קַשְׁיָא תַּקִּיף, דִּינָא רַפְיָא חָלָשׁ, וְכַד יָנְקָא הַאי דִּינָא רַפְיָא, מִדִּינָא קַשְׁיָא, כְּדֵין אִתְתַּקַּף, וְאִיהוּ תַּקִּיף.

173. Come and behold: There is harsh Judgment and mild Judgment. The harsh Judgment is strong, and the mild weak. When the mild Judgment is nourished from the harsh, it becomes powerful.

174. בְּשַׁעְתָּא דְּאִתְעֲבֵיד דִּינָא עַל יִשְׂרָאֵל, אִתְעֲבֵיד בְּהַאי דִּינָא רַפְיָא, וְלָא אִתְתַּקַּף בְּהַהוּא דִּינָא קַשְׁיָא, וְכַד דִּינָא אִתְעֲבֵיד עֲלַיְיהוּ דְּעַמִּין עעכו"ם, אִתְתַּקַּף הַאי דִּינָא רַפְיָא, בְּדִינָא קַשְׁיָא דִּלְעֵילָּא, בְּגִין לְאִתְתַּקְפָא, הה"ד, וְעָבַר ה' לִנְגּוֹף אֶת מִצְרַיִם. וְעָבַר: דְּאִתְמְלֵי עֶבְרָה וָזַעֲמָא, וְאִתְתַּקַּף בְּדִינָא קַשְׁיָא, אוּף הָכָא וְעָבַר. וְתָא חֲזֵי, בְּשַׁעְתָּא דְּמִתְכַּנְּשֵׁי עֲשָׂרָה בְּבֵי כְּנִישְׁתָּא, וְחַד מִנַּיְיהוּ אִשְׁתְּמִיט, כְּדֵין קוּדְשָׁא בְּרִיךְ הוּא אַרְגֵּיז עֲלֵיהּ.

174. When judgment is executed upon Yisrael, it is mild and not strengthened by harsh Judgment. When executed upon idolatrous nations, the mild Judgment is strengthened by the supernal harsh Judgment. This is the meaning of the verse "and Hashem will pass (Heb. *ve'avar*) through to smite Egypt." The word "*ve'avar*" also means that He was filled with wrath (Heb. *evra*) and indignation, which was supported by harsh Judgment. In this same verse, pass away MEANS THAT HE IS FILLED WITH WRATH, ALTHOUGH IT IS MILD JUDGMENT NOT POWERED BY HARSH JUDGMENT, BECAUSE IT IS EXECUTED UPON YISRAEL. And come and behold: When ten gather together in the synagogue and one of them leaves, then the Holy One, blessed be He, is angered with him. FOR THE BROTHERS OF JOSEPH WERE TEN. AFTER THEY SEPARATED FROM JOSEPH AND SIMEON THEY REMAINED NINE, AND THE HOLY ONE, BLESSED BE HE, BECAME ANGRY.

175. דָּבָר אַחֵר וְכֵן נָגֹזּוּ, כַּד מִתְעַבְּרֵי מִנַּיְיהוּ אִינוּן עוֹבָדִין בִּישִׁין, כְּדֵין וְעָבָר, מַאי וְעָבָר, ר' שִׁמְעוֹן אֲמַר בִּזְמְנָא דְנִשְׁמָתָא נָפְקַת מֵהַאי עַלְמָא, בְּכַמָּה דִינִין אִתְדָּנַת, עַד לָא תֵיעוֹל לְאַתְרָהּ, לְבָתַר, כָּל אִינוּן

נִשְׁמָתִין אִית לוֹן לְמֶעֱבַר, בְּהַךְ נְהַר דִּינוּר דְּנָגִיד וְנָפִיק, וּלְאִסְתַּחָאָה תַּמָּן, וּמַאן אִיהוּ דְּיָקוּם תַּמָּן, וְיַעֲבַר בְּלָא דְּחִילוּ, כד״א מִי יַעֲלֶה בְּהַר ה׳ וגו׳, וְנִשְׁמָתָא דְּזַכָּאָה אַעֲבַר בְּלָא דְּחִילוּ וְיָקוּם בִּמְקוֹם קָדְשׁוֹ.

175. Another explanation of the verse, "Even so they shall be cut down (Heb. *nagozu*)" is that when evil actions are removed from them (*NAGOZU* EXPLAINING AS DERIVING FROM "IT IS SOON PAST [*GAZ*]), then "it shall pass away." Who shall pass away? Rabbi Shimon answered, When the soul leaves this world, it is sentenced to several punishments before going to its place. Afterward, all the souls have to pass through and wash in the flowing The Dinur River (river of fire). Of whoever will rise and pass the river fearlessly, it is written, "Who shall ascend into the mountain of Hashem?" (Tehilim 24:3) The soul of the righteous passes without fear and "shall stand in his Holy place" (Ibid.).

176. וּמַאן דְּאִשְׁתַּדַּל בִּצְדָקָה בְּהַאי עָלְמָא, וְיָהִיב מִמָּמוֹנֵיהּ בִּצְדָקָה, כְּדֵין וְעָבַר בְּהַהוּא אֲתַר, וְלָא דָּחִיל, וְכָרוֹזָא קָרֵי לָהּ לְהַהִיא נִשְׁמָתָא, וְעִנִּיתִךְ לֹא אֲעַנֵּךְ עוֹד, מַאן דְּזָכָה לְמֶעֱבַר בְּהַאי, לֵית לֵיהּ דִּינָא יַתִּיר כְּלָל.

176. Whoever is charitable in the world and gives from his money to charity passes that place, THE DINUR RIVER, without fear. The crier proclaims before the soul, "and though I have afflicted you, I will afflict you no more" (Nachum 1:12), WHICH IS THE LAST PHRASE IN THE VERSE. For whoever merited to pass the Dinur River is free of judgments.

177. תָּא חֲזֵי, כָּל דָּא דְּיוֹסֵף עִם אֲחוֹי, וְכָל הָנֵי מִילֵי, אַמַּאי אִצְטְרִיךְ, אֶלָּא אוֹרַיְיתָא דִּקְשׁוֹט, אִיהִי אוֹרַיְיתָא, וְכָל אָרְחָהָא אָרְחִין קַדִּישִׁין, וְלֵית לָךְ מִלָּה בְּאוֹרַיְיתָא דְּלָאו אִית בָּהּ רָזִין עִלָּאִין וְקַדִּישִׁין, וְאָרְחִין לִבְנֵי נָשָׁא לְאִתְתַּקְפָא בְּהוֹ.

177. Come and behold: Why was all that passed between Joseph and his brothers RECORDED IN THE TORAH? HE ANSWERS, The Torah is of truth, all her ways are holy. There is not one word in the Torah that does not contain holy and supernal mysteries and ways in which men can be strengthened.

178. פָּתַח וַאֲמַר, אַל תֹּאמַר אֲשַׁלְּמָה רָע וגו'. תָּא חֲזֵי, קוּדְשָׁא בְּרִיךְ הוּא עֲבֵיד לֵיהּ לְבַר נָשׁ, לְאִתְתַּקְּפָא בָּהּ בְּאוֹרַיְיתָא, וּלְמֵיהַךְ בְּאֹרַח קְשׁוֹט, וְלִסְטַר יְמִינָא, וְלָא יְהַךְ לִסְטַר שְׂמָאלָא. וּבְגִין דְּבָעֵי לְהוֹ לְמֵיהַךְ לִסְטַר יְמִינָא, אִית לוֹן לְאַסְגָּאָה רְחִימוּ דָּא עִם דָּא, וְלָא יְהֵא דְּבָבוּ דָּא עִם דָּא, בְּגִין דְּלָא לְאַכְחָשָׁא יְמִינָא, דְּאִיהוּ אֲתַר דְּיִשְׂרָאֵל מִתְדַּבְּקָן בֵּיהּ.

178. He opened the discussion with the verse, "Do not say, I will repay evil" (Mishlei 20:22). Come and behold: The Holy One, blessed be He, created man so he would strengthen himself in the Torah and walk the way of truth, staying on the right side and avoiding the left. Because MEN should walk on the right side, they have to increase love between them, AS LOVE IS OF THE RIGHT SIDE, and avoid hatred among them, AS HATRED IS OF THE LEFT SIDE, so as not to weaken the right, which is the place to which Yisrael cleave.

179. וְתָא חֲזֵי, בְּגִין כָּךְ אִיהוּ יֵצֶר טוֹב וְיֵצֶר רָע, וְיִשְׂרָאֵל בָּעְיָין לְאִתְתַּקְּפָא לְיֵצֶר טוֹב עַל יֵצֶר רָע, בְּאִינוּן עוֹבָדִין דְּכַשְׁרָן, וְאִי סָטֵי בַּר נָשׁ לִשְׂמָאלָא, כְּדֵין אִתְתַּקַּף יֵצֶר רָע עַל יֵצֶר טוֹב, וּמַאן דַּהֲוָה פָּגִים, אַשְׁלֵים לֵיהּ בְּחֶטְאוֹי, דְּהָא לָא אִשְׁתְּלֵים דָּא מְנוּוְלָא, אֶלָּא בְּחֶטְאִין דִּבְנֵי נָשָׁא.

179. Come and behold: For this purpose, the Good Inclination and the Evil Inclination exist. Yisrael should make the Good Inclination master over the evil through good deeds. If a man turns to the left, the Evil Inclination overpowers the good, and the defective one, THE EVIL INCLINATION, is made whole through his sin, for the ugly one only becomes whole through men's sins.

180. וּבְגִין כָּךְ בָּעֵי בַּר נָשׁ לְאִזְדַּהֲרָא, דְּלָא יִשְׁתְּלִים הַהוּא יֵצֶר רָע בְּחֶטְאוֹי, וְיִסְתַּמַּר תָּדִיר, דְּהָא יֵצֶר טוֹב בָּעֵי לְאַשְׁלְמָא לֵיהּ בִּשְׁלֵימוּת תָּדִיר, וְלֹא יֵצֶר הָרָע. וּבְגִין כָּךְ אַל תֹּאמַר אֲשַׁלְּמָה רַע קַוֵּה אֶל ה' וְיוֹשַׁע לָךְ.

180. A man should therefore be careful lest the Evil Inclination be made whole through his sins. He should always be guarded, to make whole the Good Inclination instead of the evil. Therefore, "Do not say, I will repay (also: 'complete') evil" BECAUSE THROUGH HATRED YOU SHALL INCREASE THE POWER OF THE LEFT AND COMPLETE THE EVIL INCLINATION. Only say, "wait on Hashem, and He will save you."

181. דָּבָר אֲחֵר אַל תֹּאמַר אֲשַׁלְּמָה רַע, כְּדִכְתִיב וּמְשַׁלְּמֵי רָעָה תַּחַת טוֹבָה, לְמַעַן דְּשַׁלֵּים לֵיהּ טוֹבָה, דְּלֹא יַשְׁלֵים לֵיהּ רָע, בְּגִין דִּכְתִיב מֵשִׁיב רָעָה תַּחַת טוֹבָה לֹא תָמוּשׁ רָעָה מִבֵּיתוֹ, אֲפִילּוּ לְמַאן דְּאַשְׁלִימוּ לֵיהּ בִּישִׁין, לָא אִית לֵיהּ לְאַשְׁלָמָא בִּישָׁא, חֲלַף הַהוּא בִישׁוּ דְּשַׁלִּימוּ לֵיהּ, אֶלָּא קַוֵּה לַה׳ וְיוֹשַׁע לָךְ.

181. Another explanation of the verse, "Do not say, I will repay evil," is that it has the same meaning as the verse, "Whoever rewards evil for good" (Mishlei 17:13). One should not repay a person who did him good with evil, because "whoever rewards evil for good, evil shall not depart from his house." But even if a person caused him evil, he must not reward evil with evil, but "wait on Hashem, and He will save you."

182. וְהַאי קְרָא אוֹקְמוּהָ, בְּיוֹסֵף זַכָּאָה, דְּלָא בָּעָא לְאַשְׁלָמָא בִּישָׁא לַאֲחוֹי, בְּשַׁעְתָּא דְּנָפְלוּ בִּידוֹי. קַוֵּה לַה׳ וְיוֹשַׁע לָךְ, בְּגִין דְּהוּא הֲוָה דָּחִיל לְקוּדְשָׁא בְּרִיךְ הוּא, דִּכְתִיב זֹאת עֲשׂוּ וִחְיוּ וגו׳, וְאִיהוּ תָּדִיר הֲוָה מְחַכֶּה לְקוּדְשָׁא בְּרִיךְ הוּא.

182. This verse has been explained in relation to Joseph the Righteous, who did not wish to repay his brothers with evil when they fell into his hands, AS IT IS WRITTEN, "DO NOT SAY, I WILL REPAY EVIL; but wait on Hashem, and He will save you." For he feared the Holy One, blessed be He, as it is written, "This do, and live: I fear Elohim" (Beresheet 42:18). He always waited on the Holy One, blessed be He.

183. ר׳ אַבָּא פָּתַח וְאָמַר, מַיִם עֲמוּקִים עֵצָה בְּלֵב אִישׁ וְאִישׁ תְּבוּנָה יִדְלֶנָּה. מַיִם עֲמוּקִים עֵצָה בְּלֵב אִישׁ, דָּא קוּדְשָׁא בְּרִיךְ הוּא, בְּגִין דְּאִיהוּ עָבֵיד עֵצוֹת, דְּאַיְיתֵי טַעֲמִין לְגַלְגְּלָא גִּלְגּוּלִין עַל עַלְמָא עַל יְדָא

דְיוֹסֵף, לְקַיְּימָא הַהוּא גְזֵרָה, דְּגָזַר כַּפְנָא עַל אַרְעָא. וְאִישׁ תְּבוּנָה יִדְלֶנָּה, דָּא יוֹסֵף, דְּגַלֵּי אִינוּן עֲמִיקִין, דְּגָזַר קוּדְשָׁא בְּרִיךְ הוּא עַל עַלְמָא.

183. Rabbi Aba opened with the verse, "Counsel in the heart of man is like deep water; but a man of understanding will draw it out" (Mishlei. 20:5). "Counsel in the heart of man is like deep water" refers to the Holy One, blessed be He, who gave counsel by bringing about events by the hands of Joseph to fulfill the decree of famine upon the world. "But a man of understanding will draw it out" refers to Joseph, who revealed the deep meanings of the decree of the Holy One, blessed be He, over the world THROUGH THE INTERPRETATION OF THE DREAM.

184. תָּא חֲזֵי, יוֹסֵף לֹא דֵי לֵיהּ דְּאִיהוּ לָא שַׁלֵּים בִּישָׁא לַאֲחוֹי, אֶלָּא דַּעֲבַד עִמְּהוֹן טִיבוּ וּקְשׁוֹט, וְכָךְ אָרְחֵיהוֹן דְּזַכָּאֵי תָּדִיר, בְּגִין דָּא קוּדְשָׁא בְּרִיךְ הוּא חָיֵיס עֲלַיְיהוּ תָּדִיר, בְּעַלְמָא דֵין וּבְעַלְמָא דְּאָתֵי.

184. Come and behold: Joseph not only abstained from causing evil to his brothers, he also did kindness and truth by them. This is always the way of the righteous. Therefore, the Holy One, blessed be He, always has compassion for them in this world and the World to Come.

185. מַיִם עֲמוּקִים עֵצָה בְּלֶב אִישׁ, דָּא יְהוּדָה, וְהָא אוֹקְמוּהָ, בְּשַׁעְתָּא דְּאִתְקָרֵיב לְגַבֵּיהּ דְּיוֹסֵף, עַל עִסְקָא דְּבִנְיָמִין. וְאִישׁ תְּבוּנָה יִדְלֶנָּה דָּא יוֹסֵף.

185. "Counsel in the heart of man is like deep water" can also refer to Judah when he approached Joseph on behalf of Benjamin. The phrase, "a man of understanding will draw it out," refers to Joseph WHEN HE MADE HIMSELF KNOWN TO HIS BROTHERS.

186. ר' אַבָּא הֲוָה יָתִיב אַתַּרְעָא דְּאַבָּבָא דְּלוֹד, חָמָא חַד בַּר נָשׁ דַּהֲוָה אָתֵי, וְיָתֵיב בְּחַד קוּלְטָא דְּתָלָא דְּאַרְעָא, וַהֲוָה לָאֵי מֵאָרְחָא, וְיָתֵיב וְנָאִים תַּמָּן, אַדְּהָכֵי חָמֵי חַד חִוְיָא, דַּהֲוָה אָתֵי לְגַבֵּיהּ, נְפַק קוּסְטְפָא

דְגוֹרְדְנָא, וְקָטֵיל לֵיהּ לְחִוְיָא. כַּד אִתְעַר הַהוּא בַּר נָשׁ, חָמָא הַהוּא חִוְיָא לְקִבְלֵיהּ, דַּהֲוָה מִית, אִזְדַּקַּף הַהוּא בַּר נָשׁ, וְנָפַל הַהוּא קוּלְטָא לְעוּמְקָא דִתְחוֹתוֹי וְאִשְׁתֵּזִיב.

186. Rabbi Aba sat at the gate of the city Lod. He saw a man sitting on a ledge PROTRUDING from a mountainside. He was weary from the road, so he sat down and slept. While he was sleeping, he saw a snake coming toward him. A reptile emerged and killed the snake. When the man woke, he saw the dead snake. He stood up and the ledge, WHICH HAD BEEN TORN FROM THE MOUNTAIN, fell to the valley below. Thus, he was saved, FOR HAD HE RISEN A MOMENT LATER, HE WOULD HAVE FALLEN TOGETHER WITH THE LEDGE INTO THE VALLEY AND BEEN KILLED.

187. אָתָא ר׳ אַבָּא לְגַבֵּיהּ, אָמַר לוֹ אֵימָא לִי מָאן עוֹבָדָךְ, דְּהָא קוּדְשָׁא בְּרִיךְ הוּא רָחֵישׁ לָךְ אִלֵּין תְּרֵין נִסִּין, לָאו אִינוּן לְמַגָּנָא.

187. Rabbi Aba came to him and said: What have you done that the Holy One, blessed be He, performed for you two miracles – SAVING YOU FROM THE SNAKE AND FROM THE LEDGE THAT FELL – for these events did not happen without reason.

188. אָמַר לוֹ הַהוּא בַּר נָשׁ, כְּכָל יוֹמָאי לָא אַשְׁלִים לִי בַּר נָשׁ בִּישָׁא בְּעָלְמָא, דְּלָא אִתְפַּיְיסְנָא בַּהֲדֵיהּ, וּמְחִילְנָא לֵיהּ. וְתוּ, אִי לָא יָכִילְנָא לְאִתְפַּיְיסָא בַּהֲדֵיהּ, לָא סָלֵיקְנָא לְעַרְסִי, עַד דִּמְחִילְנָא לֵיהּ, וּלְכָל אִינוּן דִּמְצַעֲרוּ לִי, וְלָא חַיְישָׁנָא כָּל יוֹמָא לְהַהוּא בִּישָׁא דְּאַשְׁלִים לִי. וְלָאו דַּי לִי דָא, אֶלָּא דִּמְהַהוּא יוֹמָא וּלְהָלְאָה, אִשְׁתַּדַּלְנָא לְמֶעְבַּד עִמְּהוֹן טָבָא.

188. The man said: In all my days, I forgave and made peace with any man who did evil by me. If I could not make peace with him, I did not sleep on my bed before forgiving him and all those who grieved me. Thus, I did not harbor hatred all that day for the harm he did me. Moreover, from that day on, I tried to do kindness by them.

189. בָּכָה ר׳ אַבָּא וַאֲמַר, יַתִּיר עוֹבָדוֹי דְּדֵין מִיּוֹסֵף, דְּיוֹסֵף הֲווֹ אֲחוֹי

וַדַּאי, וַהֲוָה לֵיהּ לְרַחֲמָא עֲלוֹי, אֲבָל מַה דַּעֲבִיד דָּא, יַתִּיר הוּא מִיּוֹסֵף, יָאוֹת הוּא דְקוּדְשָׁא בְּרִיךְ הוּא יַרְחִישׁ לֵיהּ נִיסָא עַל נִיסָא.

189. Rabbi Aba wept and said: This man's deeds exceed those of Joseph. As for Joseph, those WHO INJURED HIM were his brothers. Assuredly, he should have pitied them FROM BROTHERHOOD. But this one behaved so TO ANY MAN, so he is greater than Joseph and is worthy to have the Holy One, blessed be He, perform one miracle after the other for his sake.

190. פָּתַח וַאֲמַר, הוֹלֵךְ בַּתֹּם יֵלֶךְ בֶּטַח וּמְעַקֵּשׁ דְּרָכָיו יִוָּדֵעַ. הוֹלֵךְ בַּתּוֹם יֵלֶךְ בֶּטַח, דָּא הַהוּא בַּר נָשׁ, דְּאָזֵיל בְּאָרְחִין דְּאוֹרַיְיתָא. יֵלֶךְ בֶּטַח, דְּלָא יָכִילוּ נִזְקֵי דְעַלְמָא לְאַבְאָשָׁא לֵיהּ. וּמְעַקֵּשׁ דְּרָכָיו יִוָּדֵעַ, מַאן יִוָּדֵעַ. דָּא הוּא מַאן דְּאַסְטֵי מֵאָרְחָא דִקְשׁוֹט, וּבָעֵי גַּבֵּי דְחַבְרֵיהּ. יִוָּדֵעַ, מַהוּ יִוָּדֵעַ: יִשְׁתְּמוֹדַע אִיהוּ בְּעֵינֵיהוֹן דְּכָל מָארֵי דְּדִינָא, דְּלָא יִתְאֲבֵיד מִנַּיְיהוּ דְּיוּקְנָא דְהַהוּא בַּר נָשׁ, בְּגִין לְאַיְיתָאָה לֵיהּ לְאַתְרָא דְּיִנְקְמוּן מִנֵּיהּ, וּבְגִין כָּךְ יִוָּדֵעַ.

190. He opened the discussion with the verse, "He that walks uprightly walks surely: but he that perverts his ways shall be found out" (Mishlei 10:9). "He that walks uprightly" refers to the man who walks the ways of the Torah. He will "walk surely" for no fiend in the world will be able to harm him. "...but he that perverts his ways shall be found out." HE ASKS: Who shall be found out? HE ANSWERS, He who deviates from the way of truth and plans to repay his friend EVIL FOR EVIL, THEREBY TRANSGRESSING THE STRICTURE IN THE VERSE, "YOU SHALL NOT AVENGE, NOR BEAR ANY GRUDGE" (VAYIKRA 19:18). The phrase, "shall be found out" means that he will be recognized by all the prosecutors, who will not forget the image of that man and will bring him to where they will execute vengeance upon him MEASURE FOR MEASURE. THE SCRIPTURE therefore READS, "shall be found out."

191. וְתָא חֲזֵי, הַהוּא דְּאָזֵיל בְּאֹרַח קְשׁוֹט, קוּדְשָׁא בְּרִיךְ הוּא חָפֵי עֲלֵיהּ, בְּגִין דְּלָא אִתְיְדַע, וְלָא אִשְׁתְּמוֹדַע, לְגַבֵּי מָארֵיהוֹן דְּדִינָא, אֲבָל מְעַקֵּשׁ דְּרָכָיו יִוָּדֵעַ, וְיִשְׁתְּמוֹדַע לְגַבַּיְיהוּ. זַכָּאִין אִינוּן בְּנֵי נָשָׁא דְּאָזְלֵי

בְּאֹרַח קְשׁוֹט, וְאָזְלֵי לְרוֹחֲצָן עַל עַלְמָא, דְּלָא דָּחֲלֵי אִינּוּן בְּעַלְמָא דֵין, וְלָא בְּעַלְמָא דְּאָתֵי.

191. Come and behold: He who walks the way of truth is hidden by the Holy One, blessed be He, so that he will not be found nor recognized by the prosecutors, "but he that perverts his ways shall be found out" and will be known to them. Happy are the men who walk the way of truth, walk surely in the world, and have no fear in this world or the World to Come.

12. "And the men were afraid, because they were brought into Joseph's house"

A Synopsis

The Zohar comments on the fear felt by Joseph's brothers. It meditates on the nature of sin and evil, and asserts that only by concentrating on the Day of Judgment at all times, and by avoiding wine, pride, and fornication, can we be free of the Evil Inclination. Whoever has sins on his hands is always afraid; thus, Joseph's brothers were full of fear when they were brought into his house.

The Relevance of this Passage

A literal interpretation of biblical text limits it to extremist views that can be misconstrued as puritanical. The Kabbalists of antiquity shed light on the deeper significance of the above verses. Fear of sin and the avoidance of wine, pride, and infidelity are not just moral values rooted in religious authority. Rather, there is a practical benefit to engaging in positive behavior. Kabbalah teaches us how to elevate all physical activity to the level of the spiritual. For example, relations between a man and wife are made more passionate when a man directs his sexual drive exclusively towards his spouse, limiting carnal activity to the spiritual confines of his marriage. Similarly, wine draws down enormous spiritual Light when used as part of a blessing, but brings alcoholism and spiritual darkness when used for self-indulgent purposes. Our eyes are opened to these insightful truths as we peruse these passages.

192. וַיִּירְאוּ הָאֲנָשִׁים כִּי הוּבְאוּ בֵּית יוֹסֵף. ר' יוֹסֵי אָמַר, וַוי לוֹן, לִבְנֵי נָשָׁא, דְּלָא יָדְעֵי וְלָא מִסְתַּכְּלִין בְּאָרְחֵי דְאוֹרַיְיתָא, וַוי לוֹן, בְּשַׁעְתָּא דְקוּדְשָׁא בְּרִיךְ הוּא יֵיתֵי לְמִתְבַּע לוֹן דִּינָא עַל עוֹבָדֵיהוֹן, וְיָקוּם גּוּפָא וְנַפְשָׁא, לְמֵיהַב חוּשְׁבָּנָא מִכָּל עוֹבָדֵיהוֹן, עַד לָא יִתְפָּרְשׁוּן נַפְשָׁא מִן גּוּפָא.

192. "And the men were afraid, because they were brought into Joseph's house" (Beresheet 43:18): Rabbi Yosi said: Woe to the men, who do not know nor reflect upon the ways of the Torah. Woe to them at the time the Holy One, blessed be He, will demand justice for their deeds, when the body and soul will rise to account for all they did before the soul separated from the body.

193. וְהַהוּא יוֹמָא, יוֹמָא דְּדִינָא אִיהוּ, יוֹמָא דְּסִפְרִין פְּתִיחָן, וּמָארֵיהוֹן דְּדִינָא קָיְימִין, בְּגִין דְּהַהוּא זִמְנָא קָיְימָא נָחָשׁ בְּקִיּוּמֵיהּ, לְנַשְׁכָא לֵיהּ, וְכָל שַׁיְיפֵי מִתְרַגְּשִׁין לְגַבֵּיהּ, וְנִשְׁמָתָא אִתְפָּרְשָׁא מִן גּוּפָא, וְאָזְלָא וְשַׁטְיָא, וְלָא יָדְעַת לְאָן אָרְחָא תְּהַךְ, וּלְאָן אֲתַר סַלְקִין לָהּ.

193. That day is the day of Judgment, when the books WHERE MEN'S DEEDS ARE WRITTEN are open, the prosecutors are in place, and the serpent is ready to bite. All the members of the body quiver before it, and the soul is separated from the body to roam and hover without knowing where it should go and to which place it will be raised.

194. וַוי לְהַהוּא יוֹמָא, יוֹמָא דְרוּגְזָא וּנְאִיצוּ הַהוּא יוֹמָא, בְּגִין כָּךְ אִבָּעֵי לֵיהּ לְבַר נָשׁ, לְאַרְגָּזָא יִצְרֵיהּ כָּל יוֹמָא, לְאַדְכָּרָא קַמֵּיהּ הַהוּא יוֹמָא, דְּיֵיקוּם בְּדִינָא דְּמַלְכָּא, דְּקָא עָאלִין לֵיהּ תְּחוֹת אַרְעָא לְאִתְרַקְּבָא, וְנִשְׁמָתָא אִתְפָּרְשָׁא מִנֵּיהּ.

194. Woe to that day, a day of ire and wrath. It behooves man, then, to face his Evil Inclination and remember that he will have to stand in the King's judgment and that he will be put beneath the ground to rot, while the soul will be separated from him.

195. וּתְנַן, לְעוֹלָם יַרְגִּיז אָדָם יֵצֶר טוֹב עַל יֵצֶר הָרָע, וְיִשְׁתַּדֵּל אֲבַתְרֵיהּ, אִי אָזֵיל מִנֵּיהּ יָאוּת, וְאִי לָאו יִשְׁתַּדֵּל בְּאוֹרַיְיתָא, דְּהָא לֵית לָךְ מִלָּה לְתַבְרָא יֵצֶר הָרָע אֶלָּא אוֹרַיְיתָא. אִי אָזֵיל מוּטָב, וְאִי לָאו יַדְכַּר לֵיהּ יוֹמָא דְמוּתָא, בְּגִין לְתַבְרָא לֵיהּ.

195. We have learned that a man should always apply himself to arousing the Good Inclinationagainst the Evil Inclination. If evil departs, that is fine; if not, he should study the Torah, for only the Torah breaks the Evil Inclination. If evil departs, that is fine; if not, man should remind it of his dying day in order to break it.

196. הָכָא אִית לְאִסְתַּכְּלָא, דְּהָא דָא הוּא יֵצֶר הָרָע, וְדָא הוּא מַלְאַךְ הַמָּוֶת, וְכִי מַלְאַךְ הַמָּוֶת מִתְבַּר מִקַּמֵּי יוֹמָא דְמוּתָא, וְהָא אִיהוּ קָטוֹלָא

דִּבְנֵי נָשָׁא הֲוֵי, וְאִשְׁתְּמַע דְּחֶדְוָה הוּא דִילֵיהּ, וּבְגִין כָּךְ אַסְטֵי לוֹן לִבְנֵי נָשָׁא תָּדִיר, בְּגִין לְאַמְשָׁכָא לוֹן לְדָא.

196. We have to study this further. The Evil Inclination is the Angel of Death. Why should the Angel of Death be broken before the day of death, seeing that it is he who delights in killing MEN? Indeed, he leads them astray to bring DEATH upon them.

197. אֶלָּא וַדַּאי מַה דְּאִתְּמָר דְּיִדְכּוֹר לֵיהּ בַּר נָשׁ הַהוּא יוֹמָא דְמוֹתָא, וַדַּאי הָכֵי הוּא, בְּגִין דְּמִתְבַּר לִבָּא דְבַר נָשׁ, דְּהָא יֵצֶר הָרָע לָא שַׁרְיָא, אֶלָּא בַּאֲתַר דְּאִשְׁתַּכַּח חֶדְוָה דְחַמְרָא, וְגַסּוּתָא דְרוּחָא, וְכַד אִשְׁתַּכַּח רוּחָא תְּבִירָא, כְּדֵין אִתְפְּרַשׁ מִנֵּיהּ, וְלָא שַׁרְיָא בַּהֲדֵיהּ, וּבְגִין כָּךְ בָּעֵי לְאַדְכָּרָא לֵיהּ יוֹמָא דְמוֹתָא, וְיִתְבַּר גּוּפֵיהּ, וְאִיהוּ אָזֵיל לֵיהּ.

197. HE ANSWERS, Surely we have learned that it behooves man to be reminded of his dying day in order to break his heart, for the Evil Inclination dwells only in a place of intoxication and pride. When a broken spirit dwells in man, evil departs and does not stay with him. One should therefore be reminded of his dying day so that his spirit will be crushed and the Evil Inclination will go away.

198. תָּא חֲזֵי, יֵצֶר טוֹב בָּעֵי חֶדְוָה דְאוֹרַיְיתָא, וְיֵצֶר רָע חֶדְוָה דְחַמְרָא, וְנִיאוּפִין וְגַסּוּתָא דְרוּחָא, וּבְגִין כָּךְ בָּעֵי בַּר נָשׁ לְאַרְגָּזָא תָּדִיר, מֵהַהוּא יוֹמָא רַבָּא, יוֹמָא דְדִינָא, יוֹמָא דְחוּשְׁבְּנָא, דְּלֵית לֵיהּ לְבַר נָשׁ לַאֲגָנָא עֲלֵיהּ, אֶלָּא עוֹבָדוֹי דְּכַשְׁרָן, דְּאִיהוּ עָבֵיד בְּהַאי עַלְמָא, בְּגִין דְּיָגֵינוּ עֲלֵיהּ בְּהַהִיא שַׁעְתָּא.

198. Come and behold: The Good Inclination requires the joy of the Torah and the Evil Inclination the joy of wine, fornication, and pride. Therefore, a man should always vex it by mention of that great day, the day of judgment, the day of reckoning, for there is nothing that protects man at that time except the good deeds that he performs in this world.

199. תָּא חֲזֵי, וַיִּירְאוּ הָאֲנָשִׁים כִּי הוּבְאוּ בֵּית יוֹסֵף, וּמַה כֻּלְּהוּ הֲווֹ גִּיבָּרִין, כֻּלְּהוּ תַּקִּיפִין, וְחַד עוּלֵימָא דְּאַיְיתֵי לוֹן לְבֵיתָא דְיוֹסֵף, דַּחֲלוּ. כַּד יֵיתֵי קוּדְשָׁא בְּרִיךְ הוּא לְמִתְבַּע לֵיהּ לְדִינָא לְבַר נָשׁ, עַל אַחַת כַּמָּה וְכַמָּה.

199. Come and behold: "And the men were afraid, because they were brought into Joseph's house." With all their might and strength, one youth who brought them into Joseph's house MADE THEM afraid. How much more SHOULD WE BE AFRAID when the Holy One, blessed be He, will demand justice of man?

200. בְּגִין כָּךְ, בָּעֵי לֵיהּ לְבַר נָשׁ, לְאִזְדַּהֲרָא בְּהַאי עָלְמָא, לְאִתְתַּקְּפָא בֵּיהּ בְּקוּדְשָׁא בְּרִיךְ הוּא, וְיַשְׁוֵי בֵּיהּ רוּחֲצָנֵיהּ, דְּאַף עַל גַּב דְּאִיהוּ חָטֵי, אִי יֶהֱדַר מִנֵּיהּ, בְּתְיוּבְתָּא שְׁלֵימָתָא, הָא תַּקִּיף אִיהוּ, וְיִתְתַּקַּף בֵּיהּ בְּקוּדְשָׁא בְּרִיךְ הוּא, כְּאִילּוּ לָא חָטָא.

200. Hence, a man should strive in this world to be strengthened by the Holy One, blessed be He, and put his trust in Him. And though he sinned, if he fully repents, THE HOLY ONE, BLESSED BE HE, is able TO OVERLOOK A WRONG AND FORGIVE HIM. And the man could fortify himself in the Holy One, blessed be He, as if he had never sinned.

201. דְּהָא שִׁבְטִין, בְּגִין דְּחָטוֹ עַל גְּנֵיבַת יוֹסֵף, הֲווֹ דַּחֲלִין, דְּאִלְמָלֵא לָא חָטוֹ, לָא הֲווֹ דָּחֲלִין כְּלַל, בְּגִין דְּחוֹבוֹי דְּבַר נָשׁ מְתַבְּרִין לִבֵּיהּ, וְלֵית לֵיהּ חֵילָא כְּלַל, מ"ט, דְּהָא הַהוּא יֵצֶר הַטּוֹב אִתְבַּר עִמֵּיהּ, וְלֵית לֵיהּ חֵילָא לְאִתְתַּקְּפָא עַל הַהוּא יֵצֶר הָרַע. וְעַל דָּא כְּתִיב, מִי הָאִישׁ הַיָּרֵא וְרַךְ הַלֵּבָב, הַיָּרֵא מֵחוֹבִין דְּבִידוֹי, דְּאִינּוּן תְּבִירָא דְּלִבָּא דְּבַר נָשׁ.

201. The tribes were afraid because they sinned in stealing Joseph. They would not have been afraid at all, had they not sinned. For man's sins break his heart and strength. Why? Because the Good Inclination is crushed within him, and he has no power to overcome the Evil Inclination. It is therefore written, "What man there is that is fearful and fainthearted" (Devarim 20:8), "that is fearful" of the sins upon his hands, which break a man's heart.

12. "And the men were afraid, because they were brought into Joseph's house"

202. וְתָא חֲזֵי, לְכַמָּה דָּרִין אִתְפְּרַע קוּדְשָׁא בְּרִיךְ הוּא, מֵאִינוּן חוֹבִין דְּשִׁבְטִין, דְּהָא לָא אִתְאֲבִיד מִקַּמֵּיהּ דְּקוּדְשָׁא בְּרִיךְ הוּא כְּלוּם, וְאִתְפְּרַע מִדָּרָא לְדָרָא, וְדִינָא קַיְימָא קַמֵּיהּ תָּדִיר, עַד דְּאִתְפְּרַע, וְשָׁרֵי דִּינָא בַּאֲתַר דְּאִצְטְרִיךְ.

202. Come and behold: The Holy One, blessed be He, exacted payments for generations for the tribes' sin OF SELLING JOSEPH, for nothing is lost before the Holy One, blessed be He, and He demands payment from one generation to the next. Judgment stands before him constantly until exacted. And judgment abides where it should BE.

203. מְנָלָן, מֵחִזְקִיָּהוּ. חִזְקִיָּהוּ חָב הַהוּא חוֹבָא, דְּגָלֵי סְתִירִין דְּקוּדְשָׁא בְּרִיךְ הוּא, לִשְׁאָר עַמִּין עעכו"ם, דְּלָא הֲוָה אִצְטְרִיךְ לְגַלָּאָה, וְקוּדְשָׁא בְּרִיךְ הוּא שַׁדַּר לֵיהּ לִישַׁעְיָהוּ, וַאֲמַר לֵיהּ, הִנֵּה יָמִים בָּאִים וְנִשָּׂא כָּל אֲשֶׁר בְּבֵיתֶךָ וַאֲשֶׁר אָצְרוּ אֲבוֹתֶיךָ עַד הַיּוֹם הַזֶּה וגו'.

203. How do we know this? From Hezekiahu, who sinned by revealing to the idolatrous nations the mysteries of the Holy One, blessed be He, which he should not have done. The Holy One, blessed be He, sent Yeshayahu, who said to him, "Behold, days are coming that all that is in your house, and that which your fathers have laid up in store until this day, shall be carried to Babylon" (Yeshayah 39:6).

204. תָּא חֲזֵי, כַּמָּה גָּרֵים הַהוּא חוֹבָא, בְּגִין דְּגַלֵּי מַה דַּהֲוָה סָתִים, דְּכֵיוָן דְּאִתְגְּלֵי, אִתְיְיהִיב דּוּכְתָּא לַאֲתַר אָחֳרָא דְּלָא אִצְטְרִיךְ, לְשַׁלְטָאָה עֲלֵיהּ, בְּגִין כָּךְ לָאו בִּרְכָה שַׁרְיָא, אֶלָּא בַּאֲתַר סָתִים. וְאוֹקְמוּהָ, מַה דְּאִיהוּ סָתִים, בִּרְכָה שַׁרְיָא עֲלוֹי, כֵּיוָן דְּאִתְגְּלֵי אִתְיְיהִיב דּוּכְתָּא, לַאֲתַר אָחֳרָא לְשַׁלְטָאָה עֲלוֹי.

204. Come and behold what that sin caused. It exposed what was hidden and, once it was revealed, an opening was given for another place, NAMELY, FOR THE OTHER SIDE TO RULE. Therefore, blessing abides only in secret places, as has been already explained. Blessings dwell on all that is undisclosed. Once it is revealed, there is an opening for another place to have dominion over it.

205. כְּתִיב כָּל מְכַבְּדֶיהָ הִזִּילוּהָ כִּי רָאוּ עֶרְוָתָהּ וְאוֹקְמוּהָ. אֲבָל כָּל מְכַבְּדֶיהָ הִזִּילוּהָ, דָּא הוּא מַלְכוּת בָּבֶל, דְּהָא מִתַּמָּן אִשְׁתַּדַּר דּוֹרוֹן לִירוּשְׁלֵם דִּכְתִיב בָּעֵת הַהִיא שָׁלַח מְרוֹדַךְ בַּלְאֲדָן בֶּן בַּלְאֲדָן מֶלֶךְ בָּבֶל סְפָרִים וּמִנְחָה אֶל חִזְקִיָּהוּ.

205. It is written, "all that honored her despise her, because they have seen her nakedness" (Eichah 1:8). This alludes to the kingdom of Babylon, where a present was sent to Jerusalem, as it is written, "At that time, Merodach Baladan, the son of Baladan, king of Babylon, sent letters and a present to Hezekiahu" (Yeshayah 39:1).

206. וּמַה כְּתִיב בְּהוֹ, שְׁלָם לְחִזְקִיָּהוּ מֶלֶךְ יְהוּדָה, וּשְׁלָם לֵאלָהָא רַבָּא וּשְׁלָם לִירוּשְׁלֵם, כֵּיוָן דְּנָפַק פִּתְקֵיהּ מִנֵּיהּ, אַהֲדַר לְלִבֵּיהּ וַאֲמַר, לָא יָאוֹת עָבְדִית לְאַקְדָּמָא שְׁלָמָא דְעַבְדָּא, לִשְׁלָמָא דְמָארֵיהּ, קָם מִכּוּרְסְיֵהּ, וּפָסַע ג׳ פְּסִיעָן, וְאַהֲדַר פִּתְקֵיהּ, וְכָתַב אָחֳרָנִין תְּחוֹתַיְיהוּ, וְכָתַב הָכֵי, שְׁלָם לֵאלָהָא רַבָּא, שְׁלָם לִירוּשְׁלֵם, וּשְׁלָם לְחִזְקִיָּה, וְדָא הוּא מְכַבְּדֶיהָ.

206. In the letters it was written, 'Peace be to Hezekiah, the king of Judah, peace be to the great Elohim, and peace be to Jerusalem'. Once he delivered the letter, he thought, I have not done well in greeting the servant before his master. He rose from his throne, took three steps, and retrieved the letter. He wrote another letter in its stead, saying, 'Peace be to the great Elohim, peace to Jerusalem, and peace be to Hezekiah'. These are "all that honored her."

207. וּלְבָתַר הִזִּילוּהָ, מ״ט הִזִּילוּהָ. בְּגִין כִּי רָאוּ עֶרְוָתָהּ, דְּאַחְזֵי לוֹן חִזְקִיָּה, דְּאִלְמָלֵא כָּךְ לֹא הִזִּילוּהָ לְבָתַר. מִגּוֹ דַּהֲוָה זַכָּאָה חִזְקִיָּהוּ יַתִּיר, אִתְעַכַּב מִלָּה מִלְּאַיְיתָאָה, וְלָא אָתָא בְּיוֹמוֹי, דִּכְתִיב כִּי יִהְיֶה שָׁלוֹם וֶאֱמֶת בְּיָמַי. וּלְבָתַר פַּקִּיד הַהוּא חוֹבָא, לִבְנוֹי אֲבַתְרֵיהּ.

12. “And the men were afraid, because they were brought into Joseph’s house”

207. Afterwards, they “despise her.” Why did they “despise her?” “Because they have seen her nakedness,” THAT IS, Hezekiah showed it to them, and were it not for that, they would not have despised her. Because Hezekiah was righteous, retribution was late in coming and came not in his days, as it is written, “But there shall be peace and truth in my days” (Yeshayah 39:8). Later, the Holy One, blessed be He, visited His children on account of that sin.

208. כְּגַוְונָא דָא, הַהוּא חוֹבָא דְּשִׁבְטִין, קָאֵים עַד לְבָתַר, בְּגִין דְּדִינָא דִלְעֵילָא, לָא יָכֵיל לְשַׁלְטָאָה עֲלַיְיהוּ, עַד דְּאִשְׁתַּכַּח שַׁעְתָּא לְאִתְפָּרְעָא, וְאִתְפְּרַע מִינַּיְיהוּ, וּבְגִין כָּךְ, כָּל מַאן דְּאִית חוֹבִין בִּידוֹי, דָּחֵיל תָּדִיר, כד״א וּפָחַדְתָּ לַיְלָה וְיוֹמָם וגו׳, וְעַל דָּא וַיִּירְאוּ הָאֲנָשִׁים כִּי הוּבְאוּ וגו׳.

208. Similarly, the sin of the tribes was deferred until a later time, for judgment above had no power over them until the time arrived to exact payment. Thus, whoever has sins on his hands is always afraid, as it is written, “And you shall fear day and night” (Devarim 28:66). Therefore, “And the men were afraid, because they were brought into Joseph’s house.”

13. "And he saw Benjamin"

A Synopsis

"Hope deferred is a heart sickness but desire fulfilled is a Tree of Life." Rabbi Chiya comments on this verse, to the effect that the negative angel Satan attends those who pray with a specific result in mind – but God quickly answers the prayers of the pure in heart. Thus, Benjamin came quickly to Joseph. The passage then digresses into a lament for the destruction of the Temple and the pains of Exile.

The Relevance of this Passage

The Evil Inclination exploits the action of prayer by stimulating feelings of self-righteousness. For this reason, most prayers go unanswered. A holier-than-thou attitude distinguishes the religious approach to prayer from the authentically spiritual perspective. The latter is replete with humility, while the religious approach fosters conceit and certitude in one's own purity and devotion. The cleansing power of this passage purifies our souls, so that we may humbly ask The Creator for what we truly need.

209. וַיִּשָּׂא עֵינָיו וַיַּרְא אֶת בִּנְיָמִין אָחִיו בֶּן אִמּוֹ וגו'. רִבִּי חִיָּיא פְּתַח וַאֲמַר, תּוֹחֶלֶת מְמוּשָּׁכָה מַחֲלָה לֵב וְעֵץ חַיִּים תַּאֲוָה בָאָה, דָּא הוּא דִּתְנַן, דְּלֵית לֵיהּ לְבַר נָשׁ, לְאִסְתַּכְּלָא בְּבָעוּתֵיהּ לְגַבֵּי קוּדְשָׁא בְּרִיךְ הוּא, אִי אָתֵי, אִי לָא אָתֵי, מ"ט. בְּגִין דְּאִי אִיהוּ אִסְתַּכֵּל בֵּיהּ, כַּמָּה מָארֵיהוֹן דְּדִינָא, אָתוֹ לְאִסְתַּכָּלָא בֵּיהּ בְּעוֹבָדוֹי.

209. "And he lifted up his eyes, and saw his brother Benjamin, his mother's son" (Beresheet 43:29). Rabbi Chiya opened the discussion with the verse, "Hope deferred makes the heart sick (lit. 'is a heart sickness'), but desire fulfilled is a Tree of Life" (Mishlei 13:12). From this verse, we have learned that a man should not, when he prays to the Holy One, blessed be He, check whether HIS SALVATION has come or not. What is the reason for this? When he looks for it, many accusers come to examine his deeds.

210. וְרָזָא אִיהוּ, דְּהָא הַהוּא אִסְתַּכְּלוּתָא, דְּאִיהוּ מִסְתַּכֵּל בְּהַהוּא בָּעוּתָא, גָּרֵים לֵיהּ לְמַחֲלַת לֵב, מַאי מַחֲלָה לֵב. דָּא אִיהוּ מַאן דְּקָאֵים תָּדִיר, עֲלֵיהּ דְּבַר נָשׁ, לְאַסְטָאָה לְעֵילָּא וְתַתָּא.

210. It is a secret that his examination during prayer causes a heart sickness.

The sickness of heart is he who always stands by man to indict him above and below, NAMELY THE SATAN.

211. וְעֵץ חַיִּים תַּאֲוָה בָּאָה, תָּנִינָן, מַאן דְּבָעֵי דְּקוּדְשָׁא בְּרִיךְ הוּא יְקַבֵּל צְלוֹתֵיהּ. יִשְׁתַּדַּל בְּאוֹרַיְיתָא, דְּאִיהִי עֵץ חַיִּים, וּכְדֵין תַּאֲוָה בָּאָה, מַאן תַּאֲוָה. דָּא הוּא דַּרְגָּא דְּכָל צְלוֹתִין דְּעַלְמָא בִּידֵיהּ, וְעָאֵיל לוֹן קַמֵּי מַלְכָּא עִלָּאָה. כְּתִיב הָכָא בָּאָה, וּכְתִיב הָתָם בָּעֶרֶב הִיא בָאָה, וְדָא הוּא תַּאֲוָה בָּאָה, בָּאָה קַמֵּי מַלְכָּא עִלָּאָה, לְאַשְׁלָמָא רְעוּתָא דְּהַהוּא בַּר נָשׁ.

211. "But desire fulfilled is a Tree of Life." We have learned that he who wants the Holy One, blessed be He, to accept his prayer, should study the Torah, which is the Tree of Life. Then, "desire is fulfilled (lit. 'comes')." Desire is the grade presiding over all the prayers in the world, NAMELY THE NUKVA. It brings them before the highest King, ZEIR ANPIN. This verse says "comes" just as elsewhere it is written, "in the evening she comes" (Ester 2:14). IN BOTH VERSES, THE WORD 'COMES' ALLUDES TO THE NUKVA. The meaning of "desire comes" is that she comes before the highest King TO BE JOINED WITH HIM in order to grant the wish of he WHO PRAYS TO FULFILL HIS REQUEST.

212. דָּבָר אֲחֵר תּוֹחֶלֶת מְמוּשָּׁכָה מַחֲלָה לֵב, דָּא הוּא אֲתַר, דְּאִתְיְיהֵיב הַהִיא מִלָּה, בַּאֲתַר אָחֳרָא, דְּלָא אִצְטְרִיךְ, וְאִתְמַשְׁכָא עַד דְּאִתְיְיהֵיב מִיָּדָא לְיָדָא, וּלְזִמְנִין דְּלָא יֵיתֵי, מ"ט, בְּגִין דְּאִתְפַּשְּׁטָא וְאִתְמַשְׁכָא בְּכָל אִינּוּן מְמַנָּן, לְנַחֲתָא לֵיהּ לְעַלְמָא.

212. Another explanation of the verse, "Hope deferred is a heart sickness" is that it refers to a place where prayer is misdirected, A PLACE CALLED "SICKNESS OF HEART." It is slow in coming and is passed from hand to hand. Sometimes SALVATION never comes. Why? Because it is passed FROM HAND TO HAND by all the chieftains to be brought down into the world.

213. וְעֵץ חַיִּים תַּאֲוָה בָּאָה, דָּא הוּא תּוֹחֶלֶת, דְּלָא אִתְמַשְׁכָא בְּגִין אִינּוּן מְמַנָּן רְתִיכִין, אֶלָּא דְּקוּדְשָׁא בְּרִיךְ הוּא יָהֵיב לֵיהּ לְאַלְתָּר, בְּגִין

דְּכַד אִתְמַשְׁכָא בֵּין אִינוּן מְמַנָּן רְתִיכִין, כַּמָּה אִינוּן מָארֵיהוֹן דְּדִינָא, דְּאִתְיְיהֵיב לוֹן רְשׁוּתָא, לְעַיְּינָא וּלְאִסְתַּכְּלָא בְּדִינֵיהּ, עַד לָא יִתְּנוּ לֵיהּ, וּמַה דְּנָפֵיק מִבֵּי מַלְכָּא וְאִתְיְיהֵיב לֵיהּ לְבַּר נָשׁ, בֵּין דְּזָכֵי, בֵּין דְּלָא זָכֵי, אִתְיְיהֵיב מִיָּד, וְדָא הוּא עֵץ חַיִּים תַּאֲוָה בָאָה.

213. "...but desire comes is a Tree of Life": When hope is not passed by all the chieftains and Chariots FROM HAND TO HAND, the Holy One, blessed be He, gives it immediately. For when it is passed by the chieftains and Chariots, numerous accusers are given permission to examine it and look at the indictments before granting him HIS SALVATION. But whatever comes from the King's house and is given to man, whether he deserves it or not, is given to him at once. This is the meaning of the phrase, "but desire comes is a Tree of Life"; IT COMES IMMEDIATELY.

214. דָּבָר אַחֵר תּוֹחֶלֶת מְמוּשָּׁכָה, דָּא יַעֲקֹב, דְּאִתְמַשְׁכָא לֵיהּ תּוֹחַלְתָּא דְּיוֹסֵף עַד זִמְנָא אָרִיךְ. וְעֵץ חַיִּים תַּאֲוָה בָאָה, דָּא הוּא בִּנְיָמִן, דְּהָא מִזִּמְנָא דְּתָבַע לֵיהּ יוֹסֵף, עַד הַהוּא זִמְנָא דְּאָתָא לְגַבֵּיהּ, לָא הֲוָה אֶלָּא זִמְנָא זְעֵיר, דְּלָא אִתְמַשְׁכָא הַהוּא זִמְנָא, הה"ד וַיִּשָּׂא עֵינָיו וַיַּרְא אֶת בִּנְיָמִין אָחִיו בֶּן אִמּוֹ. מַאי בֶּן אִמּוֹ. דִּדְיוֹקְנֵיהּ דְּאִמֵּיהּ הֲוָה בֵּיהּ, וַהֲוָה דָּמֵי דְּיוֹקְנֵיהּ לִדְיוֹקְנָא דְּרָחֵל, בְּגִין כָּךְ כְּתִיב וַיִּשָּׂא עֵינָיו וַיַּרְא אֶת בִּנְיָמִן אָחִיו בֶּן אִמּוֹ.

214. Another explanation of "hope deferred" is that it refers to Jacob whose hope to see Joseph was long deferred. And "but desire comes is a Tree of Life" refers to Benjamin, for only a short time elapsed between Joseph's request for him and his arrival; the time elapsed was short. It is written, "And he lifted up his eyes, and saw his brother Benjamin, his mother's son." Why does the scripture read, "his mother's son?" Because he had his mother's image, he was her very image. Therefore the verse reads, "And he lifted up his eyes, and saw his brother Benjamin, his mother's son."

215. רִבִּי יוֹסֵי אָמַר, וְהָא כְּתִיב בְּקַדְמֵיתָא, וַיַּרְא יוֹסֵף אִתָּם אֶת בִּנְיָמִן, וְהַשְׁתָּא כְּתִיב, וַיִּשָּׂא עֵינָיו וַיַּרְא אֶת בִּנְיָמִין אָחִיו, מַאי רְאִיָּה הָכָא. אֶלָּא חָמָא בְּרוּחָא דְקוּדְשָׁא לְבִנְיָמִן, דְּחוּלָקֵיהּ הֲוָה עִמְּהוֹן בְּאַרְעָא,

וּבְחוּלָקֵיהּ דְּבִנְיָמִן וִיהוּדָה תִּשְׁרֵי שְׁכִינְתָּא, דְּהָא חָמָא לֵיהּ לִיהוּדָה וּבִנְיָמִן דִּבְחוּלַקְהוֹן הֲוָה מַקְדְּשָׁא, וְדָא הוּא וַיַּרְא יוֹסֵף אִתָּם אֶת בִּנְיָמִן, לֵיהּ חָמָא עִמְּהוֹן, וְיוֹסֵף דַּהֲוָה אֲחוּהָ לָא חָמָא עִמְּהוֹן, בְּהַהוּא חוּלָקָא.

215. Rabbi Yosi said: It is written earlier, "And Joseph saw Benjamin with them" (Beresheet 43:16), and now "he lifted up his eyes, and saw his brother Benjamin." What did he see here? HE ANSWERS, He saw through the Holy Spirit that Benjamin will have a place in the Holy Land along with his brothers, and that the Shechinah will dwell in the place of Benjamin and Judah, for he saw the Temple standing upon their portion. This is the meaning of the phrase, "And Joseph saw Benjamin with them." But Joseph, his brother, did not see HIMSELF sharing the portion IN WHICH THE TEMPLE WOULD STAND.

216. אוּף הָכָא, וַיִּשָּׂא עֵינָיו וַיַּרְא אֶת בִּנְיָמִין אָחִיו בֶּן אִמּוֹ. מַה כְּתִיב בַּתְרֵיהּ, וַיְמַהֵר יוֹסֵף כִּי נִכְמְרוּ רַחֲמָיו אֶל אָחִיו וַיְבַקֵּשׁ לִבְכּוֹת וַיָּבֹא הַחַדְרָה וַיֵּבְךְּ שָׁמָּה.

216. When "he lifted up his eyes, and saw his brother Benjamin, his mother's son" AND SAW THE TEMPLE STANDING ON HIS PORTION, then it is written, "And Joseph made haste, for his affection was kindled towards his brother and he sought where to weep; and he entered into his chamber, and wept there" (Beresheet 43:30), BECAUSE HE SAW THE DESTRUCTION OF THE TEMPLE.

217. רִבִּי חִזְקִיָּה פְּתַח וַאֲמַר, מַשָּׂא גֵּיא חִזָּיוֹן מַה לָּךְ אֵיפֹה כִּי עָלִית כֻּלָּךְ לַגַּגּוֹת. תָּא חֲזֵי, הָא אוֹקְמוּהָ, בְּזִמְנָא דְּאִתְחָרֵיב בֵּי מַקְדְּשָׁא, וְהָווּ מוֹקְדִין לֵיהּ בְּנוּרָא, סְלִיקוּ כָּל אִינוּן כַּהֲנֵי עַל כּוֹתְלֵיהוֹן דְּמַקְדְּשָׁא, וְכָל מַפְתְּחִין בִּידַיְיהוּ, וַאֲמָרוּ, עַד הָכָא הֲוֵינָא גִּזְבָּרִין דִּילָךְ, מִכָּאן וָאֵילָךְ טוֹל דִּילָךְ.

217. Rabbi Chizkiah quoted the verse, "The burden of the valley of vision. What ails you now, that you are wholly gone up to the housetops" (Yeshayah 22:1). Come and behold: It has been said that when the Temple was destroyed and consumed by fire, all the priests went up to the roofs of the Temple with all the Temple's keys in their hands. They said "until now we have been Your treasurers, from now on take what is Yours."

218. אֲבָל תָּא חֲזֵי, גֵּיא חִזָּיוֹן: דָּא שְׁכִינְתָּא, דַּהֲוַת בְּמַקְדְּשָׁא, וְכָל בְּנֵי עַלְמָא, מִינָהּ הֲווֹ יָנְקִין, יְנִיקוּ דִּנְבוּאָה. דְּאַף עַל גָּב דְּכָל נְבִיאִין, קָא הֲווֹ מִתְנַבְּאִין מֵאֲתַר אָחֳרָא, מִגַּוָּוהּ הֲווֹ יָנְקִין נְבוּאַתְהוֹן, וְע״ד אִתְקְרֵי אִיהִי גֵּיא חִזָּיוֹן. חִזָּיוֹן: הָא אוֹקְמוּהָ, דְּאִיהוּ חֵיזוּ, דְּכָל גְּוָונִין עִלָּאִין.

218. Yet come and behold: "The valley of vision" is the Shechinah who used to be in the Temple, and all the people in the world drew prophecy from Her. And although the prophets used to prophesize from a different place, THAT IS, NETZACH AND HOD OF ZEIR ANPIN, they used to draw their prophecies from Her, THE NUKVA. BECAUSE NETZACH AND HOD OF ZEIR ANPIN GAVE PLENTY TO THE SHECHINAH, WHO GAVE THE ILLUMINATION OF NETZACH AND HOD TO THE PROPHETS, She is therefore named after prophecy "the valley of vision." It has been explained THAT SHE IS CALLED vision, because She reflects all the upper hues. THE FOUR HUES OF ZEIR ANPIN, CHOCHMAH AND BINAH, TIFERET AND MALCHUT, ARE REFLECTED ONLY IN HER. SHE IS THEREFORE CALLED VISION.

219. מַה לָּךְ אֵיפֹה כִּי עָלִית כֻּלָּךְ לַגַּגּוֹת, דְּהָא כַּד אִתְחָרַב מַקְדְּשָׁא, שְׁכִינְתָּא אָתָאת, וּסְלֵיקַת בְּכָל אִינּוּן אַתְרִין, דַּהֲוָה מְדוֹרָהּ בְּהוֹ בְּקַדְמֵיתָא, וַהֲוַת בָּכַת עַל בֵּית מְדוֹרָהּ, וְעַל יִשְׂרָאֵל דַּאֲזָלוּ בְּגָלוּתָא, וְעַל כָּל אִינּוּן צַדִּיקֵי וַחֲסִידֵי, דַּהֲווֹ תַּמָּן וְאִתְאֲבִידוּ, וּמְנָלָן, דִּכְתִּיב כֹּה אָמַר יי׳ קוֹל בְּרָמָה נִשְׁמָע נְהִי בְּכִי תַמְרוּרִים רָחֵל מְבַכָּה עַל בָּנֶיהָ, וְהָא אִתְמָר. וּכְדֵין קוּדְשָׁא בְּרִיךְ הוּא שָׁאִיל לָהּ לִשְׁכִינְתָּא, וַאֲמַר לָהּ, מַה לָּךְ אֵיפֹה כִּי עָלִית כֻּלָּךְ לַגַּגּוֹת.

219. "What ails you now, that you are wholly gone up to the housetops": When the Temple was destroyed, the Shechinah stood in all the places She used to inhabit and wept for Her apartment, for Yisrael who went into exile, and for all the righteous and the pious who perished there. How do we know this? From the words, "A voice was heard in Rama, lamentation, and bitter weeping; Rachel weeping for her children" (Yirmeyah 31:14). RACHEL

WAS THE NAME OF THE SHECHINAH, as we have already learned. The Holy One, blessed be He, then asked the Shechinah, "What ails you now, that you are wholly gone up to the housetops."

220. מַהוּ כֻּלָּךְ, דְּהָא כִּי עָלִית סַגְיָא, מַהוּ כֻּלָּךְ. לְאַכְלְלָא בַּהֲדָהּ כָּל חֵילִין וְכָל רְתִיכִין אָחֳרָנִין, דְּכֻלְּהוּ בְּכוּ עִמָּהּ, עַל חֻרְבַּן בֵּי מַקְדְּשָׁא.

220. HE ASKS: Why does it say that "you are wholly?" It would have been sufficient to say that "you are gone up TO THE HOUSETOPS." What does wholly mean? HE REPLIES: It includes all the other legions and Chariots that all wept with Her for the destruction of the Temple. IT IS THEREFORE WRITTEN "THAT YOU ARE WHOLLY GONE UP TO THE HOUSETOPS."

221. וּבְגִין כָּךְ מַה לָּךְ אֵיפֹה, אָמְרָה קַמֵּיהּ, וְכִי בָּנַי בְּגָלוּתָא, וּמַקְדְּשָׁא אִתּוֹקְדָא, וַאֲנָא מַה לִּי הָכָא, שָׁרִיאַת וַאֲמָרַת, תְּשׁוּאוֹת מְלֵאָה עִיר הוֹמִיָּה קִרְיָה עַלִּיזָה חֲלָלַיִךְ לֹא חַלְלֵי חֶרֶב וְלֹא מֵתֵי מִלְחָמָה עַל כֵּן אָמַרְתִּי שְׁעוּ מִנִּי אֲמָרֵר בַּבֶּכִי וגו׳. וְהָא אוֹקִימְנָא, דְּקוּדְשָׁא בְּרִיךְ הוּא אֲמַר לָהּ, כֹּה אָמַר יי׳ מִנְעִי קוֹלֵךְ מִבֶּכִי וגו׳.

221. Therefore, HE ASKED HER, "What ails you now..." She replied, My children are in exile and the Temple burnt, AND YOU DO NOT KNOW, and as for me, whatever shall I do here. She said: "You that are full of uproar, a tumultuous city, a joyous city: your slain men are not slain with the sword, nor dead in battle." "Therefore, said I, 'Look away from me; I will weep bitterly'" (Yeshayah 22:2, 4). We have learned that the Holy One, blessed be He, replied: "Thus says Hashem; keep your voice from weeping..." (Yirmeyah 31:15).

222. וְתָא חֲזֵי, מִיּוֹמָא דְּאִתְחָרֵיב בֵּי מַקְדְּשָׁא, לָא הֲוָה יוֹמָא, דְּלָא אִשְׁתְּכַח בֵּיהּ לְווֹטִין, בְּגִין דְּכַד בֵּי מַקְדְּשָׁא הֲוָה קַיָּים, הֲווֹ יִשְׂרָאֵל פָּלְחִין פּוּלְחָנִין וְקָרְבִין עִלָּוָון וְקָרְבָּנִין, וּשְׁכִינְתָּא שַׁרְיָא בְּבֵי מַקְדְּשָׁא עֲלַיְיהוּ, כְּאִמָּא דְּרַבְיעָא עַל בְּנַיָּיא, וַהֲווֹ כָּל אַנְפִּין נְהִירִין, עַד דְּאִשְׁתַּכָּחוּ בִּרְכָאן לְעֵילָּא וְתַתָּא, וְלָא הֲוָה יוֹמָא, דְּלָא אִשְׁתְּכַח בֵּיהּ

בִּרְכָאן וְחֶדְוָון, וַהֲווֹ יִשְׂרָאֵל שָׁרָאן לְרָחֲצָן בְּאַרְעָא, וְכָל עַלְמָא הֲוָה אִתְּזָן בְּגִינַיְיהוּ.

222. Come and behold: Since the Temple was destroyed, not a day has passed without curses. This is because as long as the Temple existed, Yisrael could worship and offer burnt offerings and sacrifices. The Shechinah hovered about them in the Temple, as a mother about her children. All faces were shining, until blessings would abide above and below. Not a day passed without blessings and delight. Yisrael dwelt securely in their land, and all the world was nourished for their sake.

223. הַשְׁתָּא דְּאִתְחָרֵיב בֵּי מַקְדְּשָׁא, וּשְׁכִינְתָּא עִמְּהוֹן בְּגָלוּתָא, לֵית לָךְ יוֹמָא דְּלָא אִשְׁתַּכַּח בֵּיהּ לְוָוטִין, וְעַלְמָא אִתְלַטְיָא, וְחֶדְוָון לָא אִשְׁתַּכָּחוּ לְעֵילָא וְתַתָּא.

223. Now that the Temple is destroyed and the Shechinah has gone with them into exile, there is not a day without curses. The world is accursed, and joys do not dwell above or below.

224. וְזַמִּין קוּדְשָׁא בְּרִיךְ הוּא, לְאַקְמָא לָהּ לִכְנֶסֶת יִשְׂרָאֵל מֵעַפְרָא, כְּמָה דְּאִתְּמָר, וּלְמֶחֱדֵי עַלְמָא בְּכֹלָּא, כד"א וַהֲבִיאוֹתִים אֶל הַר קָדְשִׁי וְשִׂמַּחְתִּים בְּבֵית תְּפִלָּתִי וגו' וּכְתִיב בִּבְכִי יָבוֹאוּ וּבְתַחֲנוּנִים אוֹבִילֵם. כְּמָה דִּבְקַדְמֵיתָא, דִּכְתִּיב בָּכֹה תִבְכֶּה בַּלַּיְלָה וְדִמְעָתָהּ עַל לֶחֱיָהּ, הָכֵי נָמֵי לְבָתַר, בִּבְכִי יִתְהַדְּרוּן, דִּכְתִּיב בִּבְכִי יָבֹאוּ וגו'.

224. In days to come, the Holy One, blessed be He, will raise the Congregation of Yisrael, THE SHECHINAH, from the dust, as it is written, "Even them will I bring to my holy mountain, and make them joyful in my house of prayer" (Yeshayah 56:7). It is also written, "They shall come with weeping, and with supplications will I lead them" (Yirmeyah 31:8). Because at first, it is written, "She weeps sore in the night, and her tears are on her cheeks" (Eichah 1:2), they will afterward return weeping FROM THE EXILE, as it is written, "They shall come with weeping."

14. "As soon as the morning was light"

A Synopsis

This verse speculates on the meaning of the phrase, "the morning was light." Drawing on many precedents from the Torah, it uses the phrase to define the healing powers of God, the bright future of the people of Israel, and the difficulties that will befall their enemies.

The Relevance of this Passage

The Light of The Creator can heal all our ailments – but we must have certainty and trust in its power, and we must be conscious of sharing this energy with all those in need. These healing forces are summoned forth as we meditate upon the primordial letters of creation.

225. הַבֹּקֶר אוֹר וְהָאֲנָשִׁים שֻׁלְּחוּ הֵמָּה וַחֲמוֹרֵיהֶם, רִבִּי אֶלְעָזָר אֲמַר, הָכָא אִית לְאִסְתַּכָּלָה, אִי אִינוּן הֲווֹ אָזְלֵי וְאִשְׁתַּדָּרוּ, מַה לָּן לְמִכְתַּב בְּאוֹרַיְיתָא, הֵמָּה וַחֲמוֹרֵיהֶם. אֶלָּא בְּגִין דִּכְתִּיב, וְלָקַחַת אוֹתָנוּ לַעֲבָדִים וְאֶת חֲמוֹרֵינוּ, בְּגִין כָּךְ, וְהָאֲנָשִׁים שֻׁלְּחוּ הֵמָּה וַחֲמוֹרֵיהֶם, בְּגִין דְּלָא יִשְׁתָּאֲרוּן אִינוּן וַחֲמוֹרֵיהוֹן, כִּדְקָאֲמָרוּ.

225. "As soon as the morning was light, the men were sent away, they and their donkeys" (Beresheet 44:3). Rabbi Elazar said: We have to study this verse carefully. If they were sent, why should the Torah add "they and their donkeys?" HE ANSWERS, Because scripture reads, "and take us for bondsmen, and our donkeys" (Beresheet 43:18), the verse "the men were sent away, they and their donkeys" teaches us that they have not stayed, nor have their donkeys.

226. פְּתַח וַאֲמַר, וַיַּשְׁכֵּם אַבְרָהָם בַּבֹּקֶר וַיַּחֲבשׁ אֶת חֲמוֹרוֹ וגו', הַהוּא בֹּקֶר דְּאַבְרָהָם הֲוָה נָהִיר, לְקַיְימָא עֲלַיְיהוּ בִּזְכוּתֵיהּ, כְּדֵין זְכוּתָא דְּאַבְרָהָם קָיְימָא עֲלַיְיהוּ, וַאֲזָלוּ בִּשְׁלָם, וְאִשְׁתְּזֵיבוּ מִן דִּינָא, בְּגִין דְּהַהִיא שַׁעְתָּא, קָיְימָא עֲלַיְיהוּ דִּינָא, לְאִתְפָּרְעָא מִנַּיְיהוּ, בַּר דִּזְכוּתָא דְּהַהוּא בֹּקֶר דְּאַבְרָהָם, אָגֵין עֲלַיְיהוּ, וְאִשְׁתַּלָּחוּ מִן דִּינָא, דְּלָא שַׁלִּיט עֲלַיְיהוּ בְּהַהוּא זִמְנָא.

226. He opened the discussion with the verse, "And Abraham rose up early in the morning, and saddled his donkey" (Beresheet 22:3). That was the morning of Abraham, WHICH IS CHESED. It shone upon THE TRIBES due to Abraham, whose merit stood for them and enabled them to go in peace and be delivered from Judgment. For at that time, Judgment impended upon them to exact payment, and only the merit of Abraham's morning protected them. Thus they were sent from that place of Judgment, for it had no power over them at the time.

227. רִבִּי יְהוּדָה פְּתַח, וּכְאוֹר בֹּקֶר יִזְרַח שֶׁמֶשׁ, דָּא הוּא נְהוֹרָא, דְּהַהוּא בֹּקֶר דְּאַבְרָהָם. יִזְרַח שֶׁמֶשׁ: דָּא הוּא שִׁמְשָׁא דְּיַעֲקֹב, דִּכְתִּיב וַיִּזְרַח לוֹ הַשֶּׁמֶשׁ. בֹּקֶר לֹא עָבוֹת, דְּהַהוּא בֹּקֶר לָא אִיהוּ עָבוֹת כָּל כָּךְ, אֶלָּא מִנֹּגַהּ מִמָּטָר, נֹגַהּ מִמָּטָר: אִיהוּ מִטְרָא דְּאָתֵי מִסִּטְרָא דְּיִצְחָק, דְּהַהוּא מִטְרָא אַפֵּיק דֶּשֶׁא מֵאָרֶץ.

227. Rabbi Yehuda continued with the verse, "And he shall be as the light of the morning" (II Shmuel 23:4): This is the light of Abraham's morning, NAMELY, THE LIGHT OF CHESED. "When the sun rises" refers to the sun of Jacob, THE LIGHT OF TIFERET, as it is written, "the sun rose upon him" (Beresheet 32:32). "In a morning without clouds" means the morning, THE LIGHT OF CHESED, is not so cloudy, BECAUSE JUDGMENTS HAVE NO HOLD UPON IT, but "clear shining after rain," WHICH MEANS the brightness that comes through rain, the rain of the side of Isaac, THE LIGHT OF GVURAH, for that rain causes that, "the grass springs out of the earth" (II Shmuel 23:4).

228. דָּבָר אַחֵר וּכְאוֹר בֹּקֶר, בְּהַהוּא נְהִירוּ דְּבֹקֶר דְּאַבְרָהָם, יִזְרַח שֶׁמֶשׁ: דָּא הוּא יַעֲקֹב, דִּנְהִירוּ דִּילֵיהּ, כִּנְהִירוּ דְּהַהוּא בֹּקֶר. בֹּקֶר לֹא עָבוֹת, בְּגִין דְּהַהוּא בֹּקֶר, לָאו אִיהוּ חָשׁוּךְ, אֶלָּא נָהִיר, דְּהָא בְּשַׁעְתָּא דְּאָתֵי בֹּקֶר, לָא שָׁלְטָא דִּינָא כְּלַל, אֶלָּא כֹּלָּא נָהִיר, בְּסִטְרָא דְּאַבְרָהָם. מִנֹּגַהּ מִמָּטָר: דָּא הוּא סִטְרָא דְּיוֹסֵף הַצַּדִּיק, דְּאִיהוּ אַמְטִיר עַל אַרְעָא, לַאֲפָקָא דִּשְׁאָה, וְכָל טִיבוּ דְּעָלְמָא.

228. Another explanation of the phrase, "as the light of the morning," MEANS THAT by the light of Abraham's morning, THE LIGHT OF CHESED, "the sun rises," which is Jacob, whose light is as that of that morning OF

ABRAHAM, BEING THE SECRET OF TIFERET, THAT SHINES WITH COVERED CHASSADIM DRAWN FROM THE LIGHT OF CHESED. The "morning without clouds" is not dark but shining, for when morning, THE LIGHT OF CHESED, comes, no judgment has sway. All is illuminating on the side of Abraham, THE RIGHT SIDE, "in the clear shining after rain": This is the side of Joseph the Righteous, who showers upon the earth, THAT IS, YESOD, WHICH GIVES PLENTY TO THE NUKVA, to produce grass and all the goodness of the world.

229. אֲמַר רַבִּי שִׁמְעוֹן, תָּא חֲזֵי, בְּשַׁעְתָּא דְּלֵילְיָא עָאל, וּפָרֵישׁ גַּדְפוֹי עַל עַלְמָא, כַּמָּה גַּרְדִּינֵי טְהִירִין, זְמִינִין לְנַפְקָא, וּלְשַׁלְטָאָה בְּעַלְמָא, וְכַמָּה מָארֵיהוֹן דְּדִינִין, מִתְעָרִין בְּכַמָּה סִטְרִין לִזְנַיְיהוּ, וְשָׁלְטֵי עַל עַלְמָא, כֵּיוָן דְּאָתֵי צַפְרָא וְנָהֵיר, כֻּלְּהוּ מִסְתַּלְּקֵי, וְלָא שָׁלְטֵי, וְכָל חַד וְחַד עָאל לְדוּכְתֵּיהּ, וְתָב לְאַתְרֵיהּ.

229. Rabbi Shimon said: Come and behold: When night falls and spreads its wings upon the world, snow-white donkeys, WHICH ARE SPIRITS IN THE SHAPES OF FEMALE DONKEYS, ARE APPOINTED TO TAKE REVENGE ON THOSE WHO TRANSGRESS RELIGION AND THE LAW. They will come out and reign over the world. Numerous accusers are aroused on several sides to rule over the world. When morning breaks, they all vanish and lose their dominion. Each comes to its FIXED position and returns to its place.

230. כד"א הַבֹּקֶר אוֹר, דָּא בֹּקֶר דְּאַבְרָהָם. וְהָאֲנָשִׁים שֻׁלְּחוּ, אִלֵּין מָארֵיהוֹן דְּדִינָא, דַּהֲווֹ שָׁלְטִין בְּלֵילְיָא. הֵמָּה וַחֲמוֹרֵיהֶם אִינוּן גַּרְדִּינֵי נִימוּסִין, דְּאַתְיָין מִסִּטְרָא דִּמְסָאֲבָא, דְּלָאו אִינוּן קַדִּישִׁין, וְלָא שָׁלְטִין, וְלָא אִתְחֲזוּן, מֵכִי אָתֵי צַפְרָא. וְאִינוּן מִסִּטְרָא דְּאִינוּן חֲמָרֵי, גַּרְדִּינֵי נִימוּסִין דְּקָאֲמָרוּ.

230. Another explanation of the phrase, "the morning was light," is that when Abraham's morning breaks, THE REIGN OF THE RIGHT BEGINS. "... the men were sent away" refers to the accusers who rule by night, "they and their donkeys": These are the female donkeys THAT ARE APPOINTED OVER THOSE WHO TRANSGRESS religion and the law. They come from the side of defilement, being unholy, and do not rule and are not seen when morning comes. The female donkeys in charge of sinners are considered the same as male donkeys, BEING OF THE SAME SPECIES.

231. דְּהָא לֵית לָךְ דַּרְגִּין עִלָּאִין. דְּלָא אִיתָאי בְּהוֹ יְמִינָא וּשְׂמָאלָא, רַחֲמֵי וְדִינָא, דַּרְגִּין עַל דַּרְגִּין קַדִּישִׁין, מִסִּטְרָא דִּקְדוּשָּׁה, וּמְסָאֲבִין, מִסִּטְרָא דִּמְסָאֲבָא, וְכֻלְּהוּ דַּרְגִּין עַל דַּרְגִּין, אִלֵּין עַל אִלֵּין.

231. There are no upper grades that are not divided into right and left, into Mercy and Judgment. There are numerous grades, holy on the side of holiness and defiled on the side of defilement. All grades stand on top of each other.

232. וּבְכָל אֲתַר דְּבֹקֶר דְּאַבְרָהָם אִתְעַר בְּעַלְמָא, כֻּלְּהוּ מִתְעַבְרֵי, וְלָא שָׁלְטֵי, בְּגִין דְּלֵית לוֹן לְקָיְימָא בִּסְטַר יְמִינָא, אֶלָּא בִּסְטַר שְׂמָאלָא. וְקוּדְשָׁא בְּרִיךְ הוּא עָבַד יְמָמָא וְלֵילְיָא, לְאַנְהָגָא כָּל חַד וְחַד לְסִטְרֵיהּ כִּדְקָא חָזֵי לֵיהּ, זַכָּאָה חוּלָקֵיהוֹן דְּיִשְׂרָאֵל, בְּעַלְמָא דֵין, וּבְעַלְמָא דְאָתֵי.

232. Wherever Abraham's morning is awakened into the world, the forces of the left are gone and have no sway, for they cannot exist on the right side, only on the left. THEREFORE, WHEN MORNING ARRIVES, WHICH IS THE REIGN OF THE RIGHT, THEY ARE FORCED TO VANISH. The Holy One, blessed be He, made day and night to give each its own proper aspect, THE RIGHT TO RULE BY DAY AND THE LEFT TO RULE BY NIGHT. Happy is the portion of Yisrael in this world and the World to Come.

233. רִבִּי חִיָּיא פְּתַח וַאֲמַר, וְזָרְחָה לָכֶם יִרְאֵי שְׁמִי שֶׁמֶשׁ צְדָקָה וּמַרְפֵּא בִּכְנָפֶיהָ. תָּא חֲזֵי, זַמִּין קוּדְשָׁא בְּרִיךְ הוּא לְאַנְהָרָא לוֹן לְיִשְׂרָאֵל, הַהוּא שִׁמְשָׁא, דְּגָנִיז קוּדְשָׁא בְּרִיךְ הוּא, מִיּוֹמָא דְּאִתְבְּרֵי עַלְמָא, מִקַּמֵּי רַשִּׁיעֵי דְעַלְמָא, כְּמָה דִכְתִיב, וַיִּמָּנַע מֵרְשָׁעִים אוֹרָם.

233. Rabbi Chiya said: "But to you who fear My name, the sun of righteousness shall arise with healing in its wings" (Malachi 3:20). Come and behold: The Holy One, blessed be He, will cause to shine upon Yisrael the sun, which, from the day the world was created, He concealed from the wicked in the world, as it is written, "And from the wicked their light is withheld" (Iyov 38:15).

234. וְהַהוּא נְהוֹרָא גָּנִיז לֵיהּ קוּדְשָׁא בְּרִיךְ הוּא, דְּכַד נָפַק בְּקַדְמֵיתָא, הֲוָה נָהִיר מִסְּיָיפֵי עָלְמָא, וְעַד סְיָיפֵי עָלְמָא, כֵּיוָן דְּאִסְתַּכַּל בְּדָרֵיהּ דֶּאֱנוֹשׁ וּבְדָרֵיהּ דְּמַבּוּל, וּבְדָרֵיהּ דְּהַפְלָגָה, וּבְכָל אִינוּן חַיָּיבַיָּא, גָּנִיז לֵיהּ לְהַהוּא נְהוֹרָא.

234. The Holy One, blessed be He, stored that light, for when it first came out, it shone from one end of the world to the other. But when He looked upon the generations of Enosh, the generation of the Flood, the generation of the Tower of Babylon and all the wicked people, He stored the light.

235. כֵּיוָן דְּאָתָא יַעֲקֹב, וְאִתְדַּבַּק בְּהַהוּא מְמַנָּא רַבְרְבָא דְעֵשָׂו, וְאַכִּישׁ לֵיהּ בְּיַרְכָא דִילֵיהּ, וַהֲוָה נְכֵי, כְּדֵין מַה כְּתִיב, וַיִּזְרַח לוֹ הַשֶּׁמֶשׁ, מַאן שֶׁמֶשׁ הַהוּא שִׁמְשָׁא דְגָנִיז, בְּגִין דְּאִית בֵּיהּ אֲסוּתָא, לְאִתְּסָאָה לֵיהּ מֵאַרְכּוּבָתֵיהּ, וּלְבָתַר אִתְּסֵי בְּהַהוּא שִׁמְשָׁא, דִּכְתִיב, וַיָּבֹא יַעֲקֹב שָׁלֵם, שָׁלֵם בְּגוּפֵיהּ דְּאִתְּסֵי.

235. When Jacob came to contend with Esau's minister, who bit his thigh, he limped. It is then written, "the sun rose upon him" (Beresheet 32:32). What sun is this? It is the sun that was stored away, which has healing in it, to heal his thigh. When he was healed through that sun, it is written, "And Jacob came to Shalem (lit. 'whole')" (Beresheet 33:18), meaning he was whole in his body and healed.

236. וְעַל דָּא, זַמִּין קוּדְשָׁא בְּרִיךְ הוּא, לְגַלָּאָה הַהוּא שִׁמְשָׁא, וּלְאַנְהָרָא לֵיהּ לְיִשְׂרָאֵל, דִּכְתִיב וְזָרְחָה לָכֶם יִרְאֵי שְׁמִי שֶׁמֶשׁ צְדָקָה, מַאי שֶׁמֶשׁ צְדָקָה. דָּא שִׁמְשָׁא דְּיַעֲקֹב, דְּאִתְּסֵי בֵּיהּ. וּמַרְפֵּא בִּכְנָפֶיהָ, דְּהַהוּא שִׁמְשָׁא, יִתְּסוּן כֻּלְּהוּ, בְּגִין דְּהָא בְּזִמְנָא דִיקוּמוּן יִשְׂרָאֵל מֵעַפְרָא, כַּמָּה חִגְּרִין, וְכַמָּה סוּמִין, יְהוֹן בְּהוֹן, וּכְדֵין קוּדְשָׁא בְּרִיךְ הוּא יַנְהִיר לוֹן הַהוּא שִׁמְשָׁא לְאִתְּסָאָה בָהּ, דִּכְתִיב וּמַרְפֵּא בִּכְנָפֶיהָ.

236. The Holy One, blessed be He, will therefore uncover that sun in the future and shine upon Yisrael, as it is written, "But to you who fear My name the sun of righteousness shall arise," the sun of righteousness being the sun with which Jacob was healed. It is "with healing in its wings," because everybody will then be healed. When Yisrael rise from the dust, many will be lame and blind. The Holy One, blessed be He, will shine the healing sun upon them, as it is written, "with healing in it wings."

237. וּכְדֵין, יִתְנְהִיר הַהוּא שִׁמְשָׁא, מִסְּיְיפֵי עָלְמָא, עַד סְיָיפֵי עָלְמָא, וּלְיִשְׂרָאֵל יְהֵא אַסְוָותָא, וְעַמִּין עעכו"ם בֵּיהּ יִתּוֹקְדוּן, אֲבָל לְיִשְׂרָאֵל מַה כְּתִיב, אָז יִבָּקַע כַּשַּׁחַר אוֹרֶךָ וַאֲרֻכָתְךָ מְהֵרָה תִצְמָח וְהָלַךְ לְפָנֶיךָ צִדְקֶךָ כְּבוֹד יי' יַאַסְפֶךָ.

237. That sun will then shine from one end of the world to the other. Yisrael will be cured, but the idolatrous nations will be burned by it. Concerning Yisrael, the verse reads, "Then shall your light break forth like the morning, and your health shall spring forth speedily; and your righteousness shall go before you; the glory of Hashem shall be your rearguard" (Yeshayah 58:8).

15. "And to Joseph were born two sons, before the years of famine came"

A Synopsis

The subject of this final passage is the nature of "the days of evil." These are not the days of old age, Rabbi Yitzchak explains, but the "illumination of the left." Man should remain chaste in a bad time and not have children, since these "strange" children would descend from the left side – thus, Joseph had his sons before the famine struck. Neither should a man go forth into the marketplace during the days of evil, since the world is full of "satanic accusers" lying in wait for the unwary.

The Relevance of this Passage

A man and woman's thoughts during sexual relations help determine the purity of their unborn child's soul. The purer our thoughts at the moment of conception, the finer the grade of soul that is drawn from the Upper Worlds. Because of social pressures and our Evil Inclination, purifying and controlling our thoughts is a formidable task. The cleansing attributes of the Hebrew letters in this passage help us to prevail over the world's negative influences, and to elevate our thoughts and desires. We draw Light to our children, which helps purify their souls.

238. אַהֲדַרְנָא לְמִילֵי קַדְמָאֵי: וּלְיוֹסֵף יֻלַּד שְׁנֵי בָנִים בְּטֶרֶם תָּבוֹא שְׁנַת הָרָעָב וגו׳. ר׳ יִצְחָק פְּתַח, וְהָיָה שְׁאֵרִית יַעֲקֹב בַּגּוֹיִם בְּקֶרֶב עַמִּים רַבִּים כְּטַל מֵאֵת ה׳ כִּרְבִיבִים עֲלֵי עֵשֶׂב אֲשֶׁר לֹא יְקַוֶּה לְאִישׁ וְלֹא יְיַחֵל לִבְנֵי אָדָם. תָּא חֲזֵי, בְּכָל יוֹמָא וְיוֹמָא, כַּד נְהוֹרָא סָלְקָא, אִתְעַר חַד צִיפֳּרָא, בְּאִילָנָא דְּגִנְתָּא דְעֵדֶן, וְקָרֵי תְּלַת זִמְנִין, וְשַׁרְבִיטָא יִזְדַּקַּף, וְכָרוֹזָא קָרֵי בְחָיִל, לְכוֹן אָמְרִין, הוּרְמָנֵי דְּבוֹרַיְירֵי, מַאן מִנְּכוֹן דְּחָמֵי וְלָא חָמֵי. דְּקַיְימָא בְּעַלְמָא, וְלָא יָדְעֵי עַל מַה קָיְימֵי, לָא מַשְׁגִּיחִין בִּיקָרָא דְמָארֵיהוֹן, אוֹרַיְיתָא קָיְימָא קַמַּיְיהוּ, וְלָא מִשְׁתַּדְּלֵי בָהּ, טַב לוֹן דְּלָא יִבָּרוֹן, עַל מַה יְקוּמוּן, בְּלָא סָכְלְתָנוּ. וַוי לוֹן, כַּד יִתְעָרוּן יוֹמֵי דְרַע עֲלַיְיהוּ, וְיִטְרְדוּן לְהוֹן מֵעָלְמָא.

238. Let us return to the former subject: "And to Joseph were born two sons before the years of famine came" (Beresheet 41:50). Rabbi Yitzchak quoted the verse, "And the remnant of Jacob shall be in the midst of many peoples like dew from Hashem, like the showers upon the grass, that tarries not for man, nor waits for the sons of men" (Michah 5:6). Come and behold: Every day, when light breaks, a bird awakens on a tree in the Garden of Eden and crows three times. The twig is straightened, and the crier loudly warns: Whoever among you see but see not; exist in the world, yet do not know why; do not care for the glory of their Master; and do not study the Torah even though it stands before you, it is better for you never to have been born. Why should you exist without understanding? Woe to you, when the days of evil shall bestir themselves against you and banish you from the world.

239. מַאן אִיוּן יוֹמִין דְּרַע, אִי סַלְקָא דַעְתָּךְ דְּאִינוּן יוֹמִין דְּסִיבוּ, לָאו הָכֵי, דְּהָא יוֹמֵי דְסִיבוּ, אִי זָכָה בִּבְנִין, וּבְנֵי בְנִין, יוֹמֵי דְטַב אִינוּן, מַאן אִינוּן יוֹמִין דְּרַע.

239. HE ASKS: What are the days of evil? Can they be days of old age? Not so, for days of old age, if man has children and grandchildren, are good days. What, then, are days of evil?

240. אֶלָּא אִינוּן, כְּמָה דְּאִתְּמָר, דִּכְתִּיב וּזְכוֹר אֶת בּוֹרְאֶךָ בִּימֵי בְחוּרוֹתֶיךָ עַד אֲשֶׁר לֹא יָבֹאוּ יְמֵי הָרָעָה, לָאו אִינוּן יוֹמִין דְּסִיבוּ, אֶלָּא רָזָא דְמִלָּה, כַּד בָּרָא קוּדְשָׁא בְּרִיךְ הוּא עַלְמָא, בָּרָא לֵיהּ בְּאַתְוָון דְּאוֹרַיְיתָא, וְכָל אָת וְאָת עָאֲלַת קַמֵּיהּ, עַד דְּאִתְקַיְימוּ כֻּלְּהוּ אַתְוָון בְּאָת בֵּי"ת. וְכָל אִינוּן אַלְפָא בֵּיתוֹת, דְּאִתְגַּלְגְּלוּ אַתְוָון, כֻּלְּהוּ קַיְימֵי לְמִבְרֵי עָלְמָא.

240. They are mentioned in the verse, "Remember now your creator in the days of your youth, before the evil days come" (Kohelet 12:1). These are not days of old age. The mystery here is that when the Holy One, blessed be He, created the world, He did it through the letters of the Torah. Each letter came before Him, until they came to be established by the letter *Bet*, WHICH IS IN THE SECRET OF BLESSING (HEB. *BERACHAH*), FOR WHICH REASON THE WORLD WAS CREATED BY IT. All the alphabets along with their various permutations, THE 231 FORWARD ALPHABETS AND THE 231 BACKWARD ALPHABETS, AS WE KNOW, are means WITH WHICH to create the world, HAVING RECEIVED THE SECRET OF BLESSING FROM THE LETTER *BET*.

241. כֵּיוָן דְּאִתְגַּלְגְּלוּ, וְאִתְחַבָּרוּ תְּרֵין אַתְוָון אִלֵּין ט״ר כַּחֲדָא, סַלְקָא טי״ת, וְלָא אִתְיַישְׁבַת, עַד דְּגָעַר בָּהּ קוּדְשָׁא בְּרִיךְ הוּא, וַאֲמַר לָהּ טי״ת טי״ת, עַל מָה אַתְּ סָלְקָא, וְלָא אִתְיַישְׁבַת בְּדוּכְתֵּיךְ, אָמְרָה קַמֵּיהּ, וְכִי עֲבַדְתְּ לִי לְמֶהֱוֵי אָת בְּרֵישָׁא דְטוֹב, דְּהָא אוֹרַיְיתָא פְּתַח בִּי כִּי טוֹב, הֵיךְ אֲנָא מִתְחַבְּרָא לְאִתְיַישְׁבָא בְּאָת רַע.

241. After the letters were permutated INTO AN ALPHABET IN WHICH THE LETTERS *Tet* and *Resh* appear together, the *Tet* ascended and would not settle together WITH *RESH*. The Holy One, blessed be He, rebuked her and said: *Tet, Tet,* why do you ascend and not settle in your place?' She replied: You have made me the first letter in the word *Tov* (good), and the Torah opened by saying "that it was good" IN THE VERSE, "AND ELOHIM SAW THE LIGHT, THAT IT WAS GOOD" (BERESHEET 1:3). How could I be united with *RESH*, WHICH IS THE FIRST LETTER IN THE WORD *Ra* (evil)?

242. אֲמַר לָהּ, תּוּב לְאַתְרֵיךְ, דְּהָא אַתְּ צְרִיךְ לָהּ, דְּהָא בַּר נָשׁ דַּאֲנָא בָּעֵי לְמִבְרֵי בְּכוֹן, תַּרְוַויְיכוּ אִתְכְּלִיל כַּחֲדָא, וְיִתְבְּרֵי, אֲבָל אַתְּ לִימִינָא, וְאִיהִי לִשְׂמָאלָא. וּכְדֵין, תָּבוּ וְאִתְיַישְׁבוּ דָּא בְּדָא כַּחֲדָא.

242. He said to her, return to your place, for you have need OF THE LETTER *RA*. For I wish to create man and include both of you together in him. Then he will be created, but with you on the right and her on the left. The letters *Tet* and *Resh* settled together with each other.

243. בְּהַהוּא שַׁעֲתָא פָּרֵישׁ לוֹן קוּדְשָׁא בְּרִיךְ הוּא, וּבָרָא לוֹן לְכָל חַד וְחַד, יוֹמִין וּשְׁנִין יְדִיעָן, אִלֵּין לִימִינָא וְאִלֵּין לִשְׂמָאלָא. אִלֵּין דִּימִינָא, אִתְקְרוּן יְמֵי הַטּוֹב, וְאִלֵּין דִּשְׂמָאלָא אִתְקְרוּן יְמֵי הָרָעָה, וְע״ד אֲמַר שְׁלֹמֹה, עַד אֲשֶׁר לֹא יָבֹאוּ יְמֵי הָרָעָה, דְּאִלֵּין מְסַחֲרִין לֵיהּ לְבַר נָשׁ, בְּחוֹבוֹי דְּאִיהוּ עָבֵיד. כֵּיוָן דְּאִתְחַבְּרוּן יוֹמִין דְּטוֹב, וְיוֹמִין דְּרַע, כְּדֵין תָּבוּ וְאִתְיַישְׁבוּ, לְאִתְכְּלָלָא בְּהוֹ בְּבַר נָשׁ.

243. The Holy One, blessed be He, then divided them, AND SEPARATED THEIR ILLUMINATION, THE ONE BEING WHOLLY GOOD AND THE OTHER WHOLLY EVIL. And He created for each certain days and years, THE SECRET OF THE 28 TIMES IN KOHELET, the ones to the right and the others to the left, FOURTEEN TIMES FOR GOOD AND FOURTEEN FOR EVIL. The ones to the right are called days of good, and the ones to the left are called days of evil. Solomon said: "before the evil days come" and encompass man on account of the sins he committed. Once the days of good and days of evil were created, *TET* AND *RESH* settled together again to be included within man.

244. וּבְגִינֵי כָּךְ אֲמַר דָּוִד, לָמָּה אִירָא בִּימֵי רָע עֲוֹן עֲקֵבַי יְסֻבֵּנִי, יְמֵי רָע וַדַּאי, וְרָזָא דָא, אִלֵּין אִקְרוּן יְמֵי רָעָב, שְׁנִין דְּרָעָב, וְאִלֵּין אִקְרוּן יְמֵי שָׂבָע, שְׁנֵי שָׂבָע.

244. David therefore asked: "Why should I fear in the days of evil, when the iniquity of my persecutors compasses me about" (Tehilim 49:6), the days of evil assuredly. There is a mystery in that THE ILLUMINATION OF THE LEFT is called days of famine and years of famine, and THE ILLUMINATION OF THE RIGHT is called days of plenty and years of plenty.

245. וְרָזָא דְמִלָּה, דְּלָא לַאֲפָקָא מַבּוּעָא דִּבְרִית קַדִּישָׁא, בְּיוֹמֵי רָעָב, בִּשְׁנַת הָרָעָב, וּבְגִין כָּךְ יוֹסֵף דְּאִיהוּ רָזָא דִבְרִית, סָתֵים מַבּוּעֵיהּ בִּשְׁנַת הָרָעָב, וְלָא יְהַב לֵיהּ דּוּכְתָּא לְאַסְגָּאָה בְּעַלְמָא, וְדָא בָּעֵי לֵיהּ לְבַר נָשׁ, דְּכַד שָׁלְטָא שְׁנַת הָרָעָב, דְּיַסְתֵּים מַבּוּעָא דִּבְרִית קַדִּישָׁא דִילֵיהּ, בְּגִין דְּלָא יְהַב לֵיהּ דּוּכְתָּא לְאַסְגָּאָה בְּעַלְמָא.

245. The secret is that one should not draw forth the source of the holy covenant, THAT IS, NOT PERFORM MARITAL DUTY, in days or years of famine. Joseph, therefore, the secret of the covenant, closed his spring in the year of famine and did not allow it to multiply in the world. HENCE THE WORDS, "AND TO JOSEPH WERE BORN...BEFORE THE YEARS OF FAMINE CAME" (BERESHEET 41:50). When the year of famine reigns, it behooves man to withhold the spring of his holy covenant and not enable THE LEFT to multiply in the world.

15. "And to Joseph were born two sons, before the years of famine came"

246. רִבִּי שִׁמְעוֹן אֲמַר, רָזָא דָא אִיהוּ רָזָא עִלָּאָה, בְּהַהִיא שְׁנַת הָרָעָב, כֵּיוָן דְּאִיהִי שָׁלְטָא, בָּעֵי לְאַסְתְּמָא מַבּוּעֵיהּ, בְּגִין דְּאִי לָא סָתֵים לֵיהּ, גָּרֵים לְאַמְשָׁכָא רוּחָא לְהַהוּא וַלְדָּא מֵהַהוּא סִטְרָא, וְיָהֵיב דּוּכְתָּא לְהַהוּא סִטְרָא, לְמִפְשֵׁי בְּעַלְמָא, סִטְרָא דִּמְסָאֲבָא בְּסִטְרָא דְּקוּדְשָׁא, וְתוּ רָזָא, דִּכְתִיב תַּחַת שָׁלֹשׁ רָגְזָה אֶרֶץ וגו'.

246. Rabbi Shimon said: It is a very deep mystery that when the year of famine, THE ILLUMINATION OF THE LEFT, has sway, it behooves man to stop his source FROM BEGETTING CHILDREN FOR TWO REASONS: (1) If he does not stop his source, he would draw upon the baby a spirit from the LEFT side, and (2) He would thus give a place to that side, thereby strengthening the side of defilement in this world at the expense of the side of holiness. Regarding this secret, the scripture also reads, "For three things the earth quakes" (Mishlei 30:21).

247. וּבְגִין כָּךְ, יוֹסֵף צַדִּיקָא, רָזָא דִּבְרִית, סָלֵיק וְסָתֵים מַבּוּעֵיהּ, בִּשְׁנַת הָרָעָב, דְּלָא לְאִתְעָרְבָא בַּהֲדָהּ כְּלַל, וּלְמֵיהַב לָהּ דּוּכְתָּא, וּמַאן דְּאַפְתַּח מַבּוּעֵיהּ בְּהַהוּא זִמְנָא, עֲלֵיהּ כְּתִיב בַּה' בָּגָדוּ כִּי בָנִים זָרִים יָלָדוּ עַתָּה יֹאכְלֵם וגו'. דְּהָא אִלֵּין אִקְרוּן בָּנִים זָרִים וַדַּאי. בַּה' בָּגָדוּ וַדַּאי. וּבְגִין כָּךְ, זַכָּאָה חוּלָקְהוֹן דְּיִשְׂרָאֵל קַדִּישִׁין, דְּלָא אִתְחַלְּפוּ דּוּכְתָּא קַדִּישָׁא, בְּדוּכְתָּא מְסָאֲבָא.

247. For that reason, Joseph the Righteous, who is the secret of the Covenant, ascended to stop his source during the year of famine, so as not to mingle at all WITH THE LEFT and prevent it from ruling OVER THE RIGHT. Of whoever lets his source flow at that time, it is written, "They have dealt treacherously against Hashem: for they have begotten strange children" (Hoshea 5:7), for the children HE BEGETS DURING THE YEARS OF FAMINE are by necessity strange children. ACCORDING TO THE FIRST REASON GIVEN BY RABBI SHIMON, HE DRAWS UPON THE BABY A SPIRIT OF THAT SIDE. Assuredly, "They have dealt treacherously against Hashem" BECAUSE, ACCORDING TO THE SECOND REASON, THEY LET THE LEFT BE STRONGER THAN THE RIGHT AND THUS BETRAYED THE NAME OF

HASHEM. Therefore, happy is the portion of holy Yisrael, who did not replace a place of holiness with that of impurity.

248. וְע״ד כְּתִיב, וּלְיוֹסֵף יֻלַּד שְׁנֵי בָנִים בְּטֶרֶם תָּבוֹא שְׁנַת הָרָעָב, דְּהָא מֵהַהוּא זִמְנָא דְּשָׁלְטָא שְׁנַת הָרָעָב, אַסְתִּים מַבּוּעֵיהּ, וְסָלֵיק מְקוֹרֵיהּ, דְּלָא לְמֵיהַב בְּנִין לְסִטְרָא מְסָאֲבָא, וְלָא לְאַחְלָפָא דוּכְתָּא דְּקוּדְשָׁא, בְּדוּכְתָּא דִּמְסָאֲבָא, וּבָעֵיבַר נָשׁ לְחַכָּאָה לְמָארֵיהּ דְּקוּדְשָׁא, כַּד יֵיתֵי וְיִשְׁלוֹט כְּדִכְתִיב וְחִכֵּיתִי לַה׳ הַמַּסְתִּיר פָּנָיו מִבֵּית יַעֲקֹב וְקִוֵּיתִי לוֹ.

248. Another explanation of the verse, "And to Joseph were born two sons before the years of famine came" is that ever since the year of famine came to rule, WHICH IS LEFT WITHOUT RIGHT, he closed his spring and raised up his source, so as not to give children to the side of defilement or exchange a holy place for an impure one, THEREBY INCREASING DEFILEMENT AT THE EXPENSE OF HOLINESS. A man should await for his Master to come and rule over the world, as it is written, "And I will wait upon Hashem, that hides His face from the house of Jacob, and I will hope for Him" (Yeshayah 8:17).

249. זַכָּאִין אִינוּן צַדִּיקַיָּא, דְּיָדְעִין אוֹרְחוֹי דְּקוּדְשָׁא בְּרִיךְ הוּא, וְנָטְרֵי פִּקּוּדֵי דְּאוֹרַיְיתָא, לְמֵיהַךְ בְּהוֹ, דִּכְתִיב, כִּי יְשָׁרִים דַּרְכֵי ה׳ וְצַדִּיקִים יֵלְכוּ בָם וּפֹשְׁעִים יִכָּשְׁלוּ בָם. וּכְתִיב וְאַתֶּם הַדְּבֵקִים בַּה׳ אֱלֹהֵיכֶם חַיִּים כֻּלְּכֶם הַיּוֹם.

249. Happy are the righteous who know the ways of the Holy One, blessed be He, observe the precepts of the Torah, and follow their course, as "the ways of Hashem are right, and the just do walk in them: but the transgressors shall stumble in them" (Hoshea 14:10) and "But you that did cleave of Hashem your Elohim are alive every one of you this day" (Devarim 4:4).

250. וּבְגִין דָּא, קוּדְשָׁא בְּרִיךְ הוּא אַזְהַר לְהוֹ לְיִשְׂרָאֵל לְאִתְקַדְּשָׁא, דִּכְתִיב וִהְיִיתֶם קְדוֹשִׁים כִּי קָדוֹשׁ אָנִי. מַאן אָנִי. דָּא קוּדְשָׁא בְּרִיךְ הוּא, מַלְכוּת שָׁמַיִם קַדִּישָׁא. מַלְכוּתָא אַחֲרָא דְּעעכו״ם, אִקְרֵי אַחֵר, דִּכְתִיב כִּי לֹא תִשְׁתַּחֲוֶה לְאֵל אַחֵר כִּי ה׳ קַנָּא שְׁמוֹ.

15. "And to Joseph were born two sons, before the years of famine came"

250. The Holy One, blessed be He, therefore admonished Yisrael to sanctify themselves, as it is written, "You shall be holy: for I Hashem your Elohim am holy" (Vayikra 19:2). HE ASKS: Who is "I?" HE ANSWERS, It is the Holy One, blessed be He, the sacred kingdom of heaven, NAMELY THE NUKVA, while the kingdom of the idolatrous nations is called other, as it is written, "For you shall worship no other El, for Hashem, whose name is Jealous, is a jealous El" (Shemot 34:14).

251. וְתָּא חֲזֵי, אֲנִי: שָׁלְטָנוּ דְּעָלְמָא דֵין, וְעָלְמָא דְּאָתֵי, וְכֹּלָּא בֵּיהּ תַּלְיָא. אַחֵר: סִטְרָא מְסָאֲבָא, אַחֵר, סִטְרָא אָחֳרָא בְּסִטְרָא מְסָאֲבָא, וְשׁוּלְטָנוּ דִּילֵיהּ בְּהַאי עָלְמָא, וְלֵית לֵיהּ בְּעָלְמָא דְּאָתֵי כְּלוּם, וּבְגִין דָּא מַאן דְּאִתְדַּבַּק בְּהַאי אֲנִי, אִית לֵיהּ חוּלָקָא בְּעָלְמָא דֵין, וּבְעָלְמָא דְּאָתֵי.

251. Come and behold: "I" is the government of this world and of the World to Come, and everything depends upon it, AS EVERYTHING DEPENDS ON THE NUKVA. Whoever cleaves to the "I," NAMELY TO THE NUKVA, has a portion in this world and the World to Come.

252. וּמַאן דְּאִתְדַּבַּק בְּהַאי אַחֵר, אִתְאֲבִיד מֵהַהוּא עָלְמָא, וְלֵית לֵיהּ חוּלָקָא בְּעָלְמָא דְּאָתֵי, וְאִית לֵיהּ חוּלָקָא בְּהַאי עָלְמָא, בְּמִסְאֲבוּ, בְּגִין דְּהַהוּא מַלְכוּ אָחֳרָא עעכו"ם, כַּמָּה אִינוּן תְּרֵיסִין גַּרְדִּינִין מִמַּנָּן בֵּיהּ, לְשַׁלְטָאָה בְּהַאי עָלְמָא.

252. Whoever cleaves to the other one, THE NUKVA OF THE HEATHEN, perishes from the world of truth, has no part in the World to Come and takes part in the impurity of this world. Yet he takes part in the defilement of this world, for the kingdom of the heathen has numerous legions of accusers through whom it rules over this world.

253. וּבְגִינֵי כָּךְ, אֱלִישָׁע אַחֵר, דְּנָחַת וְאִתְדַּבַּק בְּהַאי דַּרְגָּא, אִתְטְרֵיד מֵהַהוּא עָלְמָא דְּאָתֵי, וְלָא אִתְיְיהֵיב לֵיהּ רְשׁוּ לְמֶהְדַּר בִּתְיוּבְתָּא, וְאִתְטְרֵיד מֵהַהוּא עָלְמָא, וְעַל דָּא אִקְרֵי אַחֵר.

253. Therefore Eliah the other, who descended and clove to that grade, THE KINGDOM OF THE HEATHEN CALLED OTHER, was driven from the World to Come. He was not given permission to repent, but was expelled from the world of truth, for which reason he was named other.

254. וּבְגִין כָּךְ, בָּעֵי בַּר נָשׁ לְאִתְפָּרְשָׁא מִכָּל סִטְרִין, דְּלָא לְאִסְתָּאֲבָא, בְּהַהוּא סִטְרָא, לְמִזְכֵּי בְּהַאי עַלְמָא, וּבְעַלְמָא דְאָתֵי, וְע״ד, דָּא בְּרָכָה, וְדָא קְלָלָה, דָּא שֶׂבַע, וְדָא רָעָב, כֹּלָּא בְּהִפּוּכָא דָּא מִן דָּא. וְהָא אוֹקִימְנָא.

254. Thus, a man should separate himself from all these sides in order not to be defiled by that side and thereby merit this world and the World to Come. Thus, THIS NUKVA OF HOLINESS is a blessing and that THE NUKVA OF THE HEATHEN is a curse. The one is plenty and the other famine. They are direct opposites, as has already been explained.

255. וּבְגִין כָּךְ, בְּהַהוּא זִמְנָא דִּשְׁנַת הָרָעָב, לֵית לֵיהּ לְבַר נָשׁ, לְאִתְחֲזָאָה בְּשׁוּקָא, וְלָא לְאִתְפַּתְּחָא מַבּוּעֵיהּ לְאוֹלָדָא, לְמֵיהַב בְּנִין לְאֵל אַחֵר, וְהָא אִתְּמָר.

255. At the time of the year of famine, WHEN THE NUKVA OF THE HEATHEN REIGNED, no man should have been seen in the marketplace or let flow his source to beget children to another El, as has already been explained.

256. זַכָּאָה אִיהוּ בַּר נָשׁ, דְּאִסְתַּמַּר לְמֵיהַךְ בְּאֹרַח קְשׁוֹט, וּלְאִתְדַּבְּקָא בְּמָארֵיהּ תָּדִיר, דִּכְתִּיב וּבוֹ תִדְבָּק. וּבִשְׁמוֹ תִּשָּׁבֵעַ, וּבוֹ תִּשָּׁבֵעַ לָא כְּתִיב, אֶלָּא וּבִשְׁמוֹ, מַאי תִּשָּׁבֵעַ. כְּמָה דְּאוֹקִימְנָא, לְמֶהֱוֵי מִתְדַּבֵּק בְּרָזָא דִמְהֵימְנוּתָא.

256. Happy is the man who is careful to walk the way of truth and constantly cleaves to his Master. It is written, "To Him shall you hold fast, and by His name shall you swear" (Devarim 10:20). Note that it is not written, "by Him shall you swear," but rather "by His name," WHICH IS THE

15. "And to Joseph were born two sons, before the years of famine came"

NUKVA CALLED NAME. What then is the meaning of the words, "you swear?" HE REPLIED: As we have explained, "YOU SWEAR (HEB. *TISHAVE'A*)" MEANS cleaving to the secret of faith, THE NUKVA CALLED *SHEVA* (SEVEN) SO NAMED AFTER THE SEVEN SFIROT – CHESED, GVURAH, TIFERET, NETZACH, HOD, YESOD AND MALCHUT – WHICH SHE RECEIVES FROM BINAH, AS WILL BE EXPLAINED PRESENTLY.

257. שִׁבְעָה דַּרְגִּין לְעֵילָּא עִלָּאִין עַל כֹּלָּא, רָזָא דִּשְׁלִימוּ דִּמְהֵימְנוּתָא, וְרָזָא דְּשִׁבְעָה דַּרְגִּין דִּלְתַתָּא מִנַּיְיהוּ, דְּאִינוּן חִבּוּרָא חַד, וְקִשּׁוּרָא חַד, אִלֵּין בְּאִלֵּין, לְמֶהֱוֵי כֻּלְּהוּ חַד, וּבְגִין כָּךְ כְּתִיב, שִׁבְעַת יָמִים וְשִׁבְעַת יָמִים, י״ד יוֹם, וְכֹלָּא חַד, וְקִשּׁוּרָא חַד, וְע״ד כְּתִיב וּבִשְׁמוֹ תִּשָּׁבֵעַ, מִלְּעֵילָּא וּמִתַּתָּא.

257. There are seven grades above IN BINAH THAT ARE superior to all and constitute the secret of the wholeness of faith. THE ULTIMATE PERFECTION OF THE NUKVA IS TO ASCEND AND CLOTHE THESE SEVEN GRADES – CHESED, GVURAH, TIFERET, NETZACH, HOD, YESOD AND MALCHUT OF BINAH. The secret of the seven grades below, IN THE NUKVA HERSELF, is their union and connection with THE SEVEN UPPER ONES, so they become one. It is therefore written, "Seven days and seven days, namely, fourteen days" (I Melachim 8:65). All is one, bound as one, FOR THE SEVEN OF THE NUKVA, WHEN THEY ARE WHOLE, ASCEND AND CLOTHE THE SEVEN OF BINAH, AND THEY ARE BOUND AS ONE. And "by His name shall you swear" (Devarim 6:13) ALLUDES TO THE SEVEN above and below – THE JOINING OF THE SEVEN OF BINAH WITH THE SEVEN OF THE NUKVA INTO ONE.

258. וּמַאן דִּמְיַיחֵד אִלֵּין בְּאִלֵּין, עֲלֵיהּ כְּתִיב יִפְתַּח ה׳ לְךָ אֶת אוֹצָרוֹ הַטּוֹב אֶת הַשָּׁמַיִם, אִלֵּין אוֹצָרִין דִּלְעֵילָּא וְתַתָּא. שִׁבְעַת יָמִים וְשִׁבְעַת יָמִים כֻּלְּהוּ חַד, דִּכְתִּיב אֶת אוֹצָרוֹ הַטּוֹב אֶת הַשָּׁמַיִם, אוֹצָרוֹ חַד, וְאִיהוּ אֶת הַשָּׁמַיִם, שִׁבְעָה וְשִׁבְעָה מוּצָּקוֹת, וְאִינוּן חַד.

258. Of whoever joins these SEVEN LOWER BEINGS with the SEVEN UPPER ONES, it is written, "Hashem shall open to you His good treasure, the heaven" (Devarim 28:12), those treasures, THE SEVEN OF BINAH above and THE SEVEN OF THE NUKVA below. The seven days OF BINAH and the seven days OF THE NUKVA are as one, and it is written, "His good treasure, the heaven" and "and seven...to the seven which were upon the top of it" (Zecharyah 4:2). All of them are one.

259. רִבִּי חִיָּיא וְרִבִּי יוֹסֵי, הֲווֹ אָזְלֵי בְּאָרְחָא, אַדְּהָכֵי חָמוּ חַד בַּר נָשׁ, דַּהֲוָה אָתֵי, מִתְעַטֵּף בְּעִטּוּפָא דְּמִצְוָה, וּכְלֵי זַיְינִין קְטוּרִין תְּחוֹתוֹי, אָמַר רִבִּי חִיָּיא, בַּר נָשׁ דֵּין, חַד מִתְּרֵין אִית בֵּיהּ, אוֹ זַכָּאָה שְׁלִים אִיהוּ, אוֹ לְרַמָּאָה בְּנֵי עַלְמָא אִיהוּ.

259. Rabbi Chiya and Rabbi Yosi were walking together when they saw an armed man wearing fringes, THE TZITZIT. Rabbi Chiya said: This man is either a completely righteous man WHO WEARS A FRINGED TALIT EVEN WHILE TRAVELING or is a deceiver of men WHO CARRIES ARMS AND MIGHT BE A ROBBER, YET WEARS THE TALIT TO DECEIVE PEOPLE AND CAPTURE THEM.

260. אֲמַר לֵיהּ רִבִּי יוֹסֵי, הָא חֲסִידֵי עֶלְיוֹנִין אָמְרוּ, הֱוֵי דָן לְכָל בַּר נָשׁ לִזְכוּ. הָא תָּנִינָן, בַּר נָשׁ דְּנָפֵיק לְאָרְחָא, יִתְכַּוֵּין לִתְלַת מִלִּין, לְדוֹרוֹן, לִקְרָבָא, לִצְלוֹתָא. מִנָּלָן מִיַּעֲקֹב, דְּהָא לִתְלַת אִלֵּין אִתְכַּוֵּון, וְזָרֵיז גַּרְמֵיהּ לְדוֹרוֹן, לִקְרָבָא, לִצְלוֹתָא. וְהַאי בַּר נָשׁ, אָזֵיל בְּאָרְחָא אִיהוּ, הָא בֵּיהּ עִטּוּפָא דְּמִצְוָה, לִצְלוֹתָא. וְהָא בֵיהּ כְּלֵי זַיְינִין, לִקְרָבָא. כֵּיוָן דִּתְרֵין אִלֵּין אִית בֵּיהּ, תְּלִיתָאי לָא לְמִרְדַּף אֲבַתְרָהּ.

260. Rabbi Yosi said: The pious have said to judge every man in a favorable sense. We have learned that when a man who sets out on a journey IS AFRAID OF ROBBERS, he should meditate upon three things: a present, a war, and a prayer. How do we know this? From Jacob, who prepared himself for these three things, and was provisioned for presents, a war, and a prayer, AS IT IS WRITTEN THAT HE "SENT" (BERESHEET 32:4) ESAU A PRESENT, HE DIVIDED THE PEOPLE WITH HIM INTO TWO CAMPS LEST "ESAU COME...AND SMITE IT" IN WAR, AND HE PRAYED TO HASHEM, "DELIVER ME, I PRAY YOU, FROM THE HAND OF MY BROTHER." This man who is walking is wearing the Talit to pray and has arms for war. If he has these two, it is not necessary to look to see if he has the third, THE PRESENT. IF HE HAS THE FIRST TWO, HE MUST HAVE THE THIRD.

261. כַּד קָרֵיב לְגַבַּיְיהוּ, יַהֲבוּ לֵיהּ שְׁלָם, וְלָא אָתֵי לוֹן. אֲמַר רִבִּי חִיָּיא, הָא חַד מֵאִינוּן תְּלַת, דְּאִתְחַזְיָין לְמֶהֱוֵי בֵּיהּ, לֵית בֵּיהּ, דְּהָא לָא אַתְקֵין גַּרְמֵיהּ לְדוֹרוֹן, וּבְדוֹרוֹת שְׁלָמָא כָּלֵיל בֵּיהּ. אֲמַר רִבִּי יוֹסֵי, דִּילְמָא אִיהוּ מִשְׁתַּדֵּל בִּצְלוֹתֵיהּ, אוֹ מַרְחֵישׁ תַּלְמוּדֵיהּ. בְּגִין דְּלָא יְעָקַר לֵיהּ.

261. When he approached them, they greeted him but he did not answer. Rabbi Chiya said: It seems as if one of the three THINGS which should be upon him is absent. BECAUSE HE DOES NOT RESPOND TO OUR GREETINGS OF PEACE. THIS MEANS THAT he did not prepare a present, as a present comprises peace. Rabbi Yosi said: It may be that he is praying or reciting his study so as not to forget it.

262. אַזְלֵי כַּחֲדָא, וְלָא מַלֵּיל הַהוּא בַּר נָשׁ, בַּהֲדַיְיהוּ. לְבָתַר אִשְׁתְּמִיטוּ רִבִּי חִיָּיא וְרִבִּי יוֹסֵי, וְאִשְׁתַּדָּלוּ בְּאוֹרַיְיתָא. כֵּיוָן דְּחָמָא הַהוּא בַּר נָשׁ, דַּהֲווֹ מִשְׁתַּדְּלֵי בְּאוֹרַיְיתָא, קָרֵיב לְגַבַּיְיהוּ, וְיָהֵיב לוֹן שְׁלָם.

262. They walked with him, yet he did not talk to them. Later Rabbi Chiya and Rabbi Yosi stepped aside to study the Torah. When the man saw they were studying the Torah, he approached them and gave them greetings of peace.

263. אֲמַר לוֹן, רַבּוֹתַי, בַּמֶּה חֲשַׁדְתּוּן לִי, כַּד יַהֲבִיתוּ לִי שְׁלָם, וְלָא אֲתִיבְנָא לְכוֹ, אָמַר לוֹ ר' יוֹסֵי, דִּילְמָא צְלוֹתָא הֲוֵית אֲמַר, אוֹ מַרְחֵישׁ בְּתַלְמוּדָךְ. אֲמַר לוֹ, קוּדְשָׁא בְּרִיךְ הוּא יָדִין לְכוֹ לְכַף זְכוּ.

263. He said: Gentlemen, what did you think of when you greeted me but I did not answer. Rabbi Yosi said: WE THOUGHT you were engaged in prayer or study. He replied: May the Holy One, blessed be He, judge you favorably.

264. אֲבָל אֵימָא לְכוֹ, יוֹמָא חַד הֲוֵינָא אָזֵיל בְּאָרְחָא, אַשְׁכַּחְנָא חַד בַּר

נָשׁ, וְאַקְדִימְנָא לֵיהּ שְׁלָם, וְהַהוּא גַּבְרָא הֲוָה לְסָטִים, וְקָם עֲלַי, וְצָעַר לִי, וְאִלְמָלֵא דְאִתְתַּקַּפְנָא בֵּיהּ אִצְטָעַרְנָא. מֵהַהוּא יוֹמָא נָדַרְנָא, דְּלָא לְאַקְדָּמָא שְׁלָם, בַּר לְבַר נָשׁ זַכָּאָה, אֶלָּא אִי יְדַעְנָא בֵּיהּ בְּקַדְמֵיתָא, בְּגִין דְּיָכִיל לְצַעֲרָא לִי, וְיִתְתַּקַּף בִּי בְּחֵילָא, בְּגִין דְּאָסִיר לְאַקְדָּמָא שְׁלָם לְבַר נָשׁ חַיָּיבָא, דִּכְתִיב אֵין שָׁלוֹם אָמַר ה' לָרְשָׁעִים.

264. This I shall tell you. I met a man one day when I was walking along the road. I greeted him, but he turned out to be a robber, who fell upon me and grieved me. Had I not overcome him, I would have come to harm. Since that day, I vowed to greet only a man whom I knew was righteous, lest he might otherwise molest and overcome me. Moreover, it is forbidden to greet an evil man, as it is written, "There is no peace, says Hashem, for the wicked" (Yeshayah 48:22).

265. וְהַהִיא שַׁעְתָּא דְּחָמֵינָא לְכוּ, וְיַהֲבִיתוּ לִי שְׁלָם, וְלָא אֲתֵיבְנָא לְכוּ, חֲשִׁידְנָא לְכוּ, בְּגִין דְּלָא חָמֵינָא בְּכוּ מִצְוָה דְּאִתְחֲזֵי לְבַר, וַהֲוֵינָא כְּמוֹ כֵן מְהַדֵּר תַּלְמוּדָאי, אֲבָל הַשְׁתָּא דְּחָמֵינָא בְּכוּ, דְּאַתּוּן זַכָּאִין, הָא אָרְחָא מִתְתַּקְּנָא קָדָמַי.

265. When you greeted me, I did not respond for I suspected that YOU WERE NOT RIGHTEOUS. WHY? Because I did not see any tzitzit on you. I THEREFORE DID NOT RETURN YOUR GREETING. Besides, I was repeating my studies AND THUS COULD NOT ANSWER YOU ANYWAY. But now that I see you are righteous, the way is clear before me.

266. פָּתַח וַאֲמַר, מִזְמוֹר לְאָסָף אַךְ טוֹב לְיִשְׂרָאֵל אֱלֹהִים לְבָרֵי לֵבָב. תָּא חֲזֵי, קוּדְשָׁא בְּרִיךְ הוּא עָבַד יְמִינָא, וְעָבַד שְׂמָאלָא, לְאַנְהָגָא עָלְמָא, חַד אִקְרֵי טוֹב, וְחַד אִקְרֵי רָע, וּבִתְרֵין אִלֵּין אִתְכְּלִיל בַּר נָשׁ, וְאִתְקְרֵיב בְּכֹלָּא.

266. He then quoted the verse, "A psalm of Asaf. Truly Elohim is good to Yisrael, to such as are of a clean heart" (Tehilim 73:1). Come and behold: The Holy One, blessed be He, made right and left in order to rule over the world. The one, RIGHT, is called good, and the other, LEFT, is called evil.

Man includes them both, and in all THINGS comes closer TO HASHEM, AS THE SAGES SAID, 'WITH YOUR TWO INCLINATIONS, THE GOOD INCLINATION AND THE EVIL INCLINATION.'

267. וְהַהוּא רַע דְּאִיהוּ שְׂמָאלָא, אִתְכְּלִילוּ בֵּיהּ עַמִּין עעכו"ם, וְאִתְיְהֵב בְּסִטְרָא דִּלְהוֹן, בְּגִין דְּאִינוּן עַרְלֵי לִבָּא, וְעַרְלֵי בִּשְׂרָא, וּלְאִתְחַלְּלָא בֵּיהּ. אֲבָל בְּיִשְׂרָאֵל מַה כְּתִיב, אַךְ טוֹב לְיִשְׂרָאֵל.

267. The idolatrous nations are included within evil, the left, which was created for the defilement of their side, as they are uncircumcised of heart and uncircumcised of flesh. But of Yisrael, it is written, "Truly Elohim is good to Yisrael."

268. וְאִי תֵּימָא לְכֻלְּהוּ, לָאו, אֶלָּא לְאִינוּן דְּלָא אִתְחַלְּלֵי בְּהַדֵּי הַהוּא רָע, דִּכְתִיב לְבָרֵי לֵבָב, בְּגִין דְּדָא טוֹב, וְדָא רָע, טוֹב לְיִשְׂרָאֵל בִּלְחוֹדַיְיהוּ, וְרַע לְעַמִּין עעכו"ם. אַךְ טוֹב לְיִשְׂרָאֵל, בְּגִין לְאִדְבְּקָא בֵּיהּ, וּבְהַאי אִתְדַּבָּקוּ יִשְׂרָאֵל, בְּרָזָא עִלָּאָה, בְּרָזָא דִּמְהֵימְנוּתָא, לְמֶהֱוֵי כֹּלָּא חַד. אָמַר רִבִּי יוֹסֵי זַכָּאִין אֲנַן, דְּלָא שַׁבְּשְׁנָא בָּךְ, חֲזָא קוּדְשָׁא בְּרִיךְ הוּא שַׁדְּרָךְ לְגַבָּן.

268. You may say He is good for all Yisrael, but that is not true. He is good only to those who were not defiled with evil, as it is written, "To such as are of a clean heart." For of good and evil, good is for Yisrael alone, and evil is for the idolatrous nations alone. "Truly" He is "good to Yisrael," so they cleave to THE HOLY ONE, BLESSED BE HE. Thus, Yisrael cleaves to the supreme mystery, ZEIR ANPIN, in the secret of faith, THE NUKVA, so that all shall become one. THAT IS, BY ACHIEVING GOOD, THEY SUCCEED IN UNITING ZEIR ANPIN AND THE NUKVA AS ONE AND THEN CLEAVE TO THEM.

269. אָמַר רִבִּי יוֹסֵי, בְּגִין דְּטוֹב הוּא לְיִשְׂרָאֵל, יִשְׂרָאֵל אִית לוֹן חוּלְקָא בְּעָלְמָא דֵּין, וּבְעָלְמָא דְּאָתֵי לְמֶחֱמֵי עֵינָא בְּעֵינָא חֵיזוּ יְקָרָא, כְּמָה דִּכְתִיב, כִּי עַיִן בְּעַיִן יִרְאוּ בְּשׁוּב ה' צִיּוֹן.

269. Rabbi Yosi said: Happy are we not to have mistaken you, for it is the Holy One, blessed be He, who sent you to us. He continued, Since good is meant for Yisrael, it will then have a portion in this world and the World to Come to see the sight of glory eye to eye. It is written, "For they shall see eye to eye, Hashem returning to Zion" (Yeshayah 52:8).

בָּרוּךְ ה׳ לְעוֹלָם אָמֵן וְאָמֵן.

Blessed be Hashem forever. Amen and amen.

VAYIGASH

Names of the articles

1. "And Judah came near to him"

A Synopsis

Rabbi Elazar discusses the role and meaning of the letters of the Aleph-Bet. Just as the Torah begins with Bet, so was the world and man created with this letter. The Nukva, we are told, is as the Father, always standing by to bless. The relationship between The Creator and the Nukva is also discussed in some detail, along with its importance for the recitation of blessings.

The Relevance of this Passage

Because Bet is the first letter in the word blessing, Bet was chosen to be the instrument of Creation. The Hebrew letters are very much like DNA – they are the spiritual genetic information through which all existence comes into being. Connecting to the letters through this passage brings renewal, rejuvenation, and the connection with the creative forces of divinity that give rise to the universe as a whole.

1. וַיִּגַּשׁ אֵלָיו יְהוּדָה וגו׳, רִבִּי אֶלְעָזָר פָּתַח, כִּי אַתָּה אָבִינוּ כִּי אַבְרָהָם לֹא יְדָעָנוּ וְיִשְׂרָאֵל לֹא יַכִּירָנוּ אַתָּה ה׳ אָבִינוּ גּוֹאֲלֵנוּ מֵעוֹלָם שְׁמֶךָ. הַאי קְרָא אוֹקְמוּהָ, אֲבָל תָּא חֲזֵי, כַּד בָּרָא קוּדְשָׁא בְּרִיךְ הוּא עַלְמָא, כָּל יוֹמָא וְיוֹמָא, עָבֵיד עֲבִידְתָּא, כִּדְקָא חָזֵי, בְּכָל יוֹמָא וְיוֹמָא כְּמָה דְּאִצְטְרִיךְ, כֵּיוָן דְּאָתָא יוֹמָא שְׁתִיתָאָה, וְאִצְטְרִיךְ לְמִבְרֵי אָדָם, אָתַת אוֹרַיְיתָא קַמֵּיהּ, אָמְרָה הַאי אָדָם דְּאַתְּ בָּעֵי לְמִבְרֵי, זַמִּין הוּא לְאַרְגָּזָא קַמָּךְ, אִלְמָלֵא לָא תַּאֲרִיךְ רוּגְזָא, טַב לֵיהּ דְּלָא יִתְבְּרֵי. אֲמַר לָהּ קב״ה, וְכִי לְמַגָּנָא אִתְקְרֵינָא אֶרֶךְ אַפַּיִם.

1. "Then Judah came near to him" (Beresheet 44:18). Rabbi Elazar opened the discussion with the verse: "You are our father, though Abraham be ignorant of us, and Yisrael acknowledge us not. You, Hashem, are our Father, our Redeemer; Your name is from everlasting" (Yeshayah 63:16). This verse has already been explained, yet come and behold: When the Holy One, blessed be He, created the world, He did each day the work befitting it. When the sixth day arrived – the time for Adam to be created – the Torah came before Him and said: 'Adam, whom You want to create, will provoke You. Unless You curb Your wrath, it would be better for him not to be created.' The Holy One, blessed be He, asked: 'Am I called long-suffering for no reason?'

2. אֶלָּא, כֹּלָּא בְּאוֹרַיְיתָא אִתְבְּרֵי, וְכֹלָּא בְּאוֹרַיְיתָא אִשְׁתַּכְלֵיל, בְּגִין דְּעַד לָא בָּרָא קוּדְשָׁא בְּרִיךְ הוּא עָלְמָא, אַתְיָין כָּל אַתְוָון קַמֵּיהּ, וְעָאלוּ כָּל חַד וְחַד לְמַפְרֵעַ.

2. All was created through the medium of the Torah, and constructed by means of the Torah. AND AS THE TORAH BEGINS WITH THE LETTER *BET*, SO WAS THE WORLD CREATED WITH THE LETTER *BET*. For before the Holy One, blessed be He, created the world – THE NUKVA – all the letters were presented before Him one by one, in reverse order.

3. עָאלַת תי"ו, אֲמָרָה קַמֵּיהּ, רְעוּתָךְ לְמִבְרֵי בִּי עָלְמָא, א"ל לָאו, דְּבָךְ זְמִינִין כַּמָּה צַדִּיקַיָּא לְמֵימַת, דִּכְתִיב וְהִתְוִיתָ תָּיו עַל מִצְחוֹת הָאֲנָשִׁים וגו'. וְתָנִינָן, דִּכְתִיב וּמִמִּקְדָּשִׁי תָּחֵלּוּ אַל תִּקְרֵי מִמִּקְדָּשִׁי אֶלָּא מִמְקוּדָּשַׁי וּבְגִין כָּךְ עָלְמָא לָא יִתְבְּרֵי בָּךְ.

3. *Tav* came before Him and said: 'Would You create the world through me? The Holy One, blessed be He, responded: "No, for many righteous people are destined to die through you, in accordance with the verse, "and set a mark (Heb. *tav*) upon the foreheads of the men" (Yechezkel 9:4). We have also learned this from the verse, "and begin with My sanctuary" (Ibid. 6), in which the word 'sanctuary' should be read as 'sanctified' – WHO ARE THE RIGHTEOUS. The world therefore will not be created through you."

4. עָאלוּ תְּלַת אַתְוָון: שִׁין, קוּף, רֵישׁ, כָּל חַד וְחַד בִּלְחוֹדוֹי, א"ל קוּדְשָׁא בְּרִיךְ הוּא, לָאו אַתּוּן כְּדַאי, לְמִבְרֵי בְּכוֹ עָלְמָא, דְּהָא אַתּוּן אַתְוָון דְּאִתְקְרֵי בְּכוֹ שֶׁקֶר, וְשֶׁקֶר לָאו אִיהוּ כְּדַאי לְמֵיקַם קַמַּאי, וְהָא אוֹקְמוּהָ.

4. The three letters *Shin, Kof*, and *Resh* came before Him, each on its own. The Holy One, blessed be He said: 'It is not worthwhile to create the world by you, for you are the letters which combine to create the word 'lie' (Heb. *sheker*), and no lie deserves to rise before Me," as has already been explained.

5. **וְעָלוּ פֵּ"א צד"י, וְכֵן כֻּלְּהוּ, עַד דְּמָטוֹ אַתְוָון לְאָת כ"ף, כֵּיוָן דְּנָחַת כ"ף מֵעַל כִּתְרָא, אִזְדַּעְזָעוּ עִלָּאֵי וְתַתָּאֵי כו', עַד דְּאִתְקַיַּים כֹּלָּא בְּאָת בֵּי"ת, דְּאִיהוּ סִימָן בְּרָכָה, וּבֵיהּ אִשְׁתַּכְלֵל עַלְמָא וְאִתְבְּרֵי.**

5. Then came the letters *Pe* and *Tzadi*, and so on until the letter *Caf*. Once *Caf* descended from the Crown (Heb. *keter*), the higher and lower worlds shook until all was established using the letter *Bet*, a sign of blessing (Heb. *beracha*) – and the world was created and constructed by it.

6. **וְאִי תֵּימָא, דְּאל"ף אִיהוּ רֵישָׁא דְּכָל אַתְוָון, יָאוֹת אִיהוּ, אֶלָּא בְּגִין דְּאִתְקְרֵי בֵּיהּ אָרוּר, וּבְג"ד לָא אִתְבְּרֵי בֵּיהּ עַלְמָא, אע"ג דְּאל"ף אִיהוּ אָת דְּרָזָא עִלָּאָה, בְּגִין דְּלָא לְמֵיהַב דּוּכְתָּא לְסִטְרָא אָחֳרָא, דְּאִקְרֵי אָרוּר, לָא אִתְבְּרֵי בֵּיהּ עַלְמָא, וְאִשְׁתַּכְלֵיל בְּבֵי"ת עַלְמָא, וּבֵיהּ אִתְבְּרֵי.**

6. You may say that *Aleph* is the first letter, AND THAT THE WORLD SHOULD HAVE BEEN CREATED THROUGH IT. HE ANSWERS: True, but because the word damned (Heb. *arur*) begins with the letter Aleph, the world was not created through it. Thus, although *Aleph* pertains to a Supernal Secret, the world was not created by means of it, so that no opening – NAMELY, POWER AND STRENGTH – could be given to Other Side, called 'damned'. Rather, the world was constructed and created by Bet.

7. **תָּא חֲזֵי, כִּי אַתָּה אָבִינוּ, בְּגִין דְּהַאי עַלְמָא, בְּהַאי דַּרְגָּא אִשְׁתַּכְלֵל וְאִתְבְּרֵי, וּבַר נַשׁ בֵּיהּ אִתְבְּרֵי, וּנְפַק לְעַלְמָא.**

7. Come and behold: "You are our father" means that this world – THE NUKVA OF ZEIR ANPIN CALLED 'YOU' – was constructed and created in this grade, MARKED BY BLESSING. SIMILARLY, THE WORLD WAS CREATED AND CONSTRUCTED THROUGH *BET*, WHICH WAS A SIGN OF BLESSING. Man was also created through it – THROUGH THE SIGN OF BLESSING – and was issued into the world. THEREFORE, IN THIS RESPECT, THE NUKVA WAS CONSIDERED THE ROOT OF MAN, AND WE ADDRESS HER AS 'YOU ARE OUR FATHER' – THAT IS, 'YOU ARE OUR ROOT'. HUMANKIND TOO WAS CREATED WITH THE MARK OF BLESSING.

8. כִּי אַבְרָהָם לֹא יְדָעָנוּ, דְּהָא אע״ג דְּבֵיהּ קִיּוּמָא דְעָלְמָא, לָא אִשְׁתַּדַּל עֲלָן, כְּמָה דְּאִשְׁתַּדַּל עַל יִשְׁמָעֵאל, דַּאֲמַר לוּ יִשְׁמָעֵאל יִחְיֶה לְפָנֶיךָ. וְיִשְׂרָאֵל לֹא יַכִּירָנוּ, בְּגִין דְּכָל בִּרְכָאן דְּאִצְטְרִיךְ לְבָרְכָא לִבְנוֹי, שָׁבַק לְהַאי דַּרְגָּא לְבָרְכָא כֻּלְּהוּ.

8. The verse, "though Abraham be ignorant of us," means that although the world is sustained by him, THE SECRET OF CHESED – AS IT IS WRITTEN, "THE WORLD IS BUILT BY CHESED" (TEHILIM 89:3) – he nevertheless did not care for us as he did for Ishmael, as it is written, "O that Ishmael might live before You" (Beresheet 17:18). The verse continues, "and Yisrael acknowledge us not," for all the blessings he should have conferred on his sons, he let this grade – THE NUKVA – have to bless all. THUS, ACCORDING TO THE VERSES, "AND THIS IS THAT WHICH THEIR FATHER SPOKE TO THEM" (BERESHEET 49:28), THE NUKVA – CALLED 'THIS' – SPOKE ON BEHALF OF THEIR FATHER AND BLESSED THEM. ALSO WHEN HE BLESSED EPHRAIM AND MENASHE, HE SAID, AS IT IS WRITTEN, "THE ANGEL WHO REDEEMED ME FROM ALL EVIL" – NAMELY, THE NUKVA – "BLESS THE BOYS" (BERESHEET 48:16).

9. אַתָּה ה׳ אָבִינוּ, דְּהָא אַנְתְּ קַיְימַת עֲלָן תָּדִיר לְבָרְכָא, וּלְאַשְׁגָּחָא עֲלָן, כְּאַבָּא דְּאַשְׁגַּח עַל בְּנִין, בְּכָל מַה דְּאִצְטְרִיךְ לוֹן. גּוֹאֲלֵנוּ מֵעוֹלָם שְׁמֶךָ, דְּהָא אַנְתְּ הוּא גּוֹאֵל, דְּהָכִי אִתְקְרֵי הַמַּלְאָךְ הַגּוֹאֵל, וְדָא גּוֹאֲלֵנוּ מֵעוֹלָם שְׁמֶךָ, שְׁמֶךָ וַדַּאי. תָּנִינָן אֵין מַפְסִיקִין בֵּין גְּאוּלָּה לִתְפִלָּה, כְּמָה דְּלָא מַפְסִיקִין בֵּין תְּפִלָּה שֶׁל יָד, לִתְפִלָּה שֶׁל רֹאשׁ, דְּבָעֵי לְמֶהֱוֵי דְּכֹלָּא חַד, וְהָא אוֹקְמוּהָ.

9. "You, Hashem, are our Father" – NAMELY, THE NUKVA – always standing by to bless and care for us, like a father taking care of the needs of children; "our Redeemer; Your name is from everlasting," for You (THE NUKVA) are our Redeemer – She is called 'the angel who redeemed'. Thus, in the phrase, "our Redeemer; Your name is from everlasting," "Your name" is assuredly THE NUKVA CALLED 'THE NAME OF HASHEM'. We have learned that we should not stop between reciting the blessings, "who has redeemed Yisrael," and the Amidah; or between the blessing of the hand Tefilin and that of the head Tefilin – as has already been explained.

2. Nefesh, Ruach, and Neshamah

A Synopsis

Rabbi Yitzchak and Rabbi Yehuda explore the idea that all details in the lower world have a counterpart in the Upper World, and that the creation of Adam is the culmination the entire process of creation. The rabbis then discuss the nature of the emanations known as the Sfirot of The Creator, which gives rise to an extraordinary description of the qualities of the human soul. The three grades of the soul – Ruach, Nefesh, and Neshamah – are discussed and eventually agreed upon.

The Relevance of this Passage

Every action in this physical dimension has a corresponding influence in the Upper Worlds. In truth, both worlds are actually one reality; they are like reflections in a mirror. This passage stimulates the high spiritual realms in which the Light is aroused and then reflected back to us in the physical world to refine and perfect our souls. Perfection refers to the subjugation of the ego, and the transformation of the selfish desire to receive into a desire to receive for the sake of sharing. Because sharing is the nature of the Light, when we share we take on the nature of The Creator. In effect, we "become God." When a stone is returned to the mountain from which it was hewn, oneness is again achieved between the part and the whole. There is no distinguishing feature separating them any longer. This God-like nature is awakened within us as we connect to this passage.

10. רִבִּי יִצְחָק וְרִבִּי יְהוּדָה, הֲווֹ יַתְבֵי לֵילְיָא חַד וְלָעָאן בְּאוֹרַיְיתָא, אֲמַר ר׳ יִצְחָק לְרִבִּי יְהוּדָה, הָא תָּנִינָן דְּכַד בָּרָא קוּדְשָׁא בְּרִיךְ הוּא עַלְמָא, עֲבַד עַלְמָא תַּתָּאָה, כְּגַוְונָא דְעַלְמָא עִלָּאָה. וְכֹלָּא דָּא לָקֳבֵל דָּא. וְאִיהוּ יְקָרֵיהּ לְעֵילָּא וְתַתָּא.

10. Rabbi Yitzchak and Rabbi Yehuda were studying the Torah one night. Rabbi Yitzchak said: We have learned that when the Holy One, blessed be He, created the universe, He made the lower world after the pattern of the Supernal World, and MADE the one correspond to the other. EVERY DETAIL IN THE LOWER WORLD HAS A COUNTERPART IN THE UPPER WORLD. And He is its Glory, both above and below.

11. אֲמַר רִבִּי יְהוּדָה, הָכֵי הוּא וַדַּאי, וּבָרָא אָדָם עַל כֹּלָּא, הה״ד אָנֹכִי עָשִׂיתִי אֶרֶץ וְאָדָם עָלֶיהָ בָּרָאתִי, אָנֹכִי עָשִׂיתִי אֶרֶץ וַדַּאי, מ״ט עָשִׂיתִי

אֶרֶץ, בְּגִין דְּאָדָם עָלֶיהָ בָּרָאתִי, דְּאִיהוּ קִיּוּמָא דְעַלְמָא, לְמֶהֱוֵי כֹּלָּא בִּשְׁלִימוּ חַד.

11. Rabbi Yehuda said: Assuredly it is so, and He created Adam above all, WHO INCLUDES AND COMPLETES ALL THE PARTS OF CREATION. This is the meaning of, "I have made the earth, and created man upon it" (Yeshayah 45:12). Surely HE DOES NOT NEED TO REMIND US that He made the earth – so why is it written,"I have made the earth?" Because I "created man upon it," who exists to complete its unification into one wholeness. THAT IS, THE PURPOSE OF THE UNIVERSE, AND ITS PERFECTION IS MAN.

12. פָּתַח וַאֲמַר, כֹּה אָמַר הָאֵל ה' בּוֹרֵא הַשָּׁמַיִם וְנוֹטֵיהֶם רוֹקַע הָאָרֶץ וְצֶאֱצָאֶיהָ נוֹתֵן נְשָׁמָה לָעָם עָלֶיהָ וְרוּחַ לַהוֹלְכִים בָּהּ. הַאי קְרָא אוּקְמוּהָ, אֲבָל כֹּה אָמַר הָאֵל ה' בּוֹרֵא הַשָּׁמַיִם וְנוֹטֵיהֶם, דָּא קוּדְשָׁא בְּרִיךְ הוּא, לְעֵילָּא לְעֵילָּא, דְּאִיהוּ בּוֹרֵא הַשָּׁמַיִם, וְאַתְקִין לֵיהּ תָּדִיר, בְּכָל זִמְנָא. רוֹקַע הָאָרֶץ וְצֶאֱצָאֶיהָ, דָּא אַרְעָא קַדִּישָׁא, צְרוֹרָא דְחַיֵּי. נוֹתֵן נְשָׁמָה לָעָם עָלֶיהָ. הָאָרֶץ דָּא הִיא דְּיַהֲבָה נְשָׁמָה וגו'.

12. He opened the discussion with the verse: "Thus says El, Hashem, He that created the heavens, and stretched them out; He that spread forth the earth, and that which comes out of it; He that gives breath (also: 'soul') to the people upon it, and spirit to them that walk therein" (Yeshayah 42:5): This verse has already been explained. Nevertheless, "Thus says El, Hashem, He that created the heavens," refers to the Holy One, blessed be He, high above – NAMELY, BINAH – who "created the heavens," (ZEIR ANPIN), FOR BINAH continuously improves ZEIR ANPIN BY EMANATING AND GIVING HIM *MOCHIN*. "He that spread forth the earth, and that which comes out of it" – namely, the Holy Land, the Bundle of Life, THE NUKVA – "gives a soul to the people upon it," is the land, THE NUKVA, that confers souls.

13. אֲמַר רִבִּי יִצְחָק, כֹּלָּא אִיהוּ לְעֵילָּא, דְּהָא מִתַּמָּן נָפְקָא נִשְׁמָתָא דְחַיֵּי, לְהַאי אֶרֶץ. וְהַאי אֶרֶץ, נָקְטָא נִשְׁמָתָא לְמֵיהַב לְכֹלָּא, בְּגִין דְּהַהוּא נָהָר דְּנָגִיד וְנָפִיק, אִיהוּ יָהִיב וְעָיֵיל נִשְׁמָתִין לְהַאי אֶרֶץ, וְאִיהוּ נָקְטָא לוֹן, וְיַהֲבָא לְכֹלָּא.

13. Rabbi Yitzchak said: It is all above IN BINAH. HE DISAGREES WITH RABBI YEHUDA, WHO SAID THAT THE PHRASE, "GIVES A SOUL TO THE PEOPLE UPON IT," ALLUDES TO THE NUKVA. For from there, BINAH, the soul of life comes out into the land, THE NUKVA. The land receives the soul and issues it to all, as the river that flows (ZEIR ANPIN) RECEIVES FROM BINAH, holds all the souls and issues them to everyone in the land, THE NUKVA. She receives and distributes them to all MEN WHO ARE WORTHY OF HER.

14. תָּא חֲזֵי, כַּד בָּרָא קוּדְשָׁא בְּרִיךְ הוּא לֵיהּ לְאָדָם, אַכְנִישׁ עַפְרֵיהּ, מֵאַרְבַּע סִטְרִין דְּעָלְמָא, וַעֲבַד גַּרְמֵיהּ בַּאֲתַר דְּמַקְדְּשָׁא לְתַתָּא, וְאַמְשִׁיךְ עֲלֵיהּ נִשְׁמְתָא דְחַיֵּי מִבֵּי מַקְדְּשָׁא לְעֵילָא.

14. Come and behold: when the Holy One, blessed be He, created Adam, he gathered his dust from the four directions of the world. He created him on the site of the Lower Temple, THE SECRET OF THE NUKVA, and then drew upon him the soul of life from the Upper Temple – THE SECRET OF BINAH.

15. וְנִשְׁמְתָא אִיהִי כְּלִילָא בִּתְלַת דַּרְגִּין, וְעַל דָּא תְּלַת שְׁמָהָן אִינוּן לְנִשְׁמְתָא, כְּגַוְונָא דְרָזָא עִלָּאָה, נֶפֶ"שׁ, רוּ"חַ, נְשָׁמָ"ה. נֶפֶשׁ, הָא אוֹקְמוּהָ, דְּאִיהִי תַּתָּאָה מִכֹּלָּא. רוּחַ, אִיהוּ קִיּוּמָא, דְּשָׁלְטָא עַל נֶפֶשׁ, וְאִיהוּ דַּרְגָּא עִלָּאָה עֲלָהּ, לְקַיְימָא עֲלָהּ בְּכֹלָּא, כִּדְקָא חָזֵי. נְשָׁמָה, אִיהִי קִיּוּמָא עִלָּאָה עַל כֹּלָּא, וְשָׁלְטָא עַל כֹּלָּא, דַּרְגָּא קַדִּישָׁא, עִלָּאָה עַל כֻּלְּהוּ.

15. The soul consists of three grades and therefore has three names, just like the Supernal Secret, Nefesh, Ruach, and Neshamah. The Nefesh, as has been explained, is the lowest of them all AND COMES FROM THE NUKVA, THE LOWEST OF THE TEN SFIROT. The Ruach is its sustenance. It rules over the Nefesh, being of a higher grade, AND IS DRAWN FROM ZEIR ANPIN to sustain it well in everything – BOTH IN CHOCHMAH AND CHASSADIM. The Neshamah is the supreme existence – NAMELY, THE LIGHT OF BINAH, WHICH IS HIGHER THAN THE LIGHT OF ZEIR ANPIN AND THE LIGHT OF THE NUKVA, THE RUACH, AND THE NEFESH. It reigns over all, being a holy grade superior to all – TO RUACH AND NEFESH.

16. וְאִלֵּין תְּלַת דַּרְגִּין, כְּלִילָן בְּהוֹ בִּבְנֵי נָשָׁא, לְאִינוּן דְּזָכָאן לְפוּלְחָנָא דְּמָארֵיהוֹן. דְּהָא בְּקַדְמֵיתָא אִית בֵּיהּ נֶפֶשׁ, וְאִיהוּ תִּקּוּנָא קַדִּישָׁא לְאִתְתַּקְּנָא בָּהּ בַּר נָשׁ. כֵּיוָן דְּאָתֵי בַּר נָשׁ לְאִתְדַּכָּאָה בְּהַאי דַּרְגָּא, אִתְתַּקַּן לְאִתְעַטְּרָא בְּרוּחַ, דְּאִיהוּ דַּרְגָּא קַדִּישָׁא. דְּשָׁרְיָא עַל נֶפֶשׁ לְאִתְעַטְּרָא בֵּיהּ בַּר נָשׁ, הַהוּא דְּזָכֵי.

16. The three grades, NEFESH, RUACH AND NESHAMAH, are included within men, who attain them by serving their Master. Thus first, man has a Nefesh, a holy vessel with which to be corrected. But when he is intent on purification through this grade, man is corrected and crowned with a Ruach, the holy grade that dwells on the Nefesh, with which the deserving man is adorned.

17. כֵּיוָן דְּאִסְתַּלַּק בְּהוֹ: בְּנֶפֶשׁ וְרוּחַ, וְעָאל וְאִתְתַּקַּן בְּפוּלְחָנָא דְּמָארֵיהּ כִּדְקָא יָאוּת, כְּדֵי שַׁרְיָא עֲלֵיהּ נְשָׁמָה, דַּרְגָּא עִלָּאָה קַדִּישָׁא, דְּשָׁלְטָא עַל כֹּלָּא, בְּגִין לְאִתְעַטְּרָא בְּדַרְגָּא עִלָּאָה קַדִּישָׁא, וּכְדֵין אִיהוּ שְׁלִימָא דְּכֹלָּא, שְׁלִים בְּכָל סִטְרִין, לְמִזְכֵּי בְּעַלְמָא דְּאָתֵי, וְאִיהוּ רְחִימָא דְּקוּדְשָׁא בְּרִיךְ הוּא, כְּד״א לְהַנְחִיל אוֹהֲבַי יֵשׁ, מַאן אִינוּן אוֹהֲבַי, אִלֵּין אִינוּן דְּנִשְׁמָתָא קַדִּישָׁא בְּהוֹ.

17. Once he is elevated by Nefesh and Ruach and attains correction through proper service to his Master, Neshamah, a supernal, holy grade that reigns over everything, dwells on him so that he may be adorned by the highest holy grade and be perfect in everything, on all sides, and thereby merit the World to Come. He is then beloved of the Holy One, blessed be He, as it is written: "That I may cause those who love Me to inherit substance" (Mishlei 8:21). "...those who love Me" refers to those in whom the holy Neshamah abides.

18. אֲמַר ר׳ יְהוּדָה, אִי הָכֵי הָא כְּתִיב, כֹּל אֲשֶׁר נִשְׁמַת רוּחַ חַיִּים בְּאַפָּיו וגו׳. א״ל הָכֵי הוּא וַדַּאי, דְּהָא לָא אִשְׁתָּאַר בְּהוֹ, מִכָּל אִינוּן דַּהֲווֹ בְּהוֹ נִשְׁמָתָא קַדִּישָׁא, כְּגוֹן חֲנוֹךְ, יֶרֶד, וְכֻלְּהוּ צַדִּיקַיָּא, בְּגִין לַאֲגָנָא עַל אַרְעָא, דְּלָא יִשְׁתֵּצֵי בְּגִינַיְיהוּ, הה״ד כֹּל אֲשֶׁר נִשְׁמַת רוּחַ

חַיִּים בְּאַפָּיו מִכֹּל אֲשֶׁר בֶּחָרָבָה מֵתוּ, כְּבָר מֵתוּ, וְאִסְתַּלָּקוּ מֵעַלְמָא, וְלָא אִשְׁתָּאַר מִנְּהוֹן מַאן דְּיָגֵין עַל עַלְמָא, בְּהַהוּא זִמְנָא.

18. Rabbi Yehuda asks: If this is true, why is it written, "all in whose nostrils was the breath (Lit. 'the Neshamanh') of life..." (Beresheet 7:22)? IF THOSE WHO ATTAIN NESHAMAH ARE THE LOVERS OF THE HOLY ONE, BLESSED BE HE, WHY DID THEY DIE DURING THE FLOOD? He replied: Surely THEY LOVED THE HOLY ONE, BLESSED BE HE. From all those in whom there was a holy Neshamah, none – such as Enoch or Jered, or the other righteous Ones – remained to protect the earth so it would not be destroyed in their merit. This is the meaning of, "all in whose nostrils was the breath (lit. *'Neshamah'*) of life, of all that was on the dry land, died" – they all had already died and departed from the world, and no one remained then to protect the world.

19. תָּא חֲזֵי, כֹּלָּא אִינוּן דַּרְגִּין, אִלֵּין עַל אִלֵּין, נֶפֶ"שׁ, רוּ"חַ, נְשָׁמָ"ה, דַּרְגָּא עַל דַּרְגָּא, נֶפֶשׁ בְּקַדְמֵיתָא, וְאִיהִי דַּרְגָּא תַּתָּאָה, כִּדְקָאֲמָרָן. רוּחַ לְבָתַר, דְּשַׁרְיָא עַל נֶפֶשׁ, וְקַיְימָא עֲלָהּ. נְשָׁמָה, דַּרְגָּא דְסָלְקָא עַל כֹּלָּא, וְאוּקְמוּהָ.

19. Come and behold: There are grades upon grades, Nefesh, Ruach, and Neshamah, grade above grade; first Nefesh, being the lowest grade, as we said, then Ruach, which dwells on Nefesh and is above it. Neshamah is the highest grade, as has already been explained.

20. נֶפֶשׁ: דָּא נֶפֶשׁ דָּוִד, וְאִיהִי דְקַיְימָא לְקַבְּלָא נֶפֶשׁ, מֵהַהוּא נָהָר דְּנָגֵיד וְנָפֵיק. רוּחַ: דָּא רוּחַ דְּקַיְימָא עֲלֵיהּ דְּנַפְשָׁא, וְלֵית קִיּוּמָא לְנֶפֶשׁ, אֶלָּא בְּרוּחַ, וְדָא אִיהוּ רוּחַ, דְּשַׁרְיָא בֵּין אֶשָּׁא וּמַיָּא, וּמֵהָכָא אִתְּזָן הַאי נֶפֶשׁ.

20. Nefesh is David's Nefesh, THE NUKVA, which receives the Nefesh from the river that flows, NAMELY, FROM ZEIR ANPIN. Ruach stands over the on Nefesh, which cannot exist without the Ruach, which dwells between fire and water, NAMELY, TIFERET, THE CENTRAL COLUMN BETWEEN GVURAH, CALLED 'FIRE', AND CHESED, CALLED 'WATER'. From here Nefesh is nourished.

21. רוּחַ, קָיְימָא בְּקִיּוּמָא דְדַרְגָּא אוֹחֲרָא עִלָּאָה, דְּאִקְרֵי נְשָׁמָה, דְּהָא מִתַּמָּן נָפְקֵי נֶפֶשׁ וְרוּחַ. מִתַּמָּן אִתְּזָן רוּחַ, וְכַד נָטֵיל רוּחַ, כְּדֵין נָטְלָא נֶפֶשׁ, וְכֹלָּא חַד, וְאִתְקְרִיבוּ דָּא בְּדָא, נֶפֶשׁ אִתְקְרֵיב בְּרוּחַ, וְרוּחַ אִתְקְרֵיב בִּנְשָׁמָה, וְכֹלָּא חַד.

21. Ruach depends for its existence on yet a higher grade called 'Neshamah', which is the origin of both Ruach and Nefesh, NAMELY, THE LIGHT OF BINAH, FROM WHICH ORIGINATES THE LIGHT OF ZEIR ANPIN CALLED 'RUACH', AND THE LIGHT OF THE NUKVA CALLED 'NEFESH'. The Ruach is nourished from them. When Ruach travels, Nefesh also travels, and all is one. They approach each other, Nefesh to Ruach and Ruach to Neshamah, and are all one.

22. תָּא חֲזֵי, וַיִּגַּשׁ אֵלָיו, תִּקְרוּבְתָּא דְעַלְמָא בְּעַלְמָא, לְאִתְאַחֲדָא דָּא בְּדָא, לְמֶהֱוֵי כֹּלָּא חַד, בְּגִין דִּיהוּדָה אִיהוּ מֶלֶךְ, וְיוֹסֵף מֶלֶךְ, אִתְקְרִיבוּ דָּא בְּדָא, וְאִתְאֲחִידוּ דָּא בְּדָא.

22. Come and behold: "…came near to him" refers to the one world approaching the other world, THE ADVANCEMENT OF THE LOWER WORLD, THE NUKVA, THE ASPECT OF NEFESH CALLED 'JUDAH', TOWARD THE UPPER WORLD, YESOD OF ZEIR ANPIN, THE ASPECT OF RUACH CALLED 'JOSEPH', so that all becomes one. Because both Judah and Joseph were kings, they approached each other and joined together.

3. "For the Kings were assembled"

A Synopsis

Rabbi Yehuda and Rabbi Chiya discourse on the meeting of the Kings, Judah and Joseph, which symbolizes the union of the Supernal World – Zeir Anpin – and the Lower World of Malchut. The section explores the significance of the unity of Male and Female, and the conditions most conducive atonement for sins. The positive effects of the symbolic meeting of the Kings is emphasized.

The Relevance of this Passage

Humanity shares important attributes of the moon: like the moon, we generate no light of our own. Just as lunar light is derived from the sun, man's spiritual Light is derived from the bordering dimension known as Zeir Anpin. Light can only flow when these two worlds are enjoined, just as a lamp can only illuminate when connected to electrical current. On a metaphysical level, woman corresponds to Malchut and male denotes the realm of Zeir Anpin. Intimate relations between man and woman thus join Malchut and Zeir Anpin in this world as well as in the Upper Realms. This pleasure that accompanies this union is the Light of the Upper Worlds filling Malchut. When our consciousness is directed towards revealing this spiritual Light during sexual relations, the entire world is brightened and elevated. This section of Zohar raises our consciousness so that we can transform the sexual act into a force for bringing down Light, rather than as a tool of darkness. Moreover, the Light that is evoked through sexual union shines around the world as we meditate upon this passage.

23. ר׳ יְהוּדָה פָּתַח וַאֲמַר, כִּי הִנֵּה הַמְּלָכִים נוֹעֲדוּ, דָּא יְהוּדָה וְיוֹסֵף, בְּגִין דְּתַרְוַויְיהוּ מְלָכִים, וְאִתְקְרִיבוּ דָּא בְּדָא, לְאִתְוַוכְּחָא תַּרְוַויְיהוּ כַּחֲדָא בְּגִין דִּיהוּדָה אִתְעָרֵב בֵּיהּ בְּבִנְיָמִן, וַהֲוָה עָרֵב לְגַבֵּיהּ דַּאֲבוֹי בֵּיהּ, בְּהַאי עָלְמָא, וּבְעַלְמָא דְאָתֵי. וְעַל דָּא אִתְקְרֵיב קַמֵּיהּ דְּיוֹסֵף, לְאִתְוַוכְּחָא עִמֵּיהּ, עַל עִסְקָא דְבִנְיָמִין, דְּלָא לְמֶהֱוֵי בְּנִדּוּי, בְּהַאי עַלְמָא, וּבְעַלְמָא דְאָתֵי, כְּד״א אָנֹכִי אֶעֶרְבֶנּוּ מִיָּדִי תְּבַקְשֶׁנּוּ אִם לֹא הֲבִיאוֹתִיו אֵלֶיךָ וְהִצַּגְתִּיו לְפָנֶיךָ וְחָטָאתִי לְאָבִי כָּל הַיָּמִים, בְּהַאי עַלְמָא, וּבְעַלְמָא דְאָתֵי.

23. Rabbi Yehuda began the discussion with the verse, "For the kings were assembled" (Tehilim 48:5): These are Judah and Joseph, who were both kings. The two of them came together to dispute, because Judah became surety for Benjamin and pledged himself before his father in this world and the World to Come. He therefore came to argue with Joseph on account of Benjamin, so he would not be banned from this world and the World to Come, as it is written, "I will be surety for him; of my hand shall you require him: If I bring him not to you, and set him before you" (Berehsit 43:9), "…then I shall have sinned to my father for ever" (Beresheet 44:32) in this world and the World to Come.

24. וְעַל דָּא, כִּי הִנֵּה הַמְּלָכִים נוֹעֲדוּ עָבְרוּ יַחְדָּיו, אִתְרְגִיזוּ כַּחֲדָא, וְאִתְרְגִיזוּ דָּא בְּדָא, בְּגִינֵיהּ דְּבִנְיָמִן. מַה כְּתִיב, הֵמָּה רָאוּ כֵּן תָּמָהוּ נִבְהֲלוּ נֶחְפָּזוּ רְעָדָה אֲחָזָתַם שָׁם, לְכָל אִינוּן דַּהֲווֹ תַּמָּן.

24. Therefore, "the kings were assembled, they came on together" means that they quarreled together and were angry with each other because of Benjamin. Then, it is written, "As soon as they saw, they were astounded; they were affrighted; they rushed away. Fear took hold of them there" (Tehilim 48:6), of all them who were there.

25. חִיל כַּיּוֹלֵדָה, בְּגִין דַּהֲווֹ דַּחֲלִין, לְקָטְלָא, וּלְאִתְקְטָלָא, וְכֹלָּא בְּגִינֵיהּ דְּבִנְיָמִן, דְּהָא יוֹסֵף אִזְדַּבַּן בְּגִינֵיהּ דִּיהוּדָה, וְאִתְאֲבֵיד מֵאֲבוֹי. וְהַשְׁתָּא אִתְעָרַב בֵּיהּ בְּבִנְיָמִין, וְדָחֵיל דְּלָא יִתְאֲבֵיד, וּבְגִין כָּךְ וַיִּגַּשׁ אֵלָיו יְהוּדָה.

25. "...and pain, like a woman in travail" (Tehilim 48:7), for they were fearful lest they would kill or be killed on account of Benjamin. For Joseph was sold by Judah and was lost to his father. Now that he became surety for Benjamin, he was fearful lest he would perish. Thus, it is written, "Judah came near to him."

26. ד"א, כִּי הִנֵּה הַמְּלָכִים נוֹעֲדוּ, דָּא יְהוּדָה וְיוֹסֵף, דְּאִזְדַּמְּנוּ לְאִתְוַכְּחָא דָּא עִם דָּא, לְאִתְוַכְּחָא תַּרְוַויְיהוּ כַּחֲדָא, בְּגִין דִּיהוּדָה הֲוָה מֶלֶךְ, וְיוֹסֵף הֲוָה מֶלֶךְ, וְתַרְוַויְיהוּ אָתוּ כַּחֲדָא, לְאִתְוַכְּחָא דָּא עִם דָּא. דָּא עַל בִּנְיָמִן, וְדָא עַל בִּנְיָמִן.

26. Another explanation of the verse, "the kings were assembled," is that Judah and Joseph came to debate with each other as kings. They met to discuss, the one with the other – the one about Benjamin and the other about Benjamin. [THIS PARAGRAPH IS REDUNDANT, AND THE EXPLANATION IS CONTINUED IN THE NEXT PARAGRAPH.]

27. **כִּי הִנֵּה הַמְּלָכִים, אֲמַר ר׳ יְהוּדָה, רָזָא דִמְהֵימְנוּתָא הָכָא, דְּהָא כַּד רְעוּתָא אִשְׁתַּכַּח, וְקִשּׁוּרָא אִתְעַטַּר כַּחֲדָא, כְּדֵין תְּרֵין עָלְמִין מִתְקַשְּׁרָן כַּחֲדָא, וְאִזְדַּמְּנָן כַּחֲדָא. דָּא לְאַפְתָּחָא אוֹצָרָא, וְדָא לְלַקְטָא וּלְמִכְנַשׁ בְּגַוֵּיהּ, וּכְדֵין כִּי הִנֵּה הַמְּלָכִים נוֹעֲדוּ, תְּרֵין עָלְמִין קַדִּישִׁין, עַלְמָא עִלָּאָה, וְעַלְמָא תַּתָּאָה.**

27. Rabbi Yehuda said: "…the kings" alludes to the secret of faith, THE NUKVA. For when desire was revealed and union adorned IN MALE AND FEMALE, both the MALE AND FEMALE worlds were joined together – the one, ZEIR ANPIN, to open the treasure, TO SPREAD IT, and the other, THE NUKVA, to gather and collect PLENTY within it. Then "the kings were assembled, they came on together," both worlds, the Supernal World, ZEIR ANPIN, and the Lower World, THE NUKVA.

28. **עָבְרוּ יַחְדָּיו, רָזָא דְמִלָּה, דְּכַד מִתְחַבְּרָן כַּחֲדָא, כְּדֵין עָבְרוּ יַחְדָּיו, בְּגִין דְּכָל חִיּוּבִין דְּעַלְמָא, לָא אִתְעַבְרָן לְאִתְכַּפְּיָא, עַד דְּמִתְחַבְּרָן כַּחֲדָא, כְּדִכְתִּיב וְעוֹבֵר עַל פֶּשַׁע, וְע״ד עָבְרוּ יַחְדָּיו, עָבְרוּ: אִינּוּן חוֹבִין אִתְכַּפָּרוּ, בְּגִין דְּהָא כְדֵין כָּל אַנְפִּין נְהִירִין, וְכָל חוֹבִין אִתְעֲבָרוּ.**

28. "...they came on together (also: 'passed')," for no sin in the world is atoned for until THE MALE AND THE FEMALE are united, as it is written, "and forgives (lit. 'passes upon') the transgression" (Michah 7:18), and also "they passed together," the sins passed, because, WITH THE ILLUMINATION OF UNITY, all faces shine and all sins are atoned for.

29. **ר׳ חִיָּיא אֲמַר, רָזָא דָא בְתִקּוּנָא דְקָרְבָּנָא אִיהוּ, דְּהָא כַּד קָרְבָּנָא אִתְקְרֵיב, וְכֹלָּא מִסְתַּפְּקִין, וְכָל חַד וְחַד כִּדְקָא חָזֵי לֵיהּ, כְּדֵין אִתְקַשַּׁר כֹּלָּא כַּחֲדָא, וְכָל אַנְפִּין נְהִירִין, וְקִשּׁוּרָא חַד אִשְׁתַּכַּח, וּכְדֵין הַמְּלָכִים**

נוֹעֲדוּ, וְאִזְדַּמְּנוּ כַּחֲדָא, לְכַפָּרָא עַל חוֹבִין, לְאַעֲבָרָא עֲלַיְיהוּ, וּכְדֵין הַמְּלָכִים נוֹעֲדוּ, וְאִתְקַשְּׁרָן כַּחֲדָא, עָבְרוּ יַחְדָּיו, לְאַנְהָרָא כָּל אַנְפִּין, וּלְמֶהֱוֵי כֹּלָּא רְעוּתָא חֲדָא.

29. Rabbi Chiya said: The secret of this verse applies to correction through offering, for when a sacrifice is offered, everyone receives their provision, each according to what he deserves, and then all is joined as one, all faces shine, and one bond prevails – NAMELY, ONE UNION. Then, "the kings were assembled" to atone for transgressions and make them pass away. When, "the kings were assembled," MALE AND FEMALE, and were connected, "they passed together" – NAMELY, THEY ATONED FOR THEIR SINS so as to cause all faces to shine and make all of one accord.

30. הֵמָּה רָאוּ כֵּן תָּמָהוּ, ס"ד דְּאִינוּן מְלָכִים, אֶלָּא אִלֵּין מָארֵיהוֹן דְּדִינִין, דְּחֶדְוָה דִלְהוֹן לְמֶעְבַּד הַהוּא דִינָא, דְּאִתְפַּקְּדוּ עֲלֵיהּ, וּכְדֵין, כַּד מְלָכִים אִזְדַּמְּנוּ תַּרְוַויְיהוּ בִּרְעוּתָא חֲדָא, כְּדֵין הֵמָּה רָאוּ הַהוּא רְעוּתָא דִתְרֵין עָלְמִין, כֵּן תָּמָהוּ נִבְהֲלוּ נֶחְפָּזוּ, בְּגִין דְּכֻלְּהוּ מָארֵי דְדִינָא אִתְכַּפְיָין וּמִתְעַבְרָן מֵעַלְמָא, וְלָא יָכְלֵי לְשַׁלְטָאָה, וּכְדֵין מִתְעַבְרִין קִיּוּמֵיהוֹן, מְעַבְרִין שָׁלְטָנְהוֹן.

30. "As soon as they saw, they were astounded" (Tehilim 58:5-6). HE ASKS: Could it be that the kings SAW AND WERE ASTOUNDED? HE REPLIED: NOT THEY, but the accusers, who delight in executing justice, according to orders they receive. When the kings were assembled with mutual wishes, "they saw" the wish of both worlds, MALE AND FEMALE, and "they were astounded, they were affrighted; they rushed away" because all the accusers were subdued and passed out of the world, for they cannot rule. Both their existence and their government were then interrupted.

31. ר' אֶלְעָזָר אָמַר וַיִּגַּשׁ אֵלָיו יְהוּדָה, מ"ט יְהוּדָה. בְּגִין דְּהָכֵי אִצְטְרִיךְ, דְּאִיהוּ עָרֵב, כד"א כִּי עַבְדְּךָ עָרַב אֶת הַנַּעַר, וְרָזָא דְמִלָּה, יְהוּדָה וְיוֹסֵף הָכֵי אִצְטְרִיכוּ לְאִתְקָרְבָא כַּחֲדָא, בְּגִין דְּיוֹסֵף אִיהוּ צַדִּיק, יְהוּדָה אִיהוּ מֶלֶךְ, וְעַל דָּא וַיִּגַּשׁ אֵלָיו יְהוּדָה, בְּגִין דְּקוּרְבָא דִלְהוֹן,

דְאִתְקְרִיבוּ כַּחֲדָא, גָּרַם כַּמָּה טָבִין לְעַלְמָא, גָּרַם שְׁלָמָא לְכֻלְּהוּ שִׁבְטִין, גָּרַם שְׁלָמָא בֵּינַייהוּ, גָּרַם לְיַעֲקֹב דְּאִתְקַיַּים רוּחָא דִילֵיהּ, כְּד״א וַתְּחִי רוּחַ יַעֲקֹב אֲבִיהֶם, וְעַל דָּא קְרִיבוּ דְּדָא עִם דָּא אִצְטְרִיךְ, בְּכֻלְּהוּ סִטְרִין, לְעֵילָּא וְתַתָּא.

31. Rabbi Elazar said: "Then Judah came near to him." Why? HE ANSWERS: This is how it ought to have been, for he became surety, as it is written, "For your servant became surety for the boy." The secret is that Judah and Joseph should have approached each other simultaneously, because Joseph is righteous, NAMELY, YESOD OF ZEIR ANPIN and Judah is a king, NAMELY, MALCHUT, THE NUKVA OF ZEIR ANPIN. Therefore, "Then Judah came near to him," because their coming together produced many benefits for the world, resulted in peace among all the tribes, peace between themselves – BETWEEN JUDAH AND JOSEPH – and caused the spirit of Jacob to revive, as it is written, "the spirit of Jacob their father revived" (Beresheet 45:27). Hence, their joining together was needed by all sides, above and below.

4. "Beautiful for situation"

A Synopsis

Next, Rabbi Aba further clarifies the meaning of this important passage, relating it to Joseph, then to the Sfirot, and finally to "the Great King." In a beautiful manner, he shows how the secret of faith itself is embodied here.

The Relevance of this Passage

Ten dimensions [Sfirot] comprise our reality. The dimension known as Yesod neighbors our physical realm and it is the gateway through which all the spiritual energy of the Upper World flows into our world. Our connection to Yesod is strengthened by virtue of this passage, infusing our lives with tremendous amounts of positive energy.

32. ר׳ אַבָּא פְּתַח וַאֲמַר, יְפֵה נוֹף מְשׂוֹשׂ כָּל הָאָרֶץ הַר צִיּוֹן יַרְכְּתֵי צָפוֹן קִרְיַת מֶלֶךְ רָב. הַאי קְרָא רָזָא דִמְהֵימְנוּתָא אִיהוּ. יְפֵה נוֹף: דָּא אִיהוּ יוֹסֵף הַצַּדִּיק, דִּכְתִיב בֵּיהּ, וַיְהִי יוֹסֵף יְפֵה תֹאַר וִיפֵה מַרְאֶה. מְשׂוֹשׂ כָּל הָאָרֶץ: אִיהוּ חֶדְוָה וְחֵדוּ, לְעֵילָא וְתַתָּא. הַר צִיּוֹן יַרְכְּתֵי צָפוֹן, בְּגִין דִּבְחוּלָקֵיהּ קָאֵים מַשְׁכְּנָא דְשִׁילֹה, הַר צִיּוֹן דָּא יְרוּשָׁלַיִם. יַרְכְּתֵי צָפוֹן, הָכֵי הוּא וַדַּאי לְעֵילָא וְתַתָּא.

32. Rabbi Aba opened the discussion with the verse, "Beautiful for situation, the joy of the whole earth: Mount Zion, the uttermost parts of the north, the city of the Great King" (Tehilim 48:3). This verse is the secret of faith: "Beautiful for situation" is Joseph the Righteous, of whom scripture says, "And Joseph was good looking, and well favored" (Beresheet 39:6); he is "the joy of the whole earth," the gladness and joy above and below; "Mount Zion, the uttermost parts of the north" is his portion, JOSEPH'S PORTION, where the tabernacle of Shilo stands; "Mount Zion" is Jerusalem, NAMELY, THE NUKVA; "the uttermost parts of the north" is assuredly above and below, FOR BOTH THE UPPER TEMPLE, THE NUKVA, AND THE LOWER TEMPLE ARE CONSIDERED TO BE OF THE ASPECT OF THE NORTH, NAMELY, THE ILLUMINATION OF THE LEFT OF BINAH, THE SECRET OF THE ILLUMINATION OF CHOCHMAH.

33. קִרְיַת מֶלֶךְ רָב, אֲתַר אִיהוּ מְתַקְנָא, לְקַבֵּיל מֶלֶךְ רָב, דָּא מַלְכָּא

עִלָּאָה דְּכֹלָּא, קֹדֶשׁ הַקֳּדָשִׁים, דְּהָא מִתַּמָּן אַתְיָא כָּל נְהִירוּ, וְכָל בִּרְכָאן, וְכָל חֵידוּ דְּכֹלָּא, דְּהָא מִתַּמָּן נָהֲרִין כָּל אַנְפִּין, וּבֵי מַקְדְּשָׁא אִתְבָּרְכָא מִתַּמָּן, וְכַד אִיהִי מִתְבָּרְכָא, מִתַּמָּן נָפְקֵי בִּרְכָאן לְכָל עַלְמָא, דְּהָא כָּל עַלְמָא מִתַּמָּן אִתְבָּרְכָא.

33. "...the city of the Great King" is a place prepared for the Great King, the most high King residing over the Holy of Holies, from whom all Light, Blessings, and Joy comes, so that all faces shine and the Temple is blessed. When it is blessed, since every blessing emerges from there, the whole world is blessed from there.

5. Sixty breaths

A Synopsis

Rabbi Yehuda and Rabbi Yosi, later joined by Rabbi Elazar, discuss the meaning of King David and midnight prayer. They are joined by a "commoner," Hezekiah, whose name means, "strengthened by The Creator." He clarifies the meaning of David praying after midnight, and explores the grades of life and death, arriving at the profound understanding that it is through wisdom alone that everything in the world exists. We are introduced to the concept of the continually evolving nature of Heaven – and thus, to the continually evolving nature of perfection. Through a discussion of the Three Columns and some secrets of the Patriarchs, the rabbis return to King David, to the meaning and concept of his being alive in the present, and how such a miraculous event is possible.

The Relevance of this Passage

The mystical Light aroused during midnight prayer is invoked in our lives. This Light strengthens our soul and opens us to receive greater wisdom through spiritual learning and growth. Kabbalistic wisdom itself, including these very words, is also the sum and substance of spiritual Light. Therefore, each new lesson and each new insight makes us wiser and more pure.

34. ר׳ יְהוּדָה וְר׳ יוֹסֵי, אִעָרְעוּ בִּכְפַר חָנָן, עַד דַּהֲווֹ יָתְבֵי בֵּי אוּשְׁפִּזַיְיהוּ, אָתָא חַד בַּר נָשׁ, וְחַד מָטוּלָא דְחַמְרָא קַמֵּיהּ, וְעָאל בְּבֵיתָא. אַדְּהָכֵי, אֲמַר ר׳ יְהוּדָה לְרִבִּי יוֹסֵי, הָא תָּנִינָן, דְּדָוִד מַלְכָּא הֲוָה מִתְנַמְנֵם כְּסוּס, וְשֵׁינְתֵיהּ זְעֵיר, הֵיךְ הֲוָה קָם בְּפַלְגוּת לֵילְיָה, הַאי שִׁעוּרָא זְעֵיר אִיהוּ, וְלָא הֲוָה אִתְעַר אֲפִילּוּ בִּתְלָתוּת לֵילְיָא.

34. Rabbi Yehuda and Rabbi Yosi met in the village of Chanan. While they were sitting at the inn, a man came with a baggage-laden mule and entered the house. Rabbi Yehuda was then saying to Rabbi Yosi: We have learned that King David slept like a horse and had little sleep. If this is true, how did he wake up at midnight? The portion OF SIXTY BREATHS OF A HORSE'S SLEEP is very brief, so he would have awakened before even a third of the night was over.

35. אֲמַר לֵיהּ, בְּשַׁעְתָּא דְּעָאל לֵילְיָא, הֲוָה יָתֵיב עִם כָּל רַבְרְבֵי בֵּיתֵיהּ,

וְדָאִין דִּינָא, וְעָסֵיק בְּמִלֵּי דְאוֹרַיְיתָא, וּלְבָתַר הֲוָה נָאֵים שֵׁינְתֵיהּ עַד פַּלְגוּת לֵילְיָה, וְקָם בְּפַלְגוּת לֵילְיָא, וְאִתְעַר, וְאִשְׁתַּדַּל בְּפוּלְחָנָא דְמָארֵיהּ, בְּשִׁירִין וְתוּשְׁבְּחָן.

35. He replied: When night fell, he used to sit with the princes of his house to execute justice and study the Torah, WHICH MEANS, THAT HE DID NOT GO TO SLEEP WHEN NIGHT FELL, BUT CLOSER TO MIDNIGHT. He then slept until midnight, when he woke and rose to worship his Master with songs and hymns.

36. אַדְהָכֵי אֲמַר הַהוּא בַּר נָשׁ, וְכִי הַאי מִלָּה דְקָאַמְרִיתּוּ, הָכֵי הוּא, רָזָא דְמִלָּה הָכָא, דְּהָא דָוִד מַלְכָּא חַי וְקַיָּים, לְעָלַם וּלְעָלְמֵי עָלְמִין, וְדָוִד מַלְכָּא, הֲוָה נָטֵיר כָּל יוֹמוֹי, דְּלָא יִטְעַם טַעַם מִיתָה, בְּגִין דְּשֵׁינְתָא חַד מִשִּׁתִּין בְּמִיתָה אִיהוּ, וְדָוִד בְּגִין דוּכְתֵּיהּ דְּאִיהוּ חַי, לָא הֲוָה נָאֵים, אֶלָּא שִׁיתִּין נִשְׁמֵי, דְּעַד שִׁתִּין נִשְׁמֵי חָסֵר חַד, אִיהוּ חַי, מִתַּמָּן וּלְהָלְאָה, טָעֵים ב״נ, טַעְמָא דְמוֹתָא, וְשַׁלֵּיט בֵּיהּ סִטְרָא דְרוּחַ מְסָאֲבָא.

36. The man interposed and asks: Is this what you think? This is the secret of the matter: King David is alive and exists forever and ever. King David was careful to avoid a foretaste of death; and because sleep is a sixtieth part of death, King David, whose domain is the Living, slept only sixty breaths. For up to sixty breaths less one, it is living; from then on, man tastes death, and the side of the impure spirit reigns over him.

37. וְדָא הֲוָה נָטֵיר דָּוִד מַלְכָּא, דְּלָא יִטְעַם טַעְמָא דְמוֹתָא, וְשַׁלֵּיט בֵּיהּ סִטְרָא דְרוּחָא אָחֳרָא, בְּגִין דְּשִׁתִּין נִשְׁמֵי חָסֵר חַד, אִיהוּ רָזָא דְחַיִּים דִּלְעֵילָּא, עַד שִׁתִּין נִשְׁמֵי, דְּאִינוּן שִׁתִּין נִשְׁמֵי עִלָּאִין, וְאִילֵין רָזָא דִלְהוֹן, דְּתַלְיָין בְּהוֹן חַיֵּי, וּמִכָּאן וּלְתַתָּא, רָזָא דְמוֹתָא הוּא.

37. King David guarded himself from tasting death, lest the side of the impure spirit obtain control over him. For sixty breaths minus one are the secret of Supernal Life. The first sixty breaths are the supernal sixty breaths, whose secret is that life depends on them. From then downward, it is the secret of death.

38. וְע"ד, דָּוִד מַלְכָּא, הֲוָה מְשַׁעֵר שִׁעוּרָא דְּלֵילְיָא, בְּגִין דְּיִתְקַיֵּים בְּחַיִּים, דְּלָא יִשְׁלוֹט בֵּיהּ טַעְמָא דְּמוֹתָא. וְכַד אִתְפְּלֵיג לֵילְיָא, הֲוָה דָּוִד מִתְקַיֵּים בְּאַתְרֵיהּ, בְּגִין דְּכַד אִתְעַר פַּלְגּוּ לֵילְיָא, וְכִתְרָא קַדִּישָׁא אִתְעַר, בָּעָא דְּלָא לְאַשְׁכְּחָא לֵיהּ לְדָוִד, מִתְקַשַּׁר בַּאֲתַר אָחֳרָא, בַּאֲתַר דְּמוֹתָא.

38. Therefore King David would measure the night UNTIL MIDNIGHT, so as to remain alive, lest the foretaste of death dominate him. At midnight, David would be in his domain, IN HIS GRADE, WHICH IS LIFE AND EXISTENCE, BY WAKING UP AND UTTERING CHANTS AND HYMNS. For when midnight stirred and the Holy Crown, THE NUKVA, was awakened, David did not wish to be found connected to another domain, the domain of death.

39. בְּגִין דְּכַד אִתְפְּלֵיג לֵילְיָא, וּקְדוּשָּׁה עִלָּאָה אִתְעַר, וּבַר נָשׁ דְּנָאֵים בְּעַרְסֵיהּ, וְלָא אִתְעַר לְאַשְׁגָּחָא בִּיקָרָא דְּמָארֵיהּ, הָא אִיהוּ אִתְקַשַּׁר בְּרָזָא דְּמוֹתָא, וּמִתְדַּבַּק בַּאֲתַר אָחֳרָא, וְעַל דָּא, דָּוִד מַלְכָּא, הֲוָה קָאֵים לְאַשְׁגָּחָא בִּיקָרָא דְּמָארֵיהּ תָּדִיר, חַי לְגַבֵּי חַי, וְלָא נָאֵים בְּשֵׁינְתָא, לְטָעֳמָא טַעְמָא דְּמוֹתָא, וּבְגִין כָּךְ, הֲוָה מִתְנַמְנֵם כְּסוּס, שִׁתִּין נִשְׁמֵי, וְלָא בִּשְׁלִימוּ.

39. When midnight comes Supernal Holiness is awakened, but man is asleep in his bed and does not awaken to regard the glory of his Master; he becomes attached to the secret of death and cleaves to another domain, TO THE OTHER SIDE. King David therefore always woke at midnight, careful of the glory of his Master, alive before the Living One, and he would never sleep long enough to taste death. Thus, he slept like the sixty breaths of a horse – sixty breaths LESS ONE.

40. אָתוּ רִבִּי יְהוּדָה וְרִבִּי יוֹסֵי, וּנְשָׁקוּהָ, אֲמָרוּ לֵיהּ, מַה שְּׁמָךְ, א"ל חִזְקִיָּה, א"ל יִתְיַישַּׁר חֵילָךְ, וְיִתְתַּקַּף אוֹרַיְיתָךְ, יְתִיבוּ, אֲמַר רִבִּי יְהוּדָה, הוֹאִיל וְשָׁרֵית, אֵימָא לָן מֵהַנֵּי רָזִין עִלָּאִין דְּקָאֲמַרְתְּ.

40. Rabbi Yehuda and Rabbi Yosi came and kissed him, FOR HE

REVEALED A NEW EXPLANATION CONCERNING MIDNIGHT PRAYER. They asked him: What is your name? He replied: Hezekiah (lit. 'strengthened of Hashem'). They said to him: May you be strengthened and may your study of the Torah be augmented. They sat down. Rabbi Yehuda said: Since you have started, tell us more of the Supernal Mysteries to which You have made reference.

41. פְּתַח וַאֲמַר, ה׳ בְּחָכְמָה יָסַד אֶרֶץ כּוֹנֵן שָׁמַיִם בִּתְבוּנָה. תָּא חֲזֵי, כַּד בָּרָא קוּדְשָׁא בְּרִיךְ הוּא עַלְמָא, חָמָא דְלָא יָכֵיל לְאִתְקַיְּימָא, עַד דְּבָרָא אוֹרַיְיתָא, בְּגִין דְּמִנָּהּ נָפְקִין כָּל נִמּוּסִין עִלָּאִין וְתַתָּאִין, וּבָהּ קָיְימֵי עִלָּאֵי וְתַתָּאֵי, הה״ד ה׳ בְּחָכְמָה יָסַד אָרֶץ כּוֹנֵן שָׁמַיִם בִּתְבוּנָה, דְּהָא בְּחָכְמָה קָיְימִין כָּל קִיּוּמִין דְּעַלְמָא, וְכֻלְּהוּ נָפְקֵי מִגַּוָּהּ.

41. He opened the discussion with the verse, "Hashem by wisdom founded the earth; by understanding (Heb. *tevunah)* He established the heavens..." (Mishlei 3:19). Come and behold: When the Holy One, blessed be He, created the universe, He saw that it could not exist, FOR THE UNIVERSE WAS CREATED UNDER THE REIGN OF THE LEFT COLUMN, THE SECRET OF CHOCHMAH WITHOUT CHASSADIM, AND CHOCHMAH CANNOT ILLUMINE WITHOUT CHASSADIM. THEREFORE IT COULD NOT EXIST until He created the Torah, THE CENTRAL COLUMN CALLED 'ZEIR ANPIN', ALSO CALLED 'TORAH'. HE CAUSED THE TWO COLUMNS, RIGHT AND LEFT, TO BE INCLUDED WITHIN EACH OTHER, AND CHOCHMAH WAS INCLUDED WITHIN CHASSADIM. THEN CHOCHMAH ILLUMINATED, from the Torah – NAMELY, FROM THE CENTRAL COLUMN – all the laws issued by the Upper and Lower Worlds, which are supported by it. THIS IS THE MEANING OF YUD HEI VAV HEI AND ZEIR ANPIN, THE SECRET OF THE CENTRAL COLUMN: as it is written, "by wisdom founded the earth..." HE FOUNDED THE EARTH BY WISDOM, CLOTHING CHOCHMAH IN CHASSADIM, SO THAT THE ILLUMINATION OF CHOCHMAH REMAINED IN THE WORLD. Through wisdom everything in the world exists, and everything derives from it, AS IT IS WRITTEN, "IN WISDOM HAVE YOU MADE THEM ALL" (TEHILIM 104:24).

42. ד״א ה׳ בְּחָכְמָה יָסַד אֶרֶץ, עַלְמָא עִלָּאָה לָא אִתְבְּרֵי, אֶלָּא מִגּוֹ חָכְמָה, וְעַלְמָא תַּתָּאָה לָא אִתְבְּרֵי, אֶלָּא מִגּוֹ חָכְמָה תַּתָּאָה, וְכֻלְּהוּ

נָפְקָן מִגּוֹ חָכְמָה עִלָּאָה, וּמִגּוֹ חָכְמָה תַּתָּאָה. כּוֹנֵן שָׁמַיִם בִּתְבוּנָה. כּוֹנֵן, מַאי כּוֹנֵן. אֶלָּא, כּוֹנֵן כָּל יוֹמָא וְיוֹמָא, וְלָא פָּסֵיק, וְלָא אִתְתַּקַּן בִּזְמְנָא חָדָא, אֶלָּא בְּכָל יוֹמָא וְיוֹמָא אַתְקִין לֵיהּ.

42. Another explanation of "Hashem by wisdom founded the earth" is that the Upper World, TEVUNAH, was created only by Chochmah, and the Lower World, THE NUKVA, was created only by the lower Chochmah, CHOCHMAH CLOTHED BY THE NUKVA. Thus it seems that they were all issued from the upper and lower Chochmah. "...by understanding (Heb. *tevunah*), He established the heavens..." HE ASKS: What does it mean by "established"? HE ANSWERS: "...established" REFERS TO TEVUNAH, WHICH ESTABLISHES ZEIR ANPIN CALLED 'HEAVEN', every day. They were not mended at one time; rather, He perfects them day by day.

43. וְהַיְינוּ רָזָא דִּכְתִיב, וְשָׁמַיִם לֹא זַכּוּ בְעֵינָיו. וְכִי ס"ד, דִּגְרִיעוּתָא אִיהוּ מִשָּׁמַיִם, אֶלָּא חֲשִׁיבוּ מִשָּׁמַיִם אִיהוּ, בְּגִין חֲבִיבוּ וּרְעוּ סַגְיָא, דְּקוּדְשָׁא בְּרִיךְ הוּא רָעֵי בְּהוֹ, וַחֲבִיבוּתַיְהוּ לְגַבֵּיהּ, דְּהָא אע"ג דְּאִיהוּ מַתְקֵין לוֹן כָּל יוֹמָא וְיוֹמָא, לָא דָמֵי בְּעֵינוֹי דְּאִינוּן מִתְתַּקְּנָן כִּדְקָא יָאוֹת, בְּגִין דִּרְחִימוּתָא דִלְהוֹן לְגַבֵּיהּ, וּרְעוּתֵיהּ לְאַנְהָרָא לוֹן תָּדִיר, בְּלָא פְּסִיקוּ, דְּהָא עַלְמָא דְאָתֵי, אַפֵּיק נְהוֹרִין זְהִירִין, כָּל יוֹמָא וְיוֹמָא תָּדִיר בְּלָא פְּסִיקוּ, בְּגִין לְאַנְהָרָא לוֹן תָּדִיר, וְעַל דָּא לֹא זַכּוּ בְעֵינָיו, לֹא זַכּוּ בִּלְחוֹדוֹי לָא כְתִיב, אֶלָּא לֹא זַכּוּ בְעֵינָיו, וּבְגִין כָּךְ, כּוֹנֵן שָׁמַיִם בִּתְבוּנָה.

43. This is the secret of the verse, "and the heavens are not clean in His sight" (Iyov 15:15). Could you think it a derogation of the heavens? On the contrary, it is to the advantage of the heavens: for it is because of the love and great passion that the Holy One, blessed be He, WHO IS TEVUNAH, bears for the heavens, ZEIR ANPIN, that He views them as not perfect enough even though He perfects them daily. It is for the love of them and because of His desire to shine continuously upon them. HE EXPLAINS: The World to Come, TEVUNAH, radiates scintillating light every day without cessation to illuminate them always. Therefore, they are "not clean in His sight." It does not say 'not clean,' but rather, "not clean in His sight." THIS

INDICATES THAT, ALTHOUGH THEY ARE IN REALITY CLEAN, BECAUSE OF HIS DESIRE TO SHOWER ABUNDANCE UPON THEM, THEY ARE NOT CONSIDERED CLEAN TO HIM, AS HAS BEEN EXPLAINED. Thus, THE SCRIPTURE READS, "by understanding He established the heavens."

44. מַאן שָׁמַיִם. דָּא הוּא רָזָא דַּאֲבָהָן, וְרָזָא דַּאֲבָהָן דָּא הוּא יַעֲקֹב, דְּאִיהוּ כְּלָלָא דִלְהוֹן, בְּגִין דְּיַעֲקֹב תּוּשְׁבַּחְתָּא דַּאֲבָהָן אִיהוּ, וְאִיהוּ קָיְימָא לְאַנְהָרָא עַל עַלְמָא.

44. HE ASKS: What are the heavens IN THE VERSE, "BY UNDERSTANDING HE ESTABLISHED THE HEAVENS"? HE REPLIS: They are the secret of the Patriarchs – CHESED, GVURAH AND TIFERET. The secret of the Patriarchs is Jacob, THE CENTRAL COLUMN, TIFERET, who includes them all – AS THE CENTRAL COLUMN INCLUDES THE RIGHT AND THE LEFT, THE SECRET OF ABRAHAM AND ISAAC. For it is Jacob, the most splendid of the fathers, whose function is to shine on the world, THE NUKVA.

45. וּבְגִין דְּאִיהוּ אִסְתַּלֵּק גּוֹ עַלְמָא דְאָתֵי, נָפַק מִנֵּיהּ עֲנָפָא חָדָא, שַׁפִּירָא בְּחֵיזוּ, וְכָל נְהוֹרִין מִינֵּיהּ נָפְקִין, וְכָל שִׂבְעָא, וּמְשַׁח רְבוּ, לְאַנְהָרָא לְאַרְעָא, וּמַאן אִיהוּ. דָּא יוֹסֵף הַצַּדִּיק, דְּאִיהוּ יָהֵיב שָׂבְעָא לְכָל עַלְמָא, וְעַלְמָא מִנֵּיהּ אִתְּזָן. וּבְגִין כָּךְ, קוּדְשָׁא בְּרִיךְ הוּא כָּל מַה דְּעָבַד בְּעַלְמָא, כֹּלָּא אִיהוּ בְּרָזָא עִלָּאָה, וְכֹלָּא כִּדְקָא חָזֵי.

45. When he ascended to the World to Come, THAT IS, ASCENDED AND CLOTHED YISRAEL SABA, CALLED 'THE WORLD TO COME', THE SECRET OF COVERED CHASSADIM, WHICH IS WHY THERE IS NO PLACE IN HIM FOR THE REVELATION OF THE ILLUMINATION OF CHOCHMAH; a branch came out from him, beautiful to the sight, BY THE LIGHT OF CHOCHMAH, CALLED 'SIGHT' AND 'VISION'. And all the lights, BOTH CHOCHMAH AND CHASSADIM, radiated from it, as did the abundance and the anointing oil needed to illuminate the land, THE NUKVA. What is THIS BRANCH? It is Joseph the Righteous, who gives abundance, THE ILLUMINATION OF CHOCHMAH, to the whole world, which is sustained by him, BY THE ILLUMINATION OF CHASSADIM. Therefore whatever the Holy One, blessed be He, does has meaning, and all is as it should be.

46. אַדְהָכֵי, אָתָא רִבִּי אֶלְעָזָר, כֵּיוָן דְּחָמָא לוֹן, אֲמַר וַדַּאי שְׁכִינְתָּא הָכָא, בְּמַאי עַסְקִיתוּ. אֲמָרוּ לֵיהּ, כָּל עוֹבָדָא. אֲמַר, וַדַּאי שַׁפִּיר קָאֲמַר, אֲבָל אִינוּן שִׁתִּין נִשְׁמֵי, וַדַּאי שִׁתִּין נִשְׁמֵי אִינוּן דְּחַיִּין, בֵּין לְעֵילָּא בֵּין לְתַתָּא, מִכָּאן וּלְהָלְאָה, אִיכָּא שִׁתִּין נִשְׁמִין אָחֳרָנִין, דְּאִינוּן כֻּלְּהוּ מִסִּטְרָא דְמוֹתָא, וְדַרְגָּא דְמוֹתָא עֲלַיְיהוּ, וְאִקְרוּן דוּרְמִיטָא, וְכֻלְּהוּ טַעֲמָא דְמוֹתָא.

46. While they were talking, Rabbi Elazar came. When he saw them he said: Assuredly the Shechinah is here. What are you discussing? They told him what happened WITH THE MAN AND HIS WORDS. He said: He spoke well. HE NOW EXPLAINED ABOUT the sixty breaths. THE SIX HOURS BEFORE MIDNIGHT pertain to life, both above IN THE UPPER WORLD WHERE THE SECRET OF THE CHEST-AND-ABOVE OF THE NUKVA IS, and below IN THIS WORLD. From then on, AFTER MIDNIGHT, there are sixty other breaths, which are CHESED, GVURAH, TIFERET, NETZACH, HOD AND YESOD OF THE CHEST-AND-BELOW, all on the side of death, and the grade of death is upon them. They are called ‘Dormita’ (‘sleep’), and all of them taste of death.

47. וּבְגִין כָּךְ, דָּוִד מַלְכָּא, הֲוָה אִיהוּ מִתְדַּבֵּק בְּאִינוּן שִׁתִּין נִשְׁמִין דְּחַיִּין, וּמִתַּמָּן וּלְהָלְאָה לָא נָאִים כְּלַל, הה״ד אִם אֶתֵּן שְׁנַת לְעֵינָי לְעַפְעַפַּי תְּנוּמָה, וְעַל דָּא, שַׁפִּיר קָאֲמַר, בְּגִין דְּיָקוּם דָּוִד חַי, בְּסִטְרָא דְחַי, וְלָא בְּסִטְרָא דְמוֹתָא. יָתְבוּ כֻּלְּהוּ, וְאִשְׁתַּדְּלוּ בְּאוֹרַיְיתָא, וְאִתְחַבָּרוּ כַּחֲדָא.

47. King David therefore cleaved to the sixty breaths of life, NAMELY, THE SIX HOURS BEFORE MIDNIGHT, WHICH IS THE SECRET of ABOVE THE CHEST, WHERE THE POWER OF JUDGMENT AND DEATH, WHICH IS IN THE CHEST, CANNOT REACH. But afterward, he slept not at all. This is the meaning of, “I will not give sleep to my eyes, slumber to my eyelids” (Tehilim 132:4). Thus THAT MAN spoke well, as David should be considered alive. He is on the side of the living and not on the side of death. Then, they all joined together to study the Torah.

48. פָּתַח רִבִּי אֶלְעָזָר וַאֲמַר, ה׳ אֱלֹקֵי יְשׁוּעָתִי יוֹם צָעַקְתִּי בַלַּיְלָה נֶגְדֶּךָ. תָּא חֲזֵי, דָּוִד מַלְכָּא, הֲוָה קָם בְּפַלְגוּת לֵילְיָא, וְאִשְׁתַּדַּל בְּאוֹרַיְיתָא,

בְּשִׁירִין וְתוּשְׁבְּחָן, לְחֶדְוָה דְמַלְכָּא וּמַטְרוּנִיתָא, וְדָא הֲוָה חֶדְוָה דִמְהֵימְנוּתָא בְּאַרְעָא, בְּגִין דְּהַאי אִיהוּ שִׁבְחָא דִמְהֵימְנוּתָא, דְּאִתְחֲזֵי בְּאַרְעָא.

48. Rabbi Elazar opened the discussion with the verse: "Hashem the Elohim of my salvation, when I cry in the night before You" (Tehilim 88:2). Come and behold: King David used to rise at midnight and study the Torah and delight the King and the Queen with songs and praises. This is the joy of Faith on the earth, for it is the praise of Faith, THE SHECHINAH, that is seen on earth.

49. דְּהָא לְעֵילָּא פָּתְחֵי בְּחֶדְוָה שִׁירָתָא, כַּמָּה מַלְאָכִין עִלָּאִין, בְּכַמָּה זִינִין, דְּקָא מְשַׁבְּחָן בְּלֵילְיָא בְּכָל סִטְרִין. כה״ג לְתַתָּא בְּאַרְעָא, מַאן דִּמְשַׁבַּח לֵיהּ קוּדְשָׁא בְּרִיךְ הוּא בְּאַרְעָא בְּלֵילְיָא, רָעֵי בֵּיהּ קוּדְשָׁא בְּרִיךְ הוּא, וְכָל אִינוּן מַלְאָכִין קַדִּישִׁין, דְּקָא מְשַׁבְּחָן לֵיהּ לְקוּדְשָׁא בְּרִיךְ הוּא, כֻּלְּהוּ צַיְיתִין לְהַהוּא דְקָא מְשַׁבַּח לֵיהּ בְּלֵילְיָא בְּאַרְעָא, דְּהַאי תּוּשְׁבַּחְתָּא אִיהוּ בִּשְׁלִימוּ, לְסַלְקָא יְקָרֵי דְקוּדְשָׁא בְּרִיךְ הוּא מִתַּתָּא, וּלְזַמְּרָא בְּחֶדְוָה דְיִחוּדָא.

49. For numerous holy angels joyously begin to sing above, in different ways, praising at night on all sides, EVEN IN THE ILLUMINATION OF THE LEFT, FOR THEN THE NUKVA REIGNS, ACCORDING TO THE SECRET OF THE VERSE, "SHE RISES ALSO WHILE IT IS YET NIGHT" (MISHLEI 31:15). It is likewise below on earth, for the Holy One, blessed be He, takes pleasure in whoever on earth praises Him at night, and all the holy angels who praise the Holy One, blessed be He, listen to the man who praises THE HOLY ONE, BLESSED BE HE, at night on earth. For this chanting increases the glory of the Holy One, blessed be He, from below, and sings joyously in unison.

50. תָּא חֲזֵי, דָּוִד מַלְכָּא כָּתַב, ה׳ אֱלֹהֵי יְשׁוּעָתִי וגו׳, ה׳ אֱלֹהֵי יְשׁוּעָתִי, אֵימָתַי אִיהוּ יְשׁוּעָתִי. בְּהַהוּא יוֹמָא, דְאַקְדֵּמִית תּוּשְׁבַּחְתָּא בְּלֵילְיָא לְגַבָּךְ, כְּדֵין אִיהוּ יְשׁוּעָתִי בִּימָמָא.

50. Come and behold: King David wrote, "Hashem the Elohim of my salvation," which means, when is Hashem the Elohim of my salvation? He is my salvation by day, after I first sang to You by night. Then is He my salvation by day.

51. וְתָא חֲזֵי, דְּהָא בְּלֵילְיָא, מַאן דִּמְשַׁבַּח לְמָארֵיהּ, בְּתוּשְׁבַּחְתָּא דְּאוֹרַיְיתָא כְּדֵין אַתְקֵף בְּתְקִיפוּ בִּימָמָא, בְּסִטְרָא דִּימִינָא, דְּהָא חוּטָא חַד, נַפְקָא מִסִּטְרָא דִּימִינָא, וּכְדֵין אִתְמַשֵּׁךְ עֲלֵיהּ, וְאִתְתַּקַּף בֵּיהּ, וְע"ד אֲמַר ה' אֱלֹהֵי יְשׁוּעָתִי יוֹם צָעַקְתִּי וגו'.

51. Come and behold: Whoever sings the praises of the Torah during the night before his Master is strengthened by day on the right side, WHICH IS CHESED. THIS MEANS THAT THE CHOCHMAH HE RECEIVED BY NIGHT THROUGH THE LEFT IS CLOTHED DURING THE DAY BY CHESED, THE RIGHT SIDE. For a thread of grace comes out from the right side. It is drawn upon him, and he is strengthened by it. David therefore said: "Hashem the Elohim of my salvation, when I cry in the night before You."

52. וּבְג"כ אֲמַר, לֹא הַמֵּתִים יְהַלְלוּ יָהּ. לֹא הַמֵּתִים, בְּגִין דְּאִצְטְרִיךְ לְשַׁבְּחָא, חַי לְחַי. וּמֵת לְחַי לָאו הָכֵי, דִּכְתִיב לֹא הַמֵּתִים יְהַלְלוּ יָהּ, וַאֲנַחְנוּ נְבָרֵךְ יָהּ, דְּהָא אֲנַן חַיִּין, וְלֵית לָן חוּלָקָא בְּסִטְרָא דְּמוֹתָא כְּלַל. חִזְקִיָּהוּ אֲמַר, חַי חַי הוּא יוֹדֶךָ כָּמוֹנִי, בְּגִין דְּחַי אִתְקְרַב לְחַי. דָּוִד מַלְכָּא אִיהוּ חַי, וְקוּרְבָא דִּילֵיהּ לְחַי הָעוֹלָמִים. וּמַאן דְּאִתְקְרֵיב לְגַבֵּיהּ, אִיהוּ חַי, דִּכְתִיב וְאַתֶּם הַדְּבֵקִים בַּה' אֱלֹהֵיכֶם חַיִּים כֻּלְּכֶם הַיּוֹם, וּכְתִיב, וּבְנָיָהוּ בֶּן יְהוֹיָדָע בֶּן אִישׁ חַי רַב פְּעָלִים מִקַּבְצְאֵל.

52. Thus, he said: "The dead cannot praise Yah" (Tehilim 115:17), because it is the living who should praise the Living, and not the dead, as it is written, "The dead cannot praise Yah." "But we will bless Yah" (Ibid.), for we are living and have no part of death. Hezekiah said: "The living, the living, he shall praise You, as I do" (Yeshayah 38:19), for the living has a connection with the Living. So is King David living, and he came near the One who lives forever. And whoever approaches THE ONE LIVING FOREVER, is living, as it is written: "But you that did cleave of Hashem your Elohim are alive every one of you this day" (Devarim 4:4), and "And Benaiah the son of Jehoida, the son of a living man, of Kavtze'el" (II Shmuel 23:20).

6. "And you shall eat and be satisfied, and bless"

A Synopsis

Hezekiah resolves the apparent contradiction that exists in the scriptural injunction that we should not eat before the first prayer of the morning, and the injunction urging us to give the blessing only after the meal. This leads to greater appreciation of the weighty task that The Creator has taken on in providing his children with longevity and nourishment. We learn that the providing depends on Mazel (Eng. 'luck', here imbued with an astrological dimension), not merit – a complex and difficult mystery that is somewhat clarified here, leading to both a firmer grasp of the inherent mysteries that lie within the mystical union of Male and Female, and also to a clarification of the secrets contained within the vitally important act of Joseph and Judah approaching one another.

The Relevance of this Passage

The Hebrew word Mazel is usually translated as "luck," but it really means "sign" – as in the signs of the constellations. We are born into this world under a specific celestial influence, as determined by deeds in past lives. We can rise above any negative influences of these signs by evoking the Light through prayer, blessing, and meditation upon these mystical passages of the Zohar.

53. פְּתַח הַהוּא יוּדָאי אֲבַתְרֵיהּ, וַאֲמַר, וְאָכַלְתָּ וְשָׂבָעְתָּ וּבֵרַכְתָּ אֶת ה׳ אֱלֹקֶיךָ, וְכִי לָא מְבָרְכִינָן לֵיהּ לְקוּדְשָׁא בְּרִיךְ הוּא, עַד לָא נֵיכוּל, וְהָא אִית לָן לְאַקְדּוּמֵי בְּצַפְרָא, וּלְסַדּוּרֵי שִׁבְחָא דִּילֵיהּ כִּדְקָא יָאוּת, וּלְבָרְכָא בִּשְׁמֵיהּ, עַד לָא יְבָרֵךְ לְאַחֲרָא בְּעַלְמָא, וּכְתִיב לֹא תֹאכַל עַל הַדָּם, אָסוּר לֵיהּ לְמֵיכַל, עַד לָא יְבָרֵךְ לְמָארֵיהּ, וְהַשְׁתָּא כְּתִיב וְאָכַלְתָּ וְשָׂבָעְתָּ וּבֵרַכְתָּ.

53. The Jew then continued with the verse, "And you shall eat and be satisfied, and bless Hashem your Elohim" (Devarim 8:10). HE ASKS: Do not we bless the Holy One, blessed be He, before eating? Indeed we should rise early in the morning to recite His praises in the proper order, before we greet any other in the world. It is also written, "You shall not eat anything with the blood" (Vayikra 19:26), WHICH HAS ALREADY BEEN EXPLAINED, AS it is forbidden to eat before blessing one's Master. Yet now it is written, "And you shall eat and be satisfied, and bless," WHICH MEANS IT

BEHOOVES ONE TO BLESS ONLY AFTER THE MEAL.

54. אֶלָּא, דָּא בִּרְכָתָא דִצְלוֹתָא דְיִחוּדָא, וְדָא בִּרְכָתָא דִמְזוֹנָא, לְאַחֲזָאָה לְגַבֵּי דַרְגָּא דִמְהֵימְנוּתָא, שָׂבָע כִּדְקָא יָאוֹת. וּכְדֵין בָּעֵי לְבָרְכָא לֵיהּ כִּדְקָא יָאוֹת, דְהַהוּא דַרְגָּא דִמְהֵימְנוּתָא, יִתְרַוֵּי, וִיבָרֵךְ, וְיִתְמַלֵּא חֵידוּ מֵחַיִּין דִּלְעֵילָּא, כְּמָה דְאִצְטְרִיךְ, בְּגִין לְמֵיהַב לָן מְזוֹנֵי.

54. HE ANSWERS: The blessings we recite before eating are prayers for unity BETWEEN MALE AND FEMALE, while those we recite after eating HAVE TWO PURPOSES – (1), to show proper satiation before the grade of faith, THE NUKVA, AND (2), to bless it properly, so that THE GRADE OF FAITH shall be well watered, blessed and filled with joy from the supernal life as much as needed, and thus will confer sustenance upon us.

55. דְּהָא קָשִׁין מְזוֹנָא דְבַר נָשׁ קָמֵי קוּדְשָׁא בְּרִיךְ הוּא, כִּקְרִיעַת יַם סוּף, מ"ט. בְּגִין, דִּמְזוֹנָא דְעַלְמָא דִלְעֵילָּא הוּא, דִּתְנַן בָּנֵי חַיֵּי וּמְזוֹנֵי וכו', וּבְגִין כָּךְ, קַשְׁיָין קַמֵּיהּ מְזוֹנֵי דְעַלְמָא, דְּהָא בְּמַזָּלָא תַּלְיָא מִילְתָא, דְּמִנֵּיהּ נָפְקֵי מְזוֹנֵי, וְחַיֵּי, וּבָנֵי, וּבְגִין כָּךְ קָשִׁין קַמֵּיהּ מְזוֹנֵי דְעַלְמָא, דְּהָא לָאו בִּרְשׁוּתֵיהּ קָיְימָא, עַד דְּיִתְבָּרֵךְ אִיהוּ.

55. For providing man's food is as heavy a task for the Holy One, blessed be He, as the cleaving of the Sea of Reeds (the Red Sea). Why? Because all nourishment of the world come from above. We have learned that children, longevity, and nourishment depend NOT UPON MERIT, but upon *mazal*. Therefore daily sustenance is a heavy task for Him, for it depends upon *mazal*, from whence children, longevity, and sustenance are derived. Daily sustenance is hard for Him, because one does not have them before being blessed BY *MAZAL*.

56. כְּגַוְונָא דָא זִוּוּגִין דְעַלְמָא, קָשִׁין קַמֵּיהּ, וְכֹלָּא בְּגִין דְּרָקִיעַ וִילוֹן, לָא מְשַׁמֵּשׁ כְּלוּם. וְכ"ש אִלֵּין מִלִּין דְּקָיְימִין לְעֵילָּא בַּאֲתַר אָחֳרָא, וְעַל דָּא אִצְטְרִיךְ לְאִתְבָּרְכָא.

56. Similarly, arranging marriages is a heavy task for Him, and everything,

CHILDREN AS WELL AS LONGEVITY AND SUSTENANCE, occurs because the firmament is a curtain that serves no purpose. All the more so CHILDREN, LIFE, AND SUSTENANCE, which abide above in another place. It therefore needs to be blessed TO RECEIVE FROM THENCE.

57. תָּא חֲזֵי כָּל זִוּוּגִין דְּעַלְמָא, קָשִׁין קַמֵּיהּ הַאי דַּרְגָּא, בְּגִין דְּכַד הַאי זִוּוּגָא קַדִּישָׁא אִשְׁתַּכַּח, כָּל נִשְׁמָתִין נָפְקִין, מִגּוֹ הַאי מַזָּלָא לְעֵילָּא, דְּאִיהוּ הַהוּא נָהָר דְּנָגִיד וְנָפִיק, וְכַד תֵּיאוּבְתָּא אִשְׁתַּכַּח מִלְּרַע לְעֵילָּא, כְּדֵין פָּרְחִין נִשְׁמָתִין, וְאִתְיְיהִיבוּ כֻּלְּהוּ כְּלִילָן דְּכַר וְנוּקְבָא כַּחֲדָא, בְּהַאי דַּרְגָּא. וּלְבָתַר אִיהוּ פָּרֵישׁ לוֹן, כָּל חַד וְחַד לְאַתְרֵיהּ כִּדְקָא חָזֵי לֵיהּ. וּלְבָתַר קָשִׁין קַמֵּי הַאי דַּרְגָּא, לְחַבְּרָא לוֹן כְּקַדְמֵיתָא, בְּגִין דְּלָא מִתְחַבְּרָן, בַּר כְּאִינוּן אָרְחֵי דְּב"נ וְכֹלָּא לְעֵילָּא תַּלְיָין.

57. Come and behold: The arranging of marriages is hard for this grade, THE NUKVA, for when union occurs, WHICH BEGETS SOULS, all the souls emerge from the upper *mazal*, which is the river that flows FROM EDEN – NAMELY, YESOD OF ZEIR ANPIN. And when there is a desire TO DRAW from below upward – TO WIT, TO DRAW CHOCHMAH, WHICH IS ONLY DRAWN FROM BELOW UPWARD – the souls soar TO THE NUKVA and become in this grade comprehensive of male and female together. They are then separated, so that each goes its appointed place. Later the grade finds it hard to reunite them – THE MALE AND THE FEMALE – as before, because they are only united through men's behavior, and everything depends on what is above.

58. וְעַל דָּא קָשִׁין קַמֵּיהּ כִּקְרִיעַת יַם סוּף, דְּהָא קְרִיעַת יַמָּא, לְאִתְפַּתְּחָא בֵּיהּ שְׁבִילִין, לְעֵילָּא אִיהוּ, וּכְמָה דְּמִתְפַּתְּחִין שְׁבִילִין וְאוֹרְחִין בֵּיהּ, הָכֵי אִתְבַּקַּע וְאִתְפַּתַּח.

58. Therefore marriages are as hard for Him to arrange as the cleaving of the Red Sea, for the Red Sea was cleaved to open high roads above that then opened and cleft ways and roads below.

59. וּבְגַ"כ, כֹּלָּא תַּלְיָא לְעֵילָּא, וּבְעִינָן לְבָרְכָא לֵיהּ, וּלְמֵיהַב לֵיהּ

תּוֹקְפָּא מִתַּתָּא, בְּגִין דְּיִתְבָּרְכָא מִלְּעֵילָּא, וְיִתַתַּקַּף כִּדְקָא חָזֵי, וְעַל דָּא כְּתִיב, וּבֵרַכְתָּ אֶת ה׳, אֶת דַּיְיקָא.

59. Therefore everything depends on the high region, FOR THE NUKVA HAS NOTHING OF HERSELF AFTER SHE IS DIMINISHED, and we should bless Her, and give Her strength from below, so She will be blessed AND RECEIVE from above, FROM ZEIR ANPIN, and be well strengthened. Therefore it is written, "and bless Hashem," with the particle '*Et*' before 'Hashem', FOR IT ALLUDES TO THE NUKVA CALLED '*ET*'.

60. וּלְגַבֵּי הַאי אֲתַר, אִצְטְרִיךְ לְאַחֲזָאָה קַמֵּיהּ, שָׂבְעָא וּנְהִירוּ דְּאַנְפִּין, וּלְגַבֵּי סִטְרָא אָחֳרָא, בְּזִמְנָא דְּאִיהִי שָׁלְטָא בְּעַלְמָא, בְּעֵי לְאַחֲזָאָה קַמֵּיהּ כַּפְנָא, דְּהַהוּא דַּרְגָּא רָעָב אִיהוּ, וְאִתְחֲזֵי לְאַחֲזָאָה קַמֵּיהּ כַּפְנָא, וְלָא שׂוֹבְעָא, הוֹאִיל וְשָׂבָע לָא שָׁלְטָא בְּעַלְמָא, וְעַל דָּא, וְאָכַלְתָּ וְשָׂבָעְתָּ וּבֵרַכְתָּ אֶת ה׳ אֱלֹקֶיךָ. אֲמַר רִבִּי אֶלְעָזָר, הָכֵי הוּא וַדַּאי, וְהָכֵי אִצְטְרִיךְ.

60. We should show before this place, NAMELY, THE NUKVA, satisfaction and shining faces, and to the Other Side, when it reigns in the world, it behooves us to show ourselves famished, for the grade OF THE OTHER SIDE is hunger, and we should look hungry before it instead of well-fed, because satiation does not rule over the world BECAUSE OF IT. It is therefore written, "And you shall eat and be satisfied, and bless Hashem your Elohim," AS WHEN HOLINESS REIGNS, THERE IS PLENTY IN THE WORLD. Rabbi Elazar said: Assuredly it is so, and so should it be THAT PLENTY ABOUNDS WITH THE RULE OF HOLINESS, AND FAMINE WITH THE REIGN OF THE OTHER SIDE.

61. אֲמַר רִבִּי יְהוּדָה, זַכָּאִין אִינּוּן צַדִּיקַיָּיא, דְּקוּרְבָא דִּלְהוֹן אִיהוּ שְׁלָמָא בְּעַלְמָא, בְּגִין דְּיָדְעֵי לְיַחֲדָא יִחוּדָא, וּמְקָרְבֵי קוּרְבָא, לְאַסְגָּאָה שְׁלָמָא בְּעַלְמָא, דְּהָא יוֹסֵף וִיהוּדָה עַד לָא אִתְקְרִיבוּ דָּא עִם דָּא, לָא הֲוָה שְׁלָמָא, כֵּיוָן דְּאִתְקְרִיבוּ יוֹסֵף וִיהוּדָה כַּחֲדָא, כְּדֵין אַסְגִּיאוּ שְׁלָמָא בְּעַלְמָא, וְחֵידוּ אִתּוֹסַף לְעֵילָּא וְתַתָּא, כְּמָה דְּקוּרְבָא דִּיהוּדָה וְיוֹסֵף,

וְכֻלְּהוּ שִׁבְטִין אִשְׁתַּכָּחוּ כַּחֲדָא בֵּיהּ בְּיוֹסֵף, וְהַהוּא קוּרְבָא אַסְגֵּי שְׁלָמָא בְּעַלְמָא, כְּמָה דְּאוֹקִימְנָא דִּכְתִיב וַיִּגַּשׁ אֵלָיו יְהוּדָה.

61. Rabbi Yehuda said: Happy are the righteous, whose coming together brings peace into the world, for they know how to bring unison and approach each other to increase peace in the world. For until Joseph and Judah came near each other, there was no peace. Once they came near each other, peace increased in the world. Joy abounded above and below, when Joseph and Judah approached each other, and all the tribes joined Joseph. The coming together caused peace to abound in the world, as we have explained in relation to the verse, "And Judah came near to him."

7. "And Joseph could not restrain himself"

A Synopsis

We receive an introduction to the types of men who descended from Adam, and how each type can bring merit and benefit to the others – just as the beneficiary or "carrier" of charity gains merit in the same degree as the giver. This powerful analogy leads to further discussion of the relationship between "Charity Carrier" and the analogous Sfirot that exist above our physical realm. To assist our understanding of its inherent mystery, unity is explored as it exists within a theme of mating – specifically the mating of the Holy One with Yisrael. In the illumination following this supreme Union, all can be blessed.

The Relevance of this Passage

When a man and woman join together in sexual union within the spiritual confines of marriage, their connection creates a stirring above: the Lower World embraces the Upper World and Divine Light fills all. But the man and woman must be pure of thought and joined by love. Their union must be accompanied by a consciousness to share pleasure for the purpose of creating Light for each other and the world.

62. וְלֹא יָכוֹל יוֹסֵף לְהִתְאַפֵּק לְכָל הַנִּצָּבִים עָלָיו וגו׳, רִבִּי חִיָּיא פָּתַח וַאֲמַר, פִּזַּר נָתַן לָאֶבְיוֹנִים צִדְקָתוֹ עוֹמֶדֶת לָעַד קַרְנוֹ תָּרוּם בְּכָבוֹד. תָּא חֲזֵי, קוּדְשָׁא בְּרִיךְ הוּא בָּרָא עַלְמָא, וְאַשְׁלֵיט עֲלֵיהּ לְאָדָם, דִּיהֵא מַלְכָּא עַל כֹּלָּא.

62. "Then Joseph could not restrain himself before all them that stood by him ..." (Beresheet 45:1). Rabbi Chiya opened the discussion with the verse, "He has distributed freely, he has given to the poor; his righteousness endures for ever; his horn shall be exalted with honor" (Tehilim 112:9). Come and behold: The Holy One, blessed be He, created the world and made Adam ruler over it – to be king over all.

63. וְהַאי בַּר נָשׁ, מִתְפָּרְשָׁן מִנֵּיהּ בְּעַלְמָא, כַּמָּה זִינִין, מִנְּהוֹן צַדִּיקַיָּא, וּמִנְּהוֹן רַשִׁיעַיָּא, מִנְּהוֹן טִפְּשִׁין, וּמִנְּהוֹן חַכִּימִין, וְכֻלְּהוּ אִתְקַיְּימוּ בְּעַלְמָא, עֲתִירִין וּמִסְכֵּנִין. וְכֻלְּהוּ בְּגִין לְמִזְכֵּי אִלֵּין בְּאִלֵּין, לְמִזְכֵּי צַדִּיקַיָּא עִם רַשִׁיעַיָּא, לְמִזְכֵּי חַכִּימִין עִם טִפְּשִׁין, לְמִזְכֵּי עֲתִירִין עִם

מִסְכְּנִין דְּהָא בְּגִין כָּךְ, זָכֵי בַּר נָשׁ לְחַיֵּי עָלְמָא, וְאִתְקַשַּׁר בְּאִילָנָא דְחַיֵּי. וְלָא עוֹד, אֶלָּא דְּהָא צְדָקָה דְּאִיהוּ עָבֵיד, קָאֵים לְעָלְמִין, דִּכְתִיב וְצִדְקָתוֹ עוֹמֶדֶת לָעַד.

63. From man, four types of men branched out – some righteous and some wicked, some stupid and some wise. Of these, some were rich and some poor. They can bring merit and benefit to each other. The righteous can benefit the wicked BY CAUSING THEM TO REPENT THEIR SINS; the wise can benefit the foolish BY TEACHING THEM SENSE; the rich can benefit the poor BY SUPPORTING THEM IN THEIR NEED. Through these actions, man merits life everlasting and attaches himself to the Tree of Life. THEREFORE, THE SCRIPTURE READS, “HE HAS DISTRIBUTED FREELY, HE HAS GIVEN TO THE POOR.” Moreover, this charity he dispenses stands forever, NAMELY, THE NUKVA ESTABLISHED BY IT IS CALLED ‘EVER’, as it is written, “and his righteousness (charity) endures for ever.”

64. פִּזַּר נָתַן לָאֶבְיוֹנִים. רִבִּי אֶלְעָזָר אָמַר, כַּד בָּרָא קוּדְשָׁא בְּרִיךְ הוּא עַלְמָא, קָאֵים לֵיהּ עַל סַמְכָא חַד, וְצַדִּיק שְׁמֵיהּ, וְהַאי צַדִּיק אִיהוּ קִיּוּמָא דְעַלְמָא, וְדָא אִיהוּ דְּאַשְׁקֵי, וְזָן לְכֹלָּא. דִּכְתִיב וְנָהָר יוֹצֵא מֵעֵדֶן לְהַשְׁקוֹת אֶת הַגָּן וּמִשָּׁם יִפָּרֵד וְהָיָה לְאַרְבָּעָה רָאשִׁים.

64. “He has distributed freely, he has given to the poor.” Rabbi Elazar said: When the Holy One, blessed be He, created the universe, He established it upon one pillar named righteous, NAMELY, YESOD. The righteous is the support of the world; THAT IS, HE SUPPORTS THE NUKVA CALLED ‘WORLD’. It is he who gives water, NAMELY, THE ILLUMINATION OF CHOCHMAH, and food, THE ILLUMINATION OF CHASSADIM, to all, as it is written, “And a river went out of Eden to water the garden; and from thence it was parted, and branched into four streams” (Beresheet 2:10). THIS IS YESOD NAMED ‘RIVER’.

65. וּמִשָּׁם יִפָּרֵד, מַהוּ יִפָּרֵד. אֶלָּא, הַהוּא מְזוֹנָא וּמַשְׁקְיָא דְּהַהוּא נָהָר, נָטֵיל גִּנְתָא כֹּלָּא, וּלְבָתַר אִתְבַּדַּר הַהוּא מַשְׁקְיָא, לְד׳ סִטְרִין דְּעַלְמָא, וְכַמָּה אִינוּן דִּמְצַפָּאן לְאִתְשַׁקְיָיא וּלְאִתְזְנָא מִתַּמָּן, כְּד״א עֵינֵי כֹל

אֵלֶיךָ יְשַׂבֵּרוּ וְאַתָּה נוֹתֵן לָהֶם אֶת אָכְלָם בְּעִתּוֹ. וּבְג״כ פִּזַּר נָתַן לָאֶבְיוֹנִים, דָּא צַדִּיק. צִדְקָתוֹ עוֹמֶדֶת לָעַד, דָּא כנ״י. דִּבְגִין כָּךְ, אִיהִי קַיְימָא בְּרָזָא דִּשְׁלָם, בְּקִיּוּמָא שְׁלִים רָשָׁע יִרְאֶה וְכָעַס, דָּא מַלְכוּת עכו״ם.

65. In the verse, "and from thence it was parted," what is the meaning of the word 'parted'? HE ANSWERS: It is the food and drink from that river that the garden receives, WHICH IS THE NUKVA. Then drink is further distributed into the four directions of the universe, SO THAT ALL INHABITANTS OF THE WORLD RECEIVE WATER FROM HER AND NONE REMAINS THIRSTY. How many wait for food and drink from there, as it is written, "The eyes of all wait upon You; and You give them their food in due season" (Tehilim 145:15). Thus, the verse, "He has distributed freely, he has given to the poor," alludes to the Righteous, YESOD, WHICH DISTRIBUTES AND GIVES ALL OF CHOCHMAH AND CHASSADIM, AND SUPPORTS ALL THE POOR OF THE WORLD. The verse, "and his charity endures for ever," refers to the Congregation of Yisrael, THE NUKVA CALLED 'CHARITY', which, because SHE RECEIVES EVERYTHING FROM YESOD, stands united in the secret of peace. THUS, SHE STANDS FOREVER. "The wicked man shall see it, and be vexed," (Tehilim 112:10) alludes to the kingdom of the idolatrous, MALCHUT OF THE OTHER SIDE, WHICH THEN ENVIES THE MALCHUT OF HOLINESS.

66. תָּא חֲזֵי, מַלְכוּת שָׁמַיִם, אִיהִי בֵּי מַקְדְּשָׁא, לְקַיְימָא כָּל מִסְכְּנֵי, בְּגוֹ צִלָּא דְּשֵׁרוּתָא דִּשְׁכִינְתָּא, וְצַדִּיק דָּא אִיהוּ אִקְרֵי גַּבָּאי צְדָקָה, לְמֵיחַן וּלְמֵיזַן לְכֹלָּא, דִּכְתִיב פִּזַּר נָתַן לָאֶבְיוֹנִים, בְּגִין כָּךְ, גַּבָּאֵי צְדָקָה, נָטְלֵי אַגְרָא, לָקֳבֵיל כֻּלְּהוּ דְּיַהֲבֵי צְדָקָה.

66. Come and behold: The kingdom of heaven, THE NUKVA OF ZEIR ANPIN, is the Temple. It shelters all the poor under the shadow of the Shechinah; the righteous. YESOD OF ZEIR ANPIN is called 'charity collector', because he bestows sustenance upon everybody, NAMELY, THE POOR UNDER THE SHADOW OF THE SHECHINAH. Therefore the charity collectors receive as much a reward as those who gave them donations, BEING A CHARIOT TO YESOD OF ZEIR ANPIN CALLED 'CHARITY

COLLECTOR’, WHICH INCLUDES ALL THE SFIROT ABOVE IT.

67. תָּא חֲזֵי, וְלֹא יָכוֹל יוֹסֵף לְהִתְאַפֵּק לְכָל הַנִּצָּבִים, אִלֵּין אִינוּן, כָּל דְּקָיְימֵי, לְאִתְזָנָא וּלְאִתְשַׁקְיָיא מִנֵּיהּ. וְלֹא עָמַד אִישׁ אִתּוֹ בְּהִתְוַדַּע יוֹסֵף אֶל אֶחָיו. אִתּוֹ: דָּא כְּנֶסֶת יִשְׂרָאֵל. אֶחָיו: אִלֵּין שְׁאָר רְתִיכִין חַיָּילִין, דִּכְתִּיב בְּהוֹ לְמַעַן אַחַי וְרֵעָי. ד"א וְלֹא עָמַד אִישׁ אִתּוֹ, בְּזִמְנָא דְּקוּדְשָׁא בְּרִיךְ הוּא אָתֵי לְאִזְדַּוְּוגָא בִּכנ"י. בְּהִתְוַדַּע יוֹסֵף אֶל אֶחָיו, בְּזִמְנָא דְּקוּדְשָׁא בְּרִיךְ הוּא הֲוָה מִתְחַבֵּר בְּהוֹ בְּיִשְׂרָאֵל, בְּגִין דְּאִינוּן נָטְלֵי בִּלְחוֹדַיְיהוּ, וְלָא חִבּוּרָא דְּעַמִּין עעכו"ם בַּהֲדַיְיהוּ, בְּגִין כָּךְ בַּיּוֹם הַשְּׁמִינִי עֲצֶרֶת תִּהְיֶה לָכֶם, דְּהָא בְּזִמְנָא דָּא, אִיהוּ קוּדְשָׁא בְּרִיךְ הוּא בִּלְחוֹדוֹי, בְּחִבּוּרָא חָדָא עִם יִשְׂרָאֵל, דִּכְתִּיב בְּהוֹ אַחַי וְרֵעָי כְּמָה דְּאוּקְמוּהָ.

67. Come and behold: “Then Joseph could not restrain himself before all them that stood by him,” who waited to receive food and drink from him. YESOD, CALLED ‘JOSEPH’, COULD NOT RESTRAIN ITSELF FROM SHOWERING ABUNDANCE UPON THEM. IN THE VERSE, “And no man stood with him, while Joseph made himself known to his brethren,” the words “with him” allude to the Congregation of Yisrael, WHICH IS THE NUKVA, WITH WHOM NO ONE STOOD; “WHILE...” REFERS TO THE TIME OF MATING, AS MATING IS CALLED ‘KNOWLEDGE’; “his brethren” are the other Chariots and Legions, of whom it is written, “For my brethren and companions’ sakes” (Tehilim 122:8), BECAUSE HE MATED WITH THE NUKVA SO HE COULD GIVE THEM ABUNDANCE. WE LEARN FROM THE VERSE THAT “WHILE JOSEPH MADE HIMSELF KNOWN” – WHEN JOSEPH UNITED WITH THE SHECHINAH – HE DID IT FOR HIS BROTHERS’ SAKES, SINCE “TO” MEANS “FOR THE SAKE OF.” Another explanation of “And no man stood with him” concerns the time when the Holy One, blessed be He, approached the Congregation of Yisrael to mate with her. The verse, “while Joseph made himself known to his brethren,” refers to the time when the Holy One, blessed be He, joined Yisrael, THAT IS, WHEN THE HOLY ONE, BLESSED BE HE, WAS UNITED WITH YISRAEL, “NO MAN STOOD” OF THE OTHER NATIONS “WITH HIM,” WHEN HE MATED WITH THE NUKVA. For they alone received THE ILLUMINATION OF UNION, without connection to the other idolatrous nations. Hence it is written, “On the eighth day you shall have a solemn assembly" (Bemidbar 29:35), for at that time the Holy One, blessed be He, is united with Yisrael alone, of whom it is written, "for my brethren and companions' sakes..."

68. רִבִּי יֵיסָא פָּתַח קְרָא, בִּזְמְנָא דְקוּדְשָׁא בְּרִיךְ הוּא יוֹקִים לָהּ לִכְנֶסֶת יִשְׂרָאֵל מֵעַפְרָא, וְיִבָּעֵי לְאִנְּקָמָא נִקְמָתָא מֵעַמְמַיָּא עעכו"ם, כְּדֵין כְּתִיב וּמֵעַמִּים אֵין אִישׁ אִתִּי, וּכְתִיב הָכָא, וְלֹא עָמַד אִישׁ אִתּוֹ בְּהִתְוַדַּע יוֹסֵף אֶל אֶחָיו, כְּמָה דְאַתְּ אָמֵר וַיְנַטְּלֵם וַיְנַשְּׂאֵם כָּל יְמֵי עוֹלָם.

68. Rabbi Yisa continued: Of the time when the Holy One, blessed be He, raises the Congregation of Yisrael from the dust AT THE TIME OF REDEMPTION and wishes to take vengeance on the idolatrous nations, it is written, "And of the peoples there was no man with me" (Yeshayah 63:3). As it is written, "And no man stood with him," and "and he bore them and carried them all the days of old" (Ibid. 9).

69. וְלֹא יָכוֹל יוֹסֵף לְהִתְאַפֵּק, רִבִּי חִזְקִיָּה פָּתַח וַאֲמַר, שִׁיר הַמַּעֲלוֹת אֵלֶיךָ נָשָׂאתִי אֶת עֵינַי הַיּוֹשְׁבִי בַּשָּׁמָיִם, הַאי קְרָא אוֹקְמוּהָ וְאִתְּמָר, אֲבָל תָּא חֲזֵי, אֵלֶיךָ נָשָׂאתִי אֶת עֵינַי, וּכְתִיב אֶשָּׂא עֵינַי אֶל הֶהָרִים. אֶלָּא, דָּא לְעֵילָּא, וְדָא לְתַתָּא. אֶשָּׂא עֵינַי אֶל הֶהָרִים, דָּא לְעֵילָּא, בְּגִין לְאַמְשָׁכָא בִּרְכָאן מֵעֵילָּא לְתַתָּא, מֵאִלֵּין הָרִים עִלָּאִין, לְאַמְשָׁכָא מִנַּיְיהוּ בִּרְכָאן לִכְנֶסֶת יִשְׂרָאֵל, דְּאִתְבָּרְכָא מִנַּיְיהוּ. אֵלֶיךָ נָשָׂאתִי אֶת עֵינַי, לְמִצְפֵּי וּלְחַכָּאָה לְאִנּוּן בִּרְכָאן דְּנָחֲתוּ מִתַּמָּן לְתַתָּא.

69. "Then Joseph could not restrain himself" (Beresheet 45:1). Rabbi Chizkiyah quoted, "A song of ascents. To you I lift up my eyes, O You who dwells in the heaven" (Tehilim 123:1). This verse has already been explained, yet come and behold: It is written here, "To You I lift up my eyes;" and elsewhere, "I will lift up my eyes to the mountains" (Tehilim 121:1). WHAT IS THE DIFFERENCE? The one is above and the other below. HE EXPLAINED: "I will lift up my eyes to the mountains" above, down TO ZEIR ANPIN, to draw blessings from the Supernal Mountains above ON THE NUKVA, AS IN THE SECRET OF 'THE MOUNTAINS ARE NONE OTHER THAN THE PATRIARCHS,' WHO ARE CHESED, GVURAH AND TIFERET OF ZEIR

ANPIN, from whom blessings are drawn upon the Congregation of Yisrael. "To You I lift up my eyes," FROM DOWN BELOW IN THE NUKVA, is to yearn and wait for the blessings that come down FROM ZEIR ANPIN TO THE NUKVA.

70. הַיּוֹשְׁבִי בַּשָּׁמָיִם, דְּכָל תּוֹקְפָּהָא, וְחֵילָאָה, וְקִיּוּמָהָא, אִיהוּ בַּשָּׁמַיִם, בְּגִין דְּכַד יוֹבֵלָא, אַפְתַּח מַבּוּעֵי דְּכָל אִינּוּן תַּרְעִין, כֻּלְּהוּ קַיְימֵי בַּשָּׁמַיִם, וְכֵיוָן דְּשָׁמַיִם נָטֵיל כָּל אִינּוּן נְהוֹרִין דְּנָפְקֵי מִיּוֹבֵלָא, כְּדֵין אִיהוּ זָן וְאַשְׁקֵי לָהּ לִכְנֶסֶת יִשְׂרָאֵל, עַל יְדָא דְצַדִּיק חַד.

70. "You who dwells in the heavens." HE ASKS: IF IT REFERS TO THE NUKVA, WHY DOES IT SAY "IN THE HEAVENS," WHICH ARE ZEIR ANPIN? HE REPLIES: Because all the strength, power, and support OF THE NUKVA is in heaven, SHE RECEIVES THEM FROM ZEIR ANPIN CALLED 'HEAVEN'. For when the Jubilee, BINAH, opens the springs of all the gates – THE ABUNDANCE OF THE FIFTY GATES OF BINAH – they are all in heaven, ZEIR ANPIN. And when heaven receives all the lights from the Jubilee, it nourishes and feeds the Congregation of Yisrael, THE NUKVA, through a certain righteous One, YESOD.

71. וְכֵיוָן דְּדָא אִתְעַר לְגַבָּהּ, כַּמָּה אִינּוּן דְּקַיְימָן בְּכָל סִטְרִין, לְאִתְשַׁקְאָה וּלְאִתְבָּרְכָא מִתַּמָּן, כְּד״א הַכְּפִירִים שׁוֹאֲגִים לַטָּרֶף וּלְבַקֵּשׁ מֵאֵל אָכְלָם. וּכְדֵין, אִיהִי סָלְקָא בְּרָזָא דְרָזִין כִּדְקָא חָזֵי, וּמְקַבְּלָא עִדּוּנִין מִבַּעֲלָהּ כִּדְקָא יָאוּת, וְכֻלְּהוּ דְּקַיְימִין בְּכָל סִטְרִין עָמְדֵי בִּלְחוֹדַיְיהוּ, כְּד״א וְלֹא עָמַד אִישׁ אִתּוֹ, דִּכְתִיב וַיִּקְרָא הוֹצִיאוּ כָל אִישׁ מֵעָלַי, וּלְבָתַר דְּאִיהִי מְקַבְּלָא עִדּוּנִין מִבַּעֲלָהּ, כֻּלְּהוּ אִתְשַׁקְיָין לְבָתַר, וְאִתְזָנוּ, כְּד״א יַשְׁקוּ כָּל חַיְתוֹ שָׂדָי יִשְׁבְּרוּ פְרָאִים צְמָאָם.

71. Because YESOD is aroused toward Her, many stand on all sides to drink and be blessed from there, TO RECEIVE FROM THE ILLUMINATION OF THE UNION, as it is written, "The young lions roar after their prey, and seek their food from El" (Tehilim 104:21). She then ascends TO MATE in utmost secrecy, as is proper, and receives from Her husband delicacies that She deserves. And all those on all sides WHO WAIT TO RECEIVE FROM HER remain alone, AND DO NOT RISE WITH THE NUKVA, as it is written, "And no man stood with him," and, "and he cried, 'Cause every man to go out from me.'" Only after She receives delicacies from Her husband, NAMELY, AFTER MATING, is everybody given food and drink, as it is written, "they gave drink to every wild beast: the wild donkeys quench their thirst" (Ibid. 11).

8. "Why have You dealt ill"

A Synopsis

Moses and Elijah both said to The Creator, "Why have you brought evil?" This indicates the power of the evil side over the people of the covenant. We learn that the Prophet Elijah did not die, and continues to act as messenger to the people of the covenant to this present day. Neither Moses nor Elijah died, we' re told, but were instead brought directly into heaven immediately after shedding their bodies. The rabbis refer to a particular strength acquired by the soul when it is confronted by the powerful desire existing between man and women, and how, more than any other human, the soul of Elijah was on the side of the male.

The Relevance of this Passage

The people of the covenant are endowed with the most intense desire to receive. They can bring more Light to this world than all other nations combined, but they can bring also more darkness if they are ruled by their Evil Inclination. The strength to both recognize and subdue our negative impulses is impressed into our soul. We further receive the purifying Light of Moses and Elijah, whose influences help us rise above the desires of our physical body. We touch the divine realm of immortality and infuse our lives with this sacred and eternal energy.

72. רִבִּי יוֹסֵי פְּתַח קְרָא בְּאֵלִיָּהוּ, דִּכְתִיב וַיִּקְרָא אֶל ה׳ וַיֹּאמַר ה׳ אֱלֹהָי הֲגַם עַל הָאַלְמָנָה אֲשֶׁר אֲנִי מִתְגּוֹרֵר עִמָּהּ הֲרֵעוֹתָ לְהָמִית אֶת בְּנָהּ. תָּא חֲזֵי, תְּרֵי הֲווֹ דְּקָאָמְרִין מִלִּין לָקֳבֵיל קוּדְשָׁא בְּרִיךְ הוּא, מֹשֶׁה וְאֵלִיָּהוּ, מֹשֶׁה אָמַר, לָמָּה הֲרֵעוֹתָ לָעָם הַזֶּה. וְאֵלִיָּהוּ אָמַר, הֲרֵעוֹתָ לְהָמִית אֶת בְּנָהּ, וְתַרְוַיְיהוּ מִלָּה חָדָא קָאֲמָרוּ.

72. Rabbi Yosi opened a discussion of Elijah with the verse, "And he cried to Hashem, and said: 'Hashem my Elohim, have You also brought evil upon the widow with whom I lodge, by slaying her son?'" (I Melachim 17:20). Come and behold: There were two who said harsh words to the Holy One, blessed be He – Moses and Elijah. Moses asks: "Why have You dealt ill (lit, 'evil') with this people?" (Shemot 5:22), and Elijah said, "have You also brought evil...by slaying her son?" They both said the same thing.

73. מ״ט. אֶלָּא רָזָא אִיהוּ, מֹשֶׁה אֲמַר, לָמָּה הֲרֵעוֹתָ, מַאי טַעְמָא. אֶלָּא,

בְּגִין דְּאִתְיְהֵיב רְשׁוּ לְסִטְרָא אָחֳרָא לְשַׁלְטָאָה עֲלַיְיהוּ דְּיִשְׂרָאֵל, הֲרֵעוֹתָ: יְהַבְתְּ רְשׁוּ לְסִטְרָא אָחֳרָא דְּרַע, לְמִשְׁלַט עֲלַיְיהוּ. אֵלִיָּהוּ אָמַר הֲרֵעוֹתָ יְהַבְתְּ רְשׁוּ לְסִטְרָא דְּרַע, לִיטּוֹל נִשְׁמָתָא דְּדָא, וְדָא הוּא הֲרֵעוֹתָ, וְכֹלָּא רָזָא חָדָא.

73. HE ASKS: Why DID THEY BOTH SAY, "WHY HAVE YOU BROUGHT EVIL?" HE ANSWERS: Because permission was given to the Other Side to rule over Yisrael. Moses said "dealt evil," which means gave permission to the Other Side of evil to reign upon them. Elijah said "brought evil," WHICH ALSO MEANS THAT You allowed the Other Side to take his soul. This is why he said "brought evil." All is one mystery – "BROUGHT EVIL" IS THE SECRET OF GIVING SWAY TO THE OTHER SIDE CALLED 'EVIL'.

74. תָּא חֲזֵי, אֵלִיָּהוּ אֲמַר, הֲגַם עַל הָאַלְמָנָה אֲשֶׁר אֲנִי מִתְגּוֹרֵר עִמָּהּ, בְּגִין דְּקוּדְשָׁא בְּרִיךְ הוּא אֲמַר לֵיהּ לְאֵלִיָּהוּ, הִנֵּה צִוִּיתִי שָׁם אִשָּׁה אַלְמָנָה לְכַלְכְּלֶךָ, וְכָל מַאן דְּזָן וּמְפַרְנֵס לְמַאן דְּאִצְטְרִיךְ לֵיהּ, וְכ"ש בְּיוֹמָא דְּכַפְנָא, הָא אִתְאַחֵיד בְּאִילָנָא דְּחַיֵּי, וְגָרֵים לֵיהּ חַיִּים וְלִבְנוֹי, וְהָא אוֹקִימְנָא. וְהַשְׁתָּא אֵלִיָּהוּ אֲמַר, כָּל מַאן דְּקַיֵּים נַפְשָׁא בְּעַלְמָא, זָכֵי לֵיהּ חַיִּים, וְזָכֵי לְאִתְאַחֲדָא בְּאִילָנָא דְּחַיֵּי, וְהַשְׁתָּא שָׁלְטָא אִילָנָא דְּמוֹתָא סִטְרָא דְּרַע, עַל הָאַלְמָנָה דְּאַנְתְּ פְּקַדְתְּ לְמֵיזַן לִי, בְּגִין כָּךְ הֲרֵעוֹתָ.

74. Come and behold: Elijah said, "have You also brought evil upon the widow with whom I lodge," because the Holy One, blessed be He, said to Elijah, "behold, I have commanded a widow woman there to sustain you" (I Melachim 17:9). Whoever nourishes and sustains the needy, especially in days of famine, is united with and cleaves to the Tree of Life, and draws life unto himself and his children, as has already been explained. Now, Elijah said: Whoever sustains one soul in the world merits life and merits to be united with the Tree of Life. Yet now the tree of death, the evil side, has power over the widow, whom You commanded to sustain me. Hence HE SAID, "have You brought evil."

75. וְאִי תֵּימָא דְּרַע לָא אִתְעֲבֵיד לְבַר נָשׁ מֵעִם קוּדְשָׁא בְּרִיךְ הוּא. תָּא

חֲזֵי, בִּזְמְנָא דְבַר נָשׁ אָזֵיל לִימִינָא, נְטִירוּ דְקוּדְשָׁא בְּרִיךְ הוּא תָּדִיר לְגַבֵּיהּ, וְלָא יָכֵיל סִטְרָא אָחֳרָא לְשַׁלְטָאָה עֲלֵיהּ, וְהַאי רָע אִתְכַּפְיָא קַמֵּיהּ, וְלָא יָכֵיל לְשַׁלְטָאָה. וְכֵיוָן דִּנְטִירָא דְקוּדְשָׁא בְּרִיךְ הוּא אִתְעַבְרָא מִנֵּיהּ, בְּגִין דְּאִיהוּ אִתְדַּבַּק בְּרָע, כְּדֵין הַהוּא רָע, כֵּיוָן דְּחָמֵי דְלָאו עִמֵּיהּ נְטִירוּ, כְּדֵין שַׁלִּיט עֲלֵיהּ, וְאָתֵי לְשֵׁיצָאָה לֵיהּ, וּכְדֵין אִתְיְהֵיב לֵיהּ רְשׁוּ, וְנָטֵיל נִשְׁמָתֵיהּ.

75. HE ASKS: What if you say that no evil is brought on man by the Holy One, blessed be He. HE ANSWERS, Come and behold: When a man walks to the right, the Holy One, blessed be He, always protects him, and the Other Side cannot have mastery over him. Evil is subdued before him and cannot rule. When the protection of the Holy One, blessed be He, is removed because he cleaved to evil, then evil sees him unprotected, obtains power, and comes to destroy him. Then it is given permission to take away his soul.

76. מֹשֶׁה אֲמַר לָמָּה הֲרֵעוֹתָ, דְּאִתְיְהֵיב לֵיהּ רְשׁוּ לְסִטְרָא דְרָע, לְמִשְׁלַט עֲלַיְיהוּ דְיִשְׂרָאֵל, לְמֶהֱוֵי בְּשִׁעְבּוּדָא דִילֵיהּ. דָּבָר אַחֵר לָמָּה הֲרֵעוֹתָ, דְּחָמָא כַּמָּה מִנְהוֹן דַּהֲווֹ מֵתִין, וְאִתְמְסָרוּ בְּסִטְרָא דְרָע.

76. Moses said: "why have You dealt ill," because the evil side was given permission to reign over Yisrael, who became its slaves. Another explanation of "why have You dealt ill" is that he saw many FROM YISRAEL die and be given to the side of evil.

77. תָּא חֲזֵי, בְּשַׁעְתָּא דְטוֹב אִתְעַר, דְּאִיהוּ יְמִינָא, כָּל חֵידוּ, וְכָל טִיבוּ, וְכָל בִּרְכָאן מִשְׁתַּכְּחָן, וְכֹלָּא בַּחֲשַׁאי אִיהוּ, כְּמָה דְאוֹקְמוּהָ, דְּאָמְרֵי בשכמל"ו בַּחֲשַׁאי, וְרָזָא דָא בְּגִין דְּאִיהוּ כְּדֵין יִחוּדָא כִּדְקָא חֲזֵי.

77. Come and behold: When good, the right, is stirred, then gladness, goodness, and blessings abide, all in secrecy, as has already been explained in connection with THE SONS OF JACOB, who said 'Blessed be the name of His kingdom for ever and ever' in a whisper. There is secrecy because union is then carried out properly. THUS IT IS CLEAR WHY JOSEPH SAID AT THE

TIME OF UNION: "CAUSE EVERY MAN TO GO OUT FROM ME" – AS UNION HAS TO BE PERFORMED IN SECRECY.

78. אֲמַר רִבִּי חִיָּיא, וְכִי אֵלִיָּהוּ, כֵּיוָן דְּאִיהוּ גָּזַר, וְקוּדְשָׁא בְּרִיךְ הוּא מְקַיֵּים, וְאִיהוּ גָּזֵיר עַל שְׁמַיָּא, דְּלָא לַאֲחָתָא מִטְרָא וְטַלָּא, הֵיךְ דָּחֵיל אִיהוּ מֵאִיזֶבֶל, דְּשַׁדְּרַת לֵיהּ, דִּכְתִּיב כִּי כָעֵת מָחָר אָשִׂים אֶת נַפְשְׁךָ כְּנֶפֶשׁ אַחַד מֵהֶם, וּמִיָּד דָּחֵיל וְעָרַק עַל נַפְשֵׁיהּ.

78. Rabbi Chiya asks: How could Elijah, who, once he decreed the Holy One, blessed be He, executed such as the one that heaven will not let dew or rain fall, be afraid of Izevel, who threatened him with the words, "and more also, if I make not your life as the life of one of them by tomorrow about this time" (I Melachim 19:2). How could he take fright and immediately run for his life?

79. א"ל רִבִּי יוֹסֵי, הָא אוֹקְמוּהָ, דְּצַדִּיקַיָּא, לָא בָּעָאן לְאַטְרָחָא לְמָארֵיהוֹן, בַּאֲתַר דִּנְזָקָא אִשְׁתַּכְּחַת לְעֵינָא. כְּגַוְונָא דִּשְׁמוּאֵל, דִּכְתִּיב אֵיךְ אֵלֵךְ וְשָׁמַע שָׁאוּל וַהֲרָגָנִי, א"ל עֶגְלַת בָּקָר תִּקַּח בְּיָדֶךָ, בְּגִין דְּצַדִּיקַיָּא, לָא בָּעָאן לְאַטְרָחָא לְמָארֵיהוֹן, בַּאֲתַר דִּנְזָקָא אִשְׁתַּכַּח. אוּף הָכֵי אֵלִיָּהוּ, כֵּיוָן דְּחָמָא דִּנְזָקָא אִשְׁתַּכַּח, לָא בָּעֵי לְאַטְרָחָא לְמָארֵיהּ.

79. Rabbi Yosi replied: It has been explained that the righteous do not wish to trouble their Master, where harm is obvious to the eye. Shmuel, for example, asks, "How can I go? If Saul hears it, he will kill me. And Hashem said: Take a heifer with you ..." (I Shmuel 16:2). For the righteous do not wish to trouble their Master about obvious damage. Elijah, too, when he saw danger, did not wish to bother his Master.

80. א"ל אֲנָא מִלָּה שְׁמַעְנָא, דְּהָא בְּאֵלִיָּהוּ לָא כְתִיב בֵּיהּ וַיִּירָא וַיֵּלֶךְ אֶל נַפְשׁוֹ, אֶלָּא וַיַּרְא, רְאִיָּה חָמָא, וּמַה חָמָא, אֶלָּא חָמָא, דְּהָא מִכַּמָּה שְׁנִין אֲזַל בַּתְרֵיהּ מַלְאַךְ הַמָּוֶת, וְלָא אִתְמְסַר בִּידֵיהּ, וְהַשְׁתָּא וַיֵּלֶךְ אֶל נַפְשׁוֹ, מַאי וַיֵּלֶךְ אֶל נַפְשׁוֹ, אֲזַל לְקִיּוּמָא דְּנַפְשָׁא, וּמַאן אִיהוּ אִילָנָא דְּחַיֵּי לְאִתְדַּבְּקָא תַּמָּן.

80. He said to him, I have heard here that scripture does not say of Elijah, 'he feared (Heb. *vayira*) and went for his life,' but rather, "when he saw (Heb. *vayar*) that" (I Melachim 19, 3), which means he saw something. What did he see? He saw that the Angel of Death has been following him these many years, yet he was not delivered into his hands. And now he "went for his life (lit. '*Nefesh*')," which means that he went to the source of the sustenance of the Nefesh, which is the Tree of Life, to cleave to it, SO THE ANGEL OF DEATH WOULD NO LONGER FOLLOW HIM.

81. תָּא חֲזֵי, כֻּלְּהוּ כְּתִיב אֶת נַפְשׁוֹ, וְהָכָא כְּתִיב אֶל נַפְשׁוֹ, וְרָזָא דָא שְׁמַעְנָא, דַּאֲמַר ר"ש, כָּל נִשְׁמָתִין דְּעָלְמָא, כֻּלְּהוּ נָפְקֵי מֵהַהוּא נָהָר דְּנָגֵיד וְנָפֵיק, וְכֻלְּהוּ נָקִיט לוֹן, הַהוּא צְרוֹרָא דְחַיָּיא, וְכַד נוּקְבָא אִתְעַבְּרַת מִן דְּכוּרָא, כֻּלְּהוּ בְּתֵיאוּבְתָּא דִּתְרֵין סִטְרִין, בְּתֵיאוּבְתָּא דְּנוּקְבָא לְגַבֵּי דְּכוּרָא, וְכַד תֵּיאוּבְתָּא דִּדְכוּרָא נָפְקָא בִּרְעוּתָא, כְּדֵין אִינוּן נִשְׁמָתִין בְּקִיּוּמָא יַתִּיר, בְּגִין דְּכֹלָּא בְּתֵיאוּבְתָּא וּרְעוּ דְּאִילָנָא דְחַיָּיא. וְאֵלִיָּהוּ, בְּגִין דַּהֲוָה מֵהַהוּא רְעוּתָא, יַתִּיר מִבַּר נָשׁ אָחֳרָא, אִתְקַיַּים.

81. Come and behold: It is written everywhere else "to his Nefesh," yet here it is written, "for his Nefesh." I have heard a secret from Rabbi Shimon, who said that all the souls in the world come from the same river, YESOD OF ZEIR ANPIN. They are all received by the Bundle of Life, THE NUKVA, and the female conceives from the male when the two sides are both desirous – the female of the male, AND THE MALE OF THE FEMALE. When the male has GREAT passion, the souls are of greater endurance, because everything depends on the desire and passion of the Tree of Life, ZEIR ANPIN. Elijah, who came from that passion OF THE MALE more than other people, endured AND DID NOT DIE.

82. וּבְגִין כָּךְ אֶל נַפְשׁוֹ כְּתִיב, וְלָא כְתִיב אֶת נַפְשׁוֹ, דְּהָא אֶת נַפְשׁוֹ דָא הִיא נוּקְבָא. וְאִי תֵימָא וְאֶל הָאִשָּׁה אָמַר, כְּלָלָא דִּדְכַר וְנוּקְבָא, כַּד הִיא בְּגוֹ דְּכוּרָא, כְּדֵין וְאֶל הָאִשָּׁה אָמַר. אֶת הָאִשָּׁה, נוּקְבָא בִּלְחוֹדָהָא, וְלָא דִּדְכוּרָא. כְּגַוְונָא דָא אֶל נַפְשׁוֹ, דָּכָר בִּלְחוֹדוֹי, אֶת נַפְשׁוֹ נוּקְבָא בִּלְחוֹדָהָא וְלָא כְּלִילוּ דִּדְכוּרָא. וּבְגִין דְּאִיהוּ מִסִּטְרָא

דִּדְכוּרָא, יַתִּיר מִכָּל בְּנֵי עַלְמָא, אִתְקַיַּים בְּקִיּוּמֵיהּ יַתִּיר, וְלָא מִית כִּשְׁאָר בְּנֵי עַלְמָא, בְּגִין דְּכֹלָּא אִיהוּ מֵאִילָנָא דְחַיֵּי, וְלָא מִגּוֹ עַפְרָא, וּבְגִין דָּא אִסְתַּלַּק לְעֵילָא, וְלָא מִית כְּאֹרַח כָּל בְּנֵי עַלְמָא, דִּכְתִיב וַיַּעַל אֵלִיָּהוּ בִּסְעָרָה הַשָּׁמַיִם.

82. It is therefore written "for his Nefesh," instead of "to his Nefesh," for to (Heb. *et*) implies the female, THE NUKVA CALLED '*ET*', BUT 'FOR' ALLUDES TO THE MALE. You might say THAT IT IS WRITTEN, "for the woman He said" (Beresheet 3:16), WHO IS A FEMALE. HE REPLIED: It includes male and female, for when THE FEMALE is included within the male, then it is written, "for the woman He said," whereas "to the woman" indicates the female alone, not included with the male. Similarly, "for his Nefesh" indicates the male alone, whereas "to his Nefesh" indicates the female alone. Because Elijah is of the side of the male more than all other people in the world, he endured more than the others and did not die as did the other inhabitants of the world. For he comes from the Tree of Life and is not made of dust AS ARE THE REST OF MEN. He therefore ascended and did not die as do other people, as it is written, "and Elijah went up by a storm of wind into heaven" (II Melachim 2:11).

83. תָּא חֲזֵי, מַה כְּתִיב וְהִנֵּה רֶכֶב אֵשׁ וְסוּסֵי אֵשׁ וגו', דְּהָא כְּדֵין אִתְפַּשַּׁט גּוּפָא מִן רוּחָא, וְאִסְתַּלַּק דְּלָא כִּשְׁאָר אֹרַח בְּנֵי עַלְמָא, וְאִשְׁתְּאַר מַלְאֲכָא קַדִּישָׁא, כִּשְׁאָר קַדִּישֵׁי עֶלְיוֹנִין, וְעָבֵיד שְׁלִיחוּתָא בְּעַלְמָא, וְהָא אוֹקְמוּהָ, דְּנִסִּין דְּעָבֵד קוּדְשָׁא בְּרִיךְ הוּא בְּעַלְמָא, עַל יְדֵיהּ אִתְעֲבִידָן.

83. Come and behold the verse: "...a chariot of fire, and horses of fire" (I Melachim 2:11). The spirit shed the body, and he did not die the way of other men. He remained a holy angel like other sacred supernal beings, carrying messages in the world like an angel. It has already been explained that the miracles performed by the Holy One, blessed be He, are carried out by him.

84. וְתָא חֲזֵי, מַה כְּתִיב וַיִּשְׁאַל אֶת נַפְשׁוֹ, בְּקַדְמֵיתָא וַיֵּלֶךְ אֶל נַפְשׁוֹ,

כְּמָה דְּאִתְּמַר בְּקִיּוּמָא, וְהָכָא אֶת נַפְשׁוֹ לָמוּת, אִילָנָא דְּבֵיהּ שַׁרְיָא מוֹתָא, וְתַמָּן אִתְגְּלֵי עֲלֵיהּ קוּדְשָׁא בְּרִיךְ הוּא, כְּמָה דִּכְתִּיב צֵא וְעָמַדְתָּ בָהָר. מַה כְּתִיב בַּתְרֵיהּ, וְאַחַר הָרַעַשׁ אֵשׁ לֹא בָאֵשׁ ה׳ וְאַחַר הָאֵשׁ קוֹל דְּמָמָה דַקָּה, דָּא הוּא אֲתַר פְּנִימָאָה דְּכֹלָּא, דְּמִנֵּיהּ נָפְקִין כָּל נְהוֹרִין.

84. Come and behold the verse: "…and he requested for himself (lit. 'to his Nefesh') that he might die" (I Melachim 19:4), whereas previously it is written, "and went for his life (lit. 'for his Nefesh')" (Ibid.), which we have already explained alluded to his endurance. Here it is written, "to his Nefesh to die," to indicate the tree where death dwells, NAMELY, THE NUKVA, ACCORDING TO THE SECRET OF THE VERSE, "HER FEET GO DOWN TO DEATH" (MISHLEI 5:5). There the Holy One, blessed be He, revealed Himself to him, as it is written, "Go out and stand upon the mountain" (I Melachim 19:11), followed by the words, "and after the earthquake a fire; but Hashem was not in the fire: and after the fire a still small voice," which alludes to the innermost place, from where all lights radiate.

85. מַה כְּתִיב וַיְהִי כִּשְׁמֹעַ אֵלִיָּהוּ וַיָּלֶט פָּנָיו בְּאַדַּרְתּוֹ וְהִנֵּה אֵלָיו קוֹל וַיֹּאמֶר מַה לְּךָ פֹה אֵלִיָּהוּ וַיֹּאמֶר קַנֹּא קִנֵּאתִי, א״ל קוּדְשָׁא בְּרִיךְ הוּא עַד מָתַי אַתָּה מְקַנֵּא לִי, טְרַקְתְּ גַּלָּא דְּלָא יָכֵיל לְשַׁלְטָאָה בָּךְ מוֹתָא לְעָלְמָא, וְעַלְמָא לָא יָכֵיל לְמִסְבְּלָךְ עִם בָּנַי, א״ל כִּי עָזְבוּ בְרִיתְךָ בְּנֵי יִשְׂרָאֵל וגו׳. אֲמַר לֵיהּ חַיֶּיךָ, דִּבְכָל אֲתַר דִּבְנֵי יְקַיְּימוּ קְיָים קַדִּישָׁא, אַנְתְּ תְּהֵא זַמִּין תַּמָּן.

85. It is written, "And when Elijah heard it, he wrapped his face in his mantle...And, behold, there came a voice to him, and said: What are you doing here, Elijah? And he said: I have been very jealous" (I Melachim 19:13). The Holy One, blessed be He, said to him, "How long will you be jealous for Me." You have closed the door so that death will never have power over you and the world cannot tolerate your presence with My children, WHOM YOU ACCUSE. He answers, "because the children of Yisrael have forsaken your covenant" (Ibid. 14). He said: Upon your life, wherever people will observe the Holy Covenant, THAT IS, CIRCUMCISION, you shall be present.

86. תָּא חֲזֵי, מַה גָּרַם הַהִיא מִלָּה דְאֵלִיָּהוּ, דִּכְתִיב וְהִשְׁאַרְתִּי בְיִשְׂרָאֵל שִׁבְעַת אֲלָפִים כָּל הַבִּרְכַּיִם אֲשֶׁר לֹא כָרְעוּ לַבַּעַל וְכָל הַפֶּה אֲשֶׁר לֹא נָשַׁק לוֹ. אֲמַר לֵיהּ קוּדְשָׁא בְּרִיךְ הוּא, מִכָּאן וּלְהָלְאָה, דְּלָא יָכֵיל עָלְמָא לְמִסְבְּלָךְ עִם בָּנַי, וְאֶת אֱלִישָׁע בֶּן שָׁפָט מֵאָבֵל מְחוֹלָה תִּמְשַׁח לְנָבִיא תַּחְתֶּיךָ, יְהֵא נְבִיאָה אָחֲרָא לְגַבֵּי בָּנַי, וְאַתְּ תִּסְתַּלַּק לְאַתְרָךְ.

86. Come and behold what Elijah caused by his words. It is written, "Yet I will leave seven thousand in Yisrael, all the knees that have not bowed to the Baal, and every mouth that has not kissed him" (I Melachim 19:18). The Holy One, blessed be He, said to him, 'From now on, the world cannot endure you along with My children, BECAUSE YOU BRING ACCUSATIONS AGAINST THEM.' "...and Elijah the son of Shafat of Avel-mechola shall you anoint to be prophet in your place" (Ibid. 16). Thus, there will be another prophet for My children, and you shall go to your place.

87. וְתָא חֲזֵי, כָּל הַהוּא בַּר נָשׁ, דִּמְקַנֵּי לֵיהּ לְקוּדְשָׁא בְּרִיךְ הוּא, לָא יָכֵיל מַלְאֲכָא דְמוֹתָא לְשַׁלְטָאָה בֵּיהּ, כִּשְׁאַר בְּנֵי נָשָׁא, וְיִתְקַיֵּים בֵּיהּ שְׁלָם, וְהָא אוֹקְמוּהָ, כְּמָה דְאִתְּמָר בְּפִנְחָס, לָכֵן אֱמוֹר הִנְנִי נוֹתֵן לוֹ אֶת בְּרִיתִי שָׁלוֹם.

87. Come and behold: Any man who is jealous for the Holy One, blessed be He, is not subject to the power of the Angel of Death as are other men. Instead, peace is upon him, as was said of Pinchas: "Behold, I give to him My covenant of peace" (Bemidbar 25:12).

9. "And he fell on his brother Benjamin's neck and wept"

A Synopsis

The neck is like the Tower of David: it is not of this world, but rather of the celestial Jerusalem. Joseph weeps because he foresaw the destruction of the Temple and the exile of the tribes of Yisrael. He is able to see such things because the Holy Spirit dwells in him – although it does not dwell with his brothers. The destruction of the great Temple darkens the whole world, we learn. This was the painful foreknowledge Joseph was obliged to carry with him.

The Relevance of this Passage

Our planet contains many spiritual energy centers. These serve as portals through which the supernal Light of the Upper Worlds flows into our dimension. Israel, we are told, is the energy center of the entire planet. The city of Jerusalem is the energy source of Israel. The Holy Temple is the primal source of energy for Jerusalem. And the Holy of Holies is the Fountainhead of spiritual energy for the Temple. Reading this passage connects us to Jerusalem, the Temple, and ultimately to he Holy of Holies. This ensures that all our prayers, deeds, and meditations draw their appropriate Light from this wellspring of spiritual energy.

88. וַיִּפּוֹל עַל צַוְּארֵי בִּנְיָמִן אָחִיו וַיֵּבְךְּ וּבִנְיָמִן בָּכָה עַל צַוָּארָיו. רִבִּי יִצְחָק אֲמַר, הָא אוֹקְמוּהָ, דִּבְכָה עַל מִקְדָּשׁ רִאשׁוֹן וְעַל מִקְדָּשׁ שֵׁנִי.

88. "And he fell on his brother Benjamin's neck and wept; and Benjamin wept on his neck..." Rabbi Yitzchak said: It has been already explained that he wept for the first Temple and for the second Temple – THAT WILL BE BUILT ON BENJAMIN'S PORTION AND BE DESTROYED.

89. פְּתַח וַאֲמַר, כְּמִגְדַּל דָּוִד צַוָּארֵךְ בָּנוּי לְתַלְפִּיּוֹת אֶלֶף הַמָּגֵן תָּלוּי עָלָיו כֹּל שִׁלְטֵי הַגִּבּוֹרִים. כְּמִגְדַּל דָּוִד, מַאן מִגְדַּל דָּוִד. דָּא מִגְדַּל דָּוִד וַדַּאי, דִּבְנָה לֵיהּ דָּוִד, וְסָלֵיק לֵיהּ גּוֹ יְרוּשָׁלַיִם. אֶלָּא כְּמִגְדַּל דָּוִד, דָּא יְרוּשָׁלֵם דִּלְעֵילָּא, דִּכְתִּיב בֵּיהּ, מִגְדַּל עֹז שֵׁם ה׳ בּוֹ יָרוּץ צַדִּיק וְנִשְׂגָּב, מַאן נִשְׂגָּב. אֶלָּא הַהוּא מִגְדַּל נִשְׂגָּב, בְּגִין דְּבֵיהּ יָרוּץ צַדִּיק.

89. He opened the discussion with the verse, "Your neck is like the Tower of David built with turrets, on which there hang a thousand bucklers, all shields of mighty men" (Shir Hashirim 4:4). HE ASKS: What is the "Tower of David?" It is the Tower of David IN JERUSALEM that was built by David, NAMELY, THAT STANDS inside Jerusalem. Yet "the Tower of David" IN THE SCRIPTURE IS NOT THIS "TOWER OF DAVID," BUT is the celestial Jerusalem – NAMELY, THE NUKVA – about which it is written, "The name of Hashem is a strong tower: the righteous runs into it, and is set up on high" (Mishlei 18:10). HE ASKS: Who "is set up on high" – THE RIGHTEOUS OR THE TOWER? HE ANSWERS: the tower is, for into it the Righteous, YESOD, runs.

90. צַוָּארֵךְ: דָּא בֵּית מַקְדְּשָׁא דִלְתַתָּא, דְּאִיהוּ קָאֵים בְּתִקּוּנָא דְשַׁפִּירוּ, כְּקַדְלָא לְגוּפָא. מַה צַוָּאר, אִיהוּ שַׁפִּירוּ דְּכָל גּוּפָא, הָכֵי נָמֵי בֵּי מַקְדְּשָׁא, אִיהוּ שַׁפִּירוּ דְּכָל עַלְמָא.

90. "Your neck" is the Lower Temple, WHICH RESEMBLES THE TOWER OF DAVID, WHICH IS THE NUKVA AND IS SO CALLED because it is beautifully built, like the neck. As the neck symbolizes the beauty of the whole body, so the Temple symbolizes the beauty of the whole world.

91. בָּנוּי לְתַלְפִּיּוֹת, תִּלָּא דְּכָל בְּנֵי עַלְמָא הֲווֹ מִסְתַּכְּלָן בֵּיהּ, וְהָכֵי אוֹקְמוּהָ, תַּלְפִּיּוֹת: תֵּל דְּכָל פִּיּוֹת דְּעַלְמָא מְשַׁבְּחָן וּמְצַלָּאן לְגַבֵּיהּ.

91. The phrase, "built with turrets (Heb. *talpiot*)" means a hill on which all the children of the world look TO PRAISE AND TO PRAY. It has been explained that the word '*talpiot'* consists of the letters *Tel-Piot* (lit. 'a mound of mouths'). It is a mound which all the mouths of the world praise and pray.

92. אֶלֶף הַמָּגֵן תָּלוּי עָלָיו, אִלֵּין אֶלֶף תִּקּוּנִין, דְּמִתַּקְּנִין בֵּיהּ כִּדְקָא יָאוֹת. כֹּל שִׁלְטֵי הַגִּבּוֹרִים, דְּכֻלְּהוּ קָא אַתְיָין מִסִּטְרָא דְּדִינָא קַשְׁיָא.

92. The phrase, "on which there hang a thousand bucklers" (ibid.), refers to the thousand reconstructions fixed upon it, THAT IS, ON THE ILLUMINATION OF CHOCHMAH HINTED AT BY THE NUMBER ONE THOUSAND. AND "all shields of mighty men" are called thus because they come from the side of harsh Judgment.

93. מַה צַוָּאר כָּל תִּקּוּנִין דְּאִתְּתָא בֵּיהּ תַּלְיָין, כָּךְ בְּמַקְדְּשָׁא, כָּל תִּקּוּנִין דְּעַלְמָא, בֵּיהּ תַּלְיָין וְשַׁרְיָין. וְהָא אוֹקְמוּהָ, דִּכְתִיב עַל צַוָּארֵינוּ נִרְדָּפְנוּ, עַל בֵּי מַקְדְּשָׁא, דְּאִיהוּ צַוָּאר וְשַׁפִּירוּ דְּכָל עַלְמָא. נִרְדָּפְנוּ, יָגַעְנוּ, לְמִבְנֵי לֵיהּ תְּרֵין זִמְנִין, וְלֹא הוּנַּח לָנוּ, דְּהָא לָא שָׁבְקוּהָ לָן, וְאִתְחָרַב וְלָא אִתְבְּנֵי לְבָתַר.

93. As all a woman's jewels hang round her neck, so do all ornaments of the world hang about and dwell within the Temple. It has already been explained that the verse, "We are pursued to our necks" (Eichah 5:5) alludes to the Temple, which is the neck and beauty of the world. "We are pursued to our necks; we labor, AND HAVE NO REST," that labored building it twice – THE FIRST TEMPLE AND THE SECOND TEMPLE – "and have no rest," for we were not allowed any. The Temples were destroyed and not rebuilt.

94. מַה צַוָּאר, כֵּיוָן דְּאִשְׁתֵּצֵי, כָּל גּוּפָא אִשְׁתֵּצֵי עִמֵּיהּ, הָכֵי נָמֵי בֵּי מַקְדְּשָׁא, כֵּיוָן דְּאִיהוּ אִשְׁתֵּצֵי וְאִתְחַשַּׁךְ, כָּל עַלְמָא הָכֵי נָמֵי אִתְחַשַּׁךְ, וְלָא נָהֵיר שִׁמְשָׁא, וְלָא שְׁמַיָּא וְאַרְעָא וְכֹכְבַיָּא.

94. As when the neck is destroyed the whole body perishes, when the Temple was destroyed and darkened, the whole world became dark too, and the sun, heaven, earth, and stars did not shine.

95. בְּגִין כָּךְ, בָּכָה יוֹסֵף עַל דָּא. וּלְבָתַר דְּבָכָה עַל דָּא, בָּכָה עַל שִׁבְטִין דְּאִתְגָּלוּ, כַּד אִתְחָרֵיב בֵּי מַקְדְּשָׁא, כֻּלְּהוּ שִׁבְטִין אִתְגָּלוּ מִיָּד, וְאִתְבַּדְּרוּ בֵּינֵי עַמְמַיָּא, הה״ד וַיְנַשֵּׁק לְכָל אֶחָיו וַיֵּבְךְּ עֲלֵיהֶם, עֲלֵיהֶם וַדַּאי.

95. For that reason – FOR THE TWO TEMPLES THAT WERE DESTROYED – Joseph cried. After he wept for this, he wept for the tribes that went into exile. For shortly after the Temple was destroyed, all the tribes were sent into exile and dispersed among the nations, as it is written, "And he kissed all his brethren, and wept on them," meaning, on account of their GOING INTO EXILE.

96. עַל כֻּלָּם בָּכָה, עַל בֵּי מַקְדְּשָׁא דְּאִתְחָרֵיב תְּרֵין זִמְנִין, וְעַל אֲחוֹי עֲשֶׂרֶת הַשְּׁבָטִים, דְּאִתְגָּלוּ בְּגָלוּתָא, וְאִתְבַּדְּרוּן בֵּינֵי עַמְמַיָּא. וְאַחֲרֵי כֵן דִּבְּרוּ אֶחָיו אִתּוֹ, וְלָא כְתִיב וַיִּבְכּוּ, דְּהָא אִיהוּ בָּכָה, דְּנִצְנְצָה בֵּיהּ רוּחָא קַדִּישָׁא, וְאִינוּן לָא בָּכוּ, דְּלָא שָׁרָא עֲלַיְיהוּ רוּחַ קוּדְשָׁא.

96. He wept for everything – for the Temple that was twice destroyed and for his brothers, the ten tribes, who went into exile and were scattered among the nations. "...and after that his brethren talked with him," not 'wept'. He wept because the Holy Spirit come upon him AND HE SAW ALL THAT; but they did not weep, because the Holy Spirit did not dwell upon them – THEY DID NOT SEE IT.

10. "And the report was heard in Pharaoh's house"

A Synopsis

The Rabbis comment on the role of the voice in prayer. The hidden relationship between voice and Sfirot is explained by the fact that an inner voice can be heard, just as an outer one can – but the inner voice relates to the Sfirah of Zeir Anpin in a manner the heard voice does not. There are, we learn, many different voices, and those including the letter Vav ו, are heard differently from those without it. The rabbis conclude that when The Creator raises up the voice that is now without the Vav, the People shall come home from their long exile to worship Him at Jerusalem's holy mountain.

The Relevance of this Passage

Human speech is intimately tied to the Divine. The voice can summon forth both dark and Light forces. Different words and blessings resonate with the numerous supernal worlds that dwell on high, each realm bringing forth a particular ray of Divine Light to illuminate our existence. The ancient Kabbalists composed words and prayers that would radiate the brightest of Light in this world. This passage helps us stimulate the Light that shines in all supernal worlds. It inspires us to use our outer and inner voice to produce only positive energy.

97. וְהַקֹּל נִשְׁמַע בֵּית פַּרְעֹה. רִבִּי אַבָּא פְּתַח וַאֲמַר נִכְסְפָה וְגַם כָּלְתָה נַפְשִׁי לְחַצְרוֹת ה׳ לִבִּי וּבְשָׂרִי יְרַנְּנוּ אֶל אֵל חָי. תָּא חֲזֵי, כָּל בַּר נָשׁ דְּצַלֵּי צְלוֹתֵיהּ, קַמֵּי מָארֵיהּ, אִצְטְרִיךְ לֵיהּ, לְאַקְדָּמָא לֵיהּ בִּרְכָאן, בְּכָל יוֹמָא וְיוֹמָא, וּלְצַלֵּי צְלוֹתֵיהּ קַמֵּי מָארֵיהּ, בְּזִמְנָא דְּאִצְטְרִיךְ.

97. "...and the report (lit. 'voice') was heard in Pharaoh's house" (Beresheet 45:16). Rabbi Aba began the discussion with the verse, "My soul longs, indeed, it faints for the courts of Hashem: my heart and my flesh cry out from the living El" (Tehilim 84:3). Come and behold: When a man prays before his Master, he should first recite his daily blessings, and say his prayers at the proper times.

98. בְּצַפְרָא, לְאַחֲדָא בִּימִינָא דְּקוּדְשָׁא בְּרִיךְ הוּא. בְּמִנְחָה, לְאַחֲדָא בִּשְׂמָאלָא. וּצְלוֹתָא וּבָעוּתָא, אִצְטְרִיךְ לֵיהּ לְבַר נָשׁ, בְּכָל יוֹמָא וְיוֹמָא, בְּגִין לְאִתְאַחֲדָא בֵּיהּ, וְאוֹקִימְנָא, מַאן דְּצַלֵּי צְלוֹתֵיהּ, קַמֵּי מָארֵיהּ,

אִצְטְרִיךְ לֵיהּ, דְּלָא לְמִשְׁמַע קָלֵיהּ בִּצְלוֹתֵיהּ, וּמַאן דְּאַשְׁמַע קָלֵיהּ בִּצְלוֹתֵיהּ, צְלוֹתֵיהּ לָא אִשְׁתְּמַע.

98. In the morning, he is to be united with the right of the Holy One, blessed be He, WHICH IS CHESED. At Minchah (the afternoon prayer) he is to be united with the left OF THE HOLY ONE, BLESSED BE HE. It behooves man to pray daily, so as to be united with the Holy One, blessed be He, as has already been explained. When he prays before his Master, he must not speak out loud, for whoever speaks out loud will find his prayer is not accepted.

99. מ"ט. בְּגִין דִּצְלוֹתָא, לָאו אִיהִי הַהִיא קָלָא דְּאִשְׁתְּמַע, דְּהַהוּא קוֹל דְּאִשְׁתְּמַע לָאו הִיא צְלוֹתָא. וּמַאן אִיהִי צְלוֹתָא. דָּא קָלָא אָחֳרָא, דְּתַלְיָא בְּקָלָא דְּאִשְׁתְּמַע, וּמַאן הוּא קָלָא דְּאִשְׁתְּמַע. דָּא הַהוּא קוֹל דְּהוּא בְּוא"ו, קָלָא דְּתַלְיָא בֵּיהּ, דָּא הַהוּא קֹל בְּלָא וא"ו.

99. Why? Because the prayer is not an audible voice (Heb. *kol*), nor is the audible voice a prayer. What is then a prayer? It is a different voice that is attached to the voice that is heard. What is the voice that is heard? It is *Kol* spelled with the letter *Vav*, whereas the voice attached TO THE VOICE THAT IS HEARD is *kol* without the letter *Vav*.

100. וּבְגִין כָּךְ, לָא אִצְטְרִיךְ לֵיהּ לְבַר נָשׁ, לְמִשְׁמַע קָלֵיהּ בִּצְלוֹתֵיהּ, אֶלָּא לְצַלָּאָה בְּלַחַשׁ, בְּהַהוּא קָלָא דְּלָא אִשְׁתְּמַע, וְדָא הִיא צְלוֹתָא דְּאִתְקַבְּלַת תָּדִיר, וְסִימָנֵיךְ וְהַקֹּל נִשְׁמַע, קֹל בְּלָא וא"ו, נִשְׁמַע. דָּא הִיא צְלוֹתָא דְּהִיא בַּחֲשַׁאי, דִּכְתִּיב בְּחַנָּה, וְקוֹלָהּ לֹא יִשָּׁמַע, דָּא הִיא צְלוֹתָא דְּקוּדְשָׁא בְּרִיךְ הוּא קַבִּיל, כַּד אִתְעֲבִיד גּוֹ רְעוּתָא, וְכַוָּונָה, וְתִקּוּנָא כִּדְקָא יָאוֹת, וּלְיַחֲדָא יִחוּדָא דְּמָרֵיהּ כִּדְקָא יָאוֹת בְּכָל יוֹמָא.

100. Thus, a man should never speak out loud when he prays, but pray in a whisper, in a voice unheard, WHICH IS AN ASPECT OF THE NUKVA, THE SECRET OF PRAYER. BY OUR PRAYERS WE UNITE THE STILL VOICE WITH ZEIR ANPIN, WHICH IS THE AUDIBLE VOICE. This prayer is always accepted, BECAUSE IT IS DESIROUS OF BEING UNITED WITH ZEIR ANPIN.

This is learned from the words, "and the voice was heard," spelled without the letter Vav, in which the words "is heard" MEANS IT WAS ACCEPTED. This is a prayer said in a whisper, as is written of Hanah, "but her voice was not heard" (I Shmuel 1:13). This is the prayer that the Holy One, blessed be He, accepts – a prayer that is made willingly and intentionally, and is properly performed by a man concerned with the unity of his Master every day in the proper manner.

101. רִבִּי אֶלְעָזָר אֲמַר, קָלָא בַּחֲשַׁאי, דָּא הִיא קָלָא עִלָּאָה, דְּכָל קָלִין נָפְקִין מִתַּמָּן. אֲבָל קֹל בְּלָא ו׳, דָּא הִיא צְלוֹתָא דִלְתַתָּא, דְּאִיהִי אָזְלָא לְאִסְתַּלְּקָא בְּוא״ו, וּלְאִתְחַבְּרָא בֵּיהּ.

101. Rabbi Elazar said: A secret voice is the supernal voice, NAMELY, THE VOICE IN BINAH, from which all voices are derived. But a voice without the letter *Vav* is the prayer below, NAMELY, THE NUKVA, about to rise and be elevated to the *Vav*, WHICH IS ZEIR ANPIN, and be joined with him – TO RECEIVE CHASSADIM FROM HIM.

102. תָּא חֲזֵי, וְהַקֹּל נִשְׁמַע, דָּא הוּא קֹל בְּלָא וא״ו, דָּא הִיא קָלָא, דְּבָכַאת עַל מִקְדָּשׁ רִאשׁוֹן, וְעַל מִקְדָּשׁ שֵׁנִי. נִשְׁמַע: כְּמָה דְאַתְּ אָמֵר, קוֹל בְּרָמָה נִשְׁמָע. בְּרָמָה, מַאי בְּרָמָה. דָּא הוּא עַלְמָא עִלָּאָה, עַלְמָא דְאָתֵי, וְסִימָנֵיךְ מִן הָרָמָה וְעַד בֵּית אֵל, מִן הָעוֹלָם וְעַד הָעוֹלָם, הָכָא בְּרָמָה, דָּא עַלְמָא עִלָּאָה, דְּהָא בְּהַהִיא שַׁעְתָּא, דִּי בְּרָמָה נִשְׁמַע, כְּדֵין מַה כְּתִיב, וַיִּקְרָא ה׳ אֱלֹקִים צְבָאוֹת בַּיּוֹם הַהוּא לִבְכִּי וּלְמִסְפֵּד וגו׳.

102. Come and behold: "and the voice was heard." This is the voice without the letter *Vav*, NAMELY, THE NUKVA WHEN SEPARATED FROM ZEIR ANPIN – the voice that weeps for the first Temple and the second Temple. It is "heard" as it is written, "A voice was heard in Rama" (Yirmeyah 31:14). HE ASKS: What is "in Rama (lit. 'on high')?" HE REPLIED: It is the Supernal World, the World to Come, BINAH. This is derived from "between Rama and Bethel" (Shoftim 4:5), which means, "from everlasting to everlasting (lit. 'from world to world')." THAT IS, FROM BINAH CALLED 'RAMA', THE SUPERNAL WORLD, TO THE NUKVA CALLED 'BETHEL', THE LOWER WORLD. HERE TOO, "in Rama" refers to the Supernal World,

BINAH, for when it was heard in Rama, then it is written, "And on that day did Hashem Elohim Tzva'ot call to weeping, and to mourning" (Yeshayah 22:12).

103. וְהַקֹּל נִשְׁמַע, לְעֵילָא לְעֵילָא. מ"ט. בְּגִין, דְּוא"ו אִתְרַחַק וְאִסְתַּלַּק מִנֵּיהּ, וּכְדֵין רָחֵל מְבַכָּה עַל בָּנֶיהָ מֵאֲנָה לְהִנָּחֵם עַל בָּנֶיהָ כִּי אֵינֶנּוּ. כִּי אֵינֶנּוּ, כִּי אֵינָם מִבָּעֵי לֵיהּ. אֶלָּא כִּי אֵינֶנּוּ, וְהָא אוֹקִימְנָא, כִּי אֵינֶנּוּ: דְּבַעֲלָהּ לָא אִשְׁתַּכַּח עִמָּהּ, דְּאִלְמָלֵא בַּעֲלָהּ יִשְׁתַּכַּח עִמָּהּ, תִּתְנַחֵם עֲלַיְיהוּ, דְּהָא כְּדֵין בְּנָהָא, לָא יְהוֹן בְּגָלוּתָא, וּבְגִין דְּאֵינֶנּוּ, לָאו אִיהִי מִתְנַחֲמָא עַל בְּנָהָא, בְּגִין דִּבְנָהָא אִתְרַחֲקוּ מִנָּהּ, עַל דְּאֵינֶנּוּ עִמָּהּ.

103. "...and the voice was heard high" above, AND THEN BOTH TEMPLES WERE DESTROYED. Why WERE THEY DESTROYED? Because the letter *Vav* was gone from THE NUKVA. THUS THEY WERE SEPARATED FROM END TO END. Then it is written, "Rachel weeping for her children; she refused to be comforted for her children because he is not" (Yirmeyah 31:14). ALL HER LIGHTS WERE STOPPED, AND BECAUSE SHE THEREFORE HAD NOTHING TO GIVE TO HER CHILDREN, THEY WENT INTO EXILE. HE ASKS: WHY DOES THE VERSE READ, "because he is not," instead of, 'they are not' – THAT IS, IN THE PLURAL. HE REPLIED: It is written, "he is not," as we explained, because her husband is not with her. If her husband, ZEIR ANPIN, had been with her, she would have been comforted for her children, HER LIGHT WOULD HAVE NOT BEEN STOPPED, and her children would not be in exile. But because "he is not" with her, she is not comforted for her children, and they were removed from her.

104. תָּא חֲזֵי בֵּית פַּרְעֹה, דָּא הוּא סִימָנֵיךְ לְעֵילָא, בֵּיתָא דְּאִתְפְּרָעוּ וְאִתְגַּלְיָין מִנֵּיהּ כָּל נְהוֹרִין, וְכָל בּוּצִינִין, כָּל מַה דַּהֲוָה סָתִים, מִתַּמָּן אִתְגְּלֵי, וּבְג"כ, קוּדְשָׁא בְּרִיךְ הוּא אַפֵּיק כָּל נְהוֹרִין, וְכָל בּוּצִינִין, בְּגִין לְאַנְהָרָא לְהַהוּא קוֹל, דְּאִקְרֵי קֹל בְּלָא וא"ו.

104. Come and behold: "in Pharaoh's house" alludes to on high, BINAH, which is the house from which the lights and candles are revealed. IT ALLUDES TO THE SFIROT OF THE NUKVA CALLED 'CANDLES'. All that was hidden, is there revealed. Therefore BINAH IS CALLED 'THE HOUSE OF

PHARAOH'. The Holy One, blessed be He, then brings out all the lights and candles to shine on the voice spelled without the letter *Vav*, WHICH IS THE NUKVA.

105. תָּא חֲזֵי כַּד יָקִים קוּדְשָׁא בְּרִיךְ הוּא לְהַאי קָל מֵעַפְרָא, וְיִתְחַבַּר בְּוא"ו, כְּדֵין כָּל מַה דְּאִתְאֲבֵיד מִנַּיְיהוּ בְּזִמְנָא דְגָלוּתָא, יִתְהֲדַר וְיִתְעַדְּנוּן בִּנְהוֹרִין עִלָּאִין, דְּאִתּוֹסְפָן מִגּוֹ עַלְמָא עִלָּאָה, כְּד"א וְהָיָה בַּיּוֹם הַהוּא יִתָּקַע בְּשׁוֹפָר גָּדוֹל וּבָאוּ הָאוֹבְדִים בְּאֶרֶץ אַשּׁוּר וְהַנִּדָּחִים בְּאֶרֶץ מִצְרַיִם וְהִשְׁתַּחֲווּ לַה' בְּהַר הַקֹּדֶשׁ בִּירוּשָׁלָם.

105. Come and behold: When the Holy One, blessed be He, raises this voice, THE NUKVA, from the dust, it will join the *Vav*, WHICH IS ZEIR ANPIN. Then all that was lost TO YISRAEL at the time of exile will be returned to them. They will feast upon the supernal lights added to them from the Supernal World, as it is written, "And it shall come to pass on that day, that a great shofar shall be blown, and they who were lost in the land of Ashur, and the outcasts in the land of Egypt, shall come and worship Hashem in the holy mountain at Jerusalem" (Yeshayah 27:13).

11. "Take wagons...for your little ones"

A Synopsis

The rabbis explore the meaning of the separation of The Creator and the Shechinah – the female Divine presence – from the people of Yisrael. This parallels the separation of Joseph from Jacob. Jacob's realization that Joseph is alive continues this parallel, revealing what will come about when The Creator and the Shechinah reunite with the people.

The Relevance of this Passage

The energy summoned forth through meditation upon these Hebrew letters hastens the ultimate unification of the Shechinah and The Creator – the souls of man and the Divine. In addition, we arouse the Light of protection and joy that emanates from the Shechinah.

106. וְאַתָּה צֻוֵּיתָה זֹאת עֲשׂוּ קְחוּ לָכֶם מֵאֶרֶץ מִצְרַיִם וגו'. רִבִּי חִיָּיא פָּתַח, שִׂמְחוּ אֶת יְרוּשָׁלַיִם וְגִילוּ בָהּ כָּל אוֹהֲבֶיהָ שִׂישׂוּ אִתָּהּ מָשׂוֹשׂ וגו'. תָּא חֲזֵי, כַּד אִתְחָרַב בֵּי מַקְדְּשָׁא, וְגָרְמוּ חוֹבִין, וְאִתְגָּלוּ יִשְׂרָאֵל מֵאַרְעָא, אִסְתַּלַּק קוּדְשָׁא בְּרִיךְ הוּא לְעֵילָּא, וְלָא אַשְׁגַּח עַל חָרוּב בֵּי מַקְדְּשָׁא, וְעַל עַמֵּיהּ דְּאִתְגָּלוּ, וּכְדֵין שְׁכִינְתָּא אִתְגַּלְיָיא עִמְּהוֹן.

106. "Now, you are commanded, do this: take wagons out of the land of Egypt" (Beresheet 45:19). Rabbi Chiya opened the discussion with the verse, "Rejoice with Jerusalem, and be glad with her, all you that love her, rejoice for joy with her" (Yeshayah 66:10). Come and behold: When the Temple was destroyed and Yisrael were exiled from their land because of their sins, the Holy One, blessed be He, was gone up high and did not notice the destruction of the Temple or His exiled people. The Shechinah then went into exile with them.

107. כַּד נָחַת, אַשְׁגַּח עַל בֵּיתֵיהּ דְּאִתּוֹקַד, אִסְתַּכַּל עַל עַמֵּיהּ, וְהָא אִתְגְּלֵי, שָׁאַל עַל מַטְרוֹנִיתָא, וְאִתְתָּרְכַת, כְּדֵין וַיִּקְרָא ה' אֱלֹקִים צְבָאוֹת בַּיּוֹם הַהוּא לִבְכִי וּלְמִסְפֵּד וּלְקָרְחָה וְלַחֲגֹר שָׂק, וְהִיא גַּם הִיא מַה כְּתִיב בָּהּ, אֱלִי כִּבְתוּלָה חֲגֻרַת שַׂק עַל בַּעַל נְעוּרֶיהָ, כְּד"א כִּי אֵינֶנּוּ, בְּגִין דְּאִסְתַּלַּק מִינָהּ, וְאִשְׁתַּכַּח פֵּרוּדָא.

107. When He descended, He saw that his House was burnt. He looked for

His people and behold, they were in exile. He asked for the Lady, NAMELY, THE SHECHINAH, and learned that She was exiled. Then, it is written, "And on that day did Hashem Elohim Tzva'ot call to weeping, and to mourning, and to baldness, and to girding with sackcloth" (Yeshayah 22:12). And OF THE SHECHINAH, it is written, "Lament like a virgin girded with sackcloth for the husband of her youth" (Yoel 1:8), because "he is gone," NAMELY, HER HUSBAND. For He went away from Her, and they are apart.

108. וַאֲפִילוּ שְׁמַיָא וְאַרְעָא, כֻּלְּהוּ אִתְאַבָּלוּ, דִּכְתִיב אַלְבִּישׁ שָׁמַיִם קַדְרוּת וְשַׂק אָשִׂים כְּסוּתָם. מַלְאֲכֵי עִלָּאֵי, כֻּלְּהוּ אִתְאַבָּלוּ עֲלֵיהּ, דִּכְתִיב הֵן אֶרְאֶלָּם צָעֲקוּ חֻצָה מַלְאֲכֵי שָׁלוֹם מַר יִבְכָּיוּן. שִׁמְשָׁא וְסִיהֲרָא אִתְאַבָּלוּ, וְחָשְׁכוּ נְהוֹרֵיהוֹן, דִּכְתִיב חָשַׁךְ הַשֶּׁמֶשׁ בְּצֵאתוֹ וגו׳, וְכֹלָּא עִלָּאֵי וְתַתָּאֵי, בָּכוּ עֲלָהּ וְאִתְאַבָּלוּ. מ״ט, בְּגִין דְּשָׁלְטָא עֲלָהּ סִטְרָא אָחֳרָא, דְּשָׁלְטָא עַל אַרְעָא קַדִּישָׁא.

108. Even heaven and earth themselves mourned, as it is written, "I clothe the heavens with blackness and I make sackcloth their covering" (Yeshayah 50:3). All the high angels mourned for Her, as it is written, "Behold, the mighty ones shall cry outside; the angels of peace weep bitterly" (Yeshayah. 33:7). The sun and moon were in mourning, their lights darkened, as it is written, "the sun shall be darkened in his going forth" (Yeshayah 13:10). Everyone high and low wept for Her and mourned, because the Other Side reigned over Her, on the Holy Land.

109. פָּתַח וַאֲמַר, וְאַתָּה בֶן אָדָם כֹּה אָמַר ה׳ אֱלֹקִים לְאַדְמַת יִשְׂרָאֵל קֵץ בָּא הַקֵּץ עַל אַרְבַּע כַּנְפוֹת הָאָרֶץ, הַאי קְרָא רָזָא עִלָּאָה אִיהוּ, לְאַדְמַת יִשְׂרָאֵל קֵץ מַאי אִיהוּ, וְכִי אַדְמַת יִשְׂרָאֵל קֵץ הִיא. אֶלָּא הָכֵי הוּא וַדַּאי וְאִתְּמָר, קֵץ אִיהוּ לִימִינָא, קֵץ אִיהוּ לִשְׂמָאלָא. קֵץ לִימִינָא: דִּכְתִיב לְקֵץ הַיָּמִין. קֵץ לִשְׂמָאלָא: דִּכְתִיב, קֵץ שָׂם לַחשֶׁךְ וּלְכָל תַּכְלִית הוּא חוֹקֵר, וְדָא הוּא, קֵץ כָּל בָּשָׂר, כְּמָה דְּאִתְּמָר.

109. He opened the discussion with the verse, "you son of man, thus says Hashem Elohim to the land of Yisrael: An end, the end is come upon the four corners of the land" (Yechezkel 7:2). This verse contains a deep mystery. What does "to the land of Yisrael: An end" mean? Does it mean an end to the land of Yisrael? HE ANSWERS: Surely this is true, as we have learned. There is an end on the right and an end on the left. HE EXPLAINED: An end on the right, as it is written, "at the end of days (lit. 'right')" (Daniel 12:13), and an end on the left, as it is written, "He puts an end to darkness, and searches out all perfection" (Iyov 28:3). This is the end of all flesh, as we have learned.

110. קֵץ דִּימִינָא, הַיְינוּ דִּכְתִּיב לְאַדְמַת יִשְׂרָאֵל קֵץ. בָּא הַקֵּץ, דָּא קֵץ דִּשְׂמָאלָא. קֵץ דִּימִינָא: דָּא קֵץ דְּיֵצֶר הַטּוֹב. קֵץ דִּשְׂמָאלָא: דָּא קֵץ דְּיֵצֶר הָרָע, וְדָא אִיהוּ, דְּכַד חוֹבִין גָּרְמוּ וְאִתְגַּבְּרוּ, אִתְגְּזַר וְאִתְיְיהֵיב שָׁלְטָנָא לְמַלְכוּת הָרְשָׁעָה לְשַׁלְטָאָה, וּלְחָרְבָא בֵּיתֵיהּ וּמִקְדְּשֵׁיהּ, וְדָא הוּא דִּכְתִּיב, כֹּה אָמַר ה' אֱלֹקִים רָעָה אַחַר רָעָה הִנֵּה בָאָה, וְכֹלָּא חַד.

110. The end on the right is written of in the verse, "to the land of Yisrael: an end." "...the end is come UPON THE FOUR CORNERS OF THE LAND" refers to the end on the left. The end on the right is the end through the Good Inclination, and the end on the left is the end through the Evil Inclination, which happened when, through the increase in sins, it was decreed that the evil kingdom would be given permission to rule and destroy His house and Temple, as it is written, "Thus says Hashem Elohim! An evil, a singular evil, behold, is come" (Yechezkel 7:5).

111. וּבְגַ"כ, אִתְאַבָּלוּ עִלָּאֵי וְתַתָּאֵי, עַל דְּאִתְיְיהֵיב שָׁלְטָנוּ לְהַאי קֵץ דִּשְׂמָאלָא, וּבְגִין כָּךְ, כֵּיוָן דְּמַלְכוּ קַדִּישָׁא, מַלְכוּת שָׁמַיִם אִתְכַּפְיָא, וּמַלְכוּת חַיָּיבָא אִתְגַּבַּר, אִית לֵיהּ לְכָל בַּר נָשׁ, לְאִתְאַבְּלָא עִמָּהּ, וּלְאִתְכַּפְיָא עִמָּהּ, וּבְגִין דְּכַד אִיהִי יִזְדַּקְּפָא, וְעַלְמָא יִתְחַדֵּי, יִתְחַדֵּי אִיהוּ בַּהֲדָהּ, דִּכְתִּיב שִׂישׂוּ אִתָּהּ מָשׂוֹשׂ כָּל הַמִּתְאַבְּלִים עָלֶיהָ.

111. Therefore there was mourning above and below, for reign was given to the end of the left. Thus, because the Kingdom of Holiness, the kingdom of heaven, was humbled and the kingdom of evil prevailed, it behooves any man to mourn with it, THE HOLY KINGDOM, and be abased with it. Also, when the Holy Kingdom rises, and the world rejoices, he shall also rejoice with her, as it is written, "rejoice for joy with it, all you that did mourn for her" (Yeshayah 66:10).

112. תָּא חֲזֵי, כְּתִיב בְּהוֹ בְּמִצְרַיִם, עֶגְלָה יְפֵיפִיָּה מִצְרַיִם, וְרָזָא דְּעֶגְלָה דָּא, הֲווֹ יִשְׂרָאֵל תְּחוֹת שָׁלְטָנֵיהּ, כַּמָּה זִמְנִין, וְכַמָּה שְׁנִין, וּבְגִין דִּזְמִינִין יִשְׂרָאֵל לְשַׁלְטָאָה לְבָתַר עֲלָהּ, אִתְרְמִיז לוֹן הַשְׁתָּא עֲגָלוֹת.

112. Come and behold: It is written of Egypt "a very fair heifer" (Yirmeyah 46:20), and it is because of the secret of this heifer that Yisrael were under its rule for many years – THAT IS, FOR THE 210 YEARS THEY LIVED IN EGYPT. Because Yisrael would eventually rule over it in the future, they were now given a hint of this IN THE VERSE, "TAKE wagons (also: 'heifers') OUT OF THE LAND OF EGYPT FOR YOUR LITTLE ONES..." (BERESHEET 45:19).

113. רִבִּי אֶלְעָזָר אֲמַר, רֶמֶז רָמַז לֵיהּ יוֹסֵף לְיַעֲקֹב, עַל עֶגְלָה עֲרוּפָה, דְּהָא בְּהַהוּא פִּרְקָא אִתְפְּרַשׁ מִנֵּיהּ. וְאוֹקְמוּהָ, עֶגְלָה עֲרוּפָה, דְּאִיהִי אַתְיָא עַל דְּאִשְׁתַּכַּח קְטוֹלָא, וְלָא אִתְיְידַע מַאן קָטִיל לֵיהּ, וּבְגִין דְּלָא יִשְׁלְטוּן עַל אַרְעָא רוּחִין בִּישִׁין דְּלָא אִצְטְרִיכוּ, יַהֲבִין הַאי עֶגְלָה לְתִקּוּנָא, בְּגִין דְּלָא יִשְׁתְּמוֹדְעוּן לְגַבֵּיהּ, וְלָא יִשְׁלְטוּ עֲלַיְיהוּ.

113. Rabbi Elazar said: Joseph reminded Jacob about breaking the heifer's neck, because he went away from him when they were studying this text. It has been explained that the ritual of the heifer was carried out when a man was found slain, but the killer was not known. The heifer is then offered to pacify the evil spirits, so they would not recognize him or rule over THE LAND.

114. תָּא חֲזֵי, כָּל בְּנֵי נָשָׁא כֻּלְּהוּ עָבְרִין ע״י דְּמַלְאַךְ הַמָּוֶת, בַּר מֵהַאי, דְּאַקְדִּימוּ לֵיהּ בְּנֵי נָשָׁא, עַד לָא יִמְטֵי זִמְנָא, לְשַׁלְטָאָה בֵּיהּ, וְלִיטוֹל רְשׁוּ, דְּהָא לָא שַׁלִּיט בְּבַר נָשׁ, עַד דְּנָטִיל רְשׁוּ.

114. Come and behold: All men die by the Angel of Death, except someone who is killed by other men before the time has arrived FOR THE ANGEL OF DEATH to take hold of him and receive permission TO TAKE HIS SOUL, for the Angel of Death does not have dominion over man until he is given permission FROM ABOVE.

115. וּבְגִ"כ, אִית לֵיהּ דִּינָא לְשַׁלְטָאָה, עַל הַהוּא אֲתַר, כְּמָה דְּאַתְּ אָמֵר, לֹא נוֹדַע מִי הִכָּהוּ, ה"נ אִית לֵיהּ דִּינָא דְּלָא אִתְיְידַע, בְּגִין לְקַטְרְגָא עַל הַהוּא אֲתַר, וְע"ד וְלָקְחוּ זִקְנֵי הָעִיר הַהִיא עֶגְלַת בָּקָר וגו'. בְּגִין לְאַעֲבְרָא דִּינֵיהּ דְּהַהוּא אֲתַר, וּלְאִתְתַּקְּנָא דְּלָא יִשְׁלוֹט בֵּיהּ מְקַטְרְגָא, וּלְאִשְׁתֵּזָבָא מִנֵּיהּ.

115. Therefore the Angel of Death has the right to rule over him, as it is written, "and it be not known who has slain him" (Devarim 21:1). He also has permission, since it is unknown WHO HAS SLAIN THE VICTIM, to accuse that place, THE NUKVA. Therefore "the elders of that city shall take a heifer" (Ibid. 3), in order to remove judgment from that place and to fortify it against the Accuser's power, so it shall be saved from him.

116. תָּא חֲזֵי, יוֹסֵף כַּד אִתְפְּרַשׁ מֵאֲבוֹי, בְּלָא לְוָיָה, וּבְלָא אֲכִילָה אִשְׁתַּדַּר, וַהֲוָה מַה דַּהֲוָה, וְכַד אֲמַר יַעֲקֹב, טָרוֹף טוֹרַף יוֹסֵף, אֲמַר כִּי אֵרֵד אֶל בְּנִי אָבֵל שְׁאוֹלָה, דַּאֲנָא גָּרֵימְנָא לֵיהּ. וְתוּ, דַּהֲוֵינָא יָדַע דַּאֲחוֹי סַנְיָין לֵיהּ, וְשַׁדַּרְנָא לֵיהּ, וְרֶמֶז קָא רָמִיז לֵיהּ.

116. Come and behold: When Joseph parted from his father, he was sent without escort or without food, and whatever happened then happened. When Jacob said: "Joseph is without doubt torn in pieces" (Beresheet 37:33), he added, "For I will go down to my son mourning into Sheol" (Ibid. 35), for I caused him TO BE KILLED, HAVING SENT HIM WITHOUT ESCORT. I CANNOT SAY, "OUR HANDS HAVE NOT SHED THIS BLOOD" (DEVARIM 21:7) CONCERNING THE BREAKING OF THE HEIFER'S NECK, WHICH MEANS, "WE HAVE NOT SENT HIM UNESCORTED." I also knew his brothers hated him, yet I sent him TO THEM. JOSEPH reminded him OF THAT BY SENDING THE WAGONS (BOTH 'WAGONS' AND 'HEIFERS' ARE WRITTEN '*AGALOT*' IN HEBREW).

117. א"ל רִבִּי יְהוּדָה, אִינוּן עֲגָלוֹת ע"פ פַּרְעֹה שַׁדַּר לוֹן, דִּכְתִּיב וַיִּתֵּן לָהֶם יוֹסֵף עֲגָלוֹת עַל פִּי פַּרְעֹה. א"ל, דִּיּוּקָא דְמִלָּה, דִּכְתִּיב וְאַתָּה צֻוֵּיתָה זֹאת עֲשׂוּ. וְאַתָּה צֻוֵּיתָה דַּיְיקָא, וּבְג"כ כְּתִיב בְּה"א, מַשְׁמַע דְּיוֹסֵף תָּבַע לוֹן, וּבְג"כ וַיִּתֵּן לָהֶם יוֹסֵף עֲגָלוֹת עַל פִּי פַּרְעֹה. וְיַעֲקֹב לָא אִתְקַיַּים בְּמִלָּה, עַד דְּחָמָא לוֹן, דִּכְתִּיב וַיַּרְא אֶת הָעֲגָלוֹת אֲשֶׁר שָׁלַח יוֹסֵף לָשֵׂאת אוֹתוֹ וַתְּחִי רוּחַ יַעֲקֹב אֲבִיהֶם.

117. Rabbi Yehuda responded that the wagons were sent by the command of Pharaoh, as it is written, "and Joseph gave them wagons, according to the commandment of Pharaoh" (Beresheet 45:21). HOW CAN YOU THEN SAY THAT JOSEPH GAVE THEM A HINT BY SENDING THE WAGONS? RABBI ELAZAR replied: It is derived from the exact meaning of the verse, "Now you are commanded, do this," WHICH IS REDUNDANT, AS IT WAS PREVIOUSLY WRITTEN, "AND PHARAOH SAID TO JOSEPH, SAY TO YOUR BRETHREN..." YET "Now you are commanded" has a specific meaning and is therefore spelled with the letter *Hei* AT THE END. THIS TEACHES US THAT ITS EXACT MEANING IS that Joseph asked him TO GIVE HIM WAGONS. Thus, "and Joseph gave them wagons (also: 'heifers'), according to the commandment of Pharaoh," FOR IT WAS JOSEPH WHO GAVE, WHO ASKED OF PHARAOH. WHY DID HE DEMAND WAGONS OF PHARAOH? BECAUSE HE WISHED TO REMIND HIS FATHER OF THE PASSAGE OF THE BREAKING OF THE HEIFER'S NECK. Jacob therefore did not believe it until he saw the wagons AND TOOK THE HINT, as it is written, "and when he saw the wagons which Joseph had sent to carry him, the spirit of Jacob their father revived."

118. אר"ש, בְּקַדְמֵיתָא וַתְּחִי רוּחַ יַעֲקֹב, וּלְבָתַר וַיֹּאמֶר יִשְׂרָאֵל רַב עוֹד יוֹסֵף בְּנִי חָי. אֶלָּא בְּקַדְמֵיתָא קָרֵי לֵיהּ אוֹרַיְיתָא יַעֲקֹב, בְּגִין שׁוּתָּפוּתָא, דְּאִשְׁתַּתְּפוּ שְׁכִינְתָּא בְּהַהוּא חֵרֶם, כַּד אִזְדַּבַּן יוֹסֵף, וְהַשְׁתָּא דִּשְׁכִינְתָּא סָלְקָא, כְּדֵין אִיהוּ, וַתְּחִי רוּחַ יַעֲקֹב אֲבִיהֶם, וְדָא הוּא רָזָא דִּשְׁכִינְתָּא, וּבָתַר דְּאִיהִי קָיְימָא בְּקִיּוּמָא, כְּדֵין דַּרְגָּא דִלְעֵילָא, אִתְעֲבַר לְגַבָּהּ, דַּרְגָּא דְּאִיהוּ יִשְׂרָאֵל. מִכָּאן, דְּדַרְגָּא דִלְעֵילָא, לָא אִתְעַר לְעֵילָא, עַד דְּאִתְעַר בְּקַדְמֵיתָא לְתַתָּא, דְּהָא הָכָא וַתְּחִי רוּחַ יַעֲקֹב בְּקַדְמֵיתָא, וּלְבָתַר וַיֹּאמֶר יִשְׂרָאֵל.

118. Rabbi Shimon said: First it is written, "and the spirit of Jacob their father revived," and then it is written, "and Yisrael said: It is enough; Joseph my son is still alive." WHY DOES THE VERSE START WITH JACOB AND FINISH WITH YISRAEL? HE REPLIED: First the Torah calls him Jacob because the Shechinah took part in the vow THAT THE TRIBES TOOK NOT TO REVEAL THAT Joseph was sold. THE SHECHINAH WAS THEREFORE GONE FROM JACOB ALL THAT TIME. Now that the Shechinah has come back to him, it is written, "and the spirit of Jacob their father revived," which is the secret of the Shechinah, CALLED 'THE SPIRIT OF JACOB'. After THE SHECHINAH was established in him, the high grade went from the grade of Jacob to the grade Yisrael. From this we learn that the high grade is not awakened above until there is an awakening below. For here it is written, "and the spirit of Jacob their father revived first," WHICH REFERS TO THE AWAKENING BELOW, and then it is written, "and Yisrael said," WHICH IS THE AWAKENING ABOVE.

119. וַיֹּאמֶר אֱלֹקִים לְיִשְׂרָאֵל בְּמַרְאֹת הַלַּיְלָה, בְּמַרְאַת כְּתִיב. תָּא חֲזֵי, וַיִּזְבַּח זְבָחִים לֵאלֹהֵי אָבִיו יִצְחָק בְּקַדְמֵיתָא, בְּגִין לְאִתְעָרָא שְׂמָאלָא, בְּרָזָא דִרְחִימוּ, וּכְדֵין וַיֹּאמֶר אֱלֹקִים לְיִשְׂרָאֵל בְּמַרְאוֹת הַלַּיְלָה, בְּהַאי דַרְגָּא דְקָאֲמָרָן, דְּאִיהִי מַרְאוֹת הַלַּיְלָה.

119. "And Elohim spoke to Yisrael in the visions (Heb. *mar'ot*) of the night" (Beresheet 46:2): The word *mar'ot* is spelled without the letter *Vav,* WHICH MAKES IT SINGULAR, THUS ALLUDING TO THE GRADE OF THE NUKVA CALLED 'VISION', AND ALSO 'NIGHT'. Come and behold: The verse, "and offered sacrifices to the Elohim of his father Isaac" (Beresheet 46:1), is written first to awaken the left CALLED 'ISAAC' in the secret of love TO THE NUKVA, NUPTIAL LOVE THAT IS DRAWN FROM THE LEFT. Then "Elohim spoke to Yisrael in the visions of the night," WHICH MEANS THAT HE WAS REVEALED TO HIM, by the grade we mentioned, THE NUKVA, called "visions of the night."

120. וַיֹּאמֶר אָנֹכִי הָאֵל אֱלֹקֵי אָבִיךָ, מַאי טַעְמָא. בְּגִין דְּסִטְרָא דִקְדֻשָּׁה דִלְעֵילָא, הָכֵי הוּא, דְּהָא סִטְרָא דִמְסָאֲבָא, לָא אַדְכַּר שְׁמָא דְקוּדְשָׁא בְּרִיךְ הוּא, וְכָל סְטַר דִּקְדוּשָּׁה אִדְכַּר בִּשְׁמֵיהּ. אָנֹכִי אֵרֵד עִמְּךָ

מִצְרַיְמָה וגו׳, מִכָּאן, דִּשְׁכִינְתָּא נָחֲתַת עִמֵּיהּ בְּגָלוּתָא, וּבְכָל אֲתַר דְּיִשְׂרָאֵל אִתְגָּלוּ, שְׁכִינְתָּא אִתְגַּלְיָא עִמְּהוֹן, וְהָא אוֹקְמוּהָ.

120. "And he said: I am the El, the Elohim of your father." HE ASKS: Why DID HE MENTION HIS NAME? HE ANSWERS, Because the holy side above is wont to do so. But the side of defilement does not mention the name of the Holy One, blessed be He. Yet every side of holiness is mentioned by name. "I will go down with you into Egypt" (Beresheet 46:4). From here we understand that the Shechinah accompanied him into exile, and wherever Yisrael went into exile, the Shechinah went with them, as has already been explained.

121. תָּא חֲזֵי, כַּמָּה עֲגָלוֹת הֲווֹ. שִׁית. כְּד״א שֵׁשׁ עֶגְלוֹת צָב. ד״א, שִׁיתִּין הֲווֹ, וְכֹלָּא רָזָא חָדָא. בְּקַדְמֵיתָא כְּתִיב בָּעֲגָלוֹת אֲשֶׁר שָׁלַח יוֹסֵף, וּלְבַסּוֹף אֲשֶׁר שָׁלַח פַּרְעֹה. אֶלָּא, כֻּלְּהוּ דְּשַׁדַּר יוֹסֵף, הֲווֹ בְּחוּשְׁבָּנָא כִּדְקָא חָזֵי, וְאִינוּן דְּשַׁדַּר פַּרְעֹה יַתִּיר מִנַּיְיהוּ, לָא הֲווֹ בְּרָזָא דָא, וְלָא הֲווֹ בְּחוּשְׁבָּנָא.

121. Come and behold. HE ASKS: How many wagons were there? HE REPLIED: There were six, like the "six covered wagons" (Bemidbar 7:3). According to another explanation there were 60. All is one secret, FOR SIX ALLUDE TO THE SIX SFIROT – CHESED, GVURAH, TIFERET, NETZACH, HOD AND YESOD – AND SIXTY ALSO ALLUDES TO THE SIX SFIROT, EACH OF WHICH INCLUDED TEN, WHICH TOTALS SIXTY. HE COMMENTED, First it is written, "the wagons which Joseph had sent" (Beresheet 45:27) and then, "the wagons which Pharaoh had sent" (Beresheet 46:5). HE ANSWERS, All the wagons that Joseph sent were in proper number, and those Pharaoh sent were supernumerary, not part of the secret or part of the reckoning.

122. וְאִלֵּין וְאִלֵּין קָאתוּ, בְּגִין כָּךְ, אֲשֶׁר שָׁלַח יוֹסֵף, אֲשֶׁר שָׁלַח פַּרְעֹה, וְכַד יִפְקוּן יִשְׂרָאֵל מִן גָּלוּתָא מַה כְּתִיב, וְהֵבִיאוּ אֶת כָּל אֲחֵיכֶם מִכָּל הַגּוֹיִם מִנְחָה לַה׳ וגו׳.

122. All the wagons reached JACOB – THE WAGONS JOSEPH SENT WHICH

WERE SUPERIOR TO THE ONES PHARAOH SENT. It is therefore written, "which Joseph had sent" and "which Pharaoh had sent." When Yisrael will come out from exile, it is written, "And they shall bring all your brethren out of all the nations for an offering to Hashem" (Yeshayah 66:20), FOR THEN ALL THE NATIONS WILL BRING AN OFFERING TO HASHEM LIKE PHARAOH DID.

12. "And Joseph made ready his chariot"

A Synopsis

The rabbis continue to expound the nature of separation and its ultimate ending. We see the many ways of the Holy One, and we come to understand that His actions in Pharaoh's Egypt are fully explicable through the principles of Kabbalah, as is the potent image of the chariots evoked in the Torah's story. The rabbis conclude this section with Yisrael taking possession of the land of Goshen – an act seen as exemplifying the unworthiness of the Egyptians, who failed in their fight for the land.

The Relevance of this Passage

We have free will to choose our path in life. Two paths are always available ט the path of darkness, personified by Egypt, and the path of Light, denoted by the people of Yisrael and by Torah. We have no control or influence over the consequences and rewards that accompany these paths. We can, however, choose the path that we walk. Our self-destructive impulses impel us to constantly choose the negative path, and the negative energy blanketing our world often blinds us to the folly of our choices. The Light emitted by these verses helps brighten the spiritual landscape, revealing the doorways through which we must pass in order to attain peace, prosperity, and fulfillment.

123. וַיֶּאְסֹור יוֹסֵף מֶרְכַּבְתּוֹ, ר׳ יִצְחָק פְּתַח וַאֲמַר, וּדְמוּת עַל רָאשֵׁי הַחַיָּה רָקִיעַ כְּעֵין הַקֶּרַח הַנּוֹרָא נָטוּי עַל רָאשֵׁיהֶם מִלְמַעְלָה, הַאי קְרָא אוֹקְמוּהָ, אֲבָל תָּא חֲזֵי, אִית חַיָּה, לְעֵיל מִן חַיָּה, וְאִית חַיָּה קַדִּישָׁא, דְּקָיְימָא עַל רֵישׁ חֵיוָתָא.

123. "And Joseph made ready his chariot." Rabbi Yitzchak opened the discussion with the verse, "And over the heads of the living creatures there was the likeness of a firmament, like the color of the terrible ice, stretched out over their heads above" (Yechezkel 1:22). This verse has already been explained, yet come and behold: There is a living creature above another living creature, and a holy living creature standing over the heads of the other living creatures.

124. וְאִית חַיָּה עִלָּאָה, לְעֵילָּא עַל כָּל שְׁאָר חֵיוָתָא, וְהַאי חַיָּה שָׁלְטָא

עַל כֻּלְּהוּ, בְּגִין דְּכַד הַאי חֵיוָתָא, יָהֲבָא וְנָהֲרָא לְכֻלְּהוּ, כְּדֵין כֻּלְּהוּ נָטְלִין לְמַטְלָנוּי, וִיהִיבַת דָּא לְדָא, וְשָׁלְטָא דָּא עַל דָּא.

124. There is a living creature over all the other living creatures. It rules over them all, for when it gives OF ITS STRENGTH and shines upon them, they all travel about, derives STRENGTH FROM the other, and rule one over the other.

125. וְאִית חֵיוָתָא לְעֵילָּא עַל תַּתָּאֵי, עַל שְׁאָר חֵיוָתָא לְתַתָּא, וְכֻלְּהוּ אִתְּזָנוּ מִינָהּ, וְד׳ סִטְרֵי דְּעָלְמָא רְשִׁימִין בָּהּ, אַנְפִּין נְהִירִין יְדִיעָן לְכָל סְטַר, וְאִיהִי סָלְטָא עַל ד׳ סִטְרֵי, וְהָא אוֹקְמוּהָ, דְּאִינּוּן ג׳ לִסְטַר דָּא, וְג׳ לִסְטַר דָּא, וְכֵן לְד׳ סִטְרִין דְּעָלְמָא.

125. And there is a living creature over the lower beings, NAMELY, over the other living creatures below. They are all sustained by it, and the four winds of the world impress upon it certain faces shine upon each wind. It has power over the four winds. It has been explained that there are three of this wind and three of that wind, and so on, to the four winds of the world.

126. וְאִית רָקִיעַ לְעֵיל מִן רָקִיעַ, וְהַאי רָקִיעַ דְּשָׁלְטָא עֲלַיְיהוּ, כֻּלְּהוּ מִסְתַּכְּלָן לְגַבֵּיהּ, מַה כְּתִיב, וְתַחַת הָרָקִיעַ כַּנְפֵיהֶם יְשָׁרוֹת אִשָּׁה אֶל אֲחוֹתָהּ וגו׳, בְּגִין, דְּכֻלְּהוּ שָׁלְטִין עַל מַה דְּאִתְפְּקְדוּ, וּשְׁלִיחוּ דְּקוּסְטָא דְּקוּפְטְרָא בְּהוּ.

126. There are a series of firmaments one on top of the other, and a firmament that reigns over them. They all look to it. It is written, "And under the firmament their wings were held straight, the one toward the other" (Yechezkel 1:23), for they are all in command over what is in their charge. And there is the spreading of a rope's measurement between them.

127. וְאִינּוּן לְכָל סְטַר תִּשְׁעָה, לְד׳ סִטְרִין דְּעָלְמָא, וְאִינּוּן ל״ו בְּחוּשְׁבְּנָא, וְכַד מִתְחַבְּרָן כֻּלְּהוּ, אִתְעֲבִידוּ רְשִׁימָא חֲדָא, בְּרָזָא דִּשְׁמָא חֲדָא, בְּיִחוּדָא שְׁלִים כִּדְקָחֲזֵי.

127. There are THREE FIRMAMENTS to every wind, nine on each of the four sides of the world, 36 FIRMAMENTS in all. When they are united, they become one, NAMELY, ONE FIRMAMENT, in the secret of the one name – THE NUKVA CALLED ‘NAME’ – within the whole, as it should be.

128. וְכַד מִתְתַּקְנֵי לְגַבֵּי כָּרְסְיָא, מַה כְּתִיב וּמִמַּעַל לָרָקִיעַ אֲשֶׁר עַל רֹאשָׁם כְּמַרְאֵה אֶבֶן סַפִּיר דְּמוּת כִּסֵּא וְעַל דְּמוּת הַכִּסֵּא דְּמוּת כְּמַרְאֵה אָדָם עָלָיו מִלְמָעְלָה, וְהָא אוֹקִימְנָא דְּהַאי אֶבֶן טָבָא בְּכָרְסְיָא, דְּקָיְימָא עַל ד׳ קָיְימִין, וְעַל הַהוּא כָּרְסְיָא דְּיוֹקְנָא דְּאָדָם, לְאִתְחַבְּרָא בֵּיהּ כַּחֲדָא, וּלְאִתְבָּרְכָא כִּדְקָא יָאוֹת.

128. When they are shaped like a throne, it is written, “And above the firmament that was over their heads was the likeness of a throne, in appearance like a sapphire stone: and upon the likeness of the throne was the likeness as the appearance of a man above upon it” (Yechezkel 1:26). It has been explained that when the precious stone, THE NUKVA, is fixed into the throne that stands upon its four legs, and when the image of a man is upon the throne, ZEIR ANPIN, to be united with him, THEN THE THRONE WHICH IS THE NUKVA IS JOINED WITH THE MAN ABOVE IT, ZEIR ANPIN, and is fully blessed by him.

129. וְכַד אִיהִי מִתְתַּקְנָא לְגַבֵּיהּ דְּאָדָם, לְמֶהֱוֵי כֹּלָּא רְתִיכָא חֲדָא, לְהַאי אָדָם, כְּדֵין כְּתִיב, וַיֶּאְסֹר יוֹסֵף מֶרְכַּבְתּוֹ דָּא צַדִּיק, וַיַּעַל לִקְרַאת יִשְׂרָאֵל אָבִיו גֹּשְׁנָה. לִקְרַאת יִשְׂרָאֵל: דָּא רָזָא דְּאָדָם. גֹּשְׁנָה: תִּקְרוֹבְתָּא חֲדָא, לְאִתְקָרְבָא כַּחֲדָא, בְּקָרְבָּנָא חֲדָא, וְיִחוּדָא חֲדָא.

129. When it, THE FIRMAMENTS AND THE ANIMALS THAT ARE THE SECRET OF THE NUKVA, is fixed to form a Chariot for that man, ZEIR ANPIN, then it is written, “And Joseph made ready his chariot,” who is the righteous – YESOD OF ZEIR ANPIN, CALLED ‘JOSEPH THE RIGHTEOUS’ – “and went up to meet Yisrael his father, to Goshen.” Yisrael is the secret of Adam (man), THE MAN UPON THE THRONE, ZEIR ANPIN. “…to Goshen” is derived from their approaching (Heb. *gisha*) to be joined and united.

130. וַיֵּרָא אֵלָיו, דְּכַד אִתְחֲזֵי שִׁמְשָׁא בְּסִיהֲרָא, כְּדֵין נָהִיר סִיהֲרָא,

וְאַנְהֵיר לְכֻלְּהוּ דִּלְתַתָּא, וְכֵן כְּגַוְונָא דָא, כָּל זִמְנָא דִּקְדוּשָּׁה דִּלְעֵילָּא, שָׁרָא עַל מַקְדְּשָׁא דִּלְתַתָּא, אִתְנְהֵיר בֵּי מַקְדְּשָׁא, וְקָיְימָא בִּשְׁלֵימוּתֵיהּ, וְכַד אִסְתַּלַּק מִנֵּיהּ, וְאִתְחָרֵיב בֵּי מַקְדְּשָׁא, כְּדֵין, וַיֵּבְךְּ עַל צַוָּארָיו עוֹד, דְּבָכוּן כֹּלָּא, עַל מַקְדְּשָׁא דְּאִתְחָרֵיב. עוֹד, מַאי עוֹד. דָּא גָּלוּתָא בַּתְרָאָה.

130. "...and presented himself to him (lit. 'and he was seen to him')." THE WORDS "WAS SEEN" ARE DIFFICULT TO UNDERSTAND, FOR THEY MEAN THAT HE WAS SEEN AND THEN GONE. WHAT DOES THE VERSE MEAN? HE SAID: When the sun reflects on the moon, the moon shines, and illuminates all those below IN THE WORLD. In the same manner, as long as Supernal Holiness, THE LIGHT OF ZEIR ANPIN, hovers above the Temple below, THE NUKVA, the Temple shines and stands erect. BUT HERE IT IS WRITTEN, "AND HE WAS SEEN TO HIM," WHICH MEANS THAT THE LIGHT WAS SEEN TO HER AND THEN GONE, and after THE SUPERNAL LIGHT OF ZEIR ANPIN was gone from her, THE SCRIPTURE READS, "and wept on his neck a good while," for they all wept for the Temple that was destroyed. THE SCRIPTURE ADDS, "a good while," which means until the last exile.

131. כְּדֵין כֵּיוָן דְּחָמָא יַעֲקֹב וְאִסְתַּכַּל, דְּהָא תִּקּוּנָא דִּלְתַתָּא, אִשְׁתַּכְלֵל כְּגַוְונָא דִּלְעֵילָּא, כְּדֵין אֲמַר אָמוּתָה הַפָּעַם וגו'. כִּי עוֹדְךָ חָי, דְּאִתְקָיְימַת בְּרָזָא דִּבְרִית קַדִּישָׁא, דְּאִקְרֵי חֵי הָעוֹלָמִים, וּבְגִין כָּךְ כִּי עוֹדְךָ חָי. וְעַ"ד בְּקַדְמֵיתָא אֲמַר, רַב עוֹד יוֹסֵף בְּנִי חָי, דְּאִצְטְרִיךְ לְמֵיקַם בְּרָזָא דְּחַי, וְהָא אִתְּמָר.

131. When Jacob looked and saw that all was completed below BETWEEN MALE AND FEMALE as it is above BETWEEN ABA AND IMA, he said: "Now let me die, since I have seen your face, because you are still alive," which means, you live by the secret of the Holy Covenant called "the life of the worlds." Thus, he said, "you are still alive." He had already said before, "It is enough; Joseph my son is still alive" (Beresheet 45:28), he being the secret of the Living One, as has already been explained.

132. תָּא חֲזֵי, מַה כְּתִיב, וַיְבָרֶךְ יַעֲקֹב אֶת פַּרְעֹה, אֲמַר רִבִּי יוֹסֵי, פַּרְעֹה

אע"ג דְּאוּקְמוּהָ בְּרָזָא אוֹחֲרָא, סָמַךְ דְּקָא סַמְכִינָן בְּעַלְמָא.

132. Come and behold: "and Jacob blessed Pharaoh" (Beresheet 47:10). Rabbi Yosi said: We do agree that Pharaoh was AN EVIL KLIPAH ACCORDING TO HOMILETIC INTERPRETATION, even though it was explained in regard to another mystery THAT HE IS NOT AN EVIL KLIPAH BUT DESCENDS FROM IMA OF ATZILUT.

133. אֲבָל תָּא חֲזֵי, לְסוּסָתִי בְּרִכְבֵי פַרְעֹה דִּמִּיתִיךְ רַעְיָתִי, תָּא חֲזֵי, אִית רְתִיכִין לִשְׂמָאלָא, בְּרָזָא דְסִטְרָא אָחֳרָא, וְאִית רְתִיכִין לִימִינָא, בְּרָזָא דִלְעֵילָא דִקְדוּשָּׁה, וְאִלֵּין לָקֳבֵל אִלֵּין, אִלֵּין דְּרַחֲמֵי, וְאִלֵּין דְּדִינָא.

133. Yet come and behold: "I compare you, my love, to a mare of the chariots of Pharaoh" (Shir Hashirim 1:9). Come and behold: There are Chariots on the left in the secret of the Other Side, and Chariots on the right on the side of holiness. The ones OF HOLINESS correspond to the others. The holy ones are of Mercy, and those OF THE OTHER SIDE are of Judgment.

134. וְכַד קוּדְשָׁא בְּרִיךְ הוּא עָבֵד דִּינָא בְּמִצְרָאֵי, כָּל דִּינָא דְּעָבֵיד, כְּהַהוּא גַוְונָא, דְּאִינּוּן רְתִיכִין מַמָּשׁ, וּכְגַוְונָא דִילֵיהּ דְּהַהוּא סִטְרָא מַמָּשׁ, מַה הַהוּא סִטְרָא קָטִיל וְאַפֵּיק נִשְׁמָתִין, אוּף קוּדְשָׁא בְּרִיךְ הוּא עָבֵיד בְּהַהוּא גַוְונָא מַמָּשׁ, דִּכְתִיב וַיַּהֲרֹג ה' כָּל בְּכוֹר, וְכֵן כֹּלָּא בְּמִצְרַיִם, בְּהַהוּא גַוְונָא מַמָּשׁ, וּבְגִין כָּךְ דִּמִּיתִיךְ רַעְיָתִי, כְּגַוְונָא דִילָהּ מַמָּשׁ לְקַטְלָא, דִּכְתִיב כִּי אֲנִי ה' אֲנִי הוּא וְלֹא אַחֵר. וּלְזִמְנָא דְאָתֵי מַה כְּתִיב, מִי זֶה בָּא מֵאֱדוֹם חֲמוּץ בְּגָדִים מִבָּצְרָה וגו'.

134. When the Holy One, blessed be He, executed judgment on Egypt, He did it exactly the same way as the Chariots OF THE OTHER SIDE and in the same manner as that side. As it kills and takes souls, so the Holy One, blessed be He, did the same, as it is written, "that Hashem slew all the firstborn" (Shemot 13:15), ALTHOUGH HE IS USUALLY MERCIFUL. IN THE SAME WAY, whatever He did in Egypt was in the very same manner.

Therefore it is written, "I compare you, my love," because she is compared TO THE CHARIOTS OF PHARAOH IN KILLING AND TAKING THE SOULS OF MEN the same way THE CHARIOTS OF PHARAOH, WHO IS THE OTHER SIDE, kill, as it is written, "I am Hashem, I am He and not another." Later, it is written, "Who is this that comes from Edom, with crimsoned garments from Botzrah?" (Yeshayah 63:1). FOR THEN TOO, HASHEM WILL KILL THEM, AND NO MESSANGER.

135. תָּא חֲזֵי, מַה כְּתִיב וַיֵּשֶׁב יִשְׂרָאֵל בְּאֶרֶץ מִצְרַיִם בְּאֶרֶץ גּוֹשֶׁן וַיֵּאָחֲזוּ בָהּ וַיִּפְרוּ וַיִּרְבּוּ מְאֹד. וַיֵּאָחֲזוּ בָהּ, אַחְסָנַת עָלְמִין. וְיֵּאָחֲזוּ בָּהּ, דְּהָא לְהוֹן אִתְחֲזֵי, כְּמָה דְּאוֹקְמוּהָ. וַיִּפְרוּ וַיִּרְבּוּ מְאֹד, וַדַּאי, דְּהָא צַעֲרָא לָא שָׁרַאת בְּהוֹ, וְקַיְימֵי בְּתַפְנוּקֵי עָלְמָא, וּבְגִין כָּךְ וַיִּפְרוּ וַיִּרְבּוּ מְאֹד.

135. Come and behold: It is written, "And Yisrael dwelt in the land of Egypt in the country of Goshen; and they took possession of it, and grew and multiplied exceedingly" (Beresheet 47:27). "And took possession of it" means as a permanent heritage. "And they took possession of it" because they, AND NOT THE EGYPTIANS, were worthy of taking possession of it, as has already been explained. "...and grew and multiplied exceedingly" because surely they had nothing to vex them and they lived in royal luxury AS LONG AS THE TRIBES WERE ALIVE. They therefore grew and multiplied exceedingly.

בָּרוּךְ יי׳ לְעוֹלָם אָמֵן וְאָמֵן

Blessed be Hashem forever and ever Amen and Amen.

NOTES